£105.00

WS 736 FIT

HANDBOOK OF
Attention Deficit Hyperactivity Disorder

HANDBOOK OF
Attention Deficit Hyperactivity Disorder

Edited by
MICHAEL FITZGERALD
Trinity College Dublin, Ireland

MARK BELLGROVE
University of Queensland, Brisbane, Australia

MICHAEL GILL
Trinity College Dublin, Ireland

John Wiley & Sons, Ltd

Other Wiley Editorial Offices

John Wiley & Sons Inc., 111 River Street, Hoboken, NJ 07030, USA

Jossey-Bass, 989 Market Street, San Francisco, CA 94103-1741, USA

Wiley-VCH Verlag GmbH, Boschstr. 12, D-69469 Weinheim, Germany

John Wiley & Sons Australia Ltd, 42 McDougall Street, Milton, Queensland 4064, Australia

John Wiley & Sons (Asia) Pte Ltd, 2 Clementi Loop #02-01, Jin Xing Distripark, Singapore 129809

John Wiley & Sons Canada Ltd, 6045 Freemont Blvd, Mississauga, ONT, L5R 4J3

Wiley also publishes its books in a variety of electronic formats. Some content that appears in print may not be available in electronic books.

Anniversary Logo Design: Richard J. Pacifico

Library of Congress Cataloging-in-Publication Data
Handbook of attention deficit hyperactivity disorder / edited by Michael Fitzgerald, Mark Bellgrove, Michael Gill.
     p. ; cm.
Includes bibliographical references and index.
ISBN-13: 978-0-470-01444-8 (pbk. : alk. paper)
ISBN-10: 0-470-01444-X (pbk. : alk. paper)
1. Attention-deficit hyperactivity disorder–Handbooks, manuals, etc.   I. Fitzgerald, Michael, Dr.
  II. Bellgrove, Mark.   III. Gill, Michael, 1957-
  [DNLM: 1. Attention Deficit Disorder with Hyperactivity.   2. Risk Factors. WS 350.8.A8 H236 2007]
  RJ506.H9H3449   2007
  618.92'8589 – dc22

                                      2006036941

A catalogue record for this book is available from the British Library
ISBN 13: 978-0-470-0-14448

Typeset by SNP Best-set Typesetter Ltd., Hong Kong
Printed and bound in England by Antony Rowe Ltd, Chippenham, Wiltshire

This book is printed on acid-free paper responsibly manufactured from sustainable forestry in which at least two trees are planted for each one used for paper production.

Contents

About the Editors

Michael Fitzgerald

Michael Fitzgerald is the Henry Marsh Professor of Child and Adolescent Psychiatry at Trinity College Dublin, Ireland and was the first Professor of Child Psychiatry in Ireland. Michael has held positions at the Bethlem Royal and Maudsley Hospital London and the National Hospital for Nervous Diseases, Queen's Square, as well as King's College Hospital, London. He received an MB from University College Galway and an MD from Trinity College Dublin. Michael has special interests in ADHD and autism and has over 300 published contributions to the literature including books, peer-reviewed papers and letters to the editors. He has edited or co-edited eight books.

Mark Bellgrove

Mark Bellgrove is a University of Queensland Principal Research Fellow at the Queensland Brain Institute (QBI) and School of Psychology at the University of Queensland, Brisbane, Australia. Mark is an experimental psychologist by training and completed his Ph.D. at Monash University, Australia. Mark undertook post-doctoral training within the Departments of Psychology, Psychiatry and Institute of Neuroscience at Trinity College Dublin, Ireland, working on endophenotypes for ADHD. Subsequently, Mark returned to Australia as a National Health and Medical Research Council Howard Florey Centenary Fellow, working at the University of Melbourne. Mark has a special interest in the cognitive neuroscience of psychiatric disorders, including ADHD, autism and schizophrenia.

Michael Gill

Michael Gill is Professor and Head of the Discipline of Psychiatry within the School of Medicine and Health Sciences at Trinity College Dublin, Ireland. Michael leads the Neuropsychiatric Genetics Research Group which studies the molecular bases of a number of psychiatric conditions including programmes in ADHD, schizophrenia, and autism. Michael completed his MD at Dublin University and is a Fellow of Trinity College Dublin. Michael is a past Wellcome Trust Research Fellow and Wellcome Trust Senior Research Fellow at the Institute of Psychiatry, London. Michael has published over 200 peer-reviewed journal articles and his research has attracted major funding from national and international funding agencies.

List of Contributors

Amy F.T. Arnsten, Department of Neurobiology, Yale University, New Haven, CT, USA

Edwina Barry, School of Medicine and Health Sciences, Trinity College Dublin, Ireland

Kellie S. Bennett, School of Psychology, Curtin University of Technology, Perth, WA, Australia

John L. Bradshaw, School of Psychology, Psychiatry and Psychological Medicine, Monash University, Australia

Robert Brooks, Harvard Medical School, Needham, Mass., USA

F. Xavier Castellanos, Brooke and Daniel Neidich Professor of Child and Adolescent Psychiatry; Director, Institute for Pediatric Neuroscience; Director of Research, NYU Child Study Center; Professor of Radiology, NYU School of Medicine, USA

Stephen V. Faraone, Director, Medical Genetics Research Professor of Psychiatry and of Neuroscience and Physiology Director, Child and Adult Psychiatry Research, SUNY Upstate Medical University, Syracuse, NY, USA

Louise Gallagher, School of Medicine and Health Sciences, Trinity College Dublin, Ireland

Sam Goldstein, University of Utah School of Medicine, Salt Lake City, Utah, USA

Ziarih Hawi, School of Medicine and Health Sciences, Trinity College Dublin, Ireland

David A. Hay, School of Psychology, Curtin University of Technology, Perth, WA, Australia

Abel Ickowicz, The Hospital for Sick Children, Psychiatry Department, Toronto, Canada

A.M. Clare Kelly, Institute for Pediatric Neuroscience, NYU Child Study Center, New York, USA

Aiveen Kirley, Consultant Adult Psychiatrist, Cluan Mhuire Service, Blackrock, Co. Dublin, Ireland

Ester I. Klimkeit, Centre for Developmental Psychiatry and Psychology, School of Psychology, Psychiatry and Psychological Medicine, Monash University, Australia

Malie Lagendijk, National University of Ireland, Galway, Ireland

Florence Levy, Child and Family East, Sydney Children's Hospital Community Health Center, Randwick; Prince of Wales Hospital, Randwick, NSW, Australia

Naomi Lowe, School of Medicine and Health Sciences, Trinity College Dublin, Ireland

Paul McArdle, Newcastle University, Fleming Nuffield Unit, Jesmond, Newcastle upon Tyne, UK

Frank A. Middleton, Assistant Professor, Neuroscience and Physiology; Assistant Professor, Biomedical Sciences Program, SUNY Upstate Medical University, Syracuse, NY, USA

Redmond G. O'Connell, School of Psychology and Institute of Neuroscience, Trinity College Dublin, Ireland

Ian H. Robertson, School of Psychology and Institute of Neuroscience, Trinity College Dublin, Ireland

Russell Schachar, Department of Psychiatry, Brain and Behaviour Programme, Research Institute, The Hospital for Sick Children, Toronto, Canada

Anouk Scheres, Assistant Research Professor, Department of Psychology, University of Arizona, Tucson, Arizona, USA

Ricardo Segurado, Biostatics and Bioinformatics Unit, Department of Psychological Medicine, Cardiff University, Heath Hospital, Cardiff, Wales

Louise Sharkey, Locum Consultant Psychiatrist, Beechpark Services for Children on the Autistic Spectrum, Dublin, Ireland

Mary V. Solanto, Associate Professor, Director, ADHD Center, Department of Psychiatry, Mount Sinai School of Medicine, New York, USA

Edmund S.J. Sonuga-Barke, Professor, School of Psychology, University of Southampton, Southampton, UK

Eric T. Taylor, Department of Child and Adolescent Psychiatry, Institute of Psychiatry, King's College, London, UK

Alasdair Vance, Head Academic Child Psychiatry, Department of Paediatrics, University of Melbourne, Murdoch Children's Research Institute, Royal Children's Hospital, Parkville, Victoria, Australia

Will Wilkinson, Consultant Psychologist, Boleybeg, Barna, Co. Galway, Ireland

Susan Young, Senior Lecturer in Forensic Clinical Psychology, Department of Forensic Mental Health Science, Institute of Psychiatry, King's College, London, UK

Preface

Neuroscience seeks to decipher the mystery of the most complex of all machines, the human brain. The brain has more than 10 billion neurons in a highly interconnected web governed by complex biochemical pathways. Disorders of the brain have particularly devastating consequences for patients, families, health and financial resources. Attention Deficit Hyperactivity Disorder (ADHD) is one of these conditions. ADHD is characterised by significant symptoms of inattention, hyperactivity and impulsivity. The impact of the condition on the individual, the family and society is enormous. It is associated with extensive use of health-related resources, it is a burden on the criminal justice system and confers significant social cost in terms of educational failure, family disruption, and marital breakdown.

The major events in the life of children and adolescents are educational and ADHD undermines this part of their life, leading to many secondary complications including bullying, school failure and poor self-confidence. ADHD has multiple negative impacts on education, sense of self, social relationships, and is often associated with depression, anxiety and suicidal behaviour. Increasingly, ADHD is being appreciated as a lifelong illness in perhaps as many 60% of childhood cases. This book includes much commentary on the clinical phenomenology, genetics and both pharmacological and non-pharmacological treatment of adult ADHD. Across the lifespan ADHD impacts on many professionals including general practitioners, psychiatrists, psychologists, social workers, lawyers, judges, paediatricians, neurologists, geneticists, pharmacologists, and neuroradiologists. We hope that professionals in each of these areas will benefit from this book.

ADHD represents one of the most controversial psychiatric disorders of our time. Controversy arises for at least two reasons. First there is the public perception that ADHD is a 'new' condition and that its diagnosis rates are ever on the increase. As reviewed in this book, reports of children presenting with inattentive or hyperactive/impulsive behaviour date back to 1798 when Alexander Crichton wrote of 'mental restlessness'. Crichton wrote:

> when born with the person it becomes evident at a very early period of life, and has a very bad affect, in as much as it renders him incapable of attending with constancy to any one object of attention. But it is seldom so great a degree as to totally impede all instruction; and what is very fortunate it generally diminishes with age. (Cadell & Davis, 1976, p. 271)

Nevertheless, any psychiatric disorder is a sign of our time, and current diagnosis rates undoubtedly reflect our modern world that calls for problem-solving and analytic abilities, focus of attention and restraint of impulsivity. As Klimkeit and Bradshaw point out in Chapter 21 of this book, in certain other historical settings, the novelty seeking and impulsive behaviours of ADHD children, which in today's society are seen as maladaptive, may well have been advantageous.

Controversy also arises from the treatment of children with ADHD with potentially addictive stimulants, such as methylphenidate and dextroamphetamine. Stimulant medications have now been the mainstay treatment for ADHD for more than three decades, and an overwhelming amount of data demonstrates a beneficial impact of these drugs on core symptoms of ADHD. However, as reviewed in Chapter 13 of this book by Solanto and colleagues, newer generation, non-stimulant medications have emerged that may help to allay some of the fears surrounding stimulants. Time will tell whether these newer treatments have comparable short- and longer-term efficacy in ADHD. Nevertheless, there is a growing appreciation that therapeutic response, even to stimulants, is somewhat variable in children with ADHD and so there is a push to identify individual difference factors which may predict drug response. In this endeavour, molecular genetics and pharmacology are interfacing in a new and important way. Pharmacogenetics is the study of how individual differences in drug response might depend upon underlying genetic factors. Barry and colleagues review current knowledge in this burgeoning area of research in Chapter 16.

Perhaps more than in any other neurodevelopmental disorder, our knowledge of ADHD is expanding rapidly. This book examines ADHD at many levels and represents an up-to-date description of our knowledge and understanding of the disorder. The book is divided into three sections, dealing with research findings from the clinical, neurobiological and treatment perspectives. The book begins at the bedside by reviewing the clinical description of child and adult ADHD and its key comorbid disorders (Chapters 1–6). It then moves to the bench to examine the key neurobiological findings from the fields of genetics, neuroimaging, neuropsychology and psychopharmacology (Chapters 7–16). Finally, the book makes a return from the bedside to the bench, describing the latest non-pharmacological treatment modalities that are being informed by our growing understanding of the neurobiology of the disorder (Chapters 17–20). Thus, the book tries to bridge the gap between basic neuroscience and clinical applications.

This *Handbook of Attention Deficit Hyperactivity Disorder* particularly focuses on recent developments in Attention Deficit Hyperactivity Disorder research. Wiley has produced previous handbooks of a similar nature on autism. The aim of this ADHD Handbook is to give the reader a rapid update on recent developments on ADHD research by an international panel of contributors. We hope that this book is as useful to the student as it is to the expert.

We have relatively effective interventions for ADHD but there is a great deal of extra work to be done in devising new pharmacological and non-pharmacological treatments. There is little doubt that the future lies in rigorous scientific research. Rigorous research has led to the abandonment of earlier views of ADHD as being due to minimal brain dysfunction or parental mismanagement, for example. The book emphasises solid scientific data where this is available. While there has been much progress in defining the ADHD phenotype across the lifespan, considerable challenges lie ahead for mapping the biological pathways that may lead from gene to disorder. While this may have been unthinkable even 15 years ago, we have little doubt that in time, such scientific advances will change the landscape for clinicians and lead to improved treatment of the disorder. We are optimistic about the future of research and clinical practice in ADHD; we hope that the advances outlined in this book may inspire researchers or clinicians who are new to the area.

We would like to acknowledge the contributions of the many scientists and clinicians, from centres and universities around the world, who have taken time out of their busy schedules to contribute to this book. We would also particularly like to thank the many children with ADHD and their families, who have participated in research studies that informed this book. This book is dedicated to you all. Finally, we would like to acknowledge the editorial staff of John Wiley & Sons for their assistance and patience during the preparation of this book.

Michael Fitzgerald
Mark Bellgrove
Michael Gill

REFERENCE

Cadell T, Davis W (1976) *An Enquiry into the Nature and Origin of Mental Derangement: Comprehending a Concise System of the Physiology and Pathology of the Mind and a History of the Passions and Their Effects*. New York: AMS Press.

I Clinical Perspectives

1 The History of Attention Deficit Hyperactivity Disorder

LOUISE SHARKEY[1] AND MICHAEL FITZGERALD[2]
1. Beechpark Services for Children on the Autistic Spectrum, Dublin, Ireland;
2. Trinity College Dublin, Ireland

1.1 OVERVIEW

The condition now referred to as Attention-Deficit/Hyperactivity Disorder (DSM-IV) (American Psychiatric Association, 1994) or Hyperkinetic Disorder (ICD-10) (World Health Organization, 1992) was first described by George Still in 1901 (Still, 1902). In his lectures to the Royal Academy of Physicians he described a case series of 20 children presenting with problems of overactivity, inattention and deficits in 'volitional inhibition'. He also described symptoms of aggressiveness, defiance, resistance to discipline and dishonesty, which in today's nomenclature would be diagnosed as Oppositional Defiant Disorder or Conduct Disorder which are often comorbid with ADHD. Subsequent to Dr Still's lecture a number of different diagnostic labels were assigned to the same symptoms, including Minimal Brain Damage and Minimal Brain Dysfunction to refer to children presenting with overactivity and inattention, subsequent to a pandemic of encephalitis lethargica in 1917. The condition which we now refer to as ADHD was first included in the second edition of the *Diagnostic and Statistical Manual of Mental Disorders* (DSM) in 1968 and labelled 'Hyperkinetic Disorder of Childhood'. The definition of the condition changed in subsequent editions of DSM, in keeping with changes in diagnostic nomenclature and delineation of subtypes. The most recent edition, DSM-IV, requires pervasive symptoms of inattention or inattention, hyperactivity and or impulsivity, which are clinically impairing with an age of onset prior to age seven. The diagnostic criteria used by DSM-IV are similar to the criteria for Hyperkinetic Disorder used in the current edition of the International Classification of Diseases (ICD-10) in that specific behaviour symptoms of inattention and hyperactivity-impulsivity are recognised and both are required for a diagnosis to be made. ICD-10 does not recognise predominantly inattentive or predominantly hyperactive-impulsive subtypes, and requires symptom onset prior to age six. In addition, ICD-10 requires a direct observation of symptoms by the clinician together with parental and school reports.

The concept of the diagnosis of ADHD has evolved through a complex developmental trajectory dating back to Greek times. The focus of this chapter is to present an overview of the developmental course and unfolding of our current

Handbook of Attention Deficit Hyperactivity Disorder. Edited by M. Fitzgerald, M. Bellgrove and M. Gill.
© 2007 John Wiley & Sons Ltd

understanding of hyperactivity and attention disorders. We will present a chrono-logical account of the literature referring to symptoms of inattention, hyperactivity and impulsivity and comorbid behaviour disorders, that have contributed to our current understanding of the condition ADHD.

1.2   PREHISTORY AND HISTORY OF ATTENTION DEFICIT HYPERACTIVITY DISORDER

1.2.1   EIGHTEENTH CENTURY

The earliest literature referring to the inattentive subtype of ADHD dates back to the writings of the physician, Alexender Crichton in 1798. In his paper 'Mental Restlessness', Dr Crichton described all the essential features of the inattentive subtype of attention deficit hyperactivity disorder which were almost entirely con-sistent with the criteria for the inattentive subtype as portrayed in DSM-IV (APA, 2000) (Palmer & Finger, 2001). He saw it as a

> nervous problem which may be born with the person or be the effect of accidental disease . . . when born with the person it becomes evident at a very early period of life, and has a very bad affect, in as much as it renders him incapable of attending with con-stancy to any one object of attention. But it is seldom so great a degree as to totally impede all instruction; and what is very fortunate it generally diminishes with age. (Cadell & Davis, 1976, p. 271)

Crichton further wrote:

> every impression seems to agitate the person, and gives him or her an unnatural degree of mental restlessness. People walking up and down the room, a slight noise, too much light or too little light all destroy constant attention in such patients, in so much as it is easily excited by every impression.

He went on to say that when people are affected in such a way 'they have a par-ticular name for the state of their nerves, which is expressive enough of their feel-ings. They say they have the fidgets' (p. 272). Crichton suggested that these children needed special educational intervention.

1.2.2   NINETEENTH CENTURY

John Haslam in his book *Observations on Madness and Melancholy* (1809, p. 120), described the case of a child who from the age of two was

> mischievous and uncontrollable . . . a creature of volition and a terror of the family . . . he had limited attention span, being only attracted by 'fits and starts'. He had been several times to school and was the hopeless pupil of many masters, distinguished for their patience and rigid discipline.

This poor child also had a tendency to break things, was very oppositional and cruel to animals. While Haslam paints a picture of a young boy with conduct disorder, a diagnosis of ADHD, ODD, dyspraxia and specific learning difficulties would have to be included in the differential diagnosis.

A number of descriptions of hyperactive children mostly in the form of case reports appeared in the psychiatric literature towards the second half of the nineteenth century. The German physician Henrich Hoffman described the 'hyperkinetic syndrome' in a case report of a young boy presenting with symptoms of hyperactivity, impulsivity and inattention (Clements & Peters, 1962).

Maudsley (1867) described children as 'little more than an organic machine automatically impelled by disordered nerve centres'. He discussed their 'absence of mind' and 'an actual abnormality underlying children's problems'. Albutt (1892) reported these children as 'having an unstable nervous system'.

Clousten (1966, pp. 481–90) described a disorder which he referred to as 'simple hyperexcitability', caused by 'undue brain reactiveness to mental and emotional stimuli'. The condition he reported was characterised by symptoms of overactivity and restlessness and it primarily affected children from the age of three years until puberty. It occurred in bursts, lasting from a few months to years, adversely affecting academic performance and emotional well-being. Anorexia, weight loss and insomnia were associated features. The symptoms of 'simple hyperexcitability' that Clousten described shared a marked resemblance to DSM-IV ADHD, but also shared many of the features of early onset bipolar affective disorder. Clousten recommended a multimodal treatment approach for these children, including high dose bromides, good nutrition, fresh air, 'companionship and employment'. The aim of treatment was to 'reduce cell catabolism and the reactiveness of the cerebral cortex whilst not interfering with brain anabolism'.

In 1870 an Education Act was passed by Parliament in Britain that made school attendance compulsory. This had a significant impact on the recognition of symptoms of inattention and hyperactivity as more than just extremes of normal childhood behaviour, and brought the condition increasingly to the attention of the medical profession. This may be one of the reasons why most of the literature pertaining to ADHD dates from 1900.

1.2.3   TWENTIETH CENTURY

1900–10

The birth of the new century witnessed the birth of the recognition of a disorder which was to become the most diagnosed child psychiatric disorder. Although some attribute the first clear accounts of hyperactivity to Dr Alexander Crichton (1798), most of the psychiatric literature credits Sir George Still, a paediatrician and first professor of childhood diseases at King's College Hospital, London. In 1902 Still presented the Goulstonian lectures entitled 'Some abnormal psychical conditions in children' to the Royal College of Physicians. He described a case series of 20 children manifesting a deficit of 'moral control'. The children he described experienced extreme restlessness and an 'abnormal capacity for sustained attention', impacting on academic performance and social relationships, despite normal intellectual functioning. Their behaviour was described as violent, destructive, oppositional and non-responsive to punishment. It occurred more frequently in boys and first manifested in the early school years. The defect of moral control was not thought to be a result of adverse social circumstances which were common in society at the time, but rather was thought to be a neurobiological affliction due to 'some morbid physical condition'. He defined three subgroups of hyperactive behaviour:

> those with demonstrable gross lesions of the brain; those with a variety of acute diseases, conditions and injuries that would be expected to result in brain damage; and those with hyperactive behaviours that could not be attributed to any known cause. (Sandberg & Barton, 1996, pp. 5–7)

Alfred Tredgold (1908), a member of the English Royal Commission on Mental Deficiency, extended Still's biological theory. He suggested that some forms of brain damage, resulting from birth injury or mild anoxia, though undetected at the time, could present as behaviour problems or learning difficulties in the early school years. He was the first to propose the concept of 'minimal brain damage'. In addition to symptoms of hyperactivity and educational difficulties, the children he observed exhibited soft neurological signs and motor clumsiness.

1910–20

Neve and Turner (1913, p. 385) described Still's ideas as a 'contemporary and perhaps logical, extension of that put forward by James Crichton-Brown, as a newer neurological account of phenomena once seen as immoral, while still using the older language of morality (e.g. vicious, depraved) to describe abnormal psychological function'. In this same year the Dublin-born paediatrician, Robert Stein (1913, pp. 478–86) discussed 'children saturated with insanity while still in the womb', with 'badly built minds' and 'a kind of partial moral dementia'. He observed that children with these afflictions presented with pervasive disruptive behaviour problems, evident in the early school years resulting in educational underachievement and relationship difficulties. It is possible that the children he described would today fulfil criteria for ADHD, and his phrase 'badly built minds' could equate with current neurobiological findings underlying the disorder.

In 1917 a pandemic of encephalitis lethargica swept Europe and North America. In its aftermath clinicians encountered children who having made a full recovery from the infection, presented with overactivity, distractibility, poor impulse control and cognitive deficits. This period gave rise to theories of Minimal Brain Dysfunction (MBD) (Kessler, 1980), and is regarded by many clinicians as the beginning of North America's interest in hyperactivity (Cantwell, 1975).

1930–40

The paediatrician D.W. Winnicott (1931, p. 654) gave a very good description of the 'hyperkinetic child'. In his words

> such a fidgety child is a worry, is restless, is up to mischief if left for a moment unoccupied, and is impossible at table, either eating food as if someone would snatch it from him, or else liable to upset tumblers or spill tea . . . sleep is usually restless. . . . These children are over-excitable, or 'nervy' rather than nervous.

In 1934 Kramer-Pollnow described a condition which he referred to as '*hyperkinetische Erkrankung*' (hyperkinetic disease). The syndrome he described was characterised by symptoms of extreme restlessness, distractibility and speech disorder, 'a condition of persistent motor unrest which makes its appearance between the ages of 2 and 4 years' (reported by Hoff, 1956, pp. 537–53). Kramer-Pollnow described a case series of 15 children who were symptomatic by the age of six, and in addition to the syndrome described, presented with aggressive behaviour, impulsivity and learning difficulties. In many cases the extreme restlessness was followed by an epileptic seizure. Kramer-Pollnow clearly described a cohort of children with complex neurodevelopmental difficulties of which ADHD appears to have been a comorbid condition.

Kahn and Cohen (1934) described a case series of three children with symptoms of overactivity, impulsivity, clumsiness and soft neurological signs. They argued that the symptoms were caused by 'organic driveness, or a surplus of inner impulsion' stemming from a defect in the organisation of the brain stem, caused by trauma, birth injury or a congenital abnormality.

Although Kanner's third edition of the child psychiatry textbook (1957) made no references to hyperactivity as a diagnostic entity, he discussed a syndrome which bears a strong resemblance to the hyperactive subtype of ADHD as early as 1935. He described the 'extreme of restless, fidgety, Hyperkinetic child who is always on the go, can never sit still, always must be doing something' (Kanner, Tindal & Cox, 1935, p. 253). He subsequently described a syndrome characterised by daydreaming, lack of attention, and lack of concentration, which is similar to the DSM-IV definition of Attention Deficit Disorder.

In 1937 Charles Bradley, working at the Emma Pendleton Bradley Home in Providence, Rhode Island, USA, demonstrated the efficacy of Benzedrine, a central nervous system stimulant, in the treatment of ADHD. He administered benzedrine to children suffering with headache and noted a marked improvement in their behaviour and school performance (Bradley, 1937). This discovery marked a major milestone in the history of ADHD, and led to the use of dexamphetamine and methylphenidate in the treatment of hyperactivity.

1940–60

Despite the significant discovery of the use of psychostimulants in the treatment of ADHD, drugs were not widely used until the late 1950s. This, it was believed, was due to the psychoanalytic climate which prevailed in society during the 1940s and 1950s (Laufer *et al.*, 1957; Laufer, 1975), which resisted the idea that hyperactive behaviour had a biological basis.

1960–70

From minimal brain damage to minimal brain dysfunction

During the early 1960s several clinicians began to question the concept of brain damage as the only cause of childhood hyperactivity. Kanner recommended that 'lay persons should be discouraged from the much too frequent practice of using the term brain damage or brain injury as an everyday cliché'. Birch (1964), Herbert (1964) and Rapin (1964) questioned the assumption that brain damage caused behaviour problems on the basis that most children with behaviour problems demonstrated no physical evidence of brain damage. In 1963 the Oxford International Study Group of Child Neurology (MacKeith and Bax, 1963) stated that brain damage could not be inferred from behaviour alone, and recommended that the term 'minimal brain damage' be replaced by 'minimal brain dysfunction' (MBD). In the USA, a national task force devised an official definition (Clements, 1966):

> The term minimal brain dysfunction refers to children of near average, average or above average general intelligence with certain learning or behavioural disabilities ranging from mild to severe, which are associated with deviations of function of the central nervous system. These deviations may manifest themselves by various combinations of impairment in perception, conceptualisation, language, memory and control of attention, impulse or motor function.

The term MBD emphasised the role of organic factors in the aetiology of ADHD and challenged the prevailing psychoanalytic theories of the time that proposed that the disorder was due to poor parenting.

During the late 1950s and early 1960s, clinicians such as Laufer (1957) and Chess (1960) started introducing terms such as 'hyperkinetic behaviour syndrome'. They began to recognise the key symptoms of hyperactivity and impulsivity, and moved away from the prevailing theories of brain damage or dysfunction. The disorder hyperkinetic reaction of childhood first appeared in DSM-II *Diagnostic and Statistical Manual of Mental Disorders* in 1968 (APA, 1968). The term emphasised overactivity as the cardinal feature of the syndrome rather than minimal brain damage or dysfunction.

The 1960s also saw the development of parent and teacher rating scales for diagnostic assessment of symptoms of hyperactivity and monitoring response to treatment. These questionnaires allowed for a standardised assessment of children's behaviour in home and school settings.

1970–80

Interest in the concept of hyperactivity mushroomed in the 1970s, particularly in the USA. Symptoms such as inattention, overactivity and impulsivity began to be recognised as the core symptoms of the disorder. The shift to an emphasis on inattention began when Virginia Douglas and her team at McGill University suggested that deficits in the ability to sustain attention underlay the observed symptoms of hyperactivity and poor impulse control. She contended that these were the areas in which stimulant medication was most effective (Douglas, 1972).

The work of Douglas and her team was influential in the re-categorisation of the disorder in DSM-III (APA, 1980) as Attention Deficit Disorder with and without hyperactivity, thus emphasising the attentional aspects of the disorder, rather than hyperactivity. DSM-III defined ADD with hyperactivity as a tri-dimensional disorder characterised by developmentally inappropriate inattention, impulsivity and hyperactivity with symptoms and cut-offs to operationalise the diagnosis.

Coinciding with the work of Douglas, researchers in Northern Europe became more interested in the concept of hyperactivity as a diagnostic entity. 1977 marked the inclusion of 'Hyperkinetic syndrome of childhood' in ICD-9 (WHO, 1977), as a disorder in which the essential features are 'short attention span and distractibility'.

1980–90

DSM was revised in 1987 (DSM-III-R, APA, 1987). The revised edition listed 14 symptoms, some referring to attention and some to hyperactivity and impulsivity, requiring eight symptoms for a diagnosis. The criteria also necessitated onset of symptoms prior to age seven. DSM-III-R also included a category of Undifferentiated Attention Deficit Disorder which excluded hyperactivity and impulsivity. There was no subtyping in DSM-III-R.

1990–2005

In preparation of the ICD-10 and DSM-IV the working parties of the WHO and the APA liaised closely in drawing up diagnostic criteria for childhood hyperactivity. Although the newest editions of both systems are almost compatible, significant differences remain between the definition of Hyperkinetic Disorder (HD) and the criteria for ADHD, in their diagnostic criteria, definition of pervasiveness, the role of inattention and the inclusion of comorbidity.

The ICD definition of hyperkinetic disorder emphasises the presence of at least six inattentive, three hyperactive and one impulsive symptom in home and school settings, together with the direct observation of this behaviour (WHO, 1992). DSM in contrast requires that symptoms of hyperactivity, impulsivity or inattention must be present in two or more settings, but does not require direct observation of the symptoms by the clinician.

In addition, ICD requires that anxiety disorders, mood disorders, pervasive developmental disorders or schizophrenia pre-empt a diagnosis of hyperkinetic disorder, while DSM allows for comorbid mood, anxiety and psychotic disorders, as long as the symptoms are not better accounted for by, or occur exclusively during the course of these other diagnoses.

ICD also describes a Combined Hyperkinetic Conduct Disorder category, which is classified as ADHD plus comorbid Oppositional Defiant Disorder or Conduct Disorder in DSM. The current classification system will be described in the next chapter. While similarities and differences between the two classification systems will be discussed, the focus of the chapter will be on DSM-IV.

1.3   CONCLUSION

This chapter outlines the history of the evolution of ADHD as a valid diagnostic entity. Clinical interest in the disorder has mushroomed over the past century, and this is reflected in the systematic increase in scientific literature. The future for ADHD looks bright. The nineteenth and twentieth centuries have a lot to show for themselves. Standardised rating scales have been developed to validate the diagnosis, and multimodal treatment approaches are available. Scientific literature continues to blossom and children are being maintained in mainstream education. The twenty-first century has a lot to offer and we look forward with optimism to further developments.

1.4 REFERENCES

Albutt TC (1892) Insanity in children. In: D Hack Tuke (ed.) *A Dictionary of Psychological Medicine*. London: JA Churchill.

American Psychiatric Association (1968) *Diagnostic and Statistical Manual of Mental Disorders* (2nd edn) [DSM-II]. Washington, DC: APA.

American Psychiatric Association (1980) *Diagnostic and Statistical Manual of Mental Disorders* (3rd edn) [DSM-III]. Washington, DC: APA.

American Psychiatric Association (1987) *Diagnostic and Statistical Manual of Mental Disorders* (3rd edn, rev.) [DSM-III-R]. Washington, DC: APA.

American Psychiatric Association (1994) *Diagnostic and Statistical Manual of Mental Disorders* (4th edn) [DSM-IV]. Washington DC: APA.

Birch HG (1964) *Brain Damage in Children: The Biological and Social Aspects*. Baltimore: Williams & Wilkens.

Bradley C (1937) The behaviour of children receiving Benzedrine. *American Journal of Psychiatry* **94**: 577–85.

Cadell T, Davis W (1976). *An Enquiry into the Nature and Origin of Mental Derangement: Comprehending a Concise System of the Physiology and Pathology of the Mind and a History of the Passions and Their Effects*. New York: AMS Press.

Cantwell DP (1975) *The Hyperactive Child*. New York: Spectrum.

Chess S (1960) Diagnosis and treatment of the hyperactive child. *New York State Journal of Medicine* **60**: 2379–85.

Clements SD (1966) *Minimal Brain Dysfunction in Children: Terminology and Identification: Phase One of a Three-Phase Project*. Washington, DC: US Department of Health, Education and Welfare.

Clements SD, Peters JE (1962) Minimal brain dysfunctions in the school age child: diagnosis and treatment. *Archives General Psychiatry* **6**: 185–97.

Clousten TS (1966) Stages of over-excitability, hypersensitiveness, and mental explosiveness in children and their treatment by the bromides. *Scottish Medical and Surgical Journal* **4**: 481–90.

Conners C (1969) A teacher rating scale for use in drug studies with children. *Am J Psychiatry* **125**: 884–8.

Conners C (1997) *Conners' Rating Scale-Revised Technical Manual*. North Tonawanda, NY: Multi-Health Systems.

Crichton A (1798) *An Inquiry into the Nature and Origin of Mental Derangement*. London: T. Cadell & W. Davies.

Douglas VI (1972) Stop, look and listen: the problem of sustained attention and impulse control in hyperactive and normal children. *Canadian Journal of Behavioural Science* **4**: 259–82.

Haslam J (1809) *Observations on Madness and Melancholy including Practical Remarks on these diseases together with Cases*. London: J Callow.

Herbert M (1964) The concept and testing of brain damage in children – a review. *Journal of Child Psychology and Psychiatry* **5**: 197–217.

Hoff H (1956) *Lehrbuch der Psychiatrie*, vol. II. Basel: Benno Schwabe.

Kahn E, Cohen LH (1934) Organic driveness: a brainstem syndrome and an experience with case reports. *New England Journal of Medicine* **210**: 748–56.

Kanner L (1957) *Child Psychiatry*, 3rd edn. Springfield, IL: Charles C Thomas.

Kanner L (1959) The thirty-third Maudsley lecture: trends in child psychiatry. *J. Ment Sci* **105**: 581–93.

Laufer MW (1975). In Osler's day it was syphilis. In EJ Anthony (ed.) *Explorations in Child Psychiatry*, pp. 105–24. New York: Plenum Press.

Laufer MW, Denhoff E, Solomans G (1957) Hyperkinetic impulse disorder in children's behaviour problems. *Psychosomatic Medicine* **19**: 38–49.

MacKeith RC, Bax MCO (1963) *Minimal Cerebral Dysfunction: Papers from the International Study Group held at Oxford, September, 1962.* Little Club Clinics in Development Medicine, No 10, London: Heinemann.

Maudsley H (1867) *The Physiology and Pathology of the Mind.* London: Macmillan.

Neve M, Turner T (1995) What the doctor thought and did: Sir James Crichton-Browne (1840–1938). *Medical History* **39**(4): 399–432.

Palmer ED, Finger S (2001) An early description of Attention Deficit Hyperactivity Disorder. *Child Psychology and Psychiatry Review* **6**(2): 66–73.

Rapin I (1964) Brain damage in children. In J Brenneman (ed.) *Practice of Paediatrics*, vol. 4. Hagerstown: MD Prior.

Ross DM, Ross SA (1982) *Hyperactivity: Current Issues, Research and Theory*, 2nd edn. New York: Wiley.

Sandberg S, Barton J (1996) Historical development. In S Sandberg (ed.) *Hyperactivity Disorders of Childhood*, pp. 1–25. Cambridge: Cambridge University Press.

Stein RH (1913) Moral insanity. *Journal of Mental Science* **59**: 478–86.

Still GF (1902) The Coulstonian lectures on some abnormal psychial conditions in children. *Lancet* **1**: 1008–12, 1077–82, 1163–8.

Tredgold AF (1908) *Mental Deficiency (Amentia).* New York: W Wood.

Winnicott DW (1931) *Clinical Notes on Disorders of Childhood.* London: Heinemann.

World Health Organization (1977) *Mental Disorders: Glossary and Guide to their Classification in Accordance with the Ninth Revision of the International Classification of Diseases.* Geneva: World Health Organization.

World Health Organization (1992) The ICD 10. *Classification of Mental and Behavioural Disorders: Diagnostic Criteria for Research*, Geneva: World Health Organization.

2 Diagnosis and Classification of ADHD in Childhood

LOUISE SHARKEY[1] **AND MICHAEL FITZGERALD**[2]

1. Beechpark Services for Children on the Autistic Spectrum, Dublin, Ireland;
2. Trinity College Dublin, Ireland

2.1 OVERVIEW

Attention Deficit Hyperactivity Disorder (ADHD) is a persistent and impairing disorder resulting from abnormal levels of inattentive, hyperactive and impulsive behaviour. By definition, its onset is prior to age seven, mostly before age five. It often persists into adolescence and adult life and puts sufferers at risk of a range of adverse outcomes, including educational and occupational underachievement, antisocial behaviour and delinquency. As a condition, ADHD affects 8–12% of children worldwide (Faraone *et al.*, 2003) and represents up to 40% of referrals to child psychiatric clinics (Safer & Allen, 1976). Despite the high prevalence of this disorder ADHD remains under-diagnosed and under-treated and its validity as a diagnostic entity is frequently challenged. The focus of this chapter is to review the current understanding of the diagnosis and classification of ADHD in childhood. In addition, we will describe the rating scales used in aiding diagnosis. We begin by tracing the evolution of our understanding of the syndrome and examining the different subtypes.

2.2 WHY CLASSIFY?

Classification attempts to group cases according to distinguishing patterns of symptomatology. Classification of illness (nosology) is essential in order to categorise the observed symptoms, to communicate about the illness, to form a treatment plan, to determine prognosis and to inform scientific research. The merits of a good classification system are comprehensiveness, acceptability to users, clarity and the ability to change with emerging scientific evidence. Critics of classification argue that applying a diagnostic category stigmatises a patient and implies that all persons with this label are the same. This serves to distract from understanding the person's unique personal difficulties, which can impact on prognosis and dictate treatment regimens.

Most medical conditions can be classified on the basis of aetiology; for example, tuberculosis and coronary artery disease. While some psychiatric

Handbook of Attention Deficit Hyperactivity Disorder. Edited by M. Fitzgerald, M. Bellgrove and M. Gill.
© 2007 John Wiley & Sons Ltd

diagnoses have recognised physical aetiology (such as Down's Syndrome, Fragile X syndrome), most can be classified only on the basis of observed symptoms. This is most problematic in child psychiatry, particularly in the diagnosis of ADHD, which is viewed by some as being an extreme of normal childhood behaviour (Baughman, 2001), caused by normal childhood energy, overstressed parents or restrictive classroom curriculum (McCubbin & Cohen, 1997; Breggin, 2001).

Clinicians need a classification framework to clarify misconceptions about ADHD. Such a framework proves that psychiatrists have rules of evidence for establishing the validity of disorders and that these rules have established ADHD as a valid psychiatric diagnosis.

DSM-IV (American Psychiatric Association, 1994) and ICD-10 (American Psychiatric Association, 1994) constitute the two major psychiatric classification systems used throughout the world. The DSM system is used mainly in the USA, whereas ICD is used predominantly in Europe. ICD refers to ADHD as Hyperkinetic Disorder (HKD). While similarities and differences between the two classification systems will be outlined, for the most part we adopt the DSM convention of using the term ADHD to refer to both systems.

2.3   THE EVOLUTION OF ADHD AS A DIAGNOSTIC ENTITY

Attention Deficit Hyperactivity Disorder (ADHD) was initially described by George Still in 1901 (Still, 1902). Dr Still recounted problems of overactivity, inattention, and poor inhibitory volition in a case series of 20 children. He also observed aggressiveness, defiance, resistance to discipline, lawlessness, spitefulness and dishonesty. In today's nomenclature the latter would be diagnosed as Oppositional Defiant Disorder or Conduct Disorder, which are often comorbid with ADHD.

In 1917 a syndrome of overactivity and distractibility was described following a pandemic of Encephalitis Lethargica. Attention focused on the causal role of brain damage arising from infection and named Minimal Brain Dysfunction (Kahn & Cohen, 1934; Clements, 1966) with inattention, hyperactivity and impulsiveness seen as evidence of brain damage.

Since then successive editions of the DSM have revised the diagnostic criteria and subtyping associated with ADHD. DSM-II (APA, 1968) recognised a disorder known as Hyperkinetic Disorder of Childhood with hyperactivity as the principal symptom. DSM-III described operational criteria for diagnostic categories of ADD with and without hyperactivity, with a requirement for three inattentive, three impulsive and two hyperactive symptoms to be present to attain a diagnosis. This distinction was abolished in the revised edition that described a single list of 14 items incorporating symptoms of inattention, hyperactivity and impulsivity, with an eight-item cut off for diagnosis. This change implied that symptoms of ADHD were on a continuum from low to high numbers of symptoms. DSM-IV, based on factor analysis of field trials, returned to a categorical classification describing three subtypes of ADHD:

Table 2.1. DSM criteria for Attention Deficit Hyperactivity Disorder

A. **Either (1) or (2):**

(1) Six or more of the following symptoms of inattention have persisted for at least 6 months to a degree that is maladaptive and inconsistent with developmental level:

Inattention

(a) often fails to give close attention to details or makes careless mistakes in schoolwork, work or other activities
(b) often has difficulty sustaining attention in tasks or play activities
(c) often does not seem to listen when spoken to directly
(d) often does not follow through on instructions and fails to finish schoolwork, chores or duties in the workplace (not due to oppositional behaviour or failure to understand instructions)
(e) often has difficulty organizing tasks and activities
(f) often avoids, dislikes or is reluctant to engage in tasks that require sustained mental effort (such as schoolwork or homework)
(g) often loses things necessary for tasks or activities (e.g. toys, school assignments, pencils, books or tools)
(h) is often easily distracted by extraneous stimuli
(i) is often forgetful in daily activities

(2) Six (or more) of the following symptoms of hyperactivity-impulsivity have persisted for at least 6 months to a degree that is maladaptive and inconsistent with developmental level:

Hyperactivity

(a) often fidgets with hands or feet or squirms in seat
(b) often leaves seat in classroom or in other situations where remaining seated is expected
(c) often runs about or climbs excessively in situations in which it is inappropriate (in adolescents or adults, may be limited to subjective feelings of restlessness)
(d) often has difficulty playing or engaging in leisure activities quietly
(e) is often 'on the go' or acts as if 'driven by a motor'
(f) often talks excessively

Impulsivity

(g) often blurts out answers before questions have been completed
(h) often has difficulty awaiting turn
(i) often interrupts or intrudes on others (e.g. butts into conversations or games)

B. Some hyperactive-impulsive or inattentive symptoms that caused impairment were present before age 7 years.

C. Some impairment from the symptoms is present in two or more settings (e.g. at school (or work) and at home).

D. There must be clear evidence of clinically significant impairment in social, academic or occupational functioning.

E. The symptoms do not occur exclusively during the course of a pervasive developmental disorder, schizophrenia or other psychotic disorder and are not better accounted for by another mental disorder (e.g. mood disorder, anxiety disorder, dissociative disorder or a personality disorder).

Table 2.2. ICD 10 Diagnostic Criteria for Hyperkinetic Disorder

1. Demonstrated abnormality of attention and activity at home, for the age and developmental level of the child, as evidenced in at least three of the following attention problems:
   (a) short duration of spontaneous activities
   (b) often leaving play activities unfinished
   (c) over-frequent changes between activities
   (d) undue lack of persistence at tasks set by adults
   (e) unduly high distractibility during study, e.g. homework or reading assignment and by at least two of the following activity problems:
   (f) continuous motor activity (running, jumping, etc.)
   (g) markedly excessive fidgeting and wriggling during spontaneous activities
   (h) markedly excessive activity in situations expecting relative stillness (e.g. meal times, travel, visiting, church)
   (i) difficulty in remaining seated when required

2. Demonstrable abnormality of attention and activity at school or nursery (if applicable), for the age and developmental level of the child, as evidenced by at least two of the following attention problems:
   (a) undue lack of persistence at tasks
   (b) unduly highly distractible, i.e. often orientating towards extrinsic stimuli
   (c) overfrequent changes between activities when choice is allowed
   (d) excessively short duration of play activities and by at least two of the following activity problems:
   (e) continuous and excessive motor restlessness (running, jumping, etc.) in situations allowing free activity
   (f) markedly excessive fidgeting and wriggling in structured situations
   (g) excessive levels of off-task activity during tasks
   (h) unduly often out of seat when required to be sitting

3. Directly observed abnormality of attention or activity. This must be excessive for the child's age and developmental level. The evidence may be of any of the following:
   (a) direct observation of the criteria in 1 or 2 above, i.e. the report of parent and or teacher
   (b) observation of abnormal levels of motor activity, or off-task behaviour, or lack of persistence in activities, in setting outside home or school (e.g. clinic or laboratory)
   (c) significant impairment of performance on psychometric tests of attention

4. Does not meet criteria for pervasive developmental disorder, mania or depressive or anxiety disorder

5. Onset before the age of 6 years

6. Duration of at least 6 months

1. *Predominantly Inattentive* – the presence of six or more symptoms of inattention and fewer than six symptoms of hyperactivity-impulsivity.
2. *Predominantly Hyperactive/Impulsive* – the presence of six or more symptoms of hyperactivity-impulsivity and fewer than six symptoms of inattention and
3. *Combined* – the presence of six or more inattentive and six or more hyperactive-impulsive symptoms.

2.4 COMPARISON OF DSM-IV AND ICD-10

Historically the reported prevalence rates for ICD-9 Hyperkinetic Syndrome and DSM-III attention deficit disorder with hyperactivity (ADDH) varied by as much as a factor of 20 (Prendergast *et al.*, 1988; Szatmari *et al.*, 1989; Taylor *et al.*, 1991; Taylor & Sandberg, 1984). This variance was thought to reflect differences in diagnostic practice and conceptualisation of behaviour.

In preparation of the ICD-10 and DSM-IV the working parties of the WHO and the APA liaised closely in drawing up diagnostic criteria for childhood hyperactivity. Although the newest editions of both systems are almost compatible, significant differences remain between the definition of Hyperkinetic Disorder (HD) and the criteria for ADHD, in their diagnostic criteria, definition of pervasiveness, the role of inattention and the inclusion of comorbidity.

The ICD definition of hyperkinetic disorder emphasises the presence of at least six inattentive, three hyperactive and one impulsive symptom in home and school settings, together with the direct observation of this behaviour (American Psychiatric Association, 1994). DSM in contrast requires that symptoms of hyperactivity, impulsivity or inattention must be present in two or more settings, but does not require direct observation of the symptoms by the clinician.

In addition, ICD requires that anxiety disorders, mood disorders, pervasive developmental disorders or schizophrenia pre-empt a diagnosis of hyperkinetic disorder, while DSM allows for comorbid mood, anxiety and psychotic disorders, as long as the symptoms are not better accounted for by, or occur exclusively during the course of, these other diagnoses. ICD also describes a Combined Hyperkinetic Conduct Disorder category, which is classified as ADHD plus comorbid Oppositional Defiant Disorder or Conduct Disorder in DSM.

There is considerable overlap between cases identified by ICD and DSM diagnostic systems (Tripp *et al.*, 1999), with the majority of children diagnosed with hyperkinetic disorder also meeting criteria for ADHD. Children who meet criteria for both ADHD and HD display more severe difficulties with hyperactivity, inattention and impulsivity and this is reflected in the increased number of children in this group who meet criteria for the combined type ADHD. These children are more impaired on measures of academic and cognitive functioning and tend to be significantly younger than children meeting DSM criteria. This subgroup represents approximately 20% of those defined as ADHD by DSM and is thought to be less responsive to methylphenidate (Taylor *et al.*, 1987, 1991).

Together the cognitive and behavioural differences between the two ADHD groups suggest the ICD description of hyperkinetic disorder is identifying a more seriously impaired and younger subset of the population of children who meet diagnostic criteria for ADHD. In addition, in countries in which the ICD system is used in the diagnosis of mental disorders, children with inattention or overactivity but not both may go undiagnosed and possibly untreated.

The majority of children diagnosed with HKD also present with a delay in motor development (Taylor *et al.*, 1991). The term DAMP – disorder of attention, motor control and perception – refers to the combination of these deficits (Gillberg & Gillberg 1988, 1989). Approximately half of children with ADHD present with motor clumsiness and perceptual problems, thus meeting criteria for DAMP (Langdren *et al.*, 1996). Children meeting criteria for both DAMP plus ADHD represent a subgroup with more academic difficulties than either disorder alone.

The differences between the two diagnostic systems have implications for research. Results of studies using ICD criteria for diagnosis may be generalisable to children fulfilling DSM criteria for ADHD combined type, but may not apply to the inattentive or hyperactive-impulsive subtype. In addition, as ICD is used worldwide for recording morbidity statistics, the recording of prevalence rates is likely to be inflated in those countries using DSM for clinical diagnoses.

2.5   CATEGORICAL VS DIMENSIONAL CLASSIFICATION

There is continued debate as to whether ADHD is best regarded as a categorical or dimensional disorder. A categorical approach assumes that individuals who meet 6 out of 9 symptoms and therefore meet criteria for ADHD differ from those who meet 5 out of 9 and don't meet criteria. Using this approach the former have a discrete diagnosis that differs qualitatively from normal. A dimensional classification system of ADHD assumes that the entire population inherit some behaviours of ADHD but for some these difficulties are sufficiently severe to provide 'clear evidence of clinically significant impairment in social, academic or occupational functioning' (DSM-IV; APA, 1994). Using this approach ADHD is viewed as the extreme end of a continuum rather than a discrete entity. Affected individuals are quantitatively but not qualitatively different from unaffected individuals.

While categorical approaches are effective for communication, planning intervention and accessing resources, they may obscure quantitative differences among children with ADHD and impairment among those who are just below threshold for a diagnosis (Angold *et al.*, 1999).

Dimensional ratings of disruptive behaviour on the other hand have been shown to be better predictors of outcome and more useful for research purposes than categorical measures (Fergusson & Horwood, 1995). However, they are less effective in describing comorbidity and difficult for communication.

2.6   EVIDENCE FOR THE VALIDITY OF ADHD AS A DIAGNOSIS

Compelling evidence supports the diagnosis of attention deficit hyperactivity as a valid psychiatric disorder. Children diagnosed according to DSM or ICD criteria demonstrate a consistent pattern of symptoms and signs that clearly demarcate them from children with other behavioural disorders (Frick *et al.*, 1994; Lahey *et al.*, 1994). In addition, this pattern is associated with clinically meaningful impairments (Barkley, 1998). In general, the core symptoms of ADHD have a predictable natural history with onset in early childhood, running a chronic course and persisting into adulthood in approximately 60% (Barkley *et al.*, 2002).

Family, twin and adoption studies show ADHD is a highly heritable disorder (Faraone *et al.*, 1998) as heritable as schizophrenia and bipolar affective disorder.

Molecular genetic studies also implicate the role of genes in the aetiology of ADHD (Faraone *et al.*, 2004).

Children with ADHD show specific abnormalities on neuroimaging. These include abnormalities in the frontal-subcortical-cerebellar pathways involved in the control of attention, inhibition and motor behaviour (Faraone & Biederman, 2004).

2.7 SUBTYPES

A number of different subtypes of ADHD have been recognised, based on diagnostic criteria used, pervasiveness of symptoms, phenomenology, and patterns of comorbidity.

DSM-IV recognises three homogenous subtypes of ADHD: the inattentive (I), hyperactive-impulsive (HI) and the combined subtype (C). Each of these subtypes have distinctive patterns of comorbidity and cognitive functioning (McBurnett *et al.*, 1999; Marks *et al.*, 1999). The C and HI subtypes are more often diagnosed in boys (9.1 vs. 2.6%) and the I subtype in girls (Wolraich *et al.*, 1996). I and C subtypes are equally prevalent among school-aged children and more common than the HI subtype (Morgan *et al.*, 1996; Faraone *et al.*, 1998), which is thought to decrease with age and may actually be a developmental precursor to the C subtype (Cantwell & Baker, 1988). The C subtype tends to be associated with a younger age of symptom onset (Faraone *et al.*, 1998) and to present with higher rates of comorbid oppositional defiant disorder (ODD) and conduct disorder (CD) than the I subtype (Carlson & Mann, 2000; Lahey & Willcutt, 2002).

In contrast, ICD does not permit subtypes. To meet criteria for HKD a child must have symptoms of inattention, hyperactivity and impulsiveness.

2.7.1 SUPPORT FOR THE RELIABILITY AND VALIDITY OF ADHD SUBTYPES

Latent class analysis (LCA) of ADHD symptoms suggests multiple independent forms of ADHD. LCA reveals that specific symptoms cluster among the three DSM-IV subtypes (Hudziak *et al.*, 1998), with familial clustering of the same subtype combinations for every DSM-IV type, excluding hyperactive-impulsive and all latent classes with genetic influences contributing to patterns of subtype concordance (Rasmussen *et al.*, 2004).

2.7.2 NEUROCOGNITIVE DIFFERENCES BETWEEN THE SUBTYPES

Differences in the neurophysiological profile between the subtypes have been reported. EEG recordings of the frontal lobes of ADHD combined subtype children have shown differences in θ, α, and β bands in the frontal lobes, relative to ADHD-inattentive (ADHD-I) subtype children (Clarke *et al.*, 2001).

Differences between the subtypes have also been demonstrated on neuropsychological testing with the C-subtype showing more deficits in time reproduction (Mullins *et al.*, 2005), motor inhibition and planning relative to the I subtype who present more problems in set shifting and interference control (Klorman *et al.*, 1999, Nigg *et al.*, 2002). In addition, children in the I subtype have been described as having a sluggish cognitive tempo (Carlson & Mann, 2002) that may result in the DSM-IV inattentive symptoms such as not listening, not following through on instructions, losing things and forgetfulness. These are qualitatively different from the inattentive symptoms displayed by the C-subtype, which are characterised by deficits in response inhibition and problems with resistance to distraction and persistence of effort (Pauermeister *et al.*, 2005).

2.7.3   GENETICS

There is a growing literature to support the view that ADHD is familial and in a large part genetic. Most controlled family studies report a higher risk of ADHD in first-degree relatives of probands with ADHD than in normal controls. For example, the prevalence of ADHD among biological relatives of ADHD probands (24%) is up to three and a half times greater than normal controls (7%) (Faraone, Biederman & Friedman, 2000). In addition, depending on the population sampled, higher inattentive subtype rates (10% vs. 4%) and combined subtype rates (11% vs. 2%), but not hyperactive-impulsive rates (2% vs. 1%) have been detected among first-degree relatives of ADHD probands compared to controls. However, rates of ADHD were not higher among relatives of DSM-IV combined type probands as compared to relatives of inattentive or hyperactive-impulsive probands.

Comparison of concordance rates in monozygotic and dizygotic twins strongly support genetic influences in ADHD. Studies using LCA and DSM-IV criteria have found significant familial clustering of same subtype combinations and significant genetic influences contributing to these patterns of subtype concordance (Rasmussen *et al.*, 2004). The heritability of hyperactive-impulsive and inattentive behaviours in twin samples has been found to be as high as 90% (Hudziak *et al.*, 1998).

2.7.4   COMORBIDITY

Another source of subtype arises from the co-occurrence of other psychiatric disorders with ADHD. It appears to be the rule rather than the exception that children with hyperactivity will present with a second psychiatric disorder. There is huge diagnostic overlap between hyperactivity and other child psychiatric disorders and the nosological status of these combined conditions remains unclear. Do these children have hyperactivity or does their hyperactivity have a different meaning because it has arisen in the presence of another disorder (Ozonoff *et al.*, 1994)?

2.7.5   THE DISRUPTIVE BEHAVIOUR DISORDERS

The most common comorbid conditions are the disruptive disorders of conduct disorder (CD) and Oppositional Defiant Disorder (ODD), together affecting 40–60% of children and adolescents with ADHD (Wolraich *et al.*, 1996).

Children diagnosed with both ODD and ADHD have consistently been shown to present with more severe symptoms, more impairment, greater social deficit, higher rates of comorbidity and greater academic difficulties (Biederman *et al.*,

1996; Carlson *et al.*, 1997; Gadow & Nolan., 2002). This applies across the age ranges and suggests that ODD + ADHD may constitute a discrete clinical entity.

An increased frequency of CD or antisocial behaviours in the first-degree relatives of ADHD probands with CD, compared with ADHD probands without CD as well as cosegregation of ADHD + CD in relatives, suggests that ADHD + CD may reflect a distinct genetic group in ADHD (Faraone *et al.*, 1997).

DSM-IV classifies ADHD plus CD as two separate disorders. In contrast, ICD-10 identifies a subtype of HD plus CD. Children presenting with a diagnosis of hyperactive conduct disorder have distinct characteristics that delineate them from children with hyperactivity or CD alone. This group presents at an early age, runs a persistent course and is more vulnerable to delinquency and school failure (Loeeber *et al.*, 1990; Moffit, 1990). In addition, there is evidence of shared genetic risk factors in hyperactivity and conduct disorder (Nadder *et al.*, 1998).

2.7.6 TOURETTE'S SYNDROME AND OBSESSIVE COMPULSIVE DISORDER

In clinic samples ADHD, OCD and tics commonly co-occur. Up to 50% of individuals with Tourette's Syndrome also meet diagnostic criteria for ADHD. Children with comorbid ADHD+TS are at increased risk for externalising and internalising behaviour problems and poor social adaptation compared to children with either disorder alone (Carter *et al.*, 2000). Most of this adverse effect appears to be associated with the co-occurrence of ADHD as children with TS alone tend to do better (Carter *et al.*, 2000).

The overlap of ADHD and OCD has also been documented (Peterson *et al.*, 2001). As many as 30% of children and adolescents with OCD also satisfy diagnostic criteria for ADHD (Geller *et al.*, 1996). Findings suggest that this group represent a true comorbid state of OCD plus ADHD with significantly more impairment than either group alone (Geller *et al.*, 2002).

Family, immunological and neuroimaging studies suggest a common genetic aetiology for ADHD, OCD and tic disorders (Pauls *et al.*, 1986; Peterson *et al.*, 2000) that may be variably expressed as either one or a combination of all three disorders.

2.7.7 READING DISABILITY

Reading disabilities commonly co-occur with ADHD with up to 15% of children with the disorder affected (Adams *et al.*, 1999). Twin studies suggest that ADHD and reading disability have a common genetic aetiology, suggesting that they may be heterogenous expressions of a single genetic diathesis (Stevenson *et al.*, 1993).

2.7.8 BIPOLAR AFFECTIVE DISORDER

There is an ongoing debate as to whether juvenile mania is misdiagnosed as ADHD (Biederman *et al.*, 1998). Pre-pubertal mania is extremely rare (Costello *et al.*, 1997; Meltzer *et al.*, 2003), but behavioural difficulties fulfilling criteria for ADHD have been shown to pre-date episodes of bipolar disorder in adolescents (Strober *et al.*,

1988) and it is unclear as to whether these represent a diagnosis of ADHD or mania. Symptoms of ADHD and mania overlap. Core symptoms for both disorders include distractibility, hyperactivity, overtalkativeness and irritability. Children and adolescents with a combination of ADHD and manic symptoms are significantly more impaired than those with ADHD alone (Carlson & Kelly, 1998) and it has been speculated that they may represent a distinct clinical subtype of ADHD.

Differentiating between a diagnosis of ADHD and mania is difficult but can be assisted by assessment of the course of symptoms: bipolar disorder is a remitting and relapsing illness, whereas ADHD is chronic. Also the mania of bipolar disorder has been shown not to present before puberty. In contrast, mania comorbid with ADHD has been found to have an onset before age five years (Biederman *et al.*, 1996).

2.7.9   ANXIETY DISORDERS

Anxiety disorders co-occur in approximately 20% of children with ADHD. The most common anxiety disorders are generalised anxiety disorder, obsessive compulsive disorder, separation anxiety disorder and social phobia (Gellar *et al.*, 1996). Anxiety disorders exacerbate low self-esteem, and adversely affect cognition in children with ADHD (Manassis, Tannock & Barbosa, 2000). These children are often less resposive to stimulant medication and tend to report more severe side-effects (Tannock *et al.*, 1995) (see also Chapters 13 and 15).

2.8   PREVALENCE OF ADHD

Reports on the prevalence of ADHD/HKD have varied from 0.5% to 16% (Rowland *et al.*, 2001). The prevalence rate is affected by the diagnostic criteria used (DSM-III R, DSM-IV, ICD-10), methods of diagnosis (e.g. questionnaires or interviews), characteristics of the sample population (e.g. age and gender), number of informants used (parents only, teachers only or both), comorbidity (inclusion or exclusion of cases with a comorbid diagnosis), country and demographics of population sampled (rural vs. inner city). Community-based samples consistently reveal higher prevalence rates than school-based samples, as do inner-city populations. There is also a reported higher prevalence in lower socio-economic groups.

Comparisons of prevalence rates for various studies show that the highest prevalence is reported when using DSM criteria (Wolraich *et al.*, 1996). Studies using the DSM system, that include criteria for impairment, pervasiveness and comorbid disorders report prevalence rates between 5% and 10% (Offord *et al.*, 1987; Newman *et al.*, 1996). When more restrictive ICD-10 criteria are used and comorbid conditions are excluded, prevalence rates of 1–2% are found (Swanson *et al.*, 1998). The prevalence of ADHD plus DAMP is approximately 6% (Kadesjo & Gillberg, 1998).

Reported sex ratios for ADHD range from 3:1 to 8:1 (Lambert *et al.*, 1978). Highest rates are reported in school-aged boys, with a tendency for rates to decrease with increasing age.

2.9   GENDER

Most of the scientific literature concerning ADHD is derived from research based on studies using males, due to the greater preponderance of males in clinic-referred samples. Girls represent approximately one-fifth of referrals of cases of ADHD to child psychiatric clinics. Assuming a combined prevalence of 3%, the sex-specific prevalence of ADHD in females could be as high as 1% (Arnold, 1995, 1996). Despite this, relatively little is known about how girls with ADHD compare with boys and a review of gender comparisons reveals conflicting findings.

Most of the scientific literature cites evidence of poorer cognitive functioning in ADHD girls and more severe behaviour problems in ADHD boys. A meta-analysis of 17 clinic-based studies on ADHD gender differences by Gaub and Carlson (1997) suggested that girls with ADHD tend to be more intellectually impaired and have higher rates of mood and anxiety disorders. By contrast, boys were shown to have higher levels of hyperactivity and comorbid conduct disorder. Greene et al. (2001) found that, similarly to their male counterparts, girls with ADHD were at high risk for social impairment. Their study revealed few differences in social profiles across the genders, with the exception that boys with ADHD exhibited significantly greater social impairment at school. Biederman et al. (1999) found similarities in the core symptoms of hyperactivity, impulsivity and inattention between boys and girls, together with a preponderance of symptoms of inattention over those of hyperactivity and impulsivity in girls. Consistent with the literature (Gaub & Carlson, 1997) they cited lower rates of conduct disorder and higher rates of internalising disorders among girls with ADHD.

Wolraich et al. (1996) examined gender differences across ADHD subtypes and demonstrated higher rates of behaviour problems in boys than girls in the inattentive group, but identical rates in the other subtypes. Their findings highlight the importance of considering subtype membership when assessing ADHD gender differences. Graetz et al. (2005) extended Wolraich's findings to a non-clinical sample and demonstrated that girls with H-I subtype were no more impaired than controls without ADHD and questioned the validity of this subtype in non-referred female populations. They also showed that those with combined subtype were equally impaired as those with the inattentive. Findings of Wolraich et al. (1996) and Graetz et al. (2005) suggest that gender differences in ADHD symptom expression may possibly be overlooked in studies that collapse across type or include only those with the combined subtype.

The fact that conduct disorder is commonly associated with social impairment, family disruption and severe behaviour disturbance may be the reason why boys tend to present more frequently to the psychiatric services (Safer & Krager, 1988; Wilens & Biederman, 1992). In addition, ADHD may be unidentified in girls with comorbid mood and anxiety disorders where the focus of treatment intervention is on the latter. This is particularly problematic for the girls who show a preponderance of inattentive symptoms. This group of girls with ADHD and combined internalising disorders could represent a separate subgroup of ADHD who run a more complicated course and are less responsive to stimulant medication (Wilens & Biederman, 1992).

2.10   AGE OF ONSET

DSM-IV criteria for ADHD require evidence of impairment prior to age seven in order to make a diagnosis. This age of onset criteria (AOC) has recently been challanged on both theoretical and empirical grounds (Applegate *et al.*, 1997; Barkley & Biederman, 1997). These authors argue that because the age of onset has not been empirically validated, it should be broadened. These authors fear that the current restrictive criteria may deny diagnoses and resources to children who fail to come to the attention of the psychiatric services until middle childhood or adolescence.

Although most parents recall symptoms of ADHD prior to age seven, a substantial proportion of the inattentive group (26%) first report symptom onset after age seven (Applegate *et al.*, 1997) when increased educational demands make their symptoms more obvious. While some argue that the onset of ADHD-like symptoms in adolescence is not actually ADHD, but another Axis 1 disorder (Rucklidge & Tannock, 2002), others have pointed to the increased impairment associated with inattentive symptoms regardless of age of onset (Willoughy *et al.*, 2001).

Findings suggest that AOC has different implications depending on the subtype (Willoughby *et al.*, 2000). Children with ADHD show different patterns of comorbidity depending on age of onset. The early onset group are at increased risk for comorbid ODD and the late onset group are at increased risk for comorbid depression. However, both groups showed similar rates of comorbidity, impairment and impact on parental functioning, thus questioning the validity of the AOC as it applies to the inattentive subtype (Barkley & Biederman, 1997).

The validity of AOC as it applies to the hyperactive-impulsive subtype has also been questioned as over 90% of these children first exhibit symptoms prior to age seven.

In comparison, significant differences were noted in the combined subtype depending on age of onset. Similar to the inattentive subtype, elevated levels of combined symptoms were associated with more impairment regardless of age of onset. But those in the early onset group were at a dramatically increased risk for comorbid ODD, CD, anxiety disorders and depression. Thus for the combined subtype AOC identifies a group who experience worse clinical outcomes with more neurological pathology than their late onset peers (Taylor, 1999).

While diagnostic criteria stipulate an age of onset of ADHD symptoms prior to age seven, and it is good clinical practice to follow validated diagnostic guidelines, children do present with ADHD-like symptoms that are dated to after the age of seven. Denying these children a diagnosis deprives them of the intervention and services required to reach their full potential. In keeping with the DSM and ICD classification systems it has been recommended to classify these children as ADHD not otherwise specified and the former as ADHD.

2.11   RATING SCALES FOR ASSESSING ADHD SYMPTOMS

Rating scales for assessing ADHD symptoms serve a number of different purposes. They are useful in establishing a diagnosis, excluding differential diagnoses, screening large groups for the purpose of early intervention and monitoring treatment response. Rating scales measure quantitative differences, i.e. differences in the number or severity of symptoms and, while they are useful in aiding a diagnosis, they are no substitute for a thorough clinical assessment. Since the publication of DSM-IV and the re-conceptualisation of ADHD as consisting of three subtypes: inattentive, hyperactive and combined, scales have been developed to adequately assess these dimensions of ADHD.

In choosing a rating scale it is important to consider the scale's normative base and psychometric properties. If a scale includes youths that were not represented in the scale's normative sample, results can be difficult to interpret and may be misleading. Furthermore it is important to determine if the scale is valid for the population studied; for example, a scale based on DSM-IV criteria ensures validity for DSM-IV-defined ADHD, but not for other diagnostic criteria. Reliability will determine the scale's capacity to detect changes over time and must also be considered when choosing an appropriate scale to match a particular application.

Studies have shown that parents and teachers are the most reliable informants of the externalising behaviours of children (Loeber et al., 1991), and most of the rating scales for ADHD are completed by adult informants. Adults who rate children in different settings demonstrate only low to moderate agreement regarding the child's functioning (Achenbach et al., 1987). As DSM-IV criteria require impairment across settings, a multi-informant assessment is particularly important in establishing a diagnosis of ADHD.

Two types of rating scales are used, narrow-band scales and broad-band scales. The former are useful in forming a diagnosis or focusing on specific behaviours, while the latter are useful when considering differential diagnoses such as ODD, CD, depression, anxiety or learning disabilities. Broad-band scales such as the Child Behaviour Checklict (CBCL) (Achenbach & Rescorla, 2000) have few items per subscale so are useful for screening purposes but not for establishing a diagnosis. Also the length of these measurements makes them difficult for monitoring treatment. It is recommended that both narrow- and broad-band scales are used when conducting a comprehensive diagnostic assessment of ADHD. The narrow-band scales will form the focus of this chapter.

2.11.1 NARROW-BAND SCALES

Narrow-band scales based on DSM-IV have good face validity as their items are derived from a clear diagnostic construct for ADHD. Most require adult informants, are similar in format and have the same core subscales of inattention and hyperactivity/impulsivity. It is therefore difficult to determine if one scale is superior to another. Choosing a scale depends to a large extent on the need to screen for comorbid disorders, the intended informant (adult, adolescent), and psychometric properties of the scale itself. Following are brief summaries of the different narrow-band rating scales.

2.11.2 CONNERS' RATING SCALES-REVISED

The Conners' Rating Scale-Revised (CRS) (Conners, 1997) has the most extensive evidence base with both normative and clinical populations. CRS-R includes items specific to DSM-IV-defined ADHD and provides normative data that takes into account age and gender. Parent and teacher forms are available in full (80-item, 59-item) and abbreviated (27-item, 28-item) versions, thus facilitating repeat administration during treatment monitoring. It includes an adolescent self-report version, the Conners'-Wells' Adolescent Self Report Scale in both full and abbreviated forms. Both full and abbreviated versions share similar psychometric properties.

The parent-rated form has seven subscales and the teacher and adolescent six. The core subscales include Cognitive Problems/Inattention, Hyperactivity, Oppositional, Anxious-Shy, Perfectionism, Social Problems and for the parent form there is a seventh subscale, Psychosomatic. It also includes subscales specific to ADHD (Inattentive, Hyperactive/Impulsive and Total), global indices (Restless-Impulsive, Emotional lability and Total), and an ADHD index. T scores and percentile ranks are used, with scores above the 93rd percentile considered clinically significant.

The advantages of the CRS-R include a large normative base, good internal consistency between the subscales and strong psychometric properties. Multiple informant forms allow for a more thorough assessment and abbreviated versions facilitate treatment monitoring. However, the full form is lengthy to administer, thus restricting its use in some research protocols, and in adult informants with literacy problems.

2.11.3   IOWA CONNERS' TEACHER RATING SCALE

IOWA Conners' (Loney & Milich, 1982) is a 10-item scale, including 5 inattentive/overactive items (I/O) and 5 aggression items. It also comprises parent, teacher and adolescent report forms, although normative data are only available for the teacher version. Its brevity and sensitivity to treatment effects support its use in treatment monitoring and research. It should not, however, be used alone for diagnostic purposes.

2.11.4   SWANSON, NOLAN AND PELHAM-IV QUESTIONAIRE

The Swanson, Nolan and Pelham-IV Questionnaire (SNAP-IV) (Swanson, 1992) consists of both short and long versions in rating scale format to be completed by both parents and teachers. It does not include an adolescent self-report form. The short version of the SNAP-IV includes the core DSM-IV-derived ADHD subscales of Inattention, Hyperactivity/Impulsivity, and ODD. In addition to these subscales, the longer version includes items selected from other ADHD rating scales, in-cluding the Conners Index Questionaire (Conners, 1969), the IOWA Conners' Questionnaire (Loney & Milich, 1982) and the Swanson, Kotkin, Agler, M-Flynn and Pelham rating scale (SKAMP) (Swanson, 1992). In addition, the SNAP-IV contains 40 items extracted from DSM-IV-based criteria for internalising disorders, other externalising behaviours and motor disturbances. This facilitates a brief assessment of comorbidity.

The lack of representative normative data and published psychometric properties of the SNAP-IV is concerning. Data for age and gender are collapsed precluding interpretation of individual scores. Lack of test-retest reliability data make it difficult to interpret in clinical settings and despite its use clinically, it may be better suited to research.

2.11.5 SKAMP RATING SCALE

The SKAMP (Swanson, 1992) is a 10-item teacher-rated scale with separate sub-scales for measuring impairment due to inattention and behaviour problems. The SKAMP is included in the full version of the SNAP-IV.

There is no normative data for the SKAMP and psychometric studies are limited. Its main advantages are its brevity and sensitivity to treatment, facilitating its use in studies requiring repeated administration of scales and in treatment monitoring.

2.11.6 STRENGTHS AND WEAKNESSES OF ADHD SYMPTOMS AND NORMAL BEHAVIOUR

Strengths and Weaknesses of ADHD Symptoms and Normal Behaviour (SWAN) (Swanson *et al.*, 2001) is a modification of SNAP-IV. It is a relatively new scale which was developed in response to concerns that SNAP-IV may overidentify children with ADHD. It uses a Likert-type scale to reflect both strengths and weaknesses in a particular domain. No normative data or psychometric properties have been published for the SWAN.

2.11.7 ADHD RATING SCALE-IV

The ADHD Rating Scale-IV (ADHD RS-IV) (DuPaul *et al.*, 1998) is a parent- and teacher-rated scale directly derived from DSM-IV symptom criteria. The ADHD RS-IV consists of two subscales: Inattentive and Hyperactive/Impulsive. It has a large ethnically and geographically representative normative base and strong psychometric properties. It is particularly advantageous in clinical samples where, due to its brevity, easy scoring and sensitivity to treatment, it can be used in monitoring response to treatment.

2.11.8 VANDERBILT ADHD TEACHER RATING SCALE AND VANDERBILT ADHD PARENT RATING SCALE

The Vanderbilt ADHD Rating Scales (VARS) include both teacher (VADTRS) and parent report (VADPRS) versions (Wolraich *et al.*, 1998; Wolraich *et al.*, 2003). Like the CRS-R and SNAP-IV the VARS include items measuring ODD and CD and a subscale for anxiety and depression adapted from the Pediatric Behaviour Scale (Lindgren & Koeppel, 1987). In addition, the VADTRS includes items that assess school functioning and the VADPRS includes a comparable subscale to assess parents' perceptions of youth school and social functioning. As studies have focused on school-aged children, most of the data available relates to the VADTRS.

The VADTRS consists of four subscales relating to behaviour problems at school: Inattention, Hyperactivity/Impulsivity, Oppositional Defiant/Conduct Disorder, and Anxiety/Depression (Wolraich *et al.*, 1998), and two measuring school functioning:

Academic Performance and Behavioural Performance. The VADPRS consists of two subscales of Inattention and Hyperactivity/Impulsivity (Wolraich *et al.*, 2003b).

Preliminary studies suggest that VADTRS and VADPRS are psychometrically strong scales that could potentially be used in the assessment of ADHD. The additional subscales screen for comorbidity which may aid in devising treatment regimens. However, the VARS are new and require additional validity and normative data to establish their place among ADHD rating scales.

2.11.9   ADHD SYMPTOMS RATING SCALE

The ADHD Symptoms Rating Scale (ADHD-SRS) (Holland *et al.*, 2001) is a 56-item parent- and teacher-rated scale. Items are derived from DSM-IV. Factor analyses reveal two subscales: Inattention, Hyperactivity/Impulsivity, as well as a Total score. Normative data stratified by age and gender are available for a large representative sample. As it is a relatively new rating scale insufficient data relating to its psychometric properties are available.

2.11.10   ATTENTION DEFICIT DISORDER EVALUATION SCALE-SECOND EDITION

The Attention Deficit Disorder Evaluation Scale-Second Edition (ADDES-2) (McCarney, 1995a, 1995b) is a parent and teacher ADHD rating scale. It is based on DSM-IV and includes multiple items to tap each ADHD symptom, thus providing a thorough assessment of ADHD symptoms. Factor analyses reveal two subscales: Inattention and Hyperactivity/Impulsivity.

Few psychometric studies are available but reports based on data from the ADDES-2 manuals (McCarney, 1995a, 1995b) suggest strong psychometric functioning. Normative data are stratified by age and gender and extend down to four years of age. However, as it is a lengthy instrument, it is unsuitable for screening or monitoring response to treatment.

2.11.11   ACTeRS-SECOND EDITION

The ACTeRS-Second Edition (Ullman *et al.*, 2000) is an 11-item rating scale comprising separate parent, teacher and adolescent self-report versions. Both parent and teacher versions contain subscales for Attention, Hyperactivity, Social Skills and Oppositional Behaviour. In addition, the parent version contains a subscale for Early Childhood Problems. The adolescent self-report includes subscales for Attention, Hyperactivity/Impulsivity and Social Adjustment. Data regarding its psychometric properties is highly favourable for all three versions. However, scoring is confusing as lower scores imply greater problems and normative data is vague.

2.11.12   BROWN ATTENTION-DEFICIT DISORDER SCALES FOR CHILDREN AND ADOLESCENTS

Brown Attention-Deficit Disorder Scales for Children and Adolescents (BADDS) (Brown, 2001) measures underlying deficits in executive functioning in ADHD that are not detected by DSM-IV checklists. It was initially developed as a self-report scale for adolescents with the inattentive subtype of ADHD. It has since been updated to include separate rating scales for youths aged 3–7, 8–12 and 12–18 years old. Items in each scale are worded to reflect developmentally appropriate manifestations of ADHD. For ages 3–7 years separate versions are available for parents and teachers. There is a separate self-report scale for children aged 8–12. The adolescent version may be completed as a self-report and or a parent report.

All three versions of the BADDS include five clinically derived subscales: (1) Organising, Prioritising and Activating to work; (2) Focusing, Sustaining and Shifting Attention to Tasks; (3) Regulating Alertness, Sustaining Effort and Processing Speed; (4) Managing Frustration and Modulating Emotions; and (5) Utilising Working Memory and Accessing Recall. The versions for 3–7 year olds and 8–12 year olds include an additional subscale: Monitoring and Self-Regulating Action. A total inattentive score is obtained from the sum of these subscales.

The BADDS demonstrates strong psychometric properties across the age ranges. In addition, normative data stratified by age and gender is available for a large representative sample.

The BADDS is a unique scale which may detect nuances of ADHD that are not reflected in DSM-IV rating scales. The BADDS is especially useful for assessing the predominantly inattentive form of ADHD in conjunction with one of the narrow-band scales based on DSM-IV, such as CRS-R, SNAP-IV, ADDES-2, or the ADHD-SRS.

2.12 CONCLUSION

Ample evidence exists to support the diagnosis of ADHD as a valid psychiatric disorder. A comprehensive, multimodal clinical assessment in conjunction with validated rating scales can accurately diagnose the condition. These children have unique characteristics that distinguish them from children with other disruptive behaviour disorders. Their symptoms run a chronic course, frequently persisting into adulthood, and cause impairment in multiple areas of functioning. Inaccurate beliefs about the validity of ADHD as a diagnostic entity delay the progress of many children who do not receive adequate intervention. This suggests that a crucial part of treatment is educating parents and professionals about the nature of the disorder, and the rationale for treatment. Accurate information about the disorder should facilitate early intervention and reduce the adverse consequences that the disorder may impose on academic achievement and social interaction.

Frequent changes in diagnostic criteria suggest that the disorder and its diagnostic criteria are not fully understood and are subject to evolutionary changes in social, historical and professional practice. Uncertainty over the diagnosis of ADHD has led to the development of a number of validated rating scales to complement clinical evaluation. Many of these are in their early stages of development and require ongoing work to ensure their application in clinical practice.

2.13   REFERENCES

Achenbach TM, McConaughy SH, Howell CT (1987) Child/adolescent behavioural and emotional problems: implications of cross-informant correlations for situational specificity. *Psychol Bull* **101**: 213–32.

Achenbach TM, Rescorla LA (2000) *Manual for the ASEBA School-Age Forms & Profiles*. Burlington: University of Vermont, Research Center for Children, Youth and Families.

Adams JW, Snowling MJ, Hennessey SM, Kind P (1999) Problems of behaviour, reading and arithmetic: assessments of comorbidity using the strengths and difficulties questionnaire. *British Journal of Educational Psychology* **69**: 571–85.

American Psychiatric Association (1968) *Diagnostic and Statistical Manual of Mental Disorders* (2nd edn) [DSM-II]. Washington, DC: APA.

American Psychiatric Association (1994) *Diagnostic and Statistical Manual of Mental Disorders – IV*. Washington, DC: APA.

Angold A, Costello EJ, Farmer EM *et al.* (1999) Impaired but undiagnosed. *J Am Acad Child Adolesc Psychiatry* **38**: 129–37.

Applegate B, Lahey BB, Hart EL (1997) Validity of the age-of-onset criterion for ADHD: a report from the DSM-IV field trials. *J Am Acad Child Adolesc Psychiatry* **36**: 1211–21.

Arnold L (1995) ADHD sex differences. *J Abnorm Child Psychol* **23**: 555–69.

Arnold L (1996) Sex differences in ADHD: conference summary. *J Abnormal Child Psychology* **24**: 555–69.

Barkley RA (1998) *Attention Deficit Hyperactivity Disorder: A Handbook for Diagnosis and Treatment*. New York: Guilford.

Barkley RA, Biederman J (1997) Toward a broader definition of the age-of-onset criterion for Attention-Deficit Hyperactivity Disorder. *J Am Acad Child Adolesc Psychiatry* **36**: 1204–10.

Barkley RA, Fischer M, Smallish L, Fletcher K (2002) The persistence of Attention-Deficit Hyperactivity Disorder into young adulthood as a function of reporting source and definition of disorder. *J Abnorm Psychol* **111**: 279–89.

Baughman FA Jr (2001) Questioning the treatment for ADHD. *Science* **291**: 595.

Biederman J, Faraone SV, Mick E (1996) Attention deficit hyperactivity disorder and juvenile mania: an overlooked comorbidity? *J Am Acad Child Adolesc Psychiatry* **35**: 997–1008.

Biederman J, Faraone SV, Mick E *et al.* (1999) Clinical correlates of ADHD in females: findings from a large group of girls ascertained from paediatric and psychiatric referral sources. *J Am Acad Child Adolesc Psychiatry* **38**: 966–75.

Biederman J, Faraone SV, Milberger S (1996) Predictors of persistence and remission of ADHD into adolescence: results from a four year prospective follow-up study. *J Am Acad Child Adolesc Psychiatry* **35**: 343–51.

Biederman J, Klein RG, Pine DS, Klein DF (1998). Resolved: mania is mistaken for ADHD in prepubertal children. *J Am Acad Child Adolesc Psychiatry* **37**: 1091–9.

Breggin PR (2001) MTA Study has flaws. *Arch Gen Psychiatry* **58**: 1184.

Brown TE (2001) *Brown Attention-Deficit Disorder Scales for Children and Adolescents*. San Antonio, TX: Psychological Corporation.

Cantwell DP, Baker L (1988) Issues in the classification of child and adolescent psychopathology. *J Am Acad Child Adolesc Psychiatry* **27**: 521–33.

Carlson CL, Mann M (2000) Attention deficit/hyperactivity disorder, predominantly inattentive subtype. *Child and Adolescent Psychiatric Clinics of North America* **9**: 499–501.

Carlson CL, Mann M (2002) Sluggish cognitive tempo *J Am Acad Child Adolesc Psychiatry* **3**: 123–9.

Carlson CL, Tamm L, Gaub M (1997) Gender differences in children with ADHD, ODD, and co-occurring ADHD/ODD identified in a school population. *J Am Acad Child Adolesc Psychiatry* **36**: 1706–14.

Carlson GA, Kelly KK (1988) Manic symptoms in psychiatrically hospitalized children: what do they mean? *J Affect Disorders* **51**: 123–35.

Carter AS, O'Donnell DA, Schultz RT *et al.* (2000) Social and emotional adjustment in children affected with Gilles de la Tourette syndrome: association with ADHD and family functioning. *J Child Psychology Psychiatry* **41**: 215–33.

Clarke AR, Barry RJ, McCarthy R, Selikowitz M (2001) Electroencephalogram differences in two subtypes of attention deficit hyperactivity disorder. *Psychophysiology* **38**: 212–21.

Clements SD (1966) *Minimal Brain Dysfunction in Children: Terminology and Identification: Phase One of a Three-Phase Project.* Washington, DC: US Department of Health, Education and Welfare.

Collett BR, Ohan JL, Myers KM (2003) Ten-year review of rating scales. V: scales assessing Attention-Deficit Hyperactivity Disorder. *J Am Acad Child Adolesc Psychiatry* **42**: 1015–37.

Conners C (1969) A teacher rating scale for use in drug studies with children. *Am J Psychiatry* **125**: 884–8.

Conners C (1997) *Conners' Rating Scale-Revised Technical Manual.* North Tonawanda, NY: Multi-Health Systems.

Costello EJ, Farmer EM, Angold A *et al.* (1997) Psychiatric disorders among American, Indian and white youth in Appalachia: the Great Smoky Mountains Study. *Am J Public Health* **87**: 827–32.

DuPaul GJ, Power TJ, Anastopoulas AD, Reid R (1998) *ADHD Rating Scale-IV: Checklist, Norms and Clinical Interpretation.* New York: Guilford.

Faraone SV, Biederman J (2004) Neurobiology of Attention Deficit Hyperactivity Disorder. *Biol Psychiatry* **22**: 951–8.

Faraone SV, Biederman J, Friedman D (2000) Validity of DSM-IV Subtypes of Attention-Deficit Hyperactivity Disorder: a family study perspective. *J Am Acad Child Adolesc Psychiatry* **39**: 300–7.

Faraone SV, Biederman J, Mick E (1997) Attention deficit disorder and conduct disorder: longitudal evidence for a familial subtype. *Psychological Medicine* **27**: 291–300.

Faraone SV, Biederman J, Webber W, Russell R (1998) Psychiatric, neuropsychological, and psychosocial features of DSM IV subtypes of attention deficit hyperactivity disorder: results from a clinically referred sample. *J Am Acad Child Adolesc Psychiatry* **37**: 185–93.

Faraone SV, Perlis RH, Doyle AE *et al.* (2005) Molecular genetics of Attention Deficit Hyperactivity Disorder. *Biol Psychiatry* **57**(11): 1324–35.

Faraone SV, Sergeant J, Gillberg C, Biederman J (2003) The worldwide prevalence of ADHD: is it an American condition? *World Psychiatry* **2**: 104–13.

Fergusson DM, Horwood LJ (1995) Prevalence and comorbidity of DSM-III-R diagnosis in a birth cohort of 15 year olds. *J Am Acad Child Adolesc Psychiatry* **32**: 1127–34.

Frick PJ, Lahey BB, Applegate B (1994) DSM-IV field trials for the disruptive behaviour disorders: symptom utility estimates. *J Am Acad Child Adolesc Psychiatry* **33**: 529–39.

Gadow K, Nolan E (2002) Oppositional Defiant Disorder and Attention Deficit Hyperactivity Disorder, separate clinical entities? *Journal of Child Psychology and Psychiatry* **43**: 191–201.

Gaub M, Carlson CL (1997) Gender differences in ADHD: a meta-analysis and critical review. *J Am Acad Child Adolesc Psychiatry* **36**: 1036–46.

Geller DA, Biederman J, Faraone SV *et al.* (2002). Attention deficit/hyperactivity disorder in children and adolescents with obsessive compulsive disorder: fact or artifact? *J Am Acad Child Adolesc Psychiatry* **41**: 52–8.

Geller DA, Biederman J, Griffin S *et al.* (1996) Comorbidity of juvenile obsessive compulsive disorder with disruptive behaviour disorders. *J Am Acad Child Adolesc Psychiatry* **35**: 1637–46.

Gillberg IC, Gillberg C (1988) Children with deficits in attention, motor control and perception (DAMP): need for specialist treatment. *Acta Paediatrica Scandinavica* **77**: 450–1.

Gillberg IC, Gillberg C (1989) Children with pre-school minor neurodevelopmental disorders. IV. Behaviour and school achievement age 13. *Developmental Medicine and Child Neurology* **31**: 3–13.

Greene RW, Biederman J, Faraone SV *et al.* (2001) Social impairment with girls with ADHD: patterns, gender comparisons and correlates. *J Am Acad Child Adolesc Psychiatry* **40**: 704–10.

Goring J (2001) Social impairment in girls with ADHD: patterns, gender comparisons, and correlates. *J Am Acad Child Adolesc* **40**: 704–10.

Graetz BW, Sawyer MG, Baghurst P (2005) Gender differences among children with DSM-IV ADHD in Australia. *J Am Acad Child Adolesc Psychiatry* **44**: 159–68.

Graetz BW, Sawyer MG, Hazell PL *et al.* (2001) Validity of DSM-IV ADHD subtypes in a nationally representative sample of Australian children and adolescents. *J Am Acad Child and Adolesc Psychiatry* **40**: 1410–17.

Holland ML, Gimpel GA, Merrel KW (2001) *ADHD Symptoms Rating Scale Manual.* Wilmington, DE: Wide Range.

Hudziak JJ, Heath AC, Madden PF (1998) Latent class and factor analysis of DSM-IV ADHD: a twin study of female adolescents. *J Am Acad Child Adolesc Psychiatry* **37**: 848–57.

Kadesjo B, Gillberg C (1998) Attention deficits and clumsiness in Swedish 7-year-old children. *Developmental Medicine and Child Neurology* **40**: 796–804.

Kahn E, Cohen LH (1934) Organic driveness: a brainstem syndrome and an experience with case reports. *New England Journal of Medicine* **210**: 748–56.

Klorman R, Hazel-Fernandez LA, Shaywitz SE *et al.* (1999) Executive functioning deficits in attention deficit/hyperactivity disorder. *J Am Acad Child Adolesc Psychiatry* **38**: 1148–55.

Lahey B, Applegate B, McBurnett K *et al.* (1994) DSM IV field trials for attention deficit hyperactivity disorder in children and adolescents. *Am J Psychiatry* **151**: 1673–85.

Lahey B, Willcutt EG (2002) Validity of the diagnosis and dimensions of attention deficit/hyperactivity disorder. In PJ Jensen, JR Cooper (eds) *Attention Deficit Hyperactivity Disorder*, pp. 1–23.

Lambert NM, Sandoval J, Sassone D (1978) Prevalence of hyperactivity in elementary school children as a function of social system definers. *Am J Orthopsychiatry* **48**: 446–63.

Landgren M, Pettersson R, Kjellman B, Gillberg C (1996) ADHD, DAMP and other neurodevelopmental/psychiatric disorders in 6 year old children: epidemiology and co-morbidity. *Developmental Medicine and Child Neurology* **38**: 891–906.

Levy F, Hay D, Bennett K, McStephen M (2005) Gender differences in ADHD subtype comorbidity. *J Am Acad Child Adolesc Psychiatry* **44**: 368–76.

Lindgren S, Koeppel GG (1987) Assessing child behaviour problems in a medical setting: development of the Paediatric Behaviour Scale. In RJ Prinz (ed.) *Advances in Behavioural Assessment of Children and Families*, Vol. 3, Greenwich, CT: JAI, pp. 57–90.

Loeber R., Green SM, Lahey BB, Stouthamar-Loeber M (1991) Differences and similarities between children, mothers and teachers as informants on disruptive child behaviour. *J Abnorm Child Psychol* **19**: 75–95.

Loney J, Milich R (1982) Hyperactivity, inattention and aggression in clinical practice. In DK Routh (ed.) *Advances in Behavioural Paediatrics*, New York: Plenum.

McBurnett, K, Pfiffner LJ, Willcutt E *et al.* (1999) Experimental cross-validation of DSM-IV types of Attention Deficit/Hyperactivity Disorder. *N Am Acad Child Adolesc Psychiatry* **38**: 17–24.

McCarney SB (1995a) *The Attention Deficit Disorders Evaluation Scale, Home Version, Technical Manual*, 2nd edn. Colombia, MO: Hawthorne Educational Service.

McCarney SB (1995b) *The Attention Deficit Disorders Evaluation Scale, School Version, Technical Manual*, 2nd edn. Colombia, MO: Hawthorne Educational Service.

McCubbin M, Cohen D (1997) Empirical, ethical and political perspectives on the use of methylphenidate. *Ethical Hum Sci Serv* **1**: 81–101.

Manassis K, Tannock R, Barbosa J (2000) Dichotic listening and response inhibition in children with comorbid anxiety disorders and ADHD. *J Am Acad Child Adolesc Psychiatry* **39**: 1152–9.

Marks DJ, Himelstein J, Newcorn JH, Halperin JM (1999) Identification of AD/HD subtypes using laboratory-based measures: a cluster analysis. *J Abnormal Child Psychol* **27**: 167–75.

Meltzer H, Gatward R, Goodman R, Ford T (2003) Mental health of children and adolescents in Great Britain. *Int Review Psychiatry* **15**: 185–7.

Moffitt TE (1990) Juvenile delinquency and attention deficit disorder: boys' developmental trajectories from age 3 to age 15. *Child Development* **61**: 893–910.

Morgan A, Hynd G, Rissio C, Hall J (1996) Validity of DSM-IV ADHD predominantly inattentive and combined types: relationship to previous DSM diagnoses/subtype differences. *J Am Acad Child Adolesc Psychiatry* **35**: 325–33.

Mullins C, Bellgrove M, Gill M, Robertson I (2005) Variability in time reproduction: difference in ADHD combined and inattentive subtypes. *J Am Acad Child Adolesc Psychiatry* **44**: 169–76.

Nadder TS, Silberg JL, Eaves LJ *et al.* (1998) Genetic effects on ADHD symptomatology in 7–13 year old twins: results from a telephone survey. *Behaviour Genetics* **28**: 83–99.

Newman DL, Moffitt TE, Caspi A *et al.* (1996) Psychiatric disorder in a birth cohort of young adults: prevalence, comorbidity, clinical significance, and new case incidence from ages 11–21. *J of Consult Clin Psychology* **64**: 552–62.

Nigg JT, Blaskey LJ, Huang-Pollock CL, Rappley MD (2002) Neuropsychological executive functions and DSM-IV ADHD subtypes. *J Am Acad Child Adolesc Psychiatry* **41**: 59–66.

Offord DR, Boyle HM, Szatmari P (1987) Ontario Child Health Study. II. Six-month prevalence of disorder and rates of service utilization. *Archives of General Psychiatry* **44**: 832–6.

Ozonoff S, Strayer DL, McMahon WM, Filloux F (1994) Executive function abilities in autism and Tourette Syndrome: an information processing approach. *J Child Psychol Psychiatry* **35**: 1015–32.

Pauermeister JJ, Matos M, Reina G *et al.* (2005) Comparison of the DSM-IV combined and inattentive types of Attention-Deficit/Hyperactivity Disorder in a school-based sample of Latino-Hispanic children. *J Child Psychology Psychiatry* **46**: 166–79.

Pauls DL, Towbin KE, Lekman JF *et al.* (1986) Gilles de la Tourettes Syndrome and obsessive-compulsive disorder: evidence supporting a genetic relationship. *Arch Gen Psychiatry* **43**: 1180–2.

Peterson B, Leckman JF, Tucker D *et al.* (2000) Preliminary findings of antistreptococcal antibody titres and basal ganglia volumes in tic, obsessive-compulsive, and attention deficit/hyperactivity disorders. *Archives of General Psychiatry* **57**: 364–72.

Peterson B, Pine D, Cohen P, Brook J (2001) Prospective, longitudal study of tic, obsessive-compulsive, and Attention-Deficit/Hyperactivity Disorders in an epidemiological sample. *J Am Acad Child Adolesc Psychiatry* **40**: 685–95.

Prendergast M, Taylor E, Rapoport JL (1988) The diagnosis of childhood hyperactivity: a US-UK cross-national study of DSM-III and ICD-9. *J Child Psychol Psychiatry* **8**: 1–11.

Rasmussen ER, Neuman RJ, Heath AC *et al.* (2004) Familial clustering of latent class and DSM-IV defined attention deficit/hyperactivity disorder (ADHD) subtypes. *J Child Psychology Psychiatry* **45**: 589–99.

Rowland AS, Umbach DM, Catoe KE (2001) Studying the epidemiology of Attention-Deficit Hyperactivity Disorder: screening method and pilot results. *Can J Psychiatry* **46**: 931–40.

Rucklidge JJ, Tannock R (2001) Psychiatric, psychosocial and cognitive functioning of female adolescents with ADHD. *J Am Acad Child Adolesc Psychiatry* **40**: 530–40.

Rucklidge JJ, Tannock R (2002) Age of onset of ADHD symptoms. *J Am Acad Child Adolesc Psychiatry* **41**: 496–7.

Safer DJ, Allen RP (1976) *Hyperactive Children: Diagnosis and Management*. Baltimore, MD: University Park Press.

Safer DJ, Krager JM (1988) A survey of medication treatment for hyperactive/inattentive students. *JAMA* **260**: 2256–8.

Smith J, Johnstone S, Barry R (2003) Aiding diagnosis of Attention-Deficit/Hyperactivity Disorder and its subtypes: discriminant function analysis of event related potential data. *J Child Psychology and Psychiatry* **44**: 1067–75.

Stevenson J, Pennington BF, Gilger JW *et al.* (1993) Hyperactivity and spelling disability: testing for shared genetic aetiology. *J of Child Psychology and Psychiatry* **34**: 1137–52.

Still GF (1902) The Coulstonian lectures on some abnormal psychial conditions in children. *Lancet* **1**: 1008–12, 1077–82, 1163–8.

Strober M, Morrell W, Lampert C *et al.* (1988) A family study of bipolar I disorder in adolescence: early onset of symptoms linked to increased familial loading and lithium resistance. *J Affect Disord* **15**: 255–8.

Swanson J (1992) *School Based Assessments and Interventions for ADD Students*. Irvine, CA: KC.

Swanson J, Schuck S, Mann M (2001a) Categorical and dimensional definitions and evaluations of symptoms of ADHD: the SNAP and SWAN rating scales [ADHD website].

Swanson J, Schuck S, Mann M (2001b) Over-identification of extreme behaviour in the evaluation and diagnosis of ADHD/HKD [ADHD website].

Swanson J, Sergeant JA, Taylor E (1998) Attention deficit hyperactivity disorder and hyperkinetic disorder. *Lancet* **351**: 429–33.

Szatmari P, Offord DR, Boyle MH (1989) Ontario Child Health Study: prevalence of attention deficit disorder with hyperactivity. *J Child Psychol Psychiatry* **30**: 219–30.

Tannock R, Ickowicz A, Schachar R (1995) Differential effects of methylphenidate on working memory in ADHD children with and without comorbid anxiety. *J Am Acad Child Adolesc Psychiatry* **34**: 886–96.

Taylor E (1999) Developmental neuropsychopathology of attention deficit and impulsiveness. *Dev Psychopathol* **11**: 607–28.

Taylor E, Sandberg S (1984) Hyperactive behaviour in English schoolchildren: a questionnaire survey. *J Abnorm Child Psychol* **12**: 143–56.

Taylor E, Sandberg S, Thorley G, Gile S (1991) *The Epidemiology of Childhood Hyperactivity*. London: Oxford University Press.

Taylor E, Schachar R, Thorley G *et al.* (1987) Which boys respond to stimulant medication? A controlled trial of methylphenidate in boys with disruptive behaviour. *Psychological Medicine* **17**: 121–43.

Tripp G, Luk S, Schaughency E, Singh R (1999) DSM-IV and ICD-10: a comparison of the correlates of ADHD and Hyperkinetic Disorder. *J Am Acad Child Adolesc Psychiatry* **38**: 156–64.

Ullman RK, Sleator EK, Sprague RL (2000) *ACTeRS Teacher and Parent Forms Manual.* Champaign, IL: MetriTech.

Wilens T, Biederman J (1992) The Stimulants. *Psychiatr Clin North Am* **15**: 191–222.

Willoughby MT, Curran P, Costello J, Angold A (2000) Implications of early versus late onset of Attention-Deficit Hyperactivity Disorder symptoms. *J Am Acad Child Adolesc Psychiatry* **39**: 1512–19.

Wolraich ML (2003) Vanderbilt ADHD Teacher Rating Scale (VADTRS) and the Vanderbilt ADHD Parent Rating Scale (VADPRS) (available on line at www.nichq.org).

Wolraich ML, Feurer ID, Hannah JN *et al.* (1998) Obtaining systematic teacher reports of disruptive behaviour disorders utilizing DSM-IV. *J Abnorm Child Psychol* **26**: 141–52.

Wolraich ML, Hannah JN, Pinnock TY *et al.* (1996) Comparison of diagnostic criteria for Attention-Deficit Hyperactivity Disorder in a country-wide sample. *J Am Acad Child Adolesc Psychiatry* **35**: 319–24.

Wolraich ML, Lambert EW, Baumgaertal A *et al.* (2003a) Teachers screening for attention deficit hyperactivity disorder: comparing multinational samples on teacher ratings of ADHD. *J Abnorm Child Psychol* **31**: 445–55.

Wolraich ML, Lambert EW, Doffing MA *et al.* (2003b) Psychometric properties of the Vanderbilt ADHD diagnostic parent rating scale in a referred population. *J Pediatric Psychol* **28**: 559–67.

World Health Organization (1993) The ICD 10. *Classification of Mental and Behavioural Disorders: Diagnostic Criteria for Research*, Geneva: World Health Organization.

3 Diagnosis and Classification of ADHD in Adulthood

AIVEEN KIRLEY

Cluan Mhuire Service, Blackrock, Co. Dublin, Ireland

3.1 OVERVIEW

Adult Attention Deficit Hyperactivity Disorder (ADHD) is an increasingly recognised yet controversial disorder. Longitudinal studies indicate that ADHD, one of the most common disorders seen at child psychiatry clinics, can persist into adulthood in up to 50–75% of cases and has a prevalence of between 1% and 4.7%. Both childhood and adult ADHD have a similar profile of neuropsychological deficits. Medications used to treat ADHD are equally effective in children and in adults. Common sources of referral include young adults who are 'graduates' from child psychiatry services, parents of children with ADHD (who recognise their child's symptoms in themselves) and people who self-refer for assessment. However, unlike childhood ADHD, there is no consensus on the most valid diagnostic criteria for adult ADHD. As with most psychiatric disorders, adult ADHD remains a clinical diagnosis. This chapter focuses on diagnosis and classification of the condition and briefly describes options for management.

3.2 ADULT OUTCOMES OF CHILDHOOD ADHD

Previous chapters have detailed the psychopathology of childhood ADHD. Follow-up studies of ADHD children into adolescence and early adulthood indicate that the disorder frequently persists and is associated with significant psychopathology and dysfunction in later life. Partly because of methodological differences, earlier longitudinal studies found highly variable rates of persistence of ADHD symptoms into adolescence (50–75%) (Thorley, 1984; Klein & Mannuzza, 1991) and adulthood (4–60%) (Hechtman, 1992; Mannuzza *et al.*, 1993). Studies based on DSM-III-R (*Diagnostic and Statistical Manual of the American Psychiatric Association*, 3rd edition-revised) nomenclature and mindful of the cognitive features of the disorder have indicated higher persistence rates of 75% into young adulthood (Biederman *et al.*, 1996b; Fischer, 1997). These studies showed that the persistence of ADHD into adulthood included symptoms of inattention, disorganisation, distractibility, and impulsivity, along with academic and occupational failure. A more recent

Handbook of Attention Deficit Hyperactivity Disorder. Edited by M. Fitzgerald, M. Bellgrove and M. Gill.
© 2007 John Wiley & Sons Ltd

longitudinal study using DSM-IV criteria suggested similar persistence rates of 60–70% for childhood ADHD (Barkley *et al.*, 2002).

The above studies have highlighted the poor psychosocial functioning of this patient group with high rates of academic and occupational failure, substance abuse disorders, personality disorders and even delinquency. The ADHD adolescent and young adult is at risk for school failure, emotional difficulties, poor peer relationships, and trouble with the law (Gittelman *et al.*, 1985; Hechtman & Weiss, 1986). Factors identifiable in younger adolescents that predict the persistence of ADHD into adulthood include family history of ADHD and psychiatric comorbidity, particularly aggression or delinquency problems (Loney *et al.*, 1981; Gittelman *et al.*, 1985; Hart *et al.*, 1995).

Prevalence estimates for adult ADHD have mainly been based on studies using self-report questionnaire-based measures. A US sample of 720 adults applying for their driver's licence found a prevalence of 4.7% for adult ADHD based on DSM-IV ADHD symptoms (Murphy & Barkley, 1996b). A Dutch study (Kooij *et al.*, 2004) also using a DSM-IV based self-report questionnaire reported prevalences of 1% and of 2.5% when diagnostic criteria were relaxed from six to four inattentive or hyperactive-impulsive symptoms. A more recent population survey (Kessler *et al.*, 2005) used a combination of self-report and DSM-IV-based interview measures and reported a prevalence of 4.2% for adult ADHD. Future epidemiological studies of adult ADHD should use more structured assessment of symptoms and associated impairment to avoid the diagnostic confound of anxiety and depression symptoms.

3.3   VALIDITY OF ADULT ADHD

The validity of adult ADHD as an entity has been established and has been reviewed by Faraone *et al.* (2000a) and Spencer *et al.* (1998). Regarding descriptive validity, the consensus from most studies shows that the clinical correlates of ADHD are similar for children and adults (Spencer *et al.*, 1995; Murphy & Barkley, 1996a). Also, like their childhood counterparts, many adults with ADHD suffer from antisocial, depressive and anxiety disorders and display evidence of clinically significant impairments in histories of school failure, occupational problems and traffic accidents (Biederman *et al.*, 1994; Downey *et al.*, 1997; Heiligenstein *et al.*, 1998). Regarding predictive validity, treatment response studies show that the medications used to treat childhood ADHD are equally effective for adult ADHD (Spencer *et al.*, 1995; Levin *et al.*, 1998; Wilens *et al.*, 1999). However, there are no long-term studies on course and outcome of treatment in adult ADHD. In terms of concurrent validity, family studies provide strong support for the validity of adult ADHD. Adult relatives of ADHD children are at increased risk for ADHD (Faraone & Biederman, 1994), as are the child relatives of ADHD adults (Manshadi *et al.*, 1983; Biederman *et al.*, 1995). Both childhood and adult ADHD show a characteristic profile of neuropsychological deficits. These include impaired performance on tasks assessing vigilance, motor inhibition, executive functions (e.g. organisation, planning and complex problem-solving) and verbal learning and memory (Barkley *et al.*, 1992, 1996; Downey *et al.*, 1997).

3.4 WHY IS ADULT ADHD A CONTROVERSIAL DIAGNOSIS?

The emerging clinical entity that is adult ADHD provokes much debate among clinicians as to whether the disorder actually exists, and if so, how it should be managed and by whom. Like many psychiatric diagnoses, adult ADHD has no specific biochemical, genetic or neuropsychological marker. Making the diagnosis of adult ADHD is not straightforward. The diagnosis depends almost exclusively on the clinical history. A number of difficulties arise when taking the history that may affect the accuracy of diagnosis. These include biased recall of symptoms of ADHD in childhood and the need for a collateral history from parents of the adult presenting for assessment.

In adult ADHD, comorbidity with personality disorders, mood disorders and substance abuse disorders appears to be the rule rather than the exception. Because of this, unravelling primary and secondary diagnoses can be difficult.

Guidelines for the management of the disorder are still unclear. Methylphenidate, one of the mainstays in the treatment of childhood ADHD, has been shown to be of benefit in adult ADHD. However, in most countries, methylphenidate is not licensed for use in adults. Clinicians treating adult ADHD are faced with the dilemma of whether to prescribe off label. An even more controversial area is the usage of methylphenidate, a potentially addictive stimulant, in a patient population with high rates of substance abuse disorders.

There has been increasing coverage of ADHD by the media highlighting symptoms and behaviours that some people may recognise in themselves from childhood onwards. Critics have suggested that certain individuals in this patient group might seek the label of adult ADHD to explain life difficulties or to justify a less socially desirable diagnosis such as personality disorder or substance abuse disorder. For this reason, stringent clinical assessment of this patient group is especially relevant. Another controversial issue is the presence of adult ADHD in criminal offenders. There is growing concern that the adults with ADHD who have the least favourable outcome are among those who end up in prison. Psychiatrists are increasingly likely to be asked to assess for adult ADHD in an offender or to give an opinion as to whether the diagnosis of adult ADHD may account for diminished responsibility in criminal offences.

3.5 DIAGNOSTIC CLASSIFICATION OF ADULT ADHD

In essence, adult ADHD represents the continuation of the childhood disorder with persisting global impairment extending into adulthood. Symptoms arise from core deficits in regulation of attention, hyperactivity and impulsivity. ADHD is usually apparent from the age of seven; adult ADHD does not present *de novo* in adulthood. The Diagnostic and Statistical Manual (DSM-IV) of the American Psychiatric Association (1994) diagnostic criteria for (childhood) ADHD can be seen in Table 2.1 (Chapter 2).

Currently there are no single 'gold standard' diagnostic criteria for adult ADHD. Two different schools of thought have conceptualised adult ADHD; the Wender

Utah criteria and the DSM criteria. Their relative merits and disadvantages have been reviewed by McGough and Barkley (2004).

3.5.1 THE WENDER UTAH CRITERIA

The Wender Utah criteria for adult ADHD were proposed by Paul Wender and colleagues at the University of Utah and developed out of increasing recognition that the DSM criteria of the time (DSM-III) contained childhood symptoms not developmentally appropriate for adults. The patient and an informant (preferably a close family member) are both interviewed to assess childhood ADHD symptoms and impairment retrospectively and to assess current symptoms and functioning. According to the Wender Utah criteria, it is necessary to have ongoing impairment from childhood of both hyperactive and inattentive ADHD symptoms to be considered to have the adult diagnosis. Additionally a minimum of two out of the five following symptom clusters were proposed to be necessary to qualify for adult ADHD. These are (1) mood lability, (2) irritability and hot temper, (3) impaired stress tolerance, (4) disorganisation, and (5) impulsivity. The Wender Utah criteria have some limitations. They have diverged further from more recent revisions of DSM criteria of ADHD. As they only include patients with lifelong inattention and hyperactivity, they exclude those with the inattentive subtype of ADHD. The inclusion of diagnostic criteria such as the presence of irritability and mood lability may confound DSM-defined ADHD and comorbid conditions such as Oppositional Defiant Disorder or Bipolar Affective Disorder. Furthermore, the Wender Utah criteria do not permit the diagnosis of adult ADHD in the presence of Mood Disorder or Personality Disorder. Subsequent work has shown that these conditions are commonly comorbid with adult ADHD. As the Wender Utah criteria do not fully overlap with DSM criteria, both classification systems may potentially identify two separate sets of patients. However, Wender's approach was critical to the recognition and acceptance of adult ADHD as a valid disorder. The Wender Utah criteria have been widely used in research on adult ADHD. The criteria also set a precedent in establishing a need for retrospective assessment of childhood symptoms, and the importance of a third party informant for evaluation of childhood and adult ADHD symptoms and functioning.

3.5.2 THE DSM CRITERIA

The DSM criteria are more commonly used to diagnose adult ADHD. The criteria, based on childhood developmental norms, are adapted to identify adults with the condition. DSM-III created the category of 'attention deficit disorder, residual type' for adults diagnosed in childhood who continue to exhibit a clinically significant level of symptoms and impairment. With DSM-IV, the diagnosis of Adult ADHD is extrapolated from the diagnostic criteria shown in Table 2.1, which are based on childhood developmental norms. In other words the symptom checklist is appropriate for children but not for adults. Apart from this obvious limitation, there are other difficulties with the existing criteria. The age of onset criterion (age seven) is too strict if depending on retrospective recall of childhood symptoms by the patient or family member (i.e. if no gold standard child psychiatry diagnosis is available).

Also, DSM-IV field trials (Applegate *et al.*, 1997) have shown that a significant percentage of children who were felt to have ADHD failed to demonstrate impairment before age seven, particularly children with the inattentive subtype. Because of the practical difficulties demonstrating impairment before age seven in adults and the lack of empirical evidence supporting the age of onset criterion, some have argued that the age threshold should be raised to onset before age twelve to include the broader period of childhood (Barkley & Biederman, 1997).

As discussed in McGough and Barkley (2004), there is no scientific basis for establishing six symptoms as the appropriate threshold for adult diagnosis. Studies of adults with ADHD (Murphy & Barkley, 1996b; Heiligenstein *et al.*, 1998) concluded that significant numbers of patients with genuine impairment failed to meet the threshold of six symptoms for diagnosis and suggested that the DSM-IV criteria are too restrictive. In keeping with this hypothesis, an epidemiological study of adult ADHD (Kooij *et al.*, 2004) showed that a cutoff of four or more symptoms of inattention or hyperactivity/impulsivity was associated with significant increase in psychosocial impairment. Nevertheless, facility exists in DSM-IV for clinicians to specify 'ADHD in partial remission' for patients in whom the full diagnostic criteria, although met in childhood, are no longer fulfilled. It has been suggested (McGough & Barkley, 2004) that the settings in which impairment is evident are too narrowly defined by DSM-IV (e.g. at school (or work) and at home) and that they should be broadened to reflect the wider roles and responsibilities of adulthood. Unlike the Wender Utah criteria for adult ADHD, DSM-IV permits co-occurring psychopathology such as Mood and Anxiety Disorders in adult ADHD. The DSM-IV ADHD subtypes, Inattentive, Hyperactive and Combined are based on studies of children and adolescents with ADHD (Lahey *et al.*, 1994), which suggest that ADHD symptoms cluster around distinct inattentive or hyperactive-impulsive factors. To date, one study (Kooij *et al.*, 2004) has concluded that the same symptom model structure as specified in DSM-IV for children can be generalised to adults. Further work is necessary to validate these diagnostic subtypes on adults.

In summary, the Wender Utah criteria are more restrictive than DSM-IV criteria and more closely approximate the Combined subtype of DSM-IV ADHD. Both diagnostic systems require childhood onset of symptoms and persistence into adulthood with impairment in functioning. Both sets of criteria have their own limitations and are likely to diverge further in terms of their representativeness with further revision of DSM.

3.6 CLINICAL PRESENTATION OF ADULT ADHD

Childhood ADHD is diagnosed in far more males than females. The male:female gender ratio ranges from 3–9 males:1 female (Swanson *et al.*, 1998). However, the male:female ratio in epidemiological and adult samples is about 2 males:1 female (Millstein *et al.*, 1997). Girls with ADHD share similar symptoms as boys with ADHD but have lower rates of conduct and oppositional defiant disorder (Faraone *et al.*, 2000b). It has been suggested that referral biases may operate such that boys with oppositional and conduct problems are more likely to be clinically referred for identification of ADHD, but that these biases are less likely to be present in adulthood when patients may self-refer for diagnosis of adult ADHD.

3.6.1   REFERRAL SOURCES

In general, three types of patient groups present for assessment. They are young adults who are 'graduates' from child psychiatry services, parents of children with ADHD (who recognise their child's symptoms in themselves) and people who self-refer for assessment.

3.6.2   EVOLUTION OF ADHD SYMPTOMS FROM CHILDHOOD TO ADULTHOOD

While the same core deficits in regulation of attention, hyperactivity and impulsivity are found in adults, symptoms change both in quality and quantity from those found in childhood. Hyperactivity tends to diminish with age, impulsivity changes quality and attentional problems remain the same but are more disabling as organisational demands increase. Table 3.1 provides examples of symptoms in adulthood.

Table 3.1. Examples of adult ADHD symptoms

Adult ADHD Inattentive Symptoms
- Tasks which require detail and are tedious are stressful
- Inability to complete tasks without forgetting the objective and starting something else
- Others complain that they are not heard, sense that they are not tuned in
- Failure to follow through others' instructions, failure to keep commitments undertaken
- Recurrent errors, lateness, missed appointments and deadlines
- Putting off tasks such as responding to letters, organising papers, paying bills often due to procrastination
- Misplacing wallet, keys, assignments from work
- Subjective sense of distractibility
- Complaints of memory problems, unable to remember lists, fail to complete activities due to forgetting

Adult ADHD Hyperactivity Symptoms
- May be observed fidgeting, tapping hands or feet, changing position
- Unable to sit during conversations and meetings, strong internal feeling of restlessness when waiting
- Pacing, subjective sense of needing to do something, more comfortable with stimulating activities than sedentary
- Unwillingness to do quiet activities, may be workaholics
- Set an exhausting and frenetic pace, and may expect the same of others
- Excessive talking makes dialogue difficult, dominating conversation, may be seen as nagging, etc.

Adult ADHD Impulsive Symptoms
- Subjective sense of other people talking too slowly
- Impatient waiting for others to finish at their own pace, impatient waiting in line
- Perceived as social ineptness, difficulty watching others struggling with a task

Source: adapted from Weiss *et al.*, 1999.

Additional common symptoms include lability of mood (rapid alterations in mood over short time periods of minutes to hours), poor distress tolerance, procrastination, over-focusing (becoming absorbed in some activities to the exclusion of all others), impatience, physical and verbal aggression, and sleep problems (e.g. initial insomnia, complaints of being unable to sleep because of 'too many thoughts in my head'). Impairment is usually global and creates problems such as maintaining relationships, jobs and a stable lifestyle.

3.7 COMORBID DISORDERS

Adults with ADHD have a high likelihood of developing other mental health disorders, i.e. comorbidity tends to be the rule rather than the exception. Research indicates that up to 75% of youths with ADHD will have a lifetime comorbid illness (Biederman *et al.*, 1993). These are most commonly Anxiety Disorders (40%), Depression (25%), Polysubstance Abuse (20%), Conduct Disorder (20%), and Antisocial Personality Disorder (10%). Unravelling primary and comorbid disorders can be difficult and has been excellently reviewed by Weiss *et al.* (1999). Key points from their book are summarised below.

3.7.1 ADHD AND MOOD DISORDERS

Mood lability is the most common mood symptom associated with ADHD. Mood shifts are sustained over hours or minutes, but patients are not consistently depressed for most of the day for more than two weeks. Other mood symptoms typical of ADHD are stress intolerance, temper outbursts (two of the Utah criteria) and a tendency to react to difficult situations catastrophically. Furthermore, ADHD patients on stimulants may complain of symptoms which are medication side effects; irritability, anxiety, low mood, and insomnia. Patients may first present with ADHD and comorbid depression when they discover they do not have the emotional capacity to cope with a major life event. On clinical assessment, ADHD has always been present and represents the patient's norm whereas the mood symptoms are of recent onset. Differentiation between ADHD affective features and depression is complicated by the significant overlap between symptoms of both disorders in diagnostic classification. Information regarding the developmental course of symptoms is more useful in diagnosis. Also, suicidal ideation and consistent low mood longer than two weeks are not characteristic of ADHD.

3.7.2 ADHD AND BIPOLAR DISORDER

The relationship between ADHD and Bipolar Disorder remains confusing. ADHD and comorbid bipolar disorder represents a small subset of the entire ADHD population and of the entire population with bipolar disorder. Similar to depression, symptoms of ADHD and of mania overlap. Distractibility, hyperactivity and overtalkativeness characterise both syndromes. Differential diagnosis of ADHD and mania can be assisted by assessment of the course of symptoms; mania is an episodic illness, whereas ADHD is chronic. Also, the mania of bipolar disorder has been understood not to present until puberty or later. In contrast, mania comorbid with ADHD has been found to have an onset before age five years (Biederman *et al.*, 1996a).

3.7.3 ANXIETY DISORDERS

Anxiety disorders are commonly comorbid with adult ADHD with up to 50% of patients with the disorder affected (Biederman *et al.*, 1993). When anxiety is present with ADHD, it will exacerbate low self-esteem, stress intolerance and aspects of cognition such as impairment in working memory (Tannock, 2000). Such patients may respond suboptimally to and have difficulties tolerating stimulants (Tannock *et al.*, 1995). The overlap between inattention and anxiety can have important treatment implications. Anxiety secondary to inattention may lessen with stimulants, however, the anxiety of a primary anxiety disorder with secondary inattention may be further increased by stimulants. For this reason, thorough clinical assessment of presenting symptoms is important for treatment efficacy.

3.7.4 LEARNING DISABILITY

ADHD is associated with higher rates of repeated school years, tutoring, placement in special classes, and reading disability (Weiss & Hechtman, 1993). When these separate conditions coexist, evaluation and treatment of each condition in its own right are crucial.

3.7.5 OPPOSITIONAL DEFIANT DISORDER, CONDUCT DISORDER AND ANTISOCIAL PERSONALITY DISORDER

Oppositional defiant disorder (ODD) describes problems with being stubborn, defiant and angry. Conduct disorder (CD) describes problems with getting into trouble, with such difficulties as fighting, stealing, breaking rules or fire setting. In one study of adult ADHD clinic attenders, 29% had ODD, 20% had CD and 12% had antisocial personality disorder (Biederman *et al.*, 1993). Adult ADHD has also been shown to be over-represented in prison inmates, with reported prevalences ranging from 8% to 45% (Curran & Fitzgerald, 1999; Rosler *et al.*, 2004; Vreugdenhil *et al.*, 2004). As discussed by Weiss *et al.* (1999), the presence of comorbid antisocial features is a poor prognostic indicator in long-term outcome in ADHD. Treatment of ADHD does not lead to remission of conduct disorder or antisocial personality disorder.

3.7.6 SUBSTANCE ABUSE

Individuals with ADHD are at higher risk of developing a substance abuse disorder than the general population. Marijuana is the most commonly used drug, then followed by stimulants, cocaine and hallucinogens (Biederman *et al.*, 1995). While treating ADHD comorbid with substance abuse with stimulants is controversial, recent evidence indicates that treatment with stimulants protects against development of substance abuse. A study by Biederman *et al.* (1999) showed the risk of substance abuse in untreated ADHD between ages 15 and 27 to be 47% compared to 15% in those who received treatment and concluded if ADHD is consistently treated, that the risk of substance abuse is no greater than in the general population. The introduction of nonstimulant alternatives to methylphenidate (such as atomoxetine) provides a safer alternative if ongoing drug abuse is a concern.

3.7.7   BORDERLINE PERSONALITY DISORDER

Both ADHD and Borderline Personality Disorder (BPD) are characterised by affective instability, impulsivity, unstable relationships, and difficulties controlling anger. Differentiating between both conditions is important as ADHD and comorbid BPD has a poorer prognosis than ADHD alone and the use of stimulant medication in this patient group is curtailed by impulsivity and suicidality. Weiss *et al.* (1999) suggest some clinical features to assist in differential diagnosis. While ADHD and BPD are chronic conditions, ADHD becomes apparent in the early school years while BPD becomes most obvious in middle adolescence. Patients with BPD are not usually hyperactive or inattentive in childhood. The chronic rage, suicidality and feelings of emptiness seen in BPD are not characteristic of ADHD. The nature of impulsivity in both conditions is different. In ADHD the impulsivity is disjointed and purposeless, whereas in BPD it appears to be a more driven intent to harm. Where a borderline patient experiences emotional boredom, a patient with ADHD experiences a cognitive and sensory boredom.

3.8   ASSESSMENT OF ADULT ADHD

Similar to the majority of psychiatric disorders, assessment and diagnosis of adult ADHD are primarily achieved through taking a thorough history. Key aspects of the history are summarised in Table 3.2.

As adult ADHD is frequently comorbid with more common psychiatric conditions such as mood, anxiety and personality disorders, diagnostic difficulty can arise in deciding the nature of the primary diagnosis. In cases where symptoms of adult ADHD are superimposed on another psychiatric disorder, the clinician should carefully assess the initial presenting symptoms, the secondary symptoms and the evolution of symptoms over time. For example, ADHD is a lifelong disorder continually present from childhood, whereas mood and anxiety disorders are relapsing and remittent. ADHD is often inherited (the history reveals a positive family history of ADHD). Symptoms of ADHD are not present exclusively during the active phase of another psychiatric disorder.

It is vital to obtain a collateral history ideally from a parent or a partner. The collateral history must support the existence of symptoms with onset in childhood and persistence into adulthood.

Neuropsychological testing while supportive of the diagnosis is not diagnostic. However, it is helpful in excluding Mild Learning Disability and objectively measuring aspects of attention and concentration. Commonly performed tests include the Continuous Performance Test (sustained attention) (Conners & Jeff, 1999), Test of Everyday Attention (divided and shifting attention) (Nimmo-Smith *et al.*, 1998),

Table 3.2. Clinical assessment of adult ADHD – the history

(i) History of childhood ADHD
- Diagnosis of childhood ADHD from child psychiatry services or history highly suggestive of childhood ADHD
- Family history of ADHD
- Forensic history or evidence of conduct disorder
- Developmental history e.g. explosive, hyperactive, or dreamy (inattentive) childhood temperament, delayed speech, dyslexia
- School history (check for poor academic performance relative to ability, discipline problems, bullying, abnormal peer relations)

(ii) Onset of childhood symptoms before age 12
- According to the current DSM-IV criteria, onset must be before age 7, but this criterion is likely to be revised upwards

(iii) Persisting impairment from symptoms
- Impairment starting from childhood progressing into adulthood with global impairment in functioning (i.e. family, academic, work, relationships)

(iv) Symptoms not better accounted for by another mental disorder
- Other disorders presenting with ADHD-like behaviours include Autistic Spectrum Disorders, Tourette Syndrome, Learning Disability (see more below).

Matching Familiar Figures Test (impulsivity), Wechsler Adult Intelligence Scale (IQ) (Psychological Corporation). A more detailed discussion of neuropsychological anomalies in ADHD and assessment can be found in Chapters 12 and 22.

As with a good collateral history, school or Educational Psychology reports can be very helpful in supporting the diagnosis. Both self- and observer-reported rating scales are commonly used to quantify current and previous symptoms and to track response to treatment. Examples include the Barkley Current Behaviour Scale (Barkley & Murphy, 1997), the Barkley Childhood Behaviour Scale (Barkley & Murphy, 1997) and the Adult ADHD Self-Report Scale (ASRS) (WHO, 2003).

In summary, to make a diagnosis of adult ADHD, carefully assess the clinical presentation, take a history from multiple informants, use records to establish onset and chronicity of symptoms and look for discrepancy between IQ and achievements.

3.9   MANAGEMENT OF ADULT ADHD

Adult ADHD is managed by a combination of approaches, which comprise psychoeducation, medication, psychological strategies and management of comorbid disorders. Chapters 17 and 19 describe these therapeutic approaches in more detail.

3.9.1   PSYCHOEDUCATION

Explaining the aetiology and progression of ADHD from childhood into adulthood together with practical advice on time management and problem-solving skills can be sufficient for some patients. Usually they have suspected their diagnosis for some time and may have developed adaptive behaviours to cope with their everyday symptoms.

3.9.2 PSYCHOLOGICAL APPROACHES

Psychological interventions such as Cognitive Behavioural Therapy or Behavioural Therapy have been used to improve impulse control and time management skills. Undoubtedly they are a logical choice for management and offer an alternative to medication but their efficacy is still under-evaluated.

3.9.3 PHARMACOLOGICAL APPROACHES

Medication is used to treat patients with more severe and incapacitating symptoms of ADHD. The subject of medication remains controversial because the majority of such patients are treated with stimulants such as methylphenidate and there are concerns regarding potential for dependence. However, landmark research (Greenhill *et al.*, 2001) has clearly demonstrated the superior efficacy of medication alone or in conjunction with behavioural therapy over other treatment strategies. Further work (Biederman *et al.*, 1999) indicates that appropriate treatment with stimulants in adolescence in fact protects against the later emergence of substance abuse rather than contributes to it. However, the long-term efficacy of such medication in ADHD is still under study.

The main types of medication used in ADHD are summarised in Table 3.3 with information on dosage and common adverse effects.

(a) Methylphenidate

Most specialists in adult ADHD start treatment with methylphenidate. It acts by blocking the re-uptake of dopamine, thereby increasing dopamine neurotransmission in brain regions regulating attention such as the striatum. Methylphenidate is effective in treating ADHD symptoms with an average response rate of 70%. In

Table 3.3. Medication used in adult ADHD

Medication	Daily dose (mg)	Daily dosage effects	Common adverse effects
Stimulants			Insomnia, decreased appetite,
Methylphenidate	20–100	2–4 times	weight loss,
Dexamphetamine	10–60	2–3 times	headaches, edginess, mild ↑BP/Pulse
Noradrenergic agents Atomoxetine	40–150	1–2 times	Sleep disturbance, nausea, headache, mild ↑ BP/Pulse

Source: adapted from Wilens *et al.*, 2004.

most countries, as it is not licensed in adults, usage is off-label in patients with adult ADHD. Methylphenidate is contraindicated in cardiovascular disease, moderate to severe hypertension, hyperthyroidism, glaucoma, pregnancy and breastfeeding. It should be used with caution in patients with tics, epilepsy, and a past history of psychosis. Prior to treatment, pulse, blood pressure (BP), and full blood count (FBC) should be checked. During treatment, six monthly FBC, liver function tests (LFTs), pulse, and BP should be performed.

If medication is indicated, it is preferable to initially prescribe a short acting form of methylphenidate as dosage and side effects can be closely controlled. A suggested schedule for starting short-acting methylphenidate is described in Table 3.4.

As the dose begins to build, some patients may complain of anxiety, dysphoria, palpitations, appetite suppression or insomnia (especially if the last dose is taken after 7 pm). In this scenario, the dosage should be adjusted to that which balances optimum symptom control with the least amount of side-effects. Everyday usage may not be necessary in all patients, and medication may be required only during college term or work days. Methylphenidate differs from medications such as selective serotonin reuptake inhibitors (SSRIs) in that onset of efficacy occurs after the first dose (within 1.5 hours) and duration of action is typically 4 hours. Once the optimal dosage is established, there is an option to switch to a longer-acting form of methylphenidate (such as Concerta XL or Ritalin LA). This has the advantages of once daily dosing and a longer duration of action.

(b)   Atomoxetine (strattera)

Atomoxetine has been licensed for adult ADHD in the UK since May 2004. It improves symptoms of ADHD by blocking noradrenaline reuptake and regulating the abnormal noradrenergic neurotransmission hypothesised in ADHD. The major advantage of this medication is its non-stimulant characteristics and consequent low potential for dependence. Atomoxetine is contraindicated in narrow angle glaucoma and concomitant monoamine oxidase inhibitor (MAOI) treatment. It should be used with caution in hypertension, hypotension and cardiovascular disease. The starting dose is 40 mg mane, building by 20 mg to a maximum daily dose of 150 mg.

Table 3.4. Schedule for commencement of methylphenidate

Day	am	lunch	pm
1	5 mg	–	–
2	5 mg	5 mg	5 mg
3	5 mg	5 mg	5 mg
4	10 mg	10 mg	10 mg
5	10 mg	10 mg	10 mg
6	15 mg	15 mg	15 mg
7	15 mg	15 mg	15 mg
8	20 mg	20 mg	20 mg

Source: P. Asherson, personal communication.

(c) Other medications in adult ADHD

Other types of medication can be used to treat symptoms of adult ADHD but they are not regarded as effective as stimulants or atomoxetine. These include selective serotonin reuptake inhibitors, venlafaxine, mood stabilisers (e.g. sodium valproate), atypical antipsychotics, or more rarely anti-hypertensives (e.g. clonidine).

3.9.4 MANAGEMENT OF COMORBID DISORDERS

As comorbidity is the rule rather than the exception in adult ADHD, treatment almost always involves the treatment of comorbidity. This can require several interventions and involve a number of psychosocial and medication treatments. The most impairing condition should be first targeted, using the most effective treatment for that condition. For example, if ADHD presents with comorbid substance or alcohol abuse, the latter condition should be addressed first via detoxification/counselling/medication. When this is under control, ADHD symptoms can then be reassessed and appropriately treated.

3.10 CONCLUSION

Adult ADHD is an increasingly recognised and valid disorder. A careful clinical assessment can accurately diagnose the condition. Options for effective management of symptoms exist. As with any emergent disorder, our current understanding of adult ADHD is incomplete. More research on adult ADHD is required. Future work should refine guidelines on assessment and management in line with evidence from the literature. More long-term outcome studies on the efficacy of psychostimulants and other medications in adult ADHD are needed. Finally further education and training are necessary for clinicians to treat this complex and challenging disorder.

3.11 REFERENCES

Applegate B, Lahey BB, Hart EL *et al.* (1997) Validity of the age-of-onset criterion for ADHD: a report from the DSM-IV field trials. *J Am Acad Child Adolesc Psychiatry* **36**: 1211–21.

Barkley RA, Biederman J (1997) Towards a broader definition of the age-of-onset criterion for Attention-Deficit Hyperactivity Disorder. *J Am Acad Child Adolesc Psychiatry* **36**: 1204–10.

Barkley RA, Fischer M, Smallish L, Fletcher K (2002) The persistence of Attention-Deficit/Hyperactivity Disorder into young adulthood as a function of reporting source and definition of disorder. *J Abnorm Psychol* **111**: 279–89.

Barkley RA, Grodzinsky G, DuPaul GJ (1992) Frontal lobe functions in attention deficit disorder with and without hyperactivity: a review and research report. *J Abnorm Child Psychol* **20**: 163–88.

Barkley RA, Murphy K (1997) *Attention-Deficit Hyperactivity Disorder: A Clinical Workbook*, 2nd edn. New York: Guilford Publications.

Barkley RA, Murphy K, Kwasnik D (1996) Psychological adjustment and adaptive impairments in young adults with ADHD. *J Attention Disord* **1**: 41–54.

Biederman J, Faraone SV, Mick EA *et al.* (1996a) Attention-deficit hyperactivity disorder and juvenile mania: an overlooked comorbidity? *J Am Acad Child Adolesc Psychiatry* **35**: 997–1008.

Biederman J, Faraone SV, Milberger S *et al.* (1996b) Predictors of persistence and remission of ADHD into adolescence: results from a four-year prospective follow-up study. *J Am Acad Child Adolesc Psychiatry* **35**: 343–51.

Biederman J, Faraone SV, Spencer T *et al.* (1993) Patterns of psychiatric comorbidity, cognition, and psychosocial functioning in adults with attention deficit hyperactivity disorder. *Am J Psychiatry* **150**: 1792–98.

Biederman J, Faraone SV, Spencer T *et al.* (1994) Gender differences in a sample of adults with attention deficit hyperactivity disorder. *Psychiatry Res* **53**: 13–29.

Biederman J, Wilens T, Mick EA *et al.* (1999) Pharmacotherapy of Attention-Deficit/Hyperactivity Disorders reduces risk for substance use disorder. *Pediatrics* **105**(2): e20.

Biederman J, Wilens TE, Mick EA *et al.* (1995) Psychoactive substance use disorders in adults with attention deficit hyperactivity disorder (ADHD): effects of ADHD and comorbidity. *Am J Psychiatry* **152**: 1652–8.

Conners K, Jeff JL (1999) *ADHD in Adults and Children: The Latest Assessment and Treatment Strategies.* Kansas City, MO: Compact Clinicals.

Curran S, Fitzgerald M (1999) Attention deficit hyperactivity disorder in the prison population. *Am J Psychiatry* **156**(10): 1664–5.

Downey K, Stelson F, Pomerleau O, Giordiani (1997) Adult attention deficit hyperactivity disorder: psychological test profiles in a clinical population. *J Nerv Ment Dis* **185**: 32–8.

Faraone SV, Biederman J (1994) Is attention deficit hyperactivity disorder familial? *Harvard Rev Psychiatry* **1**: 271–87.

Faraone SV, Biederman J, Spencer T *et al.* (2000a) Attention-deficit/hyperactivity disorder in adults: an overview. *Biol Psychiatry* **48**: 9–20.

Faraone SV, Biederman J, Mick E *et al.* (2000b) Family study of girls with attention deficit hyperactivity disorder. *Am J Psychiatry* **157**: 1077–83.

Fischer M (1997) Persistence of ADHD into adulthood: it depends on whom you ask. *ADHD Rep* **5**: 8–10.

Gittelman R, Mannuzza S, Shenker R, Bonagura N (1985) Hyperactive boys almost grown up. I. Psychiatric status. *Arch Gen Psychiatry* **42**: 937–47.

Greenhill LL, Swanson JM, Vitiello B *et al.* (2001) Impairment and deportment responses to different methylphenidate doses in children with ADHD: the MTA titration trial. *J Am Acad Child Adolesc Psychiatry* **40**(2): 180–7.

Hart E, Lahey B, Loeber R *et al.* (1995) Developmental change in Attention-Deficit Hyperactivity Disorder in boys: a four-year longitudinal study. *J Abnorm Child Psychol* **23**: 729–49.

Hechtman L (1992) Long-term outcome in Attention-Deficit Hyperactivity Disorder. *Psychiatr Clin North Am* **1**: 553–65.

Hechtman L, Weiss G (1986) Controlled prospective fifteen year follow-up of hyperactives as adults: non-medical drug and alcohol use and anti-social behaviour. *Can J Psychiatry* **31**: 557–67.

Heiligenstein E, Conyers LM, Berns AR *et al.* (1998) Preliminary normative data on DSM-IV attention deficit hyperactivity disorder in college students. *J Am Coll Health* **46**: 185–8.

Heiligenstein E, Keeling RP (1999) Psychological and academic functioning in college students with attention deficit hyperactivity disorder. *J Am Coll Health* **47**: 181–5.

Kessler RC, Adler L, Ames M *et al.* (2005) The prevalence and effects of adult attention deficit/hyperactivity disorder on work performance in a nationally representative sample of workers. *J Occup Environ Med* **47**(6): 565–72.

Klein RG, Mannuzza S (1991) Long-term outcome of hyperactive children: a review. *J Am Acad Child Adolesc Psychiatry* **30**: 383–7.

Kooij JJS, Buitelaar JK, van den Oord EJ *et al.* (2004) Internal and external validity of Attention-Deficit Hyperactivity Disorder in a population-based sample of adults. *Psychol Med* **34**: 1–11.

Lahey BB, Applegate B, McBurnett K *et al.* (1994) DSM-IV field trials for attention deficit hyperactivity disorder in children and adolescents. *Am J Psychiatry* **151**: 1673–85.

Levin FR, Evans SM, McDowell DM, Kleber HD (1998) Methylphenidate treatment for cocaine abusers with adult Attention-Deficit/Hyperactivity Disorder: a pilot study. *J Clin Psychiatry* **59**: 300–5.

Loney J, Kramer J, Milich RS (1981) The hyperactive child grows up: predictors of symptoms, delinquency and achievement at follow-up. In KD Gadow, J Loney (eds) *Psychosocial Aspects of Drug Treatment for Hyperactivity*, pp. 381–416. Boulder, CO: Westview.

McGough JJ, Barkley RA (2004) Diagnostic controversies in Adult Attention Deficit Hyperactivity Disorder. *Am J Psychiatry* **161**: 1948–56.

Mannuzza S, Klein RG, Bessler A *et al.* (1993) Adult outcome of hyperactive boys: educational achievement, occupational rank and psychiatric status. *Arch Gen Psychiatry* **50**(7): 565–76.

Manshadi M, Lippmann S, O'Daniel R, Blackman A (1983) Alcohol abuse and attention deficit disorder. *J Clin Psychiatry* **44**: 379–80.

Millstein RB, Wilens TE, Biederman J *et al.* (1997) Presenting ADHD symptoms and subtypes in clinically referred adults with ADHD. *J Attent Disord* **2**: 159–66.

Murphy KR, Barkley RA (1996a) Attention deficit hyperactivity disorder in adults: comorbidities and adaptive impairments. *Compr Psychiatry* **37**: 393–401.

Murphy KR, Barkley RA (1996b) Prevalence of DSM-IV symptoms of ADHD in adult licenced drivers. *J Attent Disord* **1**: 147–62.

Nimmo-Smith I, Robertson I, Ward T, Ridgeway V (1998) *The Test of Everyday Attention.* Thames Valley Test Company.

Rosler M, Retz W, Retz-Junginger P *et al.* (2004) Prevalence of attention deficit-/hyperactivity disorder (ADHD) and comorbid disorders in young male prison inmates. *Eur Arch Psychiatry Clin Neurosci* **254**(6): 365–71.

Spencer T, Biederman J, Wilens TE *et al.* (1998) Adults with Attention-Deficit/Hyperactivity Disorder: a controversial diagnosis. *J Clin Psychiatry* 59[suppl 7]: 59–68.

Spencer T, Wilens T, Biederman J *et al.* (1995) A double-blind, crossover comparison of methylphenidate and placebo in adults with childhood-onset Attention-Deficit Hyperactivity Disorder. *Arch Gen Psychiatry* **52**: 434–43.

Swanson JM, Sergeant JA, Taylor E *et al.* (1998) Attention-defct hyperactivity disorder and hyperkinetic disorder. *Lancet* **351**: 429–33.

Tannock R (2000) Attention deficit disorders with anxiety disorders. In S Brown (ed.) *Attention Deficit Disorders and Comorbidities in Children, Adolescents and Adults.* New York: American Psychiatric Press.

Tannock R, Ickowicz A, Schachar R (1995) Differential effects of methylphenidate on working memory in ADH/HD children with and without comorbid anxiety. *J Am Acad Child Adolesc Psychiatry* **34**: 886–95.

Thorley G (1984) Review of follow-up and follow-back studies of childhood hyperactivity. *Psychol Bull* **96**: 116–32.

Vreugdenhil C, Doreleijers TA, Vermeiren R *et al.* (2004) Psychiatric disorders in a representative sample of incarcerated boys in the Netherlands. *J Am Acad Child Adolesc Psychiatry* **43**(1): 97–104.

Weiss G, Hechtman L (1993) *Hyperactive Children Grown Up: ADHD in Children, Adolescents and Adulthood*, 2nd edn. New York: Guilford Press.

Weiss M, Hechtman L, Weiss G (1999) *ADHD in Adulthood: A Guide to Current Theory, Diagnosis, and Treatment*. Baltimore, MD: The Johns Hopkins University Press.

Wilens TE, Biederman J, Spencer TJ *et al.* (1999) Controlled trial of high doses of pemoline for adults with Attention-Deficit/Hyperactivity Disorder. *J Clin Psychopharmacol* **19**: 257–64.

Wilens TE, Faraone SV, Biederman J (2004) Attention-Deficit/Hyperactivity Disorder in adults. *JAMA* **292**(5): 619–23.

4 ADHD and Comorbid Oppositional Defiant and Conduct Disorders

PAUL MCARDLE

Newcastle University, Fleming Nuffield Unit, Newcastle upon Tyne, UK

4.1 OVERVIEW

His most extraordinary quality ... was his titanic energy. He could not sit still or stay long in the same place. He walked so quickly ... that those in his company had to trot to keep up with him. When forced to do paperwork, he paced around a stand up desk. Seated at a banquet, he would eat for a few minutes, then spring up to see what was happening in the next room or to take a walk outdoors ... When he had been in one place for a while, he wanted to leave ... The most accurate image ... is of a man who throughout his life was perpetually ... restless, perpetually in movement. (Robert K Massie, *Peter the Great*)

Conduct disorder of early onset, attention deficit hyperactivity and oppositional defiant disorder share common neurodevelopmental vulnerabilities encompassing learning, language, social development and the capacity to see consequences. All may potentially be predictive of substance abuse, severely antisocial outcomes in adulthood or indeed suicide. In part, this is determined by potentially reversible environmental stresses such as unsuitable schooling, abuse, or inadequate attachment experiences. The clinician's task may be not so much differential diagnosis but one of understanding the relevant vulnerability and through relating positively and over an extended period to the child and family, pharmacotherapy, and sustained advocacy with relevant systems, attempting to construct environmental and pharmacological conditions to steer the child in a developmentally more optimal direction.

4.2 CONDUCT DISORDER AND ADHD

The emergence of attention deficit hyperactivity disorder (ADHD) as a distinct form of disruptive behaviour has marked a striking change in child psychiatry over recent decades, from a view of behaviour disorder as predominantly socially determined towards largely biological explanations (e.g. Biederman & Faraone, 2005). This process has also reduced the diagnostic role of conduct disorder (CD), previously the dominant category for child behaviour disorders, and historically understood to be, in large part, a sustained disruptive response to stresses and deficiencies within the family environment (Patterson, 1977; Keisner *et al.*, 2001).

Handbook of Attention Deficit Hyperactivity Disorder. Edited by M. Fitzgerald, M. Bellgrove and M. Gill.
© 2007 John Wiley & Sons Ltd

As currently conceptualised, ADHD is characterised by developmentally excessive levels of inattention, activity and impulsivity (APA, 1994). Although generally regarded as of early onset, some able children may cope well until, for instance, school or social demands escalate beyond their capacity to compensate, so that it may occasionally present as late as the early years of secondary school. It may also present in adulthood but usually with a long history of undiagnosed distress, disturbance and underachievement (Hesslinger *et al.*, 2003). Nevertheless, the age of onset criterion is important as it denotes a developmental disorder, a key element in the concept. Symptoms are also present in more than one setting. This is crucial to locate the problem within the child's development rather than the eye of one observer or in one dysfunctional situation (APA, 1994).

In the UK the prevalence of the combined type (with hyperactivity-impulsivity as well as inattention), broadly the equivalent of hyperkinetic disorder (Taylor *et al.*, 1991) is about 2% of primary school age boys (McArdle, Prosser & Kolvin, 2004). However, significant symptoms may be more common, hence the estimate of 5% for ADHD including predominantly inattentive and predominantly hyperactive-impulsive subtypes (APA, 1994). There is also some indication that rates vary, with higher rates of disruptive behaviour as a whole (including CD) in urban, and lower rates in small town and rural, settings (McArdle *et al.*, 2004).

The underlying neurophysiology of ADHD implicates an abnormal or at least sub-optimal functioning of possibly dorso- and infero-lateral prefrontal and adjacent sub-cortical structures, notably the striatum (Nigg, 2005). An influential view is that this gives rise to impairment in executive functioning, said to be responsible for goal-directed behaviour; unable to plan ahead, affected individuals are governed by the contingencies of the minute. Barkley (1997) also argues that an intact capacity for response inhibition, said to be linked to the inferior prefrontal cortex (Rubia *et al.*, 2005), is critical to allow time for these integrative and strategic functions to occur. Other related theories include the possibility of deficits in activation of intact neural systems or a specific aversion to delay or perhaps all three (Nigg, 2005). It is possible that there are distinct neuropsychological subtypes (Willcutt *et al.*, 2005) or that somewhat different structures or systems are called into play under different circumstances, hence the appearance of neuropsychological heterogeneity, discussed in more detail by Nigg (2005).

Peer rejection was identified as one of the early comorbidities associated with ADHD, attributed to the aversive effects on peers of impulsive behaviour interfering with play (McArdle *et al.*, 1995). However, it appears that rejection reflects an often associated social impairment (Geurts *et al.*, 2004) that persists even after the other symptoms of ADHD diminish, suggesting that it cannot be attributed solely to the core features of the syndrome (Danckaerts *et al.*, 2000). Hence, other brain systems such as those involving the 'social brain', the amygdala (associated with the emotion of fear), anterior cingulate gyrus, insula (which links language areas), and, again, the orbito- and medial-frontal cortex, may be contributing to impairment associated with the syndrome (Veit *et al.*, 2002). The prefrontal cortex is crucial to the normal integration of emotion, including normal fear, into rational decision making (Bechara *et al.*, 1999), hence, perhaps, the links between the disinhibition of ADHD and the broader realm of risk-taking. Imaging studies further point to the possibility of involvement of the cerebellum, perhaps implicated in motor and other functions (Seidman *et al.*, 2005). In addition, ADHD is attended by abnormal language development (Taylor *et al.*, 1991), possibly related to deficits in working memory (Jonsdottir *et al.*, 2005). All this suggests that in many cases, ADHD and its associated comorbidity emerge from a dysfunction of widely distributed brain systems. Indeed, in individual cases, it may be unclear whether the core symptoms or, for instance, the social or learning comorbidities are the most impairing, although the ADHD symptoms may be the most immediately treatable.

ADHD declines in prevalence with age and the underlying neural circuits appear subject to maturation. For instance, brain imaging suggests that implicated areas of the striatum, especially the caudate nucleus tend to normalise in size by mid-adolescence (Castellanos *et al.*, 2002). Indeed, some suggest that the relevant neural networks do not finish maturing until middle age (Bartzokis *et al.*, 2001). Hence, especially in severe clinical presentations it is possible to view ADHD as a component or marker of a complex neurodevelopmental dysmaturity (Rubia *et al.*, 1999) that may generally tend to improve with time (Maughan *et al.*, 2004). Nevertheless, it has also become clear that a minority of sufferers may remain significantly symptomatic well into adulthood (Kessler *et al.*, 2005).

The International Classification of Disease – 10th edition – characterises conduct disorder as 'a repetitive and persistent pattern of dissocial, aggressive, or defiant conduct'. It lists behaviours that are very similar to those in the *Diagnostic and Statistical Manual* (DSM-IV) of the American Psychiatric Association (APA, 1991) (Table 4.1). This further specifies that 'the basic rights of others or major age appropriate societal norms or rules are violated (criterion A)'. Criterion B requires that 'this disturbance in behaviour causes clinically significant impairment in social, academic or occupational functioning'. Criterion C requires that in older individuals the criteria for antisocial personality disorder are not met. In order to make the diagnosis, and since affected young people may minimise symptoms, as in the case of ADHD, it is generally recommended that information is obtained from different sources such as the school and parents.

DSM-IV further sub-classifies conduct disorder into adolescent onset, in which no symptoms were apparent before ten years of age, and childhood onset in which case at least one symptom was present before ten years of age. As early onset conduct disorder may be associated with aggression, impaired peer relationships, and higher risk of adult anti-social personality disorder, this distinction may be important for prognosis (Moffitt *et al.*, 2002). It differs from the sub-classification in ICD-10 which focuses on socialised and non-socialised conduct disorder. However, it is likely that there is overlap between respectively the socialised and adolescent onset disorder, likely to be attended by lower rates of impairment, and the non-socialised and childhood onset variety, with their greater neuro-developmental vulnerability and probably poorer prognosis (Moffitt *et al.*, 2002). Consistent with this age-related sub-classification, there is some evidence that the genes associated with early and late-onset CD are not identical (O Connor *et al.*, 1998).

Whether early or late onset, conduct disorder is associated with an increased risk of school failure and dropout, cigarette smoking (Lynskey and Ferguson, 1995), drug and alcohol misuse (Mannuzza *et al.*, 1998) and dependence (Bardone *et al.*, 1998), early

Table 4.1. DSM-IV criteria for Conduct Disorder

Criterion A includes 14 possible symptoms divided into four groups. The young person must have manifested at least three of these symptoms in the previous six months. The first group concerns aggression:

1. Often bullies, threatens or intimidates others
2. Often initiates physical fights
3. Has used a weapon that can cause serious physical harm to others
4. Has been physically cruel to people
5. Has been physically cruel to animals
6. Has stolen while confronting a victim
7. Has forced someone into sexual activity

The second group concerns destruction of property:

8. Has deliberately engaged in fire setting with the intention of causing serious damage
9. Has deliberately destroyed others' property (other than by fire setting)

The third concerns 'deceitfulness or theft':

10. Has broken into someone else's house building or car
11. Often lies to obtain goods or favors or to avoid obligations (i.e. 'cons' others)
12. Has stolen items of non-trivial value without confronting a victim (e.g. shoplifting)

The final group refers to 'serious violations of rules'

13. Often stays out at night despite parental prohibitions, beginning before age 13 years
14. Has run away from home overnight at least twice while living in parental home or parental surrogate home (or once without returning for a lengthy period)
15. Often truants from school beginning before age 13 years

---

sexual behaviour and teenage pregnancy (Kessler *et al.*, 1997), crime, completed suicide (Brent *et al.*, 1999), lasting impairment and personality dysfunction (Zoccolillo *et al.*, 1992) and a range of long-term costs to society (Knapp *et al.*, 2002). It is also responsible for the disappearance from the education, training and ultimately the labour force of a significant group of physically fit young people (Scott *et al.*, 2001, http://www.everychildmatters.gov.uk/ete/neet/). This is in an era of ageing populations when young workers, especially those with skills, are in great demand. Furthermore, there is evidence that conduct disorder is increasing in Western societies (Smith & Rutter, 1995; Collishaw *et al.*, 2004). Consequently, some argue that it is a considerable public health challenge (Angold & Costello, 2001). However, it is more than this, perhaps a social, economic and ultimately a political challenge.

Most pre-pubertal children identified as conduct disordered show predictable comorbidity (Moffitt *et al.*, 2002). For instance, deficits in verbal skills have been long recognised among conduct-disordered children (Rutter *et al.*, 1970; Lynam & Henry, 2001). These can commonly manifest as specific reading retardation or communication deficits. Tomblin *et al.* (2000) argue that 'the behaviour problems . . . arise from the presence of limited language skills and the (inability to meet) demands . . . for performance that requires verbal skills' (p. 479). Of course, this is only one factor but as the school curriculum progresses, demands escalate, contributing potentially to a breakdown of the relationship between the child and school. It appears that either a generalised language delay or a delay in comprehension of receptive language is most associated with disturbed behaviour (Beitchman, Brownlie *et al.*, 1996; Beitchman, Wilson *et al.*, 1996). Indeed, among adolescent delinquent youth (the great majority of whom are likely to have been conduct disordered) there are said to be general verbal deficits encompassing problems of language and literacy (Snowling *et al.*, 2000).

Oppositional defiant disorder (ODD) is symptomatically a close relative of conduct disorder and, according to DSM-IV, is characterised by at least four of the following symptoms: loses temper, argues with adults, actively denies or refuses adult requests, deliberately does things that annoy other people, blames others for his or her mistakes or misbehaviour, is touchy or easily annoyed by others, is angry and resentful, spiteful or vindictive. ODD shares similar correlates to conduct disorder (Burt *et al.*, 2003) and may be an early manifestation of childhood onset conduct disorder perhaps before antisocial behaviour spills into the community (Biederman *et al.*, 1996; Burke *et al.*, 2002). ODD and aggression tend both to be of early onset and to predict adult antisocial behaviour (Lahey *et al.*, 1999; Langbehn *et al.*, 1998). This suggests that ODD with its temperament- and 'personality-like' (p. 827) characteristics (Langbehn *et al.*, 1998), as well as aggressive CD, may be synonymous with or at least overlap with Moffitt's lifespan persistent or DSM's childhood onset CD.

Indeed, all three 'externalising' disorders (ADHD, CD and ODD) commonly co-occur. For instance, Maughan *et al.* (2004) demonstrated that among 5–15 year olds in the community, approaching 30% of those with CD and approaching 40% of those with ODD and CD also displayed ADHD. Among the youngest children, the comorbidity may be higher. Greene *et al.* (2002) argue that at least 80% of younger children referred with conduct disorder (mean age 10.7 years) merit a further diagnosis of ADHD. McArdle *et al.* (1995) estimated that virtually all 7–8 year olds with severe CD also displayed at least some symptoms of ADHD. Children with the combined ADHD and ODD or CD are likely to exhibit severe disturbance (Newcorn *et al.*, 2001). Maughan *et al.* (2004) further speculate on the meaning of the association between the 'negativistic, disobedient and hostile behaviour patterns indexed by ODD' (p. 619), ADHD, later CD and depression. They suggest that the presence of symptoms of ODD 'act as markers for a . . . broader construct of behavioural (and possibly emotional) dysregulation . . . (p. 620)'.

Much of the brain research most closely related to CD rather than ADHD focuses on adult antisocial personality disorder (ASPD). This is characterised by behaviour similar to CD and evidence of prior CD is a diagnostic criterion (WHO, 1992). Interestingly, the responsivity of the amygdala and orbito-frontal cortex (in ADHD research linked with response inhibition) is abnormal among the most antisocial individuals (Birbaumer *et al.*, 2005). At least superficially, their 'myopia for the future' (Bechara *et al.*, 2000, p. 2189) resembles the impulsivity of ADHD, hence the term 'disinhibitory syndromes' (p. 923) for the whole range of disruptive behaviours (Hicks *et al.*, 2004). The shared phenomenon of impulsivity may be linked with genetically influenced serotoninergic activation of a distributed cortico-subcortical circuitry (Passamonti *et al.*, 2006).

Like ADHD, ASPD with its orbito-frontal pathology may be developmental or (occasionally) acquired (Blair & Cipolotti, 2000; Anderson *et al.*, 1999). These individuals may have difficulty inhibiting behaviour inappropriate to context and case reports often also describe marked irritability and angry responses with minimal stress (Blair & Cipolotti, 2000). Indeed, it is possible to speculate that, whether the lens is focussed on ODD, ADHD, early onset conduct disorder or even ASPD, it is the same or similar dysmaturity or dysregulation that is under scrutiny. Hence, for many clinically referred children with more severe disorders, overlapping psychopathology and neurodevelopmental dysmaturity is to be expected, rather than 'pure' diagnostic groups, but with the most obvious expression through a final common pathway of dysphoria and aggression. Using an argument similar to that of Tomblin *et al.* (2000) and language development, Raine (2002) suggests that 'social and executive function demands . . . overload the late developing prefrontal cortex, giving rise to prefrontal dysfunction and a lack of inhibitory control over antisocial, violent behavior'. Overloading a young person at any age, especially in the presence of abnormalities of appraisal and control, may predispose to irritability, and in some, aggression and violence, hence the links between ADHD and disinhibitory syndromes in general and certain conduct disordered symptoms.

Accumulated evidence now points to the crucial importance of genetic influence in the origins of ADHD and CD. These have usually depended on twin studies pointing to high identical twin compared to non-identical twin concordance so that it is possible to calculate that the heritability of ADHD is in the region of 70%, i.e. 70% of the variance in the associated traits is attributable to genetic variance (Biederman & Faraone, 2005). This is clinically important as it is possible to point out to parents and others that the disorder cannot be attributable in its entirety to poor parenting, a prevailing cultural prejudice. However, genetic influences also extend to antisocial disorders. In a recent review, Moffitt (2005) argued that although there is evidence of direct environmental effects, child antisocial behaviour and parenting are both under genetic influence and, further, that genetically influenced child behaviour elicits problem parenting (although probably short of actual child mistreatment). Indeed, she challenged the convention that behaviours within the normal range of parenting could be causally related to child antisocial behaviour. Hicks *et al.* (2004) have further argued that a common genetic vulnerability underlies the whole range of antisocial disorders, child and adult. This is consistent with the view that 'the genes that influence conduct disorder symptoms are the same as those that contribute to hyperactivity' (Thapar *et al.*, 1999), although additional non-shared and shared environmental factors appear to be required for conduct disorder (Thapar *et al.*, 2001). It is also consistent with the possibility of shared neuro-developmental dysmaturity.

However, the lack of distinction between child and adolescent onset disorders may be a problem in genetic studies. It may be that the childhood onset or unsocialised disorders, whether conforming predominantly to ADHD, CD or ODD symptom patterns, that persist into adulthood are more likely to have a genetic component than the adolescent onset or socialised variety (Langbehn *et al.*, 1998). In the latter, other mechanisms, such as poor supervision or other signs of family dysfunction, peer influences and neighbourhood problems seem likely to be influential or necessary for the full syndrome to emerge (Fergusson & Horwood, 1999; Caspi *et al.*, 2000; Fergusson *et al.*, 2002; Costello *et al.*, 2003).

Indeed, even in ADHD, identical twin concordance is not perfect so that a full explanation does require acknowledgement of significant environmental influences. In an interesting study of non-concordant monozygotic twins, Castellanos *et al.* (2003) identified that ADHD affected twins had smaller caudate nuclei than their non-ADHD co-twins and suggested that this apparently non-genetic abnormality might be due to perinatal adversity. Also, extreme forms of unresponsive or hostile care may be associated with CD through the mechanism of disorganised attachment linked to 'heightened . . . distress and dysphoria' and behaviour that is characteristi-cally hostile, aggressive and antisocial (Lyons-Ruth, 1996, p. 70). Although some discount it, most clinicians would still argue that sustained parental criticism, or certain types of interaction within families that are relatively common in clinical practice, can in a practical way contribute to deviant child behaviour (Meyer *et al.*, 2000). For instance, Langbehn *et al.* (1998) argued that the expression of adolescent conduct disorder in predisposed adopted children requires an adverse adoptive family environment. Nevertheless, in order alone to lead to extreme deviance in younger children (where there is no apparent genetic predisposition), it is likely that the abnormality in relationships must also be extreme. These circumstances are uncommon and at least among younger children are probably not, alone, the usual route to symptoms of conduct disorder (O'Connor & Rutter, 2000; McArdle *et al.*, 2002a). Also, the relative importance of, and the links between, intra-familial behav-iours, family structure (for instance, as it affects supervision) and the qualities of neighbourhoods are not well known; indeed disorganised neighbourhoods are likely to have a distinct contributory role (Sampson *et al.*, 1997). However, it is clear that all relevant environmental aspects of conduct disorder are not captured by examina-tion of family 'dynamics' alone.

Focusing on ADHD, potentially influential environmental factors include early extreme psychosocial deprivation (Kreppner *et al.* 2001). Hence, there is a correla-tion between length of extreme deprivation (in this case, a Romanian orphanage) and, specifically, inattention/overactivity symptoms that cannot be attributed to general developmental level. Also, food additives may significantly increase parent-rated symptoms probably through a pharmacological mechanism (Bateman *et al.*, 2004). In addition, an ADHD-like syndrome may arise from brain injury (Bloom *et al.*, 2001), including that related to prematurity, possibly related to reduced hippo-campal volume (Abernathy *et al.*, 2002). However, the great majority of children with ADHD have not suffered extreme deprivation or head injury and the influence of food is in most cases likely to be modest or even marginal to overall impairment.

Nevertheless, in Western or Westernising societies, ADHD occurs against a back-ground of social and cultural changes that may have acted to the psychosocial detriment of children more generally (Fukuyama, 1999; Collishaw *et al.*, 2004; Timimi, 2005). These are said to include, for instance, reductions in children's scope for adventurous play and in informal social control in communities, combined with increased demands on children for academic success in a 'knowledge society' (http://ec.europa.eu/employment_social/knowledge_society/education_eu-htm). Hence, while ADHD itself has not increased in prevalence (McArdle, Prosser, Dickinson & Kolvin, 2003), it may have increased in significance. For instance, the work of Collishaw *et al.* (2004) demonstrated that the risk of comorbid conduct problems among hyperactive youth increased substantially from 1979.

Others have argued that attributes that might not have reached clinical significance or that might even have been adaptive in the past (Jensen *et al.*, 1997) may now be, for many, disadvantageous or disabling (for a further discussion see Chapter 21).

According to a developmental psychopathology model of deviance, it is possible that an array of developmental vulnerabilities renders a child difficult to raise, educate and relate to. Especially if parents are vulnerable, or if support is not forthcoming in school, such a child can elicit ineffectual coercive discipline from parents and teachers, negatively reinforcing his or her aversive behaviour (Moffitt, 2005). This effectively trains the child in defiance (Patterson, 1977). The quality of the attachment to parents in the first place and subsequently to other adults deteriorates, leading to a disorder of attachment superimposed upon an array of developmental deficits.

Interestingly, this gene–environment interaction may be particularly important in determining adverse consequences for girls (Langbehn *et al.*, 1998). Girls with ODD or CD may be even more likely to display comorbid ADHD; hence the possibility that greater developmental adversity is required for girls to be referred or to 'convert' to CD or indeed ODD (Biederman *et al.*, 2005). However, ADHD, early developmental anomalies and early onset conduct disorder occur less often in females, while the gender ratio approaches equality in adolescents (Angold *et al.*, 2002). Hence, there is a possibility that girls with CD are more likely to have the adolescent onset type that has relatively low ADHD and other neurodevelopmental comorbidity but greater emotional comorbidity such as PTSD (Reebye *et al.*, 2000).

The key point is that most young males with conduct disorder are likely to exhibit complex comorbidity that affords opportunities for in-depth assessment, comprehensibility, explanation and intervention based on a compassionate and potentially helpful rather than condemnatory framing of their presentation. For females, the likelihood of developmental deficits may be less but other pathologies, for instance, PTSD and major depression, which are more likely in females and often comorbid with CD, should be sought, as should the potentially accompanying psychosocial adversity (Crowley *et al.*, 2003).

Conceivably therefore, children with early onset CD, ODD or ADHD display a similar array of neurodevelopmental dysmaturities that differ somewhat in emphasis and that result in the symptoms of ADHD at the less severe end of the externalising spectrum. Add in a severe social communication deficit associated with lack of empathy and in addition school failure and disorganised attachment and severe CD ensues. Hence, what differentiates the conditions is not neurodevelopmental anomalies alone but their unique combination in individual cases with environmental influences, all of which require examination and formulation.

Treatment of these conditions relies on medication and psychosocial interventions. Two broad approaches to pharmacological intervention include those targeted on ADHD and those on aggression. The first are well known and epitomised by the MTA trial that demonstrated the efficacy of carefully controlled and titrated stimulant medication but also the positive usefulness on overall levels of disturbance and on ODD and CD symptoms, of combining with a psychosocial intervention (Connors *et al.*, 2001; Swanson *et al.*, 2001). There are fewer data available on direct pharmacological treatments for CD, but methylphenidate can reduce aggression, defiance and destructiveness (Klein *et al.*, 1997). Also, clinical (Soderstrom *et al.*, 2002) and trial data (Snyder *et al.*, 2002) offer evidence of the efficacy of low-dose antipsychotic medication, such as risperidone, on target symptoms of irritability and aggression.

Randomised controlled trials have also yielded evidence supportive of psychosocial interventions for comorbid hyperactivity and conduct disorder. These include parenting (Scott *et al.*, 2001), behavioural (Kazdin, 1997), psychodynamic (Fonagy and Target, 1994) and perhaps school-based group (Kolvin *et al.*, 1981; McArdle *et al.*, 2002b) interventions. Also, there is some evidence that combinations of interventions can be synergistic (Grizenko *et al.*, 1993; Kolko *et al.*, 1999; Myers *et al.*, 2000; Liddle *et al.*, 2001; Swanson *et al.*, 2001; Henggeller *et al.*, 2003). However, Kazdin (1997) has drawn attention to the high level of dropout from psychosocial interventions and the high relapse rate following cessation of intervention, although this can be reduced by active outreach (Henggeler *et al.*, 1996).

A further difficulty with psychosocial or psychotherapy intervention research is that even apparently effective interventions do not translate rapidly or even at all into practice (Weisz, 2005). In part at least this relates to the debate concerning efficacy (does it work under experimental conditions?) and effectiveness (does it work in the field?). Effectiveness studies deploy interventions that differ systematically from those that have evolved in practice, and are subject to different constraints: the type and severity of problem, seniority of intervention staff, the cost-related requirement in research that intervention and follow-up are brief, and crucially that the package is standardised and not customised to the complex circumstances and psychopathology of the patient. Indeed, the whole direction of travel: research-based evidence to practice has been subject to recent radical criticism on this basis (Westen *et al.*, 2004; Jensen *et al.*, 2005).

The authors of a recent large randomised controlled trial for cannabis-using youth (many of whom are likely to have been conduct disordered) concluded that factors held in common by the interventions assessed were likely to have been the agents of change (Dennis *et al.*, 2004). Such phenomena are likely to include the degree of engagement and retention said to 'capture' a number of patient and intervention characteristics including the quality of the relationship with the therapist that predict outcome (Hser *et al.*, 2004; Jensen *et al.*, 2005). Although this view draws to a degree on adult as well as the limited youth field, it is a view that makes intuitive sense to many clinicians. For this and similar reasons, some advocate careful study of the practice of successful clinicians (Westen *et al.*, 2004), a procedure more likely to yield interventions with external validity (Weisz *et al.*, 2005). Hence, it is likely that whatever the theoretical orientation of the clinician, that a successful clinician can engage and retain in therapy a relatively large proportion of children, young people and families and that the intervention will have a number of components. These are likely to include: medication, parental and child support and guidance, advocacy in relation to education, social support and criminal justice, and long-term involvement.

Finally, Kazdin (2000) has argued that intervention should be informed by our developing understanding of the psychopathology of these disorders. However, none of the treatment approaches that have been developed distinguish explicitly between childhood onset and adolescent onset CD, even though this seems to be an important demarcation. It may be that interventions focussed on the former would emphasise careful developmental assessment and an informed multi-modal intervention e.g. psycho-education and support for parents and schools, education in the broadest sense (including a focus on identified problems with language and literacy, coping with peers) and pharmacological interventions (for hyperactivity and aggression). For selected children, especially among those referred to services and who are often very complex, parenting interventions would represent important components of such a multi-modal programme but might be sufficient treatment for only a minority. A further point is the need to sustain interventions for these chronic conditions, either through extended follow-up or booster doses, in order to maintain gains (Kazdin, 1997).

For those with adolescent-onset disorders, the emphasis might be more on promoting association with pro-social peers and weaning away from antisocial or drug-using peers, school attendance, child–carer relationships and supervision (Liddle *et al.*, 2001; Henggeler *et al.*, 2003). It might be important also to evaluate from a child protection perspective and, perhaps especially in females, for the presence of post-traumatic symptoms. Whether differentiating the interventions for these two sub-groups in this way will determine outcome is not yet known but it may be one way that research should develop in the future.

Finally, ADHD and conduct disorder are often regarded as separate entities by clinicians, rather as they are described in diagnostic systems. However, while respecting their great value, diagnostic systems should be complemented by developmental and systemic views. These encompass the multiple overlapping characteristics and vulnerabilities often common to these disorders, their association with considerable suffering, and, despite the rhetoric (e.g. http://www.doh.gov.uk/nsf/children.htm), the key role played by rigid expectations within an often child-unfriendly, uncomprehending and intolerant adult world.

4.3 REFERENCES

Abernethy LJ, Palaniappan M, Cooke RW (2002) Quantitative magnetic resonance imaging of the brain in survivors of very low birth weight. *Archives of Disease in Childhood* **87**(4): 279–83.

American Psychiatric Association (1994) *Diagnostic and Statistical Manual of Mental Disorders*. 4th edn (DSM-IV). Washington, DC. http://www.doh.gov.uk/nsf/children.htm.

Anderson S, Bechara A, Damasio H *et al.* (1999) Impairment of social and moral behavior related to early damage in human prefrontal cortex. *Nature Neuroscience* **2**(11): 1032–7.

Angold A, Costello E (2001) The epidemiology of disorders of conduct: nosological issues and comorbidity. In J Hill, M Maughan (eds.) *Conduct Disorders in Childhood and Adolescence*. Cambridge: Cambridge University Press.

Angold A, Erkanli A, Farmer E *et al.* (2002) Psychiatric disorder, impairment, and service use in rural African American and white youth. *Archives of General Psychiatry* **59**(10): 893–901.

Bardone A, Moffitt T, Caspi A *et al.* (1998) Adult physical health outcomes of adolescent girls with conduct disorder, depression, and anxiety. *Journal of the American Academy of Child & Adolescent Psychiatry* **37**(6): 594–601.

Barkley RA (1997) *ADHD and the Nature of Self-control*. New York: Guildford Press.

Bartzokis G, Beckson M, Lu PH, Nuechterlein KH, Edwards N, Mintz J (2001) Age-related changes in frontal and temporal lobe volumes in men: a magnetic resonance imaging study. *Archives of General Psychiatry* **58**(5): 461–5.

Bateman B, Warner JO, Hutchinson E *et al.* (2004) The effects of a double blind, placebo controlled, artificial food colourings and benzoate preservative challenge on hyperactivity in a general population sample of preschool children. *Archives of Disease in Childhood* **89**(6): 506–11.

Bechara A, Damasio H, Damasio AR, Lee GP (1999) Different contributions of the human amygdala and ventromedial prefrontal cortex to decision-making. *Journal of Neuroscience* **19**(13): 5473–81.

Bechara A, Tranel D, Damasio H (2000) Characterization of the decision making of patients with ventromedial prefrontal cortical lesions. *Brain* **123**: 2189–202.

Beitchman J, Brownlie E, Inglis A *et al.* (1996) Seven-year follow up of speech and language impaired and control children: psychiatric outcome. *Journal of Child Psychology and Psychiatry* **37**(8): 961–70.

Beitchman J, Wilson B, Brownlie E *et al.* (1996) Long-term consistency in speech/language profiles: II. Behavioural, emotional and social outcomes. *Journal of the American Academy of Child and Adolescent Psychiatry* **35**(6): 815–25.

Biederman J, Faraone SV (2005) Attention-deficit hyperactivity disorder. *Lancet* **366**(9481): 237–48.

Biederman J, Faraone SV, Milberger S *et al.* (1996) Is childhood oppositional defiant disorder a precursor to adolescent conduct disorder? Findings from a four year follow-up study of children with ADHD. *Journal of the American Academy of Child and Adolescent Psychiatry* **35**(9): 1193–204.

Birbaumer N, Veit R, Lotze M *et al.* (2005) Deficient fear conditioning in psychopathy. *Archives of General Psychiatry* **62**(7): 799–805.

Blair R, Cipolotti L (2000) Impaired social response reversal: a case of acquired psychopathy. *Brain* **123**(6): 1122–41.

Bloom D, Levin H, Ewing-Cobbs L *et al.* (2001) Lifetime and novel psychiatric disorders after pediatric traumatic brain injury. *Journal of the American Academy of Child and Adolescent Psychiatry* **40**(5): 572–9.

Brent D, Baugher M, Bridge J *et al.* (1999) Age- and sex-related risk factors for adolescent suicide. *Journal of the American Academy of Child & Adolescent Psychiatry* **38**(12): 1497–505.

Burke J, Loeber R, Birmaher B (2002) Oppositional defiant disorder and conduct disorder: a review of the past 10 years, part II. *Journal of the American Academy of Child and Adolescent Psychiatry* **41**(11): 1275–93.

Burt S, Krueger R, McGue M, Iacono W (2003) Parent-child conflict and the comorbidity among childhood externalizing disorders. *Archives of General Psychiatry* **60**(5): 505–13.

Caspi A, Taylor A, Moffitt T, Plomin R (2000) Neighborhood deprivation affects children's mental health: environmental risks identified in a genetic design. *Psychological Science* **11**(4): 338–42.

Castellanos FX, Lee PP, Sharp W *et al.* (2002) Developmental trajectories of brain volume abnormalities in children and adolescents with Attention-Deficit/Hyperactivity Disorder. *JAMA* **288**(14): 1740–8.

Castellanos FX, Sharp WS, Gottesman RF *et al.* (2003) Anatomic brain abnormalities in monozygotic twins discordant for attention deficit hyperactivity disorder. *American Journal of Psychiatry* **160**(9): 1693–6.

Collishaw S, Maughan B, Goodman R, Pickles A (2004) Time trends in adolescent mental health. *Journal of Child Psychology & Psychiatry & Allied Disciplines* **45**(8): 1350–62.

Conners CK, Epstein JN, March JS *et al*. (2001) Multimodal treatment of ADHD in the MTA: an alternative outcome analysis. *Journal of American Academy of Child and Adolescent Psychiatry* **40**: 159–67.

Costello E, Compton S, Keeler G, Angold A (2003) Relationships between poverty and psychopathology: a natural experiment. *Journal of the American Medical Association* **290**(15): 2023–9.

Crowley TJ, Mikulich SK, Ehlers KM *et al*. (2003) Discriminative validity and clinical utility of an abuse-neglect interview for adolescents with conduct and substance use problems. *American Journal of Psychiatry* **160**(8): 1461–9.

Dancaerts M, Heptinstall E, Chadwick O, Taylor E (2000) A natural history of hyperactivity and conduct problems: self reported outcome. *European Child and Adolescent Psychiatry* **9**: 26–38.

Dennis M, Godley SH, Diamond S, Tims FM, Babor T, Donaldson J, Liddle H, Titus JC, Kaminer Y, Webb C, Hamilton N, Funk R (2004) The Cannabis Youth Treatment (CYT) Study: main findings from two randomized trials. *Journal of Substance Abuse Treatment* **27**(3): 197–213.

Fergusson D, Horwood L (1999) Prospective childhood predictors of deviant peer affiliations in adolescence. *Journal of Child Psychology & Psychiatry & Allied Disciplines* **40**(4): 581–92.

Fergusson D, Swain-Campbell N, Horwood L (2002) Deviant peer affiliations, crime and substance use: a fixed effects regression analysis. *Journal of Abnormal Child Psychology* **30**(4): 419–30.

Fonagy, P, Target M (1994) The efficacy of psychoanalysis for children with disruptive disorders. *Journal of the American Academy of Child and Adolescent Psychiatry* **33**(1): 45–55.

Fukuyama F (1999) *The Great Disruption and the Reconstitution of Social Order*. New York: Free Press.

Greene R, Biederman J, Zerwas S *et al*. (2002) Psychiatric comorbidity, family dysfunction, and social impairment in referred youth with oppositional defiant disorder. *American Journal of Psychiatry* **159**(7): 1214–24.

Grizenko N, Papineau D, Sayegh L (1993) Effectiveness of a multimodal day treatment program for children with disruptive behavior problems. *Journal of the American Academy of Child and Adolescent Psychiatry* **32**(1): 127–34.

Geurts HM, Verte S, Oosterlaan J, Roeyers H, Hartman CA, Mulder EJ, Berckelaer-Onnes IA, Sergeant JA (2004) Can the Children's Communication Checklist differentiate between children with autism, children with ADHD, and normal Controls? *Journal of Child Psychology and Psychiatry and Allied Disciplines* **45**(8): 1437–53.

Henggeler SW, Pickrel S, Brondino M, Crouch J (1996) Eliminating (almost) treatment dropout of substance abusing or dependent delinquents through home-based multisystemic therapy. *American Journal of Psychiatry* **153**(3): 427–8.

Henggeler SW, Rowland MD, Halliday-Boykins C *et al*. (2003) One-year follow-up of multisystemic therapy as an alternative to the hospitalization of youths in psychiatric crisis. *Journal of the American Academy of Child and Adolescent Psychiatry* **42**(5): 543–51.

Hesslinger B, Tebartz van Elst L, Mochan F, Ebert D (2003) Attention deficit hyperactivity disorder in adults-early vs. late onset in a retrospective study. *Psychiatry Research* **119**(3): 217–23.

Hicks B, Krueger R, Iacono W *et al*. (2004) Family transmission and heritability of externalizing disorders. *A Twin-Family Study Archives of General Psychiatry* **61**: 922–8.

Hser YI, Evans E, Huang D, Anglin DM (2004) Relationship between drug treatment services, retention, and outcomes. *Psychiatric Services* **55**(7): 767–74.

Jaffee S, Moffitt T, Caspi A *et al*. (2002) Influence of adult domestic violence on children's internalizing and externalizing problems: an environmentally informative twin study. *Journal of the American Academy of Child and Adolescent Psychiatry* **41**(9): 1095–103.

Jensen PS, Mrazek D, Knapp PK, Steinberg L, Pfeffer C, Schowalter J, Shapiro T, Kagan J, Leckman JF (1997) Evolution and revolution in child psychiatry: ADHD as a disorder of adaptation. *Journal of the American Academy of Child and Adolescent Psychiatry* **36**(12): 1672–9.

Jensen PS, Weersing R, Hoagwood KE, Goldman E (2005) What is the evidence for evidence-based treatments? A hard look at our soft underbelly. *Mental Health Services Research* **7**(1): 53–74.

Jonsdottir H, Bouma A, Sergeant J, Scherder E (2005) The impact of specific language impairment on working memory in children with ADHD combined subtype. *Archives of Clinical Neuropsychology* **20**(4): 443–56.

Kazdin A (1997) Treatment of conduct disorder. *Journal of Child Psychology and Psychiatry* **38**(2): 161–78.

Kazdin A (2000) Developing a research agenda for child and adolescent psychotherapy. *Archives of General Psychiatry* **57**(9): 829–35.

Keisner J, Dishion T, Poulin F (2001) A reinforcement model of conduct problems in children and adolescents: advances in theory and intervention. In J Hill, B Maughan (eds) *Conduct Disorders in Childhood and Adolescence*. Cambridge: Cambridge University Press.

Kessler RC, Adler LA, Barkley R *et al.* (2005) Patterns and predictors of Attention-Deficit/Hyperactivity Disorder persistence into adulthood: results from the national comorbidity survey replication. *Biological Psychiatry.* **57**(11): 1442–51.

Kessler RC, Berglund P, Foster C *et al.* (1997) Social consequences of psychiatric disorders, II: Teenage parenthood. American Journal of Psychiatry **154**(10): 1405–11.

Klein RG, Abikoff H, Klass E *et al.* (1997) Clinical efficacy of methylphenidate in conduct disorder with and without attention deficit hyperactivity disorder. *Archives of General Psychiatry* **54**(12): 1073–80.

Knapp M, McCrone P, Fombonne E *et al.* (2002) The Maudsley long-term follow-up of child and adolescent depression: 3. Impact of comorbid conduct disorder on service use and costs in adulthood. *British Journal of Psychiatry* **180**: 19–23.

Kolko DJ, Bukstein OG, Barron J (1999) Methylphenidate and behavior modification in children with ADHD and comorbid ODD or CD: main and incremental effects across settings. *Journal of the American Academy of Child & Adolescent Psychiatry* **38**(5): 578–86.

Kolvin I, Garside R, Nicol A, Macmillan A, Wolstenholme F, Leitch I (1981) *Help Starts Here: The Maladjusted Child in The Ordinary School.* London: Tavistock Publications.

Kreppner J, O'Connor T, Rutter M, English and Romanian Adoptees Study Team (2001) Can inattention/overactivity be an institutional deprivation syndrome? *Journal of Abnormal Child Psychology* **29**(6): 513–28.

Lahey B, Loeber R, Quay HC *et al.* (1998) Validity of DSM-IV subtypes of conduct disorder based on age of onset. *Journal of the American Academy of Child & Adolescent Psychiatry* **37**(4): 435–42.

Langbehn D, Cadoret R, Yates W *et al.* (1998) Distinct contributions of conduct and oppositional defiant symptoms to adult antisocial behavior: evidence from an adoption study. *Archives of General Psychiatry* **55**(9): 821–9.

Liddle H, Dakof G, Parker K, Diamond G, Barrett K, Tejeda M (2001) Multidimensional family therapy for adolescent drug abuse: Results of a randomized clinical trial. *American Journal of Drug & Alcohol Abuse* **27**(4): 651–88.

Lynam D, Henry B (2001) The role of neuro-psychological deficits in conduct disorders. In J Hill B Maughan (eds) *Conduct Disorders in Childhood and Adolescence*. Cambridge, Cambridge University Press.

Lynskey MT, Fergusson DM (1995) Childhood conduct problems, attention deficit behaviors, and adolescent alcohol, tobacco, and illicit drug use. *Journal of Abnormal Child Psychology* **23**(3): 281–302.

Lyons-Ruth K (1996) Attachment relationships among children with aggressive behavior problems: the role of disorganised early attachment patterns. *Journal of Consulting and Clinical Psychology* **64**(1): 64–73.

McArdle P, O'Brien G, Kolvin I (1995) Hyperactivity: prevalence and relationship with conduct disorder. *Journal of Child Psychology and Psychiatry* **36**(2): 279–305.

McArdle P, O'Brien G, Kolvin I (2000) The peer relations of children with hyperactivity and conduct disorder. *European Child and Adolescent Psychiatry* **9**(2): 91–9.

McArdle P, O'Brien G, Kolvin I (2002a) Hyperactivity and conduct disorder: exploring origins. *Irish Journal of Psychological Medicine* **19**(2): 42–47.

McArdle P, Mosely D, Quibell T, Johnson R, LeCouteur A (2002b) A randomised controlled trial of group therapy prevention of child mental health problems. *Journal of Child Psychology and Psychiatry* **43**(6): 705–12.

McArdle P, Prosser J, Dickinson H, Kolvin I (2003) Secular trends in the mental health of primary school children. *Irish Journal of Psychological Medicine* **20**(2): 56–80.

McArdle P, Prosser J, Kolvin I (2004) Epidemiology of mental disorder among primary school children in a Northern UK city. *European Child and Adolescent Psychiatry* **13**(6): 347–53.

Mannuzza S, Klein R, Bessler A, Malloy P, LaPadula M (1998) Adult psychiatric status of hyperactive boys grown up. *American Journal of Psychiatry* **155**(4): 493–8.

Maughan B, Rowe R, Messer J, Goodman R, Meltzer H (2004) Conduct disorder and oppositional defiant disorder in a national sample: developmental epidemiology. *Journal of Child Psychology & Psychiatry & Allied Disciplines* **45**(3): 609–21.

Meyer J, Rutter M, Silberg J *et al.* (2000) Familial aggregation for conduct disorder symptomatology: the role of genes, marital discord and family adaptability. *Psychological Medicine* **30**(4): 759–74.

Moffitt TE (2005) The new look of behavioral genetics in developmental psychopathology: gene–environment interplay in antisocial behaviors. *Psychological Bulletin* **131**: 533–54.

Moffitt TE, Caspi A, Harrington H, Milne B (2002) Males on the life-course-persistent and adolescence-limited antisocial pathways: follow-up at age 26 years. *Development & Psychopathology* **14**(1): 179–207.

Myers W, Burton P, Sanders P *et al.* (2000) Project back-on-track at 1 year: a delinquency treatment program for early-career juvenile offenders. *Journal of the American Academy of Child and Adolescent Psychiatry* **39**(9): 1127–34.

Newcorn JH, Halperin JM, Jensen PS *et al.* (2001) Symptom profiles in children with ADHD: effects of comorbidity and gender. *Journal of the American Academy of Child & Adolescent Psychiatry* **40**(2): 137–46.

Nigg JT (2005) Neuropsychologic theory and findings in attention deficit hyperactivity: the state of the field and salient challenges for the coming decade. *Biological Psychiatry* **57**(11): 1424–35.

O'Connor T, Neiderhiser J, Reiss D *et al.* (1998) Genetic contribution to continuity, change and co-occurrence of antisocial and depressive symptoms in adolescence. *Journal of Child Psychology and Psychiatry* **39**(3): 323–37.

O'Connor T, Rutter M (2000) Attachment disorder behavior following early severe deprivation: extension and longitudinal follow-up. English and Romanian Adoptees Study Team. *Journal of the American Academy of Child & Adolescent Psychiatry* **39**(6): 703–12.

Passamonti L, Fera F, Magariello A *et al.* (2006) Monoamine oxidase-a genetic variations influence brain activity associated with inhibitory control: new insight into the neural correlates of impulsivity. *Biological Psychiatry* **59**(4): 334–40.

Patterson GR (1977) Accelerating stimuli for two classes of coercive behaviors. *Journal of Abnormal Child Psychology* **5**(4): 335–50.

Peris T, Baker B (2000) Applications of the expressed emotion construct to young children with externalising disorder. *Journal of Child Psychology and Psychiatry* **41**(4): 457–62.

Raine A (2002) Biosocial studies of antisocial and violent behavior in children and adults: a review. *Journal of Abnormal Child Psychology* **30**(4): 311–26.

Reebye P, Moretti MM, Wiebe VJ, Lessard JC (2000) Symptoms of posttraumatic stress disorder in adolescents with a conduct disorder. Gender differences and onset patterns. *Canadian Journal of Psychiatry – Revue Canadienne de Psychiatrie* **45**(8): 746–51.

Robins L, Rutter M (eds) *Straight and Devious Pathways from Childhood to Adulthood.* Cambridge: Cambridge University Press.

Rubia K, Overmeyer S, Taylor E *et al.* (1999) Hypofrontality in attention deficit hyperactivity disorder during higher-order motor control: a study with functional MRI. *American Journal of Psychiatry* **156**(6): 891–6.

Rubia K, Smith AB, Brammer MJ *et al.* (2005) Abnormal brain activation during inhibition and error detection in medication-naive adolescents with ADHD. *American Journal of Psychiatry* **162**(6): 1067–75.

Rutter M, Tizard J, Whitmore K (1970) *Education, Health and Behaviour.* London: Longman & Green.

Sampson RJ, Raudenbush SW, Earls F (1997) Neighbourhood and violent crime: a multilevel study of collective efficacy. *Science* **277**: 918–24.

Scott S, Knapp M, Henderson J, Maughan B (2001) Financial cost of social exclusion: follow up study of antisocial children into adulthood. *British Medical Journal* **323**(7306): 191.

Seidman L, Valera E, Makris N (2005) Structural brain imaging of Attention-Deficit/Hyperactivity Disorder. *Biological Psychiatry* **57**(11): 1263–72.

Smith D, Rutter M (1995) Time trends in psychosocial disorders of youth. In M Rutter, D Smith (eds) *Psychosocial Disorders in Young People.* Chichester: John Wiley & Sons.

Snowling M, Adams J, Bowyer-Crane C, Tobin V (2000) Levels of literacy among juvenile offenders: the incidence of specific reading difficulties. *Criminal Behaviour & Mental Health* **10**(4): 229–41.

Snyder R, Turgay A, Aman M *et al.* (2002) Effects of risperidone on conduct and disruptive behavior disorders in children with subaverage IQs. *Journal of the American Academy of Child & Adolescent Psychiatry* **41**(9): 1026–36.

Soderstrom H, Rastam M, Gillberg C (2002) A clinical case series of six extremely aggressive youths treated with olanzapine. *European Child & Adolescent Psychiatry* **11**(3): 138–41.

Swanson J, Kraemer H, Hinshaw S *et al.* (2001) Clinical relevance of the primary findings of the MTA: success rates based on severity of ADHD and ODD symptoms at the end of treatment. *Journal of the American Academy of Child & Adolescent Psychiatry* **40**(2): 168–79.

Taylor E, Sandberg S, Thorley G, Giles S (1991) *The Epidemiology of Childhood Hyperactivity.* London: Oxford University Press.

Thapar A, Harrington R, McGuffin P (2001) Examining the comorbidity of ADHD-related behaviours and conduct problems using a twin study design. *British Journal of Psychiatry* **179**: 224–9.

Thapar A, Holmes J, Poulton K, Harrington R (1999) Genetic basis of attention deficit and hyperactivity. *British Journal of Psychiatry* **174**: 105–11.

Timimi S (2005) Effect of globalisation on children's mental health. *BMJ* **331**(75.7): 37–9.

Tomblin B, Zhang X, Buckwalter P (2000) The association of reading disability, behavioural disorders and language impairment among second grade children. *Journal of Child Psychology and Psychiatry* **41**(4): 473–82.

Veit R, Flor H, Erb M *et al.* (2002) Brain circuits involved in emotional learning in antisocial behavior and social phobia in humans. *Neuroscience Letters* **328**: 233–6.

Weisz JR, Doss AJ, Hawley KM (2005) Youth psychotherapy outcome research: a review and critique of the evidence base. *Annual Review of Psychology* **56**: 337–63.

Westen D, Novotny CM, Thompson-Brenner H (2004) The empirical status of empirically supported psychotherapies: assumptions, findings, and reporting in controlled clinical trials. *Psychological Bulletin* **130**(4): 631–63.

WHO (1992) *International Classification of Diseases*. Geneva. WHO.

Willcutt EG, Doyle AE, Nigg JT *et al.* (2005) Validity of the executive function theory of Attention-Deficit/Hyperactivity Disorder: a meta-analytic review. *Biological Psychiatry* **57**(11): 1336–46.

Zoccolillo M, Pickles A, Quinton D, Rutter M (1992) The outcome of childhood conduct disorder: implications for defining adult personality disorder and conduct disorder. *Psychological Medicine* **22**(4): 971–86.

5 ADHD, Autism Spectrum Disorders and Tourette's Syndrome: Investigating the Evidence for Clinical and Genetic Overlap

LOUISE GALLAGHER,[1] **MARK A. BELLGROVE,**[2] **ZIARAH HAWI,**[3] **RICARDO SEGURADO**[4] **AND MICHAEL FITZGERALD**[5]

1. School of Medicine and Health Sciences, Trinity College Dublin, Ireland; 2. School of Psychology and Queensland Brain Institute (QBI) at the University of Queensland, Brisbane, Australia; 3. School of Medicine and Health Sciences, Trinity College Dublin, Ireland; 4. Biostatics and Bioinformatics Unit, Department of Psychological Medicine, Cardiff University, Heath Hospital, Cardiff, Wales; 5. Trinity College Dublin, Ireland

5.1 OVERVIEW

ADHD, autism spectrum disorders (ASDs) and Tourette's syndrome (TS) are neurodevelopmental disorders with a complex presentation and etiology. Clinically the presentation may be confused by the presence of similar symptoms in all three conditions. What is unclear from the literature is whether these symptoms are truly the same or just appear so. This leads to the question of whether the same underlying pathophysiological processes are involved or whether there are a number of pathologies that lead to the same clinical presentation. ADHD, ASD and TS are all considered to be heritable disorders with a widely accepted genetic component to the etiology. One of the main reasons for exploring whether or not there are similarities in the phenotype and etiology is to address the question of whether there are shared genetic vulnerability factors. This chapter reviews the literature with respect to the evidence for similarities in the clinical phenotype between ADHD, ASD and TS. Subsequently there is a review of the evidence for shared genetic vulnerability focused on the published literature with respect to molecular genetics investigations in the three conditions.

Neurodevelopmental disorders are considered to be those disorders that arise as a result of abnormal early brain development. A myriad of causes, innate and acquired may result in abnormal development in the developing foetus. For example, foetal alcohol spectrum disorders (FASD) represent a relatively common cause of acquired neurodevelopmental aberration. Common neurodevelopmental disorders of childhood include autism, attention deficit hyperactivity disorder (ADHD) and Tourette syndrome (TS). All three are syndromes associated with atypical development in childhood and have significant impact on the psychological and social functioning of affected individuals.

Autism is a neurodevelopmental disorder presenting in the first three years of life with abnormalities in social interaction, communication and behaviour. Classic autism affects approximately 1 per 1000 in the population while milder autism spectrum disorders (ASD), defined as abnormalities in two of the three domains, are more common, affecting between 1 per 250–500 (Fombonne, 2002; Fombonne et al., 2001). Like many neurodevelopmental disorders, autism is commoner in males, affecting males almost four times more frequently than females. Speech and language difficulties are a central feature of autism with 50% of individuals with the core condition remaining largely non-verbal throughout their lives. Specific learning difficulties, including problems of reading, spelling and arithmetic, are commonly reported in individuals with ASD and there are higher rates of epilepsy compared with the general population. Asperger's syndrome is also included under the umbrella of ASD and refers to a subset of individuals with ASD with communication and social skills deficits and rigid and repetitive behaviours in the context of normal intellectual functioning (Asperger, 1944). While the exact causes of autism are uncertain, it is widely accepted that genetic factors play a role in the etiology. Clinical genetic studies have detected increased rates of autism in first-degree relatives of individuals with autism. The recurrence rate in siblings has been estimated at 4–10% (Bryson, Clark & Smith, 1988; Bolton et al., 1994). Identical twins are both affected far more frequently than non-identical twins. Monozygotic concordances for autism are 60–91% compared with dizygotic concordances of 0–30% (Steffenburg, Gillberg & Hellgren, 1989; Bailey et al., 1995). Thus the heritability estimates for autism are in the order of 91–93% (Bailey et al., 1995). The mode of inheritance is not Mendelian and is likely to be polygenetic with 5–15 genes of mild effect contributing to the susceptibility (Pickles et al., 1995; Risch et al., 1999).

Tourette's syndrome (TS) is a neurodevelopmental disorder of childhood that presents with multiple motor or vocal tics that have been present for at least one year. Motor tics are involuntary movements of functionally related groups of muscles in the face, limbs or trunk and at times these can develop into complex tics that involve movements of the whole body. Vocal tics are involuntary expressions, such as noises, words (sometimes obscenities) or repetitive phrases (in some cases with increasing rapidity). Prevalence estimates for TS range from 1–3% (Kadesjo & Gillberg 2000; Mason et al., 1998; Robertson, 2003). The presentation is frequently accompanied by symptoms of other neurodevelopmental disorders. Similarly to ASD and ADHD the exact causes of TS are uncertain but genetic factors are implicated. Clinical genetics studies such as twin studies have shown monozygotic (MZ) to dizygotic (DZ) concordance rates of 50–56% (MZ) to 8% (DZ) (Price et al., 1985; Hyde et al., 1992). It is widely accepted, as with ADHD and ASD, that TS is a complex genetic disorder with a strong genetic component (Walkup et al., 1996).

The genetics of ADHD have been more thoroughly described elsewhere in this book (see Chapter 8). Suffice to say that the genetics of ADHD are similar to both ASD and TS with respect to the complex polygenetic nature. Widespread efforts have attempted to elucidate the biological causes of these conditions and a variety of approaches, including genetic, neuropsychological, biochemical and animal studies, have been undertaken to this end. Once susceptibility genes for these disorders are identified, the challenge will be to tease out the functions of the protein products of these genes, how they influence brain development, how deficits in brain development contribute to neuropsychological deficits and observed clinical symptoms and the role played by environmental factors within these complex relationships.

The subject of this chapter was prompted by the clinical observation that many individuals with ADHD also appear to have symptoms frequently considered to be on the autistic spectrum and vice versa. This has not, however, been well documented in the literature; a possible reason for this might be the influence of the hierarchical rule of DSM-IV which prevents giving an Axis I diagnosis of ADHD where a diagnosis of ASD has been given. Adherence to the hierarchical rule is likely to have discouraged investigation of the overlap. This has not been the case with ADHD and TS which are well documented to occur co-morbidly (Peterson, 2001). Thus the chapter first explores the potential evidence for an epidemiological or clinical overlap between ADHD and ASD. The extant literature is also reviewed in relation to TS and ADHD. Subsequently, a discussion of the genetic susceptibility to ADHD, ASD and TS follows and the question of whether there may be shared genetic susceptibility is discussed.

5.2 EPIDEMIOLOGICAL AND CLINICAL OVERLAP BETWEEN ATTENTION DEFICIT HYPERACTIVITY DISORDER (ADHD), AUTISTIC SPECTRUM DISORDERS (ASD) AND TOURETTE SYNDROME (TS)

5.2.1 ADHD AND ASD

Clinical impression suggests that symptoms that occur in ADHD are often observed in ASD and vice versa. A literature exists that reports on the occurrence of symptoms such as hyperactivity and inattentiveness in ASD and, conversely, deficits in social interaction, oppositional behaviours and restricted and repetitive patterns of behaviour in ADHD. Longstanding debate also exists with respect to the phenomenology of the two disorders. The hierarchical rule of DSM-IV has been referred to above. This represents one extreme of the two viewpoints that are debated. It has been asserted that autistic symptoms are rare in children with hyperactivity (Rutter & Yoursov, 1994). Others, however, have argued that ADHD could occur alone or together with the triad of impairments of ASD (Wing, 1996). Increasingly co-occurrence of symptoms of autism and ADHD has been reported with rates ranging up to 80% for ASD symptoms occurring in ADHD (Yoshida, 2004). Conversely, the rates of ADHD symptoms in ASD appear to be in the order of 33% (Goldstein & Schwebach, 2004).

Before considering the clinical evidence of overlap between autism and ADHD it is worthwhile to consider what the possible mechanism for such an overlap might be. Firstly symptoms may occur in both disorders that appear to be the same but have different etiologies. This might result, for example, if symptoms specific to one disorder resulted in symptoms that were similar to the other disorder, e.g.

hyperactivity and inattention impacting on the ability to process socially relevant information in ADHD. Compounding this is the fact that symptoms observed in ADHD and autism impact on behaviours that are the result of higher cognitive processing. Thus many complex pathways may be affected that result in the apparent clinical symptom. Secondly, pleiotropy or phenotypic heterogeneity, terms referring to the phenomenon whereby phenotypic variation occurs in genetically identical organisms as a result of non-genetic factors, should also be considered. It is possible, although less likely, that in ADHD and ASD the same pathological processes result in different phenotypic presentations depending on a given set of factors, environmental or otherwise. Finally, a quantitative symptomatic theory might also be the case. This requires one to consider the symptoms occurring in both disorders in a dimensional manner and thus also the possibility that ADHD and ASD represent syndromes with clusters of symptoms that have the potential to overlap. This latter scenario gives rise to the possibility that sub-groups of individuals with ADHD may also have symptoms of ASD, and conversely that individuals with ASD may present with symptoms of ADHD.

Of course the motivation for disentangling these scenarios is a greater understanding of the pathophysiological processes underpinning both disorders. Considering that both are polygenetic disorders, then it might be that similar symptoms result from the same pathways relating to the same proteins and therefore susceptibility genes that contribute to the disorder. If ADHD and ASD are clinically and genetically related in this way, then there should also be evidence of this epidemiologically. It might, for example, be expected that relatives of individuals with ADHD have higher rates of ASD and vice versa. Unfortunately this question has not been addressed rigorously in the literature. Classic family studies in ASD have reported on the increased risk to siblings where one person with autism is affected but have not directly assessed the incidence of other neurodevelopmental disorders in family members of individuals with ASD. Increased rates of anxiety and depression are also reported (Bryson et al., 1988; Bolton et al., 1994). Family genetic studies in ADHD have similarly reported on the familiality of ADHD and that there are increased rates of antisocial disorders, major depressive disorder, substance dependence, and anxiety disorders, but not ASD (Biederman et al., 1992). Another study that investigated autistic symptoms in a sample of individuals with ADHD and in discordant siblings found that high scores on a rating scale of ASD symptoms in ADHD probands did not correlate with scores in their discordant siblings (Mulligan et al., 2005). Based on what is known about the co-occurrence of ADHD and ASD from the above family studies, one might assume that there is no connection between the two conditions.

Clinical evidence supporting apparent co-occurrence of symptoms in ASD and ADHD has been relatively scant although latterly there has been increased interest in the topic. Variable approaches have been documented. Some investigations have attempted to quantify the frequency with which ADHD and autistic symptoms appear to co-occur while others have attempted to define the symptoms that appear to overlap. Retrospective chart reviews have reported widely varying rates of comorbidity. One study reported that 17% of children with Asperger's disorder had also received an additional diagnosis of ADHD in practice (Eisenmajer et al., 1996). Another study found that the ADHD co-occurrence rate was 58% in autistic disorder and 85% in other autistic spectrum disorders such as Asperger Syndrome or Pervasive Developmental Disorder – Not Otherwise Specified (PDD-NOS) (Yoshida & Uchiyama, 2004). This study also reported higher co-occurrence rates for younger children.

Some recent studies have adopted a prospective approach using more rigorous research designs in an attempt to identify the level of comorbid symptoms in autism (Santosh & Mijovic, 2004). Individual symptom domains have been assessed such as the occurrence of deficits in social interaction or oppositional behaviours in ADHD or hyperkinesis in ASD.

5.2.2   DEFICITS OF SOCIAL INTERACTION IN ADHD

While autism is fundamentally a socio-emotional disorder, social relationship problems also occur in ADHD. Affected individuals in both disorders are less socially competent, involved in fewer social activities, and have fewer friends compared with controls (Klassen *et al.*, 2004). As adults the social problems and interpersonal difficulties continue.

While it is widely acknowledged that social skills difficulties occur in ADHD, it is disputed as to whether these deficits are secondary to the primary symptoms of ADHD, e.g. impulsivity, or if they are similar to the deficits in social interaction that occur in ASD. Wheeler and Carlson (1994) suggested that social skills deficits might be differentially mediated by symptoms typically co-occurring with each ADHD subtype, e.g. impulsivity (Wheeler, 1994). However they suggest that other social deficits, such as failing to comprehend the impact of one's actions on others, misinterpreting social information, and possessing a limited repertoire of social responses, may be closer to the autistic type of social difficulties.

Attempts have been made to better classify social deficits in ADHD. A study that compared ADHD children with a non-ADHD control group reported rates of 22% for social disability in the ADHD group (Greene *et al.*, 1999). Some specific deficits that were reported bore similarity to autistic symptoms. These were 'lack of awareness of the feelings of others' and 'difficulty forming relationships'. While these deficits were related to underlying ADHD symptoms, the authors commented that the findings might have represented a distinct symptom of autism. Similar deficits were reported in girls with ADHD in a follow-up study (Greene *et al.*, 2001). More importantly these studies reported higher rates of adverse long-term outcome, particularly substance misuse, mood disorder and conduct disorder, in individuals with social skills deficits. In another study rates of autistic symptoms in an ADHD sample were estimated using a retrospective case note-based extraction of symptoms, as reported on the Autism Criteria Checklist (Clarke *et al.*, 1999). In this study the highest mean scores on the checklist were for 'difficulties in social interaction', particularly in empathy and peer relationships. Further difficulties were reported in communication, imaginative ability, non-verbal communication and maintaining conversation. Santosh and Mijovic investigated the association of social impairment, psychopathology and environmental stressors in hyperkinetic disorder (HKD) (Santosh & Mijovic, 2004). Nine psychopathology domains were extracted from data on children with HKD and a non-HKD control group attending child and adolescent mental health services over a nine-year period. In the HKD group there were significantly greater difficulties with social reciprocity (40%), speech and language difficulties (24%) and repetitive behaviour and over-circumscribed interests (9%). Two social-impairment subtypes were defined within the study – relationship difficulty (RD) and social communication difficulty (SCD). The SCD subtype had symptoms similar to those found in ASD such as a history of speech and language disorder, repetitive behaviours, developmental difficulties, affective symptoms and conduct problems. The RD subtype was linked to conduct problems, affective symptoms and environmental stressors.

Investigations in pre-schoolers have also demonstrated higher rates of social impairment associated with ADHD possibly supporting the hypothesis that the deficits are primary (Byrne *et al.*, 1998; Shelton *et al.*, 1998; DuPaul *et al.*, 2001).

5.2.3   OPPOSITIONAL BEHAVIOURS IN ADHD AND ASD

Oppositional behaviours are common in childhood and when extreme have been described as a separate syndrome in both ICD-10 and DSM-IV known as oppositional defiant disorder (ODD). This condition is largely characterised by negative and hostile behaviour accompanied by temper tantrums, argumentativeness, defiance, being easily annoyed and annoying to others, blaming others for mistakes, being angry, resentful, spiteful or vindictive. While ODD may occur in isolation, it frequently occurs co-morbidly in ADHD and rates of up to 60% have been reported (Kadesjo *et al.*, 2003). The question of prevalence of ODD in autistic spectrum disorders has not been widely addressed, although it is widely acknowledged clinically that oppositional behaviours are frequent in autism (Gadow *et al.*, 2004; Biederman *et al.*, 2006). Features of ADHD that are associated more frequently with ODD are high levels of hyperactivity/ impulsivity symptoms (Burns & Walsh, 2002). Oppositional behaviours are common in pre-school children and peak in the second and third year. Multiple environmental factors are likely to play a strong role in the development of severe oppositional behaviours and therefore it seems unlikely that there is a direct link between ADHD and ASD. Research has, however, highlighted a putative link between the occurrence of ASD symptoms in ADHD and risk of comorbid oppositional behaviour. A recent report screened probands with ADHD and their siblings for ASD symptoms using the social and communication questionnaire (SCQ) (Mulligan *et al.*, 2005). This investigation showed that children with ADHD scored higher on the SCQ than siblings without ADHD. Children with co-morbid conduct disorder (CD) had higher SCQ scores than children with ADHD alone. Interpretation of these results is not straightforward. Lower SCQ scores in non-ADHD siblings might imply that the ASD symptoms in the ADHD group are mediated by inattention, hyperactivity or impulsivity, and not by heritability factors. The correlation between high SCQ scores and CD implies a link between ASD symptoms and oppositionality in ADHD. The direction of causation cannot be inferred but the observations suggest that there is a sub-group of individuals with ADHD who also present with ASD symptoms.

In ASD oppositional behaviours such as aggression, self-injury and temper tantrums are linked to the presence of restricted and repetitive patterns of behaviour. A recent study has also shown the relationship between these negative behaviours and the presence of restricted and repetitive patterns of behaviour in children with language impairment without autism (Dominick *et al.*, 2006). One hypothesis to explain the association between severe oppositional behaviours in the ADHD group reported above and social and communication difficulties might be the presence of restricted and repetitive patterns of behaviour. This reflects the SCD psychopathology domain described in the investigations of Santosh and Mijovic (2004) as presented above. What is clear from the literature is that the subject requires more rigorous and well-designed investigation.

5.2.4 ATTENTION AND HYPERACTIVITY IN AUTISM SPECTRUM DISORDERS

Some studies have focused on the occurrence of ADHD symptoms in ASD. A study of individuals with PDD found that 74% of children with PDD-NOS had previously been diagnosed with ADHD (Jensen *et al.*, 1997). Yoshida and Uchiyama (2004) found that ADHD co-occurred in 58% of individuals with autistic disorder and 85% of those with Asperger Syndrome / PDD-NOS; these rates were higher for younger children. Rates of up to 80% were reported in a Scandinavian study (Ehlers *et al.*, 1997) while lower but still significant rates have been reported in other studies (Ghaziuddin *et al.*, 1998). Symptoms of both hyperactivity and inattention have been reported in ASD.

According to the diagnostic criteria for ASD in DSM-IV-TR symptoms of hyperactivity are common in ASD. Goldstein and Schwebach (2004) found that in a group of children with PDD, seven out of 27 met the criteria for ADHD combined type according to the DSM-IV-TR criteria (Goldstein & Schwebach, 2004). As discussed elsewhere in this book, dopamine pathways are hypothesised to mediate hyperactivity in ADHD based on clinical response to stimulants and increasingly supported through evidence from genetics and neuroimaging studies. The underlying causes of hyperactivity observed in ASD have not been extensively investigated. Methylphenidate response in ASD appears variable based on the published reports. One report showed that a subset of individuals with ASD were responsive to methylphenidate while the remainder were unresponsive or showed increased irritability or tics that outweighed the benefit of administering the stimulant (Handen *et al.*, 2000). There have been a limited number of reviews of the efficacy of various medications in treating the hyperactivity of ASD. While stimulants and antipsychotic medications appear to improve symptoms in some cases, neither are universally efficacious (Aman, 2004).

Inattention is a core feature of ADHD combined and inattentive sub-types. Goldstein and Schwebach (2004) found that 33% of patients with PDD met diagnostic criteria for the inattentive type of ADHD (Goldstein & Schwebach, 2004). They argued that children with PDD meeting diagnostic criteria for ADHD represent a clinically distinct group from those children with PDD alone. A further study that compared a PDD and ADHD group found that scores for attentional problems on the Child Behaviour Checklist (CBCL) were similar (Luteijn *et al.*, 2000). Schatz *et al.* have also suggested a high rate of inattention in subjects with ASD based on a study that used a continuous performance test (Schatz *et al.*, 2002).

5.3 TOURETTE SYNDROME: CO-MORBIDITY IN ADHD AND AUTISM SPECTRUM DISORDERS

The presentation of Tourette syndrome (TS) is frequently accompanied by symptoms associated with other neurodevelopmental disorders. One study of comorbidity in TS found that ADHD and ASD affected about 75% of the sample (Kadesjo & Gillberg, 2000). Sixty-four per cent had ADHD and a third of these had motor clumsiness. They also noted high rates of inattention and empathy difficulties. Gillberg observed that it was unclear if the attentional deficit of ADHD was of the same quality as that encountered in TS, attributing the inattention of TS at times to an over-focus on obsessive thoughts (Gillberg, 1995). It has been reported elsewhere that 25–85% of children with TS have ADHD (Comings, 2000). Furthermore it has been noted that when ADHD and TS co-occur, social skills are impaired (Leckman & Cohen, 2002). This social-skill delay has been attributed to the ADHD symptoms as children with TS alone appear to have better social skills. Individuals with TS and comorbid ADHD also appear to present with greater rates of behavioural difficulties than those with TS alone (Carter et al., 2000). In this study social and emotional adjustment among TS children were significantly associated with ADHD diagnosis, obsessional symptom severity, and family functioning. Thus much of the social and behavioural dysfunction in children with TS appears to be ADHD specific. The corollary of this finding is that children with TS and ADHD are more impaired in their social function than those with ADHD alone (Spencer et al., 1998). A further study of aggression in ADHD found that aggressive behaviour in children with TS is observed primarily when comorbid ADHD is present (Sukhodolsky et al., 2003). It has also been reported that tics and ADHD symptoms are associated with OCD symptoms in late adolescence and early adulthood (Peterson et al., 2001). A child may present in the first instance with ADHD and subsequently present with tics. Alternatively, TS may be the first presentation and ADHD may subsequently present.

5.4 MOLECULAR GENETICS: EVIDENCE FOR OVERLAP IN GENETIC SUSCEPTIBILITY FOR ADHD, ASD AND TS

Molecular studies of ADHD, ASD and TS work from the hypothesis that these disorders are rooted in a biochemical disturbance, and therefore the pathology is best detected at this most basic level. As can be seen from the discussion above, there is some evidence that some symptoms occur in all three disorders although it remains to be resolved if these are overlapping symptom domains. Since each of these clinical syndromes is widely accepted to be highly heritable, it might be expected that perceived clinical overlap is reflected in genetic and biochemical disturbances.

As discussed previously, clinical genetic studies have demonstrated the heritability of ADHD, ASD and TS (see also Chapters 7 and 8). Based on how the disorders segregate in family studies it is thought that a polygenic mode of inheritance is likely. The exceptions to this general rule are the few families in which a single major gene appears to exist, as for example, in TS or in autism where cytogenetic abnormalities are associated in approximately 5% of cases (Fombonne, 2003). Furthermore, certain inherited conditions are associated with increased frequency of ASD and ADHD features (see below). Given polygenic inheritance, underlying genetic or biochemical disturbances for these neurodevelopmental disorders are likely to be manifold, and individually are likely to have small effects on risk.

In order to reduce phenotypic heterogeneity in molecular genetics studies there is a tendency to focus on narrow diagnostic categories. As a result, few studies have attempted to investigate the question of shared genetic vulnerability. Furthermore, the diagnostic constraints discussed above, namely the hierarchical rule of DSM-IV vis-à-vis autism and ADHD, directly impact on research investigations in these disorders. Molecular genetic investigations of these disorders have tended to take parallel approaches rather than examining points of intersection. As such, comparisons of the published literature with respect to genetic susceptibility are qualitative.

5.4.1 KNOWN GENETIC DISORDERS ASSOCIATED WITH ASD AND ADHD FEATURES

Both autism and ADHD occur more frequently in association with certain inherited neurodevelopmental disorders and this observation lends support to the role of genetic factors in the etiology. Furthermore the observation of the occurrence of symptoms of ADHD and ASD in the same conditions, such as Fragile X and Tuberous Sclerosis, might suggest shared genetic factors. Fragile X is the commonest inherited cause of intellectual disability and is associated with a characteristic physical phenotype of large ears and macro-orchidism. Autism occurs in 5–10% of individuals with Fragile X while autistic traits are not uncommon in a significant proportion of those with Fragile X (Hjalgrim, Gronskov & Brondum-Nielsen, 1998). A recent study investigated the rate of ADHD and ASD features in Fragile X and demonstrated that there was an increase in the frequency of these symptoms in individuals who had the triplet repeat and those who were carriers of the premutation (Farzin et al., 2006). Studies of FMR-1 variants in autism did not demonstrate the presence of an association (Klauck et al., 1997; Meyer et al., 1998). No studies of the FMR-1 gene have been conducted in ADHD. It has been hypothesised that neurodevelopmental genes influencing the ASD and ADHD phenotype are dysregulated by the triplet repeat expansion in Fragile X (Hagerman, 2006).

Tuberous sclerosis (TS) refers to a genetically heterogeneous group of neurocutaneous disorders characterised by benign hamartomas and abnormalities of skin and CNS. Mental retardation and seizures are commonly associated and seizures present in two-thirds of affected infants in the first year. Behavioural difficulties associated with symptoms of ASD and ADHD frequently accompany the presentation. Autistic symptomatology has been described in 17–58% of cases (Smalley et al., 1992). Symptoms of ADHD have been described in 25–50% of cases (Gillberg, Gillberg & Ahlsen, 1994). Tumor suppressor genes, TSC1 and TSC2 on chromosomes 9q34 and 16p13.3, have been implicated in the etiology of tuberous sclerosis (Fryer et al., 1987; Haines et al., 1991; Povey et al., 1994). Since TS is a genetic condition, it is possible that ASD and ADHD may be associated with abnormalities in genes involved in tuberous sclerosis. However, no association of these genes with either ASD or ADHD has been reported in the literature. It is also possible that epigenetic factors are involved with effects on the expression of other susceptibility genes for ASD or ADHD. Alternatively it may be that CNS pathology in tuberous sclerosis occurs in similar brain regions to the pathology causing ADHD or ASD and that this pathology arises through a variety of pathways.

5.4.2   GENOME-WIDE SCANS AND ADHD/AUTISM OVERLAP

Of the various types of family-genetic study designs, genetic linkage would perhaps be the design most likely to detect overlap. Genetic-linkage analysis attempts to pinpoint a broad region of the genome containing a hypothetical susceptibility locus that is inherited with the disorder in the population of affected individuals, whether it is shared by affected siblings, or passed from parent to affected child. Nowadays it is normally the case that these studies are performed on a genome-wide level, using data, for example, from each of the 23 human chromosomes. This provides the advantage that an *a priori* hypothesis of the molecular etiology is not required, as it would be if a single specific gene were being tested.

Although molecular genetic studies in autism, ADHD and TS have taken parallel approaches to the discovery of susceptibility genes, the evidence for a region of the genome harbouring a gene common to two or more of these disorders is not convincing. However, making allowances for the weak power of the studies, and employing less stringent criteria for the definition of an 'overlap', there are several chromosomes that appear to be of interest.

While no locus has universally shown evidence for linkage to either autism or ADHD three putative susceptibility loci for ADHD on chromosomes 5p13, 16p13 and 17p11 (Smalley *et al.*, 2002; Ogdie *et al.*, 2003) overlap with findings of three genome-wide scans for autism at 16p13 (Philippe *et al.*, 1999; IMGSAC, 2001; Liu *et al.*, 2001). In an independent linkage investigation in a Dutch sample of ADHD sibling pairs, putative linkage was detected at a region on 15q overlapping with a region showing evidence for linkage in both autism and reading disability (Morris *et al.*, 2000; Bakker *et al.*, 2003; Nurmi *et al.*, 2003). A further genome-wide linkage study in ADHD replicated the linkage finding at 17p11 but did not detect linkage at the loci on 5p13 and 16p13 (Arcos-Burgos *et al.*, 2004). One candidate gene for ADHD, GRIN2A (glutamate receptor, ionotropic, N-methyl D-aspartate 2A) was identified within the region on 16p. This was shown to be associated in a family-based association study in a sample of 238 individuals with ADHD (Turic *et al.*, 2004). Furthermore evidence for association with this gene and autism has also been reported (Barnby *et al.*, 2005).

Based on the observations of regions of putative overlap it has been suggested that further investigation of this potential genetic overlap between ASD and ADHD should be investigated. One attempt to do so from a genetic perspective investigated overlap in autism, ADHD and reading disability. Using a binomial test, Smalley *et al.* (2005) evaluated whether regions linked to autism, ADHD and reading disability overlap more than expected by chance using 15 genome-wide scans. Seven chromosomal regions were shown to overlap for two of the three disorders, four of which (5p13, 9q33-34, 16p13 and 17-p11-q11) show an overlap between ADHD and autism. In an attempt to draw together phenotypic and genotypic overlap the concept of 'atypical cerebral asymmetry' (ACA) was proposed as a neurobiological mechanism that might be shared across ADHD, autism and dyslexia. A quantitative linkage study using a measure of ACA found that seven chromosomal regions (2p11–12, 5p13, 7q22-33, 9q33-34, 13q22, 16p13, and 17p11-q11) showed overlap across disorders ($p = 2.4 \times 10^{-6}$). ACA showed modest linkage to two of these chromosomal regions (9q33-34 and 16p13). This investigation, while unreplicated, to date represents a first attempt to directly address the question of shared genetic susceptibility.

5.4.3   CANDIDATE GENE STUDIES

Generally other molecular approaches focus on one or more candidate genes or proteins for which a specific pathological hypothesis can be formulated. These studies attempt to establish an association between genetic polymorphisms, or protein activity or function, and the phenotype in question, and often focus on genes acting in the biochemical pathways implicated by the action of medication. Several good candidate genes for both ADHD and autism exist in the above overlapping chromosomal regions, including the dopamine beta hydroxylase gene (DBH), the Glutamate NMDA receptor subunit 2A (GRIN2A) (as discussed above) and the serotonin transporter gene (5HTT) that map to chromosomes 9q33-34, 16p13 and 17p11-q12, respectively. Although no candidate gene has been mapped to 5p13, the dopamine transporter gene has been mapped nearby, to 5p15.3.

The small numbers of genome scans which have examined linkage to TS have failed to produce any convincing evidence for overlap with the regions highlighted in either ADHD or autism. It is surprising that while there is good evidence to support a role for serotonin in TS, no studies identified linkage/association with the serotonin transporter protein located at Ch17q.

5.4.4   DOPAMINERGIC DNA VARIANTS

As discussed in Chapter 8, dopaminergic neurotransmission or dysfunction is strongly implicated in the pathophysiology of ADHD. The dopamine receptor genes DRD4 and DRD5, the dopamine transporter gene (DAT1), and the dopamine beta-hydroxylase (DBH) gene have all been confirmed to be strongly associated with ADHD, by research groups worldwide. It is generally accepted that DRD4, DRD5 and DAT1 are susceptibility loci (of minor effect) for ADHD. Investigations of these genes in autism are preliminary.

5.4.5   DRD4 AND AUTISM

As discussed elsewhere, DRD4 is widely accepted as a gene of minor effect in ADHD. A high prevalence of rare alleles within the DRD4 gene is seen in children with ADHD. This has not been the finding in a sample of individuals with autism and it has been suggested that this is an ADHD-specific finding (Grady *et al.*, 2005).

5.4.6   DOPAMINE BETA-HYDROXYLASE (DBH)

DβH is an enzyme involved in dopamine metabolism, which catalyses the conversion of dopamine to noradrenaline. A small number of studies have examined the plasma level of DβH in ADHD cases. Two studies observed a significantly lower level of DβH in a subset of children with ADHD and conduct disorder (Rogeness *et al.*, 1982; Bowden *et al.*, 1988). These biochemical studies, however, have not been followed up. In autism one study has reported that DβH levels were elevated in a small sample (Garnier *et al.*, 1986), while several studies have reported decreased DβH activity (Goldstein, 1976; Lake *et al.*, 1977). Low maternal levels of DβH have also been suggested as a possible risk factor in autism (Robinson *et al.*, 2001; Jones *et al.*, 2004), via its influence on the *in utero* environment. DBH thus represents a prime candidate gene for both disorders.

Recent genetic findings have implicated the DBH gene as a potential susceptibility locus for ADHD (Daly *et al.*, 1999; Roman *et al.*, 2002) and a trend in the same direction was also observed in a Canadian sample (Wigg *et al.*, 2002). A further case-control study reported a finding with a different allele at the associated polymorphism (Smith *et al.*, 2003), suggesting that the true ADHD susceptibility variant may lie elsewhere in the gene. Polymorphisms affecting DBH function such as the –1021C-T promoter polymorphism identified by Zabetian *et al.* (2001) have not yet been fully examined in ADHD. Despite the biochemical studies, there is no evidence for association of a genetic polymorphism at the DBH gene with autism. However, genome scans for linkage have highlighted the chromosome 9q34 region harboring this gene (IMGSAC, 2001), which is also the locus for a gene for tuberous sclerosis (TSC1) (Hunt, 1993).

5.4.7   THE DOPAMINE TRANSPORTER GENE (DAT-1)

Two lines of evidence implicate the DAT1 gene in ADHD. First, the gene product is the target of methylphenidate and other psychostimulant medications used to alleviate the symptoms of ADHD. Secondly, the DAT1-knockout mouse appears to replicate hyperactive and impulsive symptoms seen in the ADHD. Significant association between ADHD and a tandem repeat polymorphism mapped to 3′ untranslated region of the gene was reported by Cook (1995). Meta-analysis conducted by Maher and colleagues yielded a pooled odds ratio (OR) estimate of 1.27 indicating that DAT1 is susceptibility gene for ADHD of minor effect (Maher *et al.*, 2002). Several recent studies (although not all) have replicated this association (Faraone *et al.*, 2005).

One study of in vivo DAT1 ligand binding found increased activity, which was normalised by methylphenidate administration (Krause *et al.*, 2000), while another study reported no effect (Van Dyck *et al.*, 2002). Despite evidence, discussed above, that methylphenidate may be effective in reducing hyperactive behaviour in some cases of autism, to our knowledge, no study has investigated DAT1 in autism. However, as has been discussed previously, methylphenidate appears to worsen symptoms, increasing irritability and tics in a proportion of children with autism. These contrasting phenomena may indicate that the biochemical disturbances in autism are heterogeneous, sharing a common pathophysiology with ADHD in some cases.

Risperidone is an effective treatment (with or without a combined psychostimu-lant) for disruptive behaviour disorders and comorbid ADHD in children (Aman *et al.,* 2004). It is also known to be effective in the treatment of disruptive behaviour in a range of psychiatric conditions (Shea *et al.*, 2004). Recent research data have shown that risperidone is effective for the treatment of disruptive behaviour and self-injury over a six-month period (McDougle *et al.*, 2005) and that it reduces restricted and repetitive behaviours in individuals with autism. The limited data available indicate that there is an effect on the core social and communication deficits (McDougle *et al.*, 2005).

The involvement of dopamine in the pathophysiology of TS is similarly supported through the clinical improvement of symptoms in response to anti-psychotic medi-cations such as pimozide, haloperidol and risperidone (Scahill *et al.*, 2003). As might be expected, clinical response is heterogeneous and the mechanism of action of anti-psychotic medications is non-specific in the inhibition of tic or obsessive behav-iours. Investigations of dopaminergic-system genes in TS have yielded reports of correlations between genotype at genes such as DRD2, DBH, DAT1 and composite phenotypes, including ADHD and TS, and other psychiatric conditions such as substance abuse, learning disabilities, depression and anxiety (Comings, 2001). An association with DRD4 has been reported in a French-Canadian sample (Diaz-Anzaldua *et al.*, 2004) and this association was also detected in a Chinese sample of individuals with TS and ADHD but not in individuals with TS or chronic tic disor-der alone (Huang *et al.*, 2002).

5.4.8   SEROTONERGIC DNA VARIANTS AND ADHD AND AUTISM

As discussed above, the observed overlap between linkage peaks in ADHD and autism at chromosome 17p11-q11 is an interesting point of contact between the two disorders, particularly since this locus harbors the serotonin transporter gene (5-HTT), an essential component of serotonergic neurotransmission.

Decreased concentration of serotonin (hyposerotonaemia) in the blood of chil-dren with ADHD has been observed by Coleman (1971). Administration of a serotonin re-uptake inhibitor (fluoxetine) was found to reduce the hyperactivity phenotype of DAT1 knock-out mice (DAT-KO) but had no effect on the wild-type animals (Gainetdinov *et al.*, 1999). This action was presumably attributed to the increase in extracellular 5-HT concentration due to the blockade of the transporter. In autism elevated blood and platelet serotonin levels have been well documented and are the most consistently reported physiological feature in the disorder (Schain & Freedman, 1961; Cook *et al.*, 1988; Abramson *et al.*, 1989). Along with the phar-macological evidence for the usefulness of selective serotonin re-uptake inhibitors, such as fluoxetine, in ameliorating hyperactivity, anxiety, ritualistic behaviour, self-injury and aggression in autism, we can hypothesise a functional depletion of sero-tonin from the extra-cellular space due to overactivity of the re-uptake transporter.

In TS, clinical response in the reduction of obsessive-compulsive symptoms is observed with the administration of selective serotonin re-uptake inhibitors (Eapen, Trimble & Robertson, 1996). Genetic association investigations of the serotonin transporter and COMT in TS have not yielded any positive associations (Cavallini *et al.*, 2000). An investigation of serotonin binding ratios in TS with co-morbid OCD showed reduced transporter binding in untreated individuals (Muller-Vahl *et al.*, 2005). A polymorphism (44 bp insertion/deletion) located upstream of the transcriptional site of the serotonin transporter gene (5-HTT) was found to influence the expression of the gene, consequently increasing the rate of reuptake of serotonin according to the number of long alleles (Lesch *et al.*, 1996). Several studies implicated the long allele in ADHD (Hawi *et al.*, 2003), consolidating the potential importance of an over-expressed serotonin transporter as a susceptibility factor for ADHD. Although the gene has been extensively examined in autism, findings of association are not conclusive. An initial report of a positive association with the short allele has not been consistently replicated (Conroy *et al.*, 2004) with some studies finding association with the long allele (Yirmiya *et al.*, 2001), and some with neither (Kim, 2002).

From a clinical perspective it is interesting that ADHD, ASD and TS are associated with increased rates of co-morbid anxiety, depression and OCD (Peterson *et al.*, 2001). Anxiety and depression are also increased in first-degree family members suggesting heritability factors. It might therefore be hypothesised that genetic variation in genes encoding serotonin receptors or the transporter protein contributes to this vulnerability. However, this hypothesis remains untested to the best of our knowledge.

5.4.9 MAO-A AND ADHD AND AUTISM

Monoamine oxidase A (MAO-A) is an enzyme that degrades biogenic amines such as dopamine, noradrenaline and serotonin by oxidative deamination and consequently plays an important role in the modification of the efficiency of these neurotransmitter systems. It has been implicated in the aetiology of ADHD by pharmacological (Zametkin *et al.*, 1985) and animal studies (Cases *et al.*, 1995; Lawson *et al.*, 2003; Domschke *et al.*, 2005), and has been associated with the disorder in some genetic studies but not all (Lawson *et al.*, 2003; Domschke *et al.*, 2005) (see Chapter 8).

The gene has not been extensively studied in autism, however, Yirmiya *et al.* (2002) observed no association between autism and the functional VNTR at the promoter region, while Cohen *et al.* (2003) suggested that the MAO-A might act as a genetic modifier of the severity of autism in males. One study also showed evidence for association between MAO-A and TS in a French-Canadian sample (Diaz-Anzaldua *et al.*, 2004). Further work is required to clarify the role of MAO-A, if any, in the pathophysiology of ADHD, TS and autism.

5.5 SUMMARY

Similarly to what has been observed in adult neuropsychiatric disorders, such as schizophrenia and bipolar disorder, apparent clinical overlap in the symptom domains of the neurodevelopmental disorders of childhood has been observed. The published literature documents the co-occurrences of symptoms between the three conditions. An important observation regardless of the underlying etiology is that ADHD rarely occurs in isolation. It is well documented that ADHD may be accompanied by Tic disorders, Developmental Co-ordination Disorder, obsessive-compulsive symptoms and some of the symptoms of ASD. The corollary is that disorders such as TS are often accompanied by features of ADHD and hyperactivity symptoms are common in ASD. At the very least clinicians should have a high index for suspicion of co-morbidity where one neurodevelopmental disorder is present. What remains unclear from the literature is whether observed clinical overlap reflects common symptoms or is the result of a multitude of deficits that appear the same. It seems likely that clinical judgment alone is too crude to interpret this question and a standardised approach to the comparison of symptoms across disorders will be required to address this research question.

In an attempt to identify if the clinical overlap observed between these disorders is reflected in underlying biology, the relevant molecular genetic literature has been discussed. Overlapping chromosomal regions identified in genome-wide linkage studies were discussed in addition to neurotransmitter systems that appear to play a role in these disorders. In relation to the dopaminergic system, although a low DβH activity phenotype may bridge both ADHD and autism, subsequent research has diverged to the point where no direct comparisons can be made of dopaminergic dysfunction, specifically in relation to variants of DBH and DAT1. Dysfunction of dopaminergic pathways may underlie the molecular pathology of both ADHD and TS, although direct evidence for this remains to be discovered. Increased serotonin tone appears to ameliorate the behavioural effects of excessive synaptic dopamine, and there is a possibility that an abnormally upregulated serotonin transporter may underlie both ADHD and autism, although this raises the question of whether modifier genes exist which may differentiate the two diagnoses.

The sparse literature on MAO-A reflects the lack of experiments examining common candidate genes across ADHD, ASD and TS and much more work is needed to conclusively establish the molecular overlap between the disorders. At present this work is hampered by the difficulties encountered in mapping the genes for complex disorders such as these.

Given limitations of conventional research approaches, future studies might require alternative strategies in order to identify genes for these relatively common neurodevelopmental conditions. The literature with respect to the genetic investigations in disorders such as ADHD, ASD and TS clearly shows that investigations have focused on narrow phenotypic definitions. This approach is not erroneous and is based on the limitation of clinical heterogeneity within research samples. An alternative strategy might be to attempt to map genes for dimensional traits such as activity levels or inattention across disorders. This will require better endophenotypes for these traits and an attempt to measure these uniformly across disorders. This would also help to answer unresolved questions of whether co-occuring symptoms in ADHD and other neurodevelopmental conditions, such as ASD, are a manifestation of a common abnormal neurodevelopmental process.

5.6   REFERENCES

Abramson RK *et al.* (1989) Elevated blood serotonin in autistic probands and their first-degree relatives. *Journal of Autism and Developmental Disorders* **19**(3): 397–407.

Aman M (2004) Management of hyperactivity and other acting-out problems in patients with autism spectrum disorder. *Semin Pediatr Neurol* **11**(3): 225–8.

Aman M *et al.* (2004) Risperidone effects in the presence/absence of psychostimulant medicine in children with ADHD, other disruptive behavior disorders, and subaverage IQ. *Journal of Child and Adolescent Psychopharmacology* **14**(2): 243–54.

Arcos-Burgos M, Castellanos FX, Pineda D *et al.* (2004) Attention-deficit/hyperactivity disorder in a population isolate: linkage to loci at 4q13.2, 5q33.3, 11q22, and 17p11. *Am J Hum Genet.* **75**(6): 998–1014.

Asperger H (1944) Die autistischen Psychopathen im Kindersalter. *Archiv für Psychiatrie und Nervenkrankheiten* **117**: 76.

Bailey A, Le Couteur A, Gottesman I *et al.* (1995) Autism as a strongly genetic disorder: evidence from a British twin study. *Psychol Med* **25**(1): 63–77.

Bakker S, van der Meulen EM, Buitelaar JK *et al.* (2003) A whole-genome scan in 164 Dutch sib pairs with Attention-Deficit/Hyperactivity Disorder: suggestive evidence for linkage on chromosomes 7p and 15q. *Am J Hum Genet* **72**(5): 1251–60.

Barnby G, Abbott A, Sykes N *et al.* (2005) Candidate-gene screening and association analysis at the autism-susceptibility locus on chromosome 16p: evidence of association at GRIN2A and ABAT. *Am J Hum Genet* **76**(6): 950–66.

Biederman J, Faraone SV, Keenan K *et al.* (1992) Further evidence for family-genetic risk factors in attention deficit hyperactivity disorder: patterns of comorbidity in probands and relatives psychiatrically and pediatrically referred samples. *Arch Gen Psychiatry* **49**(9): 728–38.

Biederman J, Monuteaux MC, Mick E *et al.* (2006) Young adult outcome of attention deficit hyperactivity disorder: a controlled 10-year follow-up study. *Psychol Med* **36**(2): 167–79.

Bolton P, Macdonald H, Pickles A *et al.* (1994) A case-control family history study of autism. *J. Child Psychol & Psychiat* **35**: 877–900.

Bowden CL *et al.* (1988) Plasma dopamine-beta-hydroxylase and platelet monoamine oxidase in attention deficit disorder and conduct disorder. *Journal of American Academy of Child and Adolescent Psychiatry* **27**(2): 171–4.

Bryson S, Clark B, Smith I (1988) First report of a Canadian epidemiological study of autistic syndromes. *J. Child Psychol & Psychiat* **4**: 433–45.

Burns G, Walsh JA (2002) The influence of ADHD-hyperactivity/impulsivity symptoms on the development of oppositional defiant disorder symptoms in a 2-year longitudinal study. *J Abnorm Child Psychol* **30**(3): 245–56.

Byrne JM, Bawden HN, DeWolfe NA, Beattie TL (1998) Clinical assessment of psychopharmacological treatment of preschoolers with ADHD. *J Clin Exp Neuropsychol* **20**(5): 613–27.

Carter A, O'Donnell DA, Schultz RT *et al.* (2000) Social and emotional adjustment in children affected with Gilles de la Tourette's syndrome: associations with ADHD and family functioning. Attention Deficit Hyperactivity Disorder. *J Child Psychol Psychiatry* **41**(2): 215–23.

Cases O *et al.* (1995) Aggressive behavior and altered amounts of brain serotonin and norepinephrine in mice lacking MAOA. *Science* **268**: 1736–66.

Cavallini MC, Di Bella D, Catalano M, Bellodi L (2000) An association study between 5-HTTLPR polymorphism, COMT polymorphism, and Tourette's syndrome. *Psychiatry Res* **97**(2–3): 93–100.

Clarke T, Feehan C, Tinline C, Vostanis P (1999) Autistic symptoms in children with Attention Deficit Hyperactivity Disorder. *European Child and Adolescent Psychiatry* **8**: 50–5.

Cohen IL *et al.* (2003) Association of autism severity with a monoamine oxidase: a functional polymorphism. *Clinical Genetics* **64**(3): 190–7.

Coleman M (1971) Serotonin concentrations in whole blood of hyperactive children. *Journal of Pediatrics* **78**(6): 985–90.

Comings DE (2000) Attention Deficit/ Hyperactivity Disorder with Tourette Syndrome. In TE Brown (ed.) *Attention Deficit Disorder and Comorbidities in Children, Adolescents and Adults* (pp. 363–92) New York: American Psychiatric Press.

Comings DE (2001) Clinical and molecular genetics of ADHD and Tourette syndrome: two related polygenic disorders. *Annals of the New York Academy Science* **931**: 50–83.

Conroy J *et al.* (2004) Serotonin transporter gene and autism, a haplotype analysis in an Irish autistic population. *Molecular Psychiatry* **9**(6): 587–93.

Cook EH *et al.* (1988) Free serotonin in plasma: autistic children and their first-degree relatives. *Biological Psychiatry* **24**(4): 488–91.

Cook EH *et al.* (1995) Association of attention deficit disorder and the dopamine transporter gene. *American Journal of Human Genetics* **56**: 993–8.

Daly G *et al.* (1999) Mapping susceptibility loci in attention deficit hyperactivity disorder: preferential transmission of parental alleles at DAT1, DBH and DRD5 to affected children. *Molecular Psychiatry* **4**(2): 192–6.

Diaz-Anzaldua A, Joober R, Riviere JB *et al.* (2004) Tourette syndrome and dopaminergic genes: a family-based association study in the French Canadian founder population. *Mol Psychiatry* **9**(3): 272–7.

Dominick K, Davis NO, Lainhart J *et al.* (2006) Atypical behaviors in children with autism and children with a history of language impairment. *Res Dev Disabil*. **30**.

Domschke K *et al.* (2005) Association analysis of the monoamine oxidase A and B genes with Attention Deficit Hyperactivity Disorder (ADHD) in an Irish sample: preferential transmission of the MAO-A 941G allele to affected children. *American Journal Medical Genetics (Neuropsychiatric Genetics)* **143**(1): 110–14.

DuPaul GJ, McGoey KE, Eckert TL *et al.* (2001) Preschool children with Attention-Deficit/ Hyperactivity Disorder: impairments in behavioral, social, and school functioning. *J Am Acad Child Adolesc Psychiatry* **40**(5): 508–15.

Eapen V, Trimble MR, Robertson MM (1996) The use of fluoxetine in Gilles de la Tourette syndrome and obsessive compulsive behaviours: preliminary clinical experience. *Prog Neuropsychopharmacol Biol Psychiatry* **20**(4): 737–43.

Ehlers S, Nyden A, Gillberg C *et al.* (1997) Asperger syndrome, autism and attention disorders: a comparative study of the cognitive profiles of 120 children. *J Child Psychol Psychiatry* **38**(2): 207–17.

Eisenmajer R, Prior M, Leekam S *et al.* (1996) Comparison of clinical symptoms in autism and Asperger's disorder. *J Am Acad Child Adolesc Psychiatry* **35**(11): 1523–31.

Faraone SV *et al.* (2005) Molecular genetics of Attention-Deficit/Hyperactivity Disorder. *Biological Psychiatry* **57**(11): 1313–23.

Farzin F, Perry H, Hessl D *et al.* (2006) Autism spectrum disorders and Attention-Deficit/ Hyperactivity Disorder in boys with the fragile X premutation. *J Dev Behav Pediatr* **27** (2 Suppl): 137–44.

Fombonne E (2002) Epidemiological trends in rates of autism. *Mol Psychiatry* **7**(Suppl 2): S4–6.

Fombonne E (2003) Epidemiological surveys of autism and other pervasive developmental disorders: an update. *J Autism Dev Disord* **33**(4): 365–82.

Fombonne E, Simmons H, Ford T *et al.* (2001) Prevalence of pervasive developmental disorders in the British nationwide survey of child mental health. *J Am Acad Child Adolesc Psychiatry* **40**(7): 820–7.

Fryer AE, Chalmers A, Connor JM *et al.* (1987) Evidence that the gene for tuberous sclerosis is on chromosome 9. *Lancet* **1**(8534): 659–61.

Gadow K, DeVincent CJ, Pomeroy J, Azizian A (2004) Psychiatric symptoms in preschool children with PDD and clinic and comparison samples. *J Autism Dev Disord* **34**(4): 379–93.

Gainetdinov RR *et al.* (1999) Role of serotonin in the paradoxical calming effect of psychostimulants on hyperactivity. *Science* **15**(283(5400)): 397–401.

Garnier C *et al.* (1986) Dopamine-beta-hydroxylase and homovanillic acid (HVA) in autistic children. *Journal of Autism and Developmental Disorders* **16**(1): 23–9.

Ghaziuddin M, Weidmer-Mikhail E, Ghaziuddin N (1998) Comorbidity of Asperger Syndrome: a preliminary report. *J Intellect Disab Res* **42**: 279–83.

Gillberg C (1995) *Clinical Child Neuropsychiatry.* Cambridge: Cambridge University Press.

Gillberg I, Gillberg C, Ahlsen G (1994) Autistic behaviour and attention deficits in tuberous sclerosis: a population-based study. *Dev Med Child Neurol* **36**(1): 50–6.

Goldstein M (1976) Dopamine-beta-Hydroxylase studies: Dopamine-beta-Hydroxylase and endogenous total 5-hydroxyindole levels in autistic patients and controls. In *The Autistic Syndromes.* Amsterdam: North Holland Publishing Co.

Goldstein S, Schwebach AJ (2004) The comorbidity of Pervasive Developmental Disorder and Attention Deficit Hyperactivity Disorder: results of a retrospective chart review. *J Autism Dev Disord* **34**(3): 329–39.

Grady D, Harxhi A, Smith M *et al.* (2005) Sequence variants of the DRD4 gene in autism: further evidence that rare DRD4 7R haplotypes are ADHD specific. *Am J Med Genet B Neuropsychiatr Genet* **5**(136): 33–5.

Greene R, Biederman J, Faraone SV *et al.* (1999) Further validation of social impairment as a predictor of substance use disorders: findings from a sample of siblings of boys with and without ADHD. *J Clin Child Psychol* **28**(3): 349–54.

Greene R, Biederman J, Faraone SV *et al.* (2001) Social impairment in girls with ADHD: patterns, gender comparisons, and correlates. *J Am Acad Child Adolesc Psychiatry* **40**(6): 704–10.

Hagerman R (2006) Lessons from fragile X regarding neurobiology, autism, and neurodegeneration. *J Dev Behav Pediatr* **27**(1): 63–74.

Haines JL, Short MP, Kwiatkowski DJ *et al.* (1991) Localization of one gene for tuberous sclerosis within 9q32-9q34, and further evidence for heterogeneity. *Am J Hum Genet* **49**(4): 764–72.

Handen B, Johnson CR, Lubetsky M (2000) Efficacy of methylphenidate among children with autism and symptoms of Attention-Deficit Hyperactivity Disorder. *J Autism Dev Disord* **30**(3): 245.

Hawi Z *et al.* (2003) Recent genetic advances in ADHD and diagnostic and therapeutic prospects. *Expert Review of Neurotherapeutics* **3**(4): 453–64.

Hjalgrim H, Gronskov K, Brondum-Nielsen K (1998) Fragile X syndrome: diagnosis, genetics and clinical findings. *Ugeskr Laeger* **160**(37): 5330–4.

Huang Y, Liu X, Li T *et al.* (2002) Transmission disequilibrium test of DRD4 exon III 48 bp variant number tandem repeat polymorphism and tic disorder. *Zhonghua Yi Xue Yi Chuan Xue Za Zhi* **19**(2): 100–3.

Hunt ASC (1993) A prevalence study of autism in tuberous sclerosis. *Journal of Autism and Developmental Disorders* **23**(2): 323–9.

Hyde TM, Aaronson BA, Randolph C *et al.* (1992) Relationship of birth weight to the phenotypic expression of Gilles de la Tourette's syndrome in monozygotic twins. *Neurology* **42**(3 Pt 1): 652–8.

IMGSAC (2001) A genomewide screen for autism: strong evidence for linkage to chromosomes 2q, 7q, and 16p. *American Journal of Human Genetics* **69**(3): 570–81.

Jensen V, Larrieu JA, Mack KK (1997) Differential diagnosis between Attention-Deficit/Hyperactivity Disorder and pervasive developmental disorder – not otherwise specified. *Clin Pediatr (Phila)* **36**(10): 555–61.

Jones MB, Palmour RM, Zwaigenbaum L, Szatmari P (2004) Modifier effects in autism at the MAO-A and DBH loci. *Am J Med Genet B* **126**(1): 58–65.

Kadesjo B, Gillberg C (2000) Tourette's disorder: epidemiology and comorbidity in primary school children. *J Am Acad Child Adolesc Psychiatry* **39**(5): 548–55.

Kadesjo C, Hagglof B, Kadesjo B, Gillberg C (2003) Attention-deficit-hyperactivity disorder with and without oppositional defiant disorder in 3- to 7-year-old children. *Dev Med Child Neurol* **45**(10): 693–9.

Kim SJ *et al.* (2002) Transmission disequilibrium mapping at the serotonin transporter gene (SLC6A4) region in autistic disorder. *Molecular Psychiatry* **7**(3): 278–88.

Klassen A, Miller A, Fine S (2004) Health-related quality of life in children and adolescents who have a diagnosis of Attention-Deficit/Hyperactivity Disorder. *Pediatrics* **114**(5): 541–7.

Klauck SM, Munstermann E, Bieber-Martig B *et al.* (1997) Molecular genetic analysis of the FMR-1 gene in a large collection of autistic patients. *Hum Genet* **100**(2): 224–9.

Krause KL *et al.* (2000) Increased striatal dopamine transporter in adult patients with attention deficit hyperactivitydisorder, effects of methylphenidate as measured by single photon emission computed tomography. *Neuroscience Letters* **285**: 107–10.

Lake CR *et al.* (1977) Increased norepinephrine levels and decreased dopamine-beta-hydroxylase activity in primary autism. *Archives of General Psychiatry* **34**(5): 553–6.

Lawson DC *et al.* (2003) Association analysis of monoamine oxidase A and Attention Deficit Hyperactivity Disorder. *American Journal of Medical Genetics (Neuropsychiatric Genetics)* **116**: 84–9.

Leckman J, Cohen D (2002) Tic disorders. In M Rutter, E Taylor (ed.) *Child and Adolescent Psychiatry (Vol. 4)*. Oxford: Blackwell.

Lesch KP *et al.* (1996) Association of anxiety-related traits with a polymorphism in the serotonin transporter gene regulatory region. *Science* **274**(5292): 1527–31.

Liu J *et al.* (2001) A genomewide screen for autism susceptibility loci. *American Journal of Human Genetics* **69**(2): 327–40.

Luteijn EF, Serra M, Jackson S *et al.* (2000) How unspecified are disorders of children with a pervasive developmental disorder not otherwise specified? A study of social problems in children with PDD-NOS and ADHD. *Eur Child Adolesc Psychiatry* **9**(3): 168–79.

McDougle CJ, Scahill L, Aman MG *et al.* (2005) Risperidone for the core symptom domains of autism: results from the study by the autism network of the research units on pediatric psychopharmacology. *Am J Psychiatry* **162**(6): 1142–8.

Maher BS *et al.* (2002) Dopamine system genes and attention deficit hyperactivity disorder, a meta-analysis. *Psychiatric Genetics* **2**(4): 207–15.

Mason A, Banerjee S, Eapen V *et al.* (1998) The prevalence of Tourette syndrome in a mainstream school population. *Dev Med Child Neurol* **40**(5): 292–6.

Meyer GA, Blum NJ, Hitchcock W, Fortina P (1998) Absence of the fragile X CGG trinucleotide repeat expansion in girls diagnosed with a pervasive developmental disorder. *J Pediatr* **133**(3): 363–5.

Morris D, Robinson L, Turic D *et al.* (2000) Family-based association mapping provides evidence for a gene for reading disability on chromosome 15q. *Hum Mol Genet* **22**(9): 843–8.

Muller-Vahl KR, Meyer GJ, Knapp WH *et al.* (2005) Serotonin transporter binding in Tourette Syndrome. *Neurosci Lett* **385**(2): 120–5.

Mulligan A, Butler L, Sorohan J *et al.* (2005) Overlap symptoms of autism in Attention Deficit Hyperactivity Disorder. Paper presented at the World Congress in Psychiatric Genetics. *American Journal of Medical Genetics Part B: Neuropsychiatric Genetics*, Boston.

Nurmi EL, Dowd M, Tadevosyan-Leyfer O *et al.* (2003) Exploratory subsetting of autism families based on savant skills improves evidence of genetic linkage to 15q11-q13. *J Am Acad Child Adolesc Psychiatry* **42**(7): 856–63.

Ogdie M, Macphie IL, Minassian SL *et al.* (2003) A genomewide scan for Attention-Deficit/Hyperactivity Disorder in an extended sample: suggestive linkage on 17p11. *Am J Hum Genet* **72**(5): 1268–79.

Peterson B, Pine DS, Cohen P, Brook JS (2001) Prospective, longitudinal study of tic, obsessive-compulsive, and Attention-Deficit/Hyperactivity Disorders in an epidemiological sample. *J Am Acad Child Adolesc Psychiatry* **40**(6): 685–95.

Philippe A *et al.* (1999) Genome-wide scan for autism susceptibility genes. Paris Autism Research International Sibpair Study. *Human Molecular Genetics* **8**(5): 805–12.

Pickles A, Bolton P, Macdonald H *et al.* (1995) Latent-class analysis of recurrence risks for complex phenotypes with selection and measurement error: a twin and family history study of autism. *Am J Hum Genet* **57**(3): 717–26.

Povey S, Burley MW, Attwood J *et al.* (1994) Two loci for tuberous sclerosis: one on 9q34 and one on 16p13. *Ann Hum Genet* **58**(Pt 2): 107–27.

Price RA, Kidd KK, Cohen DJ *et al.* (1985) A twin study of Tourette syndrome. *Arch Gen Psychiatry* **42**(8): 815–20.

Risch N, Spiker D, Lotspeich L *et al.* (1999) A genomic screen of autism: evidence for a multilocus etiology. *Am J Hum Genet* **65**(2): 493–507.

Robertson M (2003) Diagnosing Tourette syndrome: is it a common disorder? *J Psychosom Res* **55**(1): 3–6.

Robinson PD *et al.* (2001) Genetically determined low maternal serum dopamine beta-hydroxylase levels and the etiology of autism spectrum disorders. *American Journal Medical Genetics (Neuropsychiatric Genetics)* **100**(1): 30–6.

Rogeness GA *et al.* (1982) Biochemical differences in children with conduct disorder socialized and undersocialized. *American Journal of Psychiatry* **139**(3): 307–11.

Roman T *et al.* (2002) Further evidence for the association between Attention-Deficit/Hyperactivity Disorder and the dopamine-beta-hydroxylase gene. *American Journal Medical Genetics (Neuropsychiatric Genetics)* **114**(2): 154–8.

Rutter M, Yoursov L (1994) *Child and Adolescent Psychiatry: Modern Approaches*. Oxford: Blackwell Scientific Publications.

Santosh PJ, Mijovic A (2004) Social impairment in Hyperkinetic Disorder: relationship to psychopathology and environmental stressors. *Eur Child Adolesc Psychiatry* **13**(3): 141–50.

Scahill L, Leckman JF, Schultz RT *et al.* (2003) A placebo-controlled trial of risperidone in Tourette syndrome. *Neurology* **60**(7): 1130–5.

Schain R, Freedman D (1961) Studies on 5-hydroxyindole metabolism in autistic and other mentally retarded children. *Journal of Paediatrics* **58**: 315–20.

Schatz A, Weimer AK, Trauner AD (2002) Brief report: attention differences in Asperger syndrome. *J Autism Devel Disord* **32**: 333–6.

Shea S *et al.* (2004) Risperidone in the treatment of disruptive behavioral symptoms in children with autistic and other pervasive developmental disorders. *Pediatrics* **114**(5): 634–41.

Shelton TL, Barkley RA, Crosswait C *et al.* (1998) Psychiatric and psychological morbidity as a function of adaptive disability in preschool children with aggressive and hyperactive-impulsive-inattentive behavior. *J Abnorm Child Psychol* **26**(6): 475–94.

Smalley SL, Tanguay PE, Smith M, Gutierrez G (1992) Autism and tuberous sclerosis. *J Autism Dev Disord* **22**(3): 339–55.

Smalley SL *et al.* (2002) Genetic linkage of Attention-Deficit/Hyperactivity Disorder on chromosome 16p13, in a region implicated in autism. *American Journal of Human Genetics* **71**(4): 959–63.

Smalley SL *et al.* (2005) Toward localizing genes underlying cerebral asymmetry and mental health. *American Journal Medical Genetics (Neuropsychiatric Genetics)* **135**(1): 79–84.

Smith KM *et al.* (2003) Association of the dopamine beta hydroxylase gene with attention deficit hyperactivity disorder: genetic analysis of the Milwaukee longitudinal study. *American Journal Medical Genetics (Neuropsychiatric Genetics)* **119B**(1): 77–85.

Spencer T, Biederman J, Harding M *et al.* (1998) Disentangling the overlap between Tourette's disorder and Attention Deficit Hyperactivity Disorder. *Journal of Child Psychology and Psychiatry* **39**: 1037–44.

Steffenburg S, Gillberg C, Hellgren L (1989) A twin study of autism in Denmark, Finland, Iceland and Sweden. *J Child Psychol & Psychiat* **30**: 405–16.

Sukhodolsky D, Scahill L, Zhang H *et al.* (2003) Disruptive behavior in children with Tourette's syndrome: association with ADHD comorbidity, tic severity, and functional impairment. *J Am Acad Child Adolesc Psychiatry* **42**(1): 98–105.

Turic D, Langley K, Mills S *et al.* (2004) Follow-up of genetic linkage findings on chromosome 16p13: evidence of association of N-methyl-D aspartate glutamate receptor 2A gene polymorphism with ADHD. *Mol Psychiatry* **9**(2): 169–73.

Van Dyck CH *et al.* (2002) Unaltered dopamine transporter availability in adult attention deficit hyperactivity disorder. *Am J Psychiatry* **159**(2): 309–12.

Walkup JT, LaBuda MC, Singer HS *et al.* (1996) Family study and segregation analysis of Tourette syndrome: evidence for a mixed model of inheritance. *Am J Hum Genet* **59**(3): 684–93.

Wheeler C (1994) The social functioning of children with Attention Deficit Disorder with hyperactivity and Attention Deficit Disorder without hyperactivity: a comparison of their peer relations and social deficits. *Journal of Emotional Behaviour Disorder* **2**: 2–12.

Wheeler JC, Carlson CL (1994) The social functioning of children with ADD with hyperactivity and ADD without hyperactivity: A comparison of their peer relations and social deficits. *Journal of Emotional and Behavioral Disorder* **2**(1): 2–13.

Wigg K *et al.* (2002) Attention deficit hyperactivity disorder and the gene for Dopamine Beta-hydroxylase. *American Journal Psychiatry* **159**(6): 1046–8.

Wing L (1996) *The Autistic Spectrum*. London: Constable.

Yirmiya N *et al.* (2001) Evidence for an association with the serotonin transporter promoter region polymorphism and autism. *American Journal Medical Genetics (Neuropsychiatric Genetics)* **105**(4): 381–6.

Yirmiya N *et al.* (2002) Family-based and population study of a functional promoter-region monoamine oxidase A polymorphism in autism: possible association with IQ. *American Journal Medical Genetics (Neuropsychiatric Genetics)* **114**(3): 284–7.

Yoshida Y, Uchiyama T (2004) The clinical necessity for assessing Attention Deficit/Hyperactivity Disorder (AD/HD) symptoms in children with high-functioning Pervasive Developmental Disorder (PDD). *Eur Child Adolesc Psychiatry* **13**(5): 307–14.

Zabetian CP *et al.* (2001) A quantitative-trait analysis of human plasma-dopamine beta-hydroxylase activity: evidence for a major functional polymorphism at the DBH locus. *American Journal of Human Genetics* **68**(2): 515–22.

Zametkin A *et al.* (1985) Treatment of hyperactive children with monoamine oxidase inhibitors. I. Clinical efficacy. *Archives of General Psychiatry* **42**: 962–6.

6 Forensic Aspects of ADHD

SUSAN YOUNG

Department of Forensic Mental Health Science, Institute of Psychiatry, King's College, London, UK

6.1 OVERVIEW

The association between ADHD and crime is becoming increasingly recognised and regarded with concern. High rates of antisocial behaviour in adults have been reported in studies using different methodologies, e.g. self-report, informant report and official criminal records (Satterfield, Hoppe & Schell, 1982; Hechtman & Weiss, 1986; Satterfield *et al.*, 1994; Bambinski, Hartsough & Lambert, 1999; Brassett-Grundy & Butler, 2004a, 2004b; Young, 2004; Young & Gudjonsson, 2006). Analysis of court records has revealed that ADHD is a risk for serious offences and institutionalisation (Hechtman & Weiss, 1986; Lambert, 1988; Satterfield *et al.*, 1982, 1994). Indeed Official Records from Los Angeles courts (mean age 17 years) suggest that adolescent children diagnosed with DSM-III ADHD were four to five times more likely to have been arrested and 25% more likely to be institutionalised because of delinquency than controls (Satterfield *et al.*, 1994).

Youths and adults with ADHD are likely to be vulnerable at all stages of the criminal justice process, e.g. as a suspect, witness and/or victim; within the prison and probation service and within forensic mental health services. These services are increasingly being asked to conduct assessments (either to advise the court and/or to assist in their management) and provide treatment for adult offenders, especially for individuals known to have a history of ADHD in childhood and whose symptoms appear to be persisting. However, referrals to services are more frequently made to consider the diagnosis *de novo* in adulthood (Collins & White, 2002). Court assessments are being commissioned to establish whether the diagnosis of ADHD has relevance to an offence, i.e. to negate criminal responsibility and/or to mitigate punishment. Experts are being asked to consider whether individuals with severe ADHD are fit to plead and stand trial and, if so, to advise about modifications to the trial process in order to optimise participation. Assessments are also requested from secure settings as professionals are attempting to clarify and understand detainees' behaviour and attitude, with the aim of rehabilitating and managing individuals in the settings safely and appropriately.

This chapter will review (the paucity of) investigations into ADHD and offending and discuss the role of comorbid conduct problems and outcome. The chapter will summarise data from prison studies; discuss the likely prevalence of ADHD in the prison population; consider the relationship between symptoms of ADHD and

Handbook of Attention Deficit Hyperactivity Disorder. Edited by M. Fitzgerald, M. Bellgrove and M. Gill.
© 2007 John Wiley & Sons Ltd

offending; and describe the ADHD offender 'profile'. The chapter will then examine the vulnerabilities of the ADHD offender in the criminal justice system with particular focus on arrest and detention at the police station, the trial process, incarceration and treatment.

6.2 COMORBIDITY WITH CONDUCT PROBLEMS AND ANTISOCIAL BEHAVIOUR

In order to establish the overall effect of ADHD on crime and delinquency and the degree to which this relationship may be an artefact of methodological factors across empirical studies, Pratt *et al.* (2002) conducted a meta-analysis of 20 ADHD studies. To avoid potential tautology, only studies using outcome measures of either crime and/or delinquency were included. Studies that used indicators of 'conduct disorder' as outcome measures, or used measures of conduct disorder as proxies of ADHD, were excluded. The analyses revealed a strong association between measures of ADHD and criminal/delinquent behaviour and the authors concluded that 'the effect size is sufficiently substantial as to suggest that the ADHD-crime relationship deserves theoretical explanation and that the attention-deficit condition warrants consideration in discussions of effective correctional intervention' (p. 352). They further concluded that ADHD is a factor that should be considered in the delivery of treatment services, starting with early intervention programmes and going on to rehabilitation and supervision of adult offenders.

Nevertheless, high comorbidity with conduct disorder and oppositional defiant disorder continues to lead to speculation that the real risk for the development of antisocial and criminal behaviour is associated with prior conduct problems and not symptoms of ADHD (Vitelli, 1995). Taylor *et al.* (1996) independently controlled for childhood conduct disorder in a four group design (hyperactive, conduct problem, comorbid hyperactive-conduct problem, and normal control groups) in their London epidemiological nine-year follow-up study and found that antisocial behaviour in young men (age 16–18) was not necessarily determined by childhood conduct problems. Thus the development of hyperactivity in itself may lead to negative outcomes. Indeed, Bambinski *et al.* (1999) also attempted to tease out this association in their 17-year prospective follow-up of 230 males and 75 females with childhood ADHD and conduct problems into adulthood (mean age 26 at follow-up). They found a specific association between hyperactivity-impulsivity symptoms (but not inattention) measured at nine years and later officially recorded arrests and self-reported crime for males. Thus hyperactivity-impulsivity symptoms of ADHD and early conduct problems independently predicted having an arrest record, especially when ten or more crimes were self-reported. Thus ADHD, and symptoms of hyperactivity-impulsivity in particular, contribute to the risk for criminal involvement over and above the risk associated with early conduct problems alone.

However, ADHD adults may underreport impulsive behaviour which emphasises the need to include objective measures of impulsivity and attentional control to determine subtypes (Young & Gudjonsson, 2006). Although neuropsychological tests may lack specificity between ADHD and other psychiatric disorders, e.g. anxiety, when tests are used in conjunction with a developmental and psychiatric assessment, then the assessment process will be more robust and the diagnosis more reliable. Additionally, the Matching Familiar Figures Test (Cairnes & Cammock, 1978), which is a measure of impulsivity vs reflectiveness in cognitive style, has been shown to differentiate between referrals to an adult ADHD clinic who received the diagnosis and those who did not (Young, Channon & Toone, 2000; Young & Gudjonsson, 2005). Furthermore, a positive correlation was found between error scores obtained on this measure of impulsivity and delinquency (both self-reported and parent-reported) for an ADHD group only. This association was not found between these measures for a clinical control group and normal control group.

Nevertheless comorbidity with conduct disorder in childhood has been so consistently documented that it has been suggested that hyperactivity and conduct disorder are not distinct problems, in spite of well-replicated evidence that for some children conduct disorder is a secondary consequence of hyperactivity. Taylor (1994) examined this issue in his review of the literature and concluded that the two problems are distinct but that when comorbidity occurs, then this is a group more seriously affected. Indeed, Lynham (1996) describes the comorbid group to be a unique subgroup of 'fledgling psychopaths' and one study provides some evidence to indicate that youngsters with severe problems (requiring education in special schools for children with emotional and/or behavioural difficulties) may risk the development of psychopathic traits (Colledge & Blair, 2001). However an association between ADHD and psychopathy may result from additive rather than interactive influences of childhood conduct problems and ADHD (Abramowitz, Kosson & Seidenberg, 2004). Whilst the risk for the development of psychopathy is yet to be established, it seems that ADHD and conduct disorder are clinically and genetically more severe variants of their independent disorders (Thapar, Harrington & McGuffin 2001).

6.3   ADHD IN THE PRISON POPULATION

The prevalence of adults with ADHD in prison remains unclear, although rates appear to be far higher than in the general population. There have been five adult prison studies reported in peer-reviewed journals and two studies conducted at Youth Offending Institutions (see Table 6.1). These studies, which have been conducted in the USA, Canada, Sweden, Germany, Finland and Norway, suggest that a sizeable proportion of youth inmates had childhood ADHD and many continue to be symptomatic.

Estimated prevalence rates for this population vary considerably and depend on the measures or 'cut-offs' used to determine ADHD. Most of the contemporary studies have used a version of the Wender Utah Rating Scale [WURS] to diagnose ADHD in childhood retrospectively. The 'WURS25' contains the core items described by Ward, Wender & Reimherr (1993) to show the greatest difference between patients with ADHD and normal comparison subjects, i.e. these items reflect problems concerning hyperactivity, concentration, impulsivity and mood. It has been suggested that the WURS25 has a screening ADHD 'window' of 35–45. The authors found that a score of 46 or higher correctly identified 86% of outpatients with ADHD, 99% of normal controls and 81% of outpatients with unipolar

Table 6.1. Prevalence of ADHD in offending populations

Authors	Location	Measures	Group	Age	Child Prevalence	Adult Prevalence
Eyestone & Howell (1994)	USA: Prison	Wender Adult List of Problems Wender Child List of Problems	102 male inmates	16–64	31.4% significant + 22.5% mild	33.3% significant + 20.6% mild
Haapasalo & Hamalainen (1996)	Finland: YOI	Diagnostic Interview for children and adolescents	89 inmates (sex unknown)	16–22 (mean 20)	–	Approximately 50%
Dalteg & Levander (1998)	Sweden: YOI	WURS25	75 recidivist male juveniles with conduct disorder	12–20 (follow up to age 30)	68%	–
Dalteg et al. (1999)	Sweden: Prison	WURS	51 recidivist male inmates	–	50%	25%
Vitelli (1995)	Canada: maximum security prison	WURS25	100 inmates (sex unknown)	17–70 (mean 29)	67% (WURS >= 36) 24% self-reported they took meds for ADHD	–
Rasmussen et al. (2001)	Norway: prison	WURS25 Brown ADD Scale	82 male inmates	19–57 (mean 31)	46% (WURS >= 46) 64% (WURS >= 36)	30% present + 16% probable
Retz et al. (2004) and Rosler et al. (2004)	Germany YOI	WURS25 Diagnostic Checklist of Symptoms (adults)	129 male inmates	15–28 (mean 19)	71% (WURS >= 30)	45% (DSM-IV) 21% (ICD-10) 50% mild (in partial remission)

depression. Using this methodology, the childhood prevalence rates range between 22% to 68% and this increased to 71% when a lower cut-off of 30 was applied by the German investigators (Retz *et al.*, 2004; Rosler *et al.*, 2004). Rasmussen, Almik and Levander (2001) applied the more stringent threshold of >45, and reported a rate of 46% in a Norwegian prison. In the Canadian study, investigators asked participants about assessment and treatment received in childhood, and 41% reported to have been either assessed or treated for ADHD (24% reported having taken medication for ADHD and 17% reported assessment for behavioural problems but no treatment) (Vitelli, 1995).

Consistent with an expected pattern of declining symptoms with maturity, adult rates are lower, suggesting that rates range between 25% and 50%, with higher rates appearing to apply to studies that included a younger age range. Additionally, some variation in scores may be accounted for by cultural differences in the use of the North American WURS measure and norms. The WURS use of language requires adaptation for use outside of North America, e.g. asking questions regarding 'stick-to-it-tiveness' and 'sassiness' which may not be fully understood outside of the USA. Only the Norwegian and German studies supplemented the Wender Scales with independent screens to assess ADHD symptoms in adulthood (e.g. the DSM-IV Checklist of Symptoms or the Brown Attention Deficit Disorder Scale). By using this methodology they found 30–45% of inmates were determined likely to have symptoms in adulthood consistent with the diagnosis of ADHD and a further 16–50% obtained scores falling in a lower range classified as 'mild' or 'probably' having ADHD symptoms (Rasmussen *et al.*, 2001; Retz *et al.*, 2004; Rosler *et al.*, 2004). This latter group may be in partial remission of their symptoms.

The screens suggest that around two-thirds of Youth Offending Institutions and up to half of the adult prison population may have current symptoms of ADHD to some degree of impairment. Indeed, a sizeable number of individuals may have mild symptoms, possibly being in partial remission. In June 2005, the prison population in England and Wales was estimated to be 77,628 (71,546 males and 4523 females) and a further 3373 individuals were subject to home detention curfew supervision (Home Office, National Offender Management Service Statistics, 2005). Extrapolation from these statistics suggests that in England and Wales there are up to 35,773 men who may have symptoms of ADHD. A further 1814 of the 2667 youths detained in Youth Offending Institutions may have ADHD. However, it should be borne in mind that research studies have applied self-reported questionnaires to screen for the possible presence of the disorder and only estimate rates of ADHD in the prison population. One cannot conclude from these screens that such a high proportion of prison inmates actually have the condition. Indeed, Vitelli (1995) found that 60% of inmates who had not reported disruptive behaviour in childhood exceeded a WURS25 cut-off score of 36. Thus ADHD adult screens may identify individuals whose symptoms relate to alternative explanations, e.g. long-term substance misuse, acquired head injury. Nevertheless it has been shown that, unlike children, adults can give accurate accounts of some of their symptoms (Murphy & Schachar, 2000; Young & Gudjonsson, 2005). Thus self-report questionnaires may usefully be applied as fast and cost-effective screening measures to identify individuals who may benefit from a comprehensive ADHD assessment (taking account of their developmental history) and treatment (both pharmacological and psychological).

Only one study, a brief report from Ireland, has determined individuals meeting DSM-IV criteria following a clinical psychiatric assessment. Curran and Fitzgerald (1999) found in a randomly selected group of 55 prisoners referred to a psychiatric clinic (mean age 26) that 9.1% met DSM-IV criteria for ADHD. This figure is twice as high as ADHD reported in the general population but considerably lower than that reported in other studies using screening measures. However, in view of the overall small number of prison inmates included in this evaluation, the proportion meeting the criteria for ADHD following psychiatric assessment should be treated with caution. It is unknown how many of the inmates not referred for psychiatric assessment would have met the criteria.

6.4   THE RELATIONSHIP BETWEEN SYMPTOMS OF ADHD AND OFFENDING

Studies suggest that it is activity levels or impulsive symptoms that are most likely to be related to adult crime and that this may be determined very early in life. For example, the longitudinal epidemiological study by Stevenson and Goodman (2001) investigated the association between behaviour problems in pre-school children and later adult criminality. Using official records from the Criminal Records Office, they found that activity level and management problems (among others) increased the risk of conviction of an adult offence. Consistent with the findings of Brassett-Grundy and Butler (2004b), they found family and social circumstances did not.

As children and adolescents grow up it is expected that their ADHD symptoms will remit; however, symptoms do not remit uniformly (Fischer *et al.*, 1993; Marsh & Williams, 2004) and up to two-thirds of children may retain at least one disabling symptom by age 25 (Weiss *et al.*, 1985), raising concern over the usefulness and validity of applying formal diagnostic criteria to adult functioning. The current ADHD symptom thresholds for diagnosis were derived empirically from clinical studies of children/adolescents, age 4–17 (Frick *et al.*, 1994; Lahey *et al.*, 1994) and DSM-IV may be inappropriately worded for adults with the diagnostic thresholds being too stringent when applied to adults perhaps leading to underdiagnosis of ADHD in adult populations (Murphy & Barkley, 1996).

Impulsivity has been invoked as the key clinical and cognitive problem in both children and adults with ADHD (Taylor, 1998; Young *et al.,* 2000; Colledge & Blair, 2001) and it may be that the association between ADHD and antisocial behaviour relates to unremitting impulsive symptoms of ADHD and that impulsivity, rather than inattention, is the symptom of ADHD that is most likely to be associated with antisocial and/or criminal behaviour. Indeed, Bambinski *et al.* (1999) separated DSM-IV symptoms of inattention and hyperactivity-impulsivity and found specific associations between hyperactivity-impulsivity (but not inattention) measured at age nine years and later officially recorded arrests and self-reported crime for males. The finding was irrespective of the presence of early conduct problems. This suggests that it is important to identify ADHD subtypes as a predominance of hyperactivity-impulsivity indicates higher risk for criminal outcomes.

Although the methodologies employed in the prison studies (see Table 6.1) are inconsistent and not entirely robust, these studies draw attention to the presence of individuals who obtain borderline scores on screening measures and who may be subthreshold of meeting formal diagnostic criteria, e.g. categorised as having 'mild' ADHD or 'probably' ADHD. These are likely to be individuals in partial remission of their symptoms. Little is known about the outcome for these young people who retain residual symptoms but fall short of meeting full criteria defined by formal diagnostic guidelines and which may prevent them from accessing appropriate services. The relationship between remitting symptoms and antisocial behaviour has been investigated by Young and Gudjonsson (in press) who compared clinically referred ADHD adults, with two remission groups (1) adults classified in partial remission of their symptoms and (2) adults in full remission of their symptoms. They found a decline in antisocial behaviour across the three groups yet the level of police contact and presentation to adult services remained fairly constant. Thus in spite of a reduction in antisocial behaviour, a similar amount of police contact was reported. Importantly, both the partial remission and remission groups were subthreshold for formal diagnosis of ADHD (e.g. scoring ratings of symptoms as being 'sometimes' present) and, although their self-reported symptoms appeared to be improving, they obtained similar scores on neuropsychological tests of attention and impulsivity. This means that some individuals may continue to have functional deficits which are disabling. However, the number of participants in the study is low and the sample is clinically referred, so participants may be individuals with particularly severe problems resulting in higher rates of police contact and psychiatric presentations. Ideally symptom patterns and outcomes should be investigated using a prospective epidemiological methodology.

6.5 WHO ARE THE OFFENDERS?

ADHD has been associated with onset of criminal behaviour at a young age, even prior to age 11 (Vitelli, 1995; Dalteg & Levander, 1998; Dalteg, Lindgren & Levander, 1999; Retz at al., 2004). Indeed, high rates of recidivism have been found in studies of youth detained in institutions. These youths are likely to have more severe and pervasive symptoms than older offenders detained in adult prisons and this most likely accounts for the much higher prevalence of ADHD reported in this population. For such youngsters the revolving door between prison, probation and community is most likely strongly associated with the severity of their ADHD symptoms.

The association between ADHD and crime has long been considered to relate only to males, a view which probably reflects the lower base rate for antisocial behaviour in females in the general population. An epidemiological longitudinal follow-up of the developmental risk associated with hyperactivity in teenage girls found that very few of the girls, in either the hyperactive or conduct problem group (defined by parent and teacher ratings on the Rutter A and B questionnaires) engaged in delinquent behaviours (Young *et al.*, 2005). However, there is also epidemiological evidence that, by adulthood, both men and women who had childhood ADHD are at greater risk of police contact (Hechtman, Weiss & Perlman, 1984; Rasmussen & Gillberg, 2000; Brassett-Grundy, 2004b). The findings from the 30-year follow up of ten-year-old ADHD children in the British Cohort Study [BCS-

70] suggest that type and patterns of offending may be an important distinguishing factor between males and females with ADHD, with female offending being limited to more minor offences, whereas males progress to more severe and/or persistent offending (Brassett-Grundy, 2004b). However, there is evidence to suggest that crimes of violence are a relatively low occurrence and the criminal activity of ADHD adults (gender unspecified) is more associated with recidivism of property-related or public disorder crimes (Dalteg & Levander, 1998; Bambinski *et al.*, 1999), although the evidence is not conclusive.

Two studies have reported negative outcomes irrespective of psychosocial background, suggesting that outcome is not necessarily related to family characteristics (Dalteg & Levander, 1998; Brassett-Grundy & Butler, 2004b). Dalteg and Levander (1998) studied recidivist juveniles detained in a Youth Offending Institution and found that at follow-up (age 30) ADHD was related to increased crime volume and versatility (lifetime increase in crime of 250%), markedly more pronounced school problems and worse social outcome than the non-ADHD group, in spite of a better childhood psychosocial background. These problems were present at a young age and became more pronounced in later years suggesting that ADHD symptoms markedly affect the prognosis of young offenders. Interestingly, the psychosocial background conditions of the ADHD group deteriorated in later years for children referred to a borstal institution for serious, recidivist youth offenders. This suggests that a seriously dysfunctional child can markedly disrupt family life as opposed to being the result of family dysfunction. The latter perspective may limit families' ability to access support from professional and/or community services.

The BCS-70 study controlled for pre-existing circumstances and/or background familial and personal characteristics (e.g. social class, ethnicity, birth weight, parenting style) (Brassett-Grundy, 2004b). The study, which has an attrition rate of 30% leaving 10,405 participants at follow-up, found that men and women were at higher risk of having contact with the police (i.e. arrested, cautioned or found guilty in court at least once) but only men (by age 30) had contact with the police or courts as a persistent offender (i.e. found guilty in court at least twice). It was additionally found that men were at greater risk than females of being victims of violent assault or mugging. Thus men with ADHD seem to become involved in situations that provoke aggression that may then escalate into physical violence. This may be a result of a labile temperament, poor behavioural control and an inability to delay gratification.

The crimes of people with ADHD are likely typified as impetuous, reckless opportunities for which they are easily apprehended. Crimes are likely to be motivated to satisfy an immediate need or desire. This may be financially motivated (e.g. petty theft, credit card fraud) or sensation-seeking to relieve boredom (e.g. throwing items onto train tracks). Novelty seeking may have a risk-taking element, e.g. reckless driving. Possible explanations for the association between ADHD and criminal behaviour are low tolerance of boredom and frustration and poor response inhibition. The few studies that have attempted to evaluate categories of offending for ADHD offenders (compared with non-ADHD offenders) suggest that crimes of aggression and violence are less common (e.g. Dalteg & Levander, 1998; Bambinski *et al.*, 1999). Emotional lability and poor behavioural control will mean that individuals with ADHD are provocative towards others and/or may be easily provoked into acting without thinking by others. The use of drugs and alcohol will disinhibit them further and make them even less likely to think about the consequences of their behaviour and rational alternatives. Thus youth gang fights are unlikely to be only associated with an adolescent phase as these behaviours may progress into adulthood as more serious behaviours, e.g. road rage and/or pub fights, with adults receiving convictions for actual or grievous bodily harm, manslaughter and/or murder. Crimes are unlikely to result from lengthy rumination and a hostile attitude, but are more likely to be the product of poor behavioural control. Convictions for murder imply some form of premeditation and are less likely if the individual's ADHD status was known at the time of their trial and/or was relevant to the legal issues. In the United States of America ADHD has been used as a mitigating factor in cases involving murder (Collins & White, 2002).

6.6 THE VULNERABILITIES OF THE ADHD OFFENDER IN THE CRIMINAL JUSTICE SYSTEM

Offenders with ADHD may be viewed as having four basic vulnerabilities in their liaison with the criminal justice system. Their first vulnerability is that they are not very effective criminals because they act impulsively and do not pay attention to their environment, e.g. they may not notice a CCTV camera recording their activity. This means they are likely to get caught easily. Secondly, they have to cope with arrest, detention at the police station and sometimes lengthy police interviews. Thirdly, they have to cope with the trial process. Fourthly, they may have to adapt to incarceration and prison life. One could ask why should people with ADHD be any more vulnerable or any less able to cope with these circumstances than any other defendant or convicted person. The answer is simple – they have deficits in their functional ability or capacity which cause them to have limitations in their ability to perform at an acceptable and consistent level. This is due to underlying symptoms of inattention, hyperactivity and/or restlessness, impulsivity, emotional lability, disorganisation and memory problems. Of course some people will have more severe problems than others. Some people will have deficits at a level of 'impairment' in all symptoms, others will have marked problems related to some symptoms but not others. The key is to establish the strengths and weaknesses of the individual, i.e. their functional ability, by conducting a comprehensive assessment, including a neuropsychological assessment of current functioning.

6.6.1 RECIDIVISM

It is hardly surprising that individuals with ADHD come into contact with the law. The condition is associated with educational failure, truancy, school behavioural problems, suspensions and exclusions, early drop-out from school without qualifications, occupational problems and interpersonal relationship problems. An inability to delay gratification and a desire for a state of arousal and excitement mean that people with ADHD are motivated to engage in high stimulus and sensation-seeking behaviours. Because they are easily bored and frustrated, dangerous and reckless acts may provide immediate gratification and a sense of fulfilment. This reinforces reckless behaviour. Additionally people with ADHD do not have the internal controls that may prevent them from engaging in dangerous acts as they do not effectively engage in a process of rational decision-making or consequential thinking. All these factors will increase the likelihood of a person getting in trouble by engaging in delinquent or antisocial behaviour.

The majority of crimes committed by people with ADHD are likely to be unplanned, opportunistic acts that are committed alone. This is because criminal activity is likely to be strongly associated with symptoms of impulsivity, inattention and restlessness. Feelings of restlessness will cause the individual to become quickly bored with monotonous routine tasks. The individual will find it difficult to settle down to such tasks and will have the urge to quit what they are doing and seek out a more 'interesting' occupation. This will often be a desire for thrills or 'sensation-seeking' behaviour that will satisfy a craving for excitement. Impulsivity means the individual will not stop and think about the consequences of a course of action or behaviour. An opportunity will present itself and the ADHD offender will simply act immediately on a whim without thought, e.g. theft, breaking and entering, joyriding. A labile temperament and hypersensitivity to criticism mean they may respond to perceived slights or insults in an aggressive way. Confrontations often rapidly escalate and the individual is unable to inhibit the urge to act out aggressively, e.g. by threatening a person with a weapon, physical assault and/or damage to property. Symptoms of inattention cause individuals to miss important information or cues in the environment, for example they do not notice the person observing them jump over the fence into someone's backyard and who is making a telephone call to the police; or they do not notice the CCTV in the shop.

High rates of recidivism have been reported (Satterfield *et al.*, 1982; Hechtman & Weiss, 1986; Lambert, 1988; Mannuzza *et al.*, 1989; Satterfield *et al.*, 1994) and crimes are likely to be opportunistic and unplanned. One may assume from these factors that crimes are conducted alone, and this may be the case; however, recidivistic offenders may become associated with sub-cultural deviant groups. People with ADHD have a long history of peer relationships problems and they often lack confidence about social relationships and have a poorly integrated social network. This means that membership of a deviant subgroup may be rewarding, i.e. bad friends may be better than no friends. Furthermore, they may be vulnerable to exploitation by older and more experienced criminals, who will use them as the 'front runners' in criminal activities, e.g. delivering drugs and theft to order.

6.6.2   ARREST AND DETENTION AT THE POLICE STATION

Once individuals have drawn the attention of the police, they may be arrested for questioning and detained for a period at a police station. Prior to any police interview an individual is cautioned. A problem with the caution is that it is so complex that many individuals, including some police officers, do not fully understand its meaning (Gudjonsson, 2003, p. 73). A person with ADHD may be further disadvantaged by their symptoms and pay even less attention to the caution than their peers in the general population. Attentional deficits will be exacerbated by acute feelings of distress and anxiety. Having read many transcripts of police interviews and listened to recordings of police interviews, I have noted that the caution is often rapidly outlined in a monotonous fashion by the investigating officer who then asks whether the individual has understood it. Most individuals affirm their understanding, possibly because they are familiar with the caution from television series. But this means they are familiar with the words, not that they understand them. It is rare that the police 'concept check', i.e. check the detainee's understanding of the caution by having them paraphrase or explain it. It is the middle sentence, warning of possible adverse inferences, that creates the greatest problem and this is the most important part of the caution as it advises a person of the potential ramifications of withholding information or giving false information. Detainees' understanding of their legal rights has important practical and legal implications. Detained individuals may give incorrect information or withhold information for many reasons. People with ADHD think about short-term, immediate gain. They are unable to delay gratification or anticipate longer-term rewards. This means that ADHD detainees may be strongly motivated to escape the situation and get out of the confines of the police interview room, and/or police cell by withholding important information or lying, and not realise or think about the longer-term consequences of their actions.

A second vulnerability for people with ADHD is that they may have difficulty sustaining attention during the police interview, become distracted and say the first thing that springs to mind. They may agree with suggestions of others, especially if they are juveniles who have a particular vulnerability with coping with interrogative pressure (Gudjonsson, 2003, p. 381). The police interviews of juveniles must be conducted in the presence of an Appropriate Adult, whose primary role is to ensure that the interview is conducted in a fair way. This person is likely to be a parent, and given the strong genetic link with ADHD (Levy & Hay, 2001) this will possibly be a parent with (undiagnosed) residual ADHD who will also struggle with the interview process and encourage the child to 'agree' or 'own up' so they can get out of the police station and go home. They may not wait for a solicitor to arrive which means that the police interview will proceed without the individual having legal advice. They may make admissions or give factually incorrect information which is perceived as being evasive or deliberately misleading. If the person is charged, there are two options open to the defendant: to plead guilty and attend court for sentencing or to plead not guilty and prepare for trial.

6.6.3 THE TRIAL PROCESS

In the United Kingdom, ADHD has only been very recently recognised by the courts and is consequently not commonly raised at trial or at sentencing. The lack of recognition and under-diagnosis of the disorder in adulthood by psychiatry most likely account for the fact that this is an overlooked disorder. In the USA, ADHD has been offered as the basis for mental non-responsibility (insanity defence) and diminished capacity defences. It has also been raised as a mitigating factor for sentencing purposes. The possibility that ADHD interferes with an individual's judgement and conceivably leads to reckless and unintentional behaviour underpins such defences (see Collins & White, 2002).

There are set criteria relating to the ability of an individual to plead and stand trial. In England and Wales fitness to plead and stand trial requires certain criteria to be met (R. v. Pritchard, [1836] 7 C. & P. 303). Namely, the defendant must be able to comprehend the proceedings of the trial; be able to challenge a juror to whom he might wish to object; understand the details of evidence; instruct counsel; follow proceedings and give evidence. For example, the individual has to be able to keep up with the pace of the trial; they have to sustain concentration; listen to what is being said; understand and assimilate it and, if necessary, respond by instructing counsel. For a defendant who has a severe attention deficit and who is easily distracted, this can be a challenging and difficult task. If a defendant is very impulsive this may have implications for him/her giving evidence as they may 'blurt out' the first answer in their mind, irrespective of whether it is accurate and rational. They may be inconsistent and give conflicting evidence. Emotional lability may also be a problem when testifying as they may become distressed and/or angry in the witness box, especially under cross-examination. They may not have been able to inhibit a verbally aggressive response. These vulnerabilities are likely to be misinterpreted by a jury unless these are carefully explained to them by a suitably qualified expert.

In the United Kingdom, a landmark case occurred on 12 October 2004 when the Court of Appeal quashed a conviction for murder in May 1996 on the basis of new evidence (see Gudjonsson & Young, 2006). This case set legal precedence for ADHD defendants who come before the courts, as well as for suspects interviewed by the police and illustrates how the failure to recognise and diagnose ADHD pretrial resulted in a wrongful conviction of a 15-year-old youth for murder. This 'new evidence' was that the defendant, Billy Joe Friend, had undiagnosed ADHD at the time and significant impairment in attention, impulsivity and behavioural control. These impairments meant that he was unlikely to have effectively participated in the trial proceedings or give evidence. At the time of his trial, some attentional problems were recognised but the functional impairment he experienced from his inability to sustain attention was not. These functional impairments, the severity of his condition and its implications for the trial were not highlighted in evidence.

This case demonstrated the importance of specialist psychological expertise and objective assessment of functional deficits in the assessment of ADHD. It is not enough to provide a label or diagnose the condition, but usually expert witnesses will not have the expertise to objectively assess the functional deficits. Comparison of an individual's scores with norms obtained from a 'normal' population provides information about the *severity* of functional deficits or symptoms. This is language that the courts understand as a person's functioning can be measured, and in turn indicate a level of statistically significant impairment. For example, evidence can be framed in terms of performance falling at, say, the second percentile (i.e. bottom 2% of the normative population). In other words 98% of the 'normal' population would obtain a higher score. Of course, how these functional deficits relate to legal issues will vary and range from consideration of the reliability of statements given in police interviews; the ability to follow trial proceedings; the ability to give evidence; to the question of abnormality of mind in cases of those charged with murder.

The recognition of functional deficits in people with ADHD who come before the courts may also help advise the courts of special considerations that may need to be adopted (particularly for individuals who are unmedicated and are exhibiting active symptoms) in order to facilitate the trials of people with ADHD, and perhaps prevent unnecessary (and costly) interruptions to the court process. If ADHD is diagnosed in a pre-trial court report for an individual not taking medication for ADHD, it will be important that the expert recommends a psychiatric assessment with a view to obtaining pharmacological treatment, if appropriate. During the trial, sensible precautions might include, regular breaks during the trial, avoiding lengthy questions and complex language structure, and making sure that important information is put across directly and simply. If these simple precautions are taken, the defendant may not be unfairly disadvantaged in spite of his vulnerable qualities. In this way the diagnosis can help to ensure that the defendant has a fair trial, not necessarily by making it 'undesirable' for him to give evidence at trial, or to be found unfit to plead and stand trial.

6.6.4   INCARCERATION

If individuals are convicted and receive a custodial sentence, ADHD inmates are vulnerable by finding themselves in a restrictive environment and sometimes with little stimulation. In these settings they are likely to get a reputation for being provocative, disruptive and oppositional towards both staff and other inmates. Staff may find their restless, labile temperament difficult to manage.

Young *et al.* (2003), investigated legally detained adult offenders with a primary diagnosis of personality disorder. Using screening measures on a sample of 69 males, they found 78% obtained WURS-25 scores consistent with childhood ADHD (i.e. >46) but only three people met DSM-IV adult screening criteria. However, around 29% were classified 'in partial remission'. Compared with controls, the symptomatic group (consisting primarily of individuals in partial remission) predicted a significantly greater number of critical incidents recorded in their patient notes on the wards. These incidents related to verbal aggression and damage to property. The lack of physical aggression most likely reflects that this would attract negative sanctions in this setting. In the community, physically aggressive behaviour (e.g. violent outbursts) is more likely to be expressed towards others, which in turn may attract greater police notice. The study highlighted the risk presented by personality disordered patients who may have residual ADHD symptoms. Interestingly, primary nurses did not rate a significant difference between groups on a measure of disruptive behaviour, highlighting the potential problem with relying on subjective impressions which may rely on personal likes and dislikes of individual patients concerning disruptive behaviour in this population.

Not one person in this study had been assessed for ADHD and the study illustrates how a simple screening process may usefully identify appropriate individuals for a comprehensive multidisciplinary assessment. As in the management of ADHD in childhood, pharmacotherapy has the major role in treating ADHD in adults, and when taking appropriate medications an individual is better placed to optimise psychological treatment as s/he may be better focused, less distracted and/or restless. The combination of pharmacological and psychological treatments has been shown to be efficacious by the Multimodel Treatment of Children with ADHD

Study (MTA cooperative group, 1999) and this is likely to be the case in the treatment of ADHD youth and adults (Wilens *et al.*, 1999).

However, pharmacological treatment alone, without any psychological or psycho-educational component, for offenders may well be iatrogenic. Improvement in core ADHD symptoms in a recidivistic offender will do what? Improve attentional control, make the individual less impulsive, improve planning and organisational ability. The individual may improve in their social performance and develop better social networks within the prison peer culture. They may improve their capacity to learn and retain information. They may not learn what we want them to learn. In other words pharmacological treatment for ADHD offenders may create a more effective and successful offender. One who is less likely to be caught. This devil's advocacy is indeed food for thought. I would therefore argue that it is imperative that psychological interventions are included as mainstream interventions for ADHD offenders and these have equal importance as pharmacological treatment.

Ironically, the prison setting is one that is ideal to provide rehabilitative offender programmes to ADHD adults. As in a school setting in childhood, ADHD offenders in prison find themselves in a setting that has highly imposed structure, clear rules and expectations of behaviour, and explicit sanctions (positive or negative) to reward good or inappropriate behaviour respectively. Support is structured into the system by the allocation of personal officers, psychiatric services, occupational and educational services and group programmes. If an individual with ADHD is treated with medication, they may be able to avail themselves and make better use of rehabilitation programmes designed to develop prosocial skills. Improvement in underlying symptoms is likely to better predispose individuals to engage and succeed in such programmes. This may result in a reduction of risk and accelerated move into lower security and rehabilitiation in the community (Young & Harty, 2001). (Chapter 17 provides information regarding a treatment programme for antisocial ADHD youths and adults; R&R2 for ADHD Youths and Adults, Young & Ross, 2007).

6.7 CONCLUSION

ADHD is associated not only with early offending but also with an increased likelihood of recidivist offending persisting into adult life. This risk appears to remain after taking account of comorbid conduct problems in childhood. Furthermore key comorbidities of ADHD (such as learning disorders, alcohol/substance abuse dependence disorders, depressive disorders and obsessive compulsive disorder) may have an important bearing on offending behaviour. However, ADHD symptoms are not commonly recognised within forensic settings. The information from prison studies is limited by the methodologies employed; however, it seems that a considerably greater proportion of prison inmates may have ADHD symptoms than that reported in the general population. What is concerning is that there appears to be a sizeable number of adults with unrecognised and unmet needs within the criminal justice system. If ADHD offenders are as highly recidivistic as some studies suggest, then identification and treatment – both pharmacological and psychological – should be a primary target. This is ethical practice for the individual, cost efficiency from a management perspective and potentially from a political perspective if recidivism is reduced.

Screening measures are a cost-efficient way of evaluating individuals requiring detailed assessment and investigation, i.e. a diagnostic appraisal that involves structured clinical interview and psychometric assessment from multiple informants for accurate and careful diagnosis of ADHD and associated comorbidities. A brief screening questionnaire has already been adopted by the Metropolitan (London) Police Service and is given to detainees by the police. This asks detainees specific questions to assist with the identification of vulnerability, e.g. if they require 'special help' because of reading or learning difficulties. This screening questionnaire could be adapted to include a screen for current symptoms or residual symptoms of ADHD which would alert the police that special measures may need to be adopted when interviewing this person.

Adult mental health services have been slow to take up the chalice of ADHD but gradually the condition is being understood and recognised as a developmental disorder that is not limited to childhood years. Forensic services are failing to diagnose and treat people with ADHD. However, the criminal justice system does not move so slowly and ADHD is being recognised by the courts as a valid clinical entity that has a bearing on a person's responsibility, future risk and court disposal. This is a strong 'wake-up' call to forensic services.

6.8 REFERENCES

Abramowitz CS, Kosson DS, Seidenberg M (2004) The relationship between childhood Attention Deficit Hyperactivity Disorder and conduct problems and adult psychopathy in male inmates. *Personality and Individual Differences* **36**: 1031–47.

Bambinski LM, Hartsough CS, Lambert NM (1999) Childhood conduct problems, hyperactivity-impulsivity, and inattention as predictors of adult criminal activity. *Journal of Child Psychology & Psychiatry* **40**(3): 347–55.

Brassett-Grundy A, Butler N (2004a) Attention-Deficit/Hyperactivity Disorder: an overview and review of the literature relating to the correlates and lifecourse outcomes for males and females. Bedford Group for Lifecourse & Statistical Studies Occasional Paper: No. 1. Institute of Education, University of London.

Brassett-Grundy A, Butler, N (2004b) Prevalence and adult outcomes of Attention-Deficit/ Hyperactivity Disorder: Evidence from a 30-year prospective longitudinal study. Bedford Group for Lifecourse & Statistical Studies Occasional Paper: No. 2. Institute of Education, University of London.

Cairnes E, Cammock T (1978) Development of a more reliable version of the Matching Familiar Figures test. *Developmental Psychology* **14**: 555–60.

Colledge E, Blair RJR (2001) The relationship in children between the inattention and impulsivity components of attention deficit and hyperactivity disorder and psychopathic tendencies. *Personality and Individual Differences* **30**: 1175–87.

Collins P, White T (2002) Forensic applications of attention deficit hyperactivity disorder (ADHD) in adulthood. *Journal of Forensic Psychiatry* **13**: 263–84.

Curran S, Fitzgerald M (1999) Attention Deficit Hyperactivity Disorder in the prison population. *The American Journal of Psychiatry* **156**: 1664–5.

Dalteg A, Levander S (1998) Twelve thousand crimes by 75 boys: a 20-year follow-up study of childhood hyperactivity. *Journal of Forensic Psychiatry* **9**(1): 39–57.

Dalteg A, Lindgren M, Levander S (1999) Retrospectively rated ADHD is linked to specific personality characteristics and deviant alcohol reaction. *The Journal of Forensic Psychiatry* **10**(3): 623–34.

Eyestone LL, Howell RJ (1994) An epidemiological study of Attention-Deficit Hyperactivity Disorder and major depression in a male prison population. *Bulletin of the American Academy of Psychiatry and the Law* **22**(2): 181–93.

Fischer M, Barkley RA, Fletcher KE, Smallish L (1993) The stability of dimensions of behaviour in ADHD and normal children over an 8-year follow up. *Journal of Abnormal Child Psychology* **21**: 315–37.

Frick PJ, Lahey BB, Applegate B *et al.* (1994) DSM-IV Field Trial for the Disruptive Behaviour Disorders: Symptom utility estimates, *Journal of the American Academy of Child and Adolescent Psychiatry* **33**: 529–39.

Gudjonsson GH (2003) *The Psychology of Interrogations and Confessions: A Handbook.* Chichester: John Wiley & Sons.

Gudjonsson G, Young S (2006) An overlooked vulnerability in a defendant: Attention Deficit Hyperactivity Disorder (ADHD) and a miscarriage of justice, *Legal and Criminological Psychology* **11**: 211–18.

Haapasalo J, Hamalainen T (1996) Childhood family problems and current psychiatric problems among young violent and property offenders. *Journal of the American Academy of Child and Adolescent Psychiatry* **35**(10): 1394–1401.

Hechtman L, Weiss G (1986) Controlled prospective fifteen-year follow-up of hyperactives as adults: non-medical drug and alcohol use and anti-social behaviour. *American Journal of Orthopsychiatry* **54**(1): 415–25.

Hechtman L, Weiss G, Perlman T (1984) Hyperactives as young adults: past and current substance abuse and antisocial behaviour. *American Journal of Orthopsychiatry* **54**: 415–25.

Home Office (2005) National Offender Management Service Statistics, 17 June 2005 (www.hmprisonservice.gov.uk).

Lahey BB, Applegate B, McBurnett K *et al.* (1994) DSM-IV field trials for attention deficit hyperactivity disorder in children and adolescents. *American Journal of Psychiatry* **151**(11): 1673–85.

Lambert NM (1988) Adolescent outcomes for hyperactive children: perspectives on general and specific patterns of childhood risk for adolescent educational, social and mental health problems. *American Psychologist* **43**, 786–99.

Levy F, Hay DA (2001) *Attention, Genes and ADHD.* Philadelphia, PA: Brunner-Routledge.

Lynham DR (1996) Early identification of chronic offender: who is the fledgling psychopath? *Psychological Bulletin* **120**(2): 209–34.

Mannuzza S, Klein RG, Konig PH, Giampino TL (1989) Hyperactive boys almost grown up: IV. Criminality and its relationship to psychiatric status. *Archives of General Psychiatry* **46**: 1073–9.

Marsh PJ, Williams LM (2004) An investigation of individual typologies of Attention-Deficit Hyperactivity Disorder using cluster analysis of DSM-IV criteria. *Personality and Individual Differences* **36**: 1187–95.

MTA Cooperative Group (1999) A 14-month randomized clinical trial of treatment strategies for Attention-Deficit/Hyperactivity Disorder. The Multimodal Treatment Study of Children with ADHD. *Archives of General Psychiatry* **56**(12): 1073–86.

Murphy KR, Barkley RA (1996) Prevalence of DSM-IV symptoms of ADHD in adult licensed drivers: Implications for clinical diagnosis. *Journal of Attention Disorders* **1**(3): 147–61.

Murphy P, Schachar R (2000) Use of self-ratings in the assessment of symptoms of attention deficit hyperactivity disorder in adults. *American Journal of Psychiatry* **157**: 1156–9.

Pratt TC, Cullen FT, Blevins KR *et al.* (2002) The relationship of Attention Deficit Hyperactivity Disorder to crime and delinquency: a meta-analysis. *International Journal of Police Science & Management* **4**(4): 344–60.

Rasmussen K, Almik R, Levander S (2001) Attention Deficit Hyperactivity Disorder, reading disability & personality disorders in a prison population. *Journal of the American Academy of Psychiatry and Law* **296**: 186–93.

Rasmussen K, Gillberg C (2000) Natural outcome of ADHD with developmental co-ordination disorder at age 22 years: a controlled, longitudinal, community-based study. *Journal of the American Academy of Child and Adolescent Psychiatry* **39**: 1424–31.

Retz W, Retz-Junginger P, Hengesch G *et al.* (2004) Psychometric and psychopathological characterization of young male prison inmates with and without attention deficit/hyperactivity disorder. *European Archives of Psychiatry and Clinical Neuroscience* **254**: 201–8.

Rosler M, Retz W, Retz-Junginger P *et al.* (2004) Prevalence of attention deficit/hyperactivity disorder (ADHD) and comorbid disorders in young male prison inmates. *European Archives of Psychiatry and Clinical Neuroscience* **254**: 365–71.

Satterfield JH, Hoppe CM, Schell AM (1982) A prospective study of delinquency in 110 adolescent boys with attention deficit disorder and 88 normal adolescent boys. *American Journal of Psychiatry* **139**(6): 795–8.

Satterfield T, Swanson J, Schell A, Lee F (1994) Prediction of anti-social behaviour in Attention-Deficit Hyperactivity Disorder boys from aggression/defiance scores. *Journal of American Academy of Child & Adolescent Psychiatry* **33**: 185–90.

Stevenson J, Goodman R (2001) Association between behaviour at age 3 years and adult criminality. *British Journal of Psychiatry* **179**: 197–202.

Taylor E (1994) Syndromes of attention deficit and overactivity. In M Rutter, E Taylor, L Hersov (eds) *Child and Adolescent Psychiatry: Modern Approaches*, Oxford: Blackwell Scientific Publications: 285–307.

Taylor E (1998) Clinical foundations of hyperactivity research. *Behavioural Brain Research* **94**: 11–24.

Taylor E, Chadwick O, Heptinstall E, Danckaerts M (1996) Hyperactivity and conduct problems as risk factors for adolescent development. *Journal of the American Academy of Child and Adolescent Psychiatry* **35**: 1213–26.

Thapar A, Harrington R, McGuffin (2001) Examining the comorbidity of ADHD related behaviours and conduct problems using a twin study design. *British Journal of Psychiatry* **179**: 224–9.

Vitelli R (1995) Prevalence of childhood conduct and Attention-Deficit Hyperactivity Disorders in adult maximum-security inmates. *International Journal of Offender Therapy and Comparative Criminology* **40**(4): 263–71.

Ward MF, Wender PH, Reimherr FW (1993) The Wender Utah Rating Scale: an aid in the retrospective diagnosis of Childhood Attention Deficit Hyperactivity Disorder. *American Journal of Psychiatry* **150**: 885–90.

Weiss G, Hechtman L, Milroy T, Perlman T (1985) Psychiatric status of hyperactives as adults: a controlled prospective 15-year follow-up of 63 children. *Journal of the American Academy of Child and Adolescent Psychiatry* **24**: 211–20.

Wilens TE, McDermott SP, Biederman J *et al.* (1999) Cognitive therapy in the treatment of adults with ADHD: a systematic chart review of 26 cases. *Journal of Cognitive Psychotherapy: an International Quarterly* **13**: 215–26.

Young S (2004) The YAQ-S AND YAQ-I: the development of self and informant question-naires reporting on current adult ADHD symptomatology, comorbid and associated problems. *Personality and Individual Differences* **36**(5): 1211–24.

Young S, Channon S, Toone BK (2000) Neuropsychological assessment of Attention Deficit Hyperactivity Disorder in adulthood. *Clinical Neuropsychological Assessment* **1**(4): 283–94.

Young S, Gudjonsson G (2005) Neuropsychological correlates of the YAQ-S self-reported ADHD symptomatology, emotional and social problems, and delinquent behaviour. *British Journal of Clinical Psychology* **44**: 47–57.

Young S, Gudjonsson G (2006) ADHD symptomatology and its relationship with emotional, social and delinquency problems. *Psychology, Crime and Law* **12**(5): 463–71.

Young S, Gudjonsson G (in press) Growing out of Attention-Deficit/Hyperactivity Disorder: the relationship between functioning and symptoms. *Journal of Attention Disorders.*

Young S, Gudjonsson G, Ball S, Lam J (2003) Attention Deficit Hyperactivity Disorder in personality disordered offenders and the association with disruptive behavioural problems. *Journal of Forensic Psychiatry and Psychology* **14**: 491–505.

Young S, Harty M (2001) Treatment issues in a personality disordered offender: a case of ADHD in secure services. *Journal of Forensic Psychiatry* **12**(1): 158–67.

Young S, Heptinstall E, Sonuga-Barke EJS *et al.* (2005) The adolescent outcome of hyperactive girls: self-report of psychosocial status. *Journal of Child Psychology and Psychiatry* **46**(3): 255–62.

Young S, Ross RR (2007) *R&R2 for ADHD Youths and Adults: A Prosocial Competence Training Program.* Ottawa: Cognitive Centre of Canada (cogcen@canada.com).

II Neurobiological Perspectives

7 Behaviour Genetic Approaches to the Study of ADHD

KELLIE S. BENNETT,[1] **FLORENCE LEVY**[2] **AND DAVID A. HAY**[3]

1. School of Psychology, Curtin University of Technology, Perth, WA, Australia;
2. Child and Family East, Sydney Children's Hospital Community Health Center,
Randwick; Prince of Wales Hospital, Randwick, NSW, Australia; 3. School of
Psychology, Curtin University of Technology, Perth, WA, Australia

7.1 OVERVIEW

Behaviour genetics is the study of genetic and environmental contributions to individual differences in behaviour (DiLalla, 2004). Traditionally, behaviour genetic analysis is used to ask: (1) Does ADHD run in families? (Familiality is the term to describe behaviours that present in families.) (2) Do these behaviours have a genetic component? (Heritability refers to the degree to which a behaviour is handed on to offspring). Behaviour genetics now goes much further and attempts to answer questions like: Are genetic influences consistent over development? Do the same genes contribute to related disorders (e.g. ADHD and reading) and just what are the environmental influences?

Behavioural genetic studies have been conducted to investigate both the familiality and heritability of ADHD. A large number of studies indicate that ADHD is highly familial and heritable. Familiality is examined in family and adoption studies where relationships between ADHD in family members can be examined. However, just because something runs in the family it need not be genetic. Twin studies are used to determine heritability and to quantify the relative importance of genetic and environmental influences on ADHD.

A review of behavioural genetic studies, with emphasis on those involving twins, is presented in this chapter. Most studies show that ADHD is highly heritable, but rater bias, difficulty in defining and measuring ADHD, the impact of age and gender of participants, and the comorbidity of ADHD with other behavioural disorders need to be considered when interpreting this finding. Future studies will need to combine both behavioural and molecular genetic approaches to provide more detailed answers about the source of ADHD.

7.2 FAMILIALITY OF ADHD

Family studies provide evidence of the strong familial nature of ADHD. The basic premise of familiality is that if ADHD has a strong genetic component then it should be more prevalent among biological relatives of an affected individual than

Handbook of Attention Deficit Hyperactivity Disorder. Edited by M. Fitzgerald, M. Bellgrove and M. Gill.
© 2007 John Wiley & Sons Ltd

biological relatives of controls (i.e. non-ADHD-affected individuals). Early family studies have consistently shown that there are high prevalence rates of ADHD (defined as hyperactivity) between biological parents and relatives of children with ADHD (Cantwell, 1972; Morrison & Stewart, 1973). More recent studies investigating ADHD have also identified a higher prevalence of ADHD in biological parents and children with ADHD (see Tannock, 1998 for a review). Biederman (2005) described a two-to-eightfold increase in the risk of ADHD in parents and siblings of children with ADHD. These family studies provide substantial support for the belief that ADHD is a highly familial condition. However, to address the issue of whether familial transmission of ADHD is genetic or environmental, additional evidence needs to be gathered from adoption and twin studies.

7.3   HERITABILITY OF ADHD

Family studies indicate that ADHD may have a genetic component. Adoption and twin studies allow researchers to determine the extent to which ADHD is heritable (i.e. genetic), compared to environmental (Edelbrock *et al.*, 1995).

7.3.1   ADOPTION STUDIES OF ADHD

The genetic and environmental contribution to ADHD can be identified by examining the correlation between ADHD in children who are adopted by non-relatives and ADHD in the biological parents of these children. Adopted children share genes but do not share environment with their biological parents, so any similarity between parents and children can be attributed to genes. Additionally, adopted children share the environment but not genes with their adoptive parents. Therefore, any resemblance between adoptive parents and these children can be attributed to common environment. Early studies show that adoptive relatives of children with ADHD are less likely to possess hyperactive behaviours than biological relatives of children with ADHD, indicating an underlying genetic cause (Cantwell, 1972). In a study of children with ADHD, Sprich *et al.* (2000) found 6% of adoptive parents had ADHD compared to 18% of biological parents. Adoptive parents of children with ADHD have also been shown to do better on standardised measures of attention when compared to the biological parents (Alberts-Corush *et al.*, 1986). These findings support the belief that ADHD has a genetic component.

There are some difficulties associated with the use of adoptive studies including: (1) the influence of the prenatal environment on rates of ADHD in the child (e.g. maternal smoking); (2) selective placement, when biological and adoptive parents are matched on some criteria to increase placement suitability, thereby inflating the correlation between adoptive parents and adopted children; and (3) difficulty in obtaining sufficient sample sizes in some countries, such as Australia where intra-country adoption is rare. The issue of inter-country adoption can also impact on ADHD. Rutter *et al.* (2001) found higher rates of hyperactivity in Romanian orphans who experienced severe early global deprivation prior to their adoption into UK families suggesting that early psychosocial, or perinatal such as nutrition, influences may have significant impact on aetiology.

7.3.2   TWIN STUDIES OF ADHD

Early twins studies of ADHD examined the concordance of ADHD symptoms in monozygotic (MZ) and dizygotic (DZ) twins. MZ twins occur when a single egg is fertilised and then divides into two separate embryos. MZ twins share 100% of their genes. DZ twins occur when two fertilised eggs form two zygotes. Dizygotic (DZ) twins share only 50% of their genes (the same percentage as non-twin siblings) (Waldman & Rhee, 2002).

Theoretically, results for MZ twins should correlate more closely than DZ twins if there are genetic contributions to a behaviour. Researchers expected that the MZ correlation (r), or concordant rate for a given behaviour, would be greater than that of the DZ twins if the behaviour is heritable. Conversely, the MZ and DZ correlations for a behaviour which is not genetically determined (i.e. is solely caused by environmental factors) should be similar.

Early studies comparing MZ and DZ twins have shown high heritability of hyperactivity and related disorders. Willerman (1973) studied hyperactivity in 93 MZ and 39 DZ twin pairs and found a heritability of 0.77. Comparisons between MZ and DZ twin correlations provide an estimation of the genetic effect, called heritability (h^2). Heritability is the proportion of a behaviour that is accounted for by genetic differences among individuals (Waldman & Rhee, 2002). Heritability is a common statistic used in behaviour genetics to express how much of a behaviour's variation in the population is due to genetic factors. It says nothing about any one individual. More recently modelling of twin data has made it possible to quantify the genetic contribution to a behaviour.

Behaviour geneticists use models to delineate the genetic and environmental aspects of complex behaviours. Data from different familial relationships can be combined in a comprehensive model that allows the amount of genetic and environmental contributions to a behaviour to be determined. The most common procedure is based around an ACE model (explained in Figure 7.1). This model hypothesises that additive genetic effects (A), common environment effects (C) and unique environmental effects (E), influence an individual's behaviour. Estimates of the effects of each component are derived from the model and a chi-square or other measure of goodness-of-fit is used to test how well the hypothesised model explains the data. With enough degrees of freedom, more complex models can be fitted, such as models examining the possibility that parents may exaggerate difference between their twins.

Goodman and Stevenson (1989) conducted one of the first large-scale twin studies (102 MZ, 111 DZ twin pairs) of ADHD symptoms. Using ACE modelling techniques they reported that the heritability estimates of ADHD inattention symptoms ranged from 32% to 42% (additive genetic component), the common environment effects ranged from 12% to 28%, and the unique environment effects ranged from 40% to 46%. They also investigated hyperactivity symptoms of ADHD and found heritability ranged from 42% to 100%, the common environment effects ranged from 0% to 27%, and the unique environment effects ranged from 0% to 58%. Overall this indicates that genetic effects account for approximately half of the variance in ADHD. Further details of the methodology can be found in texts such as Neale & Cardon (1992) and Hay *et al.* (2001).

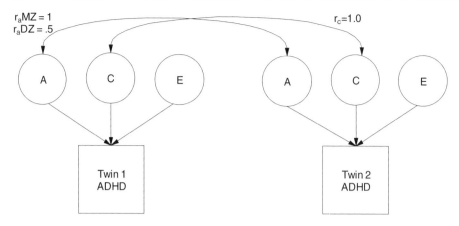

Figure 7.1. Path model of univariate ACE model of ADHD

Notes:
r_a = relationship for additive genetic influences;
r_c = relationship for common environmental influences.

A refers to the additive genetic influences on ADHD;
C refers to the common environmental influences on ADHD, that is the environmental influences that family members experience in common which make them similar to one another. These common environmental influences operate to make siblings reared together more similar than siblings reared apart.
E refers to non-shared or unique environmental influences that each family member experiences. These unique environmental effects operate to make siblings reared together, different from one another. Unique environment effects might include:

(a) different parent treatment of siblings;
(b) exposure to different peer groups;
(c) children's unique reactions to the same parental behavior.

The coefficient of the relationship for additive genetic influences (r_a) is 1 if the twins are MZ (MZ twins share 100 percent of their genes) and 0.5 if the twins are DZ (DZ twins share 50 percent of their genes). The coefficient of the relationship for common environmental influences (r_c) is 1 for MZ and DZ twins.

Several studies of ADHD, which utilise twin designs to investigate the genetic and environmental components of ADHD are reviewed (Table 7.1). This table provides an overview of 22 behavioural genetic twin studies of ADHD to allow general conclusions about the underlying genetic and environmental component of ADHD.

Twin studies of childhood behaviour problems support the conclusion that individual differences in ADHD are largely due to genetic influences. Common environment was not found to be important, while unique environmental influences were found to affect ADHD in a small way (Gillis *et al.*, 1992; Edelbrock *et al.*, 1995;

Table 7.1. Overview of 22 twin studies of ADHD

Author	MZ (N)	DZ (N)	Age years	Other	Measures	Rater	Correlation MZ	Correlation DZ	Heritability
Gillis et al. (1992)	37	37	8–10	Reading disability	Diagnostic Interview for Children and Adolescents	Mother	0.79	0.32	Highly heritable. Large genetic effect.
Edelbrock et al. (1995)	99	82	7–15		Child Behavior Checklist (attention problems)	Mother	0.68	0.29	Highly heritable. Large genetic effect.
Thapar et al. (1995)	113	85	8–16	83 OS	Rutter A (hyperactivity)	Mother	0.61	−0.10	Highly heritable. Large genetic effect.
Gjone et al. (1996)	526	389	5–15		Child Behavior Checklist (attention problems)	Mother	0.72–0.78	0.21–0.41	Highly heritable. Large genetic effect.
Levy et al. (1997)	597	602	4–12	435 OS	Australian Twin Behavior Rating Scale (DSM-III-R)	Mother	0.82	0.38	Highly heritable. Large genetic effect.
Sherman et al. (1997)	194	94	11–12		Diagnostic Interview for Children and Adolescents-R; Scale adapted from Conners' Teachers Rating Scale; Rutter B	Mother Teacher	Mother: Inattention 0.70 Mother: Hyp-imp 0.92 Teacher: Inattention 0.78 Teacher: Hyp-imp 0.69	0.30 0.32 0.57 0.42	High heritability for mother rated Inattention and Hyp-imp. Lower heritability for teacher rated Inattention and Hyp-imp.
Nadder et al. (1998)	178 M 199 F	145 M 126 F	7–13	252 OS	Interview based on Child and Adolescent Psychiatric Assessment	Mother	0.31–0.44	−0.11–0.05	Highly heritable.
Rhee et al. (1999)	493 M 541 F	291 M 261 F	3–18	457 OS 348 sibpairs	Australian Twin Behavior Rating Scale (DSM-III-R)	Mother	0.87	0.35	Highly heritable Gender differences reported.
Coolidge et al. (2000)	34 M 36 F	14 M 15 F	8.6–8.9 (mean)	13 OS	Coolidge Personality and Neuropsychological Inventory for Children	Mother	0.81	0.18	Highly heritable

Table 7.1. *Continued*

Author	MZ (N)	DZ (N)	Age years	Other	Measures	Rater	Correlation MZ	Correlation DZ	Heritability
Hudziak et al. (2000)	220	271	8–12		Child Behavior Checklist	Mother	0.66–0.69	0.20–0.26	High heritability (60–68%) for both genders. No evidence of rater bias.
Willcutt et al. (2000)	215	158	8–18	Learning difficulty, Extreme ADHD	Diagnostic Interview for Children and Adolescents	Mother	Inattention 76% Hyp-Imp 72%	30% 36%	Highly genetic for extreme ADHD scores.
Kuntsi & Stevenson (2001)	61	64	7–11		Conners' Parent Rating Scale (hyperactivity) Conners' Teacher Rating Scale	Mother Teacher	Parent 0.48 Teacher 0.57	−0.01 0.27	High genetic effects on extreme hyperactivity (Parent: heritability 71%; Teacher: heritability 57%).
Nadder et al. (2001)	458 M 564 F	277 M 255 F	8–16		Child Behavior Checklist Rutter Scale Interview (based on The Child and Adolescent Psychiatric Assessment)	Mother Father Teacher	Mother: CAPA 0.16–0.39 Mother: Rutter 0.46–0.50 Father: CAPA 0.19–0.40 Teacher 0.56–0.65	−0.16–0.0 −0.03–0.11 −0.09–0.4 0.31–0.32	High heritability. Specific measure and rater genetic factors.
Martin et al. (2002)	124 M 154 F	99 M 81 F	5–16	198 OS	Conners' Parent Rating Scale (hyperactivity) Strengths and difficulties questionnaire (hyperactivity)	Mother Teacher	Mother: Conners 0.73 Mother: SDQ 0.55 Teacher: Conners 0.81 Teacher: SDQ 0.73	0.25 −0.04 0.38 0.29	High heritability. Parents have significant non-additive genetic effects; Teacher high genetic effects.
Rietveld et al. (2003)	4106	3350	3–12	3378 OS	Child Behavior Checklist (Overactivity; Attention problems)	Mother	0.63–0.75	0.07–0.31	Overactivity and attention problems highly heritable at all ages in both genders (~75% at each age).

van Beijsterveldt et al. (2004)	1220	1445	5	2556 OS	Devereux Child Behavior Rating Scale (attention problems)	Mother Father	0.56–0.64	0.00–0.15	High heritability (76–81%); large additive genetic effects.
Hay et al. (2004)	698	462	4–12		Australian Twin Behavior Rating Scale (DSM-III-R/DSM-IV)	Mother	0.82–0.92	0.43–0.59	High heritability for Inattention and Hyp-Imp. Hyp-Imp has a common environment effect.
Kuo et al. (2004)	194	32	12–16		Child Behavior Checklist	Mother	0.64–0.71	0.38–0.51	High heritability; gender differences with common environmental influences in males.
Dick et al. (2005)	339 M 336 F	325 M 273 F	14	542 OS	Child semi-structured assessment for the genetics of alcoholism (DSM-IIIR diagnostic criteria)	Mother	0.63	0.41	Genetic effects on ADHD. Comorbidity has shared genetic and unique genetic influences.
Price et al. (2005)	2312	2279	2–4	2249 OS	Parent report (Revised Rutter Parent Scale for Pre-School Children)	Mother	0.54–0.69	−0.03–0.21	High heritability (0.78–0.81).
Kuntsi et al. (2005)	1262	1167	2–7		Revised Conners Parent Rating Scale	Mother	Male 0.86 Female 0.86	0.47 0.49	High heritability. No rater bias.
Saudino et al. (2005)	621 M 725 F	568 M 641 F	7	1159 OS	Strengths and difficulties questionnaire (hyperactivity)	Mother Teacher	Parent 0.58 Teacher 0.54–0.76	−0.05–0.02 0.23–0.40	High heritability. Evidence of greater heritability for males.

Notes:
Hyp-Imp = Hyperactivity-Impulsivity;
OS = Opposite sex twin pairs;
M = male;
F = female;
DSM-III-R – Diagnostic and Statistical Manual of Mental Disorders 3rd edition revised, 1998;
DSM-IV – Diagnostic and Statistical Manual of Mental Disorders 4th edition, 1994.

Thapar *et al.*, 1995; Gjone *et al.*, 1996; Levy *et al.*, 1997; Sherman *et al.*, 1997; Coolidge *et al.*, 2000; Hudziak *et al.*, 2000; Willcutt *et al.*, 2000; Kuntsi & Stevenson, 2001; Nadder *et al.*, 2001; Martin *et al.*, 2002; Rietveld *et al.*, 2003; Kuo *et al.*, 2004; van Beijsterveldt *et al.*, 2004; Dick *et al.*, 2005; Price *et al.*, 2005; Saudino *et al.*, 2005).

In a review of numerous studies of the heritability of ADHD, Faraone (2004) reported that approximately 80% of the aetiology of ADHD is attributable to genetic factors. Biederman (2005) also reviewed multiple studies of ADHD and found a high mean heritability of 0.77. Sherman *et al.* (1997) reported higher heritability for parent-reported hyperactivity ($h^2 = 0.91$) than for inattention ($h^2 = 0.69$). Irrespective of whether ADHD behaviours are defined as a continuum or categorised, heritability is high (75–90%) (Levy *et al.*, 2001).

High heritability estimates for ADHD imply a large genetic contribution and also a very low level of measurement error. However, several issues may impact on the estimate of the importance of genetic factors, including (1) contrast effects, (2) defining ADHD, (3) gender and age effects and (4) comorbidity.

7.3.3   CONTRAST EFFECTS

A common but not universal finding across studies of ADHD has been extremely low DZ correlations (Gjone *et al.*, 1996; Sherman *et al.*, 1997; Rietveld *et al.*, 2003; Price *et al.*, 2005). Additive genetic effects on their own cannot account for DZ correlations which are less than half that of the MZ correlations. This is particularly evident in the study by Thapar *et al.* (1995) who reported negative correlations for the DZ twins. Three possible explanations for the low DZ correlations have been suggested: (1) dominant (interactive) genetic effects, (2) sibling interaction or (3) rater bias.

Previous studies indicate that dominant genetic effects cannot explain the low DZ correlations. MZ correlations which are much higher than DZ correlations indicate sibling interaction or parent bias but can also be explained by dominant genetic effects (Rietveld *et al.*, 2003). However, dominant genetic effects would not be expected to produce negative DZ correlations as reported by Thapar *et al.* (1995). Dominant genetic effects and sibling interaction or parent bias can be distinguished by considering both MZ and DZ variance-covariance and correlations. As the reported DZ variance in studies of ADHD is often larger than the MZ variance, this does not support the hypothesis that there are dominant genetic effects in ADHD. Van Beijsterveldt *et al.* (2004) found low DZ correlations for ADHD, measured as attention problems. They also found lower variances for MZ twins than DZ twins, which suggests there is a contrast effect (sibling interaction or parent bias) in ADHD rather than dominant genetic effects.

The second possible explanation for the low DZ correlations is sibling interaction, which refers to the degree to which a twin's ADHD influences their co-twin's ADHD. Thapar *et al.* (1995) suggested that parent-rated ADHD (measured as hyperactivity) may be influenced by sibling interaction effects. However, this study only examined maternally-rated ADHD and no data from other informants (such as teachers). Therefore, it was not possible to separate the influence of actual sibling interaction from rater bias in this study.

The third possible explanation for the low DZ correlations is rater bias. Rater bias refers to prejudice in reporting on the rates of behaviour in one child by comparing them to the other child. Rater bias is the tendency to rate the behaviour of twins as more (or less) similar than they really are. Several studies of ADHD in twins have supported the finding of parent rater bias in measurement of ADHD (Simonoff et al., 1998; Nadder et al., 2001; Martin et al., 2002; Saudino et al., 2005).

Simonoff et al. (1998) examined ADHD (hyperactivity) ratings from mothers and teachers for 1644 twin pairs. They found evidence that parental reports of ADHD (measured as hyperactivity) support a rater bias effect, whereby the more hyperactive a parent rated one twin, the less hyperactive they rated the other. Additionally, Martin et al. (2002) used parent and teacher ratings to assess the extent to which rater bias influenced ADHD. Parent ratings for two measures of ADHD showed high genetic effects but indicated a bias in the rating of twins, resulting in low DZ correlations and high MZ correlations. This is consistent with previous studies (Gjone et al., 1996; Sherman et al., 1997; Rietveld et al., 2003). Examination of teacher ratings of ADHD produced a pattern of correlations that could be explained by additive genetic influences (with no rater bias). However, the difference in ratings between parent and teacher data suggests a parent rater bias, whereby parents tend to exaggerate the differences between the behaviour of their children. A bias in parent ratings was also reported by Saudino et al. (2005) who found low correlations for DZ twins when rated by parents but not when rated by teachers.

These findings support the belief that ADHD is a highly heritable disorder with a strong genetic component and a low common environmental component. However, heritability rates should be interpreted with some caution because rater bias may be operating, especially in parent (maternal) reports of twin behaviour.

7.3.4   DEFINING ADHD

One of the key elements in genetic studies is the accurate definition of the behaviour under investigation. The correct classification of individuals with ADHD is a primary concern for behavioural geneticists, as it enhances the likelihood of identifying specific genes (Leal, 2001).

There are several concerns with the definition and measurement of ADHD, such as the change in the definition of ADHD from a unitary concept (DSM-III-R, American Psychiatric Association, 1987) to categorical subtypes in DSM-IV (American Psychiatric Association, 1994). As a result, genetic studies of ADHD may not measure the same behaviours, depending on the definition adopted.

Levy et al. (1997) utilised the De Fries and Fulker regression technique (De Fries & Fulker, 1985) to examine twin data from a DSM-III-R based maternal rating scale to compare a continuum versus categorical definition of ADHD. The former places ADHD severity on a continuous scale where all individuals have some level of the behaviour, while the latter utilises a categorical cut-off point. The De Fries and Fulker technique defines heritability by the differential degree to which MZ versus DZ scores regress toward the unselected population mean. If the estimate of heritability does not change as more extreme definitions of ADHD are used, this provides evidence that a continuum model of ADHD is appropriate. Levy et al.

(1997) used this technique to show that heritability of ADHD defined as a continuum was not significantly different from that defined as a disorder. This suggested that ADHD was best measured as a continuum, whereby all individuals would have some level of ADHD symptoms, and that cut-off thresholds in the definition of DSM-III-R ADHD were somewhat arbitrary.

Differences in the definition and measurement of ADHD may account for some of the incongruence reported in previous studies of the heritability of ADHD. While contrast effects or rater bias in parental measures of ADHD have been identified in some studies of ADHD, recent studies suggest this finding could relate to the type of questionnaires used. Nadder et al. (2001) tested the genetic basis of ADHD using several different questionnaires to investigate this problem. While all measures showed that ADHD has a highly genetic basis, only the Child Behavior Checklist (Achenbach, 1991) showed no evidence of contrast or rater bias. Interestingly, the Child Behavior Checklist was developed based on a dimensional, continuous diagnostic system of child behaviour, supporting a continuum rather than dimensional definition of ADHD in this respect (Levy et al., 2001). Levy et al. (1997) did not find evidence of rater bias in their study, which utilised a large DSM-III-R based questionnaire. They argued that contrast or rater bias may be a product of the type of measure used. Kuntsi et al. (2005) suggested that studies using brief scales such as the Rutter A (Rutter et al., 1970), which has three items measuring ADHD, and the Strengths and Difficulties Questionnaire (Goodman, 1997), which has five items measuring hyperactivity, are more likely to be affected by rater bias than more detailed scales (Thapar et al., 1995; Sherman et al., 1997; Thapar et al., 2000; Martin et al., 2002; Saudino et al., 2005). The 18-item Conners' Parent Rating Scale (Goyette et al., 1978), the 18-item Australian Twin Behaviour Rating Scale (Levy et al., 1997), and the 11-item attention problems subscale of the Child Behavior Checklist (Achenbach, 1991) provide much more information, and studies using these scales have reported less parental bias (Levy et al., 1997; Kuntsi et al., 2000; Nadder et al., 2001).

One means of avoiding rater bias associated with the use of parent reports of behavioural symptoms is the use of more objective measures of ADHD. Castellanos and Tannock (2002) have discussed the use of endophenotypes in ADHD measurement. Endophenotypes are objectively measurable biological or neurological traits that are thought to be a more proximal reflection of gene function than broadly defined behaviours (Castellanos & Tannock, 2002). A number of neuropsychological tasks have been investigated as potential endophenotypes of ADHD, including attention span, impulsiveness and response inhibition (Barkley, 1997). Kuntsi and Stevenson (2001) identified a neuropsychological measure (response time variability) that shares a common genetic influence with ADHD (hyperactivity) and may be a suitable endophenotype for ADHD. They examined the bivariate heritability (h^2g) of neuropsychological tasks and hyperactivity in MZ and DZ twins. This bivariate heritability indicates the extent to which variation in one task results from the same genetic influences that impact on the other task. Results showed a genetic overlap between extreme hyperactivity and response time variability ($h^2g = 0.64$) but no evidence of a genetic overlap with extreme hyperactivity and delay time ($h^2g = -0.06$). This suggests that response time variability may be a promising endophenotype for ADHD identification. In this context, two recent studies have shown association between the 10-repeat allele of the dopamine transporter gene (DAT1) – a putative susceptibility locus for ADHD – and response time variability (Loo *et al.*, 2003; Bellgrove *et al.*, 2005). Doyle *et al.* (2005) described possible endophenotypes of ADHD, however, further research is required to accurately conclude which tasks are suitable as a measure of ADHD. The study by Kuntsi and Stevenson (2001) is one of the very few in the ADHD field that met what many would argue are essential criteria for a suitable endophenotype, namely high heritability and significant bivariate heritability with ADHD. Candidate endophenotypes for ADHD are discussed further in Chapter 12.

7.3.5   GENDER AND AGE EFFECTS

The contribution of genes and environment to ADHD in children may vary as a function of gender and age.

(a)   Gender

Mixed findings have been reported about the impact of gender on the heritability rates of ADHD. At the phenotypic level, differences between males and females have been well documented (Rutter, Caspi & Moffitt, 2003), with males tending to have higher rates of ADHD than females. Behavioural genetic studies dealing with gender differences in the aetiology of ADHD are less consistent and depend on the opposite-sex pairs often ignored in genetic analysis. Rhee *et al.* (1999) found that although the magnitude of genetic influence on ADHD was similar for males and females, there were additional specific common environment influences which were unique to females and additional specific genetic influences which were unique to males. Kuo *et al.* (2004) reported gender differences with common environmental influences in males. Alternatively, Nadder *et al.* (1998), Thapar *et al.* (2000), and Kuntsi *et al.* (2005) reported the absence of gender effects for symptoms of ADHD. The different findings may reflect varying sample characteristics, including age range of the sample. Eley and Stevenson (1999) found sex differences in internalising disorders differ across difference age ranges. However, the impact of age on gender differences in ADHD has not been well documented.

(b)   Age

Research has found that the symptoms of ADHD diminish with age (Levy, Hay & Rooney, 1996). Barkley (1997) suggested that hyperactivity-impulsivity symptoms appear at an earlier age (3–4 years), while inattention becomes apparent at a slightly later age (5–7 years). Rietveld *et al.* (2003) investigated the impact of development on the genetic contribution to ADHD. They found that the size of genetic and environmental contributions to ADHD, as measured by overactivity and attention problems, remained the same across the four age groups studied (3–12 years). Reitveld *et al.* (2004) reported that individual differences in overactivity and attention problems were mainly due to genetic factors (broad heritability 70–74%), with a small contribution from the unique environment. In another study Reitveld *et al.* (2003) reported a parental bias when children were younger (3 years) but not when older. They suggested that when the children were younger, parents were more likely to compare them to each other. However, as children got older and had more experiences outside the home, parents were more likely to compare them to non-related children than their own twin, thus reducing the bias.

Kuntsi *et al.* (2005) investigated the extent to which the same genetic influences operate throughout childhood. They found that from ages 4–7 the stability in ADHD symptoms resulted from shared genetic influences. The contribution of environmental influences to the development of ADHD symptoms was negligible.

Hay *et al.* (2001) studied the effect of development on the genetic and environmental influences on ADHD by comparing children (4–12 years) at two age points, four years apart. They found evidence of specific genetic contributions to ADHD (inattention) at different ages and little support for the role of common family environment. Thus growing-up together with all the shared environmental influences that implies does not make twins more similar in their degree of inattention. Hay *et al.* (2004) found that the genetic determinants of ADHD (inattention and hyperactivity-impulsivity) remain similar over time. However, hyperactivity-impulsivity was influenced by both genetic and common environmental effects, indicating that growing up in the same household impacts on twins' hyperactivity-impulsivity but not on inattention.

These studies suggested that despite the symptoms of ADHD decreasing as children got older, the shared genetic contribution remained high. When the subtypes of ADHD were considered separately, there was some support for environment impacting on the development of ADHD, particularly hyperactivity-impulsivity, suggesting that the behaviour of children with hyperactivity-impulsivity symptoms can directly impact on their twin, leading to similarities in both MZ and DZ twin behaviour.

7.3.6 COMORBIDITY

Individuals with ADHD commonly have other behavioural disorders including learning disorders, conduct disorder, and oppositional defiant disorder (Pliszka, 1998). ADHD has been found to coexist with other disorders in both clinical and epidemiological populations (Simonoff *et al.*, 1998). If the same genes are found to underlie multiple behaviours, there may be a biological vulnerability to behaviour problems. Therefore, it is important to understand whether this comorbidity is due to shared genes or environment. Although there have been an increasing number of studies investigating comorbidities, few have looked at the genetic overlap between ADHD and other disorders (Levy *et al.*, 2005). If there is evidence of a strong environmental basis for comorbidity, this will have important implications for treatment and intervention strategies. Twin studies allow behavioural geneticists to examine common genetic and environmental components that may underlie comorbid behaviours.

(a) Learning disorders

The issue of whether learning disabilities lead to ADHD or alternatively ADHD leads to learning disabilities has been raised, but studies investigating the comorbidity between ADHD and reading disability have shown there is a common genetic basis to these disorders (Light *et al.*, 1995; Willcutt *et al.*, 2000). Gilger *et al.* (1992) identified pairs of MZ and DZ twins in which one had a reading disability, then determined the rate of ADHD in the co-twin. High cross-concordance for MZ suggested a common genetic basis for these behaviours, although the findings were not statistically significant. Willcutt *et al.* (2000) investigated the subtypes of ADHD and reading disability and found the comorbidity between ADHD and reading disability may be explained by shared genes, particularly between the symptoms of ADHD (inattention) and reading disability. Stevenson (2001) reviewed the relationship between spelling disability and ADHD and reported a substantial overlap in the heritability of these disorders.

(b)   Conduct disorder and oppositional defiant disorder

The overlap between Conduct Disorder (CD), Oppositional Defiant Disorder (ODD), and ADHD has been well studied. These disorders have been found to commonly co-exist in both clinical and non-clinical populations (Biederman *et al.*, 1991). Family studies show that ADHD and CD co-occur in families and appear to share a common genetic aetiology (Faraone *et al.*, 1998). Studies by Stevenson (2001), Thapar *et al.* (2001) and Rhee *et al.* (2004) used behaviour genetic methods to examine genetic and environmental factors contributing to each disorder and to their comorbidity. These studies also supported the finding that ADHD and CD share a common genetic aetiology. Dick *et al.* (2005) examined 336 MZ and 295 DZ twins and found that comorbidity between CD, ADHD, and ODD may be primarily explained by common genetic influences. Coolidge (2000) examined CD, ODD and ADHD in 112 twin pairs and found that while shared genetic influences underlie the comorbidity of these behaviours, there is also evidence of unique genetic influences that underlie CD and ODD, independent of ADHD. Waldman *et al.* (2001) reported a significant overlap between symptoms of ADHD and ODD and a smaller overlap with CD.

Studies investigating the overlap between ADHD and comorbid conditions suggest shared genetic influences between ADHD and reading disorders, and between ADHD and CD and ODD. However, unique genetic influences have also been identified, indicating that these behaviours are not simply alternative behavioural symptoms of the same underlying genetic vulnerability.

7.4   SUMMARY

Family, adoption, and twin studies support the finding that ADHD is largely genetic. Common environment has been found to exert a small to negligible influence on the occurrence of ADHD. However, estimates based on parental reports need to be interpreted cautiously due to possible parental bias, especially in studies of young children. Findings must be considered in light of a number of research concerns. First, rater bias may affect the estimates of genetic and environmental influences in ADHD. Secondly, the accurate definition of the ADHD phenotype is problematic. This may be overcome in the future by the identification of suitable endophenotypes, or biological measures of ADHD.

An exciting new area of research is emerging in the field of behaviour genetics. Researchers aim to combine behavioural genetic approaches and molecular genetics to provide further evidence of a genetic influence in ADHD. Studies of DNA markers incorporated into behaviour genetic models called 'Quantitative Trait Locus (QTL) mapping' can be used to identify genomic regions associated with ADHD (Doyle *et al.*, 2005). ADHD can be thought of as a qualitative trait (the number of symptoms) and the question examined is how much particular genotypes add to or subtract from the symptom count. Cornish *et al.* (2005) have recently used QLT mapping to investigate ADHD. Specifically, they used a QTL approach to mapping genes to investigate the association between ADHD and the dopamine transporter gene, DAT1. Cornish *et al.* (2005) found a relationship between DAT1 and high ADHD scoring males which supports the belief that DAT1 may be a QTL for ADHD behaviours. Similarly, Curran *et al.* (2005) used a QTL approach to mapping genes for ADHD in a large epidemiological sample. They investigated the serotonin transporter gene and reported a significant association with ADHD. In particular, genetic variation of the serotonin transporter gene (SLC6A) was found to be associated with an index of ADHD. Studies, such as these, which investigate QTLs may ultimately help provide answers to assist in the identification of the specific genes underlying ADHD.

7.4.1 TWIN STUDIES IN THE MOLECULAR AGE

With all the current enthusiasm for molecular genetics, the days of twin studies and quantitative approaches to ADHD may seem to have passed. As we have emphasised elsewhere (Stevenson *et al.*, 2005), this is not the case. Many of the issues raised here such as whether the determinants of ADHD are the same in both girls and boys, and whether they change with age are fundamental to justifying the sampling being used for molecular studies. Issues such as rater bias which accentuate the differences within twin (or possibly sibling) pairs have major implications for such approaches as EDAC (extremely discordant and concordant pairs). Is the discordance in the genes or just in the perceptions of the rater?

Another issue is that DSM-IV was never meant to represent a classification for genetic analysis. This view has been put most strongly by the St Louis group and Rasmussen *et al.* (2004) summarises US–Australian co-operation on this issue. Latent class analysis was used to identify more discrete clusters of symptoms, the robustness of these clusters was confirmed by their replicability across US and Australian twin cohorts identified and assessed in quite different ways and finally twin methodology was used to determine the heritability of these classes.

With a behavioural category such as ADHD, where diagnosis has changed so much between DSM-III, III-R and IV, twin studies still have a major role in categorizing the phenotype.

Acknowledgments

We acknowledge the ongoing support of the Australian National Health and Medical Research Council, the Australian Twin Registry and the many families in the Australian Twin ADHD Project.

7.5 REFERENCES

Achenbach TM (1991) *Integrative Guide to the 1991 CBCL/4-18, YSR, and TRF Profiles.* Burlington, VT: University of Vermont.

Alberts-Corush J, Firestone P, Goodman JT (1986) Attention and impulsivity characteristics of the biological and adoptive parents of hyperactive and normal control children. *American Journal of Orthopsychiatry* **56**(3): 413–23.

American Psychiatric Association (1987) *Diagnostic and Statistical Manual of Mental Disorders*, 3rd edn, revised. Washington, DC: APA.

American Psychiatric Association (1994) *Diagnostic and Statistical Manual of Mental Disorders*, 4th edn. Washington, DC: APA.

Barkley RA (1997) *ADHD and the Nature of Self-Control.* New York, NY: Guildford Press.

Bellgrove MA, Hawi Z, Kirley A *et al.* (2005) Dissecting the attention deficit hyperactivity disorder (ADHD) phenotype: sustained attention, response variability and spatial attentional asymmetries in relation to dopamine transporter (DAT1) genotype. *Neuropsychologia* **43**(13): 1847–57.

Biederman J (2005) Attention-deficit/hyperactivity disorder: a selective overview. *Biological Psychiatry* **57**(11): 1215–20.

Biederman J, Newcorn J, Sprich S (1991) Comorbidity of attention deficit hyperactivity disorder with conduct, depressive, anxiety, and other disorders. *American Journal of Psychiatry* **148**: 564–77.

Cantwell DP (1972) Psychiatric illness in the families of hyperactive children. *Archive of General Psychiatry* **27**(3): 414–17.

Castellanos FX, Tannock R (2002) Neuroscience of Attention-Deficit/Hyperactivity Disorder: the search for endophenotypes. *Nature Review Neuroscience* **3**(8): 617–28.

Coolidge FL, Thede LL, Young SE (2000) Heritability and the comorbidity of attention deficit hyperactivity disorder with behavioral disorders and executive function deficits: a preliminary investigation. *Developmental Neuropsychology* **17**(3): 273–87.

Cornish KM, Manly T, Savage R *et al.* (2005) Association of the dopamine transporter (DAT1) 10/10-repeat genotype with ADHD symptoms and response inhibition in a general population sample. *Molecular Psychiatry* **10**(7): 686–98.

Curran S, Purcell S, Craig I *et al.* (2005) The serotonin transporter gene as a QTL for ADHD. *American Journal of Medical Genetics Part B (Neuropsychiatric Genetics)* **134**(1): 42–7.

De Fries JC, Fulker DW (1985) Multiple regression analysis of twin data. *Behaviour Genetics* **15**(5): 467–73.

Dick DM, Viken RJ, Kaprio J *et al.* (2005) Understanding the covariation among childhood externalizing symptoms: genetic and environmental influences on conduct disorder, attention deficit hyperactivity disorder, and oppositional defiant disorder symptoms. *Journal of Abnormal Child Psychology* **33**(2): 219–29.

DiLalla LF (2004) Behavioral genetics: background, current research, and goals for the future. In LF DiLalla (ed.) *Behavior Genetic Principles: Perspectives in Development, Personality, and Psychopathology* (pp. 3–15). Washington, DC: APA Press.

Doyle AE, Willcutt EG, Seidman LJ *et al.* (2005) Attention-deficit/hyperactivity disorder endophenotypes. *Biological Psychiatry* **57**: 1324–35.

Edelbrock C, Rende R, Plomin R, Thompson LA (1995) A twin study of competence and problem behavior in childhood and early adolescence. *Journal of Child Psychology and Psychiatry* **36**(5): 775–85.

Eley TC, Stevenson J (1999) Exploring the covariation between anxiety and depression symptoms: a genetic analysis of the effects of age and sex. *Journal of Child Psychology and Psychiatry* **40**(8): 1273–82.

Faraone SV (2004) Genetics of adult Attention-Deficit/Hyperactivity Disorder. *Psychiatric Clinics of North America* **27**: 109–21.

Faraone SV, Biederman J, Mennin D *et al.* (1998) Familial subtypes of attention deficit hyperactivity disorder: a 4-year follow-up study of children from antisocial-ADHD families. *Journal of Child Psychology and Psychiatry* **39**(7): 1045–53.

Gilger JW, Pennington BF, De Fries JC (1992) A twin study of the etiology of comorbidity: Attention-deficit hyperactivity disorder and dyslexia. *Journal of the American Academy of Child and Adolescent Psychiatry* **31**(2): 343–8.

Gillis JJ, Gilger JW, Pennington BF, DeFries JC (1992) Attention deficit disorder in reading-disabled twins: evidence for a genetic etiology. *Journal of the American Academy of Child and Adolescent Psychiatry* **20**(3): 303–15.

Gjone H, Stevenson J, Sundet JM (1996) Genetic influence on parent-reported attention-related problems in a Norwegian general population twin sample. *Journal of the American Academy of Child and Adolescent Psychiatry* **35**(5): 588–96.

Goodman R (1997) The Strengths and Difficulties Questionnaire: a research note. *Journal of Child Psychology and Psychiatry* **38**: 581–6.

Goodman R, Stevenson J (1989) A twin study of hyperactivity II: the aetiological role of genes, family relationships and perinatal adversity. *Journal of Child Psychology and Psychiatry* **30**(5): 691–709.

Goyette CH, Conners CK, Ulrich RF (1978) Normative data on revised Conners Parent and Teacher Rating Scales. *Journal of Abnormal Child Psychology* **6**(2): 221–36.

Hay DA, Bennett KS, McStephen M *et al.* (2004) Attention deficit-hyperactivity disorder in twins: a developmental genetic analysis. *Australian Journal of Psychology* **56** (2): 99–107.

Hay DA, McStephen M, Levy F (2001) Introduction to the genetic analysis of attentional disorders. In F Levy, DA Hay (eds) *Attention, Genes, and ADHD* (pp. 7–34). East Sussex: Brunner-Routledge.

Hudziak JJ, Rudiger LP, Neale MC *et al.* (2000). A twin study of inattentive, aggressive, and anxious/depressed behaviors. *Journal of the American Academy of Child and Adolescent Psychiatry* **39**(4): 469–76.

Kuntsi J, Gayan J, Stevenson J (2000) Parents' and teachers' ratings of problem behaviours in children: genetic and contrast effects. *Twin Research* **3**(4): 251–8.

Kuntsi J, Rijsdijk F, Ronald A *et al.* (2005) Genetic influences on the stability of Attention-Deficit/Hyperactivity Disorder symptoms from early to middle childhood. *Biological Psychiatry* **57**(6): 647–54.

Kuntsi J, Stevenson J (2001) Psychological mechanisms in hyperactivity: II. The role of genetic factors. *Journal of Child Psychology and Psychiatry* **42**(2): 211–19.

Kuo PH, Lin CC, Yang HJ *et al.* (2004) A twin study of competence and behavioral/emotional problems among adolescents in Taiwan. *Behavior Genetics* **34**(1): 63–74.

Leal SM (2001) Phenotypes and genetic analysis of psychiatric and neuropsychiatric traits. *American Journal of Medical Genetics* **105**: 4–7.

Levy F, Hay DA, Bennett KS, McStephen M (2005) Gender differences in ADHD subtype comorbidity. *Journal of the American Academy of Child and Adolescent Psychiatry* **44**(4): 368–76.

Levy F, Hay DA, McStephen M *et al.* (1997) Attention-deficit hyperactivity disorder: a category or a continuum? Genetic analysis of a large-scale twin study. *Journal of the American Academy of Child and Adolescent Psychiatry* **36**(6): 737–44.

Levy F, Hay DA, Rooney R (1996) Predictors of persistence of ADHD symptoms in a large-scale twin study: preliminary report. *The ADHD Report* **4**(6): 12.

Levy F, McStephen M, Hay DA (2001) The diagnostic genetics of ADHD symptoms and subtypes. In F Levy, DA Hay (eds) *Attention, Genes, and ADHD* (pp. 35–57). East Sussex: Brunner-Routledge.

Light JG, Pennington BF, Gilger JW, De Fries JC (1995) Reading disability and hyperactivity disorder: evidence for a common genetic etiology. *Developmental Neuropsychology* **11**: 323–36.

Loo SK, Specter E, Smolen A *et al.* (2003) Functional effects of the DAT1 polymorphism on EEG measures in ADHD. *Journal of the American Academy of Child and Adolescent Psychiatry* **42**(8): 986–93.

Martin N, Scourfield J, McGuffin P (2002) Observer effects and heritability of childhood Attention-Deficit Hyperactivity Disorder symptoms. *British Journal of Psychiatry* **180**: 260–5.

Morrison JR, Stewart MA (1973) The psychiatric status of the legal families of adopted hyperactive children. *Archives of General Psychiatry* **28**(6): 888–91.

Nadder TS, Silberg JL, Eaves LJ *et al.* (1998) Genetic effects on ADHD symptomatology in 7- to 13-year-old twins: results from a telephone survey. *Behavior Genetics* **28**(2): 83–99.

Nadder TS, Silberg JL, Rutter M *et al.* (2001) Comparison of multiple measures of ADHD symptomatology: a multivariate genetic analysis. *Journal of Child Psychology and Psychiatry* **42**(4): 475–86.

Neale MC, Cardon LR (1992) *Methodology for Genetic Studies of Twins and Families.* Dordrecht: Kluwer.

Pliszka SR (1998) Comorbidity of Attention-Deficit/Hyperactivity Disorder with psychiatric disorder: an overview. *Journal of Clinical Psychiatry* **7**: 50–8.

Price TS, Simonoff E, Asherson P *et al.* (2005) Continuity and change in preschool ADHD symptoms: longitudinal genetic analysis with contrast effects. *Behavior Genetics* **35**(2): 121–32.

Rasmussen ER, Neuman RJ, Heath AC *et al.* (2004) Familial clustering of latent class and DSM-IV defined Attention-Deficit/Hyperactivity Disorder (ADHD) subtypes. *Journal of Child Psychology and Psychiatry* **45**: 589–98.

Rhee SH, Waldman ID, Hay DA, Levy F (1999) Sex differences in genetic and environmental influences on DSM-III-R Attention-Deficit/Hyperactivity Disorder. *Journal of Abnormal Psychology* **108**(1): 24–41.

Rhee SH, Willcutt EG, Hartman CA *et al.* (2004) Test of alternative hypotheses explaining the comorbidity between Attention-Deficit/Hyperactivity Disorder and conduct disorder. *Behavior Genetics* **34**: 658.

Rietveld MJ, Hudziak JJ, Bartels M *et al.* (2003) Heritability of attention problems in children: I. cross-sectional results from a study of twins, age 3-12 years. *American Journal of Medical Genetics B Neuropsychiatric Genetics* **117**(1): 102–13.

Rietveld MJ, Hudziak JJ, Bartels M *et al.* (2004) Heritability of attention problems in children, longitudinal results from a study of twins, age 3 to 12. *Journal of Child Psychology and Psychiatry* **45**(3): 577–88.

Rutter M, Caspi A, Moffitt TE (2003) Using sex differences in psychopathology to study causal mechanisms: unifying issues and research strategies. *Journal of Child Psychology and Psychiatry* **44**(8): 1092–115.

Rutter M, Kreppner JM, O'Connor TG, English and Romanian Adoptees (ERA) study team (2001) Specificity and heterogeneity in children's responses to profound institutional privation. *British Journal of Psychiatry* **179**: 97–103.

Rutter M, Tizard J, Whitmore K (eds) (1970) *Education, Health and Behaviour.* London: Longman.

Saudino KJ, Ronald A, Plomin R (2005) The etiology of behavior problems in 7-year-old twins, substantial genetic influence and negligible common environmental influence for parent ratings and ratings by same and different teachers. *Journal of Abnormal Child Psychology* **33**(1): 113–30.

Sherman DK, Iacono WG, McGue MK (1997) Attention-deficit hyperactivity disorder dimensions: a twin study of inattention and impulsivity-hyperactivity. *Journal of the American Academy of Child and Adolescent Psychiatry* **36**(6): 745–53.

Simonoff E, Pickles A, Hervas A *et al.* (1998) Genetic influences on childhood hyperactivity: contrast effects imply parental rating bias, not sibling interaction. *Psychological Medicine* **28**(4): 825–37.

Sprich S, Biederman J, Crawford MH *et al.* (2000) Adoptive and biological families of children and adolescents with ADHD. *Journal of the American Academy of Child and Adolescent Psychiatry* **39**(11): 1432–7.

Stevenson J (2001) Comorbidity of reading/spelling disability and ADHD. In F Levy, DA Hay (eds), *Attention, Genes, and ADHD* (pp. 99–114). East Sussex: Brunner-Routledge.

Stevenson J, Asherton P, Hay D *et al.* (2005) Characterising the ADHD phenotype for genetic studies. *Developmental Science* **8**: 115–21.

Tannock R (1998) Attention deficit hyperactivity disorder: advances in cognitive, neurobiological, and genetic research. *Journal of Child Psychology and Psychiatry* **39**(1): 65–99.

Thapar A, Harrington R, McGuffin P (2001) Examining the comorbidity of ADHD-related behaviours and conduct problems using a twin study design. *British Journal of Psychiatry* **179**: 224–9.

Thapar A, Harrington R, Ross K, McGuffin P (2000) Does the definition of ADHD affect heritability? *Journal of the American Academy of Child and Adolescent Psychiatry* **39**(12): 1528–36.

Thapar A, Hervas A, McGuffin P (1995) Childhood hyperactivity scores are highly heritable and show sibling competition effects: twin study evidence. *Behavior Genetics* **25**(6): 537–44.

van Beijsterveldt CE, Verhulst FC, Molenaar PC, Boomsma DI (2004) The genetic basis of problem behavior in 5-year-old Dutch twin pairs. *Behavior Genetics* **34**(3): 229–42.

Waldman ID, Rhee SH (2002) Behavioral and molecular genetic studies of ADHD. In S Sandberg (ed.) *Hyperactivity and Attention Disorders in Childhood*, 2nd edn (pp. 290–335). New York: Cambridge University Press.

Waldman ID, Rhee SH, Levy F, Hay DA (2001) Causes of overlap among symptoms of ADHD, oppositional defiant disorder, and conduct disorder. In, F Levy, DA Hay, *Attention Genes and ADHD*. Philadelphia: Brunner-Routledge, 115–38.

Willcutt EG, Pennington BF, DeFries JC (2000) Etiology of inattention and hyperactivity/impulsivity in a community sample of twins with learning difficulties. *Journal of Abnormal Child Psychology* **28**(2): 149–59.

Willerman L (1973) Activity level and hyperactivity in twins. *Child Development* **44**: 288–93.

8 Molecular Genetic Aspects of Attention Deficit Hyperactivity Disorder

ZIARIH HAWI AND NAOMI LOWE

School of Medicine and Health Sciences, Trinity College Dublin, Ireland

8.1 OVERVIEW OF ADHD

Understanding of the molecular genetics of ADHD has rapidly developed over the last ten years. Ongoing research in this area is vital to our understanding of the aetiology of the disorder and may also provide insights into new therapies for individuals with ADHD. This chapter will provide a brief overview of ADHD, the neurotransmitter systems implicated in the aetiology of the disorder along with a review of the molecular genetic studies and discussion of the future direction of this field.

Attention deficit hyperactivity disorder (ADHD) is an early-onset behavioural disorder of a complex nature that occurs in approximately 1–10% of school-age children (Rhee *et al.*, 1999; Thapar *et al.*, 1999; Faraone *et al.*, 2005). Typical symptoms include inattention, excessive motor activity, impulsivity and distractibility. It is defined operationally in the *Diagnostic and Statistical Manual of Mental Disorders* (DSM) and is classified into three major subtypes; predominantly inattentive (20–30%), predominantly hyperactive (<15%) and combined (50–75%). DSM-IV diagnosed ADHD is often thought of as a discrete category; however, there is growing evidence to suggest that it may be one extreme of a continuum (Levy *et al.*, 1997). Males are more frequently diagnosed than females with ratios ranging from 2:1 to 9:1. ADHD individuals have significant behavioural and social impairment in family and peer relations. They are also at increased risk for drug abuse and dangerous behaviour such as reckless driving. The disorder persists into adulthood life in up to 60% of cases and up to 60–70% of affected individuals have comorbid or co-existing conditions. These mainly include oppositional defiant disorder, conduct disorder, depression, anxiety and obsessions, specific learning difficulties, speech and language disorders, Asperger's syndrome and Tourette's syndrome (Kewley, 1998). The exact aetiology of ADHD is not known, but it is recognised to be highly heritable with contributions from genes and environmental factors including smoking, drug abuse and birth complications. As the environmental factors will be discussed elsewhere (Chapter 9), the focus of this chapter will be on the genetic component of ADHD.

Handbook of Attention Deficit Hyperactivity Disorder. Edited by M. Fitzgerald, M. Bellgrove and M. Gill.
© 2007 John Wiley & Sons Ltd

8.2   GENETICS OF ADHD

8.2.1   FAMILY STUDIES

Family studies can only determine whether or not a disorder (or trait) is familial. Famiality may be due to either shared genes or shared environment, and other study designs are required to estimate the contribution of each. Early family studies, using older diagnostic criteria by Morrison and Stewart (1971) found that 20% of hyperactive children had a parent who was diagnosed as hyperactive compared to 5% of controls. In 1992, Biederman and colleagues reported that the relatives of individuals with ADHD were at a five times greater risk for ADHD compared to the relatives of controls. These findings were extended by Biederman *et al.* (1995) who observed that the rate of ADHD in children of adults with the disorder was significantly higher than the reported rate of ADHD among siblings of children with the disorder whose parents were unaffected. These findings suggest that the adult form of this disorder may have stronger familial etiological risk factors than the paediatric form.

8.2.2   TWIN STUDIES

Monozygotic (MZ) twins are the product of a single fertilised egg and are genetically identical, whereas fraternal or dizygotic (DZ) twins are from separate eggs and sperms and share up to 50% of their genes. Assuming that MZ and DZ twins share common environment from an early stage in life, any greater concordance shown by MZ compared with DZ twins can be attributed to genetic influence.

Twin studies consistently demonstrate greater concordance in MZ compared to DZ twins and lead to estimates of heritability (h^2) from 0.61 to 0.98. In an Australian cohort of 1,938 families with twins and siblings aged 4–12, Levy *et al.* (1997) reported heritability of 0.75 to 0.91, which was robust across familial relationships (twins, siblings, and twin-siblings) and across definitions of ADHD as part of a continuum or as a disorder with various symptom cutoffs.

Twin studies can also be applied to traits such as attention problems. Stevenson (1992) reported a substantial heritability for attention scores in ADHD. This was supported by Gjone *et al.* (1996), who found a considerable genetic influence on attention problems across sex and age using a Norwegian twin sample. Two studies reported heritabilities for hyperactivity of 0.66 and 0.72 respectively (Achenbach, 1991; Zahn-Waxler *et al.*, 1996).

8.2.3   ADOPTION STUDIES

Adoption studies can provide a separation between the effects of genes and shared environment. If a disorder has a genetic basis, the frequency of the disorder should be greater among biological relatives than among adoptive relatives. Using a measure of attention Alberts-Corush *et al.* (1986) observed that biological relatives of ADHD children performed worse than adoptive relatives of ADHD children. More recently Sprich *et al.* (2000) examined the frequency of ADHD in the first-degree adoptive relatives of adopted probands with ADHD and compared them to the first degree biological relatives of non-adopted probands with ADHD and non-adopted, non ADHD control probands. They found that 6% of the adoptive parents of adopted children had ADHD compared to 18% of the biological parents and 3% of the biological parents of the control probands. In conclusion, family, twin and adoption studies support a strong genetic component in the pathophysiology of ADHD.

8.2.4 MODE OF INHERITANCE OF ADHD

It is readily accepted that ADHD has a strong genetic component; however, the mode of inheritance is not clearly understood. Like many other psychiatric conditions, ADHD is believed to be a complex disorder with several genes of minor or moderate effect contributing to its development. Earlier linkage and recent genome-wide scans (linkage studies) have not been successful in identifying gene(s) of major effect, further supporting the notion of multiple minor risk genes in the aetiology of the disorder. As linkage-based methodologies are known to have low power to detect genes of minor or moderate effect, most of the recent ADHD molecular genetics studies have been conducted using family-based or case control association studies. These designs are considered to be the most suited to detect risk variants with small effect sizes.

8.2.5 DESIGN OF MOLECULAR GENETIC STUDIES

Molecular genetic studies of ADHD include linkage and association studies. Linkage is the phenomenon whereby alleles at loci close together on the same chromosome tend to be inherited together, due to the reduced likelihood of genetic recombination occurring between them. This relationship between the likelihood of genetic recombination and the physical distance between two loci is the basis behind family linkage studies.

Linkage studies examine the segregation of the disorder phenotype with polymorphic genetic markers using either large family pedigrees or multiple smaller families in an attempt to localise a disease gene to a chromosomal region. This approach, when applied to Mendelian genetic disorders such as Huntington's disease has been very successful. However, the situation becomes more complex for polygenetic disorders such as ADHD where the risk contribution of individual genes is much smaller. In this case, a particular DNA variant or mutation is neither necessary nor sufficient and considerable sample sizes are required to detect linkage. Linkage results are usually expressed as the logarithm of the odds ratio (LOD score). Traditionally, a score of 3 or more is accepted as evidence of linkage. The level of statistical significance in complex disorders is greater than 3 because several hypotheses, including the nature of the underlying genetic architecture, are unknown.

Association studies test if a particular DNA variant at a polymorphic locus occurs more frequently in subjects with a specific phenotype of interest (e.g. ADHD) than in the general population. The simplest design compares the frequency of the variant in samples of cases and controls. The control sample is usually matched as close as possible for age, gender, ethnicity, and socio-economic background, to avoid spurious findings due to population stratification. The frequency of the variant in cases and controls is compared and tested using a chi-square test. A statistical difference in frequencies between the groups implies a genetic association between the tested variant and the phenotype/disorder. This occurs when the variant either contributes directly to the risk of disorder, or is located very close to the risk variant.

An alternative approach uses family samples, testing for deviation from the expected transmission of DNA variants from parents to their affected offspring. For both case-control and family-based studies a measure of the increased risk from possession of the variant can be calculated. This is expressed as an odds ratio (OR) or as a relative risk (RR).

8.3   MOLECULAR GENETICS OF ADHD

8.3.1   ADHD AND LINKAGE STUDIES

As described above, ADHD is a complex disorder with unknown mode of inheritance, although the most likely model is one involving several or many genes each of minor or moderate effect. Linkage studies are known to have low power to detect genes of minor or moderate effect (Risch & Merkangas, 1996). Despite this, four recent genome-wide scans have been published showing reasonable evidence of linkage on chromosomes 4, 5, 11, 16 and 17 (Smalley *et al.*, 2002; Arcos-Burgos *et al.*, 2004). This data will inform future association studies.

8.3.2   ADHD ASSOCIATION STUDIES

Most association studies to date have followed a candidate gene approach, targeting dopaminergic, serotonergic, noradrenergic and other neurotransmitter system genes. This approach has its basis in neurobiological theories of ADHD, but is rather non-specific and covers only the obvious genes known to be involved in signal transduction and basic system functions. It is likely that this approach will become more sophisticated as knowledge of the biology of these systems increases.

8.3.3   NEUROTRANSMITTER SYSTEMS, GENES AND ADHD

Disruption in catecholamine neurotransmission (dopaminergic, serotonergic, and noradrenergic) has been hypothesised in several psychiatric and behavioural disorders including ADHD. Evidence to support catecholamine dysfunction in ADHD derives from neuropharmacology of stimulant medication, the behaviour and biochemistry of animal models, neuroimaging studies in ADHD adults and more recently from molecular studies. Of these, the dopaminergic system is the most extensively examined for its potential role in ADHD. An overview of each of the systems including details of the molecular genetic findings is provided below.

8.3.4   THE DOPAMINERGIC SYSTEM

This system is known to have a direct influence on endocrine function, motor control, reward and cognition (Vallone *et al.*, 2000). It exerts its influence through a dopamine transporter (DAT), five G-protein coupled receptors (DRD1, DRD2, DRD3, DRD4 and DRD5) and several related enzymes important for biosynthesise and degradation of dopamine such as tyrosine hydroxylase (TH), dopa decarboxylase (Dopa) and dopamine beta hydroxylase (DβH). Dopamine exerts its effects in the brain via four different dopaminergic projections, namely the tuberoinfundibular, nigrostriatal, mesocortical, and mesolimbic systems.

A complex dysregulation of the dopaminergic neurotransmission has been implicated in the pathophysiology of ADHD. This has also been linked to the mechanism of therapeutic action of stimulant drugs (such as methylphenidate) used in the treatment of ADHD. Additional evidence to support dopaminergic dysfunction in ADHD derives from the behaviour and biochemistry of animal models, neuroimaging studies in ADHD adults and more recently from molecular studies.

Several dopaminergic candidate genes have been investigated extensively. It is generally accepted that three dopaminergic genes [the dopamine transporter (DAT1), the dopamine D4 receptor (DRD4) and the dopamine D5 receptor (DRD5)] are susceptibility loci for ADHD, although biological proof is still required for all three.

(a) Dopamine transporter (DAT)

The dopamine transporter is an important regulator of extracellular dopamine and is the principal target for methylphenidate, which acts by blocking the transporter and hence the reuptake of the neurotransmitter from the synaptic cleft (Seeman & Madras, 1998). Genetically engineered mice that lack the DAT1 gene (DAT1 knock out) (paradoxically) display features such as hyperactivity and impaired attention that are characteristic of ADHD (Giros et al., 1996).

Cook et al. (1995) reported association between ADHD and a 10-repeat allele of a tandem repeat (VNTR) polymorphism mapped to the 3′ untranslated region of the gene. Since then, this has been replicated by several, but by no means all, studies (Faraone et al., 2005). A meta-analysis conducted by Maher et al. (2002) examining DAT1 association in 11 published studies with a total of 824 informative meioses, yielded a pooled odds ratio (OR) estimate of 1.27 (p = 0.06) indicating that DAT1 gene is a susceptibility loci of minor effect. A more recent analysis suggests an even smaller but significant OR of 1.13 (Faraone et al., 2005).

Heinz et al. (2000) reported that individuals heterozygous for the 10-repeat allele of DAT1 had 22% fewer dopamine transporters within the putamen compared with those homozygous for the allele. As the 10-repeat allele is considered to be the high-risk allele in ADHD, it is possible that individuals with this allele have increased transporter density, which may lead to an increased depletion of dopamine from critical synaptic regions. Dougherty et al. (1999) measured dopamine transporter density in vivo in adult ADHD, and observed an increase of 70% in the dopamine transporter density in ADHD patients compared to controls. Furthermore, Krause et al. (2000) demonstrated that methylphenidate attenuates increased striatal DAT1 availability in adult ADHD patients.

In a recent comprehensive review, Spencer et al. (2005) reported that six of eight independent imaging studies of DAT binding in ADHD show increased binding in treatment-naive children and adults with ADHD compared to controls. In addition, three studies by three different groups have reported decreased DAT binding after methylphenidate treatment. Although the exact mechanism whereby DAT1 DNA variants predispose to ADHD is not understood, the above findings suggest that the over-expression of the DAT protein in certain brain regions (involved in attention and locomotion) may result in the functional depletion of dopamine in these areas, consequently interfering with signal transduction. It should be noted that an unexplained paradox exists between the pharmacological evidence and animal studies of this gene. Blockage of DAT by medication is known to reduce hyperactivity in both humans and mice; however, knocking out the gene completely appears to have the opposite effect resulting in increased activity of the animal. This paradox is likely to be due to the fact that DAT blockage by medication is a transient action on a neurotransmitter system, which normally includes the transporter, while in the DAT1 knock-out mouse the gene and therefore its functions are absent from birth, resulting in potential compensatory actions from other neurotransmitter systems.

(b) Dopamine D4 receptor (DRD4)

The dopamine D4 receptor mediates the postsynaptic action of dopamine. DRD4 mRNA in the brain is localised to the frontal and prefrontal cortical regions, suggesting that this gene has a role in cognitive and emotional functions compared with the motor actions traditionally associated with dopamine receptors and may be involved in the control and regulation of these functions (Meador-Woodruff, 1994). Asghari *et al.* (1995) reported an almost two-fold blunted response to dopamine of DRD4 receptors in Chinese hamster ovary (CHO-K1) cell lines expressing the 7-repeat allele of the VNTR as opposed to the 4 or 2-repeat alleles.

The VNTR in the third exon of the DRD4 gene has been extensively investigated in relation to ADHD. Association between the 7-repeat allele and ADHD has been reported by many but not all groups (Faraone *et al.*, 2005). Meta-analysis of DRD4 conducted by Faraone *et al.* (2001) resulted in overall support for the association of DRD4 with ADHD with an OR of 1.4, for family-based study designs and a more significant OR = 1.9 for case control designs. Other variants have been examined for association with ADHD. Lowe *et al.* (2004a) reported association of the C allele of −616 substitution at the DRD4 promoter. This variant results in the introduction of an AP-2 (sequence specific mammalian transcription factor expressed in neural crest lineages) binding site in the promoter region of the DRD4 gene. Structural and functional analysis of DNA binding and transcription activity of the AP-2 protein has shown that these transcription factors can activate and suppress gene transcription (Williams & Tjian, 1991).

(c) Dopamine D5 receptor (DRD5)

DRD5 transduces extracellular signals, in the form of dopamine, into several intracellular responses having effects on adenylyl cyclase, intracellular Ca^{2+}, K^+ conductance and phosphatidylinositol metabolism. A high signification association between the 148 bp DRD5 allele (mapped 18.5 kb 5′ of the DRD5) was reported by Daly *et al.* (1999). Following up this finding, Lowe and colleagues (2004b) conducted a meta-analysis involving data from 14 groups. They reported significant evidence of linkage and association confirming that DRD5 is a susceptibility gene of minor effect (OR = 1.24, p = 0.00005). Interestingly, they also demonstrated evidence that the association may be confined to the inattentive and combined subtypes. This may represent the beginning of a molecular dissection of the ADHD phenotype.

(d) Dopamine β-Hydroxylase (DBH)

This is a major enzyme for dopamine metabolism and catalyses the conversion of dopamine into noradrenaline thus representing a prime candidate gene for ADHD. Daly *et al.* (1999) reported a highly significant association of the DBH gene variant with ADHD. This finding has so far been replicated in a Brazilian sample and a trend in the same direction was also observed in a Canadian sample (reviewed in Hawi *et al.*, 2003). However, two recent studies by Inkster *et al.* (2004) and Bhaduri *et al.* (2005) failed to replicate this association.

(e) Other dopamine-related genes

Molecular studies investigating polymorphisms of the dopamine DRD1, DRD2 and DRD3 receptors genes, tyrosine hydroxylase (rate-limiting in the biosynthesis of catecholamines) and dopa decarboxylase (implicated in the synthesis of dopamine and serotonin) have not been widely studied in relation to ADHD (Faraone *et al.*, 2005). More studies are needed determine their possible role (if any) in ADHD.

8.3.5   THE SEROTONERGIC SYSTEM

Serotonin (5-hydroxytryptamine, 5-HT) is known to play a central role in many biological activities such as the control of appetite, sleep, memory and learning, control of attention and locomotion, muscle contraction and endocrine regulation (Nebigil *et al.*, 2001). It exerts its effects through interaction with a variety of central nervous targets including receptors and transporters. There are at least 15 different serotonergic receptors classified into four families on the basis of structure and function. All serotonin receptors are G-protein coupled receptors except for the 5-HT_3 which is an ion channel that belongs to the family of channels gated by acetylcholine transporters, glycine and glutamate (Gingrich *et al.*, 2001). The exact function of each of these receptors is unknown. This system also comprises a serotonin transporter (5-HTT), which is Na^+ and Cl^- dependent and has 12 transmembrane domains. Enzymes such as tryptophan hydroxylase (TPH), a rate limiting enzyme in the synthesis of serotonin, and monoamine oxidase (MAO), which catalyses the conversion of serotonin (5-HT) to the serotonin metabolite 5-Hydroxyindole Acetic Acid (5-HIAA), are also members of this system.

Evidence for the serotonergic hypothesis for ADHD emerged when Coleman (1971) observed a decreased concentration of serotonin in the blood of the ADHD children. Using selective agonists of the different 5-HT receptors has shown a positive modulating effect on the functional activities of the mesotelencephalic dopaminergic system. This suggests that some of the genetic predisposition to ADHD might be due to DNA variation(s) at serotonin system genes. In addition, Fluoxetine (a selective serotonin re-uptake inhibitor) has been found to attenuate the activity of the DAT1 deficient mice (DAT-KO), but has no effect on wild type animals. This action is mediated by the increased extracellular serotonin (5-HT) that is present due to blockade of the serotonin transporter (Gainetdinov *et al.*, 1999). Furthermore, when the DAT1 knock-out mice were treated with 5-hydroxy-tryptophan or with the dietary 5-HT precursor (L-tryptophan), hyper locomotion was profoundly reduced. This occurred in the absence of change in dopamine concentration, further suggesting that the serotonergic system may also be involved in ADHD. Knock-out of serotonin gene receptors (see below) has provided further evidence on the importance of this system in the aetiology of ADHD.

(a)   5-HT transporter (5-HTT)

As mentioned above, extracellular increase in the concentration of 5-HT due to the blockage of the transporter attenuates the activity of the DAT1 knock-out mice (DAT-KO) (Gainetdinov *et al.*, 1999). In addition, reduced central serotonergic activity has been implicated in poor impulse regulation and aggressive behaviour in animals and human (Lucki, 1988). The efficiency of serotonergic signalling is controlled by the serotonin transporter, which removes serotonin from the synaptic cleft. A variant (44 bp insertion/deletion) located upstream of the transcriptional site of the transporter was found to influence the expression and consequently the reuptake function of the transporter. Individuals homozygous for the insertion variant yield a higher level of 5-HTTexpression (using transfection and luciferase assay) than those who are heterozygous or homozygous for the deletion variant (Heils *et al.*, 1996).

   Using family-based associated designs, several investigators have observed excess transmission of the insertion/insertion genotype to ADHD cases (reviewed by Hawi *et al.*, 2003). Zoroglu *et al.* (2002) observed that the deletion/deletion genotype was significantly less frequent in ADHD patients than in the controls. In contrast to these findings, Langley (2003) observed no association between the promoter (insertion/deletion) variant or the variable number tandem repeat (VNTR) with ADHD in UK sample. Overall, the evidence supports an association between the insertion variant and ADHD, similar to the association with the 10-repeat allele of DAT1.

(b)   5-HT$_{1B}$ receptor

5-HT$_{1B}$ is an autoreceptor, which is found on presynaptic serotonergic neurons and functions to modulate the release of 5-HT. The receptor is also expressed in areas involved in motor control such as the striatum, frontal cortex, medulla, hippocampus and pituitary. Pharmacological studies using the 5-HT$_{1B}$ agonist RU24969 suggest that the activation of the 5-HT$_{1B}$ receptor in mice leads to increased anxiety and locomotion in these animals. In addition, 5-HT$_{1B}$ knock-out mice displayed an increased locomotor response to cocaine acquisition and alcohol intake, along with hyperactivity and aggressive behaviour (Brunner *et al.*, 1999). The hyperlocomotion effect of this agonist was absent in the mouse lacking the 5-HT$_{1B}$, indicating that this agonist effect is mediated by this receptor. 5-HT$_{1B}$ knock-out mice display an enhanced anti-mobility response to fluoxetine compared to wild type, emphasising the important role that this receptor plays in locomotion (Mayorga *et al.*, 2001).

In a multi-centre study, Hawi *et al.* (2002) identified risk variants at the 5-HT1B gene. In support of this, Quist *et al.* (2003) and Li *et al.* (2005) also observed the same associated variant in Canadian and Han Chinese ADHD families respectively. Using a quantitative trait and a case control approach, Curran *et al.* (2003) reported the same finding in a British ADHD sample. However, using a quantitative trait measure, Mill *et al.* (2005) found no evidence to support a role for 5-HT$_{1B}$ in the distribution of ADHD symptoms scores in the general population.

(c)   5-HT$_{2A}$ receptor

This receptor has been linked to ADHD via several recent pharmacological and molecular studies. The hyperlocomotion induced by the non-competitive NMDA antagonist (MK-801) in mice was attenuated by the nonselective 5-HT$_{2A}$-antagonist ritanserine and by the selective 5-HT$_{2A}$ antagonist MDL100907 (O'Neill *et al.*, 1999). Striatal administration of serotonergic agonists causes inhibition of striatal neuronal firing possibly by a decrease in synaptic dopamine. This effect is thought to be mediated by the serotonin receptor 5-HT$_{2A}$ and may result in the decreased release or decreased synthesis of dopamine in the neuronal projections. More recently Barr *et al.* (2004) have successfully reversed the locomotor activity and highly-linearised movement in a novel environment of the DAT1-knocked animals by treatment with MDL100907.

Several variants have been identified in this gene. One of which is the HTR$_{2A}$/ Histadine452Tyrosine (His452Tyr), which maps to the C terminal end of the mature 5-HT$_{2A}$ protein. Preliminary evidence suggested that the 452Tyr form of the protein may result in desensitisation of 5-HT$_{2A}$ (Ozaki *et al.*, 1997). The possible differences in the function of His452Tyr may influence the balance of the serotonergic transmission and consequently contribute to the development of the psychiatric conditions including ADHD. Genetic studies to date have been inconclusive (Quist *et al.*, 2000; Hawi *et al.*, 2002; Li *et al.*, 2005).

(d)   Other serotonergic-related candidate genes (TPH1 and TPH2)

TPH and TPH2 are rate-limiting enzymes in the biosynthesis of serotonin (Grahame– Smith, 1964). A TPH single nucleotide polymorphism (SNP) (A218C) was examined in relation to ADHD by Tang *et al.* (2001) who reported no association with ADHD and by Li *et al.* (2003) who showed no individual variants associated but did find association with a haplotype consisting of this variant and another (6526G) in ADHD cases with learning disabilities. The discovery of TPH2, an isoform of TPH expressed specifically in the brain, rekindled interest in these candidate genes and a highly significant association between ADHD and the gene was reported by Sheehan *et al.* (2005).

8.3.6   THE NORADRENERGIC SYSTEM

Noradrenaline is a member of the catecholamine sub-grouping of biogenic amines and a key neurotransmitter of the central and peripheral nervous system. It is synthesised by dopamine beta hydroxylase (DBH) which catalyses the formation of noradrenaline from dopamine and occurs only in noradrenergic or adrenergic neurons. The noradrenergic system consists of a noradrenaline transporter (NET), several receptors and enzymes involved in the biosynthesis and degradation of noradrenaline including DBH, Phenylethanolamine N-Methyltransferase (PNMT), Catechol-O-Methytransferase (COMT) and monoamine oxidase A and B (MAO-A and MAO-B).

Noradrenergic projections are dense in the frontal cortex and cingulate gyrus. These regions form the neural substrate of an anterior attentional system that is responsible for maintaining alertness and exercising attentional control (Posner & Peterson, 1990). Several lines of evidence implicate this system in the pathophysiology of the ADHD as discussed below. Animals and humans with lesions in the pre frontal cortex (PFC) show poor attention regulation, disorganised, impulsive behaviour and hyperactivity. Noradrenaline which is secreted in the locus ceruleus and released into the PFC (Caballero & Nahata, 2003) strengthens the working memory, behavioural inhibition, and attentional functions of the PFC. Low concentration of noradrenaline in the right dorsal and orbital sections of the PFC have been associated with many ADHD symptoms such as poor concentration, increased motor activity and lack of self-control (Caballero & Nahata, 2003).

In human subjects, treatment with clonidine, which stimulates the alpha2A post-synaptic adrenergic receptors (at low level) was shown to result in increased attention lapses that were ameliorated using specific alpha2A antagonists (Smith & Nutt, 1996). This suggests that stimuli increase arousal by increasing noradrenaline release.

Drugs (such as desipramine and atomoxetine) that modulate noradrenaline transmission are also reported to be effective in the treatment of ADHD. Recent pharmacological evidence (Biederman et al., 2002) demonstrated that atomoxetine (a selective presynaptic non-stimulant that potently inhibits the noradrenaline transporter with a minimum effect on other neurotransmitter transporters or receptors) was superior to placebo in the treatment of individuals with ADHD. Biederman and Spencer (1999) reviewed the efficacy of these drugs and reported that 91% out of 33 studies showed a positive effect on the treatment of ADHD symptoms.

(a)   Noradrenergic transporter (NET)

The noradrenaline transporter is also recognised as the site of action of atomoxetine and is therefore an obvious candidate gene for ADHD. However, inconsistent findings have been reported from genetic studies (Faraone et al., 2005). A pharmacogenetic study by Yang et al. (2004) examined the medication response of methylphenidate in relation to this gene. They reported significant association between the NET gene and good response to methylphenidate for hyperactive-impulsive subscale scores but not for inattentive subscale scores. To date there have been no pharmacogenomic studies examining response to atomoxetine in ADHD.

(b)   Noradrenergic receptors (ADRA2A, ADRA2C and ADRA1C)

Comings et al. (1999) examined DNA variants of the adrenergic alpha2A receptor (ADRA2A), the adrenergic alpha2C receptor (ADRA2C), and DBH for possible association with ADHD. They observed a significant correlation between scores for

ADHD, a history of learning disabilities, and poor grade-school academic performance that was greatest for the additive effect of all three genes. Using the ADHD score regression analysis showed that each gene individually accounted for only 0.2–2.3% of the variance, however, combined, these genes accounted for 3.5% of the variance of the ADHD score.

Significant genetic association was also detected between MspI polymorphism at the ADRA2A gene for both inattentive and combined type ADHD in a Brazilian sample (Roman et al., 2003). More recently Park et al. (2005) reported a trend in the same direction in a US sample. In addition they reported significant association of the rs583668 polymorphism and ADHD. Quantitative TDT showed that this association was more significant with a dimensional measure of inattentive symptoms. Considering the fact that ADRA2A gene is a relatively small and that MspI and rs583668 variants are in a fairly strong linkage disequilibrium ($D' = 0.79$) (Park et al., 2005), it remains unclear which variant is the possible risk variant for ADHD. Alpha 1C and 2C gene polymorphisms were also examined (Barr et al., 2001) but no associations were observed.

(c)   Monoamine Oxidase A (MAO-A) and B (MAO-B)

The MAO-A and MAO-B genes are functionally related and have identical exon-intron organisation as well as a high sequence identity. Both genes are mapped to chromosome X and separated from each other by ~20 kb. MAO-A degrades biogenic amines such as dopamine, noradrenaline, adrenaline and serotonin and thereby plays a key role in the modification of signal transduction in these neurotransmitter systems. The MAO-A inhibitor tranylcypromine has been described as an effective pharmacological treatment of ADHD (Zametkin et al., 1985). Furthermore, MAO-A has also been reported to be involved in the pathogenesis of intermediate phenotypes, such as impulsivity and aggression. MAO-A knock-out mice have been observed to exhibit significantly increased aggressive behaviour accompanied by elevated levels of serotonin, noradrenaline and dopamine (Cases et al., 1995). In addition, Brunner et al. (1993) described a rare point mutation in the MAO-A gene causing a loss of function, which resulted in a highly impulsive and aggressive behavioural phenotype in many members of a large family.

Several DNA variants have been identified in the coding and control region of the gene, some with functional significance; however, the results of association studies have been inconsistent (Manuck et al., 2000; Jiang et al., 2001; Domschke et al., 2005).

Pharmacological studies provide preliminary evidence for a beneficial effect of monoamine oxidase B inhibitors such as selegiline or deprenyl in the treatment of ADHD (Feigin et al., 1996; Akhondzadeh et al., 2003). Administration of deprenyl was shown to significantly reduce impulsiveness in an animal model of ADHD (Boix et al., 1998). Molecular genetic studies have so far not shown association between MAO-B and ADHD.

(d)   Catechol-O-methyltransferase (COMT)

Several studies have examined genes involved in the regulation of dopamine synthesis and metabolism. Catechol-O-methyltransferase (COMT) catalyses the transfer of a methyl group from S-adenosylmethionine to catecholamines, including the neurotransmitters dopamine, epinephrine, and norepinephrine. This O-methylation results in degradation of the catecholamine. Several polymorphisms have been identified in this gene, with the functional Valine158Methionine (Val158Met) COMT polymorphism receiving the most attention. The Val variant degrades monoamines 3–4 times more efficiently than the Met variant. Eisenberg *et al.* (1999) reported association of ADHD with the Val variant, however, Qian *et al.* (2003) reported an association with the Met variant. In contrast, five other groups have found no association (see Hawi *et al.*, 2003). Recently, however, Bellgrove *et al.* (2005) showed that the Met variant predisposes to poor sustained attention in ADHD children.

8.3.7   OTHER CANDIDATE GENES

(a)   SNAP-25

The mouse mutant *coloboma* (congenital cleft in some part of the eye, commonly the iris) displays a three-fold excess hyperactivity compared to control littermates. *Coloboma* is a semi dominant mutation (cm/+) in which the heterozygous form results in the mutant type while the homozygous is lethal. This model was shown to be the result of a deletion of the Synaptosomal-associated protein 25 (SNAP-25) gene and can be genetically rescued by the transgene encoding SNAP-25. Synaptosomal-associated protein 25 (SNAP-25) is a presynaptic plasma membrane protein essential for synaptic vesicle fusion and neurotransmitter release. SNAP-25 along with syntaxin 1a and VAMP-2 (synaptobrevin-2) make up the core complex essential for docking and holding synaptic vesicles at the presynaptic membrane in preparation for Ca^{2+}-triggered neurotransmitter exocytosis (Sollner *et al.,* 1993). It forms a connection between the synaptic vesicles holding the transmitter and the plasma membrane at the site of fusion.

Jones *et al.* (2001) observed an increase of 40% in NA within the striatum and the nucleus accumbens of the *coloboma* mouse. Furthermore, the mRNA expression of tyrosine hydroxylase (TH) was also significantly increased in the cells of the locus ceruleus indicating that the abnormal level of NA in these regions may contribute to the hyperactive behaviour of the *coloboma*. NA depletion using the DSP-4 (N-(2-chloroethyl)-N-ethyl-2 bromobenzylamine hydrochloride) significantly reduced the hyperactivity of the *coloboma* mouse suggesting that the regulation of NA may play a central role in the hyperactive behaviour in this animal model.

Genetic association studies suggest a role for the SNAP-25 gene in ADHD susceptibility. Preliminary evidence from two variants located at the 3′ untranslated region of the gene showed excess transmission of a haplotype made of these two variants, to the ADHD cases (Barr *et al.*, 2000). Another study showed a trend towards association with the same variants (Kustanovich *et al.*, 2003). Brophy *et al.* (2002) reported significant association, but with the opposite allele to that previously reported (as part of a haplotype) by Barr *et al.* (2000). Two other studies (Mill *et al.*, 2002a; Mill *et al.*, 2004) have shown association with several variants throughout the gene including those used by Barr *et al.* (2000). Together, these observations indicate the importance of SNAP-25 (alone or in combination with other proteins) in the development of ADHD.

(b) Acetylcholine receptors

Nicotine has been shown to improve attention in ADHD individuals and to increase alertness in non-ADHD smokers and non-smokers (Levin *et al.*, 1998). Studies in rats have shown that hyperactivity induced by nicotine administration can be blocked by selective DRD1 and DRD2 antagonists (O'Neill *et al.*, 1991). In addition, smoking during pregnancy has been suggested as a risk factor for ADHD.

The nicotinic acetylcholine receptors are ligand-gated ion channels composed of multiple subunits. Two of these subunits, the alpha-4 and alpha-7 (known as CHRNA4 and CHRNA7 respectively) have been examined in ADHD association studies. The CHRNA4 gene has been the focus of two studies. However, inconsistent findings have been reported (Kent *et al.*, 2001a; Todd *et al.*, 2003) with CHRNA7 being the focus of one study that revealed no evidence for association with ADHD (Kent *et al.*, 2001b).

(c) Glutamate receptors

As with the acetylcholine receptors, the glutamate NMDA (N-methyl-D-aspartate) receptor is composed of a number of subunits, one of which is encoded for by the GRIN2A gene. This gene is located under a linkage peak (16p13) for ADHD identified in a genome-wide scan conducted by Fisher *et al.* (2002). Association was first reported between this gene and ADHD by Turic *et al.* (2004) but attempts to replicate the finding have been unsuccessful (Adams *et al.*, 2004).

8.4   ADHD GENES AND POSSIBLE THERAPEUTIC IMPLICATIONS

Identifying risk genes for ADHD will in due course, contribute significantly to our understanding of the biology of ADHD. Potentially, this could lead to a molecular basis for refining diagnostic categories. For example, it has been shown that the risk variants at DRD5 contribute to the DSM-IV inattentive and combined subtypes but not to the hyperactivity subtype. The genetic findings may also have therapeutic implications.

Recent studies have shown that the DAT1 variants (VNTR) identified as risk variants in ADHD affect the expression of the gene. Mill *et al.* (2002b) reported increased DAT expression in brain samples from individuals homozygous for the 10-repeat variant of DAT1 (considered to be a risk factor for ADHD). They suggested that possession of this variant up-regulates expression of this gene, which could influence that individual's response to methylphenidate. Several recent studies have shown association between the DAT1 10-repeat variant and a good response to methylphenidate in ADHD (Kirley *et al.*, 2003), although overall, findings are not consistent (McGough, 2005). This topic is discussed in detail in Chapter 16.

8.5   SUMMARY AND FUTURE DIRECTION

In contrast to several psychiatric conditions, the candidate gene approach has been very successful in identifying risk genes for ADHD. It is generally accepted that DRD4, DRD5 and DAT1 are risk genes for ADHD although the exact mechanism whereby this risk is mediated has yet to be elucidated. Other genes are also showing promising results although the overall picture is not fully consistent, and many findings remain to be confirmed. Inconsistency is unlikely to arise because ADHD lacks a genetic aetiology, but is rather a reflection of the extensive variability that is inherent in the studies, and the complex nature of the underlying genetic architecture of the disorder. Some variability may be attributed to ascertainment and diagnostic practices, although the majority of studies now use the DSM-IV criteria. Variation may also be due to ethnic differences and population stratification, although the family-based studies are less susceptible to the latter. In addition, ADHD is itself a highly variable disorder, with overlapping subtypes and a high rate of comorbidity with other diagnoses. Therefore, when studies examine clinically defined ADHD without any refinement of subtype or comorbidities, there is the potential for heterogeneity between samples resulting in variation in results. It would seem an obvious solution to examine more carefully defined measures of the ADHD phenotype in genetic studies. However, selecting cases may dramatically reduce the size of the study sample and therefore the power of the study. The careful assessment of the ADHD phenotype requires time and expertise and is therefore a costly undertaking.

The ADHD phenotype could be defined in terms of clinical, neuropsychological and neuroimaging measures. It is possible that specific neuropsychological or neuroimaging measures might represent aspects of the disorder that relate more closely to underlying genes. If correct, the individual gene effects would be greater for these endophenotypes, and easier to detect. This approach is covered in detail in Chapter 12.

8.6   REFERENCES

Achenbach TM (1991) *Manual for the Child Behavior Checklist/4-18 and 1991 Profile.* Burlington: University of Vermont Department of Psychiatry.

Adams J *et al.* (2004) Glutamate receptor, ionotropic, N-methyl D-aspartate 2A (GRIN2A) gene as a positional candidate for Attention-Deficit/Hyperactivity Disorder in the 16p13 region. *Molecular Psychiatry* **9**: 494–9.

Akhondzadeh S *et al.* (2003) Selegiline in the treatment of attention deficit hyperactivity disorder in children: a double blind and randomized trial. *Progress in Neuro-Psychopharmacology and Biological Psychiatry* **27**: 841–5.

Alberts-Corush J *et al.* (1986) *Manual of Behaviour Checklist and Revised Child Behaviour Profile.* Burlington: VT.

Arcos-Burgos M *et al.* (2004) Attention-deficit/hyperactivity disorder in a population isolate: linkage to loci at 4q13.2, 5q33.3, 11q22, and 17p11. *The American Journal of Human Genetics* **75**: 998–1014.

Arnsten A (1999) Development of the cerebral cortex: XIV. stress impairs prefrontal cortical function. *Journal of the American Academy of Child and Adolescent Psychiatry* **38**:
220–2.

Ashgari V *et al.* (1995) Modulation of intracellular cyclic AMP levels by different human
dopamine D4 receptor variants. *Journal of Neurochemistry* **65**: 1157–65.

Bakker SC *et al.* (2003) A whole-genome scan in 164 Dutch sib pairs with Attention-Deficit/
Hyperactivity Disorder: suggestive evidence for linkage on chromosomes 7p and 15q. *The
American Journal of Human Genetics* **72**: 1251–60.

Barr CL *et al.* (2000) Identification of DNA variants in the SNAP-25 gene and linkage study
of these variants and Attention-Deficit Hyperactivity Disorder. *Molecular Psychiatry* **5**:
405–9.

Barr CL *et al.* (2001) Attention-deficit hyperactivity disorder and the adrenergic receptors
alpha 1C and alpha 2C. *Molecular Psychiatry* **6**: 334–7.

Barr AM *et al.* (2004) The selective serotonin-2A receptor antagonist M100907 reverses
behavioral deficits in dopamine transporter knockout mice. *Neuropsychopharmacology* **29**:
221–8.

Bellgrove MA *et al.* (2005) The methionine allele of the COMT variant impairs prefrontal
cognition in children and adolescents with ADHD. *Experimental Brain Research* **163**:
352–60.

Bhaduri N *et al.* (2005) Analysis of polymorphisms in the dopamine Beta hydroxylase gene:
association with attention deficit hyperactivity disorder in Indian children. *Indian Pediatrics* **42**: 123–9.

Biederman J *et al.* (1992) Further evidence for family-genetic risk factors in attention deficit
hyperactivity disorder. Patterns of comorbidity in probands and relatives psychiatrically
and pediatrically referred samples. *Archives of General Psychiatry* **49**: 728–38.

Biederman J *et al.* (1995) High risk for attention deficit hyperactivity disorder among children
of parents with childhood onset of the disorder: a pilot study. *American Journal of Psychiatry* **152**: 431–5.

Biederman J, Spencer T (1999) Attention-deficit/hyperactivity disorder (ADHD) as a noradrenergic disorder. *Biological Psychiatry* **46**: 1234–42.

Biederman J *et al.* (2002) Efficacy of atomoxetine versus placebo in school-age girls with
Attention-Deficit/Hyperactivity Disorder. *Pediatrics* **110**: 75.

Boix F *et al.* (1998) Chronic L-deprenyl treatment alters brain monoamine levels and reduces
impulsiveness in an animal model of Attention-Deficit Hyperactivity Disorder. *Behavioural Brain Research* **94**: 153–62.

Brophy K *et al.* (2002) Synaptosomal-associated protein 25 (SNAP-25) and attention deficit
hyperactivity disorder (ADHD): evidence of linkage and association in the Irish population. *Molecular Psychiatry* **7**: 913–17.

Brunner D *et al.* (1999) Anxiety, motor activation, and maternal-infant interactions in 5-
HT1B knockout mice. *Behavioral Neuroscience* **113**: 587–601.

Brunner HG *et al.* (1993) Abnormal behavior associated with a point mutation in the structural gene for monoamine oxidase A. *Science* **262**: 578–80.

Caballero J, Nahata MC (2003) Atomoxetine hydrochloride for the treatment of Attention-
Deficit/Hyperactivity Disorder. *Clinical Therapeutics* **25**: 3065–83.

Cases O *et al.* (1995) Aggressive behaviour and altered amounts of brain serotonin and norepinephrine in mice lacking MAOA. *Science* **268**: 1763–6.

Coleman M (1971) Serotonin concentrations in whole blood of hyperactive children. *The
Journal of Pediatrics* **78**: 985–90.

Comings DE *et al.* (1999) Additive effect of three noradrenergic genes (ADRA2A, ADRA2C,
DBH) on attention deficit/hyperactivity disorder and learning disabilities in Tourette
Syndrome subjects. *Clinical Genetics* **55**: 160–72.

Cook EH *et al.* (1995) Association of attention deficit disorder and the dopamine transporter gene. *The American Journal of Human Genetics* **56**: 993–8.

Curran S *et al.* (2003) CHIP: Defining a dimension of the vulnerability to attention deficit hyperactivity disorder (ADHD) using sibling and individual data of children in a community-based sample. *American Journal of Medical Genetics Part B: Neuropsychiatric Genetics* **119**: 86–97.

Daly G *et al.* (1999) Mapping susceptibility loci in attention deficit hyperactivity isorder, preferential transmission of parental alleles at DAT1, DBH and DRD5 to affected children. *Molecular Psychiatry* **4**: 192–6.

Domschke K *et al.* (2005) Association analysis of the monoamine oxidase A and B genes with attention deficit hyperactivity disorder (ADHD) in an Irish sample: preferential transmission of the MAO-A 941G allele to affected children. *American Journal of Medical Genetics Part B: Neuropsychiatric Genetics* **134**: 110–14.

Dougherty DD *et al.* (1999) Dopamine transporter density in patients with attention deficit hyperactivity disorder. *Lancet* **354**: 2132–3.

Eisenberg J *et al.* (1999) Haplotype relative risk study of catechol-O-methyltransferase (COMT) and attention deficit hyperactivity disorder (ADHD): association of the high-enzyme activity Val allele with ADHD impulsive-hyperactive phenotype. *American Journal of Medical Genetics Part B: Neuropsychiatric Genetics* **88**: 497–502.

Faraone SV *et al.* (2001) Meta-analysis of the association between the 7-repeat allele of the dopamine D(4) receptor gene and attention deficit hyperactivity disorder. *American Journal of Psychiatry* **158**: 1052–7.

Faraone SV *et al.* (2005) Molecular genetics of Attention-Deficit/Hyperactivity Disorder. *Biological Psychiatry* **57**: 1313–23.

Feigin A *et al.* (1996) A controlled trial of deprenyl in children with Tourette's syndrome and attention deficit hyperactivity disorder. *Neurology* **46**: 965–8.

Fisher SE *et al.* (2002) A genomewide scan for loci involved in Attention-Deficit/Hyperactivity Disorder. *The American Journal of Human Genetics* **70**: 1183–96.

Gainetdinov RR *et al.* (1999) Role of serotonin in the paradoxical calming effect of psycho-stimulants on hyperactivity. *Science* **283**: 397–401.

Gingrich JA, Hen R (2001) Dissecting the role of the serotonin system in neuropsychiatric disorders using knockout mice. *Psychopharmacology (Berl)* **155**: 1–10.

Giros B *et al.* (1996) Hyperlocomotion and indifference to cocaine and amphetamine in mice lacking the dopamine transporter. *Nature* **379**: 606–12.

Gjone H *et al.* (1996) Genetic influence on parent-reported attention-related problems in a Norwegian general population twin sample. *Journal of the American Academy of Child and Adolescent Psychiatry* **35**: 588–96.

Grahame-Smith DG (1964) Tryptophan hydroxylation in brain. *Biochemical and Biophysical Research Communications* **16**: 586–92.

Hawi Z *et al.* (2002) Serotonergic system and attention deficit hyperactivity disorder (ADHD): a potential susceptibility locus at the 5-HT(1B) receptor gene in 273 nuclear families from a multi-centre sample. *Molecular Psychiatry* **7**: 718–25.

Hawi Z *et al.* (2003) Recent genetic advances in ADHD and diagnostic and therapeutic prospects. *Expert Review of Neurotherapeutics* **3**: 453–64.

Heils A *et al.* (1996) Allelic variation of human serotonin transporter gene expression. *Journal of Neurochemistry* **66**(6): 2621–4.

Heinz A *et al.* (2000) Genotype influences *in vivo* dopamine transporter availability in human striatum. *Neuropsychopharmacology* **22**: 133–9.

Inkster B *et al.* (2004) Linkage disequilibrium analysis of the dopamine beta-hydroxylase gene in persistent attention deficit hyperactivity disorder. *Psychiatric Genetics* **14**: 117–20.

Jiang S *et al.* (2001) Linkage studies between Attention-Deficit Hyperactivity Disorder and the monoamine oxidase genes. *American Journal of Medical Genetics Part B: Neuropsychiatric Genetics* **105**: 783–8.

Jones MD *et al.* (2001) Abnormal presynaptic catecholamine regulation in a hyperactive SNAP-25-deficient mouse mutant. *Pharmacology Biochemistry and Behavior* **68**: 669–76.

Kent L *et al.* (2001a) Nicotinic acetylcholine receptor alpha4 subunit gene polymorphism and attention deficit hyperactivity disorder. *Psychiatric Genetics* **11**: 37–40.

Kent L *et al.* (2001b) No association between CHRNA7 microsatellite markers and Attention-Deficit Hyperactivity Disorder. *American Journal of Medical Genetics Part B: Neuropsychiatric Genetics* **105**: 686–9.

Kewley GD (1998) Personal paper: attention deficit hyperactivity disorder is underdiagnosed and undertreated in Britain. *British Medical Journal* **316**: 1594–6.

Kirley A *et al.* (2003) Association of the 480 bp DAT1 allele with methylphenidate response in a sample of Irish children with ADHD. *American Journal of Medical Genetics Part B: Neuropsychiatric Genetics* **121**: 50–4.

Krause KL *et al.* (2000) Increased striatal dopamine transporter in adult patients with attention deficit hyperactivitydisorder, effects of methylphenidate as measured by single photon emission computed tomography. *Neuroscience Letters* **285**: 107–10.

Kustanovich V *et al.* (2003) Biased paternal transmission of SNAP-25 risk alleles in Attention-Deficit Hyperactivity Disorder. *Molecular Psychiatry* **8**: 309–15.

Langley K *et al.* (2003) No evidence of association of two 5-HT transporter gene variants and attention deficit hyperactivity disorder. *Psychiatric Genetics* **13**: 107–10.

Levin ED *et al.* (1998) Transdermal nicotine effects on attention. *Psychopharmacology* **140**: 135–41.

Levy F *et al.* (1997) Attention-deficit hyperactivity disorder: a category or a continuum? Genetic analysis of a large-scale twin study. *Journal of the American Academy of Child and Adolescent Psychiatry* **36**: 737–44.

Li J *et al.* (2003) Association between tryptophan hydroxylase gene polymorphisms and attention deficit hyperactivity disorder with or without learning disorder. *Zhonghua Yi Xue Za Zhi* **83**: 2114–18.

Li J *et al.* (2005) Serotonin 5-HT1B receptor gene and attention deficit hyperactivity disorder in Chinese Han subjects. *American Journal of Medical Genetics Part B: Neuropsychiatric Genetics* **132**: 59–63.

Lowe N *et al.* (2004a) Multiple marker analysis at the promoter region of the DRD4 gene and ADHD: evidence of linkage and association with the SNP–616. *American Journal of Medical Genetics Part B: Neuropsychiatric Genetics* **131**: 33–7.

Lowe N *et al.* (2004b) Joint analysis of the DRD5 marker concludes association with Attention-Deficit/Hyperactivity Disorder confined to the predominantly inattentive and combined subtypes. *The American Journal of Human Genetics* **74**: 348–56.

Lucki I (1998) The spectrum of behaviors influenced by serotonin. *Biological Psychiatry* **44**: 151–62.

McGough JJ (2005) Attention-deficit/hyperactivity disorder pharmacogenomics. *Biological Psychiatry* **57**: 1367–73.

Maher BS *et al.* (2002) Dopamine system genes and attention deficit hyperactivity disorder, a meta-analysis. *Psychiatric Genetics* **2**: 207–15.

Manuck SB *et al.* (2000) A regulatory variant of the monoamine oxidase-A gene may be associated with variability in aggression, impulsivity, and central nervous system serotonergic responsivity. *Psychiatry Research* **95**: 9–23.

Mayorga AJ *et al.* (2001) Antidepressant-like behavioral effects in 5-hydroxytryptamine (1A) and 5-hydroxytryptamine (1B) receptor mutant mice. *Journal of Pharmacology and Experimental Therapeutics* **298**: 1101–7.

Meador-Woodruff JH *et al.* (1994) Dopamine receptor gene expression in the human medial temporal lobe. *Neuropsychopharmacology* **10**: 239–48.

Mill J *et al.* (2002a) Association study of a SNAP-25 microsatellite and attention deficit hyperactivity disorder. *American Journal of Medical Genetics Part B: Neuropsychiatric Genetics* **114**: 269–71.

Mill J *et al.* (2002b) Expression of the dopamine transporter gene is regulated by the 3′ UTR VNTR: Evidence from brain and lymphocytes using quantitative RT-PCR. *American Journal of Medical Genetics Part B: Neuropsychiatric Genetics* **114**: 975–9.

Mill J *et al.* (2004) Haplotype analysis of SNAP-25 suggests a role in the aetiology of ADHD. *Molecular Psychiatry* **9**: 801–10.

Mill J *et al.* (2005) Quantitative trait locus analysis of candidate gene alleles associated with attention deficit hyperactivity disorder (ADHD) in five genes: DRD4, DAT1, DRD5, SNAP-25, and 5-HT1B. *American Journal of Medical Genetics Part B: Neuropsychiatric Genetics* **133**: 68–73.

Morrison JR, Stewart MA (1971) An adoption study of attention deficit/ hyperactivity/ aggression and their relationship to adult antisocial personality. *Comprehensive Psychiatry* **32**: 73–82.

Nebigil CG *et al.* (2001) Developmentally regulated serotonin 5-HT2B receptors. *International Journal of Developmental Neuroscience* **19**: 365–72.

O'Neill MF *et al.* (1991) Evidence for an involvement of D1 and D2 dopamine receptors in mediating nicotine-induced hyperactivity in rats. *Psychopharmacology* **104**: 343–50.

O'Neill MF *et al.* (1999) 5-HT2 receptor antagonism reduces hyperactivity induced by amphetamine, cocaine, and MK-801 but not D1 agonist C-APB. *Pharmacology Biochemistry and Behavior* **63**: 237–43.

Ozaki N *et al.* (1997) A naturally occurring amino acid substitution of the human serotonin 5-HT2A receptor influences amplitude and timing of intracellular calcium mobilization. *Journal of Neurochemistry* **68**: 2186–93.

Park L *et al.* (2005) Association and linkage of alpha-2A adrenergic receptor gene variants with childhood ADHD. *Molecular Psychiatry* **10**: 572–80.

Posner MI, Petersen SE (1990) The attention system of the human brain. *Annual Review of Neuroscience* **13**: 25–42.

Qian Q *et al.* (2003) Family-based and case-control association studies of catechol-O-methyltransferase in attention deficit hyperactivity disorder suggest genetic sexual dimorphism. *American Journal of Medical Genetics Part B: Neuropsychiatric Genetics* **118**: 103–9.

Quist JF *et al.* (2000) Evidence for the serotonin HTR2A receptor gene as a susceptibility factor in attention deficit hyperactivity disorder (ADHD). *Molecular Psychiatry* **5**: 537–41.

Quist JF *et al.* (2003) The serotonin 5-HT1B receptor gene and attention deficit hyperactivity disorder. *Molecular Psychiatry* **8**: 98–102.

Rhee SH *et al.* (1999) Sex differences in genetic and environmental influences on DSM-III-R Attention-Deficit/Hyperactivity Disorder. *Journal of Abnormal Psychology* **108**: 24–41.

Risch N, Merikangas K (1996) The future of genetic studies of complex human diseases. *Science* **273**: 1516–17.

Roman T *et al.* (2003) Is the alpha-2A adrenergic receptor gene (ADRA2A) associated with Attention-Deficit/Hyperactivity Disorder? *American Journal of Medical Genetics Part B: Neuropsychiatric Genetics* **120**: 116–20.

Seeman P, Madras BK (1998) Antihyperactivity medication, methylphenidate and amphetamine. *Molecular Psychiatry* **3**: 386–96.

Sheehan K *et al.* (2005) Tryptophan hydroxylase 2 (TPH2) gene variants associated with ADHD. *Molecular Psychiatry* [Epub ahead of print].

Smalley SL *et al.* (2002) Genetic linkage of Attention-Deficit/Hyperactivity Disorder on chromosome 16p13, in a region implicated in autism. *The American Journal of Human Genetics* **71**: 959–63.

Smith A, Nutt D (1996) Noradrenaline and attention lapses. *Nature* **380**: 291.

Sollner T *et al.* (1993) SNAP receptors implicated in vesicle targeting and fusion. *Nature* **362**: 318–24.

Spencer TJ *et al.* (2005) In vivo neuroreceptor imaging in Attention-Deficit/Hyperactivity Disorder: a focus on the dopamine transporter. *Biological Psychiatry* **57**: 1293–1300.

Sprich S *et al.* (2000) Adoptive and biological families of children and adolescents with ADHD. *Journal of the American Academy of Child and Adolescent Psychiatry* **39**: 1432–7.

Stevenson J (1992) Evidence for a genetic etiology in hyperactivity in children. *Behavior Genetics* **22**: 337–44.

Tang G *et al.* (2001) Lack of association between the tryptophan hydroxylase gene A218C polymorphism and Attention-Deficit Hyperactivity Disorder in Chinese Han population. *American Journal of Medical Genetics Part B: Neuropsychiatric Genetics* **105**: 485–8.

Thapar A *et al.* (1999) Genetic basis of attention deficit and hyperactivity. *British Journal of Psychiatry* **174**: 105–11.

Todd RD *et al.* (2003) Mutational analysis of the nicotinic acetylcholine receptor alpha 4 subunit gene in attention deficit/hyperactivity disorder: evidence for association of an intronic polymorphism with attention problems. *Molecular Psychiatry* **8**: 103–8.

Turic D *et al.* (2004) Follow-up of genetic linkage findings on chromosome 16p13: evidence of association of N-methyl-D aspartate glutamate receptor 2A gene polymorphism with ADHD. *Molecular Psychiatry* **9**: 169–73.

Vallone D *et al.* (2000) Structure and function of dopamine receptors. *Neuroscience and Biobehavioral* Reviews **24**: 125–32.

Williams T, Tjian R (1991) Analysis of the DNA-binding and activation properties of the human transcription factor AP-2. *Genes and Development* **5**: 670–82.

Yang L *et al.* (2004) Association of norepinephrine transporter gene with methylphenidate response. *Journal of the American Academy of Child and Adolescent Psychiatry* **43**: 1154–8.

Zahn-Waxler C *et al.* (1996) Behavior problems in five-year-old monozygotic and dizygotic twins: genetic and environmental influences, patterns of regulation, and internalization of control. *Development and Psychopathology* **8**: 103–22.

Zametkin A *et al.* (1985) Treatment of hyperactive children with monoamine oxidase inhibitors. I. Clinical efficacy. *Archives of General Psychiatry* **42**: 962–6.

Zoroglu SS *et al.* (2002) Significance of serotonin transporter gene 5-HTTLPR and variable number of tandem repeat polymorphism in attention deficit hyperactivity disorder. *Neuropsychobiology* **45**: 176–81.

9 Environmental Risk Factors and Gene–environment Interaction in Attention Deficit Hyperactivity Disorder

EDWINA BARRY AND MICHAEL GILL
School of Medicine and Health Sciences, Trinity College Dublin, Ireland

9.1 OVERVIEW

Genetic inheritance plays a considerable role in the aetiology of Attention Deficit Hyperactivity Disorder (ADHD). However, in recent times there has been renewed interest in environmental risk factors and the role of gene–environment interplay in the disorder. Individuals vary in terms of their exposure to adversity and their vulnerability to its effects, both of which are under genetic influence (Taylor & Rogers, 2005). This chapter gives an overview of published research studies of environmental risk factors for ADHD and highlights potential areas for future research. It also reviews gene–environment interplay and considers its importance in relation to ADHD.

9.2 ENVIRONMENTAL RISK FACTORS FOR MENTAL HEALTH DISORDERS: AN OVERVIEW

Environmental risk factors for ADHD were proposed well in advance of genetic risk factors. Even as early as 1902, Still's description of hyperactive behaviour as part of a minimal brain dysfunction syndrome was speculated to involve risk factors such as hypoxia during delivery. A general classification of environmental risk factors for any psychiatric disorder would include the following (Table 9.1).

It should also be borne in mind that environmental factors may be protective providing potential targets for intervention. Many claims have been made in relation to environmental 'causes' of ADHD whereas for the most part, an association has been demonstrated and causality has not been proven. Nevertheless, the work of Professor Sir Michael Rutter and others has shown that early rearing environment has important effects on psychological development and psychopathology (Rutter, 2000). In a recent article, Rutter (2005) reviewed the research design requirements needed to provide a rigorous test of environmental mediation

Handbook of Attention Deficit Hyperactivity Disorder. Edited by M. Fitzgerald, M. Bellgrove and M. Gill.
© 2007 John Wiley & Sons Ltd

Table 9.1. Environmental risk factors for mental
health disorders

Type of exposure	Example
Biological	Infection in early life
	Hypoxia
Physical	Built environment
	Head injury
Chemical	Heavy metals
	Pesticides
Diet and drugs	Food additives
	Medications
Psychosocial	Abuse and neglect
	Family structure

hypotheses and has identified three main considerations in the accurate identification of environmental risk factors:

- distinction between risk indicators and risk mechanisms (a presumed risk factor may originate from another variable which is truly associated with the outcome of interest);
- distinction between proximal versus distal risk factors (an original distal risk factor which is distant in time may be responsible for creating a chain of proximal or recent risk factors);
- identification of heterogeneity in the risk factor under study (the effects of variability in a risk factor must be considered as it may behave differently in different situations).

9.3   GENE–ENVIRONMENT INTERPLAY: AN OVERVIEW

The high heritability estimates in ADHD might suggest that there is little room left for environmental risk factors in ADHD. However, traditional heritability estimate calculations have ignored assortative mating, gene–environment correlations and gene–environment interactions and therefore heritability estimates are likely to be overestimates of direct genetic effect. In addition, lack of appreciation of the role of environmental risk factors in ADHD may lead to a failure to appreciate indirect genetic effects and a failure to identify potential targets for molecular genetic studies. The opposite argument also applies, that psychosocial research in ADHD requires an awareness of genetic factors to determine true environmental effect size.

9.3.1   GENE–ENVIRONMENT CORRELATION

Gene–environment correlation refers to an indirect path of genetic influence on the probability of exposure to a specific environment. A passive correlation implies that the genetically influenced characteristics of the parents shape the rearing environment that they create for their children. Many of the risks associated with psychosocial adversity may be genetically mediated, e.g. marital discord, family instability, parenting deficits and strengths (Weiss *et al.*, 2000). Active correlation means that the genetically influenced characteristics of the child shape the environment they select for themselves e.g. risk-taking sports and substance misuse. Evocative correlation implies that genetically influenced characteristics of the child shape their interactions with other people and the responses they elicit from others, for example, O'Connor *et al.* (1998) in a study of adopted-away children at high genetic risk for conduct disorder found that children experienced negative parenting from adoptive mothers.

9.3.2   GENE–ENVIRONMENT INTERACTION

Gene–environment interaction refers to genetically influenced individual differences in sensitivity to exposure to a specific environmental factor. Such interactions are present when the effect of an environmental risk factor depends on the individual's genotype or when the expression of an individual's genotype depends on their environmental exposure. When there is no interaction, the influence of genetic and environmental factors should not differ between subjects with different degrees of exposure. This definition refers to statistical and not biological interaction as statistically significant findings in a simple mathematical model may not be biologically relevant.

An important recent study of gene–environment interaction contributing to behavioural disturbance is that of Caspi *et al.* (2002) who demonstrated that a weak risk factor for disorder in the general population, i.e. severity of physical maltreatment in childhood had a strong influence on adult aggressive behaviour in a vulnerable subgroup of individuals with low MAO-A activity owing to a genetic polymorphism. It is important to note that in the Caspi *et al.* (2002) study, there was no main effect of the MAO-A polymorphism (a similar scenario exists for many genes in ADHD) and that interaction effects when demonstrated are independent of main effects. Moffitt (2005) using the model of gene–environment interplay in antisocial behaviour outlined six steps for testing hypotheses of measured gene–environment interplay and suggested relevant study designs for hypothesis testing. Hunter (2005) reviewed qualitative and quantitative models for the study of gene–environment interaction in human disease and highlighted the technical challenge of accessing adequate sample size. Four published gene–environment interaction studies in ADHD are presented in this chapter (Kahn *et al.*, 2003; Seeger *et al.*, 2004; Thapar *et al.*, 2005; Brookes *et al.*, 2006).

9.4   SUBSTANCE MISUSE IN PREGNANCY AND ADHD

9.4.1   PRENATAL NICOTINE EXPOSURE

Research into the consequences of prenatal nicotine exposure in humans suggests risk outcomes such as low-birth weight, spontaneous abortion, increased locomotor activity, impaired cognitive functioning (Ernst *et al.*, 2001), SIDS, cleft lip and palate and reduced child stature. Linnet *et al.* (2003) have reviewed the relationship between maternal lifestyle factors in pregnancy (including nicotine and alcohol intake) and risk of ADHD in offspring, therefore a limited review is presented here. Mick *et al.* (2002) employed a case-control study design to investigate the effects of maternal smoking, alcohol and drug use during pregnancy using a retrospective review of 280 ADHD cases of both genders and 242 non-ADHD controls. Both groups were sourced from a hospital-based child psychiatry service. Mick reported that ADHD cases were 2.1 times more likely to have been exposed to cigarettes and 2.5 times more likely to have been exposed to alcohol *in utero* than control subjects. Mick controlled for socio-economic group, family history and co-morbid conduct disorder.

Prospective studies of the relationship between prenatal nicotine exposure and later development of behavioural disorder have included the following two studies. Batstra *et al.* (2003) conducted a longitudinal study of a cohort of 1186 Dutch children aged 5.5–11 years and concluded that maternal smoking in pregnancy was associated with externalising behaviour, attention deficit and learning problems but not with internalising behaviour. Unfortunately the study design did not control for maternal alcohol or drug intake during pregnancy. Kotimaa *et al.* (2003) carried out a population-based, follow-up study of a completely ascertained population sample in Northern Finland using the 1985/1986 birth cohort. 9,357 children were followed up to 8 years of age at which time behaviour was assessed by teachers using a questionnaire. Maternal smoking was associated with hyperactivity symptoms even after adjustment for sex, family structure, socio-economic group, maternal age and alcohol use producing an odds ratio of 1.30 (1.08–1.58). Kotimaa *et al.* (2003) were also one of the first groups to take note of maternal discontinuation of smoking later in pregnancy and suggested that discontinuation of smoking or even decreased use during pregnancy might improve the behavioural outcome of children.

The link between maternal smoking in pregnancy and adverse neurodevelopmental and behavioural outcomes may not be due to direct or indirect effects of nicotine or any other component of cigarettes on the developing foetus, but is perhaps merely a marker for an underlying genetic trait. Kodl *et al.* (2004) reported that a childhood history of conduct problems is a risk factor for maternal smoking during pregnancy thus suggesting that a genetic factor transmits smoking behaviour. Maughan *et al.* (2004) in a study of childhood conduct problems concluded that much of the observed association with prenatal smoking was confounded by antisocial behaviour in both parents, depression in mothers, social disadvantage and genetic influences rather than direct effects of nicotine on childhood behavioural disorders. Therefore maternal prenatal smoking may simply be a marker of a genetic trait for ADHD or conduct disorder or antisocial personality disorder symptoms. Using a population-based sample of young adults, Kollins *et al.* (2005) identified a linear relationship between the number of self-reported ADHD symptoms and smoking behaviour measures. After controlling for social class and conduct disorder, each reported symptom of inattention and hyperactivity/impulsivity increased the likelihood of ever having smoked (odds ratios of 1.1 and 1.16 respectively). For example, an individual self-reporting the presence of six hyperactivity-impulsivity symptoms had an odds ratio of 2.95 of ever having smoked regularly.

The Milberger *et al.* (1996) study attempted to differentiate between genetic vulnerability and prenatal smoking by controlling for parental ADHD and by including siblings of children with ADHD in the model. Its results suggested that prenatal maternal smoking was associated with a fourfold higher risk of ADHD in the offspring independently of maternal disorder. Thapar *et al.* (2003) examined the relationship between smoking in pregnancy and ADHD symptoms in offspring using a population-based sample of 1452 twin pairs aged 5–16 years. The study concluded that maternal smoking still had a small but significant influence in addition to genetic effects that explained 2% of the variance in ADHD symptoms in offspring. More recently Button *et al.* (2005) examined the relationship between maternal smoking; antisocial behaviour and ADHD symptoms in offspring in order to ascertain whether maternal smoking in pregnancy is independently associated with antisocial behaviour or whether the association arises because of co-variation between antisocial behaviour and ADHD. 723 monozygotic and 1173 dizygotic twin pairs from a population-based sample were surveyed and data were analysed using structural equation modelling. The best-fitting model showed maternal prenatal smoking influencing ADHD symptoms and antisocial behaviour independently.

9.4.2 GENE–ENVIRONMENT INTERPLAY IN ADHD – KAHN *et al.* (2003)

Kahn *et al.* (2003) examined the joint effects of DAT1 DNA variants and maternal prenatal smoking on childhood hyperactivity-impulsivity and inattentiveness symptom measures. This study found that these behaviours were associated with the DAT1 polymorphism *only* in children exposed to prenatal smoking. However, this study was carried out in a general population sample recruited to measure behavioural effects of lead exposure in children living in New York. Limitations include sample population stratification and the absence of formal ADHD diagnoses. The author acknowledged that maternal smoking may reflect underlying maternal psychopathology (ADHD or other) and that additional information on maternal genotype, psychopathology and family history was needed. Brookes *et al.* (2006) investigated interaction between a common DAT1 haplotype (10/3) and maternal use of alcohol and nicotine during pregnancy. These authors did not observe any significant interaction between the 10/3 haplotype and prenatal nicotine exposure status; however, the authors noted that the study was underpowered to detect small interaction effects. Further research is needed to establish if prenatal nicotine exposure is having a direct effect on brain development in ADHD or whether the effect is mediated through a gene–environment correlation (impulsive mothers taking risks during pregnancy and transmitting their impulsive genes to their offspring) or a genuine gene–environment interaction.

No study has yet compared the relationship between maternal versus paternal prenatal smoking and transmission of high-risk genetic variants in ADHD. Interestingly Hypponen *et al.* (2004) carried out an intergenerational cohort study of the effects of grandmothers' smoking in pregnancy on birth weight (an important predictor of neurodevelopmental outcome discussed further in the section on perinatal risk factors for ADHD). Assuming heritable transmission caused the intergenerational association, grandmothers' smoking predicted a 34 g reduction in birth weight; but this effect disappeared after adjustment for maternal smoking. Therefore deficits in birth weight attributable to grandmothers' smoking were not evident in grandchildren.

9.4.3   HYPOTHESISED EFFECTS OF NICOTINE ON FOETAL BRAIN DEVELOPMENT

Direct effects of nicotine result from the binding of nicotine to foetal nicotinic acetylcholinic receptors which are present from the 8th week of gestation in humans (Hagino & Lee, 1985). Prenatal tobacco exposure selectively upregulates nicotinic receptors in rats and non-human primates (Slotkin *et al.*, 2002). This up-regulation of nicotinic acetylcholine receptors may be associated with initial supersensitivity followed by subsequent functional down-regulation. Animal studies indicate that hyperactivity in mice offspring can result from prenatal nicotine exposure (Eriksson *et al.*, 2000) possibly via dopaminergic system modulation. Noradrenergic systems have been found to be hypoactive and hyporesponsive to exogenous nicotine stimulation after prenatal exposure to nicotine (Navarro *et al.*, 1990). Drew *et al.* (2000) demonstrated that activation of nicotinic receptors enhanced amphetamine-induced release of dopamine from DAT1 in rat prefrontal cortex. The disruptions in the development of catecholaminergic systems may explain the increased incidence of ADHD in children exposed prenatally to nicotine, given the role of catecholamines in this disorder (Schweitzer *et al.*, 2000). In animal models, dopaminergic systems appear to be particularly vulnerable to a wide range of perinatal insults, resulting in persistent alterations of function in mesolimbic and mesostriatal pathways (Boksa *et al.*, 2003).

In human studies, dopamine-rich frontostriatal circuits are implicated in the pathology of ADHD. Single photon emission computerised tomography (SPECT) studies in never-medicated adults (Dougherty *et al.*, 1999) and children (Cheon *et al.*, 2003) with ADHD have shown increased striatal dopamine transporter density. Methylphenidate has been shown to reduce striatal dopamine transporter density to near normal levels in adults with ADHD (Krause *et al.*, 2000). Kirley *et al.* (2002) proposed a hypodopaminergic hypothesis of ADHD with possession of the 10-repeat DAT1 allele being associated with greater availability of DAT protein in the striatum leading to a functional hypodopaminergic state. According to this hypothesis, treatment with methylphenidate may be most effective in subjects possessing the 10-repeat DAT1 allele because it normalises DAT density (Kirley *et al.*, 2003; Bellgrove *et al.*, 2005). Interestingly, Krause *et al.* (2002) reported that never-medicated adult patients with a history of cigarette smoking showed lower DAT density values in [99mTC] TRODAT-1 SPECT scans than non-smokers with ADHD. The non-smoking medication-naïve adults with ADHD had significantly higher DAT density despite higher ADHD symptom scores in the medication-naïve smokers. Krause *et al.* (2003) postulated that nicotine may have an influence on DAT similar to that of psychostimulants. We therefore propose that mothers who abuse nicotine during pregnancy may in fact be self-medicating and that their smoking behaviour is associated with maternal DAT1 10-repeat allele homozygous status. Therefore the association between prenatal nicotine exposure and ADHD is likely to be indirectly mediated through genetic susceptibility to ADHD.

Indirect effects of cigarette smoking on the foetus include poor nutritional status of the mother due to the anorexic effects of nicotine on mother's appetite; carbon monoxide impairs oxygen delivery to foetal tissues and causes compensatory hypertrophy of the placenta. In addition, maternal smoking in pregnancy has been shown to be associated with lower serum folate concentrations (McDonald et al., 2002).

9.4.4 PRENATAL ALCOHOL EXPOSURE

High levels of maternal alcohol use in pregnancy are associated with greater risk of congenital malformations and stillbirth (Linnet et al., 2003), learning and memory deficits, ADHD (Mick et al., 2002) and Foetal Alcohol Syndrome (FAS). Centre for Disease Control and Prevention (CDC) reports (2004) from the 2002 Behavioural Risk Factor Surveillance System (BRFSS) survey of 18–44-year-old women indicate that 10% of pregnant women in the US use alcohol and approximately 2% engage in binge drinking or frequent use of alcohol during pregnancy. In addition, more than half of women who did not use birth control reported alcohol use and 12.4% reported binge drinking. Children with FAS exhibit distinctive facial features, growth retardation and cognitive/behavioural symptoms which may include ADHD symptoms. O'Malley and Nanson (2002) reviewed the link between FAS and ADHD and concluded that the quality of ADHD in children with FAS differs from that in children without FAS. In children with FAS, ADHD was more likely to be of earlier-onset, inattentive subtype, less predictable response to stimulant medication and with co-morbid developmental, psychiatric and medical conditions. The damage caused by alcohol exposure depends on the amount and duration of exposure as well as the timing of the exposure. Animal models of the effects of alcohol on neurodevelopment have shown that alcohol disrupts midline serotonergic neuronal development, disrupts L1-mediated cell adhesion, induces cell death through oxidative stress or activation of protease enzymes and disrupts cell signalling functions of growth factors that are necessary for cell differentiation and survival (Goodlett et al., 2005).

The case-control study of ADHD by Mick et al. (2002) mentioned earlier showed that twice as many children with ADHD had mothers who either drank alcohol daily or binged during pregnancy than children without ADHD. Hill et al. (2000) found that family history of alcohol dependence and not actual maternal alcohol consumption during pregnancy was associated with ADHD. Streissguth et al. (1994) showed a dose-dependent relationship between prenatal alcohol exposure and the development of neurobehavioural disorders including ADHD during the first 14 years of life. Therefore the argument is reminiscent of the relationship between prenatal nicotine exposure and risk for ADHD in offspring; does alcohol confer a direct risk for ADHD or do alcohol dependence and ADHD share genetic transmission? Again the role of gene–environment correlation could be measured by comparing the relationship between maternal versus paternal alcohol use during pregnancy and transmission of risk genotypes to offspring.

Knopik et al. (2005) interviewed the parents of 1936 female twin pairs in order to determine the relative contributions of parental smoking and drinking behaviour during and outside of pregnancy as risk factors for DSM-IV ADHD. The data were analysed using structural equation modelling to determine genetic and environmental influences of ADHD risk. The authors found that ADHD was more likely to be diagnosed in girls whose mothers or fathers were alcohol dependent, whose mothers reported heavy alcohol use during pregnancy and in those girls with low birth weight. Risk was not significantly increased in girls whose mothers smoked in pregnancy when the other risk factors were controlled for. The authors concluded that 86% of the residual variance in ADHD risk was attributable to genetic effects and 14% to non-shared environmental influences. Wilens *et al.* (2005) studied the influence of parental substance use disorder (SUD) and ADHD on ADHD in offspring in a pilot controlled study of 96 families. Children of parents with ADHD or ADHD and SUD were more likely to have ADHD compared with children of parents without ADHD or SUD. Children of parents with ADHD and SUD were at greater risk for ADHD than children of parents with SUD only. The offspring of parents with both ADHD and SUD were at highest risk for ADHD and therefore represent a subgroup that could be screened for ADHD.

9.4.5   GENE–ENVIRONMENT INTERPLAY IN ADHD – BROOKES *et al.* (2006)

In the study by Brookes *et al.* (2006) referred to earlier, interaction between prenatal alcohol exposure and a common DAT1 haplotype (10/3) was also investigated. A significant interaction was demonstrated between prenatal alcohol exposure and transmission ratios from heterozygous parents for the 10/3 risk haplotype. There was also a trend for association (p = 0.07) of the DAT1 10/3 risk haplotype with maternal alcohol consumption during pregnancy suggesting a possible gene–environment correlation. However, this finding is limited by the fact that alcohol use in pregnancy was defined by a single categorical yes/no variable in this study. Future studies require more detailed measurement of environmental exposures for example, measuring alcohol exposure *in utero* as a quantitative variable using number of units of alcohol consumed per week during pregnancy. Brookes *et al.* (2006) speculated that DAT1 DNA variants could modify the direct effects of tobacco and alcohol on the developing foetal brain and that this held implications for ADHD prevention strategies.

9.4.6   PRENATAL ILLICIT DRUG EXPOSURE

Prenatal cocaine exposure can cause a short-term withdrawal syndrome after delivery but also longer-term cognitive deficits. Prenatal cocaine exposure has been shown to be associated with a specific deficit in sustained attention on the continuous performance task (CPT) in school-aged children (Richardson *et al.*, 1996; Bandstra *et al.*, 2001). Noland *et al.* (2005) demonstrated that prenatal exposure to cannabis was associated with omission errors indicative of impaired sustained attention. It is difficult to ascertain the effects of a single drug when mothers often abuse cocaine, cannabis, alcohol and nicotine simultaneously in addition to psychological distress in mothers and social disadvantage associated with chronic drug misuse. However, in an animal model using pregnant rabbits injected with cocaine, Stanwood *et al.* (2001) demonstrated that cocaine exposure produced consistent anatomical alterations in dopamine-rich regions including the anterior cingulate cortex.

Ornoy (2003) studied the development of preschool and school-age children born to heroin-dependent parents raised at home or adopted away compared with children from low socio-economic groups (SEG) and with controls. Children born to and raised by heroin-dependent parents and children from low SEGs displayed lower intellectual skills and higher rates of inattention than control groups. High rates of ADHD were evident among school-age offspring of heroin-dependent parents whether raised at home or adopted away as well as in children from low SEG backgrounds. Intrauterine heroin exposure did not appear to confer any greater risk for ADHD than being reared in a home with socio-economic disadvantage.

9.5 PERINATAL RISK FACTORS FOR ADHD

Conflicting findings are reported regarding perinatal risk factors for ADHD (that is risk associated with events occurring immediately around the time of the birth) and their aetiological importance are modest at best (Chandola *et al.*, 1992). Chandola *et al.* examined birth records of a geographically defined birth cohort and found that referral for hyperactive behaviour was associated with social class, maternal age, antepartum haemorrhage, length of second stage of labour, 1-minute Apgar score and gender. The authors commented that these associations were not explained by socio-economic variables and that their predictive power was low. Milberger *et al.* (1997) reported a positive association between ADHD and pregnancy, delivery and infancy complications (PDICs) in their case-control study. Specific complications implicated in their study were antepartum haemorrhage, eclampsia, maternal smoking and illicit drug use, leading the authors to conclude that chronic exposure rather than acute traumatic events accounted for their findings. This study also noted that ADHD cases had a significantly higher prevalence of maternal accidents during pregnancy than controls (7% versus 1%) and it is interesting to speculate whether this 'accident proneness' reflects maternal impulsivity or inattention symptoms and underlying genotype. Ben Amor *et al.* (2005) employed an intrafamilial study design of just 50 families to compare the prevalence of PDICs in children diagnosed with ADHD and their siblings and discovered that children with ADHD had a higher rate of neonatal complications (not obstetric complications) compared with non-ADHD siblings. Studies of PDICs in ADHD have been limited by small sample size, retrospective maternal recall of obstetric complications and potential rater bias with maternal rating of child behavioural symptoms and obstetric complications. However, the evidence to date does not suggest that PDICs are likely to play a major role in the development of ADHD but may affect a subgroup of children with ADHD and other developmental disorders, e.g. dyspraxia.

9.5.1 GENE–ENVIRONMENT INTERPLAY IN ADHD – SEEGER *et al.* (2004)

Seeger *et al.* (2004) reported a gene–environment interaction in hyperkinetic conduct disorder between season of birth and the expression of a DRD4 polymorphism (7-repeat allele) in a case-control study. Mick *et al.* (1996) had previously described a seasonal pattern of birth for different subtypes of hyperkinetic disorder (HKD). There were no significant differences in seasonal birth patterns or frequencies of DRD4 7-repeat alleles between the cases and controls in this sample. However, an interaction was observed whereby children possessing the DRD4 7-repeat allele born in spring or summer were at a 2.8-fold increased risk of being diagnosed with hyperkinetic conduct disorder. The authors hypothesised that there might be an interaction between longer day lengths, the melatonin-dopamine system and the sub-sensitive postsynaptic receptor of the DRD4*7R allele during pregnancy placing offspring at risk for hypodopaminergic function and in turn ADHD. These study findings await replication and any true interaction is likely to have a very small effect size.

9.5.2   LOW BIRTH WEIGHT

Low birth weight (LBW) (less than or equal to 2500g) is a marker for high perinatal risk with most children born preterm rather than small-for-gestational age. LBW is associated with lowering of IQ (Matte *et al.*, 2001) and ADHD in some (Breslau *et al.*, 1996; Breslau & Chilcoat, 2000; Mick *et al.*, 2002) but not all studies (Goodman & Stevenson, 1989). However, the Breslau and Chilcoat (2000) study found the association between low birth weight and attention problems only in children from an urban disadvantaged setting and not in children from a middle-class suburban setting therefore suggesting an interaction between biological risk and social disadvantage. Younger mothers who substance abuse are less likely to attend antenatal care regularly and therefore obstetric complications in this group might just be a marker of social disadvantage rather than a directly causal factor of ADHD.

Very LBW or VLBW (less than or equal to 1500 g) is associated with risk for ADHD (e.g. Botting *et al.*, 1997) who found a 23% prevalence of ADHD at 12 years in VLBW children versus a 6% prevalence in controls. VLBW children are at an increased risk for a range of psychiatric disorders including depressive and anxiety disorders but there does appear to be a particular association with ADHD. Extremely LBW or ELBW (less than or equal to 1000 g) children were more likely to experience developmental delay, problems with motor co-ordination, ADHD (16% prevalence versus 6.9% in controls) but not conduct or emotional disorders according to Szatmari *et al.* (1990) in a study of 82 ELBW survivors at age 5 years. O'Callaghan & Harvey (1997) found no link between ELBW and ADHD, however, the association was reproduced in a large prospective study by Hille *et al.* (2001). While extremes of low birth weight may be a specific risk factor for ADHD, the majority of children with ADHD are of normal birth weight so this risk factor is of relevance to a minority of total ADHD cases. Tully *et al.* (2004) reported a moderating effect of maternal warmth on the association between low birth weight and children's ADHD symptoms in a study of 2232 twins. The interaction predicted mothers' and teachers' ratings of ADHD symptoms but not IQ. This study suggests a potential intervention target to prevent the development of ADHD in low birth-weight children by enhancing maternal warmth toward their child.

9.5.3   GENE–ENVIRONMENT INTERPLAY IN ADHD –
THAPAR *et al.* (2005)

Thapar *et al.* (2005) detected a significant interaction between Catechol-*O*-Methyltransferase (COMT) Val/Met genotype and birth weight which predicted early onset of conduct disorder symptoms in children with ADHD. The authors found main effects for the COMT genetic variant and birth weight as well as a significant interaction between the two. Those children with ADHD possessing the Val/Val genotype (21% of the sample) and a history of low birth weight had a higher number of conduct disorder symptoms even when the covariate of nicotine exposure during pregnancy was added to the model. The authors proposed that among children with ADHD, possession of the COMT Val/Val variant increased susceptibility to the effects of perinatal risks contributing to low birth weight. Very large sample sizes would be required to further explore how this genetic variant modifies the effect of specific perinatal risk factors for low birth weight in ADHD.

9.5.4   HYPOXIA AND ADHD: HYPOTHESISED MECHANISMS
OF ACTION

Toft (1999) proposed prenatal and perinatal striatal injury as a hypothetical cause of ADHD in preterm infants based on higher lactate levels in the striatum suggesting tissue hypoxia. As mentioned earlier, dopaminergic systems appear to be particularly vulnerable to a wide range of perinatal insults in animal experiments (Boksa & El-Khodor, 2003). Brake *et al.* (1997, 2000) studied dopamine function in response to stress in adult rats who had been exposed to a period of anoxia during caesarean section delivery and in those animals exposed to a 15-minute period of anoxia, there was evidence of persistent blunting of stress-induced dopamine release in the right but not left prefrontal cortex. In addition, as adults these rats were more spontaneously active and had increased dopamine transporter density lateralised to the right hemisphere. There was no evidence, however, that D1 or D2 receptor levels differed between birth groups (normal delivery, caesarean section with no anoxia, caesarean section with 15-minute anoxia) or cerebral hemispheres.

Lou *et al.* (2004) examined D2 and D3 receptor binding with PET scans during reaction time testing on an attention battery in six adolescents with a history of preterm delivery followed by cerebral blood flow measurements shortly after birth and a history of ADHD. The authors discovered that high dopamine receptor availability was associated with increased reaction times and reaction time variability and was also predicted by low neonatal cerebral blood flow leading the authors to conclude that cerebral ischaemia is a contributing factor in infants susceptible to ADHD. It is interesting to note that two recent studies have found an association between the 10-repeat DAT1 allele and reaction time variability in children with ADHD (Loo *et al.*, 2003; Bellgrove *et al.*, 2005). Decker *et al.* (2003) reported increased striatal expression of a vesicular monoamine transporter and D1 receptor proteins consistent with reduced dopaminergic signalling in rats exposed to intermittent neonatal hypoxia. However, in later studies (Boss *et al.*, 2005) using real-time PCR to assay gene transcription in neonatal rats exposed to the same hypoxia protocol, single ischaemic events elicited expression of stress-related genes while intermittent hypoxic insults did not. Therefore the mechanism of action of acute or chronic hypoxia in contributing to the development of ADHD is somewhat unclear, but cerebral ischaemia associated with preterm birth does appear to be a particular risk factor.

9.6   TOXINS AND ADHD

An apparent increase in the incidence of developmental disorders has led to interest in the potential contribution of environmental toxins to impaired neurodevelopment (Schettler, 2001). Neurodevelopmental effects are unknown for many industrial chemicals while for other chemicals exposure levels previously presumed safe have been revised downward. Good quality research in this field is unfortunately lacking and faces many methodological challenges. Improved monitoring of disease and exposure is essential to detect subtle, delayed effects of environmental exposures. Efforts to develop accurate biological monitoring of blood and urine for multiple chemical toxicants will improve exposure assessment in epidemiological studies. In addition, some individuals are uniquely sensitive to certain toxins because of genetic polymorphisms regulating their metabolism (Costa *et al.*, 1999). The National Children's Study (http://nationalchildrensstudy.gov/) is an ongoing longitudinal study of environmental effects on child development in the US and is expected to enrol 100,000 participants, giving it sufficient power to determine the presence or absence of exposure effects. The first research results are expected to be available in 2008.

9.6.1   LEAD

Lead is a recognised neurotoxin and a meta-analysis of cognitive damage from lead exposure concluded that there is no safe threshold for damage down to blood lead levels of 7 microgrammes/dl (Schwartz, 1994). A recent international pooled analysis found an inverse relationship between blood lead concentration and IQ score (Lanphear *et al.*, 2005). The relationship between lead exposure and ADHD is somewhat less clear. Tuthill (1996) sampled hair lead levels in 277 first-grade pupils

Table 9.2. Toxic chemicals and ADHD symptoms in humans

Toxin	Related Studies
Lead	Needleman, 1982
	Minder *et al.*, 1994
	Tuthill, 1996
	Eppright *et al.*, 1997
	Bellinger, 2005
Methylmercury	Rice, 2000a
PCBs	Jacobson & Jacobson, 2003
Phthalates	
DDT	Hardell *et al.*, 2002
Manganese	Woolf *et al.*, 2002

in the US and found a dose-response relationship between hair lead levels and negative teacher ratings of classroom attention-deficit behaviour which remained significant after controlling for potential confounders including socio-economic status. Other studies have supported an association between lead level and ADHD symptoms (e.g. Needleman, 1982; Minder *et al.*, 1994) and lead level and delinquent behaviour (Needleman *et al.*, 1996). However, Bellinger *et al.* (2005) found no relationship between teacher ratings of ADHD symptoms and blood lead level in children living in India. Eppright *et al.* (1997) screened blood lead levels in 102 children referred to an ADHD clinic in the US and found that only one patient had a mildly elevated lead level. There is no current indication for routine blood lead level screening in ADHD clinics. Patients with lead toxicity usually present with a variety of other physical symptoms in addition to ADHD symptoms. While lead is proven to induce hyperactivity in rat models (Kostas *et al.*, 1976); in human epidemiological studies of hyperactivity it is difficult to distinguish direct effects of lead exposure and social adversity associated with high lead levels, for example, living in an inner city area.

9.6.2 METHYLMERCURY

Mercury is a toxin encountered in the diet as methylmercury present in both fresh and saltwater fish. Large methylmercury exposure *in utero* is associated with seizures, developmental delay and learning disability (Amin-Zaki *et al.*, 1976). The Faroe Islands study was a prospective study designed to assess neurological and behavioural consequences of in *utero* exposure to methylmercury and PCBs via maternal consumption of contaminated fish and whale blubber. Rice (2000a) reported impairment in attention, memory, auditory processing, primary auditory function and to a lesser degree motor impairment in exposed offspring. Further cross-sectional studies in the Amazon and Madeira of methylmercury exposure *in utero* failed to find attention deficits in offspring. These preliminary findings in relation to ADHD symptoms must therefore be treated with caution.

9.6.3 POLYCHLORINATED BIPHENYLS (PCBS)

Several studies link neurodevelopmental effects of elevated levels of PCBs to lowering of intelligence in offspring (e.g. Jacobson & Jacobson, 1996). Children were exposed to PCBs in *utero* through mother's having eaten food contaminated with PCBs, e.g. Lake Michigan fish. The relationship between PCBs and ADHD is less clear though a biological mechanism is plausible though untested. As well as acting as an endocrine disruptor, PCBs also modulate dopamine synthesis, e.g. ortho-PCBs decrease dopamine synthesis while non-ortho-PCBs increase dopamine synthesis (Tilson & Kodavanti, 1997).

Jacobson and Jacobson (2003) examined the relationship between prenatal PCB exposure and child performance on neuropsychological tests of attention and information processing at age 11 in 167 children from Michigan using a prospective, longitudinal study design. Adverse effects, namely greater impulsivity, poorer concentration and poorer verbal memory (but no change in hyperactivity levels) were seen in those children who had not been breast fed, leading the study authors to speculate whether breast milk offered protection or whether better quality intellectual stimulation was provided by mothers who breast fed. Rice (2000b) reported parallels between ADHD and behavioural deficits produced by neurotoxic exposure (lead and PCBs) in monkeys and proposed that neurotoxic agents in the environment may be contributing to the rising incidence of ADHD. At this time there is insufficient evidence to definitively link PCB exposure to ADHD but it would be unwise to dismiss a potential role for PCBs as the potential of different types of PCBs to produce neurotoxic effects in humans is under-studied.

9.6.4   PHTHALATES

Phthalates are used in the manufacture of plastic bottles, cosmetics, air fresheners and can be absorbed directly through the skin, inhaled in fumes or orally ingested. Phthalate exposure has been implicated in DNA damage to human male sperm (Duty et al., 2003) and di-(2-ethylhexyl)phthalate (DEHP) exposure may shorten duration of pregnancy in humans by one week (Latini et al., 2003). Speculation exists as to whether phthalate exposure in utero may adversely affect foetal development contributing to the rising prevalence of neurodevelopmental disorders in children. At this time there is no evidence to link phthalate exposure to ADHD.

9.6.5   DDT

Hardell et al. (2002) reported the case of a 24-year-old male with a neurological impairment suggested to be ADHD who was exposed to dichlorodiphenyltrichloroethane (DDT) in utero and during breast-feeding. The mother had been exposed to DDT in pesticides in her home environment up to the age of 17 years and she was 37 years old at the time of his birth. Little history is provided in this case report to support an ADHD diagnosis and the neurodevelopmental effects of DDT are unknown. However, DDT may cause chronic neurological impairment in adults, e.g. Van Wendel de Joode et al. (2001).

9.6.6   MANGANESE EXPOSURE

Woolf et al. (2002) reported the case of a 10-year-old boy with chronic manganese exposure from drinking water who presented with inattentiveness and lack of focus in the classroom. Psychometric testing showed normal intelligence but poor verbal and visual memory. Overall the findings were consistent were manganese toxicity featuring some overlapping symptoms of cognitive impairment with ADHD.

9.7   THYROID FUNCTION AND ADHD

Mutations in the thyroid receptor-β gene (hTRβ) on chromosome 3 causing generalised resistance to thyroid hormone are a known cause of ADHD symptoms (Magner et al., 1986; Refetoff, 1990). Familial studies suggest that generalised resistance to thyroid hormone is inherited in an autosomal dominant fashion (Magner et al., 1986).

9.7.1 HYPOTHYROIDISM AND ADHD: HYPOTHESISED MECHANISMS OF ACTION

Thyroid hormone is essential for brain development and the receptor-hormone complex may influence catecholamine neurotransmitter systems. Mild hypothyroidism in the foetus during gestation and the early neonatal period is reported not to only disrupt neurotransmitter system development, but also to interfere with normal axonal growth and mitochondrial function (Haddow *et al.*, 1999). Hauser *et al.* (1998) proposed that while the mechanisms of action of toxicants such as dioxins and PCBs were poorly understood, they could act as thyroid hormone disruptors and exert their neurodevelopmental consequences at least in part via thyroid function impairment. PCBs interfere with thyroid function through a variety of mechanisms, including increased metabolism of T4 (thyroxine), interference with T4 delivery to the developing brain by displacement from the carrier protein, and interference with the conversion of T4 to T3 (triiodothyronine) (Brouwer *et al.*, 1998).

9.8 IMMUNOLOGICAL DYSFUNCTION AND ADHD

Rapp (1978) suggested an association between asthma, cutaneous allergies and ADHD resulting from food allergy. Brawley *et al.* (2004) screened 30 children with physician-diagnosed ADHD for allergic rhinitis and found that while 80% reported allergic rhinitis symptoms, 61% had at least one positive skin test result. The authors concluded that nasal obstruction and symptoms of allergic rhinitis could explain some of the cognitive patterns observed in ADHD, which might result from sleep disturbance known to occur with allergic rhinitis. Marshall (1989) hypothesised that allergic reactions result in cholinergic hyper-responsiveness and beta-adrenergic hypo-responsiveness and that these imbalances in the central nervous system lead to poorly regulated arousal levels and ADHD behaviours in some children.

Nevertheless, several studies do not support an association between asthma and ADHD, for example, McGee *et al.* (1993). Biederman *et al.* (1994) used a family-based study design to explore the association between asthma and ADHD and concluded that there was no pathophysiological link between the two disorders but that asthma and ADHD are independently transmitted in families. A further study examining the association between asthma and ADHD in girls supported the original findings that patterns of familial aggregation were most consistent with independent transmission of ADHD and asthma in families of female ADHD probands (Hammerness *et al.*, 2005).

9.9 HEAD INJURY AND ADHD

Several studies have investigated the development of secondary ADHD following head injury; for example Gerring *et al.* (1998) examined 99 children who had moderate and severe closed-head injuries and followed them up for one year. Premorbid and one-year post-injury psychiatric status was ascertained by parent and child-structured interviews and questionnaires. The pre-morbid prevalence of ADHD was 20% and a further 19% met full ADHD diagnostic criteria except for age of onset by the end of the first year. Children who developed secondary ADHD had significantly greater pre-morbid psychosocial adversity, posttraumatic affective lability and aggression, posttraumatic psychiatric co-morbidity and overall disability than children who did not develop secondary ADHD. The clinical features of secondary ADHD had more in common with personality change due to closed head injury with a deficit in behavioural inhibition being the major feature. The role of gene–environment interplay in the development of secondary ADHD following head injury warrants further investigation. It is interesting to speculate the importance of gene–environment correlation as children with ADHD are at higher risk of having accidents and potentially seek out risk situations that place them at a higher risk of experiencing a head injury. In addition, there may be a gene–environment interaction in some cases whereby children carrying risk genes of small effect for ADHD who are subsequently exposed to a head injury develop the full clinical picture of ADHD.

9.10   DIET AND ADHD

A small proportion of children with ADHD are affected by food additives and allergenic whole foods. Shannon (1922) was the original author to promote an elimination diet for the treatment of ADHD and learning disorders. Perhaps the best known dietary approach to the management of ADHD was based on Feingold's radical claims that artificial food colours, flavours, preservatives (3000 different additives) as well as naturally occurring salicylates were the primary cause of ADHD (Feingold, 1975). A recent meta-analysis by Schab and Trinh (2004) identified 15 double-blind placebo-controlled trials evaluating the effects of artificial food colours on hyperactivity in children with a diagnosis of ADHD as part of their primary analysis. Meta-analytic modelling determined the overall effect size based on standardised mean difference (i.e. the difference in outcome between the active and control arms of a randomised clinical trial in terms of the number of pooled standard deviations by which the two groups differ) of artificial food colours on hyperactivity to be 0.283 (95% CI, −0.079 to 0.488) i.e. there was a small but non-significant effect on hyperactivity.

Some researchers have speculated that sugar consumption may cause or aggravate hyperactivity. Prinz *et al.* (1980) compared the behaviour of hyperactive and control children in response to sugar intake and developed a theory that the positive effects of the Feingold diet were due to a higher protein-sugar ratio rather than to salicylates and additives. A meta-analysis by Wolraich *et al.* (1985) examining the effect of sugar on behaviour and cognition in children concluded that sugar does not affect their behaviour or cognitive performance.

The controversy then extended to sucrose and aspartame, which has been marketed since 1981 and was used as a placebo in many of the original studies examining the effects of sugar on behaviour. Wolraich *et al.* (1994) carried out a double-blind crossover trial of diets either high in sucrose and aspartame-free, low in sucrose and containing aspartame or placebo diet containing saccharin in a group of children reported to be sugar-sensitive versus a group of healthy control children. None of the three diets produced significant cognitive or behavioural change.

Crook (1994) developed a strict elimination diet eliminating sources of sugar, mould and yeast accompanied by the administration of oral antifungal agents. He maintained that frequent antibiotic usage resulted in chronic candidiasis, which in turn caused metabolic and behavioural disturbance including hyperactivity, irritability and learning disorders. His claims have not been scientifically validated.

9.11 DIETARY DEFICIENCIES AND ADHD

Dietary deficiencies that have been studied in children with ADHD but not proven as having an aetiological role are listed in Table 9.3.

9.11.1 IRON

Iron deficiency is the most common nutritional deficiency in school-aged children. Its symptoms include reduced energy and activity levels as well as reduced attention span. There is no indication for supplementation in non-iron deficient children.

9.11.2 MAGNESIUM

Kozielec and Starobrat-Hermelin (1997) screened 116 Polish children with ADHD for magnesium deficiency using hair, red blood cell and serum analysis. They reported that 95% of cases showed some type of magnesium deficiency with 33.6% having low serum levels of magnesium. Unfortunately there was no control group in this study.

9.11.3 PYRIDOXINE (VITAMIN B6)

Coleman *et al.* (1979) carried out a double-blind crossover trial of pyridoxine supplementation versus methylphenidate. The rationale for the trial was that some

Table 9.3. Dietary deficiencies associated with ADHD

Deficient nutrient	Studies in children with ADHD
Iron	
Magnesium	Kozielec & Starobrat-Hermelin, 1997
Pyridoxine	Coleman *et al.*, 1979
Zinc	Toren *et al.*, 1996
	Bekaroglu *et al.*, 1996
	Arnold *et al.*, 2000
	Bilici *et al.*, 2004
Essential fatty acids	Colquhoun & Bunday, 1981
	Mitchell *et al.*, 1987
	Stevens *et al.*, 1995
	Bekaroglu *et al.*, 1996
	Richardson & Puri, 2000

children with ADHD have low blood serotonin levels which could by boosted by B6 supplementation thus improving ADHD symptoms. Only six children took part in the trial showing an improvement in ADHD symptoms in response to B6 supplementation. B6 was not proven superior to methylphenidate but there was a trend in its favour.

9.11.4   ZINC

Zinc is an important cofactor for the metabolism of neurotransmitters, fatty acids, prostaglandins and melatonin and indirectly affects dopamine metabolism. Zinc deficiency has been found to cause a hyperactivity syndrome in rats (Halas & Stanstead, 1975). Toren *et al.* (1996) examined serum zinc levels in 43 cases of children with ADHD versus age-matched controls. The mean serum zinc level of children with ADHD was significantly lower than in controls ($\lambda^2 = 13.1$, df = 2, p < 0.002), however, the findings are questionable as the controls were volunteers without any form of psychiatric assessment. Bekaroglu *et al.* (1996) evaluated the relationship between serum free fatty acids and zinc using a case-control study design. Again the mean serum zinc levels in cases were significantly lower than those of controls and a statistically significant correlation was found between zinc and fatty acid levels in the cases. However, a criticism of this study design is that ADHD cases were often taking a stimulant medication that may have induced dietary deficiency through appetite suppression. Arnold *et al.* (2000) have reported that zinc may moderate essential fatty acid and amphetamine treatment of ADHD with low zinc status predicting poor response to amphetamine treatment of ADHD. Bilici *et al.* (2004) carried out a double-blind placebo-controlled study of zinc sulphate in the treatment of ADHD and found therapeutic response rates of the zinc and placebo groups of 28.7% and 20% respectively.

9.11.5   ESSENTIAL FATTY ACIDS

Essential fatty acids (EFAs) in the diet are linoleic acid (n-6 series) and linolenic acid (n-3 series) and are required for the normal structure and function of the nervous system. EFAs are components of phospholipids and cholesterol esters that form neuronal membranes in which receptors and ion channels are embedded. Long chain polyunsaturated fatty acids such as arachidonic acid (AA) and docosahexanoic acid (DHA) are synthesised from EFA precursors. Factors that can interfere with this process are both genetic (deficiency of conversion enzymes) and environmental (high intake of saturated fats, zinc deficiency, excess alcohol, stress hormones). Colquhoun and Bunday (1981) first proposed EFA deficiency as a possible cause of ADHD having studied hyperactive children and found an excess of males with EFA and zinc deficiency as well as an excess of associated allergic conditions such as asthma. The authors believed that the problem lay with abnormal conversion of EFAs to long chain polyunsaturated fatty acids rather than a dietary deficiency of EFAs. Interestingly zinc is an important cofactor for this conversion process. Mitchell *et al.* (1987) found significantly lower serum levels of AA, DHA and dihomogammalinolenic acid (DGLA) in 44 hyperactive subjects compared with 45 controls (the cases also had a lower mean birth weight). However, no deficiency was found of EFA precursors again suggesting that the abnormality exists in the conversion process. Stevens *et al.* (1995) found lower concentrations of key fatty acids in plasma polar lipids (e.g. AA) and red blood cell total lipids in 53 children with ADHD compared with 43 control subjects; however, there was no deficiency of EFA precursors evident. Bekaroglu *et al.* (1996) showed that mean serum free fatty acid levels were significantly lower in 45 children with ADHD than in age and sex matched controls. Richardson and Puri (2000) in a review article outlined areas for future research as (1) identification of the clinical features of children with fatty acid deficiency, (2) understanding of the role that fatty acid deficiency plays in disorders co-morbid with ADHD notably mood disorders, dyspraxia and dyslexia and (3) development of treatment guidelines.

9.12 PSYCHOSOCIAL RISK FACTORS FOR ADHD

A detailed examination of psychosocial risk factors is beyond the scope of this chapter which is restricted to a number of comments. Psychosocial research poses a considerable challenge as it is difficult to distinguish and reliably measure individual social risk factors. Many presumed risk factors are in fact just markers of adversity and do not form part of a true causal pathway. Genetic effects may operate indirectly through manipulation of the environment via gene–environment correlations. Much of the existing research refers to externalising disorders as a whole or antisocial behaviour, and it cannot be presumed that those pathways involving oppositional defiant disorder and conduct disorder equally apply to ADHD although there may be some overlap. In addition, many social factors are non-specific risk factors for a variety of mental health disorders (apart from institutional rearing discussed in the next section) and their contribution to ADHD aetiology is likely to involve gene–environment interplay.

9.12.1 SOCIAL AND DEMOGRAPHIC FACTORS

Biederman *et al.* (1995a) employed a case-control study design to investigate family environment risk factors for ADHD using Rutter's indices of adversity (severe marital discord, low social class, large family size, paternal criminality, maternal mental illness and foster care placement). They reported that the odds ratio for an ADHD diagnosis increased with the presence of an increasing number of risk indices. It is important to note that paternal criminality may reflect underlying impulsivity and that maternal mental illness, frequently a depressive illness, may be a presentation of adult ADHD. Therefore the association of social adversity with an ADHD diagnosis in offspring is likely to be due at least in part to the effects of parental genotype on the home environment they create for their offspring (gene–environment correlation), transmission of risk genotypes directly to offspring as well as direct environmental effects. Biederman *et al.* (2002) using an expanded case-control sample, examined the differential effect of environmental adversity using Rutter's indices of adversity on boys versus girls with and without ADHD. As in their previous study, all of the social adversity indices were significantly associated with ADHD in a dose-dependent relationship (except for large family size) even after controlling for parental ADHD, maternal smoking during pregnancy and gender. Gender modified the effect of adversity on learning disability and impaired social functioning with boys being more vulnerable to both than girls. However, the authors cautioned that the findings required replication in twin and adoption studies to tease apart genetic versus environmental effects.

Caspi *et al.* (2000) examined the relationship between neighbourhood deprivation and mental health disorders in a twin-study and found that environmental factors shared between family members accounted for 20% of the population variance in children's behavioural problems and that neighbourhood deprivation accounted for 5% of this shared family environment effect. Kim-Cohen *et al.* (2004) examined genetic and environmental factors influencing young children's resilience and vulnerability to economic deprivation using the E-risk study cohort. The authors reported that maternal warmth, stimulating activities and an outgoing temperament in the child promoted resilience and that resilience was in part heritable.

9.12.2   FAMILY ENVIRONMENT

With regard to family environment, non-shared environment, i.e. the environment specific to each child rather than that shared with siblings, appears to be of particular importance in influencing the development of differences rather than similarities between siblings (Plomin *et al.*, 2001). The nature of these non-shared influences and their contribution to the development of ADHD requires further study using longitudinal study designs as many of the current studies rely on cross-sectional designs and thus cannot examine the direction of effect. There is emerging evidence of interaction between family dysfunction and genotype in the development of antisocial behaviour (Button *et al.*, 2005). Many studies fail to find an association between family dysfunction and ADHD alone while there is a significant association with ODD and CD (e.g. Rey *et al.*, 2000). Some authors propose that family dysfunction is secondary to ADHD. However, an epidemiological study by Taylor *et al.* (1991) demonstrated a significant association between inconsistent parenting style and childhood hyperactivity. In the same epidemiological study carried out in East London, pervasive hyperactivity in boys was associated with reduced maternal warmth and increased levels of criticism of the child by both parents and reduced coping skills with the child's behaviour in mothers when compared with conduct disordered and random community controls. Carlson *et al.* (1995) conducted a follow-up study of 191 children up to 11 years of age and found that maternal intrusive care at six months and over-stimulation assessed at 42 months predicted children's subsequent risk of hyperactivity during middle childhood. The Swedish Adoption Twin Study of Aging found that 25% of the variance in parenting style measured using the Moos Family Environment Scale was under genetic influence (Plomin *et al.*, 1989). Pre-schoolers are especially vulnerable to negative parent–child interactions given their level of dependence on the parent, but fortunately early intervention with parent training in child behavioural management has proven effective in the management of ADHD in preschoolers (Sonuga-Barke *et al.*, 2001).

9.12.3   PARENTAL CONFLICT

Using the same case-control sample as the 1995a study, Biederman *et al.* (1995b) examined the effect of exposure to parental conflict and parental psychopathology on ADHD, ADHD co-morbid disorders and psychosocial functioning in children. Significant associations were found between parental conflict and symptom measures and psychosocial functioning in children. However, parental psychopathology was associated only with children's use of leisure time and externalising symptoms. A recent longitudinal study by Jenkins *et al.* (2005) investigating marital conflict and behavioural problems in children found that they mutually influenced each other. Marital conflict did predict change in children's behaviour, but children's behaviour particularly increased marital conflict in stepfamilies and boys were exposed to more conflict over time than girls. Interestingly, Jaffee *et al.* (2003) found that the presence of highly antisocial biological fathers in the home was associated with increased conduct problems in children and was reduced by their absence.

9.12.4   PARENTAL PSYCHOPATHOLOGY

As outlined earlier, gene–environment correlation is particularly important in this context. Several studies report an association between parental depression and ADHD in preschoolers (e.g. Cunningham & Boyle, 2002) and in school-age children (e.g. Johnston, 1996) while some do not (Biederman *et al.*, 1995b). The contribution of postnatal depression to hyperactivity may arise through poor parenting technique due to lower tolerance of infant behaviour and crying and poor parent–child interaction leading to disrupted attachment which persists despite mother's recovery from depression. Maternal postnatal depression is more likely to arise in an environment providing poor psychosocial support and thus an accumulation of psychosocial adversities may culminate in a disordered attachment pattern providing an environmental pathway for the development of ADHD. However, good quality evidence in favour of such a pathway is often lacking as studies of psychosocial risk for ADHD are often under-powered, retrospective in nature and tend to over-rely on dual maternal reporting of both depressive symptoms and child behaviour (though some do use teacher ratings of child behaviour). A large longitudinal twin study is needed to clarify the association. Sandberg (2002) reviewed the evidence supporting an inter-relationship between maternal depression, marital conflict and aggression and paternal anti-social behaviour placing a subgroup of hyperactive children at increased risk for the development of co-morbid conduct disorder.

Burt *et al.* (2005) reviewed data from the Minnesota Longitudinal Study of Parents and Children to test the hypothesis that parenting and family environmental factors mediate the association between maternal depressive symptoms and psychopathology in offspring in late adolescence in 184 families. The authors reported that analyses using a single informant and time-point showed evidence for substantial mediation, but in analyses using independent informants and multiple time-points, mediating effects were markedly reduced. In addition, gender differences were found with parenting and family environmental factors related to psychopathology in males while maternal depression related more directly to psychopathology in females. This study was not specific to ADHD but nevertheless provides an important longitudinal study model using multiple informants.

9.13 ATTACHMENT DISORDERS AND ADHD

9.13.1 INSTITUTIONAL REARING

Tizard and Hodges (1978) provided the initial evidence that early institutional rearing was associated with hyperactivity, inattention and social difficulties in eight-year-old children. It remains unclear whether institutional care represents an accumulation of social adversities or whether it acts as a specific risk factor with a lack in caregiver continuity being the key insult. Rutter and the ERA team (1998, 2001) investigated outcomes in children adopted from severely deprived orphanages in Romania into high-functioning homes in the United Kingdom (UK) compared with non-deprived UK children adopted into UK families. By the age of 6 years, more than one-third of Romanian adoptees (of both sexes) adopted after the age of two years displayed pervasive inattention and hyperactivity symptoms compared with 10% of within-UK adoptees. Furthermore, oppositional defiant disorder, conduct disorder and emotional disorders were no more common in Romanian adoptees than within-UK adoptees, i.e. there appeared to be a specific association between institutional deprivation and later inattention and hyperactivity (correlation 0.3). Malnutrition may have acted as a confounder in this study but it was less important in a later study by Roy *et al.* (2004) comparing outcomes in children removed from their biological families before the age of one year who later received good quality residential care versus foster care within the UK. Twenty-one per cent of institutionally reared children but none of the foster-care children displayed a marked lack of selective attachment to their caregivers, a feature that was strongly associated with inattention and hyperactivity symptoms.

Future research studies must consider whether institutionally reared children (irrespective of the quality of care received) develop a unique form of ADHD or whether the ADHD symptoms are all secondary to a primary attachment disorder. It is important to note that not all institutionally-reared children develop ADHD symptoms and it is tempting to speculate that the 'resilient' children possess 'low-risk' genotypes making them less vulnerable to environmental adversity. However, there is no research to date to test this hypothesis. It is unclear how this behavioural phenotype relates to the care provided by families under stress in the general community.

9.13.2 ANIMAL MODELS OF HUMAN ATTACHMENT DISORDERS

Animal models of gene–environment interaction with potential relevance for ADHD are those studies of aggressive behaviour in rhesus monkeys (Bennett *et al.*, 2002) which suggest that early experience with the caregiver may trigger gene expression. This is based on the observation that expression of a 5-HTT variant associated with decreased serotonergic function produced socially anxious and reactive behaviour *only* in peer-raised monkeys whose early environment was inadequate. The pattern of physical contact (ventral contact) a female infant monkey has with her mother or mother substitute predicts the pattern of ventral contact she will have with her own offspring in the first six months (Fairbanks, 1989; Champoux *et al.*, 1992). This cross-generational relationship was as strong for female rhesus monkeys reared by unrelated females as for females reared by their biological mothers. Suomi and Levin (1998) therefore proposed that cross-generational transmission of pattern of ventral contact, a component of mother–infant attachment in rhesus monkeys, was through non-genetic mechanisms. Research with non-human primates provides evidence for a biological basis of attachment relationships and is an important avenue for further research into gene–environment interactions and ADHD.

More recently, Brake *et al.* (2004) studied the influence of maternal separation during the first 14 days of life on mesocorticolimbic dopamine neurons and behavioural response to stimulants and stressors in adult rats. Those rats exposed to maternal separation and a lack of physical handling in early life were more hyperactive when placed in a novel setting as adults; they displayed dose-dependent heightened sensitivity to cocaine-induced locomotor activity and demonstrated a greater increase in nucleus accumbens dopamine levels in response to mild stress (a tail pinch) when compared with maternally-reared control adult rats. Quantitative autoreceptor audiography revealed a lower density of nucleus accumbens and striatal dopamine transporter sites as well as reduced D3 binding in rats who underwent maternal separation. The authors proposed that the lasting changes in dopaminergic function brought about by disruption of early postnatal care suggest a biological basis for individual differences in vulnerability to compulsive drug taking. These studies support the hypothesis that early rearing experience in animal models (and potentially in humans) can directly modulate dopaminergic and serotonergic tone and thus generate risk for later neurobehavioural disorders. It remains to be explored how this risk factor interacts with genotype to produce specific disorders such as ADHD rather than internalising disorders.

9.14 EPIGENETICS

An exciting research area is investigation of the mechanisms through which experience is translated into biology by the organism and equally how genotype is translated into experience. Epigenetics describes the study of heritable changes in gene expression that are not coded in the DNA sequence but by post-translational modifications in DNA and histone proteins. This allows one to study how social experience is transmitted across generations through non-genetic mechanisms that influence gene expression. It will also improve our understanding of normal and abnormal development and adaptation in response to social stressors.

An example of such research is that of Weaver *et al.* (2004) who studied a cross-fostering model in rats and measured maternal behaviour (high or low in terms of pup licking and grooming and arched-back nursing), behavioural changes in offspring and glucocorticoid receptor mRNA of offspring. Offspring of high-grooming and arched-back nursing mothers proved to be less fearful as adults with more modest HPA axis responses than offspring of low-grooming mothers. Cross-fostering the offspring of high and low-grooming mothers within 12 hours of birth produced adult rats with the stress-response patterns associated with their foster and not biological mothers. Increased glucocorticoid receptor mRNA in the off-spring of high-grooming mothers proved that gene expression in the HPA axis of rat pups was altered by maternal behaviour. Weaver *et al.* (2004) described this process as 'environmental programming' of gene expression and function and pro-posed that natural selection may have provided an opportunity to transmit maternal responses to the environment.

Meaney and Szyf (2005) also examined a rat model to study the consequences of variation in mother–infant interactions on the development of individual differ-ences in behavioural and endocrine responses to stress in adulthood. Differences in the DNA methylation pattern between the offspring of high- and low-grooming mothers emerged during the first week of life. These changes which were reversed by cross-fostering, persisted into adulthood and were associated with altered histone acetylation and transcription factor (nerve growth factor-induced clone A) binding to the glucocorticoid receptor promoter. Pharmacological reversal of the effects on chromatin structure eliminated the effects of maternal care on glucocorticoid recep-tor expression and HPA responses to stress. This suggests a direct relationship between epigenetic modification of the glucocorticoid receptor gene and altered stress response in offspring. These findings have implications for our understanding of the mechanisms linking early maternal behaviour and behavioural sequelae in adulthood. These findings also provide evidence that molecular mechanisms which underlie the effects of early life experience are potentially reversible in adulthood which has obvious social and therapeutic implications.

It remains to be seen whether this type of research into environmental program-ming will be replicated with other genes and other types of psychosocial stressors. Undoubtedly animal models and longitudinal studies will be invaluable to the exploration of gene–environment interplay across the lifespan. It has long been thought that parental behaviour could result in the transmission of adaptive and maladaptive responses across generations, however, in the near future; it may be possible to elucidate the molecular mechanisms underlying this phenomenon. Further understanding of these molecular mechanisms will allow for the develop-ment of targeted and timed interventions aimed at interactive risk factors to prevent the development and progression of ADHD.

9.15 CONCLUSION

Examination of gene–environment interplay in ADHD will help us to better under-stand the molecular mechanisms through which environmental risks affect gene expression and genetic risks affect environmental experience. The final pathway into ADHD is likely to involve multiple risk factors and mediating mechanisms. A variety of study designs are required as population-based twin study findings may be less applicable to samples of children with clinical ADHD diagnoses. Longitudinal study designs are preferable to the current preponderance of cross-sectional study designs. Families of children with ADHD selected for genetic studies should have detailed measurements taken of environmental exposures including toxin levels in blood and hair and biochemical screening such as zinc levels. Efforts should be made to select families exposed to extremes of psychosocial risk as families currently volunteering for research studies are more likely to be higher functioning. Trio-based genetic research studies by definition exclude families who have experienced parental conflict leading to separation and will thus underestimate environmental risk effect size. We emphasise the importance of using genetic controls in future studies of environmental risk factors for ADHD as genetic studies of this complex disorder are providing strong evidence for the importance of environmental effects as candidate risk genes are of small effect. We are on the threshold of an exciting era of renewed interest in environmental risk factor research in ADHD that can avail of advances in genetic study designs and genotyping techniques.

Researchers should follow the strategy suggested by Moffitt *et al.* (2005) for studies of gene–environment interplay using measured genes and measured environments. Her 7-step approach is summarised as follows:

1. Examine quantitative behavioural-genetic studies from twin and adoption research.
2. Identify candidate environmental risks for ADHD, for example, head injury, prenatal substance use, toxin exposure.
3. Measure the environmental risk as accurately and reliably as possible.
4. Select candidate risk genes for ADHD according to certain considerations, for example, DAT1, DRD4.
5. Test for interaction between the environmental risk factors and the candidate gene.
6. If an interaction is shown, evaluate the specificity of the relationship between the gene, the environmental risk factor and the disorder.
7. Replicate to validate findings.

9.16 SUGGESTED FURTHER READING

The reader is referred to Sandberg's (2002) book entitled *Hyperactivity and Attention Disorders of Childhood* which contains further information regarding psychosocial risk factors for ADHD.

9.17 REFERENCES

Amin-Zaki L, Ehassani S, Majeed MA *et al.* (1976) Perinatal methylmercury poisoning in Iraq. *American Journal of Diseases of Childhood* **130**: 1070–6.
Arnold LE, Pinkham SM, Votolato N (2000) Does zinc moderate essential fatty acid and amphetamine treatment of Attention-Deficit/Hyperactivity Disorder? *Journal of Child and Adolescent Psychopharmacology* **10**: 111–17.
Asherson P, Kuntsi J, Taylor E (2005) Unravelling the complexity of Attention-Deficit Hyperactivity Disorder: a behavioural genomic approach. *British Journal of Psychiatry* **187**: 103–5.

Bandstra ES, Morrow CE, Anthony JC *et al.* (2001) Longitudinal investigation of task persistence and sustained attention in children with prenatal cocaine exposure. *Neurotoxicology and Teratology* **23**: 545–9.

Batstra L, Hadders-Algra M, Neeleman J (2003) Effect of antenatal exposure to maternal smoking on behavioural problems and academic achievement in childhood: prospective evidence from a Dutch birth cohort. *Early Human Development* **75**: 21–33.

Bekaroglu M, Aslan Y, Gedik Y *et al.* (1996) Relationships between serum free fatty acids and zinc, and attention deficit hyperactivity disorder: a research note. *Journal of Child Psychology and Psychiatry* **37**: 225–7.

Bellgrove MA, Hawi Z, Kirley A *et al.* (2005) Dissecting the attention deficit hyperactivity disorder (ADHD) phenotype: Sustained attention, response variability and spatial attentional asymmetries in relation to dopamine transporter (DAT1) genotype. *Neuropsychologica* **43**: 1847–57.

Bellinger DC, Hu H, Kalaniti K *et al.* (2005) A pilot study of blood lead levels and neurobehavioural function in children living in Chennai, India. *International Journal of Occupational and Environmental Health* **11**: 138–43.

Ben Amor L, Grizenko N, Schwartz G *et al.* (2005) Perinatal complications in children with Attention-Deficit Hyperactivity Disorder and their unaffected siblings. *Journal of Psychiatry and Neuroscience* **30**: 120–6.

Bennett AJ, Lesch KP, Heils A *et al.* (2002) Early experience and serotonin transporter gene variation interact to influence primate CNS function. *Molecular Psychiatry* **7**: 118–22.

Biederman J, Milberger S, Faraone SV *et al.* (1994) Associations between childhood asthma and ADHD: issues of psychiatric comorbidity and familiality. *Journal of the American Academy of Child and Adolescent Psychiatry* **33**: 842–8.

Biederman J, Milberger S, Faraone SV *et al.* (1995a) Family-environment risk factors for Attention-Deficit Hyperactivity Disorder. A test of Rutter's indicators of adversity. *Archives of General Psychiatry* **52**: 464–70.

Biederman J, Milberger S, Faraone SV *et al.* (1995b) Impact of adversity on functioning and co-morbidity in children with Attention-Deficit Hyperactivity Disorder. *Journal of the American Academy of Child Adolescent Psychiatry* **34**: 1495–1503.

Biederman J, Faraone SV, Monuteaux MC (2002) Differential effect of environmental adversity by gender: Rutter's index of adversity in a group of boys and girls with and without ADHD. *American Journal of Psychiatry* **158**: 1556–62.

Bilici M, Yildirim F, Kandil S *et al.* (2004) Double-blind, placebo-controlled study of zinc sulphate in the treatment of attention deficit hyperactivity disorder. *Progress in Neuropsychopharmacology and Biological Psychiatry* **28**: 181–90.

Boksa P, El-Khodor BF (2003) Birth insult interacts with stress at adulthood to alter dopaminergic function in animal models: possible implications for schizophrenia and other disorders. *Neuroscience and Biobehavioural Reviews* **27**: 91–101.

Boss V, Sola A, Wen TC, Decker MJ (2005) Mild intermittent hypoxia does not induce stress responses in the neonatal rat brain. *Biology of the Neonate* **88**: 313–20.

Botting N, Powls A, Cooke RW, Marlow N (1997) Attention deficit hyperactivity disorder and other psychiatric outcomes in very low birth weight children at 12 years. *Journal of Child Psychology and Psychiatry* **38**: 931–41.

Brake WG, Boksa P, Gratton A (1997) Influence of perinatal factors on the nucleus accumbens dopamine response to repeated stress during adulthood: an electrochemical study in the rat. *Neuroscience* **77**: 1067–76.

Brake WG, Sullivan RM, Gratton A (2000) Perinatal distress leads to lateralised medial prefrontal cortical dopamine hypofunction in adult rats. *Journal of Neuroscience* **20**: 5538–43.

Brake WG, Zhang TY, Diorio J *et al.* (2004) Influence of early postnatal rearing conditions on mesocorticolimbic dopamine and behavioural responses to psychostimulants and stressors in adult rats. *European Journal of Neuroscience* **19**: 1863–74.

Brawley A, Silverman B, Kearney S *et al.* (2004) Allergic rhinitis in children with Attention-Deficit/Hyperactivity Disorder. *Annals of Allergy, Asthma and Immunology* **92**: 663–7.

Breslau N, Brown GG, Del Dotto JE, Kumar S *et al.* (1996) Psychiatric sequelae of low birth weight at 6 years of age. *Journal of Abnormal Child Psycholology* **24**: 385–400.

Breslau N, Chilcoat HD (2000) Psychiatric sequelae for low birth weight at 11 years of age. *Biological Psychiatry* **47**: 1005–11.

Brookes KJ, Mill J, Guindalini C *et al.* (2006) A common haplotype of the dopamine transporter gene associated with Attention-Deficit/Hyperactivity Disorder and interacting with maternal use of alcohol during pregnancy. *Archives of General Psychiatry* **63**: 74–81.

Brouwer A, Morse DC, Lans MC *et al.* (1998) Interactions of persistent environmental organohalogens with the thyroid hormone system: mechanisms and possible consequences for animal and human health. *Toxicology and Industrial Health* **14**: 59–84.

Burt KB, Van Dulman MH, Carlivati J *et al.* (2005) Mediating links between maternal depression and offspring psychopathology: the importance of independent data. *Journal of Child Psychology and Psychiatry* **46**: 490–9.

Button TMM, Thapar A, McGuffin P (2005) Relationship between antisocial behaviour, Attention-Deficit Hyperactivity Disorder and maternal prenatal smoking. *British Journal of Psychiatry* **187**: 155–60.

Carlson EA, Jacobvitz D, Sroufe LA (1995) A developmental investigation of inattentiveness and hyperactivity. *Child Development* **66**: 37–54.

Caspi A, Taylor A, Moffitt TE, Plomin R (2000) Neighbourhood deprivation affects children's mental health: environmental risks identified in a genetic design. *Psychological Science* **11**: 338–42.

Caspi A, McClay J, Moffitt TE *et al.* (2002) Role of genotype in the cycle of violence in maltreated children. *Science* **297**: 851–4.

CDC (2004) Alcohol consumption among women who are pregnant or who might become pregnant: United States 2002. *Morbidity and Mortality Weekly Report* Dec 24; **53**(50): 1178–81.

Champoux M, Byrne E, Delizio RD, Suomi SJ (1992) Motherless mothers revisited: Rhesus maternal behaviour and rearing history. *Primates* **33**: 251–5.

Chandola CA, Robling MR, Peters TJ *et al.* (1992). Pre- and perinatal factors and the risk of subsequent referral for hyperactivity. *Journal of Child Psychology and Psychiatry* **33**: 1077–90.

Cheon KA, Ryu YH, Kim YK *et al.* (2003) Dopamine transporter density in the basal ganglia assessed with [123I]IPT SPECT in children with attention deficit hyperactivity disorder. *European Journal of Nuclear Medicine and Molecular Imaging* **30**: 306–11.

Coleman M, Steinberg G, Tippett J *et al.* (1979) A prelimnary study of the effects of pyridoxine. *Biological Psychiatry* **14**: 741–51.

Colquhoun I, Bunday S (1981) A lack of essential fatty acids as a possible cause of hyperactivity in children. *Medical Hypotheses* **7**: 673–9.

Costa L, Li W, Richter R *et al.* (1999) The role of paraoxonase (PON1) in the detoxification of organophosphates and its human polymorphism. *Chemico-Biological Interactions* **119–20**: 429–38.

Crook WG (1994) Sugar and children's behaviour. *New England Journal of Medicine* **330**: 1901–2.

Cunningham CE, Boyle MH (2002) Preschoolers at risk for Attention-Deficit Hyperactivity Disorder and oppositional defiant disorder: family, parenting, and behavioural correlates. *Journal of Abnormal Child Psychology* **30**: 555–69.

Decker MJ, Hue GE, Caudle WM et al. (2003) Episodic neonatal hypoxia evokes executive dysfunction and regionally specific alterations in markers of dopamine signalling. *Neuroscience* **117**: 417–25.

Dougherty DD, Bonab AA, Spencer TJ et al. (1999) Dopamine transporter density in patients with attention deficit hyperactivity disorder. *Lancet* **354**: 2132–3.

Drew AE, Derbez AE, Werling LL (2000) Nicotinic receptor-mediated regulation of dopamine transporter activity in rat prefrontal cortex. *Synapse* **38**: 10–16.

Duty SM, Singh NP, Silva MJ et al. (2003) The relationship between environmental exposures to phthalates and DNA damage in human sperm using the neutral comet assay. *Environmental Health Perspectives* **111**: 1164–9.

Eppright TD, Vogel SJ, Horwitz E, Tevendale HD (1997) Results of blood lead screening in children referred for behavioural disorders. *Missouri Medicine* **94**: 295–7.

Eriksson P, Ankarberg E, Fredriksson A (2000) Exposure to nicotine during a defined period in neonatal life induces permanent changes in brain nicotinic receptors and in behaviour of adult mice. *Brain Research* **853**: 41–8.

Ernst M, Moolchan ET, Robinson MC (2001) Behavior and neural consequences of prenatal exposure to nicotine. *Journal of the American Academy of Child Adolescent Psychiatry* **40**: 630–41.

Fairbanks LA (1989) Early experience and cross-generational continuity of mother-infant contact in vervet monkeys. *Developmental Psychobiology* **22**: 669–81.

Feingold BF (1975) *Why Is Your Child Hyperactive?* New York: Random House.

Gerring JP, Brady KD, Chen A et al. (1998) Premorbid prevalence of ADHD and development of secondary ADHD after closed head injury. *Journal of the American Academy of Child and Adolescent Psychiatry* **37**: 647–54.

Goodlett CR, Horn KH, Zhou FC (2005) Alcohol teratogenesis: mechanisms of damage and strategies for intervention. *Experimental Biology and Medicine* (Maywood, N.J.) **230**: 394–406.

Goodman R, Stevenson J (1989) A twin study of hyperactivity-II. The aetiological role of genes, family relationships and perinatal adversity. *Journal of Child Psychology and Psychiatry* **30**: 691–709.

Haddow JE, Palomaki GE, Allan WC et al. (1999) Maternal thyroid deficiency during pregnancy and subsequent neuropsychological development of the child. *New England Journal of Medicine* **34**: 549–55.

Hagino N, Lee JW (1985) Effect of maternal nicotine on the development of sites for [3H] nicotine binding in the fetal brain. *International Journal of Developmental Neuroscience* **3**: 567–71.

Halas ES, Stanstead HH (1975) Some effects of prenatal zinc deficiency on behaviour of the adult rat. *Pediatric Research* **9**: 94–7.

Hammerness P, Monteaux MC, Faraone SV et al. (2005) Re-examining the familial association between asthma and ADHD in girls. *Journal of Attention Disorders* **8**: 136–43.

Hardell L, Lindstrom G, Van Bavel B (2002) Is DDT exposure during fetal period and breastfeeding associated with neurological impairment? *Environmental Research* **88**: 141–4.

Hauser P, McMillin JM, Bhatara VS (1998) Resistance to thyroid hormone: implications for neurodevelopmental research on the effects of thyroid hormone disruptors. *Toxicology and Industrial Health* **14**: 85–191.

Hill SY, Lowers L, Locke-Wellman J, Shen SA (2000) Maternal smoking and drinking during pregnancy and the risk of child and adolescent psychiatric disorders. *Journal of Studies on Alcohol* **61**: 661–8.

Hille ET, den Ouden AL, Saigal S et al. (2001) Behavioural problems in children who weigh 1000 g or less at birth in four countries. *Lancet* **357**(9269): 1641–3.

Hunter DJ (2005) Gene–environment interactions in human diseases. *Nature* **6**: 287–98.

Hypponen E, Davey Smith G, Power C (2004) Effects of grandmothers' smoking on birth weight: intergenerational cohort study. *British Medical Journal* **327**: 898–901.

Jacobson JL, Jacobson SW (1996) Intellectual impairment in children exposed to polychlorinated biphenyls in utero. *New England Journal of Medicine* **335**: 783–9.

Jacobson JL, Jacobson SW (2003) Prenatal exposure to polychlorinated biphenyls and attention at school age. *Journal of Pediatrics* **143**: 780–8.

Jaffee SR, Moffitt TE, Caspi A, Taylor A (2003) Life with (or without) father: the benefits of living with two biological parents depend on the father's antisocial behaviour. *Child Development* **74**: 109–26.

Jenkins J, Simpson A, Dunn J *et al.* (2005) Mutual influence of marital conflict and children's behaviour problems: shared and non-shared family risks. *Child Development* **76**: 24–39.

Johnston C (1996) Parent characteristics and parent-child interactions in families of nonproblem children and ADHD children with higher and lower levels of oppositional-defiant behaviour. *Journal of Abnormal Child Psychology* **24**: 85–104.

Kahn RS, Khoury J, Nichols WC, Lanphear BP (2003) Role of dopamine transporter genotype and maternal prenatal smoking in childhood hyperactive-impulsive, inattentive and oppositional behaviours. *Journal of Pediatrics* **143**: 104–10.

Kim-Cohen J, Moffitt TE, Caspi A, Taylor A (2004) Genetic and environmental processes in young children's resilience and vulnerability to socioeconomic deprivation. *Child Development* **75**: 651–68.

Kirley A, Hawi Z, Daly G *et al.* (2002). Dopaminergic system genes in ADHD: toward a biological hypothesis. *Neuropsychopharmacology* **27**: 617–19.

Kirley A, Lowe N, Hawi Z *et al.* (2003) Association of the 480 bp DAT1 allele with methylphenidate response in a sample of Irish children with ADHD. *American Journal of Medical Genetics* **121**B: 50–4.

Knopik VS, Sparrow EP, Madden PA *et al.* (2005) Contribution of parental alcoholism, prenatal substance exposure, and genetic transmission to child ADHD risk: a female twin study. *Psychological Medicine* **35**: 625–35.

Kodl MM, Wakschlag LS (2004) Does a childhood history of externalizing problems predict smoking in pregnancy? *Addictive Behaviors* **29**: 273–9.

Kollins SJ, McClernon J, Fuemeler BF (2005) Association between smoking and Attention-Deficit/Hyperactivity Disorder symptoms in a population-based sample of young adults. *Archives of General Psychiatry* **62**: 1142–7.

Kostas J, McFarland DJ, Drew WG (1976) Lead-inducing hyperactivity: chromic exposure during the neonatal period in the rat. *Pharmacology* **14**: 435–42.

Kotimaa BM, Moilanen I, Taanila A *et al.* (2003) Maternal smoking and hyperactivity in 8 year-old children. *Journal of the American Academy of Child and Adolescent Psychiatry* **42**: 826–33.

Kozielec T, Starobrat-Hermelin B (1997) Assessment of magnesium levels in children with attention deficit hyperactivity disorder (ADHD). *Magnesium Research* **10**: 143–8.

Krause KH, Dresel SH, Krause J *et al.* (2000) Increased striatal dopamine transporter in adult patients with attention deficit hyperactivity disorder: effects of methylphenidate as measures by single photon emission computed tomography. *Neuroscience Letters* **285**: 107–10.

Krause KH, Dresel SH, Krause J *et al.* (2002) Stimulant-like action of nicotine on striatal dopamine transporter in the brain of adults with attention deficit hyperactivity disorder. *International Journal of Neuropsychopharmacology* **5**: 111–13.

Krause KH, Dresel SH, Krause J *et al.* (2003) The dopamine transporter and neuroimaging in attention deficit hyperactivity disorder. *Neuroscience and Biobehavioral Reviews* **27**: 605–13.

Lanphear BP, Hornung R, Khoury J *et al.* (2005) Low-level environmental lead exposure and children's intellectual function: an international pooled analysis. *Environmental Health Perspectives* **113**: 894–9.

Latini G, De Felice C, Presta G *et al.* (2003) In utero exposure to di-(2-ethylhexyl) phthalate and duration of human pregnancy. *Environmental Health Perspectives* **111**: 1783–5.

Linnet KM, Dalsgaard S, Obel C *et al.* (2003) Maternal lifestyle factors in pregnancy, risk of attention deficit hyperactivity disorder and associated behaviours: review of the current evidence. *American Journal of Psychiatry* **160**: 1028–40.

Loo SK, Specter E, Smolen A *et al.* (2003) Functional effects of the DAT1 polymorphism on EEG measures in ADHD. *J Am Acad Child Adolesc Psychiatry* **42**: 986–93.

Lou HC, Rosa P, Pryds O *et al.* (2004) ADHD: increased dopamine receptor availability linked to attention deficit and low neonatal cerebral blood flow. *Developmental Medicine and Child Neurology* **46**: 179–83.

McDonald SD, Perkins SL, Jodouin CA, Walker MC (2002) Folate levels in pregnant women who smoke: an important gene–environment interaction. *American Journal of Obstetrics and Gynecology* **187**: 620–5.

McGee R, Stanton WR, Sears MR (1993) Allergic disorders and attention deficit disorder in children. *Journal of Abnormal Child Psychology* **21**: 79–88.

Magner JA, Petrick P, Menzes-Ferreira MM *et al.* (1986) Familial generalised resistance to thyroid hormones: report of three kindreds and correlation of patterns of affected tissues with the binding of (125I) triiodothyronine to fibroblast nuclei. *Journal of Endocrinological Investigation* **9**: 459–70.

Marshall P (1989) Attention deficit disorder and allergy: a neurochemical model of the relation between the illnesses. *Psychology Bulletin* **106**: 434–6.

Matte TD, Bresnahan M, Begg MD, Susser E (2001) Influence of variation in birth weight within normal range and within sibships on IQ at age 7 years: cohort study. *British Medical Journal* **323**: 310–14.

Maughan B, Taylor A, Caspi A, Moffitt TE (2004) Prenatal smoking and early childhood conduct problems: testing genetic and environmental explanations of the association. *Archives of General Psychiatry* **61**: 836–43.

Meaney MJ (2001) The development of individual differences in behavioural and endocrine responses to stress. *Annual Review of Neuroscience* **24**: 1161–92.

Meaney MJ, Szyf M (2005) Environmental programming of stress responses through DNA methylation: life at the interface between a dynamic environment and a fixed genome. *Dialogues in Clinical Neuroscience* **7**: 103–23.

Mick E, Biederman J, Faraone SV (1996) Is season of birth a risk factor for Attention-Deficit Hyperactivity Disorder? *Journal of the American Academy of Child and Adolescent Psychiatry* **35**: 1470–6.

Mick E, Biederman J, Faraone SV *et al.* (2002) Case-control study of attention deficit hyperactivity disorder and maternal smoking, alcohol use, and drug use during pregnancy. *Journal of the American Academy of Child and Adolescent Psychiatry* **41**: 378–85.

Milberger S, Biederman J, Faraone SV *et al.* (1996) Is maternal smoking during pregnancy a risk factor for attention deficit hyperactivity disorder in children? *American Journal of Psychiatry* **153**: 1138–42.

Milberger S, Biederman J, Faraone SV *et al.* (1997) Pregnancy, delivery and infancy complications and attention deficit hyperactivity disorder: issues of gene–environment interaction. *Biological Psychiatry* **41**: 65–75.

Minder B, Das-Smaal EA, Brand EF, Orlebeke JF (1994) Exposure to lead and specific attentional problems in schoolchildren. *Journal of Learning Disabilities* **27**: 393–9.

Mitchell EA, Aman MG, Turbott SH, Manku M (1987) Clinical characteristics and serum essential fatty acid levels in hyperactive children. *Clinical Pediatrics (Philadelphia)* **26**: 406–11.

Moffitt TE, Caspi A, Rutter M (2005) Strategy for investigating interactions between measured genes and measured environments. *Archives of General Psychiatry* **62**: 473–81.

Moffitt TE (2005) The new look of behavioral genetics in developmental psychopathology: gene–environment interplay in antisocial behaviours. *Psychological Bulletin* **131**: 533–54.

Navarro HA, Mills E, Seidler FJ *et al.* (1990) Prenatal nicotine exposure impairs beta-adrenergic function: persistent chronotropic subsensitivity despite recovery from deficits in receptor binding. *Brain Research Bulletin* **25**: 233–7.

Needleman HL (1982) The neurobehavioural consequences of low lead exposure in childhood. *Neurobehavioral Toxicology and Teratology* **4**: 729–32.

Needleman HL, Reiss JA, Tobin MJ *et al.* (1996) Bone lead levels and delinquent behaviour. *Journal of the American Medical Association* **275**: 363–9.

Noland JS, Singer LT, Short EJ *et al.* (2005) Prenatal drug exposure and selective attention in preschoolers. *Neurotoxicology and Teratology* **27**: 429–38.

O'Callaghan MJ, Harvey JM (1997) Biological predictors and co-morbidity of attention deficit and hyperactivity disorder in extremely low birth weight infants at school. *Journal of Paediatrics and Child Health* **33**: 491–6.

O'Connor TG, Deater-Deckard F, Fulker D *et al.* (1998) Gene–environment correlations in late childhood and early adolescence: antisocial behaviour problems and coercive parenting. *Developmental Psychology* **34**: 970–81.

O'Malley KD, Nanson J (2002) Clinical implications of a link between foetal alcohol spectrum disorder and Attention-Deficit Hyperactivity Disorder. *Canadian Journal of Psychiatry* **47**: 349–54.

Ornoy A (2003) The impact of intrauterine exposure versus postnatal environment in neurodevelopmental toxicity: long-term neurobehavioural studies in children at risk for developmental disorders. *Toxicology Letters* **140–1**: 171–81.

Plomin R, Asbury K, Dunn J (2001) Why are children in the same family so different? Non-shared environment a decade later. *Canadian Journal of Psychiatry* **46**: 225–33.

Plomin R, McClearn GE, Pederson NL *et al.* (1989) Genetic influence on adults' ratings of their current family environment. *Journal of Marriage and the Family* **51**: 792–803.

Prinz RJ, Roberts WA, Hantman E (1980) Dietary correlates of hyperactive behaviour in children. *Journal of Consulting & Clinical Psychology* **48**: 760–9.

Rapp DJ (1978) Does diet affect hyperactivity? *Journal of Learning Disabilities* **11**: 56–62.

Refetoff S (1990) Resistance to thyroid hormone. *Thyroid Today* **13**: 1–11.

Rey JM, Walter G, Plapp JM, Denshire E (2000) Family environment in attention deficit hyperactivity, oppositional defiant and conduct disorders. *Australian and New Zealand Journal of Psychiatry* **34**: 453–7.

Rice DC (2000a) Identification of functional domains affected by developmental exposure to methylmercury: Faroe Islands and related studies. *Neurotoxicology* **21**: 1039–44.

Rice DC (2000b) Parallels between attention deficit hyperactivity disorder and behavioural deficits produced by neurotoxic exposure in monkeys. *Environmental Health Perspectives* **108** Suppl: 405–8.

Richardson AJ, Puri BK (2000) The potential role of fatty acids in attention-deficit/hyperactivity disorder. *Prostaglandins, Leukotrienes and Essential Fatty Acids* **63**: 79–87.

Richardson GA, Conroy ML, Day NL (1996) Prenatal cocaine exposure: effects on the development of school-age children. *Neurotoxicology and Teratology* **18**: 627–34.

Roy P, Rutter M, Pickles A (2004) Institutional care: associations between overactivity and lack of selectivity in social relationships. *Journal of Child Psychology and Psychiatry* **45**: 866–73.

Rutter M (2000) Psychosocial influences: critiques, findings, and research needs. *Developmental Psychopathology* **12**: 375–405.

Rutter M (2005) Environmentally mediated risks for psychopathology: research strategies and findings. *Journal of the American Academy of Child and Adolescent Psychiatry* **44**: 3–18.

Rutter M, English and Romanian Adoptees (ERA) study team (1998) Developmental catch-up, and deficit, following adoption after severe global early privation. *Journal of Child Psychology and Psychiatry* **39**: 465–76.

Rutter M, Kreppner J, O'Connor T, ERA study team (2001) Specificity and heterogeneity in children's responses to profound privation. *British Journal of Psychiatry* **179**: 97–103.

Sandberg S (2002) Psychosocial contributions. In: S Sandberg (ed.) *Hyperactivity and Attention Disorders of Childhood*. Cambridge: Cambridge University Press.

Schab DW, Trinh NH (2004) Do artificial food colors promote hyperactivity in children with hyperactive syndromes? A meta-analysis of double-blind placebo-controlled trials. *Journal of Developmental and Behavioral Pediatrics* **25**: 423–34.

Schettler T (2001) Toxic threats to neurologic development of children. *Environmental Health Perspectives* **109** Suppl: 813–16.

Schwartz J (1994) Low-level lead exposure and children's IQ: a meta-analysis and search for a threshold. *Environmental Research* **65**: 42–55.

Schweitzer J, Anderson C, Ernst M (2000) Attention deficit hyperactivity disorder: neuroimaging and behavioral/cognitive probes. In: M Ernst, JM Rumsey (eds) *Functional Neuroimaging in Child Psychiatry*, Cambridge: Cambridge University Press.

Seeger G, Schloss P, Schmidt MH *et al.* (2004) Gene–environment interaction in hyperkinetic conduct disorder (HD+CD) as indicated by season of birth variations in dopamine receptor (DRD4) gene polymorphism. *Neuroscience Letters* **366**: 282–6.

Shannon WR (1922) Neuropathic manifestations in infants and children as a result of anaphylactic reactions to foods contained in their diet. *American Journal of Childhood Diseases* **24**: 89–94.

Slotkin TA, Oinkerton KE, Auman JT *et al.* (2002). Perinatal exposure to environmental tobacco smoke upregulates nicotinic cholinergic receptors in monkey brain. *Developmental Brain Research* **133**: 175–9.

Sonuga-Barke EJ, Daley D, Thompson M *et al.* (2001) Parent-based therapies for preschool Attention-Deficit/Hyperactivity Disorder: a randomised, controlled trial with a community sample. *Journal of the American Academy of Child and Adolescent Psychiatry* **40**: 402–8.

Stanwood GD, Washington RA, Shumsky JS, Levitt P (2001) Prenatal cocaine exposure produces consistent development alterations in dopamine-rich regions of the cerebral cortex. *Neuroscience* **106**: 5–14.

Stevens LJ, Zentall SS, Deck JL *et al.* (1995) Essential fatty acid metabolism in boys with Attention-Deficit Hyperactivity Disorder. *American Journal of Clinical Nutrition* **62**: 761–8.

Streissguth AP, Barr HM, Sampson PD, Bookstein FL (1994) Prenatal alcohol and offspring development: the first fourteen years. *Drug and Alcohol Dependency* **36**: 89–99.

Suomi SJ, Levine S (1998) Psychobiology of intergenerational effects of trauma: evidence from animal studies. In Y Daniele (ed.) *International Handbook of Multigenerational Legacies of Trauma*. New York: Plenum Press.

Szatmari P, Saigal S, Rosenbaum P *et al.* (1990) Psychiatric disorders at five years among children with birth weights less than 1000 g: a regional perspective. *Developmental Medicine and Child Neurology* **32**: 954–62.

Taylor E, Rogers JW (2005) Practitioner review: early adversity and developmental disorders. *Journal of Child Psychology and Psychiatry* **46**: 451–67.

Taylor E, Sandberg S, Thorley G, Giles S (1991) *The Epidemiology of Childhood Hyperactivity*. Maudsley Monographs 33. Oxford: Oxford University Press.

Thapar A, Fowler T, Rice F *et al.* (2003) Maternal smoking during pregnancy and attention deficit hyperactivity symptoms in offspring. *American Journal of Psychiatry* **160**: 1985–9.

Thapar A, Langley K, Fowler T, Rice F *et al.* (2005) Catechol *O*-Methyltransferase gene variant and birth weight predict early-onset antisocial behavior in children with Attention-deficit/Hyperactivity Disorder. *Archives of General Psychiatry* **62**: 1275–8.

Tilson HA, Kodavanti PR (1997) Neurochemical effects of polychlorinated biphenyls: an overview. *NeuroToxicology* **18**: 727–43.

Tizard B, Hodges J (1978) The effect of early institutional rearing on the development of eight-year-old children. *Journal of Child Psychology and Psychiatry* **19**: 99–118.

Toft PB (1999) Prenatal and perinatal striatal injury: a hypothetical cause of attention-deficit-hyperactivity disorder? *Pediatric Neurology* **21**: 602–10.

Toren P, Eldar S, Sela BA *et al.* (1996) Zinc deficiency in Attention-Deficit Hyperactivity Disorder. *Biological Psychiatry* **40**: 1308–10.

Tully LA, Arseneault L, Caspi A *et al.* (2004) Does maternal warmth moderate the effects of birth weight on twins' Attention-Deficit/Hyperactivity Disorder symptoms and IQ? *Journal of Consulting and Clinical Psychology* **72**: 218–26.

Tuthill RW (1996) Hair lead levels related to children's classroom attention deficit behaviour. *Archives of Environmental Health* **51**: 214–20.

Van Wendel de Joode, Wesseling C, Kromhout H *et al.* (2001) Chronic nervous-system effects of long-term occupational exposure to DDT. *Lancet* **357**: 1014–16.

Weaver IC, Cervoni N, Champagne FA *et al.* (2004) Epigenetic programming by maternal behaviour. *Nature Neuroscience* **7**: 847–54.

Weiss M, Hechtman L, Weiss G (2000) ADHD in parents. *Journal of the American Academy of Child and Adolescent Psychiatry* **39**: 1059–61.

Wilens TE, Hahesy AL, Biederman J *et al.* (2005) Influence of parental SUD and ADHD on ADHD in their offspring: preliminary results from a pilot-controlled family study. *American Journal of Addictions* **14**: 179–87.

Wolraich M, Milich R, Stumbo P, Schultz F (1985) Effects of sucrose ingestion on the behaviour of hyperactive boys. *Journal of Pediatrics* **106**: 675–82.

Wolraich ML, Lindgren SD, Stumbo PJ *et al.* (1994) Effects of diets high in sucrose or aspartame on the behaviour and cognitive performance of children. *New England Journal of Medicine* **330**: 301–7.

Woolf A, Wright R, Amarasiriwardena C, Bellinger D (2002) A child with chronic manganese exposure from drinking water. *Environmental Health Perspectives* **110**: 613–16.

10 The Genetics of Adult ADHD

FRANK A. MIDDLETON AND STEPHEN V. FARAONE
SUNY Upstate Medical University, Syracuse, NY, USA

10.1 OVERVIEW

Attention deficit/hyperactivity disorder (ADHD) is a cognitive and behavioural syndrome characterised by deficient attention and problem-solving, along with hyperactivity, impulsivity, and difficulty witholding incorrect responses. ADHD is usually first recognised in schoolage children. As the attention of these children wanders from one stimulus to the next, they often have difficulty absorbing information from parents and teachers. Their impulsiveness disrupts classrooms and creates problems with peers, as they blurt out answers, interrupt others, or shift from schoolwork to inappropriate activities. Their hyperactivity, often manifest as fidgeting, excessive talking, and accident proneness, is frustrating to those around them and not well-tolerated at school. As they grow older, children with ADHD are also at risk for low self-esteem, poor peer relationships, conflict with parents, delinquency, smoking, and substance abuse. Moreover, it is now recognised that as many as two-thirds of individuals with ADHD continue to experience impairing symptoms in adulthood.

While the hyperactivity and impulsivity are less prominent in adults with ADHD, the inattention and distractibility persist unabated (Biederman, Mick & Faraone, 2000; Faraone, Biederman, Spencer *et al.*, 2000; Biederman *et al.*, 2001). Furthermore, the validity of the disorder in clinically referred adults with retrospectively defined childhood-onset ADHD is supported by the fact that their clinical features, psychosocial disability, psychiatric comorbidity, neuropsychological dysfunction, familial illness and academic failure resemble those seen in children with ADHD (Faraone, Biederman, Spencer *et al.*, 2000). Given the profound impact that ADHD can have on individuals, families, and society, there is considerable interest in defining the causes of the illness. Recent advances in genetic and neuroimaging approaches have begun to yield insights into the potential pathogenetic and pathophysiological bases of ADHD. The emerging picture strongly implicates dysfunction of specific brain circuits, and the genes that regulate neurotransmitter synthesis, activity, or assembly within these circuits. In this review, much of this evidence will be presented within the context of how it could help explain key elements of adult ADHD.

Handbook of Attention Deficit Hyperactivity Disorder. Edited by M. Fitzgerald, M. Bellgrove and M. Gill.
© 2007 John Wiley & Sons Ltd

10.2 GENETIC CONTRIBUTIONS TO ADHD

The potential genetic contributions to ADHD have been the subject of several in-depth reviews and meta-analyses. Most of the genetic research completed on ADHD has taken the form of analysing the rates of familiality, the concordance rates in twin studies, the incidence in adopted children, and the potential linkage and association of chromosomal regions and candidate gene markers with the illness. We review the major findings in each of these areas in the sections that follow. A detailed review of molecular genetic findings in ADHD is provided in Chapter 8.

10.2.1 FAMILIALITY

The term familiality refers to the frequency that a disease occurs among related individuals as opposed to unrelated individuals. The occurrence of ADHD does appear to be high among relatives, supporting the concept that it runs in families (Faraone & Doyle, 2001). In fact, studies have now established the rates of familiality between children with ADHD and their parents, siblings, and twins. These rates can be compared with the rates of occurrence in children who are adopted into families with ADHD.

(a) Parents

There have been a number of studies that have examined the rate of ADHD in families (reviewed in Faraone & Doyle, 2001). Only eight of these studies provided information about rates of ADHD among the parents of ADHD probands (Faraone & Tsuang, 1995). However, both earlier and more recent studies offer agreement with each other (Morrison & Stewart, 1971; Cantwell, 1972; Biederman et al., 1990; Schachar & Wachsmuth, 1990; Frick et al., 1991; Faraone et al., 1992). Specifically, these studies find that the parents of ADHD children have a two- to eight-fold increase in the risk for ADHD compared with unrelated adults. This elevated risk thus confirms the familiality of ADHD, and also provides further evidence for the validity of the diagnosis in adults.

(b) Siblings

In addition to the studies demonstrating increased risk in the parents of ADHD children, other studies report elevated rates of ADHD among the siblings of ADHD probands (Manshadi et al., 1983; Pauls et al., 1983; Biederman et al., 1990; Faraone et al., 1992; Welner et al., 1977). In fact, the first double-blind case-control family study of DSM-III ADD (Biederman et al., 1990) found siblings of ADHD children to be at high risk for ADD after statistically correcting for gender and generation of relative, intactness of family, and social class. These results were replicated in a double-blind study of DSM-III-R ADHD for both boys (Biederman et al., 1992; Faraone et al., 1992) and girls (Faraone, Biederman, Mick et al., 2000). Taken together, studies of first-degree relatives suggest that ADHD is familial. Studies of more distant relatives are consistent with this idea as well (Faraone & Tsuang, 1995).

(c) Twin studies

A subtype of family studies have been performed using twins. There are two types of twins: identical or monozygotic twins receive identical copies of their parents' DNA and thus share 100% of their genes in common. In contrast, fraternal or dizygotic twins are no more genetically alike than siblings and therefore share only 50% of their genes. If ADHD is strongly influenced by genetic factors then the risk to co-twins of ill probands should be greatest for MZ twins, and the risk for DZ twins should exceed the risk to controls but not that of siblings. Twin data are also used to estimate heritability, which measures the degree to which a disorder is influenced by genetic factors. Heritability ranges from zero to one with higher levels indicating a greater degree of genetic determination (see Chapter 7 for an in-depth review).

Several twin studies have provided evidence of genetic influence on hyperactive and inattentive symptom dimensions. Goodman and Stevenson (Goodman & Stevenson, 1989a, 1989b) found the heritability of hyperactivity to be 64%. In a re-analysis of these data, Stevenson (1992) reported that the heritability of mother-reported activity levels was 75%, with the heritability of a psychometric measure of attention at 76%. In a study of ADHD in twins who also had reading disability, Gilger, Pennington and DeFries (1992) estimated the heritability of attention-related behaviours to be 98%. In a study of 288 male twin pairs from the Minnesota Twin Family Study, Sherman and colleagues (Sherman, Iacono & McGue, 1997) examined inattentive and impulsive/hyperactive symptoms using both mother and teacher reports. Within both raters, the heritability of the impulsivity/hyperactivity dimension exceeded that of the inattention dimension, with mothers' ratings producing a heritability of 91% for impulsivity/hyperactivity and 69% for inattention and teacher ratings yielding a heritability of 69% for impulsivity/hyperactivity and 39% for inattention.

(d) Adoption studies

Like twinning, the occurrence of adoption provides another useful opportunity to evaluate the familiality of ADHD (Faraone & Tsuang, 1995) because unlike biological children, adoptive children can only confer risk via environmental influences. Thus, by examining both the adoptive and the biological relatives of ill probands, it is possible to dissociate genetic and environmental sources of familial transmission. Early studies showed that the adoptive relatives of hyperactive children are less likely to have hyperactivity or associated disorders than are the biological relatives of hyperactive children (Cantwell, 1975; Morrison & Stewart, 1973). In a more recent study, Sprich et al. (2000) found that the adoptive relatives of adopted ADHD probands had rates of ADHD and other associated disorders that were lower than those observed in the biological relatives of non-adopted ADHD probands and similar to those found in relatives of control probands. Biological relatives of ADHD children also do more poorly on standardised measures of attention than do adoptive relatives of ADHD children (Alberts-Corush, Firestone & Goodman, 1986). These data are consistent with the direct familial studies, lending further support to the concept of ADHD heritability.

10.2.2   FAMILIALITY OF PERSISTENT ADHD

If adult ADHD is valid, it would be expected that the children of ADHD adults would have an elevated prevalence of ADHD (Faraone & Tsuang, 1995; Faraone, Tsuang & Tsuang, 1999). This has been found by two family studies of adult ADHD (Manshadi et al., 1983; Biederman et al., 1995). These studies both produced the same intriguing result: the risk of ADHD among children of ADHD adults was much higher than the risk for ADHD among relatives of children with ADHD. For example, a 57% prevalence of ADHD among children of ADHD adults was found, a result which was much higher than the 15% prevalence of ADHD among siblings of ADHD children (Biederman et al., 1995). These results are somewhat counter-intuitive. If adult ADHD is an uncertain diagnosis, fraught with the difficulties of retrospective recall and self-referral biases, there should be more false positive cases of ADHD among adults than among children. If that were the case, then evidence for familial transmission should be lower in families sampled through adults compared with those sampled through children. The opposite is true.

The high familial loading of adult ADHD suggests that genes, or other familial risk factors, actually influence the etiology of remitting ADHD less than that of persistent ADHD. This 'persistence' hypothesis was tested in two ways. In a prospective study, 140 ADHD boys and 120 non-ADHD boys were examined at a baseline assessment and completed a four-year follow-up study. By mid-adolescence, 85% of the ADHD boys continued to have the disorder, while 15% remitted. The prevalence of ADHD was significantly higher among the relatives of persistent ADHD probands compared to relatives of remitted ADHD probands (Biederman et al., 1996). Parents of persistent ADHD probands were 20 times more likely to have ADHD than parents of controls whereas parents of non-persistent ADHD probands showed only a fivefold increased risk. Similarly, siblings of persistent ADHD probands were 17 times more likely to have ADHD than siblings of controls whereas siblings of non-persistent ADHD probands showed only a fourfold increased risk (Faraone, Biederman & Monuteaux, 2000). In a retrospective study, ADHD adolescents having retrospectively reported childhood onset ADHD were compared with ADHD children. The relatives of adolescent probands had higher rates of ADHD compared with the relatives of child probands (Biederman et al., 1998). Thus, a prospective study of children and a retrospective study of adolescents suggest that, when ADHD persists into adolescence and adulthood, it is highly familial.

Taken together, these data suggest that, from a familial perspective, not only is the adult ADHD diagnosis valid, but it might actually be more biologically proba-tive than the childhood diagnosis. This idea makes a straightforward prediction: when selecting families through ADHD children, the evidence for familial transmis-sion should be greater when examining the risk to adult relatives than it is when examining the risk to non-adult relatives. To test this prediction, Faraone, Biederman, Spencer et al. (2000) analysed ADHD symptom data collected by structured inter-views from the members of 280 ADHD and 242 non-ADHD families. For past and current symptoms, ADHD families showed significantly more familial aggregation for adult relatives than for non-adult relatives. The results were similar for inatten-tive and hyperactive-impulsive symptoms and for relatives with and without psychi-atric comorbidity.

Faraone, Biederman, Spencer *et al.* (2000) also considered the possibility that ADHD in children biases the self-reports of ADHD in their adult relatives. The adult relatives of ADHD children are usually aware of the ADHD symptoms in the proband child. That knowledge may bias them to report ADHD symptoms in themselves. If that occurs, then the rates of ADHD among adult relatives of ADHD children would be spuriously high, leading to the incorrect conclusion that adult ADHD is more familial than child ADHD. But if ADHD adults are biased to over-report symptoms, then the adult relatives of ADHD children should have had a greater number of symptoms than the child relatives. That was not the case. In fact, the adult relatives tended to report fewer symptoms, although the difference was not statistically significant.

This evidence against reporter bias is consistent with a prior report from a different sample even if the data cannot rule out the possibility of some biased reports of ADHD in adults. That study (Faraone, Biederman & Mick, 1997) hypothesised the following: If having an ADHD child biased an adult to report ADHD symptoms, then ADHD adults having ADHD children should have reported more symptoms than ADHD adults who did not have ADHD children. It compared symptom rates between 26 clinically referred ADHD adults who had ADHD children and 49 clinically referred ADHD adults who did not have ADHD children. It rejected the hypothesis by showing that the number of symptoms reported by ADHD adults did not differ between those who did and did not have ADHD children. An additional finding indicated that no individual symptom was more frequent among the ADHD adults who had ADHD children compared with those who did not have ADHD children. Moreover, having an ADHD child did not bias ADHD adults to over-report ADHD symptoms.

10.2.3 SEGREGATION ANALYSIS STUDIES

With these background data in hand regarding the rates of familiality of ADHD, it becomes possible to determine whether the occurrence of ADHD in multigenerational families appears to be transmitted according to standard Mendelian principles for single or multiple allele disorders. For example, if a disorder can be caused by a mutation in a single copy of a gene located on one of the first 22 chromosomes, it is said to be an autosomal dominant disorder. If only one parent carries the mutation, autosomal dominant diseases should occur in approximately half the children in any given generation. On the other hand, if two independent autosomal dominant mutations at different loci must be inherited to produce a disease, then only one-fourth of the offspring will be expected to show the trait, and the trait is said to be polygenic. In contrast to autosomal dominant mutations, if a disease is conferred in an autosomal recessive manner, then affected offspring must inherit a disease-causing allele from each parent. For both autosomal dominant and recessive illnesses, the expected incidence of the disease in each generation is further complicated by the degree of penetrance that disease alleles exhibit.

Major deviations from expected frequencies suggest alternative or mixed models. In ADHD, an early approach to determining the mode of inheritance of the disorder was reported by Morrison and Stewart (1974) who concluded that ADHD was a polygenic disorder, caused by inheritance of multiple disease causing alleles.

In contrast, Deutsch *et al.* (1990) reported evidence for a single dominant gene regulating the transmission of ADHD and minor physical anomalies in 48 families. Similarly, Faraone *et al.* (1992) also reported that the familial distribution of ADHD was consistent with the effects of a single major gene. Other similar findings have since been reported in a twin study by Eaves *et al.* (1997) and a pedigree study by Hess *et al.* (1995). The studies by Deutsch *et al.* and Faraone *et al.* favouring a single gene model predicted that only about 40% of children carrying the putative ADHD gene would develop ADHD. This finding, along with other features of the genetic epidemiology of ADHD, suggests that such a gene likely interacts with other genes and environmental factors to produce ADHD. Moreover the segregation studies indicate that about 2% of people without the ADHD gene would develop ADHD, suggesting that non-genetic forms of ADHD might exist.

10.3   MOLECULAR GENETIC STUDIES

Given the evidence for heritability and the promising segregation analysis results, much research is now devoted to trying to define the location and identity of the putative ADHD genes. To accomplish this, researchers have focused on three separate, but complementary methods: cytogenetic analysis, whole genome linkage analysis, and candidate gene analysis.

10.3.1   CYTOGENETIC STUDIES

Cytogenetic studies examine the physical appearance and number of chromosomes using specialised staining techniques, or the arrangement and copy number of specific genes along the length of these chromosomes with fluorescent probes. Changes in the number or gross structure of chromosomes such as in trisomy or monosomy usually lead to very early-onset disorders having severe clinical manifestations (e.g. mental retardation, gross physical anomalies, or neonatal lethality). While there have been no systematic studies of gross chromosomal anomalies in ADHD, there are several reports of these conditions being associated with hyperactivity and/or inattention in children. Examples include the Fragile-X syndrome, duplication of the Y-chromosome in boys, and loss of an X-chromosome in girls. In contrast to whole chromosome duplications and deletions, there is also a considerable body of evidence that partial deletions and duplications can lead to the production of behavioural syndromes (such as Prader-Willi syndrome or Velocardiofacial syndrome) which share some symptomatic overlap with ADHD. These associations are intriguing but rare. Thus, they can account for only a very small proportion of ADHD cases.

   In the absence of data implicating any gross chromosomal abnormalities in ADHD, researchers have turned to whole genome linkage analysis and candidate gene analysis. The genome scan examines all chromosomal locations without *a priori* predictions regarding what genes underlie susceptibility to ADHD. In contrast, the candidate gene approach examines one or more genes based upon some theory (hopefully backed by empirical evidence) about the nature of the disorder. Both approaches have yielded promising results.

10.3.2 WHOLE GENOME LINKAGE SCANS

In a typical whole genome scan, at least one generation of affected and unaffected individuals from multiple pedigrees are genotyped with a common set of markers. The markers are used to define the regions of chromosomes that are shared by individuals with the disease, and not shared by the subjects without the disease. The regions which are shared among affected individuals are said to be linked. The standard measure of significance in a linkage study is the LOD score, which is the logarithm of the odds favouring linkage compared to no linkage. To date, there have been only a small number of published whole genome scans of ADHD (see Table 10.1). In one of the first studies, involving 126 sib-pairs, LOD scores exceeding 1.5 were reported for regions on 5p12, 10q26, 12q23, and 16p13. In a follow-up study of 203 families, a LOD score of 4.2 implicated a susceptibility locus for ADHD in 12-cM region on chromosome 16p13 (Smalley *et al.*, 2002), and a further analysis of 270 total families produced a LOD score of 2.98 on 17p11 (Ogdie *et al.*, 2003). In contrast to these findings, a separate study (Bakker *et al.*, 2003) involving 164 affected sib pairs reported LOD scores of 3.04 on 7p, 2.05 on 9q, and 3.54 on 15q. Finally, a third separate study (Arcos-Burgos *et al.*, 2004) analysed 16 multigenerational pedigrees and reported individual pedigree LOD scores of 1.72 for 2q37, 2.41 for 5q33.3, 1.72 for 8p23, 1.67 for 9q33, 2.45 for 11q22, 2.83 for 17p11, 1.73 for 18p and 1.72 for 19p13.2.

Although it is premature to draw definitive conclusions from these whole genome scans, there are suggestions of shared genetic liability for ADHD in at least two separate populations on 17p11. In a few of these studies, the authors attempted to identify candidate genes, based on their known functions in the brain. We

Table 10.1. Neurotransmission genes implicated by whole genome scans of ADHD

Study	Region	LOD	Potential genes of interest at these loci
Columbia[3]	5q33.3	2.4	MEGF protein, Sorting nexing 24, Synphilin
Netherlands[2]	7p13	3.0	Dopa decarboxylase, Cordon-bleu homolog
Netherlands[2]	9q33	2.1	DA beta hydroxylase, LIM homeobox 6
Columbia[3]	11q22	2.5	APP beta-secretase, Down syndrome cell adhesion molecule like-protein 1b,
USA[1]	12p13	2.6	Neurotrophin 3, Synaptobrevin 1, ERC protein 1, Betaine/GABA transporter
Netherlands[2]	15q15	3.5	Nicotinic receptor alpha 7 subunit, Connexin-36, Meis2, SNAP23, MAP1A
USA[1]	16p13	3.7	Nudel, Stannin, NMDA2A receptor
USA[1]	17p11	3.0	Peripheral myelin protein 22, Tektin 3, Adenosine A2b receptor, Nuclear receptor co-repressor
Columbia[3]	17p11	2.8	

1. UCLA study of 270 sib-pairs (Ogdie *et al.*, 2003)
2. Dutch study of 164 sib-pairs (Bakker *et al.*, 2003)
3. Columbian study of 14 three-generation pedigrees (Arcos-Burgos *et al.*, 2004)
Source: adapted from Faraone *et al.*, 2006.

independently reviewed the genes in each of these reported linkage regions and identified several we feel might be most critical to consider because they are known to be involved in the development of the brain, are expressed at moderate to high levels in the forebrain, or are involved in neurotransmission of neurotransmitter metabolism (Table 10.1). Notably, at each of the loci, there were actually several genes which met these criteria. Some of these genes are critically involved in catecholamine or cholinergic signalling or are related to the candidate genes discussed in the next section.

10.3.3　CANDIDATE GENE STUDIES

In contrast to the relatively few whole genome scans of ADHD, there have been numerous candidate gene studies of ADHD published to date, and some of these are also beginning to yield tantalising clues regarding the causes of the disorder. These studies were initially driven by the pathophysiological theories about ADHD, much of which derives from the large pharmacotherapy literature about the disorder. Drugs that effectively treat ADHD are either dopamine reuptake inhibitors (e.g. the stimulants) or norepinephrine reuptake inhibitors (e.g. tricyclic antidepressants, atomoxetine). In contrast, drugs that work in the nicotinic system have a less robust therapeutic effect, and those that are primarily serotonergic are not helpful for ADHD patients.

In performing a case-control association study, investigators test for changes in the distribution of allele frequencies in a group of unrelated ADHD subjects compared to a matched group of unrelated control subjects. Generally, in a well-balanced study, it is possible to achieve significant results with allele frequency changes of 10% or greater, or two-fold increases in the frequency of rare alleles in the affected subjects. The other manner of performing candidate gene association studies is family-based, and involves looking across large sets of genotyped parents and offspring for evidence of overtransmission of specific alleles to affected subjects. In this case, the transmitted to untransmitted ratio is often the most informative.

According to a survey of family-based and case-control studies, the strongest findings to date have been reported for the monoamine oxidase A gene, the SNAP-25 gene, the 5HT-1B gene, some of the nicotinic receptor genes (particularly alpha 4), three genes involved in DA signalling or metabolism, the DRD4 and DRD5 receptors, and the DA transporter gene (see review by Faraone et al., 2001; LaHoste et al., 1996). In addition to these neurotransmitter-related genes, Hauser et al. (1993) demonstrated that a rare familial form of ADHD is associated with generalised resistance to thyroid hormone (GRTH), a disease caused by mutations in the thyroid receptor-b gene. The thyroid receptor-b gene cannot, however, account for many cases of ADHD because the prevalence of GRTH disease is very low among ADHD patients (1 in 2500) (Weiss et al., 1993) and, among GRTH pedigrees, the association between ADHD and the thyroid receptor-b gene has not been consistently found (Weiss et al., 1994).

Faraone and colleagues (2005) recently reviewed the results of all major case-control and family-based candidate gene association studies and determined that only a small number of genes have shown significant findings in three or more studies. These genes (listed in Table 10.2) include the Dopamine D4 receptor, the

Table 10.2. Pooled odds ratios for gene variants examined in three or more association studies

Gene	N Studies	Sample Size	OR	95% CI
FB: DRD4 (VNTR, 7-repeat)	17	1112 Inf. Trans	1.16	1.03–1.31
CC: DRD4 (VNTR, 7-repeat)	13	1910 cases, 5614 cntrls	1.45	1.27–1.65
FB: DRD5 (CA repeat, 148 bp)	14	1980 Inf. Trans	1.24	1.12–1.38
FB: SLC6A3 (VNTR, 10-repeat)	14	1765 Inf. Trans	1.13	1.03–1.24
FB: DBH (TaqI A)n	3	476 Inf. Trans	1.33	1.11–1.59
FB: SNAP25 (T1065G)	5	731 Inf. Trans	1.19	1.03–1.38
CC: SLC6A4 (5HTTLPR long)	3	386 cases, 818 cntrls	1.31	1.09–1.59
FB: HTR1B (G861C)	2	281 Inf. Trans	1.44	1.14–1.83

CC = Case Control, FB = Family-Based; OR = Odds Ratio; Inf. Trans = Informative transmissions
Source: adapted from Faraone *et al.*, 2005.

Dopamine D5 receptor, the Dopamine transporter gene, the Dopamine beta-hydroxylase gene, the Serotonin transporter gene, the Serotonin HTR1B receptor, and a gene involved in synaptic vesicle fusion and release – SNAP25.

(a) DRD4

The gene most strongly implicated in ADHD above all else is the D4 dopamine receptor gene (DRD4). In their analysis Faraone *et al.* reported that, despite some variation across studies, when data from analyses of the exon III polymorphism are pooled, the association with ADHD remains statistically significant (case-control odds ratio = 1.45 (95% CI 1.27–1.65); family based OR = 1.16 (95% CI 1.03–1.31). In addition to the VNTR, a small number of studies have assessed other DRD4 polymorphisms, but these data have not been conclusive.

These molecular genetic data are bolstered by other considerations suggesting that DRD4 is relevant for ADHD. Notably, both noradrenaline and dopamine are potent agonists of DRD4 (Lanau *et al.*, 1997). In vitro studies had found DRD4-7 to mediate a blunted response to dopamine (Van Tol *et al.*, 1992; Asghari *et al.*, 1995), although the biological significance for ADHD is not clear given the small effects found in these studies (Paterson, Sunohara & Kennedy, 1999). In addition, the distribution of DRD4 mRNA in the brain suggests it plays a role in cognitive and emotional functions, functions implicated in the pathophysiology of ADHD (Paterson, Sunohara & Kennedy, 1999).

A link between DRD4 and one of the core features of ADHD, hyperactivity, was implicated by a knockout mouse study. When that study disabled DRD4 in a knock-out mouse model, dopamine synthesis increased in the dorsal striatum and the mice showed locomotor supersensitivity to ethanol, cocaine, and methamphetamine. (Rubinstein *et al.*, 1997). DRD4 knockout mice also show reduced novelty-related exploration (Dulawa *et al.*, 1999), which is consistent with human data suggesting a role for DRD4 in novelty-seeking behaviours.

(b) DAT

The dopamine transporter gene (DAT) was initially considered a suitable candidate for ADHD because stimulant medications are known to block the transporter as one mechanisms of action for achieving their therapeutic effects (Spencer, Biederman & Wilens, 2000). Using a family-based association study, Cook *et al.* (1995) first reported an association between ADHD and the 480-bp allele of a DAT1VNTR polymorphism located in the 3′ untranslated region. Waldman's pooled analysis of all family-based studies showed a statistically significant effect (Waldman, 2001) while the several ensuing studies of this gene were individually inconclusive.

Barr *et al.* (2001) examined additional polymorphisms in intron 9 and exon 9 in 102 nuclear families with an ADHD proband. When tested individually, they did not find significant evidence for the biased transmission of the alleles of either the VNTR or the other polymorphisms. There was a trend for the biased transmission of the 480-bp allele of the VNTR. When they tested haplotypes comprising the three polymorphisms, they found significant biased transmission of one of the haplotypes that included the 480-bp VNTR allele.

In mice, eliminating DAT gene function through the knockout procedure leads to two features suggestive of ADHD: hyperactivity and deficits in inhibitory behaviour. Moreover, the DAT knockout mouse shows reductions in hyperactivity with stimulant treatment (Giros *et al.*, 1996; Gainetdinov *et al.*, 1999). Similar findings were seen in DAT knockdown model in which DAT activity was reduced to 10 percent of normal (Zhuang *et al.*, 2001). These mouse models show the potential complexities of gene-disease associations. The loss of the DAT gene has many biological effects: increased extracellular dopamine, a doubling of the rate of dopamine synthesis (Gainetdinov *et al.*, 1998), decreased dopamine and tyrosine hydoxylase in striatum (Jaber *et al.*, 1999), and a nearly complete loss of functioning of dopamine autoreceptors (Jones *et al.*, 1999). Because ADHD is believed to be a hypodopaminergic disorder, it is the decreased striatal dopamine that may be most relevant to the disorder.

In humans, Dougherty *et al.* (1999) measured dopamine transporter density in striatum by single photon emission computed tomography (SPECT) with the Iodine-123-labelled altropane. They found the dopamine transporter to be elevated by about 70% in ADHD adults. This finding was replicated by Krause *et al.* (2000) using a different ligand ([Tc-99m]TRODAT-1). These authors also showed that after treatment with methylphenidate (a stimulant used therapeutically with ADHD), ligand binding to the DAT was reduced to normal levels. In contrast, van Dyck *et al.* (van Dyck *et al.*, 2002) did not find altered dopamine transporter levels in a SPECT study of ADHD adults as assessed by striatal [(123)I]beta-CIT binding.

(c) DRD5

Kirley *et al.* (2001) presented a pooled analysis of five family-based studies examining the association between ADHD and the 148bp variant of DRD5. Not all studies find a significant association, yet all report an odds ratio greater than 1.0. As a group, the meta-analysis concludes that there is a statistically significant association.

Notably, the DRD5 148bp allele has also been associated with oppositional defiant disorder (Vanyukov *et al.*, 2000), which is diagnosed in more than half of clinically referred ADHD children (Biederman, Newcorn & Sprich, 1991).

Four human studies of ADHD have examined the catechol-O-methyltransferase (COMT) gene, the product of which is involved in the breakdown of dopamine and norepinephrine. One study (Eisenberg *et al.*, 1999) found that ADHD was associated with the Val allele, while others have found no association between the COMT polymorphism and ADHD in Irish (Hawi *et al.*, 2000), Turkish (2000) and Canadian (Barr *et al.*, 1999) samples. The positive finding is intriguing despite the negative finding because the Val allele leads to high COMT activity and an increased breakdown of catecholamines.

(d) MAO

Another study (Jiang *et al.*, 2000) found an association with the DXS7 locus of the X chromosome, a marker for MAO which encode enzymes that metabolise dopamine and other neurotransmitters. Finally, Comings and colleagues (Comings *et al.*, 1999) revealed associations and additive effects of polymorphisms at three noradrenergic genes (the adrenergic alpha 2A, adrenergic alpha 2C, and dopamine-beta-hydroxylase) on ADHD symptoms in a sample of individuals with Tourette's syndrome. They discovered no association between the tyrosine hydroxylase gene and ADHD in this sample (Comings *et al.*, 1995).

(e) SNAP-25

Some investigators have used the coloboma mouse model to investigate the genetics of ADHD. These mice have the coloboma mutation, a hemizygous two centimorgan deletion of a segment on chromosome 2q that includes the gene encoding SNAP-25, a neuron-specific protein involved in neurtransmitter vesicle transport and release. The mutation leads to spontaneous hyperactivity (which is reversed by stimulants), delays in achieving complex neonatal motor abilities, deficits in hippocampal physiology, possibly contributing to learning deficiencies, and deficits in Ca2+-dependent dopamine release in dorsal striatum (Wilson, 2000). Hess *et al.* (1992) suggested that interference with SNAP-25 might mediate the mouse's hyperactivity. As predicted by this hypothesis, when these investigators bred a SNAP-25 transgene into coloboma mice, their hyperactivity was reduced. Other work further suggested that reduced SNAP-25 expression leads to striatal dopamine and serotonin deficiencies, which may be involved in hyperactivity (Raber *et al.*, 1997).

Hess *et al.* (1995) tested the idea that the human homolog of the mouse coloboma gene could be responsible for ADHD by completing linkage studies of ADHD families using markers on human chromosome 20p11-p12, which is syntenic to the coloboma deletion region. They used five families for which segregation analysis suggested that ADHD was due to a sex-influenced, single gene. No significant linkage was detected between ADHD and markers on chromosome 20p11–p12 through this analysis. In contrast, Barr *et al.* (2000) reported a positive association between ADHD and SNAP-25.

(f) 5HTR

Compared with dopaminergic and noradrenergic systems, serotonergic systems have received relatively little attention in ADHD research. This is due to the fact that measures of serotonin metabolism are minimally related to the clinical efficacy of the medicines which treat ADHD (Zametkin & Rapoport, 1987), and serotonergic drugs are not efficacious for treating ADHD (Spencer, Biederman & Wilens, 2000). Nonetheless, some evidence does implicate serotonin in this disorder. For example, as previously mentioned, Gainetdinov et al. (1999) showed that DAT knockout mice showed decreased locomotion in response to stimulants. However, they also demonstrated that the effects of stimulants on these mice were mediated by serotonergic neurotransmission. In another study, mice lacking the 5HT1B receptor showed reduced anxiety and remained hyperactive throughout their life (Brunner et al., 1999). Building on these data, Hawi (2001) presented a meta-analysis of five family-based studies examining the association between ADHD and the 861G variant of a 5HT1B gene polymorphisms. Although only one study found a significant association, three of four reported an odds ratio greater than 1.0 and, as a group, the meta-analysis concludes that there is a statistically significant association.

10.4 ANIMAL MODEL STUDIES

10.4.1 LOW-DOSE MPTP-TREATED MONKEYS

Given profiles of drugs that treat ADHD and the positive associations, it is not surprising that the dopaminergic and noraderenegic systems have received the most attention in animal models of ADHD. One approach has been the use of 6-hydroxy-dopamine to lesion dopamine pathways in developing rats. Because these lesions created hyperactivity, they were thought to provide an animal model of ADHD (Shaywitz, Cohen, & Shaywitz, 1978). Disruption of catecholaminergic transmission with chronic low-dose N-methyl-4-phenyl-1,2,3,6-tetrahydropyridine (MPTP), a neurotoxin, creates an animal model of ADHD in monkeys. In this latter work, MPTP administration to monkeys caused cognitive impairments on tasks thought to require efficient frontal-striatal neural networks, the same networks implicated in ADHD (Faraone & Biederman, 1998). These cognitive impairments mirrored those seen in monkeys with frontal lesions, and occur in the absence of prominent motor impairments seen with higher doses of MPTP (Schneider & Kovelowski, 1990; Schneider & Roeltgen, 1993). Like ADHD children, MPTP-treated monkeys show attention deficits and task impersistence. Methylphenidate and the dopamine D2 receptor agonist LY-171555 reverse the behavioural deficits but not the cognitive dysfunction (Roeltgen & Schneider, 1994; Schneider, Sun & Roeltgen, 1994).

10.4.2 SHR RAT

Several investigators have also used the spontaneously hypertensive rat (SHR) as an animal model of ADHD due to the SHR's locomotor hyperactivity and impaired discriminative performance. Studies using SHR have implicated dopaminergic and noradrenergic systems. For example, the dopamine D2 receptor agonist, quinpirole, caused significantly greater inhibition of DA release from caudate-putamen but not from nucleus accumbens or prefrontal cortex slices in SHR compare with control mice (Russell *et al.*, 1995). In another study dopamine release secondary to electrical stimulation was significantly lower in caudate-putamen and prefrontal cortex slices of SHR compared with control mice. These findings were attributed to increased autoreceptor-mediated inhibition of dopamine release in caudate-putamen slices but not in the prefrontal cortex. Another study showed that the altered presynaptic regulation of dopamine in SHR led to the down regulation of the dopamine system (Russell *et al.*, 2000). The authors hypothesised that this may have occurred early in development as a compensatory response to abnormally high DA concentrations.

Other SHR studies have implicated an interaction between the noradrenergic and dopaminergic system in the nucleus accumbens, but have ruled out the idea that a dysfunctional locus coeruleus and A2 nucleus impairs dopaminergic transmission in the nucleus accumbens via alpha 2-adrenoceptor mediated inhibition of dopamine release (de Villiers *et al.*, 1995). Papa *et al.* (1998) used molecular neuroanatomical techniques to assess the neural substrates of ADHD-like behaviours in the SHR rat. Their data showed the cortico-striato-pallidal system to mediate these behaviours. King *et al.* (2000) showed that exposure to excess androgen levels early in development led to decreased catecholamine innervation in frontal cortex and enhanced expression of ADHD-like behaviours. Carey *et al.* (1998) used quantitative receptor autoradiography and computer-assisted image analysis to show a higher density of low affinity D1 and D5 dopamine receptors in the caudate-putamen, the nucleus accumbens and the olfactory tubercle of SHR. Stimulant treatment normalised these receptors by decreasing the number of binding sites and increasing affinity to the control level.

10.5 INTEGRATING GENETIC DATA WITH NEUROIMAGING DATA IN A NEUROANATOMICAL CONTEXT

There are now considerable data implicating dopaminergic, adrenergic, and cholinergic systems, as well as synaptic transmission machinery, in the pathophysiology and possibly the pathogenesis of ADHD. In order to provide a framework for interpreting these data, we recently reviewed the molecular genetic and neuroimaging data on ADHD (Faraone *et al.* (in presss); Table 10.3). Interestingly, among the brain areas most consistently implicated in both structural and functional brain imaging studies are regions of the prefrontal cortex, basal ganglia, and cerebellum which are interconnected via polysynaptic frontal-subcortical circuits (Figure 10.1; reviewed in Middleton & Strick, 2000).

In simplest terms, both the basal ganglia and cerebellum can be said to consist of an 'input layer' of processing, that receives direct or second-order projections from the cerebral cortex, and an 'output layer' of processing that projects back to the cerebral cortex via the thalamus. Moreover, the information from most cortical areas remains largely segregated in through the subsequent stages of processing in the basal ganglia and cerebellum and thus can be said to form parallel anatomical

Table 10.3. Neuroimaging studies implicating frontal subcortical circuits in ADHD

Study	Diagnosis	Method	Findings
Nasrallah *et al.* (1986)	HYP n = 24	CT	sulcal widening, cerebellar atrophy
Aylward *et al.* (1996)	ADHD+TS n = 10 (pure)	MRI	smaller left globus pallidus
Singer *et al.* (1993)	ADHD+TS n = 18	MRI	smaller left globus pallidus
Castellanos *et al.* (1996)	ADHD n = 57	MRI	smaller right prefrontal cortex, right right caudate, globus pallidus; and cerebellum
Filipek *et al.* (1997)	ADHD n = 15	MRI	smaller left caudate, right frontal cortex, and bilateral peribasal ganglia and parietal-occipital regions
Castellanos *et al.* (1994)	ADHD n = 50	MRI	smaller caudate, caudate asymmetry
Mataro *et al.* (1997)	ADHD n = 11	MRI	smaller left caudate, larger right caudate
Berquin *et al.* (1998)	ADHD n = 46	MRI	smaller cerebellar posterior vermis (lobules VIII–X)
Mostofsky *et al.* (1998)	ADHD n = 12	MRI	smaller cerebellar posterior vermis (lobules VIII–X)
Semrud-Clikeman *et al.* (2000)	ADHD n = 10	MRI	reversed asymmetry of the caudate, smaller left caudate, and smaller right frontal lobe
Castellanos *et al.* (2001)	ADHD n = 50	MRI	smaller cerebellar posterior vermis (lobules VIII–X)
Castellanos *et al.* (2002)	ADHD n = 152	MRI	ADHD associated with smaller brain volumes in all regions. Volume differences were unrelated to stimulant treatment
Sowell ER *et al.* (2003)	ADHD n = 27	MRI	reduced size in dorsal PFC and anterior temporal cortex, increased size of posterior temporal and inferior parietal cortices
Castellanos *et al.* (2003)	ADHD, MZ twins 9 discordant pairs	MRI	reduced size of caudate in affected twin
Lou *et al.* (1984)	ADD n = 11	rCBF	hypoperfusion in frontal cortex and caudate, hyperperfusion in occipital cortex
Lou *et al.* (1989)	ADHD n = 6 pure/18 total	rCBF	hypoperfusion in right striatal region, hyperperfusion in occipital cortex, left sensorimotor and primary auditory regions
Lou *et al.* (1990)	ADHD n = 9 pure/17 total	rCBF	hypoperfusion – striatal and posterior periventricular regions, hyperperfusion – visual, sensorimotor and auditory regions

Table 10.3. *Continued*

Study	Diagnosis	Method	Findings
Amen *et al.* (1997)	ADHD n = 54	SPECT	decreased perfusion in the prefrontal cortex with intellectual stress
Gustafsson (2000)	ADHD n = 28	SPECT	low rCBF in the temporal and cerebellar regions and high rCBF in the subcortical and thalamic regions
Kim *et al.* (2002)	ADHD n = 40	SPECT	decreased blood flow in lateral PFC, middle temporal cortex, orbital PFC, cerebellar cortex, some parietal and occipital areas
Zametkin *et al.* (1990)	ADHD n = 19 pure/25 total	PET	lower glucose metabolism in premotor, dorsal prefrontal cortex, right thalamus, caudate, hippocampus and cingulate
Schweitzer *et al.* (2003)	ADHD n = 10	PET	subjects off MPH had increases in rCBF bilaterally in the precentral gyri, left caudate nucleus, and right claustrum; subjects on MPH had increased rCBF in the cerebellar vermis
Ernst *et al.* (1998)	ADHD n = 17	PET ^{F18}DOPA	decreased medial and left prefrontal DA metabolism in adults (but not striatum or nigra)
Ernst *et al.* (1999)	ADHD n = 10	PET ^{F18}DOPA	increased DOPA decarboxylase activity in midbrain of 10 children
Vaidya *et al.* (1998)	ADHD n = 10	fMRI	greater frontal activation and reduced striatal activation on go/no go tasks; reversed by MPH
Rubia *et al.* (1999)	ADHD n = 7	fMRI	during go/no go task, reduced activity of right mesial prefrontal cortex, right inferior prefrontal cortex and left caudate
Jin *et al.* (2001)	ADHD n = 12	PMRS	neuronal loss and/or dysfunction around globus pallidus, affecting cholinergic projections

and functional circuits (Middleton & Strick, 2000). For example, the dorsal prefrontal cortex is known to project to neurons in the dorsomedial pontine nuclei, that subsequently innervate crus II and the posterior vermis in the cerebellar cortex. These regions of the cerebellar cortex, in turn, innervate the ventral dentate nucleus, which projects, via the thalamus, back to the dPFC, thus completing a closed loop circuit that can subserve cognitive functions.

When considering all of the structural and functional imaging data on ADHD, it is striking how consistently abnormalities in the various components of this frontal-subcortical circuitry have been reported. Interestingly, superimposed on this circuitry at the level of the input layer of processing for both the basal ganglia and

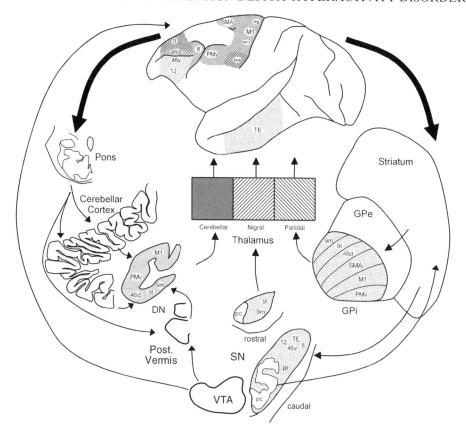

Figure 10.1 Frontal-subcortical circuits involving the basal ganglia and cerebellum

Note: Information from cortical areas to the basal ganglia and cerebellum is maintained in anatomically distinct circuits. Some areas have circuits with either the basal ganglia or cerebellum, while others have circuits with both. DA modulates both types of circuitry (via the SNpc and VTA), as do noradrenergic and cholinergic inputs (not shown). Numbers indicate cortical areas. Cross-hatching of different cortical areas indicates their participation in loops with the globus pallidus, substantia nigra, dentate nucleus, or a combination of these, based on anatomical tracing studies in non-human primates (reviewed in Middleton & Strick, 2000). We point out that many of these structures have been reported to display structural or functional changes in ADHD subjects.

Abbreviations: 8, area 8 (frontal eye field); 9l, lateral area 9; 9m, medial area 9; 12, area 12 (lateral orbitofrontal cortex); 46d, dorsal area 46; 46v, ventral area 46; DN, dentate; GPe, external globus pallidus; GPi, internal globus pallidus; IP, interpositus nucleus; M1, primary motor cortex; PMv, ventral premotor area; SMA, supplementary motor area; SNpr, substantia nigra pars reticulata; SNpc, substantia nigra pars compacta; TE, area TE of inferotemporal cortex; VTA, ventral tegmental area.

cerebellum, there is an often overlooked feature that involves common modulatory influences by mesencephalic dopamine (DA) neurons. It is well known that the pars compacta cells of the substantia nigra (SNpc) provide the major source of DA for the striatum and other basal ganglia nuclei, and that dysfunction of this input produces much of the symptomatology of Parkinson's disease. On the other hand, DA neurons adjacent to the SNpc – in the ventral tegmental area (VTA) – have prominent projections to the cerebral cortex and also the posterior vermis in non-human primates (see Lewis *et al.*, 1988; Melchitzky & Lewis, 2000). In fact, in the human cerebellum, the posterior vermis lobules VIII, IX, and X (pyramis, uvula, and nodulus) comprise the major target for innervation by DA fibres from the VTA. Such fibres display mossy fibre-like projections that pass into the granule layer, and appear to ramify on Purkinje cells. At the level of the cerebral cortex, the DA inputs are richest to area 9 in the dPFC, and are themselves strongly modulated during adolescent development (Rosenberg & Lewis, 1995).

Along with the strong DA modulation of prefrontal-subcortical circuits, the noradrenergic and cholinergic projection systems are also positioned to modulate the same circuitry reviewed above, and do so with a similar bias in their distribution. Thus, much of the prefrontal-subcortical brain circuitry most involved in formal cognitive function and response inhibition is strongly modulated at nearly every level by the same systems which appear to be so heavily involved in ADHD. We have previously proposed (Faraone *et al.*, in press) that the PFC normally exerts control over the premotor areas and participates in subcortical circuits that facilitate response selection (basal ganglia) and error detection (cerebellum), but that in ADHD, primary or secondary PFC dysfunction leads to less control of motor outputs and impaired cognitive performance. By virtue of the prominent DA innervation of the prefrontal-subcortical circuitry, however, boosting PFC function through enhancement of DA transmission is possible at multiple levels.

In view of the obvious relevance of the underlying circuitry for explaining some of the localised findings reported in neuroimaging studies in ADHD, we have wondered whether any of the putative ADHD candidate genes discussed in this review show any relationship in their expression pattern with the underlying circuitry that supports cognitive function. We analysed this in two general means. First, we reviewed and analysed all published reports where the expression patterns of the genes in question were easily obtained and interpreted (Table 10.4). And secondly, we have begun to employ gene expression profiling of anatomically disected brain regions in the non-human primate. The first analysis indicated clear evidence for the presence of several of the putative ADHD candidate genes within multiple regions of the PFC, basal ganglia, and cerebellum (Table 10.4). The results of our second analysis, focused on expression levels of 20 different ADHD candidate genes within the cerebellar circuitry are presented in Figure 10.2. Notably, only those genes with strong modulation in at least one region are shown. Other genes (e.g. DRD4, CHRNA7) displayed no difference in expression between motor and cognitive regions. We note that several of the putative ADHD candidate genes show apparent enrichment in cognitive circuitry (e.g. 5HTR1B, 5HT transporter, and Thyroid receptor b) while others are clearly enriched in motor components of this circuitry (e.g. SNAP-25 and MAO-A). While preliminary, one of the predictions that derives from this work is that mutations or dysregulation of the genes that are specifically enriched in cognitive circuitry could produce profound cognitive impairments, while impairments in genes with higher levels of expression in motor circuits should produce more of an apparent effect on motor function. Likewise, pharmacological modulation of gene products that are specifically enriched in the

Table 10.4. Distribution patterns of selected candidate genes in prefrontal-subcortical circuits

	PFC	Basal Ganglia	Cerebellum
Thyroid receptor-b	High cingulated cortex	unknown	High levels of ThyR-b in vermis, ventral dentate nucleus
DRD3	Islets of Calleja; anterior cingulate	Accumbens; SNpc	Highest in vermis, lobules VIII–X
DRD4*	Pyramidal cells; modulate NMDA responses	Striatonigral, striatopallidal projection neurons; SNpc	Molecular layer and white matter
DRD5*	Pyramidal cells	Striosome and matrix projection neurons; SNpc	Molecular layer
DAT*	Many layers – esp. III	SNpc; lateral striatal components > medial	Vermis lobules VIII–X, adjacent to Purkinje cells
DBH*	Dorsomedial convexity (incl. areas 8B, 9, 24) highest, layer V highest	Core and shell of accumbens; globus pallidus	Locus coeruleus projections dense to vermis
Alpha 2 Adrenergic	Cingulate, orbital PFC, layer VI cells	GP, SN, striatum, accumbens	Transient expression in granule cells
HTR-1B*	Cingulate – upper layers	Striatal cells; ventral striatum in opioid positive striosomes	Purkinje cells (PCs)
Nicotinic AchR	Cingulate-moderate, low elsewhere	Moderate – low in caudate and putamen	High alpha 7, beta 2, moderate alpha 4, present in PCs and GCs

*genes that also show strong evidence for association in ADHD.

cognitive circuitry should be expected to boost cognitive function without affecting motor function.

10.6 SUMMARY

We have reviewed the evidence obtained from a large number of studies which clearly indicate there is a strong genetic component to ADHD in general and adult ADHD in particular. Genome-wide linkage studies and candidate gene association studies both implicate some of the same genes and chromosomal 'hotspots' as potentially harbouring disease causing alleles. Examination of the patterns of gene expression of several of the putative ADHD candidate genes indicates that their dysfunction could be expected to produce localised effects on either the cognitive or motor components of different frontal subcortical loops which have been

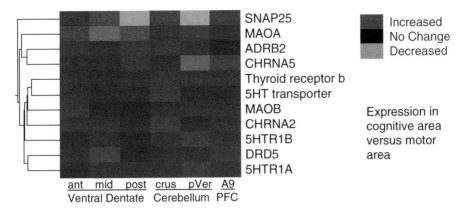

SNAP25
MAOA
ADRB2
CHRNA5
Thyroid receptor b
5HT transporter
MAOB
CHRNA2
5HTR1B
DRD5
5HTR1A

■ Increased
■ No Change
■ Decreased

Expression in
cognitive area
versus motor
area

ant   mid   post   crus   pVer   A9
Ventral Dentate   Cerebellum   PFC

Figure 10.2 The relative expression of putative ADHD candidate genes in cerebello-prefrontal circuitry that is involved in attention and cognitive function and the target of dense cholinergic and dopaminergic innervation

Note: Each of the expression levels in these cognitive regions is normalized relative to the levels in matching cortical and subcortical areas that subserve purely motor function, through connections with the primary motor cortex (these areas include the anterior, middle and posterior portions of the dorsal dentate, the anterior medial cerebellar cortex, the anterior vermis, and the primary motor cortex itself. The colouring of these genes indicates the areas of high relative expression (red) or low relative expression (green) in these cognitive regions compared to the matching motor areas. We note that several of the putative ADHD candidate genes show apparent enrichment in cognitive circuitry (e.g. 5HTR1B, 5HT transporter, and Thyroid receptor b), while others are clearly enriched in motor components of this circuitry (e.g., SNAP-25 and MAO-A). A9, area 9 of PFC; ant, anterior; mid, middle; post, posterior; pVer, posterior vermis.

consistently implicated by ADHD neuroimaging studies. The cognitive loops, in particular, also show a striking bias of being modulated at many levels by dense dopaminergic and noradrenergic inputs. Thus, we appear to have come full circle in our view of ADHD. Clearly, more work is needed to continue to integrate the vast amounts of accumulating molecular genetic and neurobiological data in a comprehensive understanding of ADHD. However, from what we now know, it appears highly valid to consider ADHD as a neurobiological disorder in need of research into its cause.

10.7 REFERENCES

Alberts-Corush J, Firestone P, Goodman JT (1986) Attention and impulsivity characteristics of the biological and adoptive parents of hyperactive and normal control children. *American Journal of Orthopsychiatry* **56**(3): 413–23.

Amen D, Carmichael B (1997) High-resolution brain SPECT imaging in ADHD. *Annals of Clinical Psychiatry* **9**: 81–6.

Arcos-Burgos M, Castellanos FX, Pineda D *et al.* (2004) Attention-deficit/hyperactivity disorder in a population isolate: linkage to loci at 4q13.2, 5q33.3, 11q22, and 17p11. *American Journal of Human Genetics* **75**(6): 998–1014.

Asghari V, Sanyal S, Buchwaldt S *et al.* (1995) Modulation of intracellular cyclic AMP levels by different human dopamine D4 receptor variants. *Journal of Neurochemistry* **65**(3): 1157–65.

Aylward EH, Reiss AL, Reader MJ *et al.* (1996) Basal ganglia volumes in children with Attention-Deficit Hyperactivity Disorder. *Journal of Child Neurology* **11**: 112–15.

Bakker SC, van der Meulen EM, Buitelaar JK *et al.* (2003) A whole-genome scan in 164 Dutch sib pairs with Attention-Deficit/Hyperactivity Disorder: suggestive evidence for linkage on chromosomes 7p and 15q. *American Journal of Human Genetics* **72**: 1251–60.

Barr CL, Feng Y, Wigg K *et al.* (2000) Identification of DNA variants in the SNAP-25 gene and linkage study of these polymorphisms and Attention-Deficit Hyperactivity Disorder. *Molecular Psychiatry* **5**(4): 405–9.

Barr CL, Wigg K, Malone M *et al.* (1999) Linkage study of catechol-O-methyltransferase and Attention-Deficit Hyperactivity Disorder. *American Journal of Medical Genetics* **88**(6): 710–13.

Barr CL, Xu C, Kroft J *et al.* (2001) Haplotype study of four polymorphisms at the dopamine transporter locus confirm linkage to attention deficit hyperactivity disorder. *Biological Psychiatry* **49**(4): 333–9.

Berquin PC, Giedd JN, Jacobsen LK, Hamburger SD, Krain AL, Rapoport JL, Castellanos FX (1998) Cerebellum in attention-deficit hyperactivity disorder: a morphometric MRI study. *Neurology* **50**: 1087–93.

Biederman J, Faraone SV, Keenan K *et al.* (1990) Family-genetic and psychosocial risk factors in DSM-III attention deficit disorder. *Journal of the American Academy of Child and Adolescent Psychiatry* **29**(4): 526–33.

Biederman J, Faraone SV, Keenan K *et al.* (1992) Further evidence for family-genetic risk factors in attention deficit hyperactivity disorder. Patterns of comorbidity in probands and relatives in psychiatrically and pediatrically referred samples. *Archives of General Psychiatry* **49**(9): 728–38.

Biederman J, Faraone SV, Mick E *et al.* (1995) High risk for attention deficit hyperactivity disorder among children of parents with childhood onset of the disorder: a pilot study. *American Journal of Psychiatry* **152**: 431–5.

Biederman J, Faraone SV, Milberger S *et al.* (1996) Predictors of persistence and remission of ADHD: results from a four-year prospective follow-up study of ADHD children. *Journal of the American Academy of Child and Adolescent Psychiatry* **35**(3): 343–51.

Biederman J, Faraone SV, Taylor A *et al.* (1998). Diagnostic continuity between child and adolescent ADHD: findings from a longitudinal clinical sample. *Journal of the American Academy of Child and Adolescent Psychiatry* **37**(3): 305–13.

Biederman J, Mick E, Faraone SV (2000) Age-dependent decline of symptoms of attention deficit hyperactivity disorder: Impact of remission definition and symptom type. *American Journal of Psychiatry* **157**(5): 816–18.

Biederman J, Mick E, Faraone SV, Burback M (2001) Patterns of remission and symptom decline in conduct disorder: a four-year prospective study of an ADHD sample. *Journal of the American Academy of Child and Adolescent Psychiatry* **40**(3): 290–8.

Biederman J, Newcorn J, Sprich S (1991) Comorbidity of attention deficit hyperactivity disorder with conduct, depressive, anxiety, and other disorders. *American Journal of Psychiatry* **148**(5): 564–77.

Berquin PC, Giedd JN, Jacobsen LK *et al.* (1998) Cerebellum in Attention-Deficit Hyperactivity Disorder: a morphometric MRI study. *Neurology* **50**: 1087–93.

Brunner D, Buhot MC, Hen R, Hofer M (1999) Anxiety, motor activation, and maternal-infant interactions in 5HT1B knockout mice. *Behavioral Neuroscience* **113**(3): 587–601.

Cantwell DP (1972) Psychiatric illness in the families of hyperactive children. *Archives of General Psychiatry* **27**: 414–17.

Cantwell DP (1975) Genetics of hyperactivity. *Journal of Child Psychology and Psychiatry* **16**: 261–4.

Carey MP, Diewald LM, Esposito FJ *et al.* (1998) Differential distribution, affinity and plasticity of dopamine D-1 and D-2 receptors in the target sites of the mesolimbic system in an animal model of ADHD. *Behavioural Brain Research* **94**(1): 173–85.

Castellanos FX, Giedd JN, Berquin PC *et al.* (2001) Quantitative brain magnetic resonance imaging in girls with Attention-Deficit/Hyperactivity Disorder. *Archives of General Psychiatry* **58**: 289–95.

Castellanos FX, Giedd J, Eckburg P *et al.* (1994) Quantitative morphology of the caudate nucleus in attention deficit hyperactivity disorder. *Amercan Journal of Psychiatry* **151**: 1791–6.

Castellanos FX, Giedd J, Marsh W *et al.* (1996) Quantitative brain magnetic resonance imaging in attention deficit hyperactivity disorder. *Archives of General Psychiatry* **53**: 607–16.

Castellanos FX, Lee PP, Sharp W *et al.* (2002) Developmental trajectories of brain volume abnormalities in children and adolescents with Attention-Deficit/Hyperactivity Disorder. *Journal of the American Medical Association* **288**: 1740–8.

Castellanos FX, Sharp WS, Gottesman RF *et al.* (2003) Anatomic brain abnormalities in monozygotic twins discordant for attention deficit hyperactivity disorder. *American Journal of Psychiatry* **160**: 1693–6.

Comings D, Gade-Andavolu R, Gonzalez N *et al.* (1999) Additive effect of three naradenergic genes (ADRA2A, ADRA2C, DBH) on attention-deficit hyperactivity disorder and learning disabilities in Tourette syndrome subjects. *Clinical Genetics* **55**(3): 160–72.

Comings D, Gade R, Muhleman D, Sverd J (1995) No association of a tyrosine hydroxylase gene tetranucleotide repeat polymorphism in autism, Tourette Syndrome, or ADHD. *Biological Psychiatry* **37**(7): 484–6.

Cook EH, Stein MA, Krasowski MD *et al.* (1995) Association of attention deficit disorder and the dopamine transporter gene. *American Journal of Human Genetics* **56**: 993–8.

Deutsch CK, Matthysse S, Swanson JM, Farkas LG (1990) Genetic latent structure analysis of dysmorphology in attention deficit disorder. *Journal of the American Academy of Child and Adolescent Psychiatry* **29**: 189–94.

de Villiers AS, Russell VA, Sagvolden T *et al.* (1995) Alpha 2-adrenoceptor mediated inhibition of [3H]dopamine release from nucleus accumbens slices and monoamine levels in a rat model for Attention-Deficit Hyperactivity Disorder. *Neurochemical Research* **20**(4): 427–33.

Dougherty DD, Bonab AA, Spencer TJ *et al.* (1999) Dopamine transporter density is elevated in patients with ADHD. *Lancet* **354**(9196): 2132–3.

Dulawa SC, Grandy DK, Low MJ *et al.* (1999) Dopamine D4 receptor-knock-out mice exhibit reduced exploration of novel stimuli. *Journal of Neuroscience* **19**(21): 9550–6.

Eaves LJ, Silberg JL, Meyer JM, Maes HH, Simonoff E, Pickles A, Rutter M, Neale MC, Reynolds CA, Erikson MT, Heath AC, Loeber R, Truett KR, Hewitt JK (1997) Genetics and developmental psychopathology: 2. The main effects of genes and environment on behavioral problems in the Virginia Twin Study of Adolescent Behavioral Development. *Journal of Child Psychology and Psychiatry* **38**: 965–80.

Eisenberg J, Mei-Tal G, Steinberg A *et al.* (1999) Haplotype relative risk study of catechol-O-methyltransferase (COMT) and attention deficit hyperactivity disorder (ADHD): association of the high-enzyme activity Val allele with ADHD impulsive-hyperactive phenotype. *American Journal of Medical Genetics* **88**(5): 497–502.

Ernst M, Zametkin A, Matochik JA *et al.* (1998) DOPA decarboxylase activity in attention deficit hyperactivity disorder adults. a [fluorine-18]fluorodopa positron emission tomographic study. *Journal of Neuroscience* **18**: 5901–7.

Ernst M, Zametkin AJ, Matochik JA *et al.* (1999) High midbrain [18F]DOPA accumulation in children with attention deficit hyperactivity disorder. *American Journal of Psychiatry* **156**: 1209–15.

Faraone SV, Biederman J (1998) Neurobiology of Attention-Deficit Hyperactivity Disorder. *Biological Psychiatry* **44**(10): 951–8.

Faraone SV, Biederman J, Chen WJ *et al.* (1992) Segregation analysis of attention deficit hyperactivity disorder: Evidence for single genc transmission. *Psychiatric Genetics* **2**: 257–75.

Faraone SV, Biederman J, Feighner JA, Monuteaux MC (2000) Assessing symptoms of attention deficit hyperactivity disorder in children and adults: which is more valid? *Journal of Consulting and Clinical Psychology* **68**(5): 830–42.

Faraone S, Biederman J, Mick E (1997) Symptom reports by adults with attention deficit hyperactivity disorder: are they influenced by attention deficit hyperactivity disorder in their children? *Journal of Nervous and Mental Diseases* **185**(9): 583–4.

Faraone SV, Biederman J, Mick E *et al.* (2000) Family study of girls with attention deficit hyperactivity disorder. *American Journal of Psychiatry* **157**(7): 1077–83.

Faraone SV, Biederman J, Monuteaux MC (2000) Toward guidelines for pedigree selection in genetic studies of attention deficit hyperactivity disorder. *Genetic Epidemiology* **18**(1): 1–16.

Faraone SV, Biederman J, Spencer T *et al.* (2000) Attention deficit hyperactivity disorder in adults: an overview. *Biological Psychiatry* **48**(1): 9–20.

Faraone SV, Doyle AE (2001) The nature and heritability of Attention-Deficit/Hyperactivity Disorder. *Child and Adolescent Psychiatric Clinics of North America* **10**(2): 299–316, viii–ix.

Faraone SV, Doyle AE, Mick E, Biederman J (2001) Meta-analysis of the association between the dopamine D4 gene 7-repeat allele and attention deficit hyperactivity disorder. *American Journal of Psychiatry* **158**: 1052–7.

Faraone SV, Middleton FA, Biederman J (in press) An integrated neurobiological model of attention deficit hyperactivity disorder. In *ADHD Reference Book*. Veritas Institute for Medical Education.

Faraone, SV, Perlis RH, Doyle AE, Smoller JE, Goralnick JJ, Holmgren MA, Sklar P (2005) Molecular genetics of attention deficit hyperactivity disorder. *Biological Psychiatry* **57**: 1313–23.

Faraone SV, Tsuang MT (1995) Methods in Psychiatric Genetics. In M Tohen, MT Tsuang, GEP Zahner (eds) *Textbook in Psychiatric Epidemiology* (pp. 81–134). New York, NY: John Wiley.

Faraone SV, Tsuang D, Tsuang MT (1999) *Genetics and Mental Disorders: A Guide for Students, Clinicians, and Researchers*. New York, NY: Guilford.

Filipek PA, Semrud-Clikeman M, Steingrad R *et al.* (1997) Volumetric MRI analysis: comparing subjects having Attention-Deficit Hyperactivity Disorder with normal controls. *Neurology* **48**: 589–601.

Frick PJ, Lahey BB, Christ MG, Green S (1991) History of childhood behavior problems in biological relatives of boys with attention deficit hyperactivity disorder and conduct disorder. *Journal of Clinical Child Psychology* **20**(4): 445–51.

Gainetdinov RR, Jones SR, Fumagalli F *et al.* (1998) Re-evaluation of the role of the dopamine transporter in dopamine system homeostasis. *Brain Research. Brain Research Reviews* **26**(2–3): 148–53.

Gainetdinov RR, Wetsel WC, Jones SR *et al.* (1999) Role of serotonin in the paradoxical calming effect of psychostimulants on hyperactivity. *Science* **283**: 397–402.

Gilger JW, Pennington BF, DeFries C (1992) A twin study of the etiology of comorbidity: attention deficit hyperactivity disorder and dyslexia. *Journal of the American Academy of Child and Adolescent Psychiatry* **31**(2): 343–8.

Giros B, Jaber M, Jones SR *et al.* (1996) Hyperlocomotion and indifference to cocaine and amphetamine in mice lacking the dopamine transporter. *Nature* **379**(6566): 606–12.

Goodman R, Stevenson J (1989a) A twin study of hyperactivity: I. An examination of hyperactivity scores and categories derived from Rutter teacher and parent questionnaires. *Journal of Child Psychology and Psychiatry* **30**(5): 671–89.

Goodman R, Stevenson J (1989b) A twin study of hyperactivity: II. The aetiological role of genes, family relationships and perinatal adversity. *Journal of Child Psychology and Psychiatry* **30**(5): 691–709.

Gustafsson P, Thernlund G, Ryding E *et al.* (2000) Associations between cerebral blood-flow measured by single photon emission computed tomography (SPECT), electroencephalogram (EEG), behaviour symptoms, cognition and neurological soft signs in children with Attention-Deficit Hyperactivity Disorder (ADHD). *Acta Paediatrica* **89**: 830–5.

Hawi Z (2001) *The UK/Ireland study of 5HT1B polymorphisms.* Paper presented at the Third Annual ADHD Molecular Genetics Network Meeting, Boston, MA.

Hawi Z, Millar N, Daly G *et al.* (2000) No association between catechol-O-methyltransferase (COMT) gene polymorphism and attention deficit hyperactivity disorder (ADHD) in an Irish sample. *American Journal of Medical Genetics (Neuropsychiatric Genetics)* **96**: 282–4.

Hess EJ, Jinnah HA, Kozak CA, Wilson MC (1992) Spontaneous locomotor hyperactivity in a mouse mutant with a deletion including the Snap gene on chromosome 2. *Journal of Neuroscience* **12**(7): 2865–74.

Hess EJ, Rogan PK, Domoto M *et al.* (1995) Absence of linkage of apparently single gene mediated ADHD with the human syntenic region of the mouse mutant Coloboma. *American Journal of Medical Genetics* **60**(6): 573–9.

Jaber M, Dumartin B, Sagne C *et al.* (1999) Differential regulation of tyrosine hydroxylase in the basal ganglia of mice lacking the dopamine transporter. *European Journal of Neuroscience* **11**(10): 3499–511.

Jiang S, Xin R, Wu X *et al.* (2000) Association between attention deficit disorder and the DXS7 locus. *American Journal of Medical Genetics (Neuropsychiatric Genetics)* **96**: 289–92.

Jin Z, Zang YF, Zeng YW *et al.* (2001) Striatal neuronal loss or dysfunction and choline rise in children with Attention-Deficit Hyperactivity Disorder: a 1H-magnetic resonance spectroscopy study. *Neurosci Letters* **315**: 45–8.

Jones SR, Gainetdinov RR, Hu XT *et al.* (1999) Loss of autoreceptor functions in mice lacking the dopamine transporter. *National Neuroscience* **2**(7): 649–55.

Kim BN, Lee JS, Shin MS *et al.* (2002) Regional cerebral perfusion abnormalities in attention deficit/hyperactivity disorder. Statistical parametric mapping analysis. *European Archives of Psychiatry and Clinical Neuroscience* **252**: 219–25.

King JA, Barkley RA, Delville Y, Ferris CF (2000) Early androgen treatment decreases cognitive function and catecholamine innervation in an animal model of ADHD. *Behavioural Brain Research* **107**(1–2): 35–43.

Kirley A (2001) *The DRD5 gene and ADHD: The Case for a Collaboration.* Paper presented at the Third Annual ADHD Molecular Genetics Network Meeting, Boston, MA.

Krause K, Dresel SH, Krause J *et al.* (2000) Increased striatal dopamine transporter in adult patients with attention deficit hyperactivity disorder: effects of methylphenidate as measured by single photon emission computed tomography. *Neuroscience Letters* **285**(2): 107–10.

LaHoste GJ, Swanson JM, Wigal SB, Glabe C, Wigal T, King N, Kennedy JL (1996) Dopamine D4 receptor gene polymorphism is associated with attention deficit hyperactivity disorder. *Molecular Psychiatry* **1**: 121–4.

Lanau F, Zenner M, Civelli O, Hartman D (1997) Epinephrine and norepinephrine act as potent agonists at the recombinant human dopamine D4 receptor. *Journal of Neurochemistry* **68**(2): 804–12.

Lewis DA, Foote SL, Goldstein M, Morrison JH (1988) The dopaminergic innervation of monkey prefrontal cortex: a tyrosine hydroxylase immunohistochemical study. *Brain Research* **449**(1–2): 225–43.

Lou H, Henriksen L, Bruhn P (1984) Focal cerebral hypoperfusion in children with dysphasia and/or attention deficit disorder. *Archives of Neurology* **41**, 825–9.

Lou H, Henriksen L, Bruhn P (1990) Focal cerebral dysfunction in developmental learning disabilities. *Lancet* **335**: 8–11.

Lou HC, Henriksen L, Bruhn P *et al.* (1989) Striatal dysfunction in attention deficit and hyperkinetic disorder. *Archives of Neurology* **46**: 48–52.

Manshadi M, Lippmann S, O'Daniel R, Blackman A (1983) Alcohol abuse and attention deficit disorder. *Journal of Clinical Psychiatry* **44**: 379–80.

Mataro M, Garcia-Sanchez C, Junque C *et al.* (1997) Magnetic resonance imaging measurement of the caudate nucleus in adolescents with Attention-Deficit Hyperactivity Disorder and its relationship with neuropsychological and behavioral measures. *Archives of Neurology* **54**: 963–8.

Melchitzky DS, Lewis DA (2000) Tyrosine hydroxylase- and dopamine transporter-immunoreactive axons in the primate cerebellum. Evidence for a lobular- and laminar-specific dopamine innervation. *Neuropsychopharmacology* **22**(5): 466–72.

Middleton FA, Strick PL (2000) Basal ganglia and cerebellar loops: motor and cognitive circuits. *Brain Research. Brain Research Reviews* **31**(2–3): 236–50.

Morrison JR, Stewart MA (1971) A family study of the hyperactive child syndrome. *Biological Psychiatry* **3**: 189–95.

Morrison JR, Stewart MA (1973) The psychiatric status of the legal families of adopted hyperactive children. *Archives of General Psychiatry* **28**(June): 888–91.

Morrison JR, Stewart MA (1974) Bilateral inheritance as evidence for polygenicity in the hyperactive child syndrome. *Journal of Nervous and Mental Disorders* **158**: 226–8.

Mostofsky S *et al.* (1998) Evaluation of cerebellar size in Attention-Deficit Hyperactivity Disorder. *Journal of Child Neurology* **13**: 434–9.

Nasrallah HA, Loney J, Olson SC *et al.* (1986) Cortical atrophy in young adults with a history of hyperactivity in childhood. *Psychiatry Research* **17**: 241–6.

Ogdie MN, Macphie IL, Minassian SL *et al.* (2003) A genomewide scan for Attention-Deficit/Hyperactivity Disorder in an extended sample: suggestive linkage on 17p11. *American Journal of Human Genetics* **72**: 1268–79.

Papa M, Berger DF, Sagvolden T *et al.* (1998) A quantitative cytochrome oxidase mapping study, cross-regional and neurobehavioural correlations in the anterior forebrain of an animal model of Attention Deficit Hyperactivity Disorder. *Behavioural Brain Research* **94**(1): 197–211.

Paterson AD, Sunohara GA, Kennedy JL (1999) Dopamine D4 receptor gene: novelty or nonsense? *Neuropsychopharmacology* **21**(1): 3–16.

Pauls DL, Shaywitz SE, Kramer PL *et al.* (1983) Demonstration of vertical transmission of attention deficit disorder. *Annals of Neurology* **14**: 363.

Raber J, Mehta PP, Kreifeldt M *et al.* (1997) Coloboma hyperactive mutant mice exhibit regional and transmitter-specific deficits in neurotransmission. *Journal of Neurochemistry* **68**(1): 176–86.

Roeltgen DP, Schneider JS (1994) Task persistence and learning ability in normal and chronic low dose MPTP-treated monkeys. *Behavioral Brain Research* **60**(2): 115–24.

Rosenberg DR, Lewis DA (1995) Postnatal maturation of the dopaminergic innervation of monkey prefrontal and motor cortices: a tyrosine hydroxylase immunohistochemical analysis. *Journal of Comparative Neurology* **358**(3): 383–400.

Rubia K, Overmeyer S, Taylor E *et al.* (1999) Hypofrontality in attention deficit hyperactivity disorder during higher-order motor control: a study with functional MRI. *American Journal of Psychiatry* **156**: 891–6.

Rubinstein M, Phillips TJ, Bunzow JR *et al.* (1997) Mice lacking dopamine D4 receptors are supersensitive to ethanol, cocaine, and methamphetamine. *Cell* **90**(6): 991–1001.

Russell VA (2000) The nucleus accumbens motor-limbic interface of the spontaneously hypertensive rat as studied in vitro by the superfusion slice technique. *Neuroscience and Biobehavioral Reviews* **24**(1): 133–6.

Russell VA, de Villiers A, Sagvolden T *et al.* (1995) Altered dopaminergic function in the prefrontal cortex, nucleus accumbens and caudate-putamen of an animal model of Attention-Deficit Hyperactivity Disorder – the spontaneously hypertensive rat. *Brain Research* **676**(2): 343–51.

Russell VA, de Villiers AS, Sagvolden T, Lamm MC, Taljaard JJ (2000) Methylphenidate affects striatal dopamine differently in an animal model for attention-deficit/hyperactivity disorder – the spontaneously hypertensive rat. *Brain Research Bulletin* **53**: 187–92.

Schachar R, Wachsmuth R (1990) Hyperactivity and parental psychopathology. *Journal of Child Psychology and Psychiatry* **31**(3): 381–92.

Schneider JS, Kovelowski CJ d (1990) Chronic exposure to low doses of MPTP. I. Cognitive deficits in motor asymptomatic monkeys. *Brain Research* **519**(1–2): 122–8.

Schneider JS, Roeltgen DP (1993) Delayed matching-to-sample, object retrieval, and discrimination reversal deficits in chronic low dose MPTP-treated monkeys. *Brain Research* **615**(2): 351–4.

Schneider JS, Sun ZQ, Roeltgen DP (1994) Effects of dopamine agonists on delayed response performance in chronic low-dose MPTP-treated monkeys. *Pharmacology, Biochemistry and Behavior* **48**(1): 235–40.

Schweitzer JB, Lee DO, Hanford RB *et al.* (2003) A positron emission tomography study of methylphenidate in adults with ADHD: alterations in resting blood flow and predicting treatment response. *Neuropsychopharmacology* **26**: 26.

Semrud-Clikeman M, Steingard RJ, Filipek P *et al.* (2000) Using MRI to examine brain-behavior relationships in males with attention deficit disorder with hyperactivity. *Journal of the American Academy of Child and Adolescent Psychiatry* **39**: 477–84.

Shaywitz SE, Cohen DJ, Shaywitz BA (1978) The biochemical basis of minimal brain dysfunction. *The Journal of Pediatrics* **92**(2): 179–87.

Sherman D, Iacono W, McGue M (1997) Attention deficit hyperactivity disorder dimensions: a twin study of inattention and impulsivity hyperactivity. *Journal of the American Academy of Child and Adolescent Psychiatry* **36**(6): 745–53.

Singer HS, Reiss AL, Brown JE (1993) Volumetric MRI changes in basal ganglia of children with Tourette's syndrome. *Neurology* **43**: 950–6.

Sowell ER, Thompson PM, Welcome SE *et al.* (2003) Cortical abnormalities in children and adolescents with Attention-Deficit Hyperactivity Disorder. *Lancet* **362**: 1699–707.

Spencer T, Biederman J, Wilens T (2000) Pharmacotherapy of attention deficit hyperactivity disorder. *Child and Adolescent Psychiatric Clinics of North America* **9**(1): 77–97.

Sprich S, Biederman J, Crawford MH *et al.* (2000) Adoptive and biological families of children and adolescents with ADHD. *Journal of the American Academy of Child and Adolescent Psychiatry* **39**(11): 1432–7.

Stevenson J (1992) Evidence for a genetic etiology in hyperactivity in children. *Behavior Genetics* **22**(3): 337–44.

Tahir E, Curran S, Yazgan Y *et al.* (2000) No association between low and high activity catecholamine-methl-transferase (COMT) and Attention deficit hyperactivity disorder (ADHD) in a sample of Turkish children. *American Journal of Medical Genetics (Neuropsychiatric Genetics)* **96**: 285–8.

Vaidya C, Austin G, Kirkorian G *et al.* (1998) Selective effects of methylphenidate in attention deficit hyperactivity disorder: a functional magnetic resonance study. *Proceedings of the National Academy of Sciences (USA)* **95**: 14494–9.

van Dyck CH, Quinlan DM, Cretella LM *et al.* (2002) Unaltered dopamine transporter availability in adult attention deficit hyperactivity disorder. *Am J Psychiatry* **159**(2): 309–12.

Van Tol HH, Wu CM, Guan HC *et al.* (1992) Multiple dopamine D4 receptor variants in the human population. *Nature* **358**(6382): 149–52.

Vanyukov MM, Moss HB, Kaplan BB *et al.* (2000) Antisociality, substance dependence, and the DRD5 gene: a preliminary study. *American Journal of Medical Genetics* **96**(5): 654–8.

Waldman I (2001) *Meta-Analysis of the DAT-ADHD Association.* Paper presented at the Third Annual ADHD Molecular Genetics Network Meeting, Boston, MA.

Weiss RE, Stein MA, Trommer B, Refetoff S (1993) Attention-deficit hyperactivity disorder and thyroid function. *Journal of Pediatrics* **123**: 539–45.

Weiss RE, Stein MA, Duck SC, Chyna B, Phillips W, O'Brien T, Gutermuth L, Refetoff S (1994) Low intelligence but not attention deficit hyperactivity disorder is associated with resistance to thyroid hormone caused by mutation R316H in the thyroid hormone receptor beta gene. *Journal of Clinical Endocrinology and Metabolism* **78**: 1525–8.

Welner Z, Welner A, Stewart M *et al.* (1977) A controlled study of siblings of hyperactive children. *Journal of Nervous and Mental Disease* **165**: 110–17.

Wilson MC (2000) Coloboma mouse mutant as an animal model of hyperkinesis and attention deficit hyperactivity disorder. *Neuroscience and Biobehavioral Reviews* **24**(1): 51–7.

Zametkin AJ, Nordahl TE, Gross M *et al.* (1990) Cerebral glucose metabolism in adults with hyperactivity of childhood onset. *New England Journal of Medicine* **323**: 1361–6.

Zametkin AJ, Rapoport JL (1987) Noradrenergic hypothesis of attention deficit disorder with hyperactivity: a critical review. In HY Meltzer (ed.) *Psychopharmacology: The Third Generation of Progress* (pp. 837–42). New York: Raven Press.

Zhuang X, Oosting RS, Jones SR *et al.* (2001) Hyperactivity and impaired response habituation in hyperdopaminergic mice. *Proceedings of the National Academy of Sciences of the United States of America* **98**(4): 1982–7.

11 Functional Neuroimaging of Reward and Motivational Pathways in ADHD

A.M. CLARE KELLY,[1] ANOUK SCHERES,[2] EDMUND S.J. SONUGA-BARKE[3] AND F. XAVIER CASTELLANOS[4]

1. *Institute for Pediatric Neuroscience, NYU Child Study Center, New York, USA;*
2. *Department of Psychology, University of Arizona, Tucson, Arizona, USA;*
3. *School of Psychology, University of Southampton, Southampton, UK; 4. NYU School of Medicine, USA*

11.1 OVERVIEW

The evolving field of research on Attention-Deficit/Hyperactivity Disorder (ADHD) has now moved beyond the search for a common core dysfunction towards a recognition of ADHD as a heterogeneous disorder of multiple neuropsychological deficits and hypothesised causal substrates (e.g. Faraone & Biederman, 1998; Todd, 2000; Nigg, 2001; Castellanos & Tannock, 2002; Sonuga-Barke, 2002, 2003). The variety of topics and research areas covered by the chapters of this book attests to this important theoretical and empirical progression but also to the realisation of the complexity implied by such an undertaking.

That ADHD is a heterogeneous disorder is apparent at almost every level of analysis, from the implication of multiple genes (Chapters 7, 8 and 10), the identification of multiple sites of neural dysfunction (Chapters 12 and 14), and a wide range and varying degrees of cognitive deficits (Chapter 12); to vast differences in the behavioural expression of the disorder, including clinical presentation (Chapters 2 and 3), to variation in response to treatment, particularly drug treatments such as methylphenidate (Chapters 13 and 15). This phenotypic, genetic and neuropsychological heterogeneity poses a formidable challenge as investigators attempt to discern the many factors that contribute to the development and expression of ADHD. Indeed, subtypes based on the DSM-IV symptom dimensions of Inattention or Hyperactivity/Impulsivity have not proved to be particularly fruitful means of clarifying neurobiological or nosological questions. Translational approaches, such as the pursuit of endophenotypes, have been suggested as a strategy to delineate putative causal mechanisms that may serve to organise our clinical and neuroscientific perspectives in a manner similar to that used to organise the

Handbook of Attention Deficit Hyperactivity Disorder. Edited by M. Fitzgerald, M. Bellgrove and M. Gill.
© 2007 John Wiley & Sons Ltd

Periodic Table of the Elements based on their fundamental physical and chemical properties (Castellanos & Tannock, 2002, see also Chapter 12). Although attempting to assemble even a preliminary 'Table of Neurocognitive Elements' is premature, we believe that we can start on this ambitious agenda by building on the advances emerging from basic neuroscience and imaging studies. One area which may prove particularly fruitful is the investigation of how variations in the circuitry and the cellular and molecular mechanisms involved in motivational processes are linked to the symptoms of ADHD or underlying genetic risk factors. This chapter will focus on delineating such mechanisms and their relevance to understanding ADHD.

11.2 EXECUTIVE DYSFUNCTION AND EVOLVING NEUROCOGNITIVE MODELS OF ADHD

ADHD research over the past decade was energised by the hypothesis that deficits in executive function (EF), in particular, inhibitory control, form the core neurocognitive deficit in ADHD (Barkley, 1997). However, the substantial resulting literature (as reviewed by Homack & Riccio, 2004; Romine *et al.*, 2004; Boonstra *et al.*, 2005; Martinussen *et al.*, 2005; van Mourik *et al.*, 2005; Willcutt *et al.*, 2005) demonstrates that no specific EF deficit is sufficient to account for dysfunction across all or most individuals with ADHD (Nigg *et al.*, 2005). Quantitatively, the explanatory power of single EF deficits calculated using meta-analytic techniques demonstrates that the association between ADHD diagnosis and deficits in planning, attention switching, working memory, or sustained attention is moderate at best (Nigg *et al.*, 2005; Willcutt *et al.*, 2005; Castellanos *et al.*, 2006). For example, Nigg *et al.* (2005) reviewed the evidence for executive dysfunction in ADHD across three samples comprising almost 900 children, about one-third of whom were children with combined type ADHD and two-thirds controls. They examined performance on several neuropsychological measures of EF including the Stop Signal Reaction Time (SSRT), Reaction Time variability, and performance on the Stroop, Continuous Performance and Trailmaking tasks. Task measures were clustered to assess dysfunction on the putative executive functions of inhibitory control, vigilance/sustained attention, and attentional control. Defining 'abnormal' or 'impaired' performance on a given neuropsychological measure as performance worse than that of 90% of control subjects (i.e. below the 10th percentile, see Figure 11.1(i), they observed that no more than half of the children with ADHD could be classified as 'impaired'. More specifically, on one of the most frequently used measures of inhibitory EF deficit in ADHD, the SSRT, fewer than 50% of the total ADHD sample were 'impaired' in their performance (see Figure 11.1(ii)). Furthermore, while nearly 80% of children with ADHD demonstrated a deficit on at least one EF measure, the same was true of almost 50% of control subjects (Nigg *et al.*, 2005). The authors conclude that while between 35% and 50% of children with combined type ADHD exhibit impaired performance on common neuropsychological tests of EF (as defined by control sample performance), the remaining 50% to 65% of children with the diagnosis do not.

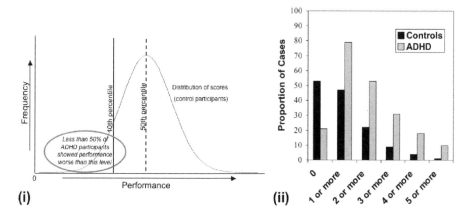

Figure 11.1. (i) Schematic representation of the distribution of scores and performance percentiles on any given measure and (ii) the proportion of Control and ADHD participants demonstrating performance above the 10th percentile on different numbers of EF tasks (based on Nigg et al., 2005)

11.2.1 MULTIPLE PATHWAYS TO DYSFUNCTION: 'HOT' AND 'COOL' EXECUTIVE FUNCTION

In response to evidence for the cognitive and neurobiological heterogeneity of ADHD, an alternative view emphasising multiple etiologic 'pathways' in ADHD has been proposed by a number of investigators (Sonuga-Barke, 2002, 2003, 2005; Nigg et al., 2005). This view suggests that the causal substrates of ADHD comprise multiple neural pathways that are dissociable anatomically and neuropsychologically. In the earliest version of such a model, Sonuga-Barke proposed that a minimum of two pathways would be necessary to account for ADHD (Sonuga-Barke, 2002, 2003). Accordingly termed the 'dual pathway' model, it posits that deficits in executive processes are mediated through ventrolateral and dorsolateral cortical-striatal circuitry, and are distinct from differences in motivational performance, which are mediated by mesolimbic (medial and orbital prefrontal) ventral striatal circuits. Support for this model is provided by studies demonstrating that cognitive deficits such as inhibition are distinct from (i.e., uncorrelated with) the tendency to choose a smaller immediate reward rather than a larger delayed reward (Solanto et al., 2001; Sonuga-Barke et al., 2003). The dual pathway model maps onto and supports the distinction between 'hot' and 'cool' executive function in ADHD cognition and in development (Zelazo et al., 2002). 'Cool' executive function (EF) refers to top-down processes that are relatively purely cognitive in nature, which are typically elicited by abstract, decontextualised problems. Examples of 'cool' EF include working memory, sustained attention, or task set switching. In contrast, 'hot' EF refers to cognitive processes that also have an affective, motivational, or incentive/ reward component, and include processes such as affective decision-making (e.g. decision-making under conditions of risk). 'Hot' EF comprises both top-down and bottom-up processes, although the latter are likely to weigh more heavily in 'hot' EF than in circumstances that evoke 'cool' EF.

While EF in general is purported to rely on discrete cortico-striatal-thalamo-cortical loops (Alexander *et al.*, 1986; McFarland & Haber, 2002; Heyder *et al.*, 2004; Chudasama & Robbins, 2006), 'cool' and 'hot' aspects of EF may be dissociated according to the trajectory of their associated neural pathways. Thus, 'cool' EF is primarily subserved by a dorsal pathway connecting the thalamus and the dorsal striatum to lateral (including inferior prefrontal) and dorsolateral PFC, while 'hot' EF is mediated by more ventromedial pathways connecting mesolimbic reward circuitry, including the amygdala and ventral striatum, to orbitofrontal and medial PFC (Haber *et al.*, 2000; Haber, 2003). The distinction between dorsal and ventral pathways is admittedly simplistic. Clearly, 'cool' EF comprises a range of cognitive functions, which may be dissociated based on their functional localisation to various portions of frontal cortex. For example, 'cool' functions such as working memory (e.g. d'Esposito *et al.*, 2000; Curtis & d'Esposito, 2003) and inhibition (e.g. Aron *et al.*, 2004; Chambers *et al.*, 2005) are differentially localised to dorsal and ventral portions of the lateral surface of the frontal lobes, with further differentiation associated with the component processes of those functions (e.g. maintenance and manipulation in working memory). There is a similar diversity of 'hot' executive functions, which reflect the interaction of top-down processes associated with orbital and ventromedial PFC and more primitive, bottom-up motivational mechanisms involved in mediating the effects of rewards and punishments, linked to the ventral striatum.

Pervasive 'cool' EF deficits, which are present in a subset of children with ADHD (Nigg *et al.*, 2005; Willcutt *et al.*, 2005), are thus likely to be closely linked to dysfunction in regions of the frontostriatal pathway, such as dorsolateral or ventrolateral prefrontal cortex (dlPFC, vlPFC) and anterior/dorsal regions of caudate and putamen. Conversely, dysfunction in regions such as the ventral striatum or amygdala may adversely affect bottom-up 'hot' motivational processes, reflected in abnormalities in sensitivity to performance incentives (rewards), temporal delays before receipt of rewards (Delay Aversion), and environmental cues. These abnormalities in turn can impact top-down cognitive processes to produce deficits in 'hot' EF. As a consequence of these theoretically dissociable paths for dysfunction, and consistent with the empirical evidence suggesting heterogeneity of neuropsychological deficits in ADHD, individuals with ADHD may be expected to manifest varying degrees of deficits, reflecting primarily cognitive dysfunction, primarily motivational dysfunction, or a combination of these. Because distinctions between 'hot' and 'cool' are a matter of degree rather than being clearly demarcated, dysfunctional interactions between cognitive and motivational processes are perhaps particularly likely, and successful goal-directed behaviour is likely to require a combination of effective 'hot' and 'cool' EF (Hongwanishkul *et al.*, 2005).

The predominant focus of ADHD research has been on 'cool' EF, assessed by tasks such as Continuous Performance Tasks (CPT), GO/NOGO, Stop task (the SSRT measure), Stroop, Eriksen Flanker, and working memory tasks (Homack & Riccio, 2004; Romine *et al.*, 2004; Boonstra *et al.*, 2005; Martinussen *et al.*, 2005; van Mourik *et al.*, 2005) and studies have demonstrated that specific 'cool' EF deficits are associated with dysfunction in particular regions of the dorsal frontostriatal pathway, including the anterior cingulate cortex (Bush *et al.*, 1999), the caudate and putamen (Casey *et al.*, 1997; Durston *et al.*, 2003; Vaidya *et al.*, 2005) and ventral prefrontal cortex/inferior frontal gyrus (Aron & Poldrack, 2005; Rubia *et al.*, 2005). These studies have contributed considerably to the view that ADHD is a neuro-biologically and neuropsychologically heterogeneous disorder, and to the recognition that individuals with ADHD will demonstrate varying degrees of impairment in these 'cool' executive functions (e.g. Nigg, 2005; Nigg *et al.*, 2005). Furthermore, these studies have spurred progress in the search for endophenotypes for ADHD, with the proposal of several 'cool' executive functions as candidate endopheno-types, including inhibition (Slaats-Willemse *et al.*, 2003; Aron & Poldrack, 2005), working memory (Castellanos & Tannock, 2002; Westerberg *et al.*, 2004), reaction time variability (Manor *et al.*, 2002; Toplak *et al.*, 2003; Castellanos *et al.*, 2005), and sustained attention (Chapter 12).

In contrast to recent progress in delineating the role of 'cool' executive functions and their corresponding neurobiological substrates in ADHD, 'hot' EF in ADHD remains relatively unexplored. A notable exception has been the theory articulated by Sagvolden *et al.* (2005) which hypothesises that the full range of combined type ADHD symptoms can be traced to a hypofunctioning dopaminergic system that results in a shorter and steeper delay-of-reinforcement gradient and deficient behav-ioural extinction. Their 'dynamic developmental theory' is grounded primarily in basic science observations gleaned from study of the spontaneously hypertensive rat (SHR). This translational model provides an ambitious framework within which many methodological and conceptual issues remain to be fully articulated, as pointed out in many of the accompanying commentaries and responses to the Sagvolden *et al.* (2005) paper. In addition, the theory is partially, but not wholly supported by data from studies of the SHR (e.g. Johansen and Sagvolden, 2005a, 2005b; Johansen *et al.*, 2005). While we are enthusiastic regarding the long-term value and importance of translational research in bridging from rodent model systems to human symptomatology and vice versa, the availability of neuroimaging techniques also provides heretofore unavailable access to neuroanatomic structure and cere-bral function in humans. In this chapter, we will focus on the neural substrates of bottom-up reward and reinforcement processing, examining the behavioural, func-tional and anatomic evidence for the role of dysfunction in these motivational processes in ADHD, in light of emerging perspectives from basic neuroscience, neuropsychological studies, and functional neuroimaging.

11.2.2 'HOT' MOTIVATIONAL FUNCTIONS: REWARD AND DELAY

The notion that ADHD is secondary to abnormalities in reward-related circuitry has a long history (Wender, 1972; Douglas & Parry, 1983; Haenlein & Caul, 1987; Iaboni *et al.*, 1997; Sagvolden *et al.*, 1998; Douglas, 1999; Tripp & Alsop, 1999, 2001; Blum *et al.*, 2000; Castellanos & Tannock, 2002; Sonuga-Barke, 2002, 2003, 2005; Ernst *et al.*, 2003; Sagvolden *et al.*, 2005). However, empirical evidence for this hypothesis remains somewhat equivocal. There are many different aspects to reward such as magnitude, immediacy, and probability (Williams & Taylor, 2004), and the contribution of each of these aspects to reward sensitivity in ADHD has not been studied comprehensively. While some studies (e.g. Douglas & Parry, 1983; Douglas,

1999) have suggested that children with ADHD are unusually sensitive to rewards, behavioural studies of reward sensitivity in ADHD have not yielded consistent group differences in behavioural facilitation or suppression as a result of rewards or punishments. A qualitative review of this literature was recently provided by Luman *et al.* (2005) and is briefly summarised here.

Luman *et al.* (2005) examined 22 studies, comprising behavioural data collected from almost 1200 children, which compared ADHD and control participants on tasks involving rewards and punishments, in order to chart the behavioural effects of reinforcement contingencies in ADHD. Just over half of the studies reviewed demonstrated a differential effect of reward contingencies on performance between ADHD and control groups, suggesting a greater positive impact of reward on performance in ADHD participants, relative to control participants. Interestingly, a number of studies that included physiological measures of heart rate and skin conductance suggested that children with ADHD were generally psychophysiologically *less sensitive* to reinforcement contingencies than control children. Overall, the picture provided by Luman *et al.* is that of a complex literature that does not provide clear support for, nor clear evidence against, a role for dysfunctional reward and motivational processing in ADHD.

Given the wide range of paradigms, measures, and methods used, it should not be surprising that the ADHD reward literature is mostly inconclusive (Luman *et al.*, 2005). The most consistent finding in the 'hot' motivational domain that has been identified is the preference for immediate over-delayed rewards exhibited by individuals with ADHD relative to controls (Rapport *et al.*, 1986; Sonuga-Barke *et al.*, 1992; Schweitzer& Sulzer-Azaroff, 1995; Barkley *et al.*, 2001; Kuntsi *et al.*, 2001; Solanto *et al.*, 2001; Tripp & Alsop, 2001, Luman *et al.*, 2005; Bitsakou *et al.*, 2006; but also see negative reports, e.g. Scheres *et al.*, 2006). These studies have generally found that children with ADHD prefer rewards that minimise time on task while control children tend to maximise their total reward. That is, children with ADHD demonstrate a hypersensitivity to reward-related delay and delay-predictive cues, and difficulties in waiting and working for rewards. This leads them to escape or avoid delay when they can (Solanto *et al.*, 2001; Sonuga-Barke *et al.*, 2004), a tendency that has been termed *Delay Aversion* (Sonuga-Barke *et al.*, 1992; Sonuga-Barke, 2002). Like deficits in 'cool' EF, Delay Aversion has been linked to putative alterations in dopamine-modulated basal ganglia/anterior cortical circuits (Sagvolden *et al.*, 2005), but in the distinct 'hot' EF circuit that links the ventral striatum to ventromedial and orbitofrontal cortex (Sonuga-Barke, 2005). To our knowledge, however, this link has not been explicitly assessed on a neurobiological level.

Clearly, the examination of reward-related processing in ADHD is complex, a fact that is reflected in discrepancies and inconsistencies in results across studies. In addition, we currently lack empirical knowledge concerning the functioning of the neurobiological substrates of reward-related processing in ADHD. As a result, the neural foci of motivational processes, such as Delay Aversion have yet to be identified experimentally. *We suggest that what has been lacking in this research area is an attempt to explicitly probe the neural circuitry underlying task performance.* We suggest that the use of neuroimaging techniques to probe the neural circuitry underlying reward-related processing in ADHD constitutes an important step towards an empirical delineation of the neurobiological substrates of reward-related processing in ADHD.

11.3 THE NEURAL CIRCUITRY OF REWARD

Broadly defined, rewarding stimuli are those an organism will work to attain. The brain regions most commonly activated by rewarding stimuli include the midbrain, ventral and dorsal striatum (including the nucleus accumbens – NAcc), amygdala, orbitofrontal cortex (OFC) and other areas of prefrontal cortex (PFC) (McClure et al., 2004b; Knutson & Cooper, 2005) and may be considered nodes of a motivational processing pathway. Goal-directed behaviour is mediated by information processing in several parallel thalamo-cortico-striatal loops which begin with midbrain dopaminergic neurons in the substantia nigra and ventral tegmental area and spiral through the striatum and thalamus to areas of frontal cortex (Alexander et al., 1986; Alexander & Crutcher, 1990; Haber et al., 2000; Schultz, 2002; Haber, 2003). These ascending circuits may be differentiated into 'hot' and 'cool' processing pathways on the basis of their functional projections, with connections between ventral striatum and areas of orbital and medial frontal cortex forming a pathway for motivational processing (Haber et al., 2000). The basal ganglia are a crucial component of these neural pathways, linking two neural circuits. A striato-nigral-striatal network circuit channels information flow between ventromedial (limbic) central (associative) and dorsolateral (motor) regions of the striatum, while a thalamo-cortical-thalamic network relays information to the cortex. Within each of these networks, information is channelled from limbic to cognitive to motor circuits (Haber, 2003). This pattern of information flow and the interactions between the parallel pathways provide a basis through which emotion/motivation related 'hot' pathways influence 'cool' cognitive pathways, which, in turn, influence behaviour through their input to motor pathways (see Figure 11.2).

In this section, we will first focus on the functions of the bottom-up 'hot' motivational pathway centred on the ventral striatum. Later in the chapter, we will discuss the top-down processing pathways and their interactions. It is important to mention that while we focus on the role of dopamine in reward-related process, a clear role for other neurotransmitters, such as serotonin, has also been demonstrated (e.g. Robbins, 2005; Chudasama & Robbins, 2006). However, dopamine has been identified as having a central role in the pathophysiology of ADHD (e.g. Sagvolden & Sergeant, 1998; Biederman & Faraone, 2002; Castellanos & Tannock, 2002; Sagvolden et al., 2005).

11.3.1 DOPAMINE AND BOTTOM-UP REWARD SIGNALS: INCENTIVE SALIENCE AND REWARD ANTICIPATION

The seminal work of Schultz and colleagues (Schultz & Romo, 1990; Schultz et al., 1993; Hollerman & Schultz, 1998; Schultz, 1998, 2001, 2002; Schultz et al., 1998) established that midbrain dopamine (DA) neurons code for rewarding stimuli by demonstrating brief increases in phasic activation following the occurrence of rewards. Importantly, this response is only observed when rewards are different

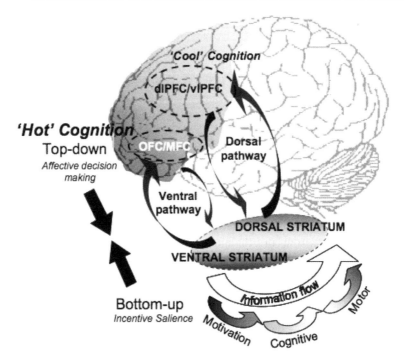

Figure 11.2. Schematic model of the dorsal and ventral neural pathways associated with 'Cool' and 'Hot' cognition

from predictions. That is, there is a change in the phasic activity of DA neurons when there is a discrepancy or 'error' between the prediction of the reward and its occurrence. This change in phasic activity is termed the 'reward prediction error' (Schultz, 1998). When a reward occurs that is unpredicted, the prediction error is positive and is signalled by an increase in DA activity. If a predicted reward is omitted, the prediction error is negative (activation is depressed). Experimental work has shown that this depression in DA firing occurs when animals fail to obtain reward because of erroneous behaviour, when reward delivery is blocked, or when reward delivery is unexpectedly delayed (Schultz *et al.*, 1993; Hollerman & Schultz, 1998; Schultz, 2002). The reward prediction error thus functions as an important behavioural learning signal that *indicates the need to modify behaviour in order to reduce the discrepancy between predictions and outcomes* (Schultz, 2001). Predictions and behaviour continue to change on the basis of the reward prediction error signal until the outcome occurs as predicted (i.e. learning asymptotes), at which time the prediction error becomes zero (Schultz, 2001).

An important characteristic of the reward prediction error signal is that, during learning, the response transfers from the reward itself to reward-predicting stimuli (cues) (Schultz *et al.*, 1998). That is, DA neurons (particularly afferents to the ventral striatum) signal the *anticipation* of a possible reward by responding to cues that predict the occurrence of the reward, rather than the occurrence of the reward itself (Schultz, 2001). The DA reward prediction error thus appears to constitute a bottom–up signal that assigns 'incentive salience', or motivational value to objects and actions. Incentive salience is then used in action selection such that more valuable actions are more likely to be selected (McClure *et al.*, 2003). In order to be useful for behaviour, however, incentive salience needs to be supplemented by additional information. Neurons in other regions of the striatum, in the frontal cortex and amygdala also process reward information and provide more differentiated information for identifying and anticipating rewards and organising goal-directed behaviour (Schultz, 2002). In particular, the OFC appears to discriminate between different types of rewards; neurons in the OFC respond differentially to preferred versus non-preferred rewards (Critchley & Rolls, 1996; Tremblay & Schultz, 1999; Padoa-Schioppa & Assad, 2006), suggesting that OFC neurons contribute to the 'liking' (hedonic) component of reward-seeking behaviour. Regions of orbitofrontal and ventromedial frontal cortex also show activation during the outcome period of a reward task (e.g. Knutson *et al.*, 2001b), showing greater activation for positive than negative outcomes (Knutson *et al.*, 2003; O'Doherty *et al.*, 2003a; Rogers *et al.*, 2004), suggesting that these areas also perform an evaluative role. In contrast, neurons in the midbrain and ventral and dorsal striatum do not appear to discriminate between different rewards or signal the pleasure associated with a particular reward, but instead provide the 'wanting' component, the motivational component of reward-seeking behaviour (McClure *et al.*, 2003; Schultz, 2002). This bottom-up motivational signal provided by the activity of DA neurons in the midbrain and striatum then influences pathways involved in higher cognitive processes by means of interactions between ascending thalamo-cortico-striatal loops projecting to areas of PFC (Schultz, 2001; Haber, 2003). It is in this way that bottom-up DA reward signals interact with top-down signals from other areas of the brain to produce successful goal-directed behaviour.

11.3.2 HUMAN NEUROIMAGING STUDIES OF BOTTOM-UP REWARD-RELATED PROCESSING

While the foundational work in this area was carried out with animals such as rats and non-human primates, recent investigations have observed the reward prediction error response in humans using fMRI (Knutson *et al.*, 2000; Berns *et al.*, 2001; McClure *et al.*, 2003). By examining changes in activation in the brain during performance of a task in which participants work to receive a reward, an increase in activation in areas of the mesolimbic reward circuit, including the ventral striatum/NAcc and amygdala, has been observed to coincide with the occurrence of the reward, while a depression of activation occurs when an expected reward is omitted (Delgado *et al.*, 2000; Berns *et al.*, 2001; McClure *et al.*, 2003; Ramnani *et al.*, 2004; Ernst *et al.*, 2005). These responses were observed regardless of whether the reward is a primary stimulus such as food, or a conditioned reward such as money. Reward-related activation in the ventral striatum/NAcc has also been observed to scale with reward magnitude, with more activation being associated with larger rewards (Knutson *et al.*, 2001a; Galvan *et al.*, 2005; Knutson *et al.*, 2005).

More recently, studies have focused on the transfer of incentive salience activation from the time of reward occurrence to reward-predicting cues, a response that has been termed 'reward anticipation' (Knutson *et al.*, 2001a; Pagnoni *et al.*, 2002; McClure *et al.*, 2003; O'Doherty *et al.*, 2003b; Galvan *et al.*, 2005). This work is based on Schultz's (2001) observation that DA neurons (particularly in the ventral striatum) signal the anticipation of a possible reward, rather than the delivery of the reward itself. For example, Knutson and colleagues (Knutson *et al.*, 2001b) examined activations related to reward anticipation as distinct from reward delivery with fMRI in normal adult volunteers. Participants were first presented with a cue that signalled either a potentially rewarded response, an unrewarded response, or no response requirement. In reward trials, participants were then required to respond to a target while it was on screen in order to receive the monetary reward. In the non-rewarding trials, there was no reward, regardless of the response, and in the non-response trials, participants were required to refrain from responding. Feedback regarding success (win/no win) on that trial was then provided.

By examining separately activation related to the cue presentation and activation related to feedback, Knutson *et al.* (2001b) were able to dissociate activations related to reward anticipation and reward outcome. They observed robust activations associated with reward anticipation in the NAcc while reward delivery was associated with activation in the ventral medial prefrontal cortex. Activation in the NAcc was depressed when a reward was omitted because a participant had failed to respond in time, consistent with Schultz's observation of a negative reward error signal. These and similar findings have been repeated in several other neuroimaging studies (e.g. Knutson *et al.*, 2001a; O'Doherty *et al.*, 2002; Pagnoni *et al.*, 2002; McClure *et al.*, 2004b; O'Doherty, 2004).

11.3.3 THE VENTRAL STRIATUM MAINTAINS INCENTIVE SALIENCE OVER DELAYS

The neuroimaging studies of reward anticipation discussed in the preceding paragraphs suggest that the ventral striatum, the NAcc in particular, is a crucial structure in the brain's response to delayed rewards, through the anticipatory activity of DA neurons. Given the robust behavioural evidence for Delay Aversion in ADHD (e.g. Sonuga-Barke *et al.*, 1992; Barkley *et al.*, 2001; Kuntsi *et al.*, 2001; Solanto *et al.*, 2001; Tripp & Alsop, 2001; Bitsakou *et al.*, 2006), the investigation of the effects of delayed reward on ventral striatal/NAcc neurons should be informative to our understanding of the disorder.

Models of the relationship between dysfunctional reward circuitry and symptoms such as Delay Aversion provide a framework for such investigations. As discussed earlier in this chapter, Sagvolden *et al.* (e.g. Sagvolden *et al.*, 1998; Johansen *et al.*, 2002; Sagvolden *et al.*, 2005) have proposed a comprehensive theory of ADHD which hypothesises that hypofunctioning dopamine systems give rise to the altered reinforcement processes, deficient attentional responses and poor executive functioning that underlie a majority of the behavioural symptoms associated with the disorder. More specifically, the theory proposes that hypofunction of the mesolimbic DA reward system, and consequent low levels of DA activity in areas such as the NAcc, result in altered reinforcement processes, which take the form of a shorter and steeper delay-of-reinforcement gradient, and deficient behavioural extinction. This predicts that the time window within which a behaviour will become associated with its consequences (e.g., a reward) is shortened in children with ADHD, giving rise to impulsiveness. Delay Aversion in ADHD is suggested to be a result of this shorter delay-of-reinforcement gradient, as even short delays between a behaviour and its reward may be too long to reinforce the behaviour (Sagvolden *et al.*, 2005).

While the dynamic developmental theory (Sagvolden *et al.*, 2005) hypothesises a link between reduced DA activity, a shorter delay-of-reinforcement gradient and Delay Aversion in ADHD, it does not explicitly associate deficient reward-related *anticipatory* activity in areas such as the NAcc with Delay Aversion. In a model that makes this potential link explicit, Tripp & Wickens (Wickens & Tripp, 2005) have proposed that in children with ADHD, the DA reward anticipation signal is diminished. They suggest that the transfer of the DA response from a reward to its predictive cue fails to develop normally in children with ADHD. This means that the delay-bridging anticipatory activity of DA cells is weaker for children with ADHD than for normal children, making them increasingly likely to engage in behaviours that result in immediate reinforcement (e.g. choosing the smaller, immediate reward).

While the two theories vary somewhat in the perspective within which they frame predictions, they have in common a hypothesised link between hypofunctioning mesolimbic reward circuitry (particularly reduced DA activity in the NAcc) in ADHD and behavioural phenomena such Delay Aversion. Despite the evidence supporting dysfunction of prefrontal cortical-striatal circuitry provided by neuroimaging investigations of ADHD (Aylward *et al.*, 1996; Castellanos *et al.*, 1996; Casey *et al.*, 1997; Filipek *et al.*, 1997; Mataro *et al.*, 1997; Bush *et al.*, 1999; Rubia *et al.*, 1999; Teicher *et al.*, 2000; Durston *et al.*, 2003), the neural circuitry underlying motivational phenomena such as Delay Aversion in ADHD has not been directly assessed using neuroimaging. The failure to probe the neural substrates of reward using neurobiologically informed paradigms may account in part for our difficulty in resolving the question of precisely how reward-related neuronal systems are abnormal in ADHD. Nonetheless, the development of theories concerning the role of dysfunctional reward circuitry in ADHD, such as those of Sagvolden *et al.* (Sagvolden *et al.*, 1998; Sagvolden *et al.*, 2005), Sonuga-Barke (Sonuga-Barke, 2002, 2003), and Wickens and Tripp (Wickens & Tripp, 2005), set out a clear research path for neuroimaging assays of their hypotheses.

The translational nature of this approach suggests this will be a fruitful research path. Studies have demonstrated that lesions to the NAcc cause rats and chickens to prefer small immediate rewards to larger delayed rewards (Cardinal *et al.*, 2001; Cardinal *et al.*, 2002; Izawa *et al.*, 2005). A lesion to the NAcc core similarly impaired instrumental learning in rats when reinforcement was delayed and also impaired performance of a previously learned instrumental response when reinforcement was delayed (Cardinal & Cheung, 2005). In light of these findings, Cardinal and colleagues propose that the function of the NAcc is to bridge action-outcome delays – both during and subsequent to learning. That is, they suggest that the NAcc maintains a working memory-type representation of incentive salience over a delay, in order to facilitate reward-seeking behaviour. It is this delay-bridging maintenance of incentive salience that is proposed to be diminished in ADHD (Wickens & Tripp, 2005). In the following sections, we highlight what we believe are the salient research questions and hypotheses that can be addressed by pursuing these links through neuroimaging examinations of reward and delay-related processing in ADHD.

11.4 NEW RESEARCH DIRECTIONS

The preceding discussion prompts us to assert that the investigation of the neural circuitry of reward processing in ADHD represents a fruitful avenue of research, one which has the potential to both generate and answer a new set of questions about the dysfunctions that might underpin 'hot' motivational aspects of cognition in ADHD.

11.4.1 NEUROIMAGING OF INCENTIVE SALIENCE AND REWARD ANTICIPATION IN ADHD

One of the principal research questions is whether there are differences in brain activations related to reward processing between ADHD and normal individuals. Scheres *et al.* (in press) recently addressed this question by using fMRI to examine the areas activated when adolescents with and without ADHD performed the reward-anticipation paradigm developed by Knutson *et al.* (Knutson *et al.*, 2000, 2001a, 2001b). The ADHD group comprised six adolescents with combined-type ADHD and five with inattentive-type ADHD, and there were eleven gender-, age- and IQ-matched healthy controls. The hypothesis that the ADHD and control groups would differ in the magnitude of striatal activation during reward anticipation was supported. Relative to controls, adolescents with ADHD demonstrated reduced ventral striatal activation during reward anticipation, and this reduction became more pronounced with increasing reward magnitudes (20c – $1 – $5). In addition, a significant negative correlation was observed between ventral striatal activation and levels of hyperactivity/impulsivity in the sample as a whole (i.e. including both ADHD and control participants), while no such correlation was found for symptoms of inattention. These findings provide preliminary support for the hypothesis that ADHD is associated with hyporesponsiveness of the ventral striatum during reward anticipation, and further, suggest that this hyporesponsiveness is specifically related to hyperactive/impulsive behaviours.

It is possible that the ventral striatal hyporesponsiveness observed in the ADHD group is the result of a dopaminergic deficiency in the mesolimbic circuit, which may have acted to diminish the perceived saliency of anticipated rewards in the ADHD sample (Johansen *et al.*, 2002; Volkow *et al.*, 2004). This hypothesis is consistent with a study (Ernst *et al.*, 1999) which examined midbrain dopaminergic activity in children with ADHD using pharmacological PET and the dopaminergic tracer fluro-DOPA ([^{18}F]DOPA). This tracer is an analogue of dihydroxy-phenylalanine (DOPA), the DA precursor, and imaging the tracer using PET provides information on DA synthesis and storage processes (Ernst *et al.*, 1999). High accumulations of the tracer were observed in the right midbrain of children with ADHD, and higher levels of the tracer were associated with increased symptom severity. High levels of [^{18}F]DOPA indicate enhanced DA synthesis, which could reflect a number of processes: higher enzyme activity, increased density of DA cell bodies and terminals, or both (Ernst *et al.*, 1999). Ernst *et al.* note that this kind of enhanced activity has been observed previously in response to low extracellular levels of DA (Abercrombie *et al.*, 1990; Torstenson *et al.*, 1997), and to the blockade of DA receptors (Hadjiconstantinou *et al.*, 1993; Zhu *et al.*, 1993). Replication of such findings is essentially impossible given current trends in research ethics (Wendler *et al.*, 2005), which makes it difficult to determine how to integrate these data with recent findings which suggest that ADHD in adults is associated with increased striatal DAT density (Spencer *et al.*, 2005), and the observation that therapeutic doses of methylphenidate increase the concentration of dopamine in striatum by blocking DAT (Volkow *et al.*, 2001). Finally, methylphenidate has been shown to increase extracellular levels of dopamine in striatum during math test performance in ADHD, in association with increased motivation (Volkow *et al.*, 2004). One way in which this dopamine hypothesis could be addressed indirectly in children would be to assess the effects of stimulant administration on activation in the ventral striatum during reward anticipation in participants with ADHD.

11.4.2 NEUROIMAGING OF DELAY AVERSION

In addition to providing encouraging support for the hypothesis that reward-related processing is dysfunctional in ADHD, Scheres *et al.*'s findings provide a basis from which to develop further research questions and hypotheses. One such question is, what is the interaction between incentive salience and delay? If we take the view, outlined in the previous section, that the ventral striatum/NAcc serves to maintain a working memory-type representation of incentive salience, what might be the impact of delay on ventral striatal activation? Might Delay Aversion in ADHD be related to a weaker/more rapidly dissipating signal in the ventral striatum/NAcc over a delay imposed prior to reward presentation, as has been suggested (e.g. Wickens & Tripp, 2005)? What is the effect of uncertain delays or rewards? Such questions might be investigated using a reward anticipation paradigm (e.g. one based on the work of Knutson and colleagues), combined with an immediate/ delayed reward manipulation. While we believe this approach may be informative with regard to the neural bases of reward processing and Delay Aversion in ADHD, there are a number of caveats to any such investigation.

Caveat #1: One must account for the potential impact of apparently extraneous environmental contingencies on reward processing. The potential influence of such contingencies has been suggested by two recent behavioural studies (Scheres *et al.*, 2006; Solanto *et al.*, 2001). Scheres *et al.* (2006) examined temporal discounting in children (aged 6–11) and adolescents (aged 12–17) with and without ADHD. Temporal discounting (TD) refers to the decrease of subjective reward value as a function of increasing delay (Monterosso & Ainslie, 1999; Critchfield & Kollins, 2001). It may be a more sensitive measure of reward-related processes than previously used paradigms such as the Choice Delay Task, as TD functions capture the trade-off between reward magnitude and delay (Myerson *et al.*, 2001). However, TD in ADHD has received little research attention. In the TD task employed by Scheres *et al.* (2006), participants chose between small immediate rewards and larger delayed rewards, and the size of the rewards (real money) and the delay were parametrically varied so that the subjective value of the large delayed reward could be plotted as a function of delay (a discounting function). The large reward (10 cents) was delayed by between 0 and 30 seconds (0, 5, 10, 20, and 30 s), and the immediate reward varied in magnitude (0, 2, 4, 6, 8 and 10 cents). The primary hypothesis of the study was that ADHD participants would show steeper temporal discounting than controls.

Contrary to expectations, however, there were no differences between children and adolescents with ADHD and controls in temporal discounting of real monetary rewards. This result stands in contrast to previous studies that demonstrated increased preference for smaller, immediate rewards in ADHD (e.g. Sonuga-Barke *et al.*, 1992; Barkley *et al.*, 2001; Kuntsi *et al.*, 2001; Solanto *et al.*, 2001; Tripp & Alsop, 2001; Bitsakou *et al.*, 2006). Several methodological issues may account for the negative finding of this study and its divergence from previous studies which used more standard choice-delay tasks, with only one choice (e.g. 2 cents now or 10 cents after 30 seconds) repeated several times (e.g. Sonuga-Barke *et al.*, 1992; Solanto *et al.*, 2001). These issues demonstrate the crucial but perhaps subtle impact of reward and environmental contingencies on reward-related behaviour, and highlight the need to distinguish between real and hypothetical rewards and delays (e.g. Barkley *et al.*, 2001), to be cautious regarding the provision of rewards following the practice trials (as this may have increased the incentive salience of the task, an effect that was also observed by Solanto *et al.* 2001), and to be aware of the use of varying reward magnitudes and delays, which, in this study, may have decreased monotony as well as decreasing the intensity of the delay effect (Scheres *et al.*, 2006). These issues emphasise that reward-related processes and reward learning involve highly sensitive neural mechanisms, a primary function of which is to associate subtle cues in the environment with the attainment of rewards. Thus, subtle and apparently extraneous environmental and contextual factors can have considerable impact on reward-related behaviour, an important consideration which we should attempt to incorporate into our study designs.

Caveat #2: Another important consideration for neuroimaging investigations of reward-related processing in ADHD is that we sometimes may not observe a significant difference in behavioural performance between the ADHD and control groups. Nonetheless, when brain activations are examined, meaningful differences may be observed, as has been demonstrated by several studies in which the groups being compared performed at equivalent levels (e.g. Ring *et al.*, 1999; Cabeza *et al.*, 2002; Park *et al.*, 2003; Sohn *et al.*, 2004; Cannon *et al.*, 2005; Valera *et al.*, 2005). This was also the case in the neuroimaging study (discussed above), which demonstrated ventral striatal hypoactivation in individuals with ADHD during reward anticipation, despite there being no differences in behavioural performance between the ADHD and control groups (Scheres *et al.*, in press). Similarly, Ernst *et al.* (2003) showed that adults with childhood-onset ADHD had lower levels of activation than a control group in limbic areas such as the hippocampus and in the anterior cingulate during the performance of a risky decision-making task (the Iowa Gambling Task), in the absence of performance differences between the groups. These findings demonstrate that neuroimaging can provide insights inaccessible to purely behavioural analyses (Rubia, 2002).

Nonetheless, this situation represents a 'catch-22' situation for any neuroimaging researcher: in the absence of differences in overt behaviour, and more specifically, behavioural impairment in an ADHD group, what is the meaning of differences in brain activation? On the other hand, differences in overt behaviour may confound interpretations of differences in activation, as those activation differences may be secondary to behavioural differences such as lower accuracy rates, or slower/more variable reaction times (Murphy & Garavan, 2004). Indeed, it has been argued that activation differences between groups cannot be reliably interpreted unless the clinical and control groups are matched on performance (Callicott *et al.*, 1998).

This issue is complicated further if we are to examine neuropsychologically impaired subtypes – the selection of a subgroup within an ADHD sample who demonstrate significantly impaired performance relative to controls. If this strategy is to be employed in neuroimaging studies, and groups are mismatched on perform-ance, we must be able to rule out potentially confounding factors such as poor motivation, lack of understanding or lack of cooperation, before differences in activation can be interpreted reliably. Another potential solution is the use of para-metric designs, as these provide a within-subject comparison (control) that can aid in the interpretation of group differences in activation (Brown & Eyler, 2006).

These issues aside, careful examination of differences in activation and brain-behaviour relationships are vital to our understanding of neurobiology of ADHD. For example, Fassbender and Schweitzer (2006) recently reviewed the neuroimag-ing evidence for compensatory neural activations in ADHD. They suggest that the literature is consistent with an ADHD-related pattern of hypoactivity in prefrontal and midline areas of the brain and concurrently, greater recruitment or hyperactiva-tion of more posterior visual, spatial and motor regions during task performance. However, little is known about the putative dysfunctions and compensatory mech-anisms underlying these patterns of hypo- and hyperactivity, highlighting the need for considerable further research.

Caveat #3: It is also necessary to think carefully about the role of reward-related delay in ADHD. The prediction that children with ADHD would show a steeper decline in NAcc activation over the delay prior to reward seems to follow logically from the evidence suggesting that NAcc dopamine firing to future rewards is reduced in ADHD (Scheres *et al.*, in press). However, it is also possible that delay represents a 'motivational commodity' to ADHD children in and of itself, independent of its effects on reward salience. For instance, at the heart of the concept of Delay Aversion is the hypothesis that delay has a powerful negative salience for children with ADHD. That is, children with ADHD experience the imposition of a delay prior to receipt of rewards as punishing, and escaping the delay is negatively rein-forcing. If this hypothesis is correct, then the inclusion of a delay before rewards will have two competing effects in terms of overall salience for the ADHD child: it will reduce the motivational salience (subjective magnitude) of the reward, and at the same time it will increase the salience of the delay. These responses should be dissociable on a neural level, however, as the NAcc appears to respond to posi-tive, rewarding events, rather than to punishments (in humans, e.g. Knutson *et al.*, 2001a, but see animal studies for conflicting evidence, e.g. Schoenbaum & Setlow, 2003; Wilson & Bowman, 2005), while other areas of the striatum and the amygdala appear to respond to both positive and negative outcomes (Delgado *et al.*, 2003; McClure *et al.*, 2004b). Nonetheless, it is important to bear in mind that both valance and salience will impact upon the functional activations observed and the inclusion of experimental manipulations to tease apart their separate influence should be considered.

11.4.3   HOW CAN WE CHARACTERISE THE DISTINCTIVE CONTRIBUTION OF 'HOT' AND 'COOL' PROCESSES AND THEIR INTERACTIONS TO ADHD?

We have emphasised that interaction between 'hot' and 'cool' processing pathways is necessary for successful goal-directed behaviour, and we have suggested that Haber's (Haber *et al.*, 2000; Haber, 2003) description of the striato-nigral-striatal and thalamo-cortico-thalamic networks provides the anatomic basis through which emotion/motivation-related 'hot' EF pathways influence 'cool' EF pathways. Information flow through non-reciprocal components of these spiralling circuits is unidirectional, suggesting a hierarchy of emotion/motivation affecting cognitive processing which can regulate motor outputs (Haber, 2003). Such a hierarchy may be particularly relevant to the understanding of ADHD and related disorders (Castellanos *et al.*, 2006) – as Haber points out: 'parallel circuits and integrative circuits must work together, so that the coordinated behaviours are maintained and focused (via parallel networks), but also can be modified and changed according to appropriate external and internal stimuli (via integrative networks). Indeed, both the inability to maintain and to focus in the execution of specific behaviours, as well as the inability to adapt appropriately to external and internal cues, are key deficits in basal ganglia diseases which affect these aspects of motor control, cognition and motivation' (Haber, 2003, p. 325).

   Haber's description of distinct but interacting circuits prompts the examination of the loci and consequence of their interactions, and the role dysfunctional interactions might play in ADHD. A potentially crucial locus of this interaction is the anterior cingulate cortex (ACC), part of the thalamo-cortical-striatal pathway (Sonuga-Barke, 2005). The ACC has been implicated in conflict-and error-monitoring processes, and more specifically, through its interconnections with PFC, in signalling the requirement for and implementing cognitive control (MacDonald *et al.*, 2000; Kerns *et al.*, 2004; Ridderinkhof *et al.*, 2004; Brown & Braver, 2005). The ACC is thus well suited to the role of integrating bottom-up reward-related signals with top-down signals in order to indicate the need for changes in behaviour and for the implementation of cognitive control. In support of this suggestion, a recent study (Cohen *et al.*, 2005) demonstrated increased connectivity between the ACC and areas implicated in reward-related processing, including the NAcc and OFC, when participants were faced with high-relative to low-risk decisions. Furthermore, a recent study (Magno *et al.*, 2006) demonstrated dissociable roles for the ACC and NAcc in signalling the requirement for control and signalling response to absence of reward. Those authors suggest that the NAcc responds to primary reward-related information while the ACC uses this information in the signalling and implementation of behavioural change. There is consistent evidence for hypoactivation of the

ACC in ADHD (Bush *et al.*, 1999, Dickstein *et al.*, 2006; Fassbender & Schweitzer, 2006), emphasising the requirement to investigate the ACC as a potential locus of dysfunction in the interactions between 'cool' and 'hot' EF pathways in ADHD.

A recent paper also provides other clues regarding the interactions between 'hot' and 'cool' pathways. McClure *et al.* (2004a) demonstrated that the ventral striatum, medial OFC and medial PFC showed greater activation when subjects were required to choose between small immediate and larger delayed rewards, while dlPFC, lateral OFC and parietal cortex showed greater levels of activation when participants chose the larger delayed reward over the small immediate reward. The authors suggest decision-making is governed by a competition between the more automatic appetitive processes of the ventral striatum-OFC circuit and reasoning and planning processes in fronto-parietal cortex. When the ventral striatal-OFC circuit 'wins' this competition, impatient or impulsive choice results (McClure *et al.*, 2004a).

In consideration of these findings, we suggest that an important avenue for research will be the identification and examination of potential loci of dysfunction along the 'hot' and 'cool' pathways and the neural systems for motor production with which they interact (see also Nigg & Casey, 2005). Key research questions that arise from this focus include: what is the impact of affective/'hot' processes on 'cool' EF such as decision-making? Conversely, how do 'cool' EF processes and cognitive control impact upon reward-related and motivational processes?

The potential avenues for empirical research outlined in this section may serve as the foundation for new directions in the field of ADHD research. In the next section we briefly outline what might be the focus of some of these future directions.

11.5   FUTURE DIRECTIONS

In this chapter we have outlined the evidence suggesting that decrements in 'hot' EF – reward-related and motivational processes, constitute a significant and measurable deficit in ADHD, and are distinct from deficits in other 'cool' cognitive EF processes. Pursuit of the research directions laid out in the preceding section will enable the empirical delineation of the deficits in motivational processes implicated in ADHD, and their underlying neural substrates. The development of new paradigms (Bitsakou *et al.*, 2006; Muller *et al.*, 2006) which attempt to incorporate more sensitive measures of Delay Aversion than those employed previously, is a promising step in this direction. One component of these future investigations may be the examination of 'hot' EF deficits as potential ADHD endophenotypes. The endophenotype approach has been described in detail in other chapters (Chapter 12) and in previous papers (Castellanos & Tannock, 2002). Further investigations are needed to establish whether deficits in specific 'hot' EF processes are endophenotypic for ADHD.

In highlighting the potential for examinations of 'hot' motivational processes in ADHD we have also drawn attention to a caveat – reward-related processes and reward learning involve highly sensitive neural mechanisms, a primary function of which is to associate subtle cues in the environment with the attainment of rewards. There is thus a clear requirement that those working in the area of reward research develop an awareness of the influence of apparently extraneous environmental and contextual factors in their research.

The potential for examination of interactions between 'hot' and 'cool' EF and their underlying neural substrates represents a promising new direction for ADHD research. That ADHD individuals demonstrate hypoactivation in the ACC is an increasingly robust finding (Bush et al., 1999; Dickstein et al., 2006; Fassbender & Schweitzer, 2006), prompting the question of how this hypoactivity might impact on the implementation of cognitive control ('cool' EF) and the interactions between 'hot' and 'cool' EF processes.

As we have emphasised throughout the chapter (see also Chapter 12), the use of neuropsychologically impaired subtypes may constitute a break-through in the characterisation of the neural substrates of ADHD (Nigg, Willcutt et al., 2005). This implies the identification of a subgroup within an ADHD research sample who show a significant decrement in performance, relative to controls (e.g., as employed by Johnson et al., 2007). This subgroup may have a specific deficit in the neurocognitive function of interest, which is not shared by other members of the ADHD sample, but which contributes to the expression of the disorder. Comparisons between this subgroup and controls, or between this subgroup and the 'unimpaired' ADHD group, on measures of interest, should then be informative with regard to the behavioural, cognitive or neurobiological correlates of the specific deficit in the 'impaired' ADHD subgroup. The inclusion of secondary measures of impulsivity, hyperactivity, and other symptoms (e.g. questionnaires such as the Barratt Impulsiveness Scale) will aid in the examination of the potential relationships between these dissociable deficits and real-world behaviours. These steps will enable us to construct neurobiological dimensional profiles of ADHD that will improve on current symptom-based distinctions (Castellanos et al., 2006). Moreover, by defining neuropsychologically impaired subgroups, the heterogeneity of a sample will be reduced, which may clarify some of the inconsistencies in behavioural findings to date. For example, a recent study observed that the preference for small immediate over larger delayed rewards demonstrated by children with ADHD was uncorrelated with the Stop Signal Reaction Time (SSRT), suggesting that inhibitory deficits and delay aversion are dissociable processes (Solanto et al., 2001). Furthermore, performance on either task was only moderately associated with ADHD, but taken together, performance on both tasks correctly classified almost 90% of children with ADHD.

Once we have formed a picture of the patterns of neuropsychologically and neurologically dissociable deficits (a 'Table of Neurocognitive Elements', something which will require considerable further research), we should be able to measure those deficits in any sample of ADHD individuals by assessing them on a battery of tasks which tap the identified span of deficits. This, in turn, may feed into the development of targeted neurorehabilitative interventions (see Chapter 20). Without demonstrable (significant) impairment on a given cognitive ability, cognitive remediation techniques aimed at that ability would fail to show significant improvement across an ADHD sample, as a subset of that sample will not have been impaired on that function in the first place. Thus the establishment of neuropsychological subtypes of ADHD is a critical step in moving the field of research forward, both in terms of basic research, and in terms of the design of rehabilitative interventions.

Finally, the DA reward prediction system, and in particular the ventral striatum and NAcc, are central to the understanding of substance abuse and addiction. Drugs such as opiates, nicotine, cocaine and amphetamine increase DA concentration by either increasing its release or blocking its reuptake (Schultz, 2001). Work with animal models suggests that DA neurons in the ventral striatum respond to these drugs in a similar way to natural rewards. Thus natural reward and drug-seeking behaviour might share a common path in the influence of the reward message on goal-directed behaviour (Schultz, 2001). Increasing knowledge about neurophysiological reward mechanisms may therefore help provide us with a better understanding of the mechanism of action of addictive drugs. This possibility is of great relevance to the study of ADHD, as we know that individuals with a diagnosis of ADHD are more susceptible to substance abuse than the general population (e.g. Biederman *et al.*, 1995; Biederman *et al.*, 1999). Substance abuse in ADHD has been interpreted by some as self-medication, and it has been suggested that treatment with psychostimulants may decrease the risk for substance abuse in ADHD (Wilens, 2004). The link between the dysfunctional reward processing mechanisms and the development of substance abuse disorder represents an important new frontier in ADHD research.

11.6 SUMMARY

In this chapter we have provided an outline of some of the main avenues of investigation, and potential research hypotheses, in the examination of reward and motivational processes in ADHD. We have emphasised that the heterogeneity intrinsic to the disorder demands a multi-faceted approach, one which bridges the key areas of ADHD research, particularly those that examine dysfunction in 'cool' EF and those that examine deficits in reward-related and other motivational processes ('hot' EF). In addition, we have emphasised the need to examine the potential foci of interaction between these distinct but intertwined processing pathways. It is in this way that we believe the field will move forward to provide a deeper understanding of the etiological processes underlying ADHD, and provide targets for neurocognitive interventions.

11.7 REFERENCES

Abercrombie ED, Bonatz AE, Zigmond MJ (1990) Effects of L-dopa on extracellular dopamine in striatum of normal and 6-hydroxydopamine-treated rats. *Brain Res* **525**: 36–44.

Alexander GE, Crutcher MD (1990) Functional architecture of basal ganglia circuits: neural substrates of parallel processing. *Trends Neurosci* **13**: 266–71.

Alexander GE, Delong MR, Strick PL (1986) Parallel organization of functionally segregated circuits linking basal ganglia and cortex. *Annu Rev Neurosci* **9**: 357–81.

Aron AR, Poldrack RA (2005) The cognitive neuroscience of response inhibition: relevance for genetic research in Attention-Deficit/Hyperactivity Disorder. *Biol Psychiatry* **57**: 1285–92.

Aron AR, Robbins TW, Poldrack RA (2004) Inhibition and the right inferior frontal cortex. *Trends Cogn Sci* **8**: 170–7.

Aylward EH, Reiss AL, Reader MJ *et al.* (1996) Basal ganglia volumes in children with Attention-Deficit Hyperactivity Disorder. *J Child Neurol* **11**: 112–15.

Barkley RA (1997) Behavioral inhibition, sustained attention, and executive functions: constructing a unifying theory of ADHD. *Psychol Bull* **121**: 65–94.

Barkley RA, Edwards G, Laneri M *et al.* (2001) Executive functioning, temporal discounting, and sense of time in adolescents with attention deficit hyperactivity disorder (ADHD) and oppositional defiant disorder (ODD). *J Abnorm Child Psychol* **29**: 541–56.

Berns GS, McClure SM, Pagnoni G, Montague PR (2001) Predictability modulates human brain response to reward. *J Neurosci* **21**: 2793–8.

Biederman, J, Faraone SV (2002) Current concepts on the neurobiology of Attention-Deficit/Hyperactivity Disorder. *J Atten Disord* **6**(Suppl 1): S7–16.

Biederman J, Wilens T, Mick E *et al.* (1995) Psychoactive substance use disorders in adults with attention deficit hyperactivity disorder (ADHD): effects of ADHD and psychiatric comorbidity. *Am J Psychiatry* **152**: 1652–8.

Biederman J, Wilens T, Mick E *et al.* (1999) Pharmacotherapy of Attention-Deficit/Hyperactivity Disorder reduces risk for substance use disorder. *Pediatrics* **104**: e20.

Bitsakou P, Antrop I, Wiersema JR, Sonuga-Barke EJ (2006) Probing the limits of delay intolerance: preliminary young adult data from the Delay Frustration Task (DeFT). *J Neurosci Methods* **151**: 38–44.

Blum K, Braverman ER, Holder JM *et al.* (2000) Reward deficiency syndrome: a biogenetic model for the diagnosis and treatment of impulsive, addictive, and compulsive behaviors. *J Psychoactive Drugs* **32**(Suppl): i–iv, 1–112.

Boonstra AM, Oosterlaan J, Sergeant JA, Buitelaar JK (2005) Executive functioning in adult ADHD: a meta-analytic review. *Psychol Med* **35**: 1097–1108.

Brown GG, Eyler LT (2006) Methodological and conceptual issues in functional magnetic resonance imaging: applications to schizophrenia research. *Annual Review of Clinical Psychology* **2**: 51–81.

Brown JW, Braver TS (2005) Learned predictions of error likelihood in the anterior cingulate cortex. *Science* **307**: 1118–21.

Bush G, Frazier JA, Rauch SL *et al.* (1999) Anterior cingulate cortex dysfunction in Attention-Deficit/Hyperactivity Disorder revealed by fMRI and the Counting Stroop. *Biol Psychiatry* **45**: 1542–52.

Cabeza R, Anderson ND, Locantore JK, McIntosh AR (2002) Aging gracefully: compensatory brain activity in high-performing older adults. *Neuroimage* **17**: 1394–1402.

Callicott JH, Ramsey NF, Tallent K *et al.* (1998) Functional magnetic resonance imaging brain mapping in psychiatry: methodological issues illustrated in a study of working memory in schizophrenia. *Neuropsychopharmacology* **18**: 186–96.

Cannon TD, Glahn DC, Kim J *et al.* (2005) Dorsolateral prefrontal cortex activity during maintenance and manipulation of information in working memory in patients with schizophrenia. *Arch Gen Psychiatry* **62**: 1071–80.

Cardinal RN, Pennicott DR, Sugathapala CL *et al.* (2001) Impulsive choice induced in rats by lesions of the nucleus accumbens core. *Science* **292**: 2499–2501.

Cardinal RN, Parkinson JA, Lachenal G *et al.* (2002) Effects of selective excitotoxic lesions of the nucleus accumbens core, anterior cingulate cortex, and central nucleus of the amygdala on autoshaping performance in rats. *Behav Neurosci* **116**: 553–67.

Cardinal RN, Cheung TH (2005) Nucleus accumbens core lesions retard instrumental learning and performance with delayed reinforcement in the rat. *BMC Neurosci* **6**(9).

Casey BJ, Castellanos FX, Giedd JN *et al.* (1997) Implication of right frontostriatal circuitry in response inhibition and Attention-Deficit/Hyperactivity Disorder. *J Am Acad Child Adolesc Psychiatry* **36**: 374–83.

Castellanos FX, Giedd JN, Marsh WL *et al.* (1996) Quantitative brain magnetic resonance imaging in Attention-Deficit Hyperactivity Disorder. *Arch Gen Psychiatry* **53**: 607–16.

Castellanos FX, Sonuga-Barke EJ, Milham MP, Tannock R (2006) Characterizing cognition in ADHD: beyond executive dysfunction. *Trends Cogn Sci* **10**: 117–23.

Castellanos FX, Sonuga-Barke EJ, Scheres A *et al.* (2005) Varieties of Attention-Deficit/Hyperactivity Disorder-related intra-individual variability. *Biol Psychiatry* **57**: 1416–23.

Castellanos FX, Tannock R (2002) Neuroscience of Attention-Deficit/Hyperactivity Disorder: the search for endophenotypes. *Nat Rev Neurosci* **3**: 617–28.

Chambers CD, Bellgrove MA, Stokes MG *et al.* (2005) Executive 'brake' failure following deactivation of human frontal lobe. *J Cogn Neurosci*.

Chudasama Y, Robbins TW (2006) Functions of frontostriatal systems in cognition: comparative neuropsychopharmacological studies in rats, monkeys and humans. *Biological Psychology* **73**(1): 19–38.

Cohen MX, Heller AS, Ranganath C (2005) Functional connectivity with anterior cingulate and orbitofrontal cortices during decision-making. *Brain Res Cogn Brain Res* **23**: 61–70.

Critchfield TS, Kollins SH (2001) Temporal discounting: basic research and the analysis of socially important behavior. *J Appl Behav Anal* **34**: 101–22.

Critchley HD, Rolls ET (1996) Olfactory neuronal responses in the primate orbitofrontal cortex: analysis in an olfactory discrimination task. *J Neurophysiol* **75**: 1659–72.

Curtis CE, d'Esposito M (2003) Persistent activity in the prefrontal cortex during working memory. *Trends Cogn Sci* **7**: 415–23.

Delgado MR, Locke HM, Stenger VA, Fiez JA (2003) Dorsal striatum responses to reward and punishment: effects of valence and magnitude manipulations. *Cogn Affect Behav Neurosci* **3**, 27–38.

Delgado MR, Nystrom LE, Fissell C *et al.* (2000) Tracking the hemodynamic responses to reward and punishment in the striatum. *J Neurophysiol* **84**: 3072–7.

d'Esposito M, Postle BR, Rypma B (2000) Prefrontal cortical contributions to working memory: evidence from event-related fMRI studies. *Exp Brain Res* **133**: 3–11.

Dickstein SG, Bannon K, Castellanos FX, Milham MP (2006) The neural correlates of attention deficit hyperactivity disorder: an ALE meta-analysis. *Journal of Child Psychology and Psychiatry and Allied Disciplines* **47**(10): 1051–62.

Douglas VI (1999) Cognitive control processes in Attention-Deficit/Hyperactivity Disorder. In HC Quay, AE Hogan (eds) *Handbook of Disruptive Behavior Disorders*. New York: Plenum Press.

Douglas VI, Parry PA (1983) Effects of reward on delayed reaction time task performance of hyperactive children. *J Abnorm Child Psychol* **11**: 313–26.

Durston S, Tottenham NT, Thomas KM *et al.* (2003) Differential patterns of striatal activation in young children with and without ADHD. *Biol Psychiatry* **53**: 871–8.

Ernst M, Grant SJ, London ED *et al.* (2003) Decision making in adolescents with behavior disorders and adults with substance abuse. *Am J Psychiatry* **160**: 33–40.

Ernst M, Nelson EE, Jazbec *et al.* (2005) Amygdala and nucleus accumbens in responses to receipt and omission of gains in adults and adolescents. *Neuroimage* **25**, 1279–91.

Ernst M, Zametkin AJ, Matochik JA *et al.* (1999) High midbrain [18F]DOPA accumulation in children with attention deficit hyperactivity disorder. *Am J Psychiatry* **156**: 1209–15.

Faraone SV, Biederman J (1998) Neurobiology of Attention-Deficit Hyperactivity Disorder. *Biol Psychiatry* **44**: 951–8.

Fassbender C, Schweitzer JB (2006) Is there evidence for neural compensation in attention deficit hyperactivity disorder? A review of the functional neuroimaging literature. *Clin Psychol Rev.*

Filipek PA, Semrud-Clikeman M, Steingard RJ *et al.* (1997) Volumetric MRI analysis comparing subjects having Attention-Deficit Hyperactivity Disorder with normal controls. *Neurology* **48**: 589–601.

Galvan A, Hare TA, Davidson M *et al.* (2005) The role of ventral frontostriatal circuitry in reward-based learning in humans. *J Neurosci* **25**: 8650–6.

Haber SN (2003) The primate basal ganglia: parallel and integrative networks. *J Chem Neuroanat* **26**: 317–30.

Haber SN, Fudge JL, McFarland NR (2000) Striatonigrostriatal pathways in primates form an ascending spiral from the shell to the dorsolateral striatum. *J Neurosci* **20**: 2369–82.

Hadjiconstantinou M, Wemlinger TA, Sylvia CP *et al.* (1993) Aromatic L-amino acid decarboxylase activity of mouse striatum is modulated via dopamine receptors. *J Neurochem* **60**: 2175–80.

Haenlein M, Caul WF (1987) Attention deficit disorder with hyperactivity: a specific hypothesis of reward dysfunction. *J Am Acad Child Adolesc Psychiatry* **26**: 356–62.

Heyder K, Suchan B, Daum I (2004) Cortico-subcortical contributions to executive control. *Acta Psychol (Amst)* **115**: 271–89.

Hollerman JR, Schultz W (1998) Dopamine neurons report an error in the temporal prediction of reward during learning. *Nat Neurosci* **1**: 304–9.

Homack S, Riccio CA (2004) A meta-analysis of the sensitivity and specificity of the Stroop Color and Word Test with children. *Arch Clin Neuropsychol* **19**: 725–43.

Hongwanishkul D, Happaney KR, Lee WS, Zelazo PD (2005) Assessment of hot and cool executive function in young children: age-related changes and individual differences. *Dev Neuropsychol* **28**: 617–44.

Iaboni F, Douglas VI, Ditto B (1997) Psychophysiological response of ADHD children to reward and extinction. *Psychophysiology* **34**: 116–23.

Izawa E, Aoki N, Matsushima T (2005) Neural correlates of the proximity and quantity of anticipated food rewards in the ventral striatum of domestic chicks. *Eur J Neurosci* **22**: 1502–12.

Johansen EB, Aase H, Meyer A, Sagvolden T (2002) Attention-deficit/hyperactivity disorder (ADHD) behaviour explained by dysfunctioning reinforcement and extinction processes. *Behav Brain Res* **130**: 37–45.

Johansen EB, Sagvolden T (2005a [formerly b]) Behavioral effects of intra-cranial self-stimulation in an animal model of Attention-Deficit/Hyperactivity Disorder (ADHD). *Behav Brain Res* **162**: 32–46.

Johansen EB, Sagvolden T (2005b [formerly a]) Slower extinction of responses maintained by intra-cranial self-stimulation (ICSS) in an animal model of Attention-Deficit/Hyperactivity Disorder (ADHD). *Behav Brain Res* **162**: 22–31.

Johansen EB, Sagvolden T, Kvande G (2005) Effects of delayed reinforcers on the behavior of an animal model of Attention-Deficit/Hyperactivity Disorder (ADHD). *Behav Brain Res* **162**: 47–61.

Johnson KA, Kelly SP, Bellgrove MA *et al.* (2007) Response variability in Attention Deficit Hyperactivity Disorder: evidence for neuropsychological heterogeneity. *Neuropsychologia* **45**(4): 630–8.

Kerns JG, Cohen JD, Macdonald AW *et al.* (2004) Anterior cingulate conflict monitoring and adjustments in control. *Science* **303**: 1023–6.

Knutson B, Adams CM, Fong GW, Hommer D (2001a) Anticipation of increasing monetary reward selectively recruits nucleus accumbens. *J Neurosci* **21**: RC159.

Knutson B, Cooper JC (2005) Functional magnetic resonance imaging of reward prediction. *Curr Opin Neurol* **18**: 411–17.

Knutson B, Fong GW, Adams CM *et al.* (2001b) Dissociation of reward anticipation and outcome with event-related fMRI. *Neuroreport* **12**: 3683–7.

Knutson B, Fong GW, Bennett SM *et al.* (2003) A region of mesial prefrontal cortex tracks monetarily rewarding outcomes: characterization with rapid event-related fMRI. *Neuroimage* **18**: 263–72.

Knutson B, Taylor J, Kaufman M *et al.* (2005) Distributed neural representation of expected value. *J Neurosci* **25**: 4806–12.

Knutson B, Westdorp A, Kaiser E, Hommer D (2000) FMRI visualization of brain activity during a monetary incentive delay task. *Neuroimage* **12**: 20–7.

Kuntsi J, Oosterlaan J, Stevenson J (2001) Psychological mechanisms in hyperactivity: I. Response inhibition deficit, working memory impairment, delay aversion, or something else? *J Child Psychol Psychiatry* **42**: 199–210.

Luman M, Oosterlaan J, Sergeant JA (2005) The impact of reinforcement contingencies on AD/HD: a review and theoretical appraisal. *Clin Psychol Rev* **25**: 183–213.

McClure SM, Berns GS, Montague PR (2003) Temporal prediction errors in a passive learning task activate human striatum. *Neuron* **38**: 339–46.

McClure SM, Laibson DI, Loewenstein G, Cohen JD (2004a) Separate neural systems value immediate and delayed monetary rewards. *Science* **306**: 503–7.

McClure SM, York MK, Montague PR (2004b) The neural substrates of reward processing in humans: the modern role of FMRI. *Neuroscientist* **10**: 260–8.

MacDonald AW III, Cohen JD, Stenger VA, Carter CS (2000) Dissociating the role of the dorsolateral prefrontal and anterior cingulate cortex in cognitive control. *Science* **288**: 1835–8.

McFarland NR, Haber SN (2002) Thalamic relay nuclei of the basal ganglia form both reciprocal and nonreciprocal cortical connections, linking multiple frontal cortical areas. *J Neurosci* **22**: 8117–32.

Magno E, Foxe JJ, Molhom S *et al.* (2006) The anterior cingulate and error avoidance. *J Neurosci* **26**(18): 4769–73.

Manor I, Tyano S, Mel E *et al.* (2002) Family-based and association studies of monoamine oxidase A and attention deficit hyperactivity disorder (ADHD): preferential transmission of the long promoter-region repeat and its association with impaired performance on a continuous performance test (TOVA). *Molecular Psychiatry* **7**: 626–32.

Martinussen R, Hayden J, Hogg-Johnson S, Tannock R (2005) A meta-analysis of working memory impairments in children with Attention-Deficit/Hyperactivity Disorder. *J Am Acad Child Adolesc Psychiatry* **44**: 377–84.

Mataro M, Garcia-Sanchez C, Junque C *et al.* (1997) Magnetic resonance imaging measurement of the caudate nucleus in adolescents with Attention-Deficit Hyperactivity Disorder and its relationship with neuropsychological and behavioral measures. *Arch Neurol* **54**: 963–8.

Monterosso J, Ainslie G (1999) Beyond discounting: possible experimental models of impulse control. *Psychopharmacology (Berl)* **146**: 339–47.

Muller UC, Sonuga-Barke EJ, Brandeis D, Steinhausen HC (2006) Online measurement of motivational processes: introducing the Continuous Delay Aversion Test (ConDAT). *J Neurosci Methods* **151**: 45–51.

Murphy K, Garavan H (2004) Artifactual fMRI group and condition differences driven by performance confounds. *Neuroimage* **21**: 219–28.

Myerson J, Green L, Warusawitharana M (2001) Area under the curve as a measure of discounting. *J Exp Anal Behav* **76**: 235–43.

Nigg JT (2001) Is ADHD a disinhibitory disorder? *Psychol Bull* **127**: 571–98.

Nigg JT (2005) Neuropsychologic theory and findings in Attention-Deficit/Hyperactivity Disorder: the state of the field and salient challenges for the coming decade. *Biol Psychiatry* **57**: 1424–35.

Nigg JT, Casey BJ (2005) An integrative theory of attention-deficit/hyperactivity disorder based on the cognitive and affective neurosciences. *Dev Psychopathol* **17**: 785–806.

Nigg JT, Willcutt EG, Doyle AE, Sonuga-Barke EJ (2005) Causal heterogeneity in Attention-Deficit/Hyperactivity Disorder: do we need neuropsychologically impaired subtypes? *Biol Psychiatry* **57**: 1224–30.

O'Doherty JP (2004) Reward representations and reward-related learning in the human brain: insights from neuroimaging. *Curr Opin Neurobiol* **14**: 769–76.

O'Doherty JP, Critchley H, Deichmann R, Dolan RJ (2003a) Dissociating valence of outcome from behavioral control in human orbital and ventral prefrontal cortices. *J Neurosci* **23**: 7931–9.

O'Doherty JP, Dayan P, Friston K *et al.* (2003b) Temporal difference models and reward-related learning in the human brain. *Neuron* **38**: 329–37.

O'Doherty JP, Deichmann R, Critchley HD. Dolan RJ (2002) Neural responses during anticipation of a primary taste reward. *Neuron* **33**: 815–26.

Padoa-Schioppa C, Assad JA (2006) Neurons in the orbitofrontal cortex encode economic value. *Nature* **441**: 223–6.

Pagnoni G, Zink CF, Montague PR, Berns GS (2002) Activity in human ventral striatum locked to errors of reward prediction. *Nat Neurosci* **5**: 97–8.

Park DC, Welsh RC, Marshuetz C *et al.* (2003) Working memory for complex scenes: age differences in frontal and hippocampal activations. *J Cogn Neurosci* **15**: 1122–34.

Ramnani N, Elliott R, Athwal BS, Passingham RE (2004) Prediction error for free monetary reward in the human prefrontal cortex. *Neuroimage* **23**: 777–86.

Rapport MD, Tucker SB, Dupaul GJ *et al.* (1986) Hyperactivity and frustration: the influence of control over and size of rewards in delaying gratification. *J Abnorm Child Psychol* **14**: 191–204.

Ridderinkhof KR, Ullsperger M, Crone EA, Nieuwenhuis S (2004) The role of the medial frontal cortex in cognitive control. *Science* **306**: 443–7.

Ring HA, Baron-Cohen S, Wheelwright S *et al.* (1999) Cerebral correlates of preserved cognitive skills in autism: a functional MRI study of embedded figures task performance. *Brain* **122**(Pt 7): 1305–15.

Robbins TW (2005) Chemistry of the mind: neurochemical modulation of prefrontal cortical function. *J Comp Neurol* **493**: 140–6.

Rogers RD, Ramnani N, Mackay C *et al.* (2004) Distinct portions of anterior cingulate cortex and medial prefrontal cortex are activated by reward processing in separable phases of decision-making cognition. *Biol Psychiatry* **55**: 594–602.

Romine CB, Lee D, Wolfe ME *et al.* (2004) Wisconsin Card Sorting Test with children: a meta-analytic study of sensitivity and specificity. *Arch Clin Neuropsychol* **19**: 1027–41.

Rubia K (2002) The dynamic approach to neurodevelopmental psychiatric disorders: use of fMRI combined with neuropsychology to elucidate the dynamics of psychiatric disorders, exemplified in ADHD and schizophrenia. *Behav Brain Res* **130**: 47–56.

Rubia K, Overmeyer S, Taylor E *et al.* (1999) Hypofrontality in attention deficit hyperactivity disorder during higher-order motor control: a study with functional MRI. *Am J Psychiatry* **156**: 891–6.

Rubia K, Smith AB, Brammer MJ *et al.* (2005) Abnormal brain activation during inhibition and error detection in medication-naive adolescents with ADHD. *American Journal of Psychiatry* **162**: 1067–75.

Sagvolden T, Aase H, Zeiner P, Berger D (1998) Altered reinforcement mechanisms in Attention-Deficit/Hyperactivity Disorder. *Behav Brain Res* **94**: 61–71.

Sagvolden T, Johansen EB, Aase H, Russell VA (2005) A dynamic developmental theory of Attention-Deficit/Hyperactivity Disorder (ADHD) predominantly hyperactive/impulsive and combined subtypes. *Behav Brain Sci* **28**: 397–419; discussion 419–68.

Sagvolden T, Sergeant JA (1998) Attention deficit/hyperactivity disorder – from brain dysfunctions to behaviour. *Behav Brain Res* **94**: 1–10.

Scheres A, Dijkstra M, Ainslie E *et al.* (2006) Temporal and probabilistic discounting of rewards in children and adolescents: Effects of age and ADHD symptoms. *Neuropsychologia* **44**(11): 2092–103.

Scheres A, Milham MP, Knutson B, Castellanos FX (in press) Ventral striatal hyporesponsiveness during reward anticipation in Attention Deficit/Hyperactivity Disorder. *Biol Psychiatry*.

Schoenbaum G, Setlow B (2003) Lesions of nucleus accumbens disrupt learning about aversive outcomes. *J Neurosci* **23**: 9833–41.

Schultz W (1998) Predictive reward signal of dopamine neurons. *J Neurophysiol* **80**: 1–27.

Schultz W (2001) Reward signaling by dopamine neurons. *Neuroscientist* **7**: 293–302.

Schultz W (2002) Getting formal with dopamine and reward. *Neuron* **36**: 241–63.

Schultz W, Apicella P, Ljungberg T (1993) Responses of monkey dopamine neurons to reward and conditioned stimuli during successive steps of learning a delayed response task. *J Neurosci* **13**: 900–13.

Schultz W, Romo R (1990) Dopamine neurons of the monkey midbrain: contingencies of responses to stimuli eliciting immediate behavioral reactions. *J Neurophysiol* **63**: 607–24.

Schultz W, Tremblay L, Hollerman JR (1998) Reward prediction in primate basal ganglia and frontal cortex. *Neuropharmacology* **37**: 421–9.

Schweitzer JB, Sulzer-Azaroff B (1995) Self-control in boys with attention deficit hyperactivity disorder: effects of added stimulation and time. *J Child Psychol Psychiatry* **36**: 671–86.

Slaats-Willemse D, Swaab-Barneveld H, de Sonneville L *et al.* (2003) Deficient response inhibition as a cognitive endophenotype of ADHD. *Journal of the American Academy of Child and Adolescent Psychiatry* **42**: 1242–8.

Sohn MH, Goode A, Koedinger KR *et al.* (2004) Behavioral equivalence, but not neural equivalence – neural evidence of alternative strategies in mathematical thinking. *Nat Neurosci* **7**: 1193–4.

Solanto MV, Abikoff H, Sonuga-Barke E *et al.* (2001) The ecological validity of delay aversion and response inhibition as measures of impulsivity in AD/HD: a supplement to the NIMH multimodal treatment study of AD/HD. *J Abnorm Child Psychol* **29**: 215–28.

Sonuga-Barke EJ (2002) Psychological heterogeneity in AD/HD – a dual pathway model of behaviour and cognition. *Behav Brain Res* **130**: 29–36.

Sonuga-Barke EJ (2003) The dual pathway model of AD/HD: an elaboration of neurodevelopmental characteristics. *Neurosci Biobehav Rev* **27**: 593–604.

Sonuga-Barke EJ (2005) Causal models of Attention-Deficit/Hyperactivity Disorder: from common simple deficits to multiple developmental pathways. *Biol Psychiatry* **57**: 1231–8.

Sonuga-Barke EJ, Dalen L, Remington B (2003) Do executive deficits and delay aversion make independent contributions to preschool Attention-Deficit/Hyperactivity Disorder symptoms? *J Am Acad Child Adolesc Psychiatry* **42**: 1335–42.

Sonuga-Barke EJ, de Houwer J, de Ruiter K *et al.* (2004) AD/HD and the capture of attention by briefly exposed delay-related cues: evidence from a conditioning paradigm. *J Child Psychol Psychiatry* **45**: 274–83.

Sonuga-Barke EJ, Taylor E, Sembi S, Smith J (1992) Hyperactivity and delay aversion – I. The effect of delay on choice. *J Child Psychol Psychiatry* **33**: 387–98.

Spencer TJ, Biederman J, Madras BK *et al.* (2005) In vivo neuroreceptor imaging in Attention-Deficit/Hyperactivity Disorder: a focus on the dopamine transporter. *Biol Psychiatry* **57**: 1293–1300.

Teicher MH, Anderson CM, Polcari A *et al.* (2000) Functional deficits in basal ganglia of children with Attention-Deficit/Hyperactivity Disorder shown with functional magnetic resonance imaging relaxometry. *Nat Med* **6**: 470–3.

Todd RD (2000) Genetics of attention deficit/hyperactivity disorder: are we ready for molecular genetic studies? *Am J Med Genet* **96**: 241–3.

Toplak ME, Rucklidge JJ, Hetherington R *et al.* (2003) Time perception deficits in Attention-Deficit/Hyperactivity Disorder and comorbid reading difficulties in child and adolescent samples. *Journal of Child Psychology and Psychiatry and Allied Disciplines* **44**: 888–903.

Torstenson R, Hartvig P, Langstrom B *et al.* (1997) Differential effects of levodopa on dopaminergic function in early and advanced Parkinson's disease. *Ann Neurol* **41**: 334–40.

Tremblay L, Schultz W (1999) Relative reward preference in primate orbitofrontal cortex. *Nature* **398**: 704–8.

Tripp G, Alsop B (1999) Sensitivity to reward frequency in boys with attention deficit hyperactivity disorder. *J Clin Child Psychol* **28**: 366–75.

Tripp G, Alsop B (2001) Sensitivity to reward delay in children with attention deficit hyperactivity disorder (ADHD). *J Child Psychol Psychiatry* **42**: 691–8.

Vaidya CJ, Bunge SA, Dudukovic NM, Zalecki CA (2005) Altered neural substrates of cognitive control in childhood ADHD: Evidence from functional magnetic resonance imaging. *American Journal of Psychiatry* **162**: 1605–13.

Valera EM, Faraone SV, Biederman J *et al.* (2005) Functional neuroanatomy of working memory in adults with Attention-Deficit/Hyperactivity Disorder. *Biological Psychiatry* **57**: 439–47.

van Mourik R, Oosterlaan J, Sergeant JA (2005) The Stroop revisited: a meta-analysis of interference control in AD/HD. *J Child Psychol Psychiatry* **46**: 150–65.

Volkow ND, Wang G, Fowler JS *et al.* (2001) Therapeutic doses of oral methylphenidate significantly increase extracellular dopamine in the human brain. *J Neurosci* **21**: RC121.

Volkow ND, Wang GJ, Fowler JS *et al.* (2004) Evidence that methylphenidate enhances the saliency of a mathematical task by increasing dopamine in the human brain. *Am J Psychiatry* **161**: 1173–80.

Wender PH (1972) The minimal brain dysfunction syndrome in children. I. The syndrome and its relevance for psychiatry. II. A psychological and biochemical model for the syndrome. *J Nerv Ment Dis* **155**: 55–71.

Wendler D, Belsky L, Thompson KM, Emanuel EJ (2005) Quantifying the federal minimal risk standard: implications for pediatric research without a prospect of direct benefit. *JAMA* **294**: 826–32.

Westerberg H, Hirvikoski T, Forssberg H, Klingberg T (2004) Visuo-spatial working memory span: A sensitive measure of cognitive deficits in children with ADHD. *Child Neuropsychology* **10**: 155–61.

Wickens JR, Tripp G (2005) Altered sensitivity to reward in children with ADHD: dopamine timing is off. Commentary on Sagvolden *et al.* A dynamic developmental theory of Attention-Deficit/Hyperactivity Disorder. *Behav Brain Sci* **28**, 445–6.

Wilens TE (2004) Attention-deficit/hyperactivity disorder and the substance use disorders: the nature of the relationship, subtypes at risk, and treatment issues. *Psychiatr Clin North Am* **27**: 283–301.

Willcutt EG, Doyle AE, Nigg JT *et al.* (2005) Validity of the executive function theory of Attention-Deficit/Hyperactivity Disorder: a meta-analytic review. *Biol Psychiatry* **57**: 1336–46.

Williams J, Taylor E (2004) Dopamine appetite and cognitive impairment in attention deficit/ hyperactivity disorder. *Neural Plast* **11**: 115–32.

Wilson DI, Bowman EM (2005) Rat nucleus accumbens neurons predominantly respond to the outcome-related properties of conditioned stimuli rather than their behavioral-switching properties. *J Neurophysiol* **94**: 49–61.

Zelazo PD, Mueller U, Goswami U (2002) Executive function in typical and atypical development. In U Goshwami (ed.) *Handbook of Childhood Cognitive Development.* Oxford: Blackwell.

Zhu MY, Juorio AV, Paterson IA, Boulton AA (1993) Regulation of striatal aromatic L-amino acid decarboxylase: effects of blockade or activation of dopamine receptors. *Eur J Pharmacol* **238**: 157–64.

12 Genes, Cognition and Brain Activity: The Endophenotype Approach to ADHD

MARK A. BELLGROVE,[1] **IAN H. ROBERTSON**[2] **AND MICHAEL GILL**[3]

1. School of Psychology and Queensland Brain Institute (QBI), at the University of Queensland, Brisbane, Australia; 2. School of Psychology and Institute of Neuroscience, Trinity College Dublin, Ireland; 3. School of Medicine and Health Sciences, Trinity College Dublin, Ireland

12.1 OVERVIEW

Molecular genetic studies of attention deficit hyperactivity disorder (ADHD) have made progress towards identifying genes that may confer susceptibility to the disorder (Chapter 8). These advances have largely been made on the basis of aetiological models of ADHD that suggest dysfunction within multiple neurotransmitter systems. The efficacy of stimulants in treating the behavioural features of ADHD led to the initial search for candidate genes involved in dopaminergic signalling. However, in a disorder that is thought to be oligogenic, and indeed multi-factorial, the effect of an individual gene on the ADHD phenotype is likely to be small. In part, for these reasons, researchers have emphasised the utility of quantitative indices of disease risk or liability, termed endophenotypes (Swanson *et al.*, 2000; Castellanos & Tannock, 2002; Gottesman & Gould, 2003). Endophenotypes are traits that may be closer to dysfunction in discrete neural systems than might be the case for the broad phenotype. Since the endophenotype is thought to be less removed from the relevant gene effect than diagnosis, endophenotypes may provide greater sensitivity for genetic studies (Almasy & Blangero, 2001). The goal of this chapter is to use knowledge from cognitive neuroscience to constrain genotype/phenotype associations. When research is guided by a cognitive-neuroanatomical model progress can be made in determining how a gene might contribute to variation in the development of brain mechanisms modulating a discrete cognitive process (Bellgrove *et al.*, in press) (see Figure 12.1). This approach extends traditional molecular genetic studies towards studies in which the gene hypothetically influences the development of a cognitive, neural or other biological process and variation within that process in turns confers susceptibility to the disorder. Here we review the cognitive neuroscience of attention, response inhibition and working memory as exemplar processes that may lie between gene and disorder.

Handbook of Attention Deficit Hyperactivity Disorder. Edited by M. Fitzgerald, M. Bellgrove and M. Gill.
© 2007 John Wiley & Sons Ltd

12.2   THE ENDOPHENOTYPE APPROACH

The application of endophenotypes to complex disorders that show a non-Mendelian inheritance pattern is not new. A number of areas of clinical medicine have identified quantitative traits that are predictive of disorder. For example, blood pressure and cholesterol levels may serve as predictors for cardiovascular disease (Leboyer *et al.*, 1998; Almasy & Blangero, 2001). In psychiatry, however, the application of the endophenotype approach is relatively new (Leboyer *et al.*, 1998; Almasy & Blangero, 2001; Castellanos & Tannock, 2002; Gottesman & Gould, 2003). The approach is perhaps best validated in adult psychiatry, where deficits in cognitive, oculomotor and physiological measures have been reported in probands with schizophrenia and their unaffected relatives. For example, parents of probands with a family history of schizophrenia show an aberrant electrophysiological response (P50) to repeated auditory stimuli. The P50 waveform is associated with DNA variation at the α7-nicotinic receptor gene which lies within a linkage region for schizophrenia (15q14) (Freedman *et al.*, 1997; Freedman, Adler, & Leonard, 1999).

The above examples indicate that any one of a number of different measures might operate as an endophenotype. Thus candidate endophenotypes may include markers of cognitive, biochemical, endocrinological, neuroanatomical or neurophysiological function. A key criteria, however, is that the endophenotype is continuously quantifiable and shows variation within the normal population (Leboyer *et al.*, 1998; Almasy & Blangero, 2001; Castellanos & Tannock, 2002). Additionally, the endophenotype should segregate with disease or disease severity, demonstrate a familial risk profile with unaffected siblings presenting with a subthreshold form of the trait, and variation in the endophenotype should be heritable (Waldman, 2005).

Since the study of suitable endophenotypes for ADHD is only recently underway, many measures have either not been shown to meet, or do not meet, all the proposed objective criteria for endophenotypes (Almasy & Blangero, 2001; Castellanos & Tannock, 2002). Nevertheless, significant advances have recently been made toward establishing heritability estimates, familial risk profiles, and molecular genetic correlates of a number of candidate cognitive phenotypes, such as attention (Bellgrove *et al.*, 2006), response variability (Castellanos *et al.*, 2005), response inhibition (Nigg, 2001; Slaats-Willemse *et al.*, 2003) and working memory (Ando, Ono & Wright, 2001).

12.3   CANDIDATE ENDOPHENOTYPES FOR ADHD

Historically, the study of cognition in ADHD has been driven by the application of paradigms from cognitive neuropsychology that owe much to the functional localisation perspective of cognition. Thus, inferences regarding frontal pathology in ADHD have been made based upon the performance of children on tests that are sensitive to lesions of the frontal lobe. Theories of information-processing deficits in ADHD have proved influential but such theories are limited in what they can tell us about where and how the brain implements these processes (van der Meere

& Sergeant, 1988; Sergeant, Oosterlaan & van der Meere, 1999). Nevertheless, the discipline's rigorous and reliable measurement of function, such as the dissociable components of working memory (Baddeley & Hitch, 1974), means that cognitive phenotypes can be defined with precision. More recently, the application of functional brain imaging has meant that researchers are increasingly interested in the way in which cognitive processes are instantiated in the human brain. Such advances in cognitive neuroscience integrate converging evidence from human and non-human primate lesion studies, psychopharmacology, neuroanatomy and neurophysiology to define neural circuits that subserve distinct aspects of cognition. This knowledge can assist in constraining and guiding the study of endophenotypes for ADHD. This review is selective in that it focuses on cognitive and neural mechanisms that at least partially satisfy the requirements for an endophenotype, are grounded in neuroscience and show preliminary evidence of association to candidate genes for ADHD.

12.3.1   ATTENTION

(a)   Cognitive neuroscience of attention

Recent advances in cognitive neuroscience suggest that attention is subserved by discrete neural systems that, while allowing interaction, function relatively independently. Convergent evidence from neuropsychology, neuroimaging, lesion studies, animal studies and pharmacology support a view that attention comprises at least three modular components (Posner & Peterson, 1990).

The first component is a *sustained attention* or *alertness* system that is centred on fronto-parietal regions, particularly of the right hemisphere, and is responsible for achieving and maintaining sensitivity to incoming stimuli (Pardo, Fox & Raichle, 1991; Paus *et al.*, 1997; Sturm *et al.*, 1999). Attention may be maintained over relatively short periods, or over longer periods, as may be required in continuous performance tasks (CPTs). Pharmacological challenge studies indicate that drugs that block noradrenergic transmission can impair alertness and sustained attention, over both short and longer periods, in humans and monkeys (Smith & Nutt, 1996; Witte & Marrocco, 1997).

The second component is an *orienting* system that acts to prioritise the processing of sensory events at certain locations in space. This system relies upon the superior parietal lobe and temporo-parietal junction, with additional involvement from the frontal-eye fields. A distinction may be made between goal-directed or endogenous orienting and stimulus-driven or exogenous orienting. The former operates when attention is oriented based upon a cue that is predictive of, for example, a target location. The latter may operate when attention is oriented by a sudden-onset peripheral stimulus. Some evidence suggests that cholinergic signalling may influence goal-directed orienting (Parasuraman *et al.*, 2005) whereas catecholamine signalling may influence stimulus-driven orienting (Corbetta & Shulman, 2002). Acquired damage to the right-hemisphere orienting system results in the syndrome of unilateral spatial neglect, in which the ability to detect and act upon contralesional stimuli (most typically in the left visual field) is impaired (Robertson & Marshall, 1993).

The third component is an *executive attention* system, involving the anterior cingulate, lateral prefrontal cortex and the basal ganglia (particularly caudate nucleus) that is responsible for exercising control over lower-level cognitive functions and resolving conflicts of thought, emotion or responses (Posner & DiGirolamo, 2000). A large amount of evidence, including that from studies of patients with dopamine depletion, such as Parkinson's disease, supports the view that dopamine is a dominant neuromodulator of the executive attention system. An important implication of attention systems that are dissociable (in terms of behaviour, neuroanatomy and neurochemistry) is that these dissociations might be reflected in underlying genetics.

(b) Attention in ADHD

While inattention comprises a core component of ADHD symptomatology, many commentators have noted that attention research in ADHD has failed to identify a significant pattern of impairment (Barkley, 1997; Tannock, 1998), and have suggested that attention deficits may arise due to deficits in other cognitive domains such as inhibition or working memory (Barkley, 1997). Notwithstanding the importance of inhibition and working memory for ADHD (see below), we contend that attention deficits in ADHD can be identified and parsimoniously described using the above cognitive-neuroanatomical model of attention.

Executive attention in ADHD

Neuropsychological research over the last decade with children, adolescents and adults who have ADHD has suggested deficits in each of these attentional systems. On tasks requiring *executive attention*, such as the Stroop or Eriksen flanker task, in which subjects must ignore an irrelevant yet attention-capturing dimension of a stimulus, children and adolescents with ADHD are often adversely affected by incongruent configurations, indicative of a failure to use executive control to resolve conflict (Everett *et al.*, 1991; Barkley, Grodzinsky & DuPaul, 1992; Grodinsky & Diamond, 1992; Carter *et al.*, 1995a; Seidman *et al.*, 1997; Jonkman *et al.*, 1999; Swanson *et al.*, 2000; Shallice *et al.*, 2002; Konrad *et al.*, 2005). This behavioural impairment appears to be underpinned by reduced activity with the anterior cingulate in both children and adults with ADHD (Bush *et al.*, 1999; Konrad *et al.*, 2005).

Sustained attention in ADHD

In ADHD research, *sustained attention* has typically been investigated using variants of the continuous performance task (CPT) in which participants must monitor a stream (auditory or visual) in order to detect a rare target. Studies employing sustained attention tasks have revealed that children, adolescents and adults with ADHD are poorer and slower at detecting targets and are more variable in their reaction time (Seidman *et al.*, 1998; Epstein *et al.*, 2001; Shallice *et al.*, 2002; O'Connell *et al.*, 2004). Willcutt *et al.* (2005) conducted a meta-analysis of CPT studies in ADHD and reported moderate-large effect sizes for both errors of commission and omission (weighted mean effect size (d') = 0.51; 0.64, respectively). Konrad *et al.* (2005) recently examined the functional neuroanatomy of the alerting network in medication-naïve children with ADHD. While the children with ADHD tended to have longer RTs on trials on which a target was not preceded by a warning cue – indicative of an impaired alerting response – this difference was not significant. The children with ADHD showed less activation in the brainstem on trials without a warning cue, than on those with a warning cue, whereas the controls showed the reverse pattern. This finding is interesting as the activation focus was maximal at the ponto-mesencephalic junction which bears the noradrenergic locus coeruleus. Nigg *et al.* also reported an impaired alerting response for un-cued left visual field targets in ADHD, consistent with a right-hemisphere noradrenergic deficit (Nigg, Swanson, & Hinshaw, 1997).

Attentional orienting in ADHD

Evidence for dysfunction to the *orienting network* in ADHD comes from two sources: studies that have employed clinical tests of neglect and those that have employed visual orienting paradigms from cognitive neuroscience. A number of studies have reported asymmetrical impairments of attention on clinical tests of neglect, such as letter cancellation or line bisection. On cancellation tasks, children with ADHD have been found to cancel fewer targets in the left visual field (Voeller & Heilman, 1988). On line bisection tasks, children with ADHD have been reported to bisect lines further towards the right of centre (Sheppard *et al.*, 1999). This pattern of impairment is also seen after damage to right frontal and parietal cortices and to subcortical structures such as the putamen and basal ganglia and suggests a subtle left-sided inattention in ADHD. A number of investigators have also examined the integrity of the orienting system in ADHD using endogenous and exogenous cuing paradigms. Huang-Pollock and Nigg (2003) review the visual orienting literature in ADHD and conclude that any such deficits are of small effect size and will require large samples in order to detect meaningful differences.

Methodological shortcomings within this literature, such as the failure to exclude comorbid reading disorder which itself may be associated with impaired attentional orienting (Facoetti *et al.*, 2001), and to exclude trials on which an eye movement was made, may have further reduced effect sizes. Nevertheless, within this literature, a number of groups have reported asymmetrical impairments in the control of visual orienting (Swanson *et al.*, 1991; Carter *et al.*, 1995b; Nigg *et al.*, 1997). Konrad *et al.* (2005) showed a trend for children with ADHD to be impaired when reorienting their attention from an invalidly cued location in order to detect a target in the contralateral hemi-field. This slower reorienting response was associated with greater activity in the right putamen in the children with ADHD, relative to controls. Moreover, ADHD children with higher symptom levels showed less activity within the putamen during reorienting. This study provides preliminary evidence for disruption within a broad right-hemisphere spatial attentional system, including the putamen, in ADHD.

(c)   Attention as an endophenotype for ADHD

Sustained attention

A number of lines of evidence suggest that *sustained attention/alertness* may be a valid endophenotype for ADHD. First, meta-analyses show that most studies (77%) detect reliable differences between ADHD and control groups on measures of sustained attention, such as the number of omission errors (Willcutt *et al.*, 2005). Secondly, preliminary evidence for a familial-risk profile for sustained attention/ alertness has recently emerged. Using an affected-sibling pair design within an ADHD cohort, Slaats-Willemse *et al.* (2005) recently showed significant sib-pair correlations for aspects of sustained attention. Another study, reported numerically greater sustained attention deficits in an unaffected sibling group relative to controls (Slaats-Willemse *et al.*, 2003). Nigg *et al.* reported that both ADHD probands and their biological parents had a poorer alerting response to left visual targets, consistent with a right-hemisphere noradrenergic deficit (Nigg *et al.*, 1997). Thirdly, behaviour genetic studies show that sustained attention measures are moderately heritable (0.46–0.72) with generally higher correlations in monozygotic relative to dizygotic twin pairs (Groot *et al.*, 2004).

Drawing on these lines of evidence, a number of studies have recently examined sustained attention in ADHD in relation to catecholamine candidate genes. Loo *et al.* (2003) and Bellgrove *et al.* (2005) reported an effect of the 10-repeat allele of variable number of tandem repeat (VNTR) polymorphism of the DAT1 gene on measures of sustained attention, with errors of commission, omission and response variability being higher in 10-repeat homozygotes. Bellgrove *et al.* (2006) also reported an effect of the A2 allele of a Taq I polymorphism of the gene (DBH) encoding dopamine beta hydroxylase (DβH) on sustained attention. DβH is the enzyme converting dopamine to noradrenaline and is critical to the regulation of catecholamines within the brain. The A2 allele has been associated with ADHD in a number of studies (Daly *et al.*, 1999; Roman *et al.*, 2002). Bellgrove *et al.* found that ADHD children who were homozygous for the A2 allele had poorer sustained attention than ADHD children who did not possess this allele. The association between sustained attention and DBH gene variants is particularly interesting given catecholamine theories of prefrontal function (Posner & Peterson, 1990; Arnsten, 1998; Aston-Jones *et al.*, 1998) and ADHD (Pliszka, McCracken & Maas, 1996). No studies have yet examined whether catecholamine gene variants modulate task-related brain activity within the above-defined fronto-parietal sustained attention network.

Reaction-time variability

A ubiquitous finding from reaction time studies of ADHD, including those employing sustained attention tasks, such as the CPT, is that of increased response time variability (see Johnson *et al.*, 2007). Rather than reflecting uninteresting random noise, it has been suggested that response time variability could be a marker for frontal brain pathology (Stuss *et al.*, 2003; Bellgrove, Hester & Garavan, 2004). Castellanos and colleagues (2005) recently suggested that response time variability may be a reflection of a catecholaminergic deficiency within frontostriatal structures which impairs the ability to modulate very low-frequency fluctuations in neuronal activity. This scenario could give rise to the relatively frequent lapses of attention which may underpin deficits such as sustained attention in ADHD. A number of investigators have sought to determine whether intra-individual reaction time variability may be a suitable candidate endophenotype for ADHD (Kuntsi & Stevenson, 2001; Castellanos & Tannock, 2002). For example, using a twin-study design, Kuntsi and colleagues demonstrated shared genetic effects for both dimensionally defined hyperactivity and response time variability. This study thus provides important first evidence that response time variability may be causally related to hyperactivity. A number of studies have also reported higher response time variability in children with ADHD carrying risk variants for the DAT1 and DRD4 genes (Loo et al., 2003; Bellgrove et al., 2005b; Bellgrove, Hawi, Lowe et al., 2005d). Although these findings are important, what exactly response time variability reflects at a neural level remains unclear. While some have argued that response time variability may underpin sustained attention deficits and reflect a primarily frontostriatal pathology (Bellgrove et al., 2004, 2005b; Castellanos et al., 2005), others suggest that it is a reflection of sub-optimal activation states (Kuntsi & Stevenson, 2001).

Executive attention

A number of recent studies have examined the genetics of executive attention. Fan et al. (2001) examined the heritability of attentional networks, including executive attention, using a flanker task under various cuing conditions. To index executive attention, these authors contrasted reaction times to a central target arrowhead (left or right pointing) under conditions where flanking arrowheads were either congruent or incongruent. Greater reaction time differences between the incongruent and congruent conditions are indicative or a poorer ability to resolve conflict between stimuli and responses. Twenty-six monozygotic and 26 dizygotic twin pairs performed the combined flanker/cued reaction time task. Correlations within the monozygotic pairs (r = 0.73) were higher than in the dizygotic pairs (0.28), with the latter not significant. Formal analyses of heritability demonstrated that the executive attention index was highly heritable (additive genetic variance $h^2 = 0.72$). A range of other studies have demonstrated moderate-high heritability estimates for tasks that tap executive attention (Carmelli et al., 2002; Swan & Carmelli, 2002; Anokhin, Heath & Ralano, 2003; Coolidge, Thede & Jang, 2004). Fossella et al. recently examined the efficiency of executive attention in relation to four catecholamine candidate genes – DRD4, DAT, COMT and MAOA – in a sample of 220 healthy individuals (Fossella et al., 2002). Modest associations were reported between executive attention and the A allele of the DRD4 –521 SNP, and two polymorphisms of the gene encoding monoamine oxidase (MAOA). Using fMRI, Fan and colleagues also examined the influence of DRD4 (–1217G insertion/deletion) and MAOA (30-bp repeat in the promoter region) polymorphisms on the efficiency with which the brain implements executive attention (Fan et al., 2003). Activation differences by genotype were detected in the dorsal anterior cingulate when 16 healthy subjects resolved response conflict. The dorsal anterior cingulate is a key node of the executive attention network and is thought to be dysfunctional in ADHD (Bush *et al.*, 1999). The finding that genotypic differences in brain activity can be observed with sample sizes as small as 16 provides important support for the endophenotype approach and the assumption that intermediate phenotypes may have greater power to detect genetic associations. In a seminal study, Swanson *et al.* examined the effect of the DRD4 VNTR on executive attention in children and adolescents with ADHD (Swanson *et al.*, 2000). Contrary to predictions, ADHD individuals carrying the 7-repeat 'risk variant' out-performed those without this variant. This apparent paradox is discussed further below.

Attentional orienting

As mentioned above, a number of studies have documented a subtle inattention towards the left of space in children with ADHD, resembling a sub-clinical form of 'left-neglect'. This presentation is most commonly seen after lesions to the right hemisphere, particularly the parietal lobe, but also sub-cortical regions, such as the putamen. Sheppard *et al.* reported that left-sided inattention in ADHD could be ameliorated by methylphenidate (Sheppard *et al.*, 1999). Since the dopamine transporter is a primary site of action for methylphenidate, Bellgrove *et al.* (2005b, 2005c) asked whether left-sided inattention in ADHD might relate to variation in the dopamine transporter gene (DAT1). The 10-repeat allele of a variable number of tandem repeats (VNTR) situated within the 3' untranslated (3' UTR) region of this gene has been repeatedly associated with ADHD and may have functional significance. In two separate studies, Bellgrove *et al.* asked children with ADHD to perform standard clinical tests of neglect – the Greyscales task (2005b) and the Landmark task (2005c).

In the Landmark task participants are presented with a pre-bisected line and asked which end of the line is the shorter. In cases of left-neglect, there is a pathological bias of attention away from the left-side and so the left-hand extremity of the line is poorly represented. This scenario leads to the subjective judgment that the left end of the line is the shorter. Bellgrove *et al.* asked 43 right-handed children with ADHD to perform this task and genotyped them for the DAT1 VNTR. As hypothesised, children who were homozygous for the 10-repeat allele displayed left-sided inattention, whereas heterozygotes did not. Furthermore, the extent of spatial attentional asymmetry related to dimensional measures of DSM inattentiveness. Given the high expression of the dopamine transporter within the striatum (Krause *et al.*, 2003) and high densities of DAT-immunoreactive axons within the posterior parietal cortex (Lewis *et al.*, 2001), Bellgrove *et al.* (2005c) proposed that 10-repeat allele might confer susceptibility to a broad disruption of right-hemisphere spatial attentional networks, including the striatum and parietal lobe. It should be noted, however, that a number of studies have failed to document left-sided inattention in ADHD or robust dysfunction within visual orienting systems more generally (Huang-Pollock & Nigg, 2003). One possibility is that neuropsychological heterogeneity within ADHD samples could reduce the effect sizes associated with such measures (Nigg *et al.*, 2005). We are currently pursuing the hypothesis that dysfunction within visual orienting systems could be associated with a subgroup of children with ADHD who have high symptom levels and for whom the 10-repeat DAT1 allele is a genetic risk factor.

12.3.2   RESPONSE INHIBITION

(a)   Cognitive neuroscience of response inhibition

Response inhibition refers to the ability in everyday circumstances to inhibit inappropriate action when environmental circumstances dictate that such behaviour is no longer appropriate. Such control is typically thought to be exercised by an executive system responsible for forming strategies and setting goals, and a subordinate system responsible for interpreting and implementing the necessary commands (Logan & Cowan, 1984; see also Shallice, 1988). The cognitive mechanisms of response inhibition have been studied within cognitive psychology for many years (Logan, 1994; Logan & Cowan, 1984; Logan, Schachar & Tannock, 1997). Within this literature response inhibition is often measured using the *stop-signal paradigm* (Figure 12.1). In the stop-signal paradigm an established pattern of responding to a *go-signal* must be inhibited upon presentation of an immediately-subsequent and countermanding *stop-signal*. Typically the *go-task* is a choice-reaction-time (CRT) task, requiring, for example, left and right button presses upon presentation of the letters 'X' and 'O' respectively (Logan *et al.*, 1997). The *stop-task*, typically a tone, signals that participants must suppress their response to the *go-signal*, and this typically occurs in 25% of trials. Varying the delay between the presentation of the go- and stop-signals allows the *stop-signal reaction time (SSRT)* to be derived. The SSRT is a measure of the speed of the inhibitory process, with longer SSRTs reflecting poorer inhibitory capacity.

The stop-signal paradigm can be contrasted to classic go/no-go tasks in which participants are instructed to respond upon presentation of a particular stimulus (e.g., a red square) but not upon presentation of an alternative stimulus (e.g., a green square). Typically, the go-stimuli are presented more frequently than the no-go-stimuli, allowing the development of a response tendency. The stop-signal paradigm is unique, however, in that it allows a specific definition of the conditions triggering the control (i.e. presentation of a *stop-signal*), the changes that result from executing the inhibitory act (i.e. inhibition of the response), and the latency associated with executing the inhibitory act (i.e. SSRT) (Logan, 1994).

More recently the neural basis of response inhibition in the human brain has been investigated. Human lesion and neuroimaging studies now support the view that response inhibition is achieved throughout a neural network including the inferior and middle frontal gyri (IFG and MFG, respectively) and the inferior parietal lobe (Konishi *et al.*, 1998; Garavan, Ross & Stein, 1999; Rubia *et al.*, 2001; Aron *et al.*, 2003). Activation foci may also be seen in midline regions, such as the anterior cingulate (Rubia *et al.*, 2001), although such activations may reflect ancillary processes such as monitoring response conflict (Carter *et al.*, 1998) or error detection (Garavan *et al.*, 2003), rather than response inhibition *per se*. Aron and colleagues (2003) examined response inhibition using the stop-signal paradigm in patients who had acquired lesions to the medial frontal area, orbital frontal, inferior frontal, middle frontal or superior frontal gyri. Right hemisphere lesions were associated with longer SSRTs and damage within the right IFG (pars opercularis) was specifically associated with longer SSRTs. Split brain (Funnell, Gazzaniga & Garavan, 2004) and functional imaging studies confirm a dominant role of the right-hemisphere in response inhibition (Garavan *et al.*, 1999; Ford *et al.*, 2004; Kelly *et al.*,

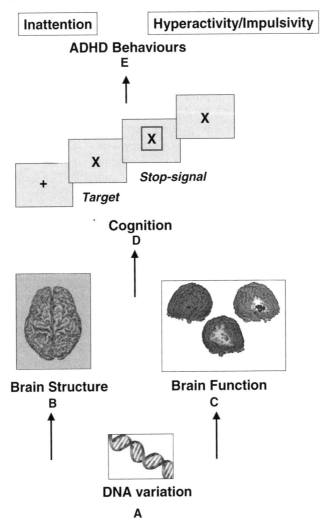

Figure 12.1. An example of the edophenotype approach to ADHD: Response Inhibition. Response inhibition can be measured using the stop-signal paradigm in which a response to a *Target* is inhibited upon the presentation of a *Stop-signal*. Stop-signal reaction time, or *SSRT*, is a measure of response inhibition. Familial influences on response inhibition have been observed in ADHD. Figure 12.1 depicts a hypothetical causal model in which [A] DNA variation (e.g., DRD4, DAT1) confers risk to [B] structural and/or [C] functional changes in areas of the brain that are important for response inhibition, such as the inferior frontal gyrus. Variation in the processing efficiency within these neural networks gives rise to [D] response inhibition deficits (e.g., increased SSRT) and thence [E] the symptoms of ADHD

2004). Moreover, using the neural disruption technique of transcranial magnetic stimulation, Chambers *et al.* recently demonstrated that disruption to the pars opercularis of the right IFG, but not nearby middle frontal areas, specifically impaired response inhibition (Chambers *et al.*, 2006). While these studies indicate a critical role for the right IFG in response inhibition, this cognitive function is clearly instantiated within a broad neural network.

Recent functional neuroimaging studies also support a role for subcortical areas, such as the striatum and basal ganglia, in response inhibition. These areas form nodes within re-entrant frontostriatal loops: projections from prefrontal areas including the dorsolateral prefrontal cortex, orbitofrontal and anterior cingulate cortices, are channelled through the striatum and basal ganglia before reaching the nuclei of the thalamus. Projections from the thalamus back to the prefrontal cortical areas in turn close these frontostriatal loops (DeLong et al., 1990; Alexander, 1995; Bradshaw, 2001). Vink et al. (2005) recently examined the role of the striatum in response inhibition using fMRI and a stop-signal task that parametrically manipulated the likelihood of a stop-trial occurring. Vink et al. reported that activation in the striatum became more pronounced as the requirement for inhibition became more likely. Moreover, activity in the striatum was greater on trials that had been successfully, versus unsuccessfully, inhibited. Kelly et al. (2004) showed a dissociation of prefrontal and striatal activity as a function of event-rate in a go/no-go task: when event rate was fast, significant activation was seen in the IFG and striatum, whereas a slower event rate was associated with activity in the anterior dorsal and polar prefrontal cortex and left inferior parietal cortex. This study suggests that IFG and striatal areas are particularly active under task circumstances that maximally challenge response inhibition. Activations in the striatum and basal ganglia have also been seen in fMRI studies of response inhibition in healthy children and adolescents (Vaidya et al., 1998; Durston et al., 2003; Booth et al., 2005).

(b)   Response inhibition in ADHD

Morphological studies that have employed MRI have identified abnormalities within nodes of the response inhibition network in ADHD (see also Chapter 10). Reduced volumes of the prefrontal cortex (including IFG), caudate and globus pallidus, particularly on the right, have been reliably reported (Aylward et al., 1996; Casey et al., 1997; Castellanos et al., 1994; Castellanos et al., 1996; Filipek et al., 1997; Sowell et al., 2003). Correlations between prefrontal morphology and behavioural measures of response inhibition have also been found (Casey et al., 1997). To date, 10 studies have employed fMRI while ADHD and control subjects performed response inhibition tasks (Vaidya et al., 1998; Rubia et al., 1999; Teicher et al., 2000; Durston et al., 2003; Schulz et al., 2004; Tamm et al., 2004; Booth et al., 2005; Rubia et al., 2005; Vaidya et al., 2005; Pliszka et al., 2006). These studies have revealed under-activation in the caudate nucleus and globus pallidus of children with ADHD, relative to controls (Vaidya et al., 1998; Rubia et al., 1999; Durston et al., 2003; Booth et al., 2005). Under-activation within the IFG has been reported in children (Booth et al., 2005) and adolescents with ADHD (Rubia et al., 1999). Hypo-activation of the anterior/mid-cingulate and hyperactivation of the left temporal gyrus was reported in one study of adolescents with ADHD (Tamm et al., 2004). Increased frontal activation in ADHD has been reported in children (Vaidya et al., 1998) and adolescents who were asymptomatic at the time of scanning but had a childhood-diagnosis of ADHD (Schulz et al., 2004). Using T2 relaxometry, Teicher and colleagues demonstrated higher T2 relaxation times (indicative of hypoperfusion) bilaterally in the putamen of children with ADHD, that were subsequently modified by MPH (Teicher et al., 2000). In general these studies converge upon a view of response inhibition, particularly in children with ADHD, which is characterised by dysfunctional frontostriatal inhibitory networks. Structural and functional deficits within the IFG, caudate and basal ganglia are reliably observed and may form the pathophysiological substrate of response inhibition deficits in ADHD. Functional deficits within this inhibitory network may require the recruitment of additional and compensatory brain areas by children and adolescents with ADHD (Durston *et al.*, 2003; Tamm *et al.*, 2004).

(c) Response inhibition as an endophenotype for ADHD

A number of lines of evidence suggest response inhibition as a good candidate endophenotype for ADHD (Castellanos & Tannock, 2002; Aron & Poldrack, 2005). First, a wealth of data supports the existence of response inhibition deficits in children, adolescents and adults with ADHD. This has led to theories positing the primacy of behavioural inhibition deficits for the aetiology of the disorder (Barkley, 1997; Nigg, 2001). Meta-analyses indicate that response inhibition deficits in ADHD are of moderate to large effect sizes and are thus reliably observed (Willcutt *et al.*, 2005). While response inhibition deficits may not be specific to ADHD (see Pennington & Ozonoff, 1996; Geurts *et al.*, 2004), on balance, it appears that such deficits may segregate with the disorder.

A number of studies have now examined response inhibition in familial ADHD (Seidman *et al.*, 2000; Crosbie & Schachar, 2001; Schachar *et al.*, 2005) or in affected or unaffected siblings of ADHD probands (Slaats-Willemse *et al.*, 2003; Slaats-Willemse *et al.*, 2005). Crosbie and Schachar asked 54 children with ADHD and 26 comparison children to perform the stop-signal task. Of the children with ADHD, 27 were defined as having relatively poorer response inhibition, based upon an SSRT that was 3.8 standard deviations above the mean of published normative values. A further group of 27 children with ADHD were defined as having relatively good inhibition, based upon SSRTs that were in the normative range. Family history of ADHD was established via a clinician interview regarding current and past family history of psychiatric disorder and ADHD. Crosbie and Schachar found higher prevalence rates of ADHD in the families of those children with poor response inhibition, relative to those with better response inhibition, or the matched control cohort. Thus by using family history as a proxy for genetic risk, Crosbie and Schachar identified that response inhibition deficits are associated with familial ADHD. Subsequent studies by Slaats-Willemse and colleagues have identified that response inhibition deficits, as identified by a go/no-go task, are pronounced in the unaffected siblings of ADHD probands with a positive family history for ADHD (Slaats-Willemse *et al.*, 2003). Further, evidence for familial clustering of response inhibition deficits was found by demonstrating strong correlations between performance indices in affected sibling pairs (Slaats-Willemse *et al.*, 2005). The above studies thus provide important evidence of familial risk profiles for response inhibition deficits and support its candidacy as an endophenotype.

A number of studies have indicated that response inhibition deficits can be ameliorated by stimulants, such as methylphenidate that act on catecholamine systems (Aron *et al.*, 2003; Scheres *et al.*, 2003). *A priori*, one might therefore predict that catecholamine candidate genes for ADHD might relate to response inhibition deficits. Our own work has approached this issue by examining sustained attention and response inhibition in ADHD in relation to the dopamine D4 receptor (DRD4) gene (Bellgrove *et al.*, 2005d). D4 receptors are preferentially expressed in the prefrontal cortex (Primus *et al.*, 1997) and are hypothesised to play a key role in the neuromodulation of cognitive control. The DRD4 gene (a member of the D2-like dopamine receptor family) is mapped to the short arm of chromosome 11 at 11p15.5. It encodes a seven trans-membrane protein that is expressed on postsynaptic neurons of the dopamine system's pathways. A number of variants within the DRD4 gene have been tested for association with ADHD. The best replicated association is with the 7-repeat allele of a variable number of tandem repeats (VNTR) located within a coding region of the gene (Faraone *et al.*, 2001)(see also Chapter 8). It has been reported that the 7-repeat allele mediates a blunted response to dopamine (Asghari *et al.*, 1995); however, more recent studies have questioned the functionality of this variant (Jovanovic, Guan & Van Tol, 1999). Evidence of functionality does, however, exist for a single nucleotide polymorphism (SNP) located within the promoter region of the gene. The A allele of a −521 SNP has been shown to alter gene transcription by up to 40% relative to the G allele (Okuyama *et al.*, 1999). Lowe and colleagues (2004) recently reported a trend for the A allele to be associated with ADHD.

Bellgrove *et al.* (2005d) asked children and adolescents with ADHD to perform a go/no-go task in which they were required to inhibit their response to a target digit (a 3) that occurred randomly in a stream of 1-9 digits. In line with a number of other studies (Swanson *et al.*, 2000; Manor *et al.*, 2002), carriers of the 7-repeat allele of the VNTR performed significantly better on the go/no-go task than those ADHD probands without this allele. This result is interesting as it suggests that the 7-repeat allele of the VNTR is associated with ADHD but is not associated with neuropsychological deficit. This relationship goes against the notion that this variant confers susceptibility to dysfunction within the neural networks sub-serving, in this case, response inhibition. How might this contradiction be explained? One explanation is that the 7-repeat allele characterises a particular subgroup of ADHD without neuropsychological deficit, perhaps in association with a range of other genetic and non-genetic abnormalities (Swanson *et al.*, 2000). In a separate analysis, ADHD probands who were homozygous for the A allele of the −521 SNP showed response inhibition deficits relative to heterozygotes (Bellgrove *et al.*, 2005d). Within the Irish population at least, these two DRD4 variants are not in strong linkage disequilibrium (see Chapter 8), and so it seems possible that associations with the 7-repeat allele of the VNTR are independent of those with the A allele of the −521 SNP. Other studies have, however, demonstrated relationships between other candidate genes, such as DAT1, and response inhibition capacity (Cornish *et al.*, 2005).

How might variation in the DRD4 (or DAT1) gene influence the neural substrates of response inhibition? As reviewed above, structural and functional changes within prefrontal and sub-cortical areas have been implicated in the response inhibition deficits of ADHD. D4 receptors are known to be heavily expressed in prefrontal areas (Primus *et al.*, 1997), while the dopamine transporter is heavily expressed in the striatum (Krause *et al.*, 2003). Durston *et al.* (2005) made use of this regionally selective expression to examine prefrontal and striatal grey matter volumes, in relation to DRD4 and DAT1 gene variants in children with ADHD, their unaffected siblings and controls. Individual variation in brain structure is highly heritable (Winterer & Goldman, 2003; Winterer *et al.*, 2005), suggesting that brain morphometry measures, such as grey matter volumes within selected regions, may be a useful endophenotype. These authors reported a significant effect of the

DAT1 VNTR genotype on caudate volume, with 10-repeat homozygotes having smaller volumes than those carrying the 9-repeat allele. This effect was most pronounced in children with ADHD, relative to their unaffected siblings and controls. There was no effect of DAT1 genotype on prefrontal grey matter volumes. Other studies have also reported that transporter densities are elevated in the striatum of children and adults with ADHD (Dresel *et al.*, 2000; Krause *et al.*, 2000; Cheon *et al.*, 2003). Heinz *et al.* (2000) reported that 10-repeat homozygotes had higher striatal transporter densities, relative to 9-repeat carriers (see also Cheon *et al.*, 2005 for studies in ADHD children), however, others have failed to replicate this result. At this stage, however, the relationship between elevated striatal transporter densities in ADHD, reduced caudate volumes and the 10-repeat DAT1 allele remains unclear. Madras *et al.* (2005) hypothesised that elevated DAT densities might 'represent hypertrophy of dendritic trees or dopaminergic neurons [and be], a result of inadequate pruning during neurodevelopment' (p. 1404). If that is true, then morphometric changes in the caudate, in relation to DAT1, may represent a plastic change to an altered dopaminergic state.

By contrast to the effects of DAT1 on caudate volumes, Durston *et al.* (2005) reported an effect of the DRD4 VNTR on prefrontal, but not striatal, grey matter volumes. Individuals who were homozygous for the 4-repeat allele had smaller prefrontal volumes than those carrying other alleles of the VNTR, such as the 7-repeat. No interaction between ADHD status and genotype was found. The study of Durston *et al.* takes important first steps in linking candidate genes to an intermediate phenotype of cerebral grey matter volumes. By utilising the cognitive specificity of functional magnetic resonance imaging, researchers will now be able to ask how genotype influences the level of activation within discrete brain regions.

In summary, substantial evidence suggests that deficient response inhibition may be reliably associated with ADHD and may be familial. Response inhibition deficits in children with ADHD are likely to reflect immaturity to ventral frontostriatal circuitry, including the inferior frontal gyrus (IFG). While the involvement of other neurotransmitter systems, such as serotonin and noradrenaline, in response inhibition seems plausible (Passamonti *et al.*, 2005; Rubia, Lee *et al.*, 2005), preliminary evidence suggests that DRD4 gene variants may be associated with response inhibition deficits in ADHD. Based upon these data, one may propose a genetic-physiological hypothesis as part of the pathophysiology of ADHD: Genetic variation within catecholaminergic genes (*a priori* DRD4, DAT1) influences the development of ventral frontostriatal circuitry sub-serving response inhibition. Variation within this system may in turn confer susceptibility to ADHD (Figure 12.1). With the advent of imaging genomics (Hariri & Weinberger, 2003), testing this hypothesis is feasible using validated response inhibition paradigms to activate ventral frontostriatal circuity in both genotyped healthy control and ADHD populations.

12.3.3   WORKING MEMORY

(a)   Cognitive neuroscience of working memory

Working memory (WM) is viewed as a limited capacity system that is responsible for the temporary storage and processing of information (Baddeley & Hitch, 1974;

Baddeley & Salla, 1996). In allowing information to be stored and manipulated 'on-line' WM facilitates a range of higher-order cognitive processes, such as fluid intelligence, reasoning ability and language comprehension. Baddeley's model of WM originally described two peripheral slave systems, the phonological loop and visuospatial sketchpad, which were controlled by a modality-free central executive. Processes of passive storage and active rehearsal within each of these slave systems were seen as distinct. Storage is measured as capacity and reflects the amount of information that a subject can recall immediately. Information that is stored is vulnerable to interference and/or decay over time. Rehearsal refers to processes that refresh and maintain representations. Within the phonological loop, verbal information may be stored in the phonological store and can be protected from decay by a process of sub-vocal rehearsal via the articulatory control process (Baddeley & Hitch, 1974; Baddeley & Salla, 1996).

Neuropsychological investigations with brain-damaged patients have generally supported the separability of these slave systems by documenting cases who experience difficulty with verbal but not spatial WM and vice versa (Gathercole, 1994). D'Esposito and Postle (1999) reviewed the literature on WM deficits after prefrontal lesions and observed that lesions to the PFC, particularly Brodmann's areas 9 and 46, impaired rehearsal but not storage processes.

A range of neuroimaging studies have attempted to isolate where in the human brain verbal and spatial representations might be *maintained*. Broadly speaking, a left-hemisphere network comprising the ventrolateral prefrontal cortex (VLPFC) (near the IFG), parietal and motor areas, in addition to the right cerebellum, appears to be important in maintaining information in verbal WM. Within this network, the left inferior parietal cortex along with the right inferior cerebellum may be the locus of the phonological store, while the left VLPFC and right superior cerebellum may be involved in rehearsal processes (Smith & Jonides, 1999; Fletcher & Henson, 2001; Chen & Desmond, 2005). With respect to spatial WM, a similar network of areas, this time predominantly in the right hemisphere, is associated with the maintenance of visuospatial information. Thus areas including the right VLPFC, the right posterior parietal, right anterior occipital and right premotor cortices are important for maintaining visuospatial information (Fletcher & Henson, 2001). Fletcher and Henson (2001) have proposed that visuospatial information may be stored in occipital cortex and the spatial organisation of the stimuli represented via associations between occipital and parietal cortex. These associations may be rehearsed by selective attentional processes engaging the right superior parietal cortex, premotor cortex and right frontal cortex (see also Awh, Anllo-Vento & Hillyard, 2000). Sub-cortical activation foci have also been observed in the caudate nucleus during delayed-response tasks when spatially coded mnemonic information must be integrated with motor preparation to guide behaviour (Postle & d'Esposito, 1999).

A critical aspect of human cognition involves the ability to use or *manipulate* stored mnemonic information to guide future action. Many researchers agree that the prefrontal cortex plays a vital role in those executive process that fall under the rubric of Baddeley's central executive (d'Esposito *et al.*, 1995; Smith & Jonides, 1999). Within the functional imaging literature, executive control over the contents of WM has been examined under a number of different task circumstances. N-back tasks have frequently been employed to investigate areas of the brain associated with the manipulation of information stored in verbal WM. In N-back tasks participants are required to monitor a continuous sequence of stimuli and to make their response based upon the correspondence between a current item and an item that was presented n items previously in the sequence. When n is equal to zero, the participant is simply required to respond upon the presentation of a target stimuli. At this working memory load the task requires little on-line manipulation. However, when $n > 0$ the task becomes taxing and requires both maintenance of the previous n stimuli plus updating whenever a new stimulus item occurs (Fletcher & Henson, 2001). Typically, researchers vary the working memory load (i.e. n) between 0 and 3 and observe which areas of the brain are sensitive to this load effect. As above, left-hemisphere sites corresponding to the maintenance of verbal information in the N-back task include the VLPFC, left premotor/supplementary motor areas and left motor cortex. Additional bilateral activation associated with the manipulation of verbal information within WM was found in DLPFC (see also Derrfuss *et al.*, 2005 for involvement of the VLPFC in N-back tasks). Some investigators have also noted tendencies towards lateralised activity within DLPFC for verbal versus spatial N-back tasks. Activations within left inferior parietal regions have also been observed in N-back tasks (Ravizza *et al.*, 2004), suggesting that executive control is unlikely to be the exclusive dominion of the frontal cortex. As we shall see below, dopaminergic genotypes have been reported to modulate task-related frontal activation during N-back tasks (Egan *et al.*, 2001).

Another paradigmatic measure of executive working memory systems is dual-task performance (Baddeley & Salla, 1996; Shah & Miyake, 1996). Dual-task performance involves the switching between two sets of information and task-demands that are relevant to each task. A number of imaging studies have now shown that compared to the performance of a single-task, dual-task paradigms reliably activate the DLPFC (Brodman's areas 9 and 46) (d'Esposito *et al.*, 1995; Kubler *et al.*, 2003) and anterior cingulate (d'Esposito *et al.*, 1995) with additional involvement from parietal areas (Klingberg, 1998; Garavan *et al.*, 2000; Kubler *et al.*, 2003; Wylie, Javitt, & Foxe, 2004). Recent lesion studies also suggest the involvement of the right IFG and cerebellum in aspects of task-switching (Aron *et al.*, 2004; Berger *et al.*, 2005).

In summary, recent fMRI work largely supports the hypothesis that verbal and spatial information is stored in left and right parietal cortices, respectively. Right inferior and right superior cerebellar areas are also thought to play a role in the processes of storage and rehearsal, respectively, within verbal WM. Manipulating information stored in WM (as exemplified by N-back and task-switching) is achieved via a predominantly fronto-parietal network.

(b)   Working memory in ADHD

In-line with theoretical models of ADHD emphasising WM dysfunction (Barkley, 1997; Levy & Farrow, 2001), recent meta-analysis suggest that WM impairments are reliably impaired in children and adolescents with ADHD (Martinussen *et al.*, 2005). Although deficits in multiple components of WM were found (including maintenance and manipulation within both verbal and spatial WM) effect sizes associated with case/control differences were most pronounced for spatial storage and spatial central executive measures. WM deficits may be particularly relevant to ADHD given the robust association between measures of WM and academic achievement and the likely militating effects of WM deficits for cognitively based treatments. To date only two functional imaging studies of WM have been conducted in ADHD, both with adult participants (Schweitzer *et al.*, 2000; Valera *et al.*, 2005).

Schweitzer and colleagues (2000) asked six unmedicated male adults with ADHD who had current and childhood histories of inattention, impulsivity and hyper-activity, and six healthy men to perform the Paced Auditory Serial Addition Task (PASAT) under $[^{15}O]$ H_2O PET conditions. Subjects were presented with single digits binaurally every 2.4 seconds and were required to add each number to the preceding number. Across four repetitions of the addition task scans, men without ADHD showed significant increases in blood flow in the anterior cingulate and medial frontal regions and decreases in the left middle frontal regions. In contrast, men with ADHD showed significant decreases in left middle temporal lobe and increases in left parahippocampal gyrus and bilateral cerebellum. Temporal lobe and frontal activations in the control subjects are consistent with the recruit-ment of a phonological loop for subvocal rehearsal and the operation of executive control processes. The failure of the ADHD subjects to activate a similar network suggests dysfunctional verbal WM processes and the recruitment of an alternative network, which perhaps relies more heavily on visual imagery to perform the addi-tion task.

Valera *et al.* (2005) recently employed a 2-back task under blocked-fMRI condi-tions with 20 adults with ADHD and 20 healthy controls. The researchers presented sequences of capital letters centrally in pseudorandom order. In a vigilance control task, participants were required to respond to every letter, with the constraint that they pressed an alternative button every time an X was presented (25% of occa-sions). For the 2-back task the target was any letter that was identical to the letter that preceded it by two trials. Despite the ADHD and control participants perform-ing comparably, the ADHD group showed less activation in the 2-back minus vigi-lance task comparison than the controls in the posterior cerebellum and inferior occipital cortex. How the ADHD participants performed the task as accurately as controls with lower activity within the cerebellum is, however, puzzling. Since the cerebellum shows greater activity under heightened task difficulty (i.e. WM load) (Chen & Desmond, 2005) a more difficult task may have obviated performance differences. Nevertheless, given well-documented reductions in the volume of the cerebellum in ADHD (Castellanos *et al.*, 2002), the results of Valera *et al.* (2005) are consistent with the hypothesis that dysfunction to the posterior cerebellum may mediate verbal WM impairments in ADHD.

(c) Working memory as an endophenotype for ADHD

As reviewed above, WM deficits (perhaps particularly spatial) are reliably observed in children and adolescents with ADHD and are predictive of poor functional outcome. While familial-risk profiles for WM deficit are yet to be established in ADHD, much evidence suggests that the components of WM (maintenance and manipulation) are heritable (Ando *et al.*, 2001; Wright *et al.*, 2001).

Ando and colleagues (2001; see also Wright *et al.*, 2001) employed spatial and verbal WM span tasks (see Shah & Miyake, 1996) within a twin design. The dual-tasks employed (rotation-arrow task and verification-word task) are validated and reliable measures of WM and allow indices of storage and executive capacity to be measured. Measures of spatial and verbal cognitive ability were also employed to ascertain the contribution of WM to spatial and verbal thinking. The heritability estimates for each of the four WM scores were moderate (43–49%) and the heritability estimates for spatial and verbal cognitive ability were high (65%). Bedard and colleagues (2004) recently reported that methylphenidate (MPH) improved maintenance and manipulation of information within spatial WM in school-age children with ADHD. These results are consistent with the known action of MPH on frontostriatal and frontoparietal circuits sub-serving maintenance and manipulation within WM (Mehta *et al.*, 2000). The effect of MPH on spatial WM is also consistent with theories postulating catecholamine modulation of prefrontal function (Arnsten, 1998) (see also Chapter 14).

A number of lines of evidence also suggest associations between dopaminergic candidate genes and WM performance and/or task-related brain activity. Catechol-O-methyltransferase (COMT) catalyses the inactivation of monoaminergic neurotransmitters, such as dopamine and noradrenaline, by an extraneuronal transfer of a methyl group to catechol compounds (Tehunen *et al.*, 1994). A single nucleotide polymorphism (472G/A) results in an amino acid change from valine to methionine at position 108 or 158 of the coding sequence of the soluble or membrane-bound COMT protein, respectively (Lachman *et al.*, 1996). The valine variant is associated with a three- to fourfold higher enzymatic activity than the methionine variant (Lachman *et al.*, 1996). While it has been argued that this polymorphism has a regionally selective effect on the prefrontal cortex, accounting for more than 60% of dopamine turnover, recent studies have shown functional effects of this polymorphism on striatal and limbic areas (Karoum, Chrapusta & Egan, 1994). In their programme of research examining whether the COMT Val/Met polymorphism might be a risk factor for schizophrenia, Egan and colleagues have reported an association between WM performance (as assessed by perseverative errors on the Wisconsin Card Sorting Task (WCST) and the COMT Val/Met polymorphism (Egan *et al.*, 2001). Specifically, schizophrenic and healthy controls who were homozygous for the valine variant, had poorer WM than those with the Val/Met or Met/Met genotypes, presumably because the high activity variant reduced dopamine to levels that are suboptimal for WM. Other studies have reported an influence of the COMT Val/Met polymorphism on tasks involving visuospatial processing, working memory, attention, cognitive flexibility and inhibition (Bilder *et al.*, 2002; Goldberg *et al.*, 2003; Diamond *et al.*, 2004). A number of studies have also examined whether the COMT Val/Met polymorphism influences the efficiency with which prefrontal cortical networks implement verbal WM. Egan *et al.* (2001) reported that COMT genotype modulated task-related brain activation in dorsolateral prefrontal and anterior cingulate areas when performing a 2-back task. However, Ho *et al.* recently failed to confirm the association between COMT Val/Met genotype and either WM performance or task-related brain activation (Ho *et al.*, 2005). A number of studies have tested for association of this variant with ADHD, however, the results have been largely negative (Hawi *et al.*, 2000; Manor *et al.*, 2000; Bellgrove *et al.*, 2005a). Given the uncertain role of the COMT Val/Met polymorphism in ADHD, we suggest that association between this variant and verbal WM is unlikely to clarify the aetiological mechanisms of ADHD (compared with Castellanos & Tannock, 2002).

In our view a far better case can be made for a genotype/phenotype relationship between polymorphisms of the gene encoding dopamine beta hydroxylase (DβH) and spatial WM impairments in ADHD. DßH is the enzyme catalysing the conversion of dopamine to noradrenaline and is critical to catecholamine regulation in the brain. Neurons containing DβH project from the subcortical locus coeruleus to frontoparietal cortex and are therefore capable of modulating spatial WM (Foote & Morrison, 1987). An association between ADHD and allele 2 of a Taq I polymorphism (maps to intron 5) of the DBH gene has been reported (Daly *et al.*, 1999; Roman *et al.*, 2002). Since the original report of this association by Daly *et al.*, other functional polymorphisms, such as a promoter SNP (-1021 C-T) and exonic SNP (G444A), have been identified but not yet rigorously tested for association with ADHD. Dysregulated noradrenergic function has been implicated in aetiological models of ADHD (Pliszka *et al.*, 1996; Viggiano *et al.*, 2004) and animal models of prefrontally-mediated WM (Arnsten, Steere & Hunt, 1996).

Parasuraman and colleagues (Parasuraman *et al.*, 2005) recently reported that a G to A substitution at 444 within exon 2 of the DBH gene, is associated with spatial working memory in healthy subjects. The A allele of this variant is associated with lower plasma and cerebrospinal fluid (CSF) levels of DßH, relative to the G allele. However, the -1021 C-T promoter SNP has recently been identified as the main variant controlling plasma DßH levels, with the T allele associated with lower plasma levels of DßH (Cubells & Zabetian, 2004). No studies have yet tested for association of this variant with spatial working memory measures.

In summary, measures of WM are heritable and reliably distinguish ADHD children from healthy controls. Participants with ADHD appear particularly impaired on the aspects of WM that require the maintenance and manipulation of spatial material within WM. Deficits in spatial WM are consistent with the predominantly right-hemisphere structural and functional anomalies reported in the condition. Deficits in the executive control of attention within WM are entirely consistent with frontal lobe theories of ADHD. Given the critical dependence of the prefrontal cortex on the ratio of dopamine to noradrenaline, the DBH gene may be particularly important to ADHD. Association with the intronic Taq I polymorphism provides preliminary evidence for an aetiological role of this gene in ADHD. Testing of other functional variants, such as the -1021-C-T SNP will be an important next step. Given the predominant right-hemisphere projections of noradrenergic neurons, we hypothesise that DBH gene variants may influence the development of fronto-parietal, and possibly cerebellar, networks subserving (spatial) WM. Variation within this system may again confer risk to aspects of ADHD.

12.4 FUTURE AVENUES FOR ENDOPHENOTYPE RESEARCH IN ADHD

12.4.1 ALTERNATIVE ENDOPHENOTYPES

As reviewed herein, the research literature on endophenotypes for ADHD has, to date, largely focused on behavioural measures of cognition. A small number of studies have also attempted to forge links between genes and either brain structure (MRI) or activity (fMRI). One neglected area of research is the application of electrophysiological measures within genetic studies of ADHD. Electroencephalography (EEG) provides information about the electrical activity of the brain, recorded over the scalp. Although lacking spatial resolution, EEG can provide valuable information regarding the time-course of neural activity and is thought to reflect the background state of the brain. Much research has demonstrated that a substantial portion of the variance in the EEG signal is explained by additive genetic factors, with heritability estimates for EEG power in the alpha, beta and theta bands in the range of 79–89%. EEG as a physiological technique has a number of advantages that make it suitable for genetic studies including high test-retest stability for many measures (0.6–0.9), low cost, and measures that are culturally unbiased (Winterer & Goldman, 2003). EEG studies of children with ADHD have revealed a relatively consistent picture that includes an excess of slow-wave EEG activity (predominantly theta) and increased theta/beta and theta/alpha ratios that are more predominant in children with ADHD combined than inattentive type. These results are generally in accord with theories that propose cortical hypoarousal in ADHD (Sergeant, 2000). Despite the established heritability of many EEG measures, we are not aware of any published studies that have attempted to establish familial-risk profiles for EEG measures (e.g. theta/beta or theta/alpha ratios) in ADHD. One recent study examined the effect of the DAT1 polymorphism on EEG power in the theta and beta bands as well as the theta/beta ratio (Loo *et al.*, 2003). Participants in this study were also administered a single 10 mg dose of methylphenidate in a double-blind, placebo-controlled study. Although no direct effect of DAT1 genotype on the EEG measures was found, an interaction between genotype and medication was seen for the EEG measures. Specifically, children who were homozygous for the 10-repeat allele showed an increase in central and parietal beta power and the decrease in the theta/beta ratio from the placebo to medication condition. The reverse pattern occurred for children who were either heterozygous for the 10-repeat or did not possess this allele. This study, although preliminary, is interesting as it suggests medication-related changes in EEG power that vary by genotype.

As suggested earlier, biochemical markers may also act as endophenotypes for psychiatric disorders. For example, dopamine beta hydroxylase (DβH) exists in the plasma as a stable heritable trait. The DBH gene appears to be a quantitative trait locus influencing plasma DβH activity with a single nucleotide polymorphism (1021-C/T SNP) located in the promoter region of the gene thought to be the primary controller of plasma DβH levels (Cubells & Zabetian, 2004). Given catecholamine theories of ADHD (Pliszka *et al.*, 1996), a number of studies have investigated whether plasma DβH levels are aberrant in children with ADHD (Rogeness *et al.*, 1982; Bowden, Deutsch & Swanson, 1988). In general these studies seem suggest that plasma DβH may be lowered in children with ADHD who also have comorbid conduct disorder (Rogeness *et al.*, 1982). A number of studies have tested for association between polymorphisms of the DBH gene and ADHD (Daly *et al.*, 1999; Roman *et al.*, 2002; Wigg *et al.*, 2002; Smith *et al.*, 2003; Zhang *et al.*, 2004; Bhaduri *et al.*, 2005). As reviewed earlier, the best replicated association is with an intron 5 SNP (Taq 1) of no known function (Daly *et al.*, 1999; Roman *et al.*, 2002). One recent study has examined the association of the functional 1021-C/T SNP and ADHD with and without disruptive behavioural disorder (DBD) (Zhang *et al.*, 2004). This study reported over-transmission of the T allele (associated with lower plasma DβH) from parents to children with ADHD plus DBD, whereas the C allele was over-transmitted to ADHD children without DBD. Although preliminary these results seem broadly in line with the biochemical results reported by Rogeness and colleagues. Future studies should attempt to conduct genotype-controlled studies of plasma DβH activity in ADHD with and without DBD. Given recent reports of associations between DBH gene polymorphisms and sustained attention and spatial working memory (Parasuraman *et al.*, 2005; Bellgrove *et al.*, 2006), it will also be of interest to examine the relationship between genes, biochemical markers and cognitive function.

12.4.2 DEALING WITH NEUROPSYCHOLOGICAL HETEROGENEITY

In psychiatry, clinical and neuropsychological heterogeneity is the rule rather than the exception. Recent commentary has focused upon whether children with ADHD who present with neuropsychological impairment may represent a distinct subgroup with its own aetiology (Nigg *et al.*, 2005). The corollary of this assertion is that ADHD children presenting with neuropsychological impairment may have a distinct set of genetic risk factors, and this poses significant challenges to the design of genetic association studies. Although we are not aware of any genetic research in ADHD that has attempted to isolate distinct genetic mechanisms in children with and without cognitive impairment, lessons may be learned from schizophrenia research. Hallmayer *et al.* (2005) recently found genetic evidence for a distinct subtype of schizophrenia that was characterised by pervasive cognitive deficit. These authors performed a broad-based neuropsychological test battery and defined the performance of probands with schizophrenia and their first-degree relatives, relative to that of a healthy control cohort. This procedure defined a generalised pervasive cognitive deficit as an endophenotype in some, but not all, probands with schizophrenia and their families. Notably, linkage to a region of chromosome 6 was observed for families with the 'cognitive deficit' phenotype but not for families without this phenotype. This study therefore provided evidence for a 'relatively homogeneous, familial and genetically distinct subtype [of schizophrenia]' (p. 475). The application of a similar approach within ADHD research may help to resolve long-standing debates regarding the existence of attention deficits, for example, and may substantially increase the power of genetic association studies.

Acknowledgements

Dr Bellgrove is supported by a Howard Florey Centenary Fellowship from the National Health and Medical Research Council of Australia. Ongoing research from Drs Bellgrove, Robertson and Gill is supported by the Irish Health Research Board (HRB) and Science Foundation Ireland (SFI).

12.5   REFERENCES

Alexander GE (1995) Functional neuroanatomy of the basal ganglia. In MM Robertson, V Eapen (eds) *Movement and Allied Disorders in Childhood* (pp. 257–77) Chichester: John Wiley & Sons.

Almasy L, Blangero J (2001) Endophenotypes as quantitative risk factors for psychiatric disease: rationale and study design. *Am J Med Genet* **105**(1): 42–4.

Ando J, Ono Y, Wright MJ (2001) Genetic structure of spatial and verbal working memory. *Behav Genet* **31**(6): 615–24.

Anokhin AP, Heath AC, Ralano A (2003) Genetic influences on frontal brain function: WCST performance in twins. *Neuroreport* **14**(15): 1975–8.

Arnsten AF (1998) Catecholamine modulation of prefrontal cortical cognitive function. *Trends in Cognitive Sciences* **2**(11): 436–47.

Arnsten AF, Steere JC, Hunt RD (1996) The contribution of alpha 2-noradrenergic mechanisms of prefrontal cortical cognitive function. Potential significance for Attention-Deficit Hyperactivity Disorder. *Archives of General Psychiatry* **53**(5): 448–55.

Aron AR, Dowson JH, Sahakian BJ, Robbins TW (2003) Methylphenidate improves response inhibition in adults with Attention-Deficit/Hyperactivity Disorder. *Biological Psychiatry* **54**(12): 1465–8.

Aron AR, Fletcher P, Bullmore ET *et al.* (2003) Stop-signal inhibition disrupted by damage to the right inferior frontal gyrus in humans. *Nature Neuroscience* **6**(2): 115–16.

Aron AR, Monsell S, Sahakian BJ, Robbins TW (2004) A componential analysis of task-switching deficits associated with lesions of left and right frontal cortex. *Brain* **127**(Pt 7): 1561–73.

Aron AR, Poldrack RA (2005) The cognitive neuroscience of response inhibition: relevance for genetic research in attention deficit/hyperactivity disorder. *Biological Psychiatry.*

Asghari V, Sanyal S, Buchwaldt S *et al.* (1995). Modulation of intracellular cyclic AMP levels by different human dopamine D4 receptor variants. *J Neurochem* **65**(3): 1157–65.

Aston-Jones G, Rajkowski J, Ivanova S *et al.* (1998) Neuromodulation and cognitive performance: recent studies of noradrenergic locus ceruleus neurons in behaving monkeys. *Adv Pharmacol* **42**: 755–9.

Awh E, Anllo-Vento L, Hillyard SA (2000) The role of spatial selective attention in working memory for locations: evidence from event-related potentials. *J Cogn Neurosci* **12**(5): 840–7.

Aylward EH, Reiss AL, Reader MJ *et al.* (1996) Basal ganglia volumes in children with Attention-Deficit Hyperactivity Disorder. *Journal of Child Neurology* **11**(2): 112–15.

Baddeley A (1996) Cognition, neurology, psychiatry: golden triangle or Bermuda triangle? *Cognitive Neuropsychiatry* **1**: 185–9.

Baddeley A, Hitch GJ (1974) Working memory. In GH Bower (ed.) *The Psychology of Learning and Motivation* (Vol. 8, pp. 47–89). New York: Academic Press.

Baddeley A, Salla SD (1996) Working memory and executive control. *Philosophical Transcations of the Royal Society of London* **351**: 1397–1404.

Barkley RA (1997) Behavioral inhibition, sustained attention, and executive functions: constructing a unifying theory of ADHD. *Psychological Bulletin* **121**(1): 65–94.

Barkley RA, Grodzinsky G, DuPaul GJ (1992) Frontal lobe functions in attention deficit disorder with and without hyperactivity: a review and research report. *J Abnorm Child Psychol* **20**(2): 163–88.

Bedard AC, Martinussen R, Ickowicz A, Tannock R (2004) Methylphenidate improves visual-spatial memory in children with Attention-Deficit/Hyperactivity Disorder. *J Am Acad Child Adolesc Psychiatry* **43**(3): 260–8.

Bellgrove MA, Domschke K, Hawi Z et al. (2005a) The methionine allele of the COMT polymorphism impairs prefrontal cognition in children and adolescents with ADHD. *Experimental Brain Research* **163**(3): 352–60.

Bellgrove MA, Gill M, Hawi Z et al. (2005b) Dissecting the Attention Deficit Hyperactivity Disorder (ADHD) phenotype: sustained attention, response variability and spatial attentional asymmetries in relation to Dopamine Transporter (DAT1) Genotype. *Neuropsychologia* **43**(13): 1847–57.

Bellgrove MA, Hawi Z, Gill M, Robertson IH (2006) The cognitive genetics of attention deficit hyperactivity disorder (ADHD): sustained attention as a candidate phenotype. *Cortex* **42**: 838–45.

Bellgrove MA, Hawi Z, Kirley A et al. (2005c) Association between Dopamine Transporter (DAT1) genotype, left-sided inattention, and an enhanced response to methylphenidate in Attention-Deficit Hyperactivity Disorder. *Neuropsychopharmacology* **30**: 2290–7.

Bellgrove MA, Hawi Z, Lowe N et al. (2005d) DRD4 gene variants and sustained attention in attention deficit hyperactivity disorder (ADHD): effects of associated alleles at the VNTR and -521 SNP. *American Journal of Medical Genetics Part B: Neuropsychiatric Genetics* **136**(1): 81–6.

Bellgrove MA, Hester R, Garavan H (2004) The functional neuroanatomical correlates of response variability: evidence from a response inhibition task. *Neuropsychologia* **42**(14): 1910–16.

Berger A, Tzur G, Constantini S et al. (2005) Task switching after cerebellar damage. *Neuropsychology* **19**(3): 362–70.

Bhaduri N, Sinha S, Chattopadhyay A et al. (2005) Analysis of polymorphisms in the dopamine Beta hydroxylase gene: association with attention deficit hyperactivity disorder in Indian children. *Indian Pediatr* **42**(2): 123–9.

Bilder RM, Volavka J, Czobor P et al. (2002) Neurocognitive correlates of the COMT Val(158)Met polymorphism in chronic schizophrenia. *Biol Psychiatry* **52**(7): 701–7.

Booth JR, Burman DD, Meyer JR et al. (2005) Larger deficits in brain networks for response inhibition than for visual selective attention in attention deficit hyperactivity disorder (ADHD). *J Child Psychol Psychiatry* **46**(1): 94–111.

Bowden CL, Deutsch CK, Swanson JM (1988) Plasma dopamine-beta-hydroxylase and platelet monoamine oxidase in attention deficit disorder and conduct disorder. *J Am Acad Child Adolesc Psychiatry* **27**(2): 171–4.

Bradshaw JL (2001) *Developmental Disorders of the Frontostriatal System: Neuropsychological, Neuropsychiatric and Evolutionary Perspectives*. Hove, East Sussex: Psychology Press Ltd.

Bush G, Frazier JA, Rauch SL et al. (1999) Anterior cingulate cortex dysfunction in Attention-Deficit/Hyperactivity Disorder revealed by fMRI and the Counting Stroop. *Biol Psychiatry* **45**(12): 1542–52.

Carmelli D, Swan GE, DeCarli C, Reed T (2002) Quantitative genetic modeling of regional brain volumes and cognitive performance in older male twins. *Biol Psychol* **61**(1–2): 139–55.

Carter CS, Braver TS, Barch DM *et al.* (1998) Anterior cingulate cortex, error detection, and the online monitoring of performance. *Science* **280**: 747–9.

Carter CS, Krener P, Chaderjian M *et al.* (1995a) Abnormal processing of irrelevant information in attention deficit hyperactivity disorder. *Psychiatry Res* **56**(1): 59–70.

Carter CS, Krener P, Chaderjian M *et al.* (1995b) Asymmetrical visual-spatial attentional performance in ADHD: evidence for a right hemispheric deficit. *Biol Psychiatry* **37**(11): 789–97.

Casey BJ, Castellanos FX, Giedd JN *et al.* (1997) Implication of right frontostriatal circuitry in response inhibition and Attention-Deficit/Hyperactivity Disorder. *Journal of the American Academy of Child and Adolescent Psychiatry* **36**(3): 374–83.

Castellanos FX, Giedd JN, Eckburg P *et al.* (1994) Quantitative morphology of the caudate nucleus in attention deficit hyperactivity disorder. *Am J Psychiatry* **151**(12): 1791–6.

Castellanos FX, Giedd JN, Marsh WL *et al.* (1996) Quantitative brain magnetic resonance imaging in Attention-Deficit Hyperactivity Disorder. *Archives of General Psychiatry* **53**(7): 607–16.

Castellanos FX, Lee PP, Sharp W *et al.* (2002) Developmental trajectories of brain volume abnormalities in children and adolescents with Attention-Deficit/Hyperactivity Disorder. *Journal of the American Medical Association* **288**(14): 1740–8.

Castellanos FX, Sonuga-Barke EJS, Scheres A *et al.* (2005) Varieties of Attention Deficit/Hyperactivity Disorder-related intra-individual variability. *Biological Psychiatry.*

Castellanos FX, Tannock R (2002) Neuroscience of Attention-Deficit/Hyperactivity Disorder: the search for endophenotypes. *Nat Rev Neurosci* **3**(8): 617–28.

Chambers CD, Bellgrove MA, Stokes MG *et al.* (2006) Executive 'brake failure' following deactivation of human frontal lobe. *Journal of Cognitive Neuroscience* **18**(3): 444–55.

Chen SH, Desmond JE (2005) Temporal dynamics of cerebro-cerebellar network recruitment during a cognitive task. *Neuropsychologia* **43**(9): 1227–37.

Cheon KA, Ryu YH, Kim YK *et al.* (2003) Dopamine transporter density in the basal ganglia assessed with [123I]IPT SPET in children with attention deficit hyperactivity disorder. *Eur J Nucl Med Mol Imaging* **30**(2), 306–11.

Cheon KA, Ryu YH, Kim JW, Cho DY (2005) The homozygosity for 10-repeat allele at dopamine transporter gene and dopamine transporter density in Korean children with attention deficit hyperactivity disorder: relating to treatment response to methylphenidate. *Eur Neuropsychopharmacol* **15**(1): 95–101.

Coolidge FL, Thede LL, Jang KL (2004) Are personality disorders psychological manifestations of executive function deficits? Bivariate heritability evidence from a twin study. *Behav Genet* **34**(1): 75–84.

Corbetta M, Shulman GL (2002) Control of goal-directed and stimulus-driven attention in the brain. *Nat Rev Neurosci* **3**(3): 201–15.

Cornish KM, Manly T, Savage R *et al.* (2005) Association of the dopamine transporter (DAT1) 10/10-repeat genotype with ADHD symptoms and response inhibition in a general population sample. *Mol Psychiatry.*

Crosbie J, Schachar R (2001) Deficient inhibition as a marker for familial ADHD. *Am J Psychiatry* **158**(11): 1884–90.

Cubells JF, Zabetian CP (2004) Human genetics of plasma dopamine beta-hydroxylase activity: applications to research in psychiatry and neurology. *Psychopharmacology (Berl)* **174**(4): 463–76.

Daly G, Hawi Z, Fitzgerald M, Gill M (1999) Mapping susceptibility loci in Attention Deficit Hyperactivity Disorder: preferential transmission of parental alleles at DAT1, DBH and DRD5 to affected children. *Molecular Psychiatry* **4**: 192–6.

DeLong MR, Alexander GE, Miller WC, Crutcher MD (1990) Anatomical and functional aspects of basal ganglia-thalamocortical circuits. In AJ Franks, JW Ironside, HS Mindham *et al.* (eds) *Function and Dysfunction in the Basal Ganglia* (pp. 3–32). Manchester: Manchester University Press.

Derrfuss J, Brass M, Neumann J, von Cramon DY (2005) Involvement of the inferior frontal junction in cognitive control: meta-analyses of switching and Stroop studies. *Hum Brain Mapp* **25**(1): 22–34.

d'Esposito M, Detre JA, Alsop DC *et al.* (1995) The neural basis of the central executive system of working memory. *Nature* **378**(6554): 279–81.

d'Esposito M, Postle BR (1999) The dependence of span and delayed-response performance on prefrontal cortex. *Neuropsychologia* **37**(11): 1303–15.

Diamond A, Briand L, Fossella J, Gehlbach L (2004) Genetic and neurochemical modulation of prefrontal cognitive functions in children. *Am J Psychiatry* **161**(1): 125–32.

Dresel S, Krause J, Krause KH *et al.* (2000) Attention deficit hyperactivity disorder: binding of [99mTc]TRODAT-1 to the dopamine transporter before and after methylphenidate treatment. *European Journal of Nuclear Medicine* **27**(10): 1518–24.

Durston S, Fossella JA, Casey BJ *et al.* (2005) Differential effects of DRD4 and DAT1 genotype on fronto-striatal gray matter volumes in a sample of subjects with attention deficit hyperactivity disorder, their unaffected siblings, and controls. *Mol Psychiatry*.

Durston S, Tottenham NT, Thomas KM *et al.* (2003) Differential patterns of striatal activation in young children with and without ADHD. *Biol Psychiatry* **53**(10): 871–8.

Egan MF, Goldberg TE, Kolachana BS *et al.* (2001) Effect of COMT Val 108/158 Met genotype on frontal lobe function and risk for schizophrenia. *Proceedings of the National Academy of Science* **98**(12): 6917–22.

Epstein JN, Johnson DE, Varia IM, Conners CK (2001) Neuropsychological assessment of response inhibition in adults with ADHD. *Journal of Clinical & Experimental Neuropsychology* **23**(3): 362–71.

Everett J, Thomas J, Cote F *et al.* (1991) Cognitive effects of psychostimulant medication in hyperactive children. *Child Psychiatry Hum Dev* **22**(2): 79–87.

Facoetti A, Turatto M, Lorusso ML, Mascetti GG (2001) Orienting of visual attention in dyslexia: evidence for asymmetric hemispheric control of attention. *Exp Brain Res* **138**(1): 46–53.

Fan J, Fossella J, Sommer T *et al.* (2003) Mapping the genetic variation of executive attention onto brain activity. *Proceedings of the National Academy of Sciences (USA)* **100**(12): 7406–11.

Fan J, Wu Y, Fossella JA, Posner MI (2001) Assessing the heritability of attentional networks. *BMC Neuroscience* **2**: 14.

Faraone SV, Doyle AE, Mick E, Biederman J (2001) Meta-analysis of the association between the 7-repeat allele of the dopamine D(4) receptor gene and attention deficit hyperactivity disorder. *Am J Psychiatry* **158**(7): 1052–7.

Filipek PA, Semrud-Clikeman M, Steingard RJ *et al.* (1997) Volumetric MRI analysis comparing subjects having Attention-Deficit Hyperactivity Disorder with normal controls. *Neurology* **48**(3): 589–601.

Fletcher PC, Henson RNA (2001) Frontal lobes and human memory: insights from functional neuroimaging. *Brain* **124**L 849–81.

Foote SL, Morrison JH (1987) Extrathalamic modulation of cortical function. *Annu Rev Neurosci* **10**: 67–95.

Ford JM, Gray M, Whitfield SL *et al.* (2004) Acquiring and inhibiting prepotent responses in schizophrenia: event-related brain potentials and functional magnetic resonance imaging. *Arch Gen Psychiatry* **61**(2): 119–29.

Fossella J, Sommer T, Fan J *et al.* (2002). Assessing the molecular genetics of attention networks. *BMC Neurosci* **3**(1): 14.

Freedman R, Adler LE, Leonard S (1999) Alternative phenotypes for the complex genetics of schizophrenia. *Biol Psychiatry* **45**(5): 551–8.

Freedman R, Coon H, Myles-Worsley M *et al.* (1997) Linkage of a neurophysiological deficit in schizophrenia to a chromosome 15 locus. *Proc Natl Acad Sci USA* **94**(2): 587–92.

Funnell M, Gazzaniga M, Garavan H (2004) Hemispheric lateralization of inhibitory control and task set in split-brain patients. Paper presented at the Cognitive Neuroscience Society Annual Meeting, San Francisco.

Garavan H, Ross TJ, Kaufman J, Stein EA (2003) A midline dissociation between error-processing and response-conflict monitoring. *Neuroimage* **20**(2): 1132–9.

Garavan H, Ross TJ, Li SJ, Stein EA (2000) A parametric manipulation of central executive functioning. *Cereb Cortex* **10**(6): 585–92.

Garavan H, Ross TJ, Stein EA (1999) Right hemisphere dominance for inhibitory control: an event-related functional MRI study. *Proceedings of the National Academy of Sciences,USA*, **96**: 8301–6.

Gathercole SE (1994) Neuropsychology and working memory: a review. *Neuropsychology* **8**(4): 494–505.

Geurts HM, Verte S, Oosterlaan J *et al.* (2004) How specific are executive functioning deficits in attention deficit hyperactivity disorder and autism? *J Child Psychol Psychiatry* **45**(4): 836–54.

Goldberg TE, Egan MF, Gscheidle *et al.* (2003) Executive subprocesses in working memory: relationship to Catechol-O-methyltransferase Val158Met genotype and schizophrenia. *Archives of General Psychiatry* **60**: 889–96.

Gottesman II, Gould TD (2003) The endophenotype concept in psychiatry: etymology and strategic intentions. *Am J Psychiatry* **160**(4): 636–45.

Grodinsky GM, Diamond R (1992) Frontal lobe functioning in boys with Attention-Deficit Hyperactivity Disorder. *Developmental Neuropsychology* **8**: 427–45.

Groot AS, de Sonneville LM, Stins JF, Boomsma DI (2004) Familial influences on sustained attention and inhibition in preschoolers. *J Child Psychol Psychiatry* **45**(2): 306–14.

Hallmayer JF, Kalaydjieva L, Badcock J *et al.* (2005) Genetic evidence for a distinct subtype of schizophrenia characterized by pervasive cognitive deficit. *Am J Hum Genet* **77**(3).

Hariri AR, Weinberger DR (2003) Imaging genomics. *Br Med Bull* **65**(1): 259–70.

Hawi Z, Millar N, Daly G *et al.* (2000) No association between catechol-O-methyltransferase (COMT) gene polymorphism and attention deficit hyperactivity disorder (ADHD) in an Irish sample. *Am J Med Genet* **96**(3): 282–4.

Heinz A, Goldman D, Jones DW *et al.* (2000) Genotype influences in vivo dopamine transporter availability in human striatum. *Neuropsychopharmacology* **22**: 133–9.

Ho BC, Wassink TH, O'Leary DS *et al.* (2005) Catechol-O-methyl transferase Val158Met gene polymorphism in schizophrenia: working memory, frontal lobe MRI morphology and frontal cerebral blood flow. *Mol Psychiatry* **10**(3): 229, 287–98.

Huang-Pollock CL, Nigg JT (2003) Searching for the attention deficit in attention deficit hyperactivity disorder: the case for visuospatial orienting. *Clinical Psychology Review* **23**: 801–30.

Johnson KJ, Kelly SP, Bellgrove MA *et al.* (2007) Fast Fourier transform analysis of response variability in ADHD: evidence for neuropsychological heterogeneity. *Neuropsychologia* **45**(4): 630–8.

Jonkman LM, Kemner C, Verbaten MN *et al.* (1999) Perceptual and response interference in children with Attention-Deficit Hyperactivity Disorder, and the effects of methylphenidate. *Psychophysiology* **36**(4): 419–29.

Jovanovic V, Guan HC, Van Tol HH (1999) Comparative pharmacological and functional analysis of the human dopamine D4.2 and D4.10 receptor variants. *Pharmacogenetics* **9**(5): 561–8.

Karoum F, Chrapusta SJ, Egan MF (1994) 3-Methoxytyramine is the major metabolite of released dopamine in the rat frontal cortex: reassessment of the effects of antipsychotics on the dynamics of dopamine release and metabolism in the frontal cortex, nucleus accumbens, and striatum by a simple two pool model. *J Neurochem* **63**(3): 972–9.

Kelly AM, Hester R, Murphy K *et al.* (2004) Prefrontal-subcortical dissociations underlying inhibitory control revealed by event-related fMRI. *Eur J Neurosci* **19**(11): 3105–12.

Klingberg T (1998) Concurrent performance of two working memory tasks: potential mechanisms of interference. *Cereb Cortex* **8**(7): 593–601.

Konishi S, Nakajima K, Uchida I *et al.* (1998) No-go dominant brain activity in human inferior prefrontal cortex revealed by functional magnetic resonance imaging. *European Journal of Neuroscience* **10**: 1209–13.

Konrad K, Neufang S, Hanisch C *et al.* (2005) Dysfunctional attentional networks in children with attention deficit/hyperactivity disorder: evidence from an event-related functional magnetic resonance imaging study. *Biol Psychiatry*.

Krause K-H, Dresel SH, Krause J *et al.* (2000) Increased striatal dopamine transporter in adult patients with attention deficit hyperactivity disorder: effects of methylphenidate as measured by single photon emission computed tomography. *Neuroscience Letters* **285**: 107–10.

Krause K-H, Dresel SH, Krause J *et al.* (2003) The dopamine transporter and neuroimaging in attention deficit hyperactivity disorder. *Neuroscience & Biobehavioral Reviews* **27**(7): 605–13.

Kubler A, Murphy K, Kaufman J *et al.* (2003) Co-ordination within and between verbal and visuospatial working memory: network modulation and anterior frontal recruitment. *Neuroimage* **20**(2): 1298–1308.

Kuntsi J, Stevenson J (2001) Psychological mechanisms in hyperactivity: II. The role of genetic factors. *J Child Psychol Psychiatry* **42**(2): 211–19.

Lachman HM, Papolos DF, Saito T *et al.* (1996) Human catechol-O-methyltransferase pharmacogenetics: description of a functional polymorphism and its potential application to neuropsychiatric disorders. *Pharmacogenetics* **6**(3): 243–50.

Leboyer M, Bellivier F, Nosten-Bertrand M *et al.* (1998) Psychiatric genetics: search for phenotypes. *Trends Neurosci* **21**(3): 102–5.

Levy F, Farrow M (2001) Working memory in ADHD: prefrontal/parietal connections. *Current Drug Targets* **2**(4): 347–52.

Lewis DA, Melchitzky DS, Sesack SR *et al.* (2001) Dopamine transporter immunoreactivity in monkey cerebral cortex: regional, laminar, and ultrastructural localization. *J Comp Neurol* **432**(1): 119–36.

Logan GD (1994) On the ability to inhibit thought and action: a user's guide to the stop signal paradigm. In D Dagenbach, TH Carr (eds) *Inhibitory Processes in Attention, Memory, and Language* (pp. 189–239). San Diego: Academic Press.

Logan GD, Cowan WB (1984) On the ability to inhbit thought and action: a theory of an act of control. *Psychological Review* **91**(3): 295–327.

Logan GD, Schachar RJ, Tannock R (1997) Impulsivity and inhibitory control. *Psychological Science* **8**(1): 60–4.

Loo SK, Specter E, Smolen A *et al.* (2003) Functional effects of the DAT1 polymorphism on EEG measures in ADHD. *J Am Acad Child Adolesc Psychiatry* **42**(8): 986–93.

Lowe N, Kirley A, Mullins C *et al.* (2004) Multiple markers analysis at the promoter region of the DRD4 gene and ADHD: evidence of linkage and association with the SNP-616. *American Journal of Medical Genetics Part B: Neuropsychiatric Genetics* **131B**(1): 33–7.

Madras BK, Miller GM, Fischman AJ (2005) The Dopamine Transporter and Attention-Deficit/Hyperactivity Disorder. *Biological Psychiatry*.

Manor I, Kotler M, Sever Y *et al.* (2000) Failure to replicate an association between the catechol-O-methyltransferase polymorphism and attention deficit hyperactivity disorder in a second, independently recruited Israeli cohort. *Am J Med Genet* **96**(6): 858–60.

Manor I, Tyano S, Eisenberg J *et al.* (2002) The short DRD4 repeats confer risk to attention deficit hyperactivity disorder in a family-based design and impair performance on a continuous performance test (TOVA). *Mol Psychiatry* **7**(7): 790–4.

Martinussen R, Hayden J, Hogg-Johnson S, Tannock R (2005) A meta-analysis of working memory impairments in children with Attention-Deficit/Hyperactivity Disorder. *J Am Acad Child Adolesc Psychiatry* **44**(4): 377–84.

Mehta MA, Owen AM, Sahakian BJ *et al.* (2000) Methylphenidate enhances working memory by modulating discrete frontal and parietal lobe regions in the human brain. *J Neurosci* **20**(6): RC65.

Nigg JT (2001) Is ADHD a disinhibitory disorder? *Psychological Bulletin* **127**(5): 571–98.

Nigg JT, Swanson JM, Hinshaw SP (1997) Covert visual spatial attention in boys with attention deficit hyperactivity disorder: lateral effects, methylphenidate response, and results for parents. *Neuropsychologia* **35**(2): 165–76.

Nigg JT, Willcutt EG, Doyle AE, Sonuga-Barke EJ (2005) Causal heterogeneity in Attention-Deficit/Hyperactivity Disorder: do we need neuropsychologically impaired subtypes? *Biol Psychiatry* **57**(11): 1224–30.

O'Connell RG, Bellgrove MA, Dockree PM, Robertson IH (2004) Reduced electrodermal response to errors predicts poor sustained attention performance in attention deficit hyperactivity disorder. *Neuroreport* **15**(16): 2535–8.

Okuyama Y, Ishiguro H, Toru M, Arinami T (1999) A genetic polymorphism in the promoter region of DRD4 associated with expression and schizophrenia. *Biochem Biophys Res Commun* **258**(2): 292–5.

Parasuraman R, Greenwood P, Kumar R, Fossella J (2005) Beyond heritability: neurotransmitter genes differentially modulate visuospatial attention and working memory. *Psychological Science* **16**(3): 200–7.

Pardo JV, Fox PT, Raichle ME (1991) Localisation of a human system for sustained attention by Positron Emission Tomography. *Nature* **349**: 61–4.

Passamonti L, Fera F, Magariello A *et al.* (2005) Monoamine oxidase – a genetic variation's influence on brain activity associated with inhibitory control: new insight into the neural correlates of impulsivity. *Biol Psychiatry.*

Paus T, Zatorre RJ, Hofle N *et al.* (1997) Time-related changes in neural systems underlying attention and arousal during the performance of an auditory vigilance task. *Journal of Cognitive Neuroscience* **9**(3): 392–408.

Pennington BF, Ozonoff S (1996) Executive functions and developmental psychopathology. *Journal of Child Psychology and Psychiatry* **37**(1): 51–87.

Pliszka SR, Glahn DC, Semrud-Clikeman M *et al.* (2006) Neuroimaging of inhibitory control areas in children with attention deficit hyperactivity disorder who were treatment naive or in long-term treatment. *Am J Psychiatry* **163**(6): 1052–60.

Pliszka SR, McCracken JT, Maas JW (1996) Catecholamines in Attention-Deficit Hyperactivity Disorder: current perspectives. *J Am Acad Child Adolesc Psychiatry* **35**(3): 264–72.

Posner MI, DiGirolamo GJ (2000) Cognitive neuroscience: origins and promise. *Psychological Bulletin* **126**(6): 873–89.

Posner MI, Peterson SE (1990) The attention system of the human brain. *Annual Review of Neuroscience* **13**: 35–42.

Postle BR, d'Esposito M (1999) Dissociation of human caudate nucleus activity in spatial and nonspatial working memory: an event-related fMRI study. *Brain Res Cogn Brain Res* **8**(2): 107–15.

Primus RJ, Thurkauf A, Xu J *et al.* (1997) II. Localization and characterization of dopamine D4 binding sites in rat and human brain by use of the novel, D4 receptor-selective ligand [3H]NGD 94-1. *J Pharmacol Exp Ther* **282**(2): 1020–7.

Ravizza SM, Delgado MR, Chein JM *et al.* (2004) Functional dissociations within the inferior parietal cortex in verbal working memory. *Neuroimage* **22**(2): 562–73.

Robertson IH, Marshall JC (eds) (1993) *Unilateral Neglect: Clinical and Experimental Studies.* Hillsdale, NJ: Lawrence Erlbaum & Associates.

Rogeness GA, Hernandez JM, Macedo CA, Mitchell EL (1982) Biochemical differences in children with conduct disorder socialized and undersocialized. *Am J Psychiatry* **139**(3): 307–11.

Roman T, Schmitz M, Polanczyk GV *et al.* (2002) Further evidence for the association between Attention-Deficit/Hyperactivity Disorder and the dopamine-beta-hydroxylase gene. *Am J Med Genet* **114**(2): 154–8.

Rubia K, Lee F, Cleare AJ *et al.* (2005) Tryptophan depletion reduces right inferior prefrontal activation during response inhibition in fast, event-related fMRI. *Psychopharmacology (Berl)* **179**(4): 791–803.

Rubia K, Overmeyer S, Taylor E *et al.* (1999) Hypofrontality in attention deficit hyperactivity disorder during higher-order motor control: a study with functional MRI. *American Journal of Psychiatry* **156**(6): 891–6.

Rubia K, Russell T, Overmeyer S *et al.* (2001) Mapping motor inhibition: conjunctive brain activations across different versions of go/no-go and stop tasks. *Neuroimage* **13**(2): 250–61.

Rubia K, Smith AB, Brammer MJ *et al.* (2005) Abnormal brain activation during inhibition and error detection in medication-naive adolescents with ADHD. *Am J Psychiatry* **162**(6): 1067–75.

Schachar RJ, Crosbie J, Barr CL *et al.* (2005) Inhibition of motor responses in siblings concordant and discordant for Attention Deficit Hyperactivity Disorder. *Am J Psychiatry* **162**(6): 1076–82.

Scheres A, Oosterlaan J, Swanson J *et al.* (2003) The effect of methylphenidate on three forms of response inhibition in boys with AD/HD. *J Abnorm Child Psychol* **31**(1): 105–20.

Schulz KP, Fan J, Tang CY *et al.* (2004) Response inhibition in adolescents diagnosed with attention deficit hyperactivity disorder during childhood: an event-related FMRI study. *Am J Psychiatry* **161**(9): 1650–7.

Schweitzer JB, Faber TL, Grafton ST *et al.* (2000) Alterations in the functional anatomy of working memory in adult attention deficit hyperactivity disorder. *Am J Psychiatry* **157**(2): 278–80.

Seidman LJ, Biederman J, Faraone SV *et al.* (1997) Toward defining a neuropsychology of attention deficit-hyperactivity disorder: performance of children and adolescents from a large clinically referred sample. *J Consult Clin Psychol* **65**(1): 150–60.

Seidman LJ, Biederman J, Monuteaux MC *et al.* (2000) Neuropsychological functioning in nonreferred siblings of children with attention deficit/hyperactivity disorder. *J Abnorm Psychol* **109**(2): 252–65.

Seidman LJ, Biederman J, Weber W *et al.* (1998) Neuropsychological function in adults with Attention-Deficit Hyperactivity Disorder. *Biological Psychiatry*, **44**(4), 260–68.

Sergeant, J. (2000). The cognitive-energetical model: An empirical approach to Attention-Deficit Hyperactivity Disorder. *Neuroscience & Biobehavioral Reviews* **24**: 7–12.

Sergeant J, Oosterlaan J, van der Meere J (1999) Information processing and energetic factors in ADHD. In H Quay, A Hogan (eds), *Handbook of Disruptive Behavior Disorders* (pp. 75–103). New York: Kluwer Academic.

Shah P, Miyake A (1996) The separability of working memory resources for spatial thinking and language processing: an individual differences approach. *Journal of Experimental Psychology: General* **125**: 4–27.

Shallice T (1988) *From Neuropsychology to Mental Structure.* New York: Cambridge University Press.

Shallice T, Marzocchi GM, Coser S. *et al.* (2002) Executive function profile of children with attention deficit hyperactivity disorder. *Dev Neuropsychol* **21**(1): 43–71.

Sheppard DM, Bradshaw JL, Mattingley JB, Lee P (1999) Effects of stimulant medication on the lateralisation of line bisection judgements of children with Attention Deficit Hyperactivity Disorder. *Journal of Neurology, Neurosurgery and Psychiatry* **66**: 57–63.

Slaats-Willemse D, Swaab-Barneveld H, De Sonneville L, Buitelaar J (2005) Familial clustering of executive functioning in affected sibling pair families with ADHD. *J Am Acad Child Adolesc Psychiatry* **44**(4): 385–91.

Slaats-Willemse D, Swaab-Barneveld H, De Sonneville L *et al.* (2003) Deficient response inhibition as a cognitive endophenotype of ADHD. *J Am Acad Child Adolesc Psychiatry* **42**(10): 1242–8.

Smith A, Nutt D (1996) Noradrenaline and attention lapses. *Nature* **380**: 291.

Smith EE, Jonides J (1999) Storage and executive processes in the frontal lobes. *Science* **283**: 1657–61.

Smith KM, Daly M, Fischer M *et al.* (2003) Association of the dopamine beta hydroxylase gene with attention deficit hyperactivity disorder: genetic analysis of the Milwaukee longitudinal study. *Am J Med Genet* **119B**(1): 77–85.

Sowell ER, Thompson PM, Welcome SE *et al.* (2003) Cortical abnormalities in children and adolescents with Attention-Deficit Hyperactivity Disorder. *Lancet* **362**(9397): 1699–707.

Sturm W, de Simone A, Krause BJ *et al.* (1999) Functional anatomy of intrinsic alertness: evidence for a fronto-parietal-thalamic-brainstem network in the right hemisphere. *Neuropsychologia* **37**(7): 797–805.

Stuss DT, Murphy KJ, Binns MA, Alexander MP (2003) Staying on the job: the frontal lobes control individual performance variability. *Brain* **126**(Pt 11): 2363–80.

Swan GE, Carmelli D (2002) Evidence for genetic mediation of executive control: a study of aging male twins. *J Gerontol B Psychol Sci Soc Sci* **57**(2): P133–43.

Swanson J, Oosterlaan J, Murias M *et al.* (2000) Attention deficit/hyperactivity disorder children with a 7-repeat allele of the dopamine receptor D4 gene have extreme behavior but normal performance on critical neuropsychological tests of attention. *PNAS* **97**(9): 4754–9.

Swanson J, Posner M, Potkin S *et al.* (1991) Activating tasks for the study of visual-spatial attention in ADHD children: a cognitive anatomic approach. *J Child Neurol* **6**(Suppl): S119–27.

Tamm L, Menon V, Ringel J, Reiss AL (2004) Event-related FMRI evidence of frontotemporal involvement in aberrant response inhibition and task switching in Attention-Deficit/Hyperactivity Disorder. *J Am Acad Child Adolesc Psychiatry* **43**(11): 1430–40.

Tannock R (1998) Attention Deficit Hyperactivity Disorder: advances in cognitive, neurobiological, and genetic research. *Journal of Child Psychology and Psychiatry* **39**(1): 65–99.

Tehunen J, Salminen M, Lundstrom K *et al.* (1994) Genomic organization of the human catechol-O-methyltransferase gene and its expression from two distinct promoters. *European Journal of Biochemistry* **223**: 1049–59.

Teicher MH, Anderson CM, Polcari A *et al.* (2000) Functional deficits in basal ganglia of children with Attention-Deficit/Hyperactivity Disorder shown with functional magnetic resonance imaging relaxometry. *Nature Medicine* **6**(4): 470–3.

Vaidya CJ, Austin G, Kirkorian G et al. (1998) Selective effects of methylphenidate in attention deficit hyperactivity disorder: a functional magnetic resonance study. *Proceedings of the National Academy of Sciences of the United States of America* **95**(24): 14494–9.

Vaidya CJ, Bunge SA, Dudukovic NM et al. (2005) Altered neural substrates of cognitive control in childhood ADHD: evidence from functional magnetic resonance imaging. *Am J Psychiatry* **162**(9): 1605–13.

Valera EM, Faraone SV, Biederman J et al. (2005) Functional neuroanatomy of working memory in adults with Attention-Deficit/Hyperactivity Disorder. *Biol Psychiatry* **57**(5): 439–47.

van der Meere J, Sergeant J (1988) Focused attention in pervasively hyperactive children. *J Abnorm Child Psychol* **16**(6): 627–9.

Viggiano D, Ruocco LA, Arcieri S, Sadile AG (2004) Involvement of norepinephrine in the control of activity and attentive processes in animal models of attention deficit hyperactivity disorder. *Neural Plast* **11**(1–2): 133–49.

Vink M, Kahn RS, Raemaekers M et al. (2005) Function of striatum beyond inhibition and execution of motor responses. *Hum Brain Mapp* **25**(3): 336–44.

Voeller KK, Heilman KM (1988) Attention deficit disorder in children: a neglect syndrome? *Neurology* **38**(5): 806–8.

Waldman ID (2005) Statistical approaches to complex phenotypes: evaluating neuropsychological endophenotypes for Attention-Deficit/Hyperactivity Disorder. *Biol Psychiatry* **57**(11): 1347–56.

Wigg K, Zai G, Schachar R et al. (2002) Attention deficit hyperactivity disorder and the gene for dopamine Beta-hydroxylase. *Am J Psychiatry* **159**(6): 1046–8.

Willcutt EG, Doyle AE, Nigg JT et al. (2005) Validity of the executive function theory of ADHD: a meta-analytic review. *Biological Psychiatry*.

Winterer G, Goldman D (2003) Genetics of human prefrontal function. *Brain Res Brain Res Rev* **43**(1): 134–63.

Winterer G, Hariri AR, Goldman D, Weinberger DR (2005) Neuroimaging and human genetics. *Int Rev Neurobiol* **67PB**: 325–83.

Witte EA, Marrocco RT (1997) Alteration of brain noradrenergic activity in rhesus monkeys affects the alerting component of covert orienting. *Psychopharmacology (Berl)* **132**(4): 315–23.

Wright M, De Geus E, Ando J et al. (2001) Genetics of cognition: outline of a collaborative twin study. *Twin Res* **4**(1): 48–56.

Wylie GR, Javitt DC, Foxe JJ (2004) Don't think of a white bear: an fMRI investigation of the effects of sequential instructional sets on cortical activity in a task-switching paradigm. *Hum Brain Mapp* **21**(4): 279–97.

Zhang HB, Wang YF, Li J et al. (2004) [Association of dopamine beta-hydroxylase polymorphism with attention deficit hyperactivity disorder in children]. *Beijing Da Xue Xue Bao* **36**(3): 290–3.

13 The Psychopharmacology of ADHD

MARY V. SOLANTO,[1] **RUSSELL SCHACHAR**[2] **AND ABEL ICKOWICZ**[2]

1. Department of Psychiatry, Mount Sinai School of Medicine; 2. Department of Psychiatry, University of Toronto

13.1 OVERVIEW

ADHD is a common condition that is first detected in young children and persists in many individuals through childhood and adolescence and even into adulthood. At each age, ADHD is associated with substantial impairment, and the presence of ADHD increases risk for development of secondary comorbidity (Jensen, Martin & Cantwell, 1997), injuries (Brehaut *et al.*, 2003), impairment and use of medical services (Miller *et al.*, 2004a). Medication has been a mainstay of treatment for three or more decades. The beneficial effects of amphetamine were discovered serendipitously by Charles Bradley in 1937 (Bradley, 1937). Methylphenidate (MPH) was licensed in the US in 1955. Numerous randomised clinical trials conducted since 1970 and enrolling thousands of children leave little doubt that medication has a beneficial impact on the core behavioural manifestations of ADHD and that they have a favourable cost-benefit profile when compared with the benefits and costs of non-pharmacological interventions.

Nevertheless, questions remain about the breadth of the therapeutic effects of stimulants, their ability to mitigate the most worrisome of adverse outcomes (substance use disorder, antisocial behaviour, and scholastic failure), their role in treating special populations such as the very young and those with low intellectual function, and their long-term effects.

ADHD is a controversial condition with some arguing that the scientific evidence does not merit its status as a valid medical condition. It goes without saying that critics of ADHD as a valid entity will be considerably distressed by the use of medication to treat ADHD. The unsubstantiated nature of these arguments has been pointed out by an International Consensus of leading scientists in the field of ADHD (Barkley, 2002a).

13.2 PREVALENCE OF MEDICATION USE

For many years, MPH (marketed as Ritalin) and, to a much lesser extent, dextroamphetamine (Dexedrine) were the most frequently prescribed treatment for ADHD in North America (Swanson, Lerner, & Williams, 1995; Safer, Zito & Fine, 1996).

Handbook of Attention Deficit Hyperactivity Disorder. Edited by M. Fitzgerald, M. Bellgrove and M. Gill.
© 2007 John Wiley & Sons Ltd

Tricyclic antidepressants and alpha-2 noradrenergic agonists such as clonidine (Catapres) and guanfacine (Tenex) served as second-line drug treatments in cases with inadequate or adverse response to stimulants (Swanson *et al.*, 1995).

In recent years, long-acting stimulant preparations of MPH such as Concerta, Ritalin-LA and of amphetamine (Adderall-XR) have become the norm because of the increased convenience of once daily dosing and its potential impact on adherence. In 2002, a selective beta-adrenergic reuptake inhibitor, atomoxetine (Strattera) was approved. Modafinil is a dopaminergic agonist that is currently marketed as Provigil to treat narcolepsy that appears to also have some beneficial effects in the treatment of ADHD.

In a recent study of American children, parental report was used to assess the prevalence of ADHD and drug treatment (Visser & Lesesne, 2005). This survey found that 4.4 million children, age 4–17 years (11.0% of males; 4.4% of females) had a history of an ADHD diagnosis. Of these children, 56% or 2.5 million were taking medication. That means that 4.3% of children had been diagnosed with ADHD and were taking medication (see also Cox *et al.*, 2003). Prevalence was highest among males age 12 years (9.3%) and among females age 11 years (3.7%). The rate of treated ADHD was highest in non-Hispanic, primarily English-speaking children with insurance. This prevalence represents a substantial increase over the last decade from an estimated prevalence of 1.5 million American children (Safer *et al.*, 1996; Robison *et al.*, 2001). The prevalence of medication use is lower in Canada and Australasia than it is in the United States, but rates are beginning to rise (Miller *et al.*, 2004b). The prevalence of treated ADHD in the United Kingdom was estimated to be 5.3 per 1000 boys in 1999 – a rate that is one-tenth of that in North America (Jick, Kaye & Black, 2004). It should be noted that criteria for ADHD, termed 'Hyperkinetic Disorder' in the current edition of the International Classification of Diseases (ICD-10) (World Health Organization, 1990), used mainly in Europe, are somewhat more stringent than the DSM-IV criteria for ADHD (American Psychiatric Association, 1994). Notably, *direct* observation of symptoms by the clinician are required in addition to report of symptoms by parent and teacher, and symptoms must have had onset *before* the age of *6 years*, compared to *by* age *7 years* in the DSM-IV. The ICD-10 furthermore, does not recognise the 'Predominantly Inattentive' and 'Predominantly Hyperactive-Impulsive' subtypes of ADHD, which are considered 'subthreshold' cases. These differences in diagnostic criteria may contribute to a lower rate of identification and treatment in the UK and other European countries.

The steady rise in rate of medication usage in the US is attributable to a number of factors. Community physicians rely heavily on medication for treatment of ADHD. ADHD is being diagnosed more frequently among children with the inattentive symptoms only, among girls, and among preschoolers, adolescents, and adults (Goldman *et al.*, 1998). The duration of treatment of each patient may be increasing along with increasing awareness of the developmental adversity associated with the disorder. Increasing prevalence of medication use may also be linked to lack of availability in the community of well-crafted, non-drug treatments which, in any case, are less effective, more expensive and generally less cost-effective (Jensen *et al.*, 2005). The role of medication is expanding as the general public and practitioners become more familiar and accepting of medication for children. Wide variation in rates of medication use among communities has been observed and is thought to be a function of the availability of treatment rather than of overuse of medication (Visser & Lesesne, 2005). One might even argue based on population-based studies that ADHD often goes unidentified and untreated (Goldman et al., 1998b). We do not know all the reasons for therapeutic choices, but parent and patient preference, affluence and the availability of non-drug treatments are likely to influence these decisions (Bokhari, Mayes & Scheffler, 2005).

The increase in paediatric psychotropic drug treatment in the US may also be attributable in part to the passage of the Food and Drug Modernization Act (FDAMA) of 1997 which included, among other provisions, a six-month extension on patent exclusivity for post-marketing studies on the safety and efficacy of a given drug in children. Since a six-month patent extension may result in additional proceeds to the company in the millions of dollars, this provision constituted a powerful incentive to conduct new research on effects of stimulants and other drugs in children (FDA, 1997). Subsequently, the Pediatric Research Equity Act, which became effective in December 2003, required that all new drug applications submitted to the FDA include assessment of the safety and efficacy of the new product in all relevant paediatric populations for all claimed indications (FDA, 2003). These initiatives served to greatly heighten interest in and awareness of paediatric drug treatment within industry and in the community at large.

The drugs currently available to treat ADHD will be discussed in turn, beginning with the stimulants since they are the most widely researched and still the most widely used drug treatment alternative. The first section is devoted to the treatment of school-age children using stimulants and non-stimulants, with separate sections devoted to the pharmacological treatment of preschoolers, adolescents and adults. A listing of all drugs used to treat ADHD, along with important usage parameters, appears in Table 13.1.

13.3 STIMULANTS

13.3.1 ACUTE EFFECTS IN CHILDREN

Stimulant medication has been used extensively for four decades and is generally regarded by practitioners as the drug of first choice for the treatment of ADHD (Greenhill et al., 2002). The acute effects of MPH have been extensively investigated in numerous, placebo-controlled, randomised trials. These studies confirm that stimulants confer significant short-term benefit (Spencer et al., 1996; Jadad et al., 1999) with effect sizes of 0.8 to 1.3 for improvement in deportment and impairment (Greenhill et al., 2001). The effect size is the difference in mean outcome score between placebo and medication, divided by the variability (standard deviation) of scores in the total sample. Careful titration to the optimal dose and active management of medication double the number of cases that show near-normal ADHD levels over the effect achieved by medication management as typically practised in the community (Swanson et al., 2001). The overall positive response rate to MPH is about 77% (Barkley, 1977; Spencer et al., 1996; Greenhill et al., 2001). If both

Table 13.1. Medications commonly used for ADHD

Medication	Dosing (paediatric)			Onset/ ≈ duration	Common side effects	Contraindications and interactions
	Initial (mg)	Usual (mg)	Doses per day			
Methylphenidate						
Ritalin, Methylin, Rubifen IR[1]	5–10 mg	10–20 mg	2–3	30–60 min/ ≈ 4 hr	Appetite suppression, stomachaches, headaches, irritability, weight loss, mild increase in blood pressure (BP) and heart rate (HR), growth deceleration?, exacerbation of tics?	Cardiovascular disease, glaucoma, use of monoamino oxidase inhibitors
Concerta	18–27 mg	27–54 mg	1	30–60 min/ ≈ 12 hr		
Metadate CD	10 mg					
Methylin ER	10 mg	10–40 mg	1	30–90 min/ ≈ 6–8 hr		
Ritalin LA	20 mg	20–40 mg	1	30–60 min/ ≈ 8 hr		
Rubifen SR	20 mg	20–40 mg	1	30–90 min/ ≈ 8 hr		
Focalin	2.5–5 mg	2.5–10 mg	2–3	30–60 min/ ≈ 4 hr		
Daytrana (methylphenidate-transdermal)	10 mg	10–30 mg	1	60–90 min/ ≈ 9 hr		
Amphetamines						
Dexedrine	2.5–5 mg	5–10 mg	2–3	30–60 min/ ≈ 4–6 hr	Appetite suppression, stomachaches, headaches, irritability, weight loss, mild increase in BP and HR, growth deceleration?, exacerbation of tics?	Cardiovascular disease, glaucoma, use of monoamino oxidase inhibitors
Dexedrine Spansules	10 mg	10–20 mg	1	60–90 min/ ≈ 6–9 hr		
Adderall	5–10 mg	5–30 mg	1–2	30–60 min/ ≈ 4–6 hr		
Adderall XR	5–10 mg	10–30 mg	1	60–90 min/ ≈ 12 hr		
Atomoxetine						
Strattera	0.5 mg/kg/ day	1.2 mg/kg/ day	1–2	May require several days of treatment to observe onset, effects may last 24 hours	Nausea, vomiting and other GI symptoms, appetite suppression, fatigue, mild increase in BP and HR	Liver impairment, glaucoma, use of monoamine oxidase inhibitors. Safety in pregnancy has not been established

Drug	Starting dose	Dose range	Doses/day	Onset/duration	Side effects	Contraindications/cautions
Modafinil Provigil/Alertec	100 mg	100–300	1–2	30–90 min, duration of effect variable but typically less than 24 hours	Insomnia, headache, decreased appetite, nausea, mild increase in HR and BP, overconfidence	Cardiovascular safety has not been established. Concomitant use with psychostimulants, TCAs and monoamine oxidase inhibitors not recommended
Bupropion Wellbutrin SR	1/3 to 1/2 of target dose	3–7 mg/kg/day	1–2	May require several days of treatment to observe onset, effects may last less than 24 hours on SR preparation	Weight loss, insomnia, agitation, anxiety, irritability, dry mouth, seizures	Bulimia, anorexia nervosa, seizures, abrupt discontinuation of alcohol/benzodiazepines, use of monoamine oxidase inhibitors
Wellbutrin XL			1			
Alpha adrenergic agonists						
Clonidine Catapres, Dixarit	1/3 of target dose	0.003–0.008 mg/kg/day	2–4	60–90 min Children metabolize Clonidine more rapidly than adults and may require 3 to 4 doses per day.	Sedation, hypotension, bradycardia, headaches, dizziness, stomachaches, nausea. Rebound hypertension on abrupt discontinuation.	Depression, cardiovascular disorders, renal or liver disease, pregnancy
Guanfacine Tenex	1/3 of target dose	0.015–0.05 mg/day	1–2	60–90 min	Less sedation with guanfacine	

¹IR = Immediate-release.

MPH and d-amphetamine are tried and higher than typical doses are administered, the rate of behavioural response may be as high as 95% (Elia *et al.*, 1991). As many as 25% of children may respond better to one stimulant than to another (Elia *et al.*, 1991).

When treated with stimulants, children are immediately and substantially less restless, impulsive and inattentive (Schachar *et al.*, 1997). Stimulants decrease oppositional and aggressive behaviour as well as reducing the core manifestations of ADHD (MTA Cooperative Group, 1999a). There is also evidence that covert antisocial behaviours such as stealing are also decreased by stimulants (Hinshaw *et al.*, 1992; Klein *et al.*, 1997).

Limited research in children to date indicates that children with the Predominantly Inattentive subtype of ADHD are as responsive to MPH as children with the Combined type (Barkley, DuPaul & McMurray, 1991; Solanto *et al.*, submitted-b; Stein *et al.*, 2003).

Stimulants improve performance on a wide range of important attention skills as measured on laboratory tasks. Medicated children perform tasks with increased accuracy and are better able to identify their errors (Krusch *et al.*, 1996). They can better hold information in short-term 'working memory,' withhold and stop their motor responses when necessary, focus on complex tasks and switch set flexibly (Denney & Rapport, 2001). In addition to improving performance when narrowness of attentional focus is an asset, stimulants facilitate performance on tasks demanding divergent thinking and creativity (Solanto and Wender, 1989). Treated children are better able to perform on ecologically relevant tasks as well as on boring, simple or repetitive tasks such as the continuous performance test (Losier, McGrath & Klein, 1996). Improvements are observed in driving ability in adults (Barkley *et al.*, 2005), academic accuracy and productivity (Rapport *et al.*, 1994; Evans, Pelham & Smith, 2001) and scores on intelligence testing (Gimpel *et al.*, 2005). Stimulants also improve mathematical computation and word discovery (Douglas *et al.*, 1986), verbal retrieval, letter search and arithmetic (Tannock *et al.*, 1989b). Across laboratory studies of cognition, positive effects of stimulants are most consistently seen on simple, automatised functions, such as vigilance, reaction time and motor inhibitory control (Losier *et al.*, 1996; Solanto, 1998) and more variably demonstrated across higher order measures of executive functioning. Thus, for example, whereas motor inhibitory control, as measured by the Stop Signal Task (Scheres *et al.*, 2003; Tannock *et al.*, 1989a), is reliably increased by MPH, cognitive inhibitory control in the form of resistance to distraction, as measured by the Stroop Color-Word naming test or the Eriksen Flanker task, was improved in one recent study (Langleben *et al.*, 2006) but not others (Scheres *et al.*, 2003; Bedard *et al.*, 2004).

In the vast majority of treated children, there is no evidence that any component of cognition is consistently impaired by stimulants either through over-focusing or increased perseverative thoughts or actions (Solanto & Wender, 1989; Douglas *et al.*, 1995; Mehta, Goodyer & Sahakian, 2004), or through interference in recall of information that was learned while medicated (state-dependent learning) (Becker-Mattes *et al.*, 1985). On the other hand, several studies have found specific cognitive processes that do not show stimulant-related improvement, including speed of naming letters or digits; story length or comprehension (Tannock,

Martinussen, & Frijters, 2000; Francis, Fine & Tannock, 2001; Bedard, Ickowicz & Tannock, 2002; Bedard *et al.*, 2003; Bedard *et al.*, 2004) and individual children may exhibit some over-focusing and perseveration. The clinical or theoretical implications of these observations are unclear. Further research into cognitive effects of stimulants is warranted to ensure that there are no, as yet undetected, adverse cognitive effects in the complete range of doses that are used in clinical practice and to increase our understanding of the mechanism whereby these drugs work in ADHD. Moreover, it is important to monitor the response of individual patients.

Interpersonal relations with peers (Hinshaw *et al.*, 1989; MTA Cooperative Group, 1999a) and parents are improved by stimulants. In a pivotal study, Barkley and Cunningham (1979) coded the behaviour of mothers and their children with and without ADHD during free play and while performing a task. Mothers of unmedicated children with ADHD made more comments that were critical or controlling than did mothers of children without ADHD. Following a single dose of MPH administered to children with ADHD, children became more compliant and mothers evidenced a decrease in directive comments. These results clearly demonstrated that the mothers' directive behaviour was *in response to rather than the cause of* their children's non-compliance. Subsequent research similarly reported decreased maternal criticism and increased maternal warmth and mother–child contact following medication (Schachar *et al.*, 1997).

The majority of medicated children feel that medication is helpful and the quality of their social interactions is improved although not necessarily normalised (Whalen *et al.*, 1989; Whalen & Henker, 1991; Hoza *et al.*, 2005). Medication does not seem to engender the belief that success is attributable to external factors rather than to one's own personal effort (Pelham *et al.*, 1992). When medicated, children persist more in the face of difficult tasks and failure experiences and expend more effort to obtain rewards (Milich *et al.*, 1991).

13.3.2 RESPONSE OF COMORBID SUBGROUPS

Few predictors of stimulant response have been identified to guide clinical decision making. Among school-age ADHD children, more favourable stimulant response is often observed among younger patients. Increasing severity was a positive predictor of outcome in one study (Taylor *et al.*, 1987) but a negative predictor in another (Buitelaar *et al.*, 1995). Children with comorbid anxiety symptoms seem to have a unique physiological response to acute administration of MPH (Urman *et al.*, 1995). Although early studies suggested these children may respond less well to stimulants than do children with ADHD without anxiety (Pliszka, 1989; DuPaul, Barkley & McMurray, 1994; Buitelaar *et al.*, 1995; Tannock, Ickowiz & Schachar, 1995) (see also Chapter 15), more recent and larger-scaled studies have failed to confirm that such differences exist either acutely (Diamond, Tannock, & Schachar, 1999; Gadow *et al.*, 2002) or in the longer term (Jensen *et al.*, 2001a; Thiruchelvam, Charach & Schachar, 2001). In the NIMH-sponsored Multimodal Treatment Study of ADHD (MTA) (Jensen *et al.*, 2001a), children with one or more comorbid conditions (68% of the sample) responded to stimulants as well as those with ADHD alone. However, children with an anxiety disorder plus another disruptive behaviour disorder (ODD or CD) derived increased benefit from the combination of behavioural treatment and stimulant medication relative to medication alone than did children without these comorbidities (Jensen *et al.*, 2001a).

Greater number of depressive symptoms among parents predicts a lesser response to stimulants among their children, an effect which highlights the necessity of treating ADHD in the context of the family (Owens *et al.*, 2003). The beneficial effects of stimulant treatment do not vary with ethnicity or social class (Arnold *et al.*, 2003) although these factors can affect the ability of the patient's family to participate in treatment (Rieppi *et al.*, 2002).

Traditional belief and practice have been that the stimulants are unsuitable for children with tics or with a family history of tic disorder because of the potential of these drugs to cause an increase in tics. However, two controlled prospective studies of stimulants enrolling a total of 56 children with ADHD and comorbid Tourette Disorder followed from 2 to 4 years, did not find a significant long-term increase in tics in the samples as a whole (Castellanos *et al.*, 1997; Gadow *et al.*, 1997; Law & Schachar, 1999), However, one-third of the participants in the study by Castellanos discontinued stimulant treatment because of a worsening of tics, which was reversed upon discontinuation of drug treatment. Thus, there may be a subgroup of children with tic disorder for whom MPH produces an unacceptable worsening of tics.

MPH is safe and effective in children with ADHD and a comorbid seizure disorder after the seizures have been controlled using an anti-epileptic agent (Gross-Tsur *et al.*, 1997).

Children with ADHD and low IQ show positive behavioural and cognitive responses to stimulants. Yet their response is less robust than that of normal-IQ ADHD children (Handen *et al.*, 1990; Handen *et al.*, 1992; Aman, Buican & Arnold, 2003; Owens *et al.*, 2003) and they experience more adverse effects (Handen *et al.*, 1991). Studies examining a range of dosages (0.15, 0.30, 0.60 mg/kg t.i.d.) found that, similarly to ADHD children without low IQ, they responded better both cognitively and behaviourally to higher doses (Pearson *et al.*, 2003, 2004a, 2004b). There is a small body of literature which demonstrates favourable stimulant response among children whose ADHD symptoms developed following traumatic brain injury although the effect is less marked and less consistent (Jin & Schachar, 2004; Siddall, 2005).

13.3.3 LONG-ACTING STIMULANT PREPARATIONS

Long-acting preparations are useful for non-adherent parents and patients, for situations where taking medication at school is deemed socially unacceptable and for individuals who dislike the waxing and waning nature of stimulant effects. These preparations were developed because of poor adherence especially for the midday dose of immediate-release medication and because of the potentially adverse social impact of taking medication to manage behaviour while in school. Adherence is a major concern in the treatment of all conditions in medicine and is certainly a factor that influences the effectiveness of stimulant treatment (Thiruchelvam *et al.*, 2001; Charach, Ickowicz & Schachar, 2004; Sanchez *et al.*, 2005).

There are multiple extended action preparations of stimulant medications (Table 13.1). Each preparation includes some provision to deliver an initial dose of stimulant followed by a slower release of medication with the goal of extending the pharmacodynamic effects over the entire day. Each preparation achieves this goal using a slightly different technology and dosing strategy. Concerta employs an osmotic pump system (OROS) which delivers an increasing dose of methylphenindate to yield an ascending plasma profile of methylphenindate across the day (Swanson et al., 2003). Controlled studies indicated that a higher dosage of MPH in the afternoon was necessary to achieve the same control of symptoms as in the morning, possibly because of the development of tachyphylaxis, or acute tolerance, after the morning dose (Swanson et al., 1999). In a randomised, controlled study, OROS MPH and MPH immediate-release (IR) t.i.d. were each significantly more effective than placebo and non-significantly from each other (Wolraich et al., 2001). Adderall-XR, a long-acting formulation of d- and l- amphetamine salts, employs 2 sets of beads – immediate and 4-hour delayed-release – to achieve the same ascending profile (Greenhill et al., 2003). The formulations differ with respect to the total length of coverage they provide during the day: Ritalin-LA and Metadate-CD, for example, are 8-hour preparations, whereas Concerta and Adderall-XR are 10–12 hour formulations. The preparations also differ with respect to the percentage of immediate-release MPH they contain: Concerta, 22%; Metadate-CD; 30%; Ritalin-LA 50%; Adderall: 50%, and Focalin XR 50%. Thus, the choice of the best formulation may depend in part on the time of day when the child's symptoms are most pronounced. Children who need better coverage in the morning may benefit more from a formulation with a higher percentage of immediate-release MPH. An alternate management strategy is to add a small IR dose of MPH in the morning to accompany a long-acting formulation in order to achieve better morning coverage, or in the late afternoon to achieve better after-school coverage without interfering with sleep.

Direct comparison of effects of long-acting preparations on behaviour in a laboratory classroom indicated that treatment effects are directly related to the pharmacokinetics of the medication. That is, Metadate is more effective than Concerta during the morning, as would be expected given its higher percentage of immediate-release methylphenindate; the two preparations are equivalent during the afternoon and Concerta, as intended by its 12-hour release mechanism, is more effective in the early evening (Swanson et al., 2004). Long-acting preparations appear to be as safe and effective in long-term treatment as immediate release formulations. For example, OROS R methylphenindate was effective for up to 24 months with minimal effects on growth, tics, vital signs, or laboratory test values (Wilens et al., 2005).

Use of a long-acting preparation increases the likelihood that the child's after-school behaviour with respect to both social interactions with peers and parents, as well as homework performance, is improved, thereby avoiding long-term adverse effects on social (Taylor et al., 1996; Schachar et al., 1997) and academic outcomes. A recent randomised open-label trial enrolling 145 children with ADHD showed that remission rates at 8 weeks were higher for OROS-MPH (Concerta) (44%) than for immediate-release b.i.d. (4%) or t.i.d. (25%) MPH (Steele et al., 2006). In addition, analysis of a national healthcare database showed that over one year's time, the rates of accidents and injury, emergency room visits, hospital days, were reduced for those patients receiving OROS-MPH compared to those receiving IR formulations (Lage & Hwang, 2004).

13.3.4   ADVERSE EFFECTS

The most common adverse effects of stimulants are loss of appetite, weight loss, headache, and delayed sleep onset (Barkley *et al.*, 1990b; Greenhill, Halperin & Abikoff, 1999). Controlled research has not established a clear cause-effect relationship between stimulants and development of new tics (Palumbo *et al.*, 2004). In most patients, all of these adverse effects can be managed by decreasing the total daily dose of medication or reducing the amount given late in the day. Therefore, fewer than 10% of patients discontinue treatment because of adverse effects during the acute phase of treatment (Barkley *et al.*, 1990b; Greenhill *et al.*, 1999). Dextroamphetamine may cause more insomnia and emotional symptoms than MPH (Efron, 1999). Parents may feel that their children are less enthusiastic and more withdrawn than they were without medication. Some parents report a rebound phenomenon in the late afternoon by which they mean that their child's behaviour is worse when medication wears off than it would have been at that time of day had the child not taken medication. One controlled study failed to capture such an effect (Johnston *et al.*, 1988). Nonetheless, rebound can be managed by administering a small dose late in the day to cover the rebound period or by administering an extended release preparation. Typically, one half of the usual IR dose is given.

No reduction in height over long periods of treatment has been demonstrated reliably (Klein & Mannuzza, 1988; Schertz *et al.*, 1996; Spencer *et al.*, 1996). Short-term inhibition of growth was noted in the MTA study; children who received stimulant treatment continuously for two years were on average, 2.0 cm (0.78 in) shorter in height and 2.50 kg (5.5 lb) lighter in weight than those who did not receive stimulant treatment over that time. However, the data also revealed that children with ADHD are significantly taller than children without ADHD. Thus, even after two years on stimulants, their average height was not less than expected based on national norms (MTA, 2004). Most recently, Spencer *et al.* (2006a) examined the effects of OROS methyphenidate (Concerta) on growth in 178 children ages 6 to 13 years who were treated for at least 21 months. Weight did not increase and BMI decreased slightly in the first four months of treatment. At month 21, children were on average 0.23 cm shorter than expected in height and 1.23 kg less in weight. Drug holidays did not reduce any impact on growth, highlighting the need for more data concerning the usefulness of this clinical practice.

A rare adverse effect is the occurrence of psychotic symptoms, such as hallucinations, usually involving insects, snakes or worms. However, there is little systematic data on the occurrence of hallucinations in children receiving stimulants. A chart review of 98 children found that 9 children developed psychotic symptoms during stimulant treatment (Cherland & Fitzpatrick, 1999). Hallucinations generally resolve upon discontinuation of the drug. Over a five-year period (1999–2003) 1000 cases of hallucinations were reported to the FDA. The FDA Pediatric Advisory Committee estimated an occurrence of 2–5% and recently recommended more prominent placement of an existing warning concerning the possibility of hallucinations during stimulant treatment.

A concern raised about the effects of long-term stimulant exposure in the treatment of ADHD is the possibility of increased liability to drug abuse later in life (Laviola *et al.*, 1999; Vitiello, 2001). Under some experimental conditions, repeated exposure to amphetamine-like stimulants can have enduring effects in experimental animals (see for review Robinson & Becker, 1986; Vanderschuren & Kalivas, 2000; Robinson & Berridge, 2001) as well as in humans (Sax & Strakowski, 2001; Strakowski *et al.*, 2001). Progressive enhancement of some stimulant-induced behaviours with repeated administration, a process referred to as behavioural sensitisation or reverse tolerance, can persist after prolonged periods of abstinence. Animal studies with behavioural paradigms such as drug self-administration, indicate that repeated administration of psychomotor stimulants might also enhance the reinforcing properties of these drugs. However, most animal research to date has used doses of stimulants that are far in excess of those used clinically. When oral or i.p. doses are used in young animals to produce maximum plasma levels and duration of action that more closely approximate those seen clinically (Gerasimov *et al.*, 2001; Kuczenski & Segal, 2005), studies have either failed to produce sensitisation (Kuczenski & Segal, 2002) or have shown that early exposure to MPH actually *reduced* sensitivity in adulthood to cocaine's reinforcing effects (Carlezon, Mague & Andersen, 2003; Mague, Andersen & Carlezon, 2005). Moreover, there was no evidence of sensitisation as a function of repeated doses of MPH (Swanson *et al.*, unpublished) during the MTA titration trial (Greenhill *et al.*, 2001). In addition, there is no evidence of increased risk of later addiction in medicated ADHD children (Wilens *et al.*, 2003). Indeed, by reducing symptoms of ADHD in childhood and adolescence and thereby enhancing cognitive, social and emotional functioning, stimulants could conceivably *decrease* risks for the development of abuse of drugs, alcohol and tobacco. There is, furthermore, evidence that the use of these substances might reflect, in part, self-medication for ADHD.

Cardiovascular effects

Amphetamines have peripheral [alpha]- and [beta]-adrenergic actions and all stimulants have sympathomimetic effects that can lead to increases in systolic blood pressure (SBP) and diastolic blood pressure (DBP) and pulse at therapeutic doses. However, the cardiovascular effects of immediate-release (IR) amphetamine and MPH formulations that have been documented in children and adolescents appear to be modest and are not judged to be of significant clinical concern. In the most recent long-term follow-up of 229 children who received at least 21 months of treatment with OROS MPH, the increase in SBP was statistically but not clinically significant (from 104.7 +/- 8.1 mm at baseline to 108.1 +/- 8.7 at end of study). One subject was dropped because of elevated blood pressure; otherwise no subject experienced clinically significant changes in vital signs (Wilens *et al.*, 2005).

In February, 2006, the Drug Safety and Risk Management Advisory Committee of the US Food and Drug Administration (FDA) reviewed data from a five-year period (1999–2003) concerning the frequency of adverse events reported to the FDA for individuals taking stimulants (FDA, 2006). The data, obtained from the Adverse Event Reporting System, showed that among the 2.5 million children and adolescents treated with stimulants in the US, there were 19 cases of sudden death, which is equal to a rate of 0.00076%, and an additional 18 non-fatal cardiac-related problems. Among 1.0 million adults (over 18 years of age) taking stimulants, there were 6 cases of sudden death, equivalent to a rate of 0.0006%. On the basis of these data, a panel of consultants to the Committee narrowly voted (8 to 7) to recommend that a 'Black Box' warning for adults be added to ADHD drugs. Ultimately, the Committee decided that the risk did not warrant a Black Box, but did vote to include a more prominent warning about cardiovascular risk due to increased blood pressure resulting from stimulant treatment.

In evaluating these data, it is important to bear in mind several points. First, since there was, of course, no control group, it is not possible to attribute these deaths with any certainty to the effects of the stimulants. In fact, this sudden death rate is lower than the expected rate of sudden unexplained death for this age group in the population at large: 26.25 deaths among 2.5 million youth over a five-year period (Wren, O'Sullivan & Wright, 2000). Secondly, there was evidence on autopsy of undiagnosed congenital heart disease in five of these cases, which may have accounted for an unusual response to stimulant treatment or may have been the cause of death without reference to the drug. Even if one acknowledges that there may be under-reporting to the FDA by as much as a factor of 10–100, the risk of serious cardiac adverse response remains extremely small. This small but serious risk should be managed by screening patients for possible pre-existing cardiac abnormalities before beginning stimulant treatment and monitoring heart rate and blood pressure regularly during the course of treatment.

13.3.5   MECHANISM OF ACTION OF STIMULANTS

Amphetamine has a chemical structure closely resembling that of norepinephrine (NE) and dopamine (DA) and is the parent compound of its own structural class. MPH is a piperidine derivative that is structurally related to amphetamine. Both amphetamine and MPH are chiral compounds for which the primary psychoactive properties reside in the d- rather than the l-isomer (Srinivas et al., 1992). Pharmacokinetic and pharmacodynamic studies in children show that MPH has a $T_{1/2} = 3$ hours and a $T_{max} = 1.5$ hr and that the modal effective dose of 10 mg yields a serum level of 8–10 ng/ml (Swanson et al., 1999; Swanson & Volkow, 2001). The presence of food in the stomach does not affect absorption or elimination. D-amphetamine has a longer $T_{1/2}$ and T_{max}, than does MPH, corresponding in one study in children to 6.8 hr and 3–4 hr, respectively (Brown et al., 1979).

Both MPH and d-amphetamine bind to and inhibit the dopamine transporter (DAT) and the norepinephrine transporter (NET) in pre-synaptic dopaminergic and noradrenergic neurons, respectively. These transporter molecules effectuate the reuptake of NE or DA into the pre-synaptic cell where it is available for re-release. Thus inhibition of these transporter molecules has the effect of potentiating the action of dopamine and NE in the synapse. D-amphetamine binds reversibly to the transporter and thereby facilitates the release of DA, whereas MPH, which binds irreversibly, does not increase DA release. Although both MPH and d-amphetamine also inhibit MAO, this action does not appear to play a significant role in the clinical effects of the stimulants.

Recent studies in animals using low, clinically relevant doses, have shown that both d-amphetamine and MPH increase NE and NA levels in prefrontal cortex (PFC) (Berridge et al. 2006) and hippocampus, and increase DA in striatum, and nucleus accumbens (Kuczenski & Segal, 2001; Kuczenski & Segal, 2002). It is noteworthy that neither drug had any effect on serotonin (Kuczenski & Segal, 2001). The latter finding, which is consistent with the failure of SSRIs to yield significant clinical benefit in children with ADHD (Pliszka, 2001) argues against a significant role of serotonin in mediating clinical effects of the stimulants (Volkow et al., 2000).

Pivotal studies using Positron Emission Tomography (PET) have helped to elucidate the effects of MPH in humans. Binding of radio-labelled methylphenindate was much higher in striatum than in cortex or cerebellum. A dose of methylphenidate in the therapeutic range (0.25 mg/kg) occupied 50% of total brain DAT (Volkow et al., 1998) and produced increased levels of extracellular DA (Volkow et al., 2001). Two factors appear to be positively related to abusability of stimulants: the rate of uptake of the drug into the brain and the rate of clearance (Swanson & Volkow, 2003). Following oral administration, radio-labelled MPH (reaches a peak concentration in the brain after 60–120 minutes, compared to 8–10 minutes following i.v. administration (Volkow et al., 1995). Self-reported feelings of being 'high' parallel the fast rate of uptake into striatum (Volkow et al., 1996). When administered intravenously, MPH has a far slower rate of clearance than does i.v. cocaine, with respective half-lives of 90 minutes and 20 minutes (Volkow et al., 1995; Volkow et al., 1996). The slower clearance may reduce the likelihood that MPH will be repeatedly self-administered in attempts to maintain a 'high', as is typical in cocaine use (Volkow & Swanson, 2003; Volkow et al., 2005).

The regions targeted by MPH and d-amphetamine – particularly the PFC and the striatum – correspond to those believed to play a role in the etiology of ADHD. It is well known from both animal and human studies that both NE and DA are essential to the cognitive function of the PFC (Arnsten, 2001; Arnsten & Dudley, 2005). Lesions to the PFC result in poor regulation of attention, disorganised behaviour, impulsivity and hyperactivity, and impaired executive function, which closely resemble the primary symptoms of ADHD (Stuss, Eskes & Foster, 1994). Many, but not all, children (Nigg, 2005) and adults (Hervey, Epstein & Curry, 2004) with ADHD perform more poorly on neuropsychological measures of focused and sustained attention, visual-spatial organisation and memory, inhibitory control, and working memory. Furthermore, anatomical MRI studies have shown smaller PFC volume in children (Castellanos et al., 1996; Filipek et al., 1997; Seidman, Valera & Makris, 2005) and adults (Seidman, 2005; Seidman, Valera & Bush, 2004). The projection zones of the caudate – the basal ganglia and the corpus callosum are also of smaller size in children with ADHD (Hynd et al., 1993; Aylward et al., 1996; Filipek et al., 1997; Castellanos et al., 1996; Castellanos et al., 2003). Stimulant medication increases activation of the PFC while simultaneously improving response inhibition on a go/no-go task in children with ADHD (Vaidya et al., 1998). As described, stimulants also enhance performance on some measures of executive functioning.

Poor regulation of impulses and activity level is, by definition, characteristic of the combined type of ADHD (American Psychiatric Association, 1994). Furthermore, individuals with ADHD may have reduced sensitivity to positive reinforcement such that they are more reward-seeking and such that naturally occurring positive contingencies, particularly those that are delayed in time, are less likely to effectively govern their behaviour (Luman, Oosterlaan & Sergeant, 2004). MPH may act therapeutically by increasing the activation of DA substrates for motor behaviour in the dorsal striatum (caudate and putamen) and by increasing response to reward in the ventral striatum (nucleus accumbens) (see Chapter 11 for further discussion of reward circuitry in ADHD). In this context, it is relevant that a recent PET study of normal human volunteers found that MPH increased the reward salience of a mathematics task compared to a neutral task while simultaneously increasing extracellular DA in the striatum (Volkow *et al.*, 2004).

The locus coeruleus (LC) may also be involved in the etiology of ADHD and response to stimulants. The LC is a subcortical noradrenergic nucleus that broadly innervates many structures within the CNS and is itself regulated by downward projections from PFC. The LC has been shown to be important in the regulation of arousal and attention (Berridge, 2001). In studies with monkeys, both hypo- and hyper-arousal of the LC, associated with low and high levels of NE release, respectively, are associated with a poor signal:noise ratio for response to stimuli, and concomitant poor attention.

The volume of the midline cerebellar vermis has consistently been found to be smaller in children with ADHD (Castellanos *et al.*, 1996; Berquin *et al.*, 1998; Mostofsky *et al.*, 1998; Castellanos *et al.*, 2001). Children with ADHD frequently have deficits in fine motor control suggestive of cerebellar dysfunction (Whitmont & Clark, 1996). More recently, it has been postulated that cerebellar dysfunction is important in time estimation and utilisation deficits in ADHD (Radonovich & Mostofsky, 2004). An MRI study comparing children with ADHD with their unaffected siblings and normal controls reported that right PFC volume was decreased in both the ADHD children and their unaffected siblings whereas volumetric reduction in cerebellum was limited to the children with ADHD. These results suggested that the cerebellum was more specifically linked than PFC to the pathophysiology expressed in ADHD (Durston *et al.*, 2004). Cerebellum is richly innervated by noradrenergic afferents whereas DA is found in only trace amounts (Glaser, 2006); thus, stimulant effects on cerebellum, if present, would be likely mediated by effects on NE. MPH has been shown to improve motor-timing deficits in ADHD (Rubia *et al.*, 2003).

Rate-dependency

Stimulant effects in humans may be predictable on the basis of the phenomenon of rate-dependency, shown for the effects of stimulants in animals (Dews & Wenger, 1977). Rate-dependency predicts an inverse relationship between the baseline level of a given variable and the level of that variable on drug, such that low rates are increased whereas higher baseline rates are increased to a lesser extent or are decreased. Robbins (1979) re-analysed data from several studies of stimulant effects in children and adults, and demonstrated a negative linear slope for the relationship between change in activity level on drug and baseline level activity. Statistical problems with the rate-dependency formulation (Gonzalez & Byrd, 1977; Swanson, 1988) appear to have been addressed in a more recent study by Teicher demonstrating rate-dependency for attention and activity level in children's response to stimulants after correction for regression-to-the-mean artifacts (Teicher *et al.*, 2003).

13.3.6   LIMITATIONS OF STIMULANT MEDICATION.

Despite many demonstrated advantages, there are also important limitations of stimulant treatment. There is no evidence that even prolonged therapy leads to the internalisation of self-control which persists even when medication is discontinued. Rather, the beneficial effects of stimulant therapy dissipate rapidly upon discontinuation of treatment (Brown et al., 1986; MTA, 2004).

Marked variation in response is evident both across individuals and outcomes. Although beneficial behavioural impact is observed in more than 70% of treated children (for review see Spencer et al., 1996), only about half of children show normalisation of teacher-rated behaviour (Rapport et al., 1994; Swanson et al., 2001). Although academic productivity and classroom behaviour may improve, stimulants have only a limited impact on school grades (Rapport et al., 1994). One quarter of children with ADHD who are aggressive before treatment show no increase in prosocial behaviour or in processing of social information (Pelham et al., 1991). Although negative, disruptive, and aggressive behaviours are reduced by stimulants, as perceived by other children as well as by adults (Hinshaw et al., 1989), prosocial behaviours are not increased (Hinshaw et al., 1989; Hoza et al., 2005) and peer status, while improved, is not normalised (Whalen et al., 1989). In addition, stimulant medication may induce an increase in socially inhibited behaviour, social withdrawal and dysphoria (Barkley & Cunningham, 1979; Buhrmester et al., 1992; Granger, Whalen & Henker, 1993). Consequently, the medicated child may be perceived as socially less responsive which could, in turn, decrease the extent to which a child is liked by peers or adults (Whalen & Henker, 1991).

Although there is substantial evidence supporting the effectiveness of stimulants over short and intermediate duration of treatment, there is far less evidence with respect to important issues such as long-term risks and benefits of stimulants even though the majority of treated children receive stimulants for three years or more. The first long-term follow-up study of children with ADHD found that treated children were more likely than their untreated peers to have enhanced self-esteem and social adjustment in adulthood (Hechtman, Weiss & Perlman, 1984). However, neither this nor other studies produced evidence that effective treatment with medication in childhood improves other important outcomes such as scholastic achievement or the risk of developing antisocial behaviour later in life (Charles & Schain, 1981; Richters et al., 1995). Of course, the same can be said for other treatments in medicine and psychiatry. The lack of information is a result of the ethical and practical difficulties of obtaining quality evidence through the conduct of randomised control trials with prolonged and therefore clinically relevant duration of treatment. With the exception of the MTA study, discussed later in this chapter, there have been few long-term studies (e.g. duration greater than 12 weeks) of medications. Most published long-term studies have had significant methodological flaws such as uncertain medication status at post-testing, inclusion of an atypical sample of ADHD subjects, a limited range of outcome measures and failure to consider side-effects (Schachar & Tannock, 1993; Jadad et al., 1999). In addition, it is often the case that the children who are most severely affected, and thus at greatest risk for long-term negative outcomes, are also those that receive the most stimulant treatment. In non-randomised long-term treatment studies, this can result in an apparent positive association between stimulant use and long-term negative or unimproved outcomes that may be only partially correctable statistically.

Whereas a few early studies suggested that tolerance to stimulant effects occur in some children (Charles, Schain & Guthrie, 1979), more recent, methodologically advanced, long-term treatment studies (reviewed in Greenhill, 2001) have failed to find evidence of appreciable tolerance to the beneficial effects of stimulants.

13.3.7   ACCEPTABILITY OF STIMULANT TREATMENT

Any treatment, regardless of its virtues, is useful only to the extent it is accepted and utilised by the patient. Many families and children feel that any kind of psychotropic medication is an unacceptable option. Some families believe that the problems do not reside in the child but rather in the child's key relationships either at home or at school. Others feel that the child's problems arise from their learning difficulties and that learning difficulties demand academic, not pharmacological, interventions. Other families are concerned about the biological or ethical implications of treating young children with drugs or about the risk for drug dependence later in life and are not persuaded by the available research evidence. Non-compliance is a significant problem with drug treatment of ADHD as it is with drug treatments for other emotional and behavioural disorders. Non-compliance becomes a more serious problem in the treatment of adolescents (Charach et al., 2004). Psychoeducation of patients and their families concerning the symptom manifestations, impairment, and short- and long-term outcomes associated with ADHD, as well as the rationale, benefits, and risks associated with pharmacological treatment thus constitutes an extremely important part of the professional–patient interaction in the management of this condition.

13.4   NON-STIMULANT MEDICATIONS

13.4.1   ATOMOXETINE

Atomoxetine is the first non-stimulant medication approved for the treatment of ADHD by drug regulatory agencies in the USA, Australia, Canada, the United Kingdom, and several other countries. Atomoxetine is a highly selective noradrenergic reuptake inhibitor. It does not increase DA activity in the nucleus accumbens nor in the striatum suggesting reduced abuse potential and lack of induction or aggravation of tic/motor activity. simultaneously, it was found to increase DA in the prefrontal cortex by indirect mechanisms, with potential benefit for cognitive functions (Bymaster et al., 2002). Atomoxetine is rapidly absorbed after oral administration, with plasma concentrations peaking within 1–2 hours. It is metabolised by the cytochrome P450 system, particularly CYP-2d6 (Ring et al., 2002).

Atomoxetine has been shown to be superior to placebo in the treatment of ADHD in children, adolescents, and adults (Michelson et al., 2001; Michelson et al., 2002; Michelson et al., 2003) and was shown to prevent return of symptoms following discontinuation better than placebo (Michelson et al., 2004). Although the effects of atomoxetine have been shown to emerge on day one (Kelsey *et al.*, 2004), full benefits appear to accrue over 2–6 weeks (Michelson *et al.*, 2002), suggesting the patient should be maintained at the full therapeutic dose for at least several weeks in order to determine the drug's full effect. Once a day and twice a day dosing appear to be equally effective (Michelson *et al.*, 2002; Kelsey *et al.*, 2004).

Direct comparisons in children of the efficacy of atomoxetine to that of methylphenindate (Michelson *et al.*, 2004) and amphetamine (Wigal *et al.*, 2004) have yielded effect sizes for atomoxetine of 0.62 compared with 0.91 and 0.95 for IR and long-acting stimulants, respectively (Faraone *et al.*, 2003). An earlier open-label study showed comparable therapeutic benefits, as well as safety and tolerability, for atomoxetine and MPH (Kratochvil *et al.*, 2002). In studies with adults, the effect size reported for atomoxetine compared to placebo is .35–.40 (Michelson *et al.*, 2003), which is smaller than that typically reported for stimulants in adults. Further head-to-head comparative studies between atomoxetine and the stimulants in all age groups are clearly needed.

Atomoxetine has been studied in the treatment of patients with ADHD and comorbid anxiety (Sumner *et al.*, 2005). Patients with both ADHD and an anxiety disorder were randomised to either atomoxetine (n = 87) or placebo (n = 89) in a double-blind, placebo-controlled manner for 12 weeks of treatment. At the end of the treatment period, atomoxetine led to a significant reduction in ratings of symptoms of both ADHD and anxiety relative to placebo, showing the drug to be efficacious in the treatment of both conditions. This study is of interest because treatment algorithms for ADHD with comorbid anxiety have recommended treatment of ADHD first with stimulants, then addition of a selective serotonin reuptake inhibitor (SSRI) for treatment of the anxiety (Pliszka *et al.*, 2000). However, the SSRI fluvoxamine was shown not to be superior to placebo for the treatment of anxiety when added to a stimulant in a small sample (n = 25) of children with ADHD and comorbid anxiety (Abikoff *et al.*, 2005). This small study does not invalidate this practice, but the above results of Sumner (2005) suggest that using atomoxetine for the treatment of ADHD with comorbid anxiety is a viable alternative approach.

Atomoxetine was also studied in a sample of adolescents with ADHD and comorbid depression (Emslie *et al.*, 2005). After a placebo induction period patients were randomised to either atomoxetine (n = 72) or placebo (n = 70). Atomoxetine was superior to placebo on measures of ADHD but no differences between the placebo and atomoxetine-treated groups were found on measures of depressive symptoms.

Once-daily administration of atomoxetine is safe and effective in improving core ADHD symptoms, associated oppositional defiant behaviours, psychosocial functioning and quality of life in ADHD children and adults according to parent and teacher, and self-reports (Weiss & Tannock, 2005). However, individuals with comorbid ADHD and ODD may require a higher dose. The comorbid group showed improvement compared with placebo at 1.8 mg/kg/day but not 1.2 mg/kg/day. In contrast, youths without ODD showed improvement at 1.2 mg/kg/day and no incremental benefit at 1.8 mg/kg/day (Newcorn *et al.*, 2005). Atomoxetine does not cause worsening of motor symptoms in patients with ADHD with comorbid tic disorders or Tourette's syndrome (Allen *et al.*, 2002; McCracken *et al.*, 2003). Atomoxetine administration in animals does not engender repeated self-administration observed with MPH and amphetamine preparations; as a result, it might lack the reinforcing effects that are thought to increase potential for abuse (Wee & Woolverton, 2004).

Safety and tolerability of atomoxetine

Discontinuation due to adverse events is low and does not differ from what is found with placebo treatment (atomoxetine 5.9%, placebo 0%, p = .096). Adverse events reported significantly more frequently with atomoxetine than placebo were decreased appetite, somnolence, and fatigue. The initial period of weight loss is followed by an apparently normal rate of weight gain. Adverse events tend to appear early in the course of treatment with atomoxetine and then decline (Michelson *et al.*, 2002; Spencer *et al.*, 2003). Atomoxetine has also been associated with small increases in children in systolic (2.8 +/− 10.2 mm) and diastolic (2.1 +/− 9.6 mm) blood pressure and pulse (7.8 +/− 12.0) that plateau during treatment and resolve upon discontinuation (Wernicke *et al.*, 2003). One-year follow-up data in 169 children and adolescents showed no discontinuations due to cardiovascular-related events (Wernicke *et al.*, 2003). Studies examining abrupt discontinuation of atomoxetine treatment in children, adolescents, and adults report an absence of symptom rebound and low rates of discontinuation-emergent adverse events (Wernicke *et al.*, 2004); therefore, tapering of doses is not necessary when atomoxetine is discontinued.

One of the three oxidative metabolic pathways involved in the systemic clearance of atomoxetine is primarily mediated by the polymorphically expressed enzyme cytochrome P450 (CYP) 2D6. Consequently, there are individuals who exhibit active metabolism (CYP-2D6 extensive metabolisers) and those (5–10% of the North American population) who exhibit poor metabolism (CYP-2D6 poor metabolisers) for atomoxetine. The oral bioavailability and clearance of atomoxetine are influenced by the activity of CYP-2D6. Compared to poor metabolisers, in extensive metabolisers, atomoxetine has a substantially shorter plasma half-life, faster plasma clearance, and lower average steady-state plasma concentrations. Poor metabolisers experience 2–3 fold higher peak plasma concentrations of atomoxetine. Atomoxetine's mean plasma half-life is 5.2 hours and 21.6 hours for extensive metabolisers and poor metabolisers respectively (Sauer *et al.*, 2003). Upon multiple dosing there is plasma accumulation of atomoxetine in poor metabolisers, but very little accumulation in extensive metabolisers. Nevertheless, the frequency and severity of adverse events are similar regardless of CYP-2D6 phenotype. It is important to take into account that atomoxetine is metabolised by CYP-2D6 when considering concomitant use of medications using the same metabolic pathway.

Problematic side effects associated with atomoxetine are not common, and serious safety concerns are rare. However, in the first two years of post-marketing experience during which 2 million patients received atomoxetine, there were two reported cases of serious liver injury (markedly elevated hepatic enzymes and bilirubin) associated with atomoxetine treatment. Upon discontinuation of atomoxetine both patients recovered and did not require liver transplants. Because of likely under-reporting, the true incidence of these events cannot be accurately estimated. They may occur several months into treatment, and laboratory abnormalities may continue to worsen for several weeks after atomoxetine's discontinuation. Treatment with atomoxetine should be permanently suspended in patients with jaundice or laboratory evidence of liver injury. Liver enzyme levels should be assessed at the first sign of liver dysfunction (e.g. prurius, dark urine, jaundice, upper right quadrant tenderness, or unexplained 'flu-like' symptoms).

A recent reanalysis of reports of suicidal ideation in all antidepressant-like medications found that five youths under the age of 12 years, of a total of 1357 taking atomoxetine, reported having suicidal thoughts, two of which were clinically significant. Only one child reported self-harm, and there were no reports of medical damage or death. This rate of suicidality is substantially less than the 2% reported for all antidepressants. A warning about suicidal risk was added to the product information in Canada and in the US.

13.4.2   OTHER NON-STIMULANTS

(a)   Modafinil

Modafinil has a clinical profile similar to conventional stimulants such as MPH, despite a structurally and pharmacologically different mechanism of action. Modafinil selectively targets neuronal pathways in the sleep/wake centres in the hypothalamus mediated by the orexin/hypocretin neurotransmitter system (Stahl, 2002). Modafinil is readily absorbed, reaching maximum plasma concentrations at 2–4 hours after administration and pharmacokinetic steady state within 2–4 days. The elimination half-life is approximately 12–15 hours. It is primarily metabolised in the liver, with subsequent excretion in the urine; metabolism is largely via amide hydrolysis, with lesser contributions from cytochrome P450-mediated oxidative pathways. In patients who are renally or hepatically compromised, the elimination processes can be slowed (Robertson & Hellriegel, 2003). Evidence from preclinical in vitro and in vivo studies, human laboratory studies, and post-marketing experiences examining the potential abuse liability of modafinil suggests that modafinil has limited potential for large-scale abuse (Myrick et al., 2004).

Initial randomised, double blind, placebo-controlled studies of the use of modafinil to treat children and adolescents with ADHD showed significant improvements in the core symptoms of the disorder (Rugino & Samsock, 2003; Biederman et al., 2005). In the larger of these studies (Biederman et al., 2005), 248 subjects were randomly assigned in a 2:1 ratio, and 246 were treated for nine weeks with modafinil (n = 164) or placebo (n = 82). Modafinil significantly improved the core symptoms of ADHD both at school and home (effect size: 0.69) The most commonly reported adverse events in the modafinil group were insomnia (29%), headache (20%), and decreased appetite (16%). Three per cent of modafinil-treated patients and 4% of placebo-treated patients discontinued treatment because of adverse events (Biederman et al., 2005). In adults with ADHD modafinil produced a similar pattern of cognitive enhancement to that observed in healthy adults, with improvements on tests of short-term memory span, visual memory, spatial planning, and stop-signal motor inhibition (Turner et al., 2004).

The primary indication of modafinil is the treatment of narcolepsy. Use in ADHD is off-label. An application to the FDA from the manufacturer to seek an indication for ADHD was turned down in August, 2006, due to concerns about possible induction of Stevens–Johnson Syndrome, a rare allergic reaction.

(b) Tricyclic antidepressants

Tricyclic antidepressants (TCAs) such as desipramine, clomipramine and imipramine are superior to placebo in treating ADHD but have somewhat less impact than stimulants on the behavioural and cognitive manifestations of ADHD (for review see Popper, 1997; Pliszka, 2003). They increase plasma noradrenaline by blocking its re-uptake, but have virtually no effect on the dopaminergic system. This may explain why TCAs have a favourable impact on the behavioural manifestations of ADHD but a less beneficial effect on cognitive and academic performance (Gualtieri, Keenan & Chandler, 1991). In particular, they lack the robust beneficial impact on attention that is observed with stimulants. Unlike the typical response to this antidepressant when it is used to treat depression, the effects of TCAs on ADHD are apparent within two or three days.

Common adverse effects of TCAs include dry mouth, blurred vision, constipation, dizziness, sedation, perspiration, and tremors. These medications may also increase heart rate and blood pressure, and have been associated with prolongation of electrocardiogram conduction parameters indicating intraventricular conduction delay of the right bundle branch block type. There have also been reports of delirium and increased heart rate in adolescents who take TCAs and smoke marijuana (Mannion, 1999; Wilens, Biederman & Spencer, 1997). Serious questions have been raised about the clinical role of TCAs because of a small number of sudden deaths of apparently healthy children with no history of cardiovascular problems who were taking this medication (Riddle et al., 1991). These sudden deaths are rare, seem impossible to predict even with careful monitoring (Biederman et al., 1993) and may not exceed the incidence of sudden death in the general paediatric population. The mechanism of these cardiac effects is unknown but they may be conduction abnormalities caused in predisposed individuals by change in parasympathetic and sympathetic input to the heart (Riddle et al., 1991; Walsh et al., 1994). Adverse cardiac effects might be exaggerated by drug–drug interaction when combining tricyclic antidepressants with other medications. An electrocardiogram (ECG) should be done before and after each significant increase in dose to monitor for changes in cardiac conduction. TCAs should be discontinued if a patient demonstrates any ECG abnormality. Monitoring serum levels is not necessary (Pliszka, 2003).

(c) Alpha-2 agonists

Alpha-2 agonists (clonidine and guanfacine) have been widely prescribed to patients with ADHD – for the disorder itself, for comorbid aggression, comorbid tic disorder or to address sleep difficulties. These agents show some effectiveness in the treatment of ADHD although there have been few randomised controlled trials. Clonidine (Catapres) reduces behavioural symptoms of ADHD and improves the sleep disturbance that occasionally arises with stimulant treatment (Hunt, Minderra & Cohen, 1985; Hunt, 1987). A randomised controlled study conducted by the

Tourette's Syndrome Study Group (Tourette's Syndrome Study, 2002) provides support for the use of clonidine and methylphenindate, alone and in combination for the treatment of ADHD children with comorbid tics. A meta-analysis of 11 studies of clonidine in the treatment of ADHD revealed a large degree of variability in both methods and measured outcomes (Connor, Fletcher & Swanson, 1999). Open-label studies showed a larger effect than controlled studies; overall the review documented a moderate degree of efficacy for clonidine in the treatment of ADHD. Although clonidine is commonly used for its sedative effects to counter stimulant-induced insomnia, this practice has not been evaluated.

Clonidine is generally well-tolerated. Common adverse effects include fatigue and hypotension especially at the outset of treatment, as well as depressive symptoms (Pliszka, 2003). Abrupt withdrawal may cause transient hypertension. There are no long-term data on safety and efficacy. Moreover, there have been four cases of sudden death reported in children taking methylphenindate and clonidine together, and several reports of nonfatal cardiac events in children taking clonidine alone or in combination (Cantwell, Swanson & Conner, 1997).

Guanfacine (Tenex) is another alpha-2 adrenergic agonist that has proven effective and safe in a small number of subjects with ADHD (Horrigan & Barnhill, 1995; Hunt, Arnsten & Asbell, 1995). One small double-blind trial showed the superiority of guanfacine over placebo in the treatment of children with ADHD and comorbid tics (Scahill et al., 2001). Guanfacine appears to cause less sedation and hypotension than clonidine. A gradual titration is required for both clonidine and guanfacine, and, clinical consensus suggests the alpha-agonists are more successful in treating hyperactive/impulsive symptoms than inattention symptoms, although this remains to be proven by clinical trials.

(d) Bupropion

Bupropion (Wellbutrin) is an antidepressant with a pharmacological profile similar to stimulants. Presumably, it acts by decreasing whole body NE turnover (Golden et al., 1988). Conners et al. (1996) reported significant improvement in symptoms of ADHD with bupropion without any concomitant deterioration in cognitive performance or serious side effects. A direct comparison found that bupropion was less effective than MPH in improving attention but otherwise had comparable effects (Barrickman et al., 1995). In that study, the majority of subjects preferred MPH to bupropion because, unlike bupropion, MPH can be taken on week-days only and because many subjects had previous positive response to MPH. Due to concerns about the emergence of seizures in some patients (Johnston et al., 1991; Dunlop, 2000), the risk for which may be increased if buproprion is combined with other medications (Ickowicz, 2002), bupropion is contraindicated in patients with a current seizure disorder. It can be given in both IR and long-acting forms, but may not come in pill sizes small enough for children who weigh less than 25 kg.

(e) Other medications

Carbamazepine is an anticonvulsant that is structurally related to tricyclic antidepressants. Seventy per cent of patients experienced improvement in ADHD symptoms with this medication (Silva, Munoz & Alpert, 1996). Carbemazepine has little effect on the aggressive symptoms of children with a primary diagnosis of conduct disorder (Cueva, 1996). The most common side effects are sedation, ataxia, tremor, headache, diplopia, poor coordination, slurred speech and dizziness that were all mild and transient. Carbemazepine can cause hematological changes and liver abnormalities and monitoring of these systems is indicated.

Neuroleptics used to treat ADHD-related symptoms improved behavioural symptoms in fewer than half of the affected children and adolescents, according to a review of earlier studies (Gittelman-Klein, 1987). Improvement in cognition was even less apparent. Given the serious risks associated with both acute and long-term use of these drugs (e.g. sedation, dystonic reactions, tardive dyskinesia, and neuro-leptic malignant syndrome), the use of antipsychotics for the management of ADHD is restricted to extreme cases of patients whose severe symptoms and impairment persist, even after exhaustive investigation of alternative treatments known to be both safer and more effective.

13.5 COMBINATIONS, AUGMENTATION AND SUBGROUP SPECIFIC TREATMENT

Treatment with a single drug is the optimal goal of treatment. Occasionally, combinations must be considered because of suboptimal clinical response, side effects, or the presence of some troubling comorbid condition such as tics, Tourette' syndrome or anxiety disorder. Combinations of therapies are especially relevant for treatment of the most complex of cases, of adults, and of the very young and over the long term. Few combinations have been adequately studied.

13.5.1 MULTIMODAL TREATMENTS

Various combinations of treatments have been used in the hope that a greater proportion of patients will show normalisation across a wider range of outcomes than is typically achieved with stimulants alone (Hoza *et al.*, 2005). Unfortunately, there is relatively little systematic evaluation of combined treatments for ADHD (Jadad *et al.*, 1999). One major exception is the Multimodal Treatment Study of ADHD (MTA). The MTA study is a large multi-site study in the United States and Canada which assessed the relative effectiveness of drug and non-drug treatments delivered individually and in combination in 579 school-aged children with ADHD (MTA Cooperative Group, 1999a, 1999b). Four treatment strategies were compared: drug treatment (MPH for 90% of participants), drug treatment combined with an intensive behavioural intervention strategy, behavioural intervention alone, and a typical community-based intervention. The behavioural intervention consisted of parent management training, teacher behavioural consultation and a classroom aide, and an intensive summer camp programme managed according to behavioural principles. All subjects received the same assessment, but those in the community-based intervention were referred to facilities in the community. The other treatments were administered by the study team. The community-based intervention was treatment as usual. It turned out that 61% of those who were assigned to this treatment arm received at least one prescription for medication; however, medication management for this group occurred, on average, at lower doses and with less frequent follow-up than was the treatment administered within the MTA medication management arm.

Behavioural treatment, when administered without medication, was generally equivalent to that of community-based treatment even though community treatment involved medication in two-thirds of cases. The combination treatment and medication management alone were substantially superior to behavioural treatment alone and the community control for core ADHD symptoms. For other functional domains (social skills, academics, parent–child relations, anxiety, and client satisfaction) results suggested slight advantages of combined treatment over the single treatments (medication management, behavioural) and community care. Carefully crafted behavioural intervention with intensive medication management yielded a somewhat greater effect of treatment on core symptoms in that more children in this group (68%) were 'normalised' with combined treatment than with medication management alone (56%) (Conners *et al.*, 2001; Swanson *et al.*, 2001). The primary benefit of combined parent training and medication may be reduction of secondary impairments such as the conflict between parents and children in subgroups of ADHD cases with emotional symptoms or poor parent–child relationships (MTA Cooperative Group, 1999a, 1999b). Combined treatment achieved improvement equivalent to medication alone but with slightly lower doses of medication (31 mg vs. 38 mg), which may be a potential advantage to some children. Parental attitudes and disciplinary practices appeared to mediate improved response to the behavioural and combined interventions (Jensen *et al.*, 2001b).

Many children in the community-based intervention received medication, but they were less improved than those who received medication from study physicians. This finding suggests that medication management that is intensive and coupled with supportive counseling is superior to the medication treatment most children receive in the community. There are many unanswered questions about the optimal timing, intensity and duration of psychological interventions (Cunningham, 1999; Pelham & Waschbusch, 1999).

13.6 TREATMENT OF PRESCHOOL AGE CHILDREN

Stimulants are used regularly for preschool-age ADHD and their use is increasing in this age group in spite of the fact that regulatory agencies have not approved their use in children under six years of age. Far less is known about medication effects in the very young ADHD child than the school-aged child. Only a few studies addressing safety and efficacy of these medications in preschool age children have been published.

Connor (2002) conducted a review of the literature extending back to 1970 and identified nine controlled studies of stimulant treatment and two controlled trials of stimulant side effects in preschool ADHD children. These studies involved 206 subjects and used doses of methylphenindate in the 0.15 to 1.0 mg/kg/day range. Eight of the nine studies supported the efficacy of methylphenindate relative to placebo in the treatment of preschoolers with ADHD. Therapeutic benefits were observed in measures of cognition, interpersonal interactions, and hyperactive-impulsive behaviours. However, in contrast to school-aged children with ADHD, greater variability of stimulant response was observed in ADHD-affected preschoolers. ADHD preschool children also experienced slightly more and different types of stimulant-induced side effects compared with older children. Studies of preschoolers with significant developmental delays suggested this sub-group is prone to higher rates of side effects including social withdrawal, irritability, and crying (Handen *et al.*, 1999).

The NIMH recently funded a comprehensive study known as the Preschool ADHD Treatment Study (PATS). PATS enrolled 303 children aged 3–5 years. Children who received a diagnosis of ADHD were assigned first to receive Parent Training. Those who were unimproved at the end of this period (92.5%) were eligible to continue to the medication phases of the study: a 1-week open-label safety titration; a 5-week double-blind placebo-controlled titration trial evaluating weekly doses of placebo, 1.25 mg, 2.5 mg., 5.0 mg, and 7.5 mg tid; followed by a 4-week randomised parallel group efficacy study (n = 165) in which half the children were randomly assigned to receive their optimal dose, as determined in the titration trial, and the other half were assigned to receive placebo. Subjects completing the efficacy phase then entered a 40-week long-term outcome study.

Preliminary results (Greenhill *et al.*, 2004) have confirmed earlier reports supporting the effectiveness of MPH in preschoolers with ADHD. However, preschool ADHD children appear to respond best to relatively lower doses of methylphendate with a mean optimal dose of 0.75 mg/kg/day, in contrast to 1 mg/kg/day found to be optimal in the MTA study with school-age children. In addition, the effect sizes for pre-schoolers at their optimal dose, relative to placebo, were approximately one-half of those seen in school-aged children in the MTA study. However, the conservative limitation on the maximum dose in the pre-school titration study may have also constrained the determination of the optimal dose and the maximum effect size. Relative to the school-aged children in the MTA study, the preschool group showed a higher rate of emotional adverse events, including crabbiness, irritability, and proneness to crying. A pharmacokinetic sub-study indicated that methylphenindate was metabolised more slowly in preschoolers than in school-age children (Wigal *et al.*, 2004), and this finding may explain, at least in part, why preschool age children may respond better to lower doses and may be more vulnerable to adverse events associated with stimulant use.

In the studies described above, it was noted that preschoolers had high rates of irritability and crying while on placebo. Because these may be misinterpreted as stimulant side effects, it is important the preschoolers receive a careful baseline evaluation of these behaviours before stimulant treatment is initiated. High rates of behaviour reported as stimulant side effects are found for children receiving a placebo, necessitating a baseline evaluation for medication side effects before stimulants are initiated.

Recognising the limitations of the research literature, available evidence to guide practice would suggest that stimulants are beneficial and relatively safe for carefully diagnosed ADHD preschool children aged 3 years and older. However, information regarding dose response and vulnerability of adverse effects would indicate that dose titration of any stimulant should be approached conservatively (Kratochvil, 2006).

13.7   TREATMENT OF ADHD IN ADOLESCENTS

It has been well established that ADHD persists into adolescence in a majority of childhood cases (Barkley *et al.*, 1990a), however, the unique challenges of diagnosis and management in this population (Wolraich *et al.*, 2005) are relatively under-researched. Both stimulant (Smith *et al.*, 1998; Evans *et al.*, 2001; Wilens, 2004a; Spencer *et al.*, 2006b) and non-stimulant (Michelson *et al.*, 2002; Wilens *et al.*, 2006b) medications have been shown to be effective in the adolescent age group and include positive effects on cognition (Klorman *et al.*, 1991; Klorman *et al.*, 1992). However, adolescents are particularly sensitive to any conditions that might make them appear or feel 'different' from their peers and may be less accepting of clinical care. Even when successfully medicated in childhood, adolescents may question both the validity of the diagnosis and the need for continued medication. Reduced compliance with medication has been shown as children progress into their teen years (Thiruchelvam *et al.*, 2001). One useful approach with adolescents in this situation is to ally with them in a 'Let's see' approach and have the adolescent complete self-reports of concentration, performance, and behaviour in school while on and off medication in order to decide together, on the basis of self-report as well as objective indices such as grades, whether the medication confers a favourable cost:benefit ratio.

Clinician concerns about the likelihood of diversion or misuse of stimulant medication in the adolescent age group were addressed recently in a 10-year longitudinal follow-up study of youth with ADHD (Wilens *et al.*, 2006a). When studied in late adolescence (mean age 20.8 +/- 5 years), 11% of the 55 youths receiving medication for ADHD reported selling their medication, compared with none of the 43 subjects in a control group receiving psychotropic medication for other purposes. An additional 22% of those in the ADHD group reported misusing their medications, compared with 5% of the control group. Comorbidity with conduct or substance use disorders accounted for the diversion and misuse, suggesting that non-stimulant alternatives may be preferable when prescribing for this subgroup of adolescents with ADHD.

13.8   TREATMENT OF ADHD IN ADULTS

The recognition that ADHD frequently persists into adulthood (Weiss & Hechtman, 1986; Mannuzza *et al.*, 1993; Mannuzza *et al.*, 1998; Barkley, 2002b; Biederman *et al.*, 2006b) spurred the investigation of the effects of medication in this age-group. Several studies have shown that IR MPH is effective in reducing DSM-IV ADHD symptoms in adults as rated by clinicians (Wilens, Spencer & Biederman, 2002; Spencer, Biederman & Wilens, 2004). Response rates – up to 78% – were highest in studies employing the highest MPH dosages (up to 1.1 mg/kg/day) (Spencer *et al.*, 2004, 2005). Plasma level of the drug is unrelated to the behavioural response (Spencer *et al.*, 1995). As is true for children with ADHD, MPH improved sustained attention, spatial working memory, and inhibitory control in adults with ADHD (Boonstra *et al.*, 2005; Turner *et al.*, 2005). Long-acting OROS MPH (Concerta) was shown to be effective in one recently completed study and was associated with statistically significant but clinically insignificant increases in SBP (3.5 +/− 11.8 mm Hg), DBP (4.0 +/− 8.5 mm Hg), and heart rate (4.5 +/− 10.5 bpm) (Biederman *et al.*, 2006a).

Amphetamine is also effective in adults with ADHD – both in the form of standard d-amphetamine (Paterson *et al.*, 1999; Taylor & Russo, 2001) and in the form of mixed amphetamine salts (Adderall) (Horrigan & Barnhill, 2000; Spencer *et al.*, 2001). In the study by Spencer *et al.* (2001), positive response rate to Adderall was 70% and the maximum and mean total daily doses were 60 mg and 54 mg, respectively, administered in two daily doses. Adderall-XR was shown to be effective in a 10-week open-label study (Goodman *et al.*, 2005). Follow-up of cardiovascular effects up to 24 months found small, clinically insignificant increases in SBP (2.3 +/− 12.5 mm Hg), DBP (1.3 +/− 9.2 mm Hg), and pulse (2.1 +/− 13.4 bpm). Seven subjects of the total of 223 discontinued treatment due to cardiovascular adverse events (hypertension, n = 5; palpitation/tachycardia, n = 2) (Weisler *et al.*, 2005). Pharmacokinetic studies showed T-max of 4.2 hours for plasma d-amphetamine following a single oral dose of Adderall-XR (Clausen, Read & Tulloch, 2005).

Cardiovascular risks and FDA warnings that are relevant to adults have been discussed previously in this chapter.

13.8.1   STIMULANTS AND SUBSTANCE ABUSE IN ADULTS

It is well established that ADHD itself confers a greater than expected risk to develop alcohol or substance abuse, which occurs in as many as 55% of adults with ADHD. Conversely, ADHD is estimated to occur in 10–30% of substance-abusing adults (Kalbag & Levin, 2005; Wilson & Levin, 2005). Research concerning the effects of stimulant treatment in adults co-morbid for both ADHD and substance abuse is limited to one controlled study by Schubiner (2002) which failed to find significant effects of MPH on clinician-rated DSM-IV inattentive or hyperactive-impulsive symptoms. There was no evidence of worsening of substance abuse symptoms as a result of medication treatment. This is an area of active research investigation, with clinical trials underway. Current clinical recommendations for treatment of comorbid adults emphasise stabilisation of the substance abuse symptoms first, followed by treatment of ADHD symptoms with one of the non-stimulants (atomoxetine or bupropion) before progressing, with close monitoring, to stimulants if necessary (Wilens, 2004b; Kalbag & Levin, 2005).

Contrasting with an extensive literature in children examining the effects of stimulant treatment on multiple domains of functioning (e.g. academic, social, emotional) in multiple settings (home, school), there is little systematic information in adults concerning drug effects of either the stimulants or atomoxetine in such functional domains as social competence, occupational performance, and organisation/time-management. Clinical experience suggests that even optimised drug treatment may be insufficient to address problems of organisation/time-management and social competence, and that a multi-modal approach, incorporating targeted psychosocial interventions (Safren *et al.*, 2005; Solanto *et al.*, in press) is needed. Also needed are comparisons of the effects of the available medications on comorbid symptoms commonly seen in adults such as anxiety and depression, as well as studies examining modulation of drug effects on primary ADHD symptoms as a function of comorbidity.

13.8.2 NON-STIMULANT TREATMENT OF ADULTS

Atomoxetine is an effective intervention for adults with ADHD. Following an initial small double-blind trial showing effectiveness and tolerability of atomoxetine in adults (Spencer *et al.*, 1998), a pair of placebo-controlled, randomised drug trials enrolling a total of 536 patients provided more information about the dose–response relationship (Michelson *et al.*, 2003). Atomoxetine was titrated up to 60 mg, 90 mg, or 120 mg, as needed and as tolerated. At end point, 90 mg and 120 mg were each optimally effective for 35–40% of patients whereas 60 mg was optimally effective for only 20–25%. The treatment effect size for the active drug compared to placebo in the two studies was 0.35 and 0.40, respectively. This effect size is smaller than that shown for studies of children with ADHD treated with atomoxetine (0.63–0.77), and also smaller than that typically shown across studies for the stimulants in children and adults (Spencer *et al.*, 1996). In addition to reduction of the core DSM-IV ADHD symptoms, 'associated features' of emotional dysregulation, including temper, affective lability and emotional overreactivity were significantly reduced (Reimherr *et al.*, 2005). No improvement was seen in cognitive interference control on the Stroop (Faraone *et al.*, 2005). Across studies, the profile of adverse events was different from that typically seen with the stimulants and included, in addition to insomnia and decreased appetite, dry mouth, nausea, constipation, dizziness, sweating, dysuria, sexual problems, and palpitations. Modest increases in heart rate (5.3 +/− 11.0) and in systolic (2.9 +/− 10.9 mm) and diastolic (1.8 +/− 8.5) blood pressure (Wernicke *et al.*, 2003) were well tolerated, and atomoxetine was not associated with prolongation of the QT interval (Simpson & Plosker, 2004).

Before the introduction of atomoxetine to the market, the tricyclic antidepressant desipramine (Wilens *et al.*, 1995) and the atypical catecholaminergic antidepressant buproprion (Wilens *et al.*, 2001) were the primary stimulant alternatives used to treat ADHD in adults; each was shown to be effective in one placebo-controlled clinical trial. Although the degree of clinical improvement was not as robust as seen with the stimulants or atomoxetine, these drugs may be alternatives for those unresponsive to, or unable to tolerate the first-line interventions.

13.9 MANAGEMENT

It is widely agreed that stimulants are a first-line treatment for ADHD because of their high efficacy, good safety record, and the substantial body of literature that has been accumulated to support its role in treating ADHD. The combination of medication and intensive psychosocial intervention, at least those that have been extensively evaluated, confers a modest added benefit as described above. Recent research makes it abundantly clear that medication management requires careful titration to an optimal dose, evaluation of drug effects across multiple domains (social, behavioural, academic) and settings (home, school), monthly follow-up visits, close management to ensure rapid response to treatment-emergent adverse effects, and supportive interventions that, among other things, might improve the understanding of the disorder and its treatment, facilitate communication with schools and therefore enhance compliance (Vitiello *et al.*, 2001).

Clinical management is guided by the knowledge that ADHD is a chronic condition that affects most aspects of a child's life and that is, in turn, shaped by a wide range of biological, psychological and social factors. Consequently, a comprehensive assessment is the logical starting point for management. This assessment must identify core ADHD symptoms, associated impairments in language and learning and the concurrent emotional and behavioural conditions that frequently accompany the disorder. A good assessment builds a solid treatment alliance based on a clear understanding of the issues that concern a particular family. Thorough assessment ensures that all comorbidities will be identified and taken into account in a comprehensive treatment plan. The treatment plan must consider the child's social context including the quality of current schooling, nature of parenting practices and the extent of parental psychopathology. The longitudinal nature of the disorder dictates the need for a consistent case manager. Treatment must be flexible both in kind and in intensity to reflect social, physiological and cognitive developments and variations in the life situations of each child and family.

Infrequently will medication be prescribed as a sole treatment. For some children and families, medication will be an undesirable therapeutic option. For others, medication may be unnecessary or premature. However, in clinical practice, physicians do encounter families who are not ready or capable of undertaking treatments other than those involving medication. For many of these families, a period of behavioural improvement resulting from successful drug therapy may provide the impetus for entry into other, essential non-pharmacological components of therapy. Some families may not consider non-drug interventions until they observe that an immediate increase in academic productivity does not necessarily translate into better grades at the end of the year and teacher reports of improved behaviour do not ensure improved family relationships in the evenings. Other families may be too chaotic to employ medications appropriately and non-drug interventions may need to be instituted first or under very close supervision. Some families are more content with the decision to use medication if it follows a period of counselling or behavioural intervention (Slimmer & Brown, 1985).

Given their longer track record and larger effect sizes, the stimulants should still be considered the first-line intervention for ADHD, with exceptions for cases of active or potential stimulant abuse, tics, cardiovascular risk factors, and previous adverse response to stimulants. If one stimulant fails to produce desired benefits or causes side effects that are unacceptable, one should try another. The long-acting preparations of the psychostimulants play an important role when compliance is an issue or when the waxing and waning effect of shorter acting preparations is undesirable.

Typical starting doses and target doses for the IR and long-acting stimulants, atomoxetine and other drugs used for the treatment of ADHD are presented in Table 13.1. Concerta is typically started at 18 mg, with dosage increments of 18 mg and Adderall-XR is started at 10 mg and increased by 5 mg. For both IR and long-acting stimulants, dosage adjustments may be made at intervals of 3 days to 1 week depending on the extent and quality of feedback available from parents and teachers. Feedback should be obtained orally from parents and from completion by parents and teachers of standardised behaviour rating checklists such as the Vanderbilt checklist of DSM-IV symptoms of disruptive behaviour disorders (Wolraich *et al.*, 2003). The parent is also asked to monitor sleep, appetite, personality changes, and moodiness, and any other behaviour problems. The dosage is increased as outlined as long as there is room for improvement and the medication is reasonably well tolerated. The aim of the titration is to identify the dose that achieves the best behavioural response at school for both morning and afternoon and has relatively few or no side effects at home.

Both the American Academy of Child and Adolescent Psychiatry (2002) and the American Academy of Pediatrics (2001) have published practice guidelines for medication treatment of ADHD. The Texas Medication Algorithm for Pharmacotherapy of ADHD was recently revised and updated (Pliszka *et al.*, 2006). An excellent handbook for physicians for management of ADHD is also available (Arnold, 2004).

Various authorities have described the advantages of a double-blind, placebo-controlled trial as the process by which medication is initiated even in typical clinical practice (Vitiello *et al.*, 2001). In many children, higher doses do not necessarily confer optimal overall treatment (Chacko *et al.*, 2005). A systematic trial involves double-blind administration of various doses of mediation and placebo in random order. Systematic trials are not particularly complicated and can be organised in typical clinical practice. The arguments against the use of a systematic trial are that there appears to be little systematic and sustained placebo effect and doses determined by systematic trial tend to be similar to those determined by open titration. Consequently, the extra cost of a double-blind trial might not be justified. However, many parents are reassured by the rigor of a systematic trial (Fine & Johnston, 1993) and this alone could be ample justification.

The presence of physical complaints such as headaches and insomnia must be assessed before the start of medication. Otherwise, these symptoms may be construed incorrectly as side effects once treatment starts. Side effects must be monitored continuously because some may have a late onset (Schachar *et al.*, 1997). Some side effects such as over-focusing, dysphoria and dystonia are subtle and unreliably reported by teachers and parents. Direct observation is important. A useful strategy for monitoring medication effects is to have the child attend follow-up visits at a time of peak medication effect. Systematic observation for tics, stereotypic movements, perseveration, over-focusing and other side effects can be conducted during the course of these routine office visits in addition to obtaining the reports of parents and teachers. Regular contact with the child's teacher is useful and can be organised by having the parents take a behaviour rating and side effects scale to the teacher before follow-up visits. In many cases, the parents actually do not see the child during the time of peak medication effects as medication is taken so as to be effective during school hours.

Atomoxetine may be considered as the first medication for ADHD in persons with an active substance abuse problem, or comorbid anxiety. Atomoxetine is preferred if the patient experiences severe side effects to stimulants such as mood lability or tics (Biederman, Spencer & Wilens, 2004). Atomoxetine can also be dosed every 12 hours to achieve very late evening coverage. Atomoxetine can be given in the late afternoon or evening, whereas stimulants generally cannot; atomoxetine may have less pronounced effects on appetite and sleep than do stimulants, though they may produce relatively more nausea or sedation.

13.10 SUMMARY

Medications are an important part of the clinical armamentarium of treatment for ADHD in children, teens and adults. Goals for the future include a fuller understanding of the mechanisms of actions of these drugs so as to better maximise their therapeutic benefits and minimise adverse effects. Much more research is needed on the effects of combinations of medications to treat comorbid conditions or to treat individuals who do not show an adequate response of primary symptoms to a single medication. Another major challenge is to develop methods to identify *a priori* those individuals who will respond best to a given drug; this will likely involve applications of the growing fields of pharmacogenetics and neuroimaging, discussed elsewhere in this book (see Chapters 10, 11, 16 and 22). Finally, the long-term effects of the medications, particularly those recently introduced to the market, as well as the effects of the stimulants when used continuously from childhood through adulthood, must be more thoroughly investigated.

13.11 REFERENCES

Abikoff H, McGough J, Vitiello B *et al.* (2005) Sequential pharmacotherapy for children with comorbid attention-deficit/hyperactivity and anxiety disorders. *Journal of the American Academy of Child & Adolescent Psychiatry* **44**(5): 418–27.

Allen AJ, Wernicke J, Dunn D *et al.* (2002) Safety and efficacy of atomoxetine in pediatric CYP2D6 extensive versus poor metabolizers. Paper presented at the Society of Biological Psychiatry, Philadelphia, PA.

Aman MG, Buican B, Arnold LE (2003) Methylphenidate treatment in children with borderline IQ and mental retardation: analysis of three aggregated studies. *Journal of Child & Adolescent Psychopharmacology* **13**(1): 29–40.

American Academy of Child and Adolescent Psychiatry (2002) Practice parameter for the use of stimulant medication in the treatment of children, adolescents, and adults. *Journal of the American Academy of Child and Adolescent Psychiatry* **41**(2 (Suppl)): 26S–49S.

American Academy of Pediatrics (2001) Clinical practice guideline: treatment of the school-aged child with Attention-Deficit/Hyperactivity Disorder. *Pediatrics* **108**: 1033–44.

American Psychiatric Association (1994) *Diagnostic and Statistical Manual of Mental Disorders* (4th edn, DSM-IV). Washington, DC: APA.

Arnold LE (2004) *Contemporary Diagnosis and Management of Attention-Deficit/Hyperactivity Disorder* (3rd edn). Newtown, PA: Handbooks in Health Care Co.

Arnold LE, Elliot M, Sachs L *et al.* (2003) Effects of ethnicity on treatment attendance, stimulant response/dose, and 14-month outcome in ADHD. *Journal of Consulting & Clinical Psychology* **71**(4): 713–27.

Arnsten AF (2001) Dopaminergic and noradrenergic influences on cognitive functions mediated by prefrontal cortex. In MV Solanto, AFT Arnsten, FX Castellanos (eds) *Stimulant Drugs and ADHD: Basic and Clinical Neuroscience* (pp. 185–208). New York: Oxford University Press.

Arnsten AF, Dudley AG (2005) Methylphenidate improves prefrontal cortical cognitive function through alpha2 adrenoceptor and dopamine D1 receptor actions: Relevance to therapeutic effects in Attention Deficit Hyperactivity Disorder. *Behavioral and Brain Functions* **1**(1): 2.

Aylward EH, Reiss AL, Reader MJ *et al.* (1996) Basal ganglia volumes in children with Attention-Deficit Hyperactivity Disorder. *Journal of Child Neurology* **11**: 112–15.

Barkley RA (1977) A review of stimulant drug research with hyperactive children. *Journal of Child Psychology and Psychiatry* **18**: 137–65.

Barkley RA (2002a) International Consensus Statement on ADHD. *Clinical Child and Family Psychology Review* **5**: 89–111.

Barkley RA (2002b) Major life activity and health outcomes associated with Attention-Deficit/Hyperactivity Disorder. *Journal of Clinical Psychiatry* **63**: 10–15.

Barkley RA, Cunningham CE (1979) The effect of methylphenidate on the mother-child interactions of hyperactive children. *Archives of General Psychiatry* **36**: 201–8.

Barkley RA, DuPaul GJ, McMurray MB (1991) Attention deficit disorder with and without hyperactivity: Clinical response to three dose levels of methylphenidate. *Pediatrics* **87**: 519–31.

Barkley RA, Fischer M, Edelbrock CS, Smallish L (1990a) The adolescent outcome of hyperactive children diagnosed by research criteria: I. An 8-year prospective follow-up study. *Journal of the American Academy of Child and Adolescent Psychiatry* **29**: 546–57.

Barkley RA, McMurray MB, Edelbrock CS, Robbins K (1990b) Side effects of methylphenidate in children with attention deficit hyperactivity disorder: a systematic placebo-controlled investigation. *Pediatrics* **86**: 184–92.

Barkley RA, Murphy KR, O'Connell T, Connor DF (2005) Effects of two doses of methylphenidate on simulator driving performance in adults with attention deficit hyperactivity disorder. *Journal of Safety Research* **36**(2): 121–31.

Barrickman LL, Perry PJ, Allen AJ *et al.* (1995) Bupropion versus methylphenidate in the treatment of Attention-Deficit Hyperactivity Disorder. *Journal of the American Academy of Child and Adolescent Psychiatry* **34**(5): 649–57.

Becker-Mattes A, Mattes JA, Abikoff H, Brandt L (1985) State-dependent learning in hyperactive children receiving methylphenidate. *American Journal of Psychiatry* **142**: 455–9.

Bedard AC *et al.* (2004) Methylphenidate improves visual-spatial memory in children with Attention-Deficit/Hyperactivity Disorder. *Journal of the American Academy of Child and Adolescent Psychiatry* **43**(3): 260–8.

Bedard AC, Ickowicz A, Logan GD *et al.* (2003) Selective inhibition in children with Attention-Deficit Hyperactivity Disorder off and on stimulant medication. *Journal of Abnormal Child Psychology* **31**(3): 315–27.

Bedard AC, Ickowicz A, Tannock R (2002) Methylphenidate improves Stroop naming speed, but not response interference, in children with attention deficit hyperactivity disorder. *Journal of Child & Adolescent Psychopharmacology* **12**(4): 301–9.

Berquin PC, Giedd JN, Jacobsen LK *et al.* (1998) The cerebellum in Attention-Deficit/Hyperactivity Disorder: a morphometric study. *Neurology* **50**: 1087–93.

Berridge CW (2001) Arousal- and attention-related actions of the locus coeruleus-noradrenergic system: potential target in the therapeutic actions of amphetamine-like stimulants. In MV Solanto, FX Castellanos, AFT Arnsten (eds) *Stimulant Drugs and ADHD: Basic and Clinical Neuroscience*. New York: Oxford University Press.

Berridge CW, Devilbiss DM, Andrzejewski ME *et al.* (2006) Methylphenidate preferentially increases catecholamure neurotransmission within the prefrontal cortex at low doses that enhance cognitive function. *Biological Psychiatry* **60**(10): 1111–20.

Biederman J, Baldessarini RJ, Goldblatt A *et al.* (1993) A naturalistic study of 24-hour electrocardiographic recordings and echocardiographic findings in children and adolescents treated with desipramine. *Journal of the American Academy of Child and Adolescent Psychiatry* **32**(4): 805–13.

Biederman J, Mick E, Surman C *et al.* (2006a) A randomized, placebo-controlled trial of OROS methylphenidate in adults with Attention-Deficit/Hyperactivity Disorder. *Biological Psychiatry* **59**(9): 829–35.

Biederman J, Monuteaux MC, Mick F *et al.* (2006b) Young adult outcome of attention deficit hyperactivity disorder: a controlled 10-year follow-up study. *Psychological Medicine* **36**(2): 167–79.

Biederman J, Spencer T, Wilens T (2004) Evidence-based pharmacotherapy for Attention-Deficit Hyperactivity Disorder. *International Journal of Neuropsychopharmacology* **7**(1): 77–97.

Biederman J, Swanson JM, Wigal SB *et al.* (2005) Efficacy and safety of modafinil film-coated tablets in children and adolescents with Attention-Deficit/Hyperactivity Disorder: results of a randomized, double-blind, placebo-controlled, flexible-dose study. *Pediatrics* **116**(6): e777–84.

Bokhari F, Mayes R, Scheffler RM (2005) An analysis of the significant variation in psychostimulant use across the U.S. *Pharmacoepidemiology & Drug Safety* **14**(4): 267–75.

Boonstra AM, Kooij JJ, Oosterlaan J *et al.* (2005) Does methylphenidate improve inhibition and other cognitive abilities in adults with childhood-onset ADHD? *Journal of Clinical and Experimental Neuropsychology*, **27**(3): 278–98.

Bradley C (1937) The behavior of children receiving Benzedrine. *American Journal of Psychiatry* **94**: 577–85.

Brehaut JC, Miller A, Raina P, McGrail KM (2003) Childhood behavior disorders and injuries among children and youth: a population-based study. *Pediatrics* **111**(2): 262–9.

Brown GL, Hunt RD, Ebert MH *et al.* (1979) Plasma levels of d-amphetamine in hyperactive children. *Psychopharmacology* **62**(2): 133–40.

Brown RT, Borden KA, Wynne ME *et al.* (1986) Methylphenidate and cognitive therapy with ADD children: a methodological reconsideration. *Journal of Abnormal Child Psychology* **14**(4): 481–97.

Buhrmester D, Whalen CK, Henker B *et al.* (1992) Prosocial behavior in hyperactive boys: effects of stimulant medication and comparison with normal boys. *Journal of Abnormal Child Psychology* **20**(1): 103–21.

Buitelaar JK, Van der Gaag J, Swaab-Barneveld H, Kuiper M (1995) Prediction of clinical response to methylphenidate in children with Attention-Deficit Hyperactivity Disorder. *Journal of the American Academy of Child and Adolescent Psychiatry* **34**(8): 1025–32.

Bymaster FP, Katner JS, Nelson DL *et al.* (2002) Atomoxetine increases extracellular levels of norepinephrine and dopamine in prefrontal cortex of rat: a potential mechanism for efficacy in Attention Deficit/Hyperactivity Disorder. *Neuropsychopharmacology* **27**: 699–711.

Cantwell DP, Swanson J, Conner DF (1997) Case study: adverse response to clonidine. *Journal of the American Academy of Child and Adolescent Psychiatry* **36**: 539–44.

Carlezon WAJ, Mague SD, Andersen SL (2003) Enduring behavioral effects of early exposure to methylphenidate in rats. *Biological Psychiatry* **54**(2): 1330–7.

Castellanos FX, Giedd JN, Berquin PC *et al.* (2001) Quantitative brain magnetic resonance imaging in girls with Attention-Deficit/Hyperactivity Disorder. *Archives of General Psychiatry* **58**: 289–95.

Castellanos FX, Giedd J, Elia J *et al.* (1997) Controlled stimulant treatment of ADHD and comorbid Tourette's Syndrome: Effects of stimulant and dose. *Journal of the American Academy of Child and Adolescent Psychiatry* **36**: 589–96.

Castellanos FX, Giedd JN, Marsh WL *et al.* (1996) Quantitative brain magnetic resonance imaging in Attention-Deficit Hyperactivity Disorder. *Archives of General Psychiatry* **53**: 607–16.

Castellanos FX, Sharp WS, Gottesman RF *et al.* (2003) Anatomic brain abnormalities in monozygotic twins discordant for attention deficit hyperactivity disorder. *American Journal of Psychiatry* **160**: 1693–6.

Chacko A, Pelham WE, Gnagy EM *et al.* (2005) Stimulant medication effects in a summer treatment program among young children with Attention-Deficit/Hyperactivity Disorder. *Journal of the American Academy of Child & Adolescent Psychiatry* **44**(3): 249–57.

Charach A, Ickowicz A, Schachar R (2004) Stimulant treatment over five years: adherence, effectiveness, and adverse effects. *Journal of the American Academy of Child and Adolescent Psychiatry* **43**(5): 559–67.

Charles L, Schain R (1981) A four-year follow-up study of the effects of methylphenidate on the behavior and academic achievement of hyperactive children. *Journal of Abnormal Child Psychology* **9**(4): 495–505.

Charles L, Schain RJ, Guthrie D (1979) Long-term use and discontinuation of methylphenidate with hyperactive children. *Developmental Medicine and Child Neurology* **21**(6): 758–64.

Cherland E, Fitzpatrick R (1999) Psychotic side effects of psychostimulants: a 5-year review. *Canadian Journal of Psychiatry* **44**(8): 811–13.

Clausen SB, Read SC, Tulloch SJ (2005) Single- and multiple-dose pharmacokinetics of an oral mixed amphetamine salts extended-release formulation in adults. *CNS Spectrums* **10**(12 Suppl 20): 6–15.

Conners CK, Casat CD, Gualtieri CT *et al.* (1996) Bupropion hydrochloride in attention deficit disorder with hyperactivity. *Journal of the American Academy of Child & Adolescent Psychiatry* **35**(10): 1314–21.

Conners CK, Epstein JN, March JS *et al.* (2001) Multimodal treatment of ADHD in the MTA: an alternative outcome analysis. *Journal of the American Academy of Child & Adolescent Psychiatry* **40**(2): 159–67.

Connor DF (2002) Preschool attention deficit hyperactivity disorder: a review of prevalence, diagnosis, neurobiology, and stimulant treatment. *Journal of Developmental & Behavioral Pediatrics* **23**(1 Suppl): S1–9.

Connor DF, Fletcher KE, Swanson JM (1999) A meta-analysis of clonidine for symptoms of Attention-Deficit Hyperactivity Disorder. *Journal of the American Academy of Child & Adolescent Psychiatry* **38**(12): 1551–9.

Cox ER, Motheral BR, Henderson RR, Mager D (2003) Geographic variation in the prevalence of stimulant medication use among children 5 to 14 years old: results from a commercially insured US sample. *Pediatrics* **111**(2): 237–43.

Cueva JE, Overall JE, Small AM *et al.* (1996) Carbamazepine in aggressive children with conduct disorder: a double-blind and placebo-controlled study. *Journal of the American Academy of Child and Adolescent Psychiatry* **35**(4): 480–90.

Cunningham CE (1999) In the wake of the MTA: charting a new course for the study and treatment of children with Attention-Deficit Hyperactivity Disorder. *Canadian Journal of Psychiatry – Revue Canadienne de Psychiatrie* **44**(10): 999–1006.

Denney CB, Rapport MD (2001) The cognitive pharmacology of stimulants in children with ADHD. In MV Solanto, AFT Arnsten, FX Castellanos (eds) *Stimulant Drugs and ADHD: Basic and Clinical Neuroscience* (pp. 283–302). New York: Oxford University Press.

Dews PB, Wenger GR (1977) Rate-dependency of the behavioral effects of amphetamine. In T Thompson, PB Dews (eds) *Advances in Behavioral Pharmacology* (Vol. 1, pp. 167–227). New York: Academic Press.

Diamond IR, Tannock R, Schachar RJ (1999) Response to methylphenidate in children with ADHD and comorbid anxiety. *Journal of the American Academy of Child & Adolescent Psychiatry* **38**(4): 402–9.

Douglas VI, Barr RG, Desilets J, Sherman E (1995) Do high doses of methylphenidate impair flexible thinking in Attention-Deficit Hyperactivity Disorder? *Journal of the American Academy of Child and Adolescent Psychiatry* **34**: 877–85.

Douglas VI, Barr RG, O'Neill ME, Britton BG (1986) Short-term effects of methylphenidate on the cognitive, learning and academic performance of children with attention deficit disorder in the laboratory and the classroom. *Journal of Child Psychology and Psychiatry* **27**: 191–211.

Dunlop H (2000) Bupropion (Zyban, sustained-release tablets): update. *CMAJ Canadian Medical Association Journal* **162**(1): 106–7.

DuPaul GJ, Barkley RA, McMurray MB (1994) Response of children with ADHD to methylphenidate: interaction with internalizing symptoms. *Journal of the American Academy of Child and Adolescent Psychiatry* **33**: 894–903.

Durston S, Hulshoff Pol HE, Schnack HG *et al.* (2004) Magnetic resonance imaging of boys with Attention-Deficit/Hyperactivity Disorder and their unaffected siblings. *Journal of the American Academy of Child and Adolescent Psychiatry* **43**: 332–40.

Efron D (1999) Methylphenidate versus dextroamphetamine in ADHD. *Journal of the American Academy of Child and Adolescent Psychiatry* **38**: 500.

Elia J, Borcherding BG, Rapoport JL, Keysor CS (1991) Methylphenidate and dextroamphetamine treatments of hyperactivity: are there true nonresponders? *Psychiatry Research* **36**(2): 141–55.

Emslie GJ, Bangs ME, Spencer TJ *et al.* (2005) Atomoxetine in adolescents with ADHD and comorbid depression. Paper presented at the American Psychiatric Association, Atlanta, GA.

Evans S, Pelham WE, Smith BH (2001) Dose-response effects of methylphenidate on ecologically-valid measures of classroom performance and classroom behavior in adolescents with ADHD. *Experimental and Clinical Psychopharmacology* **9**: 163–75.

Faraone SV, Biederman J, Spencer T *et al.* (2005) Atomoxetine and Stroop task performance in adult Attention-Deficit/Hyperactivity Disorder. *Journal of Child and Adolescent Psychopharmacology* **15**(4): 664–70.

Faraone SV, Spencer TJ, Alcadri M *et al.* (2003) Comparing the efficacy of medications used for ADHD using meta-analysis. Paper presented at the Annual Meeting of the American Psychiatric Association, San Francisco, CA.

FDA (1997) *The FDA Modernization Act of 1997*. Available: http://www.fda.gov/cber/fdama. htm [22 April 2006].

FDA (2003) *How to Comply with the Pediatric Research Equity Act*. Available: http://www. fda.gov/cder/guidance/6215dft.pdf [2006, May 15].

FDA (2006) *Review of AERS Data for Marketed Safety Experience during Stimulant Therapy: Death, sudden death, cardiovascular SAEs (including stroke)*. FDA [9 May 2006, available at http://www.fda.gov/ohrms/dockets/ac/06/briefing/2006–4210b_08_01_ReviewAERSdata. pdf].

Filipek PA, Semrud-Clikeman M, Steingard RJ (1997) Volumetric MRI analysis comparing subjects having Attention-Deficit Hyperactivity Disorder with normal controls. *Neurology* **48**: 589–601.

Fine S, Johnston C (1993) Drug and placebo side effects in methylphenidate-placebo trial for attention deficit hyperactivity disorder. *Child Psychiatry & Human Development* **24**(1): 25–30.

Francis S, Fine J, Tannock R (2001) Methylphenidate selectively improves story retelling in children with attention deficit hyperactivity disorder. *Journal of Child & Adolescent Psychopharmacology* **11**(3): 217–28.

Gadow KD, Nolan EE, Sverd J *et al.* (2002) Anxiety and depression symptoms and response to methylphenidate in children with Attention-Deficit Hyperactivity Disorder and tic disorder. *Journal of Clinical Psychopharmacology* **22**(3): 267–74.

Gadow KD, Sverd J, Sprafkin J *et al.* (1997) Efficacy of methylphenidate for attention deficit hyperactivity in children with tic disorder. *Archives of General Psychiatry* **52**: 444–55.

Gerasimov MR, Franceschi M, Volkow ND *et al.* (2001) Comparison between intraperitoneal and oral methylphenidate administration: a microdialysis and locomotor activity study. *The Journal of Pharmacology and Experimental Therapeutics* **295**: 51–7.

Gimpel GA, Collett BR, Veeder MA *et al.* (2005) Effects of stimulant medication on cognitive performance of children with ADHD. *Clinical Pediatrics* **44**(5): 405–11.

Gittelman-Klein R (1987) Pharmacotherapy of childhood hyperactivity: an update. In HY Meltzer (ed.) *Psychopharmacology: The Third Generation of Progress* (pp. 1215–24). New York: Raven Press.

Glaser P (2006) Cerebellar neurotransmission in Attention-Deficit/Hyperactivity Disorder: does dopamine neurotransmission occur in the cerebellar vermis? *Journal of Neuroscience Methods* **151**(1): 62–7.

Golden RN, Markey SP, Risby ED *et al.* (1988) Antidepressants reduce whole-body norepinephrine turnover while enhancing 6-hydroxymelatonin output. *Archives of General Psychiatry* **45**(2): 150–4.

Goldman LS, Genel M, Bezman RJ, Slanetz PJ (1998) Diagnosis and treatment of Attention-Deficit/Hyperactivity Disorder in children and adolescents. *Journal of the American Medical Association* **279**: 1100–7.

Gonzalez FA, Byrd LD (1977) Mathematics underlying the rate-dependency hypothesis. *Science* **195**: 546–50.

Goodman DW, Ginsberg L, Weisler RH *et al.* (2005) An interim analysis of the Quality of Life, Effectiveness, Safety, and Tolerability (Q.U.E.S.T.) evaluation of mixed amphetamine salts extended release in adults with ADHD. *CNS Spectrums* **10**(12 Suppl 20): 26–34.

Granger DA, Whalen CK, Henker B (1993) Perceptions of methylphenidate effects on hyperactive children's peer interactions. *Journal of Abnormal Child Psychology* **21**(5): 535–49.

Greenhill LL (2001) Clinical effects of stimulant medication in ADHD. In MV Solanto, AFT Arnsten, FX Castellanos (eds) *Stimulant Drugs and ADHD: Basic and Clinical Neuroscience* (pp. 31–71). New York, NY: Oxford University Press.

Greenhill LL, Halperin JM, Abikoff H (1999) Stimulant medications. *Journal of the American Academy of Child and Adolescent Psychiatry* **38**(5): 503–12.

Greenhill LL, Pliszka S, Dulcan MK *et al.* (2002) Practice parameter for the use of stimulant medications in the treatment of children, adolescents, and adults [see comment]. *Journal of the American Academy of Child and Adolescent Psychiatry* **41**(2 Suppl): 26S–49S.

Greenhill LL, Swanson JM, Steinhoff K *et al.* (2003) A pharmacokinetic/pharmacodynamic study comparing a single morning dose of Adderall to twice-daily dosing in children with ADHD. *Journal of the American Academy of Child and Adolescent Psychiatry* **42**(10): 1234–341.

Greenhill LL, Swanson JM, Vitiello B *et al.* (2001) Impairment and deportment responses to different methylphenidate doses in children with ADHD: the MTA titration trial. *Journal of the American Academy of Child and Adolescent Psychiatry* **40**(2): 180–7.

Greenhill LL, Vitiello B, Abikoff HB *et al.* (2004) Outcome results from the NIMH, multisite, preschool ADHD treatment study (PATS). Paper presented at the Annual Meeting of the American Academy of Child and Adolescent Psychiatry, Washington, DC.

Gross-Tsur V, Manor O, van der Meere J *et al.* (1997) Epilepsy and attention deficit hyperactivity disorder: is methylphenidate safe and effective? *Journal of Pediatrics* **130**(4): 670–4.

Gualtieri CT, Keenan PA, Chandler M (1991) Clinical and neuropsychological effects of desipramine in children with attention deficit hyperactivity disorder. *Clinical Psychopharmacology* **11**(3): 155–9.

Handen BL, Breaux AM, Gosling A *et al.* (1990) Efficacy of methylphenidate among mentally retarded children with attention deficit hyperactivity disorder [see comments]. *Pediatrics* **86**(6): 922–30.

Handen BL, Breaux AM, Janosky J *et al.* (1992) Effects and noneffects of methylphenidate in children with mental retardation and ADHD. *J Am Acad Child Adolesc Psychiatry* **31**(3): 455–61.

Handen BL, Feldman H, Gosling A *et al.* (1991) Adverse side effects of methylphenidate among mentally retarded children with ADHD. *Journal of the American Academy of Child & Adolescent Psychiatry* **30**(2): 241–5.

Handen BL, Feldman HM, Lurier A, Murray PJ (1999) Efficacy of methylphenidate among preschool children with developmental disabilities and ADHD. *Journal of the American Academy of Child & Adolescent Psychiatry* **38**(7): 805–12.

Hechtman L, Weiss G, Perlman T (1984) Young adult outcome of hyperactive children who received long-term stimulant treatment. *Journal of the American Academy of Child and Adolescent Psychiatry* **23**(3): 361–9.

Hervey AS, Epstein JN, Curry JF (2004) Neuropsychology of adults with Attention-Deficit/Hyperactivity Disorder: a meta-analytic review. *Neuropsychology* **18**(3): 485–503.

Hinshaw SP, Heller T, McHale JP (1992) Covert antisocial behavior in boys with Attention-Deficit Hyperactivity Disorder: external validation and effects of methylphenidate. *Journal of Consulting and Clinical Psychology* **60**(2): 274–82.

Hinshaw SP, Henker B, Whalen CK *et al.* (1989) Aggressive, prosocial, and nonsocial behavior in hyperactive boys: dose effects of methylphenidate in naturalistic settings. *Journal of Consulting & Clinical Psychology* **57**(5): 636–43.

Horrigan JP, Barnhill LJ (1995) Guanfacine for treatment of Attention-Deficit Hyperactivity Disorder in boys. *Journal of Child and Adolescent Psychopharmacology* **5**: 215–23.

Horrigan JP, Barnhill LJ (2000) Low-dose amphetamine salts and adult Attention-Deficit/Hyperactivity Disorder. *Journal of Clinical Psychiatry* **61**: 414–17.

Hoza B, Gerdes AC, Mrug S *et al.* (2005) Peer-assessed outcomes in the multimodal treatment study of children with Attention-Deficit Hyperactivity Disorder. *Journal of the American Academy of Child and Adolescent Psychiatry* **34–86**(1): 74.

Hunt RD (1987) Treatment effects of oral and transdermal clonidine in relation to methylphenidate: an open pilot study in ADD-H. *Psychopharmacology Bulletin* **23**: 111–14.

Hunt RD, Arnsten AFT, Asbell MD (1995) An open trial of guanfacine in the treatment of attention deficit hyperactivity disorder. *Journal of the American Academy of Child and Adolescent Psychiatry* **34**: 50–4.

Hunt RD, Minderra R, Cohen DJ (1985) Clonidine benefits children with attention deficit disorder: report of a double-blind crossover trial. *Journal of the American Academy of Child and Adolescent Psychiatry* **24**: 617–29.

Hynd GW, Hern KL, Novey ES *et al.* (1993) Attention deficit hyperactivity disorder and asymmetry of the caudate nucleus. *Journal of Child Neurology* **8**: 339–47.

Ickowicz A (2002) Bupropion-methylphenidate combination and grand mal seizures. [see comment]. *Canadian Journal of Psychiatry – Revue Canadienne de Psychiatrie* **47**(8): 790–1.

Jadad A, Boyle M, Cunningham C *et al.* (1999) *Treatment of Attention-Deficit/Hyperactivity Disorder.* Agency for Healthcare Research and Quality. Available: http://www.ncbi.nlm.nih.gov/books/bv.fcgi?rid = hstat1.chapter.14677 [28 May 2006].

Jensen PS, Garcia, JA, Glied S *et al.* (2005) Cost-effectiveness of ADHD treatments: findings from the multimodal treatment study of children with ADHD. *American Journal of Psychiatry* **162**(9): 1628–36.

Jensen PS, Hinshaw SP, Kraemer HC *et al.* (2001a) ADHD comorbidity findings from the MTA study: comparing comorbid subgroups. *Journal of the American Academy of Child & Adolescent Psychiatry* **40**(2): 147–58.

Jensen PS, Hinshaw SP, Swanson JM *et al.* (2001b) Findings from the NIMH Multimodal Treatment Study of ADHD (MTA): implications and applications for primary care providers. *Journal of Developmental and Behavioral Pediatrics* **22**(1): 60–73.

Jensen PS, Martin D, Cantwell DP (1997) Comorbidity in ADHD: Implications for research, practice, and DSM-V. *Journal of the American Academy of Child and Adolescent Psychiatry* **36**: 1065–79.

Jick H, Kaye J, Black C (2004) Incidence and prevalence of drug-treated attention deficit disorder among boys in the UK. *British Journal of General Practice* **54**(502): 345–7.

Jin C, Schachar R (2004) Methylphenidate treatment of Attention-Deficit/Hyperactivity Disorder secondary to traumatic brain injury: a critical appraisal of treatment studies. *Cns Spectrums* **9**(3): 217–26.

Johnston C, Pelham WF, Hoza J, Sturges J (1988) Psychostimulant rebound in attention deficit disordered boys. *Journal of the American Academy of Child and Adolescent Psychiatry* **27**(6): 806–10.

Johnston JA, Lineberry CG, Ascher JA *et al.* (1991) A 102-center prospective study of seizure in association with bupropion [see comments]. *Journal of Clinical Psychiatry* **52**(11): 450–6.

Kalbag AS, Levin FR (2005) Adult ADHD and substance abuse: diagnostic and treatment issues. *Substance Use and Misuse* **40**(13–14): 1895–7.

Kelsey DK, Sumner CR, Casat CD *et al.* (2004) Once-daily atomoxetine treatment for children with Attention-Deficit/Hyperactivity Disorder, including an assessment of evening and morning behavior: a double-blind, placebo-controlled trial. *Pediatrics* **114**(1): e1–8.

Klein RG, Abikoff H, Klass E *et al.* (1997) Clinical efficacy of methylphenidate in conduct disorder with and without attention deficit hyperactivity disorder. *Archives of General Psychiatry* **54**: 1073–80.

Klein RG, Mannuzza S (1988) Hyperactive boys almost grown up. III. Methylphenidate effects on ultimate height. *Archives of General Psychiatry* **45**(12): 1131–4.

Klorman R, Brumaghim JT, Fitzpatrick PA, Borgstedt A (1991) Methylphenidate speeds evaluation processes of attention deficit disorder adolescents during a continuous performance task. *Journal of Child Psychology and Psychiatry* **19**: 262–83.

Klorman R, Brumaghim JT, Fitzpatrick PA, Borgstedt AD (1992) Methylphenidate reduces abnormalities of stimulus classification in attention deficit disorder adolescents. *Journal of Abnormal Psychology* **101**: 130–8.

Kratochvil CJ, Egger H, Greenhill LL, McGough JJ (2006) Pharmacological management of preschool ADHD. *Journal of the American Academy of Child and Adolescent Psychiatry* **45**(1): 115–18.

Kratochvil CJ, Heiligenstein JH, Dittmann R *et al.* (2002) Atomoxetine and methylphenidate treatment in children with ADHD: a prospective, randomized, open-label trial. *Journal of the American Academy of Child and Adolescent Psychiatry* **41**(7): 883–4.

Krusch DA, Klorman R, Brumaghim JT *et al.* (1996). Methylphenidate slows reactions of children with Attention Deficit Disorder during and after an error. *Journal of Abnormal Child Psychology* **24**: 633–50.

Kuczenski R, Segal DS (2001) Locomotor effects of acute and repeated threshold doses of amphetamine and methylphenidate: relative roles of dopamine and norepinephrine. *Journal of Pharmacology and Experimental Therapeutics* **296**: 876–83.

Kuczenski R, Segal DS (2002) Exposure of adolescent rats to oral methylphenidate: preferential effects on extracellular norepinephrine and absence of sensitization and cross-sensitization to methamphetamine. *Journal of Neuroscience* **22**: 7264–71.

Kuczenski R, Segal DS (2005) Stimulant actions in rodents: implications for Attention-Deficit/Hyperactivity Disorder treatment and potential substance abuse. *Biological Psychiatry* **57**(11): 1391–6.

Lage M, Hwang P (2004) Effect of methylphenidate formulation for attention deficit-hyperactivity disorder on patterns and outcomes of treatment. *Journal of Child and Adolescent Psychopharmacology* **14**: 575–81.

Langleben DD, Monterosso J, Elman I *et al.* (2006) Effect of methylphenidate on Stroop Color-Word task performance in children with attention deficit hyperactivity disorder. *Psychiatry Research* **141**(3): 315–20.

Laviola G, Adriani W, Terranova ML, Gerra G (1999) Psychobiological risk factors for vulnerability to psychostimulants in human adolescents and animal models. *Neuroscience & Biobehavioral Reviews* **23**(7): 993–1010.

Law SF, Schachar RJ (1999) Do typical clinical doses of methylphenidate cause tics in children treated for Attention-Deficit Hyperactivity Disorder? *Journal of the American Academy of Child and Adolescent Psychiatry* **38**: 944–51.

Losier BJ, McGrath PJ, Klein RM (1996) Error patterns on the continuous performance test in non-medicated and medicated samples of children with and without ADHD: a meta-analytic review. *Journal of Child Psychology and Psychiatry* **37**: 971–87.

Luman M, Oosterlaan J, Sergeant JA (2004) The impact of reinforcement contingencies on ADHD: a review and theoretical appraisal. *Clinical Psychology Review*.

McCracken JT, Sallee FR, Leonard HL *et al.* (2003). Improvement of ADHD by Atomoxetine in children with tic disorders. Paper presented at the Annual Meeting of the American Academy of Child and Adolescent Psychiatry, Miami, FL.

Mague SD, Andersen SL, Carlezon WAJ (2005) Early developmental exposure to methylphenidate reduces cocaine-induced potentiation of brain stimulation reward in rats. *Biological Psychiatry* **57**(2): 120–5.

Mannion V (1999) Case report: adverse effects of taking tricyclic antidepressants and smoking marijuana. *Canadian Family Physician* **45**: 2683–4.

Mannuzza S, Klein RG, Bessler A *et al.* (1993) Adult outcome of hyperactive boys: educational achievement, occupational rank, and psychiatric status. *Archives of General Psychiatry* **50**: 565–76.

Mannuzza S, Klein RG, Bessler A *et al.* (1998) Adult psychiatric status of hyperactive boys grown up. *American Journal of Psychiatry* **155**: 493–8.

Mehta MA, Goodyer IM, Sahakian BJ (2004) Methylphenidate improves working memory and set-shifting in ADHD: relationships to baseline memory capacity. *Journal of Child Psychology and Psychiatry* **45**(2): 293–306.

Michelson D, Adler L, Spencer T *et al.* (2003) Atomoxetine in adults with ADHD: two randomized, placebo-controlled studies. *Biological Psychiatry* **15**: 112–20.

Michelson D, Allen AJ, Busner J *et al.* (2002) Once-daily atomoxetine treatment for children and adolescents with attention deficit hyperactivity disorder: a randomized, placebo-controlled study. *American Journal of Psychiatry* **159**(1): 1896–1901.

Michelson D, Buitelaar JK, Danckaerts M *et al.* (2004) Relapse prevention in pediatric patients with ADHD treated with atomoxetine: a randomized, double-blind, placebo-controlled study. *Journal of the American Academy of Child & Adolescent Psychiatry* **43**(7): 896–904.

Michelson D, Faries D, Wernicke J *et al.* (2001) Atomoxetine in the treatment of children and adolescents with Attention-Deficit/Hyperactivity Disorder: a randomized, placebo-controlled, dose-response study. *Pediatrics* **108**(5): E83.

Milich R, Carlson CL, Pelham WE, Jr, Licht BG (1991) Effects of methylphenidate on the persistence of ADHD boys following failure experiences. *Journal of Abnormal Child Psychology* **19**(5): 519–36.

Miller AR, Brehaut JC, Raina P *et al.* (2004a) Use of medical services by methylphenidate-treated children in the general population. *Ambulatory Pediatrics* **4**(2): 174–80.

Miller AR, Lalonde CE, McGrail KM (2004b) Children's persistence with methylphenidate therapy: a population-based study. *Canadian Journal of Psychiatry – Revue Canadienne de Psychiatrie* **49**(11): 761–8.

Mostofsky SH, Reiss AL, Lockhart P, Denckla MB (1998) Evaluation of cerebellar size in Attention-Deficit Hyperactivity Disorder. *Journal of Child Neurology* **13**: 434–9.

MTA Cooperative Group (1999a) A 14-month randomized clinical trial of treatment strategies for Attention-Deficit/Hyperactivity Disorder. *Archives of General Psychiatry* **56**: 1073–86.

MTA Cooperative Group (1999b) Moderators and mediators of treatment response for children with Attention-Deficit/Hyperactivity Disorder. *Archives of General Psychiatry* **56**: 1088–96.

MTA Cooperative Group (2004) The NIMH MTA follow-up: changes in effectiveness and growth after the end of treatment. *Pediatrics* **113**(4): 762–9.

Myrick H, Malcolm R, Taylor B, LaRowe S (2004) Modafinil: preclinical, clinical, and post-marketing surveillance – a review of abuse liability issues. *Annals of Clinical Psychiatry* **16**(2): 101–9.

Newcorn JH, Spencer TJ, Biederman J *et al.* (2005) Atomoxetine treatment in children and adolescents with Attention-Deficit/Hyperactivity Disorder and comorbid oppositional defiant disorder. *Journal of the American Academy of Child and Adolescent Psychiatry* **44**(3): 240–8.

Nigg JT (2005) Neuropsychologic theory and findings in Attention-Deficit/Hyperactivity Disorder: the state of the field and salient challenges for the coming decade. *Biological Psychiatry* **57**(11): 1424–35.

Owens EB, Hinshaw SP, Kraemer HC *et al.* (2003) Which treatment for whom for ADHD? Moderators of treatment response in the MTA. *Journal of Consulting & Clinical Psychology* **71**(3): 540–52.

Palumbo D, Spencer T, Lynch J *et al.* (2004) Emergence of tics in children with ADHD: impact of once-daily OROS methylphenidate therapy. *Journal of Child and Adolescent Psychopharmacology* **14**(2): 185–94.

Paterson R, Douglas C, Hallmayer J *et al.* (1999) A randomised, double-blind, placebo-controlled trial of dexamphetamine in adults with attention deficit hyperactivity disorder. *Australian and New Zealand Journal of Psychiatry* **33**: 494–502.

Pearson DA, Lane DM, Santos CW *et al.* (2004a) Effects of methylphenidate treatment in children with mental retardation and ADHD: individual variation in medication response. *Journal of the American Academy of Child & Adolescent Psychiatry* **43**(6): 686–98.

Pearson DA, Santos CW, Casat CD *et al.* (2004b) Treatment effects of methylphenidate on cognitive functioning in children with mental retardation and ADHD. *Journal of the American Academy of Child & Adolescent Psychiatry* **43**(6): 677–85.

Pearson DA, Santos CW, Roache JD *et al.* (2003) Treatment effects of methylphenidate on behavioral adjustment in children with mental retardation and ADHD. *Journal of the American Academy of Child & Adolescent Psychiatry* **42**(2): 209–16.

Pelham WE, Milich R, Cummings EM *et al.* (1991) Effects of background anger, provocation, and methylphenidate on emotional arousal and aggressive responding in Attention-Deficit Hyperactivity Disordered boys with and without concurrent aggressiveness. *Journal of Abnormal Child Psychology* **19**(4): 407–26.

Pelham WE, Murphy DA, Vannatta K *et al.* (1992) Methylphenidate and attributions in boys with Attention-Deficit Hyperactivity Disorder. *Journal of Consulting & Clinical Psychology* **60**(2): 282–92.

Pelham WE, Waschbusch DA (1999) Behavioral intervention in Attention-Deficit/Hyperactivity Disorder. In HC Quay, AE Hogan (eds) *Handbook of Disruptive Behavior Disorders* (pp. 255–78). New York: Kluwer Academic/Plenum Publishers.

Pliszka SR (1989) Effect of anxiety on cognition, behavior, and stimulant response in ADHD. *Journal of the American Academy of Child and Adolescent Psychiatry* **28**: 882–7.

Pliszka SR (2001) Comparing the effects of stimulant and non-stimulant agents on catecholamine function: Implications for theories of ADHD. In MV Solanto, AFT Arnstein, FX Castellanos (eds) *Stimulant Drugs and ADHD: Basic and Clinical Neuroscience* (pp. 332–52). New York: Oxford University Press.

Pliszka SR (2003) Non-stimulant treatment of Attention-Deficit/Hyperactivity Disorder. *CNS Spectrums* **8**(4): 253–8.

Pliszka SR, Greenhill LL, Crimson ML *et al.* (2000) The Texas Children's Medication Algorithm Project: report of the Texas consensus conference panel on medication treatment of childhood attention deficit/hyperactivity disorder. Part I. Attention-deficit/hyperactivity disorder. *Journal of the American Academy of Child and Adolescent Psychiatry* **39**: 908–19.

Pliszka SR, Crismon ML, Hughes CW *et al.* (2006) The Texas Children's Medication Algorithm Project: revision of the algorithm for pharmacotherapy of Attention-Deficit/Hyperactivity Disorder. *Journal of the American Academy of Child and Adolescent Psychiatry* **45**(6): 642–57.

Popper CW (1997) Antidepressants in the treatment of Attention-Deficit/Hyperactivity Disorder. *Journal of Clinical Psychiatry* **58** (Suppl 14): 14–29; discussion 30–1.

Radonovich KJ, Mostofsky SH (2004) Duration judgments in children with ADHD suggest deficient utilization of temporal information rather than general impairment in timing. *Neuropsychology, Development, and Cognition. Section C, Child Neuropsychology* **10**(3): 162–72.

Rapport MD, Denney C, DuPaul GJ, Gardner MJ (1994) Attention deficit disorder and methylphenidate: Normalization rates, clinical effectiveness, and response prediction in 76 children. *Journal of the American Academy of Child and Adolescent Psychiatry* **33**: 882–93.

Reimherr FW, Marchant BK, Strong RE *et al.* (2005) Emotional dysregulation in adult ADHD and response to atomoxetine. *Biological Psychiatry* **58**(2): 125–31.

Richters JE, Arnold LE, Jensen PS *et al.* (1995) NIMH collaborative multisite multimodal treatment study of children with ADHD: I. Background and rationale. *Journal of the American Academy of Child and Adolescent Psychiatry* **34**(8): 987–1000.

Riddle MA, Nelson JC, Kleinman CS *et al.* (1991) Sudden death in children receiving Norpramin: a review of three reported cases and commentary. *Journal of the American Academy of Child and Adolescent Psychiatry* **30**(1): 104–8.

Rieppi R, Greenhill LL, Ford RR *et al.* (2002) Socioeconomic status as a moderator of ADHD treatment outcomes. *Journal of the American Academy of Child and Adolescent Psychiatry* **41**: 269–77.

Ring BJ, Gillespie JS, Eckstein JA, Wrighton SA (2002) Identification of the human cytochromes P450 responsible for atomoxetine metabolism. *Drug Metabolism & Disposition* **30**(3): 319–23.

Robbins TW, Sahakian BJ (1979) 'Paradoxical' effects of psychomotor stimulant drugs in hyperactive children from the standpoint of behavioural pharmacology. *Neuropharmacology* **18**: 931–50.

Robertson PJ, Hellriegel ET (2003) Clinical pharmacokinetic profile of modafinil. *Clinical Pharmacokinetics* **42**(2): 123–37.

Robinson TE, Becker JB (1986) Enduring changes in brain and behavior produced by chronic amphetamine administration: a review and evaluation of animal models of amphetamine psychosis. *Brain Research Reviews* **11**: 157–98.

Robinson TE, Berridge KC (2001) Incentive-sensitization and addiction. *Addiction* **96**: 103–14.

Robison LM, Sclar DA, Skaer TL, Galin RG (2001) Is the prevalence of Attention-Deficit Hyperactivity Disorder increasing among US girls? Trends in diagnosis and the prescribing of stimulants. Paper presented at the NCDEU, Miami, FL.

Rubia K, Noorloos J, Smith A *et al.* (2003) Motor timing deficits in community and clinical boys with hyperactive behavior: the effect of methylphenidate on motor timing. *Journal of Abnormal Child Psychology* **31**(3): 301–13.

Rugino TA, Samsock TC (2003) Modafinil in children with Attention-Deficit Hyperactivity Disorder. *Pediatric Neurology* **29**(2): 136–42.

Safer DJ, Zito JM, Fine EM (1996) Increased methylphenidate usage for attention deficit disorder in the 1990's. *Pediatrics* **98**: 1084–8.

Safren SA, Otto MW, Sprich S *et al.* (2005) Cognitive-behavioral therapy for ADHD in medication-treated adults with continued symptoms. *Behavioral Research and Therapy* **43**(7).

Sanchez RJ, Crismon ML, Barner JC *et al.* (2005) Assessment of adherence measures with different stimulant among children and adolescents. *Pharmacotherapy* **25**(7): 909–17.

Sauer JM, Ponsler GD, Mattiuz EL *et al.* (2003) Disposition and metabolic fate of atomoxetine hydrochloride: the role of CYP2D6 in human disposition and metabolism. *Drug Metabolism & Disposition* **31**(1): 98–107.

Sax KW, Strakowski SM (2001) Behavioral sensitization in humans. *Journal of Addiction Disorders* **20**(3): 55–65.

Scahill L, Chappell PB, Kim YS *et al.* (2001) A placebo-controlled study of guanfacine in the treatment of children with tic disorders and attention deficit hyperactivity disorder. *American Journal of Psychiatry* **158**(7): 1067–74.

Schachar RJ, Tannock R (1993) Childhood hyperactivity and psychostimulants: a review of extended treatment studies. *J Child Adolescent Psychopharmacol* **3**(2): 81–97.

Schachar RJ, Tannock R, Cunningham C, Corkum PV (1997) Behavioral, situational, and temporal effects of treatment of ADHD with methylphenidate. *Journal of the American Academy of Child & Adolescent Psychiatry* **36**(6): 754–63.

Scheres A, Oosterlaan J, Swanson J *et al.* (2003) The effect of methylphenidate on three forms of response inhibition in boys with ADHD. *Journal of Abnormal Child Psychology* **31**(1): 105–20.

Schertz M, Adesman AR, Alfieri NE, Bienkowski RS (1996) Predictors of weight loss in children with attention deficit hyperactivity disorder treated with stimulant medication. *Pediatrics* **98**(4 Pt 1): 763–9.

Schubiner H, Saules KK, Arfken CL *et al.* (2002) Double-blind placebo-controlled trial of methylphenidate in the treatment of adult ADHD patients with comorbid cocaine dependence. *Experimental and Clinical Psychopharmacology* **10**(3): 286–94.

Seidman LJ (2005) Cortical abnormalities in adults with ADHD assessed with structural MRI. Paper presented at the Annual Meeting of the American Academy of Child and Adolescent Psychiatry, Toronto, Ontario, Canada.

Seidman LJ, Valera EM, Bush G (2004) Brain function and structure in adults with Attention-Deficit/Hyperactivity Disorder. *Psychiatric Clinics of North America* **27**(2): 323–47.

Seidman LJ, Valera EM, Makris N (2005) Structural brain imaging of Attention-Deficit/Hyperactivity Disorder. *Biological Psychiatry* **57**(11): 1263–72.

Siddall OM (2005) Use of methylphenidate in traumatic brain injury. *Annals of Pharmaco-therapy* **39**(7–8): 1309–13.

Silva RR, Munoz DM, Alpert M (1996) Carbamazepine use in children and adolescents with features of Attention-Deficit Hyperactivity Disorder: a meta-analysis. *Journal of the American Academy of Child and Adolescent Psychiatry* **35**(3): 352–8.

Simpson D, Plosker GL (2004) Atomoxetine: a review of its use in adults with attention deficit hyperactivity disorder. *Drugs* **64**(2): 205–22.

Slimmer LW, Brown RT (1985) Parents' decision-making process in medication administration for control of hyperactivity. *Journal of School Health* **55**(6): 221–5.

Smith B, Pelham WE, Gnagy E *et al.* (1998) Equivalent effects of stimulant treatment for Attention-Deficit Hyperactivity Disorder during childhood and adolescence. *Journal of the American Academy of Child and Adolescent Psychiatry* **37**: 314–21.

Solanto MV (1998) Neuropsychopharmacological mechanisms of stimulant drug action in attention deficit/hyperactivity disorder: a review and integration. *Behavioural Brain Research* **94**: 127–52.

Solanto MV, Marks DJ, Mitchell K *et al.* (in press) Development of a new psychosocial treatment for adults with ADHD. *Journal of Attention Disorders.*

Solanto MV, Newcorn JN, Yail L *et al.* (submitted). Stimulant drug response in ADHD, Predominantly inattentive subtype.

Solanto MV, Wender EH (1989) Does methylphenidate constrict cognitive functioning? *Journal of the American Academy of Child and Adolescent Psychiatry* **26**: 897–902.

Spencer T, Wilens T, Biederman J *et al.* (1995) A double-blind, crossover comparison of methylphenidate and placebo in adults with childhood-onset attention deficit hyperactivity disorder. *Archives of General Psychiatry* **52**: 434–43.

Spencer T, Biederman J, Wilens T *et al.* (1996) Pharmacotherapy of Attention-Deficit Hyperactivity Disorder across the life cycle. *Journal of the American Academy of Child and Adolescent Psychiatry* **35**(4): 409–32.

Spencer T, Biederman J, Wilens T *et al.* (1998) Effectiveness and tolerability of tomoxetine in adults with attention deficit hyperactivity disorder. *Am. J. Psychiatry* **155**: 693–5.

Spencer T, Biederman J, Wilens T *et al.* (2001) Efficacy of a mixed amphetamine salts compound in adults with ADHD. *Archives of General Psychiatry* **58**: 775–82.

Spencer T, Biederman J, Wilens T (2004) Stimulant treatment of adult Attention-Deficit/Hyperactivity Disorder. *Psychiatric Clinics of North America* **27**(2): 361–72.

Spencer T, Biederman J, Wilens T *et al.* (2005) A large, double-blind, randomized clinical trial of methylphenidate in the treatment of adults with Attention-Deficit/Hyperactivity Disorder. *Biological Psychiatry* **57**(5): 456–63.

Spencer TJ, Faraone SV, Biederman J *et al.* (2006a) Does prolonged therapy with a long-acting stimulant suppress growth in children? *Journal of the American Academy of Child and Adolescent Psychiatry* **45**(5): 527–37.

Spencer TJ, Ruff DR, Feldman PD, Michelson D (2003) Long-term effects of atomoxetine on growth in children and adolescents with ADHD. Paper presented at the European Society for Child and Adolescent Psychiatry (ESCAP), Paris, France.

Spencer TJ, Wilens TE, Biederman J *et al.* (2006b) Efficacy and safety of mixed amphetamine salts extended release (Adderall XR) in the management of Attention-Deficit/Hyperactivity Disorder in adolescent patients: a 4-week, randomized, double-blind, placebo-controlled, parallel-group study. *Clinical Therapeutics* **28**(2): 266–79.

Srinivas NR, Hubbard JW, Quinn D, Midha KK (1992) Enantioselective pharmacokinetics and pharmacodynamics of dl-threo-methylphenidate in children with attention deficit hyperactivity disorder. *Clinical Pharmacology and Therapeutics* **52**: 561–8.

Stahl SM (2002) Psychopharmacology of wakefulness: pathways and neurotransmitters. *Journal of Clinical Psychiatry* **63**(7): 551–2.

Steele M *et al.* (2006) A randomized, controlled effectiveness trial of OROS-methylphenidate compared to usual care with immediate-relase methylphenidate in attention deficit-hyperactivity disorder. *Canadian Journal of Clinical Pharmacology* **13**: e50–62.

Stein M, Sarampote CS, Waldman ID *et al.* (2003) A dose-response study of OROS methylphenidate in children with Attention-Deficit/Hyperactivity Disorder. *Pediatrics* **112**: e404.

Strakowski SM, Sax KW, Rosenberg HL *et al.* (2001) Human response to repeated low-dose d-amphetamine: evidence for behavioral enhancement and tolerance.

Stuss DT, Eskes GA, Foster JK (1994) Experimental neuropsychological studies of frontal lobe functions. In F Boller, H Spinnier, JA Hendler, H Sinnier (eds) *Handbook of Neuropsychology: The Frontal Lobes* (pp. 149–85) Oxford: Elsevier.

Sumner CS, Donnelly C, Lopez FA *et al.* (2005) Atomoxetine treatment for pediatric patients with ADHD and comorbid anxiety. Paper presented at the American Psychiatric Association, Altanta, GA.

Swanson JM (1988) What do psychopharmacological studies tell us about information processing deficits in ADD/Hyperactive children? In J Sergeant, L Bloomingdale (eds) *Attention: Criteria, Cognition, Intervention* (Vol. 5). New York: Pergamon Press.

Swanson JM, Greenhill LL, Vitiello B *et al.* (unpublished). An evaluation of sensitization to clinical doses of methylphenidate. Presented in December 1999 at Washington DC conference on stimulant effects in ADHD (Ben Vitiello, organizer).

Swanson JM, Gupta S, Guinta D *et al.* (1999) Acute tolerance to methylphenidate in the treatment of attention deficit hyperactivity disorder in children. *Clinical Pharmacology and Therapeutics* **66**: 295–305.

Swanson JM, Gupta S, Lam A *et al.* (2003) Development of a new once-a-day formulation of methylphenidate of Attention-Deficit/Hyperactivity Disorder: proof-of-concept and proof-of-product studies. *Archives of General Psychiatry* **60**: 204–11.

Swanson JM, Kraemer HC, Hinshaw SP *et al.* (2001) Clinical relevance of the primary findings of the MTA: success rates based on severity of ADHD and ODD symptoms at the end of treatment. *Journal of the American Academy of Child & Adolescent Psychiatry* **40**(2): 168–79.

Swanson JM, Lerner M, Williams L (1995) More frequent diagnosis of attention deficit hyperacitivity disorder. *New England Journal of Medicine* **333**: 944.

Swanson JM, Volkow ND (2001) Pharmacokinetic and pharmacodynamic properties of methylphenidate. In MV Solanto, AFT Arnsten, FX Castellanos (eds) *Stimulant Drugs and ADHD: Basic and Clinical Neuroscience* (pp. 259–82). New York: Oxford University Press.

Swanson JM, Volkow ND (2003) Serum and brain concentrations of methylphenidate: implications for use and abuse. *Neuroscience and Biobehavioral Reviews* **27**(7): 615–21.

Swanson JM, Wigal SB, Wigal T *et al.* (2004) A comparison of once-daily extended-release methylphenidate formulations in children with Attention-Deficit/Hyperactivity Disorder in the laboratory school (the Comacs Study). *Pediatrics* e206–16.

Tannock R, Ickowiz A, Schachar R (1995) Differential effects of methylphenidate on working memory in ADHD children with and without comorbid anxiety. *Journal of the American Academy of Child and Adolescent Psychiatry* **34**: 886–96.

Tannock R, Martinussen R, Frijters J (2000) Naming speed performance and stimulant effects indicate effortful, semantic processing deficits in attention deficit hyperactivity disorder. *Journal of Abnormal Child Psychology* **28**: 237–52.

Tannock R, Schachar RJ, Carr RP *et al.* (1989a) Effects of methylphenidate on inhibitory control in hyperactive children. *Journal of Abnormal Child Psychology* **17**: 473–91.

Tannock R, Schachar RJ, Carr RP, Logan GD (1989b) Dose response effects of methylphenidate on academic performance and overt behavior in hyperactive children. *Pediatrics* **84**: 648–57.

Taylor E, Chadwick O, Heptinstall E, Danckaerts M (1996) Hyperactivity and conduct problems as risk factors for adolescent development. *Journal of the American Academy of Child and Adolescent Psychiatry* **35**(9): 1213–26.

Taylor E, Schachar R, Thorley G *et al.* (1987) Which boys respond to stimulant medication? A controlled trial of methylphenidate in boys with disruptive behaviour. *Psychological Medicine* **17**: 121–43.

Taylor FB, Russo J (2001) Comparing guanfacine and dextroamphetamine for the treatment of adult Attention-Deficit/Hyperactivity Disorder. *Journal of Clinical Psychopharmacology* **21**: 223–8.

Teicher MH, Polcari A, Anderson CM *et al.* (2003) Rate dependency revisited: understanding the effects of methylphenidate in children with Attention Deficit Hyperactivity Disorder. *Journal of Child and Adolescent Psychopharmacology* **13**(1): 41–51.

Thiruchelvam D, Charach A, Schachar RJ (2001) Moderators and mediators of long-term adherence to stimulant treatment in children with ADHD. *Journal of the American Academy of Child & Adolescent Psychiatry* **40**(8): 922–8.

Tourette's Syndrome Study G (2002) Treatment of ADHD in children with tics: a randomized controlled trial [see comment]. *Neurology* **58**(4), 527–36.

Turner DC, Blackwell AD, Dowson JH *et al.* (2005) Neurocognitive effects of methylphenidate in adult Attention-Deficit/Hyperactivity Disorder. *Psychopharmacology (Berl)* **178**(2–3): 289–95.

Turner DC, Clark L, Dowson J *et al.* (2004) Modafinil improves cognition and response inhibition in adult Attention-Deficit/Hyperactivity Disorder. *Biological Psychiatry* **55**(10): 1031–40.

Urman R, Ickowicz A, Fulford P, Tannock R (1995) An exaggerated cardiovascular response to methylphenidate in ADHD children with anxiety. *Journal of Child and Adolescent Psychopharmacology* **5**(1): 29–37.

Vaidya CJ, Austin G, Kirkorian G *et al.* (1998) Selective effects of methylphenidate in attention deficit hyperactivity disorder: a functional magnetic resonance study. *Proceedings of the National Academy of Science* **95**: 14494–5.

Vanderschuren LJ, Kalivas PW (2000) Alterations in dopaminergic and glutamatergic transmission in the induction and expression of behavioral sensitization: a critical review of preclinical studies. *Psychopharmacology (Berl.)* **151**(2–3): 99–120.

Visser S, Lesesne C (2005) Mental health in the United States: prevalence of diagnosis and medication treatment for Attention-Deficit/Hyperactivity Disorder – United States, 2003. *Morbidity and Mortality Weekly Report: Center for Disease Control* **54**(34): 842–7.

Vitiello B (2001) Long-term effects of stimulant medications on the brain: Possible relevance to the treatment of Attention Deficit Hyperactivity Disorder. *Journal of Child and Adolescent Psychopharmacology* **11**(1): 25–34.

Vitiello B, Severe JB, Greenhill LL *et al.* (2001) Methylphenidate dosage for children with ADHD over time under controlled conditions: Lessons from the MTA. *Journal of the American Academy of Child and Adolescent Psychiatry* **40**: 188–96.

Volkow ND, Ding YS, Fowler JS *et al.* (1995) Is methylphenidate like cocaine? Studies on their pharmacokinetics and distribution in the human brain. *Archives of General Psychiatry* **52**: 456–63.

Volkow ND, Gatley SJ, Fowler JS, Wang G-J (2000) Serotonin and the therapeutic effects of Ritalin. *Science* **288**: 11a.

Volkow ND, Swanson JM (2003) Variables that affect the clinical use and abuse of methylphenidate in the treatment of ADHD. *American Journal of Psychiatry* **160**(11): 1909–18.

Volkow ND, Wang G-J, Fowler JS *et al.* (1998) Therapeutic doses of oral methylphenidate induce significant levels of dopamine transporter occupancies in the human brain. *American Journal of Psychiatry* **155**: 1325–31.

Volkow ND, Wang G, Fowler JS *et al.* (2001) Therapeutic doses of oral methylphenidate significantly increase extracellular dopamine in the human brain. *Journal of Neuroscience* **15**: RC121.

Volkow ND, Wang GJ, Fowler JS, Ding YS (2005) Imaging the effects of methylphenidate on brain dopamine: new model on its therapeutic actions for Attention-Deficit/Hyperactivity Disorder. *Biological Psychiatry* **57**(11): 1410–15.

Volkow ND, Wang GJ, Fowler JS *et al.* (2004) Evidence that methylphenidate enhances the saliency of a mathematical task by increasing dopamine in the human brain. *American Journal of Psychiatry* **161**: 1173–80.

Volkow ND, Wang GJ, Gatley SJ *et al.* (1996) Temporal relationships between the pharmacokinetics of methylphenidate in the human brain and its behavioral and cardiovascular effects. *Psychopharmacology (Berl)* **123**(1): 26–33.

Walsh BT, Giardina EG, Sloan RP *et al.* (1994) Effects of desipramine on autonomic control of the heart. *Journal of the American Academy of Child & Adolescent Psychiatry* **33**(2): 191–7.

Wee S, Woolverton WL (2004) Evaluation of the reinforcing effects of atomoxetine in monkeys: comparison to methylphenidate and desipramine. *Drug & Alcohol Dependence* **75**(3): 271–6.

Weisler RH, Biederman J, Spencer TJ, Wilens TE (2005) Long-term cardiovascular effects of mixed amphetamine salts extended release in adults with ADHD. *CNS Spectrums* **10**(12 Suppl 20): 35–43.

Weiss G, Hechtman L (1986) *Hyperactive Children Grown Up*. New York: Guilford Press.

Weiss M, Tannock R, Kratochvil C *et al.* (2005) A randomized, placebo-controlled study of once-daily atomoxetine in the school setting in children with ADHD. *Journal of the American Academy of Child and Adolescent Psychiatry* **44**(7): 647–55.

Wernicke JF, Adler L, Spencer T *et al.* (2004) Changes in symptoms and adverse events after discontinuation of atomoxetine in children and adults with attention deficit/hyperactivity disorder: a prospective placebo-controlled assessment. *Journal of Clinical Psychopharmacology* **24**(1): 30–5.

Wernicke JF, Faries D, Girod D *et al.* (2003) Cardiovascular effects of atomoxetine in children, adolescents, and adults. *Drug Safety* **26**(10): 729–40.

Whalen C, Henker B, Buhrmester D *et al.* (1989) Does stimulant medication improve the peer status of hyperactive children? *Journal of Consulting and Clinical Psychology* **57**: 545–9.

Whalen CK, Henker B (1991) Social impact of stimulant treatment for hyperactive children. *Journal of Learning Disabilities* **24**(4): 231–41.

Whitmont S, Clark C (1996) Kinaesthetic acuity and fine motor skills in children with attention deficit hyperactivity disorder: a preliminary report. *Developmental Medicine and Child Neurology* **38**: 1091–8.

Wigal S, McGough J, McCracken JT *et al.* (2004) Analog classroom study of amphetamine XR and atomoxetine for ADHD. Paper presented at the Annual Meeting of the American Academy of Child and Adolescent Psychiatry, Washington, DC.

Wigal SB *et al.* (2004) Pharmacokinetics (PK) of methylphenidate (MPH) in preschoolers with ADHD. Paper presented at the Annual Meeting of the American Academy of Child and Adolescent Psychiatry, Washington, DC.

Wilens TE (2004a) Safety and efficacy of OROS methylphenidate in adolescents with ADHD. Paper presented at the American Psychiatric Association.

Wilens TE (2004b) Impact of ADHD and its treatment on substance abuse in adults. *Journal of Clinical Psychiatry* **65**(suppl 3): 38–45.

Wilens TE, Biederman J, Mick E, Spencer T (1995) A systematic assessment of tricyclic antidepressants in the treatment of adult Attention-Deficit Hyperactivity Disorder. *Journal of Nervous and Mental Disease* **184**: 48–50.

Wilens TE, Biederman J, Spencer TJ (1997) Case study: adverse effects of smoking marijuana while receiving tricyclic antidepressants. *Journal of the American Academy of Child & Adolescent Psychiatry* **36**(1): 45–8.

Wilens TE, Faraone SV, Biederman J, Gunawardene S (2003) Does stimulant therapy of Attention-Deficit/Hyperactivity Disorder beget later substance abuse? A meta-analytic review of the literature. *Pediatrics* 179–85.

Wilens TE, Gignac M, Swezey A *et al.* (2006a) Characteristics of adolescents and young adults with ADHD who divert or misuse their prescribed medications. *Journal of the American Academy of Child and Adolescent Psychiatry* **45**(4): 408–14.

Wilens TE, Kratochvil C, Newcorn JH, Gao H (2006b) Do children and adolescents with ADHD respond differently to atomoxetine? *Journal of the American Academy of Child and Adolescent Psychiatry.*

Wilens TE, McBurnett K, Stein M *et al.* (2005) ADHD treatment with once-daily OROS methylphenidate: final results from a long-term open-label study. *Journal of the American Academy of Child and Adolescent Psychiatry* **44**(10): 1015–23.

Wilens TE, Spencer TJ, Biederman J *et al.* (2001) A controlled clinical trial of buproprion for attention deficit hyperactivity disorder in adults. *American Journal of Psychiatry* **158**: 282–8.

Wilens TE, Spencer TJ, Biederman J (2002) A review of the pharmacotherapy of adults with Attention-Deficit/Hyperactivity Disorder. *Journal of Attention Disorders* **5**: 189–202.

Wilson JJ, Levin FR (2005) Attention-deficit/hyperactivity disorder and early-onset substance use disorders. *Journal of Child and Adolescent Psychopharmacology* **15**(5): 751–63.

Wolraich ML, Greenhill LL, Pelham W *et al.* (2001) Randomized, controlled trial of oros methylphenidate once a day in children with Attention-Deficit/Hyperactivity Disorder. *Pediatrics* **108**(4): 883–92.

Wolraich ML, Lambert W, Doffing MA *et al.* (2003) Psychometric properties of the Vanderbilt ADHD diagnostic parent rating scale in a referred population. *Journal of Pediatric Psychology* **28**(8): 559–67.

Wolraich ML, Wibbelsman CJ, Brown TE *et al.* (2005) Attention-deficit/hyperactivity disorder among adolescents: a review of the diagnosis, treatment, and clinical implications. *Pediatrics* **115**: 1734–46.

World Health Organization (1990) *International Classification of Diseases* (10th edn). Geneva: WHO.

Wren C, O'Sullivan JJ, Wright C (2000) Sudden death in children and adolescents. *Heart* **83**(4): 410–13.

14 Catecholamines and the Prefrontal Cortical Regulation of Behaviour and Attention

AMY F.T. ARNSTEN

Department of Neurobiology, Yale University, New Haven, CT, USA

14.1 OVERVIEW

Attention Deficit Hyperactivity Disorder (ADHD) is characterised by symptoms of inattention (poor sustained attention, distractibility, increased susceptibility to interference), hyperactivity and poor impulse control. These symptoms have long been associated with impaired function of the prefrontal cortex (PFC), a higher cortical region especially sensitive to levels of catecholamines. This chapter provides a brief review of PFC physiology, and catecholamine regulation of PFC function as they relate to ADHD. Basic research has demonstrated that noradrenaline (NA) has a critical beneficial influence on PFC regulation of behaviour and attention through actions at post-synaptic α2A-adrenoceptors, while dopamine (DA) improves PFC function through moderate stimulation of D1/D5 receptors. Recent research suggests that catecholamine stimulation of D4 receptors is also critical for optimal PFC function. Thus, genetic changes in molecules utilised in catecholamine transmission may disrupt essential modulatory influences in PFC and induce symptoms associated with ADHD. Pharmacological treatments that normalise catecholamine transmission would ameliorate these deficits and strengthen PFC regulation of behaviour and attention.

14.2 THE ROLE OF PFC IN THE REGULATION OF BEHAVIOUR AND ATTENTION

The PFC guides behaviour, thought and affect using working memory, i.e. the ability to keep in mind an event that has just happened, or bring to mind information from long-term stores, and use this representational knowledge to inhibit inappropriate actions or thoughts and to plan effective actions. These processes are the bases of the so-called executive functions, including regulation of attention, planning, impulse control, mental flexibility, and the initiation and monitoring of action, including self-monitoring. Lesions to the PFC produce symptoms such as forgetfulness, distractibility, impulsivity and/or perseveration, and disorganisation.

Handbook of Attention Deficit Hyperactivity Disorder. Edited by M. Fitzgerald, M. Bellgrove and M. Gill.
© 2007 John Wiley & Sons Ltd

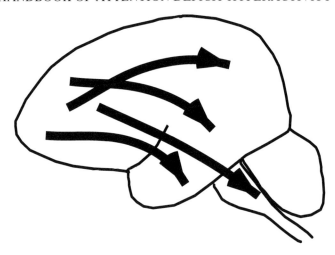

Figure 14.1. A schematic depiction of the multiple descending projections from PFC to posterior cortical and subcortical structures. The PFC is ideally positioned to regulate attention and motor responding. Many of the projections are reciprocal in nature (not shown)

The neural basis of these executive functions is the subject of intensive analysis. Anatomical tracing studies have revealed intricate and highly organised circuits, with parallel inputs from sensory and affective structures (Goldman-Rakic, 1987). The PFC also has extensive descending projections that allow amplification or inhibition of posterior cortical and subcortical processing (schematically illustrated in Figure 14.1). These pathways include projections to sensory areas for gating of distraction (Cavada & Goldman-Rakic, 1989; Barbas *et al.*, 2005), and motor areas for regulation of movement (Selemon & Goldman-Rakic, 1985; Bates & Goldman-Rakic, 1993). The PFC also has projections to catecholamine nuclei in brainstem to regulate its own modulatory state and that of the rest of the brain (Arnsten & Goldman-Rakic, 1984; Sara & Herve-Minvielle, 1995; Jodo *et al.*, 1998; Carr & Sesack, 2000). The PFC is thus ideally suited for this regulatory role.

14.2.1   PFC AND ATTENTION REGULATION

The PFC plays a critical role in the regulation of attentional processes, suppressing responses to distracting stimuli, inhibiting interference from irrelevant memories and thoughts, and allowing us to divide or sustain attention, especially under conditions where concentration is challenged by long delays or 'boring' repetition. Early studies of monkeys with dorsolateral PFC lesions discovered that their animals had become more vulnerable to distraction or other types of interference e.g. (Malmo, 1942; Bartus & Levere, 1977). More recent studies have found that PFC lesions in monkeys and rats can impair attentional regulation on set-shifting tasks (Dias *et al.*, 1996; Muir *et al.*, 1996). As with animal studies, patients with PFC lesions are easily distracted (Woods & Knight, 1986; Godefroy & Rousseaux, 1996), are impaired at gating sensory stimuli (Knight *et al.*, 1989; Yamaguchi & Knight, 1990), have poor concentration and organisation, and are more vulnerable to disruption from proactive interference (Thompson-Schill *et al.*, 2002). PFC lesions impair the ability to sustain attention, particularly over a long delay (Wilkins *et al.*, 1987). Lesions of the dorsolateral PFC impair the ability to shift attentional set (Manes *et al.*, 2002). PFC lesions also impair divided attention, and these attentional deficits have been associated with lesions in the left, superior PFC (Godefroy & Rousseaux, 1996). Data from imaging studies in noninjured subjects are consistent with data observed in lesioned patients (Bunge *et al.*, 2003).

14.2.2 PFC MEDIATES BEHAVIOURAL INHIBITION

The PFC plays a critical role in behavioural inhibition. In humans, the right hemisphere appears specialised for this function (for review, see Aron *et al.*, 2004). Both imaging (Konishi *et al.*, 1999; Rubia *et al.*, 2003) and lesion studies indicate that the right PFC in humans is critical for inhibitory abilities, e.g. performance of the Stop or Go-No Go tasks. Indeed, temporary deactivation of the right PFC by transcranial magnetic stimulation in normal human subjects can induce reversible deficits in inhibitory control (Chambers *et al.*, 2006). The importance of the PFC to inhibitory control has also been shown in monkeys with lesions (Petrides, 1986), electrophysiological (Watanabe, 1986) and imaging studies (Morita *et al.*, 2004). The orbital and ventral PFC may perform this same inhibitory function in the affective domain (Dias *et al.*, 1996), thus permitting appropriate social behaviours in both animals and humans (e.g. Iversen and Mishkin, 1970; Stuss *et al.*, 1992; Anderson *et al.*, 1999; Raine *et al.*, 2000). There is also an old literature demonstrating that PFC lesions cause locomotor hyperactivity in monkeys (Kennard *et al.*, 1941; French, 1959; Gross, 1963; Gross & Weiskrantz, 1964). Thus, the locomotor symptoms of ADHD, often thought of in terms of striatal mechanisms, may also have an important PFC component.

14.2.3 THE NEURONAL BASIS OF PFC EXECUTIVE FUNCTION

Electrophysiological studies in monkeys performing working memory tasks have shown that PFC neurons are able to hold modality-specific information 'on-line' over a delay and use this information to guide behaviour in the absence of environmental cues (Goldman-Rakic, 1995). As shown in Figure 14.2 (top traces), many PFC neurons show spatially-tuned firing during the delay period of a spatial delayed response task, firing more for the preferred direction (left graph) than for nonpreferred directions (right graph). Delay-related firing of PFC neurons was first discovered by Fuster, who emphasised the ability of the PFC to reactivate memories from long-term stores when the information became appropriate to present goals (Fuster, 1973). Fuster also emphasised the importance of delay-related cell firing for temporal integration and the ability to organise complex sequences to achieve a goal (Fuster, 1985). Thus it is clear that delay-related firing during working memory tasks is relevant to executive functions. More recently, PFC neurons have been shown to hold 'on-line' an abstract rule that is used to govern action (Wallis *et al.*, 2001). A unique feature of PFC neurons is their ability to hold information 'on-line' in the presence of interference: PFC neurons can maintain delay-related

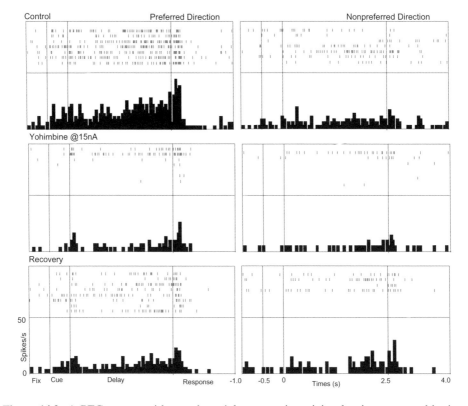

Figure 14.2. A PFC neuron with tuned spatial mnemonic activity that is suppressed by iontophoretic application of yohimbine, a compound that blocks endogenous NA stimulation of alpha-2-adrenoceptors. These data replicate those of Dr Bao-Ming Li (Li *et al.*, 1999). The neuron was recorded from area 46 of the PFC in a monkey performing a spatial working memory task, oculomotor delayed response. The neuron shows slight firing during fixation and cue presentation, and greatly increased firing during the delay period. This neuron is highly tuned under control conditions (top panel), showing increased firing during the delay period to its preferred direction (left panels) and reduced firing to nonpreferred spatial positions (right graphs). Following iontophoresis of yohimbine (middle panel), firing to the preferred direction is greatly suppressed, thus eroding spatial tuning. As yohimbine's effects wear off (bottom panel), the neuron returns to its normal firing pattern. The alpha-2A-adrenoceptor agonist, guanfacine, shows the opposite effect, increasing delay-related firing to the preferred direction (not shown). Recordings by Dr Min Wang, Arnsten Lab, Dept. Neurobiology, Yale Medical School

activity in the presence of distracting stimuli (Miller *et al.*, 1993). Electrophysiological data have also indicated that delay-related firing underlies behavioural inhibition, as examined in an anti-saccade task in which monkeys must look away from a remembered visual stimulus (Funahashi *et al.*, 1993). Thus, delay-related activity is observed both when an animal must make a memory-guided action, and when an animal must withold a prepotent response based on representational knowledge. As described below, the strength of delay-related firing depends critically on the local neurochemical environment, and thus genetic alterations influencing this environment may have dramatic effects on PFC neuronal responding.

14.3   EVIDENCE OF PFC DYSFUNCTION IN ADHD

Evidence from a variety of perspectives demonstrates that PFC function is weaker in subjects with ADHD (reviewed in Arnsten *et al.*, 1996; Barkley, 1997). Neuropsychological analyses have shown that patients with ADHD are impaired on the same tasks as those with PFC lesions; e.g. tasks of behavioural inhibition, reward reversal and working memory (Itami & Uno, 2002; Bedard *et al.*, 2003; McLean *et al.*, 2004). Numerous structural imaging studies have shown reduced size of the PFC in ADHD patients, particularly in the right hemisphere (Castellanos *et al.*, 1996; Casey *et al.*, 1997; Filipek *et al.*, 1997; Giedd *et al.*, 2001; Kates *et al.*, 2002; Hill *et al.*, 2003; Sowell *et al.*, 2003). Imaging studies have also shown evidence of inefficient or reduced blood flow or metabolism in PFC of ADHD patients, deficits which correspond with poor PFC cognitive function (Rubia *et al.*, 1999; Yeo *et al.*, 2000). There is also suggestive evidence of reduced catecholamine inputs to the PFC in adults with ADHD based on fluoro-dopa PET imaging (Ernst *et al.*, 1998). However, the sensitivity of the latter technology is not ideal for the very delicate catecholamine innervation of cortex, and thus most studies of this kind have focused on striatum. Intriguingly, genetic studies suggest that ADHD children with a methionine substitution in COMT, an enzyme that catabolises catecholamines, actually do worse on PFC tasks (Bellgrove *et al.*, 2005b). The important interactions between cognitive abilities, brain structural changes and genetic characterisation are just beginning to emerge. Imaging studies have also shown evidence of inefficient or reduced blood flow or metabolism in PFC of ADHD patients, deficits which correspond with poor PFC cognitive function.

14.4   GENETIC CHANGES IN ADHD ARE OFTEN LINKED TO CATECHOLAMINES

ADHD is highly heritable, and genetic studies have confirmed an association between a number of genes related to catecholamines and ADHD (reviewed by Hawi *et al.*, Chapter 8 and in Faraone *et al.*, 2005). Genetic studies have indicated association with a variety of genes related to both DA – the DA transporter, and DA D1, D5 and D4 receptors – and NA – the synthetic enzyme dopamine beta hydroxylase (DBH), and the D4 receptor, which has high affinity for NA as described by Van Tol *et al.* (1991). Patients with ADHD show a greater prevalence of the 7 repeat allele of a tandem repeat polymorphism of the D4 receptor that renders this receptor less effective. Intriguingly, recent studies have associated allelic variation in the D4 receptor gene with PFC volume (Durston *et al.*, 2005), and with performance of a sustained attention task (Bellgrove *et al.*, 2005a). These genetic alterations in catecholamine signalling are of particular interest, given that both DA and NA have profound effects on PFC cognitive function.

14.5 CATECHOLAMINES HAVE PROFOUND INFLUENCES ON PFC EXECUTIVE FUNCTIONS

Patricia Goldman-Rakic first established that catecholamines have a critical influence on PFC working memory function (Brozoski et al., 1979). Depletion of both DA and NA from the PFC was as detrimental to performance as removing the PFC itself. Although the original paper emphasised the importance of DA influences in PFC, it is now known that both DA and NA are critical to PFC function.

It should be noted that the research summarised below was conducted in young adult or aged monkeys; there are no data on the modulatory influences of catecholamincs on PFC cognitive function in juvenile monkeys. As there are age-related changes in monoamine innervation of primate PFC (Brown et al., 1979), including increased DA innervation in adolescence (Rosenberg & Lewis, 1994), there may be interesting differences in catecholamine mechanisms in the juvenile PFC.

14.5.1 DOPAMINE

There are two families of DA receptors, D1 (D1 and D5 subtypes) and D2 (D2, D3 and D4 subtypes). As pharmacological agents cannot distinguish between D1 and D5 receptor subtypes, all information described as 'D1' may be relevant to either the D1 and/or D5 receptor.

(a) D1 receptor family

Much research has focused on the critical role of DA at the D1 family of receptors, the predominant DA receptor type in the PFC. Stimulation of D1 receptors follows an inverted 'U'-shaped dose-response function: Either too little (Sawaguchi & Goldman-Rakic, 1994) or too much (Zahrt et al., 1997) D1 receptor stimulation impairs PFC function in rats (Granon et al., 2000), monkeys (Arnsten & Goldman-Rakic, 1998), and possibly humans (Kimberg et al., 1997). Thus, low doses of D1 agonists improve working memory and attention regulation (Cai & Arnsten, 1997; Granon et al., 2000), while high levels of DA release, e.g. during stress exposure, impair PFC function (Murphy et al., 1996). Most recently this inverted 'U' has been observed in regard to COMT genotype in humans, and has been related to D1 actions (Mattay et al., 2003). Intriguingly, electrophysiological studies in monkeys have also observed an inverted 'U' response of PFC neurons to D1 receptor stimulation (Vijayraghavan et al., 2007). Low levels of D1 receptor stimulation enhance spatial tuning by selectively inhibiting cell firing to nonpreferred spatial directions, while higher doses erode tuning by inhibiting firing to all directions (ibid.). Thus, D1 receptor stimulation is essential for reducing input 'noise'. This interpretation is consistent with previous findings showing that modest levels of D1 receptor blockade increase neuronal firing (Williams & Goldman-Rakic, 1995). In contrast, extensive blockade of D1 receptors with high doses of D1 receptor antagonist shuts down cell firing, likely due to insufficient D1 activation of basic excitatory processes, e.g. (Henze et al., 2000; Young & Yang, 2004). It will be very important to identify the relative contributions of D1 vs. D5 receptor actions in future animal studies.

(b)   D2 receptor family

The influences of the D2 family of DA receptors (D2, D3, D4) on PFC function are less well understood. Stimulation of the D2 receptor subtype increases response-related firing of PFC neurons, which may be involved in corollary discharge, i.e. alerting the brain that it has made a response (Wang *et al.*, 2004). This work has been related to the efficacy of D2 blockers in schizophrenia, but has not been related to ADHD. There is limited evidence from rat studies that excessive D2 receptor stimulation in PFC can impair working memory (Druzin *et al.*, 2000), while D2 receptor blockade seems to have little impairing effect under control conditions (Sawaguchi & Goldman-Rakic, 1994).

The D4 receptor is of particular interest given its association with ADHD. As noted above, NA has high affinity for the D4 receptor – higher affinity than for the any of the adrenergic receptors (Van Tol *et al.*, 1991). Thus, the D4 receptor should actually be considered a catecholamine receptor rather than a DA receptor. D4 receptor stimulation can inhibit GABAergic transmission in PFC (Wang *et al.*, 2002), and thus is in a potentially powerful position to alter PFC function. Recent data from monkeys performing working memory tasks has also shown that D4 receptor blockade can lead to reduced PFC pyramidal cell firing, possibly the result of excessive GABAergic inhibition of pyramidal cells (Wang & Arnsten, unpublished). As the 7 repeat allele of a DRD4 polymorphism that is associated with ADHD represents a weakened form of the receptor, subjects with this genetic alteration may similarly have insufficient PFC pyramidal cell control over behaviour and attention.

14.5.2   NORADRENALINE

NA has marked effects on PFC function, and these actions may have particular relevance to ADHD. As with DA, low to moderate levels of NA have important beneficial effects on PFC function, whereas high concentrations of NA released during stress contribute to impaired PFC function. However, in contrast to DA, the beneficial vs. detrimental actions can be dissociated at distinct adrenoceptors, where beneficial effects involve alpha-2A, and detrimental effects alpha-1 and beta-1 actions. A more detailed discussion of NA effects on PFC function can be found in a recent review (Arnsten & Li, 2005).

(a)   Alpha-2-adrenoceptors

Alpha-2 adrenoceptor agonists improve working memory and behavioural inhibition, and/or protect against distractibility in mice (Franowicz *et al.*, 2002), rats (Tanila *et al.*, 1996), monkeys (Arnsten *et al.*, 1988; Rama *et al.*, 1996), and humans (Jakala *et al.*, 1999a; Jakala *et al.*, 1999b). The efficacy of these agents to enhance PFC cognitive function can be completely dissociated from the sedating properties of these compounds at higher doses (Arnsten *et al.*, 1988). The PFC-enhancing effects occur through actions at post-synaptic, alpha-2 adrenoceptors. (Arnsten & Goldman-Rakic, 1985; Cai *et al.*, 1993) of the alpha-2A subtype (Franowicz *et al.*, 2002). These cognitive-enhancing effects are mediated by alpha-2A-adrenoceptor coupling to Gi, inhibiting adenylyl cyclase production of cAMP (Ramos *et al.*, 2003; Ramos & Arnsten, 2006). SPECT imaging of monkeys performing a delayed response task shows that systemic administration of guanfacine – an alpha-2 adreno-receptor agonist – increases regional cerebral blood flow in the dorsolateral PFC, the same brain region that is critical for spatial working memory (Avery *et al.*, 2000). Infusions of guanfacine directly into this same region of the PFC produce a delay-related improvement in working memory performance in young adult monkeys (Mao *et al.*, 1999), while infusions of the alpha-2 antagonist, yohimbine, impair performance (Li and Mei, 1994). Similar results are seen at the cellular level, where iontophoresis of an alpha-2 agonist onto PFC neurons in monkeys performing a spatial working memory task increases delay-related firing for the preferred direction, while application of yohimbine suppresses firing (Li *et al.*, 1999). Thus, in contrast to D1 receptor stimulation which suppresses 'noise', alpha-2 receptor stimulation in PFC strengthens working memory by increasing 'signals'. This effect is dramatically shown in Figure 14.2 (middle traces), whereby iontophoresis of yohimbine blocks endogenous NA actions at alpha-2 receptors and potently erodes delay-related firing.

Studies in monkeys indicate that many of the symptoms of ADHD can be recreated by blocking alpha-2 NA receptors in the PFC. In addition to the weakened working memory and delay-related activity described above, infusions of the alpha-2 antagonist, yohimbine, into PFC increase impulsivity as measured by errors of commission on a go/no-go task (Ma *et al.*, 2003). ADHD patients also show errors of commission on a go-no go task, and methylphenidate ameliorates these errors (Trommer *et al.*, 1991). Most recently, yohimbine infusions into the dorsolateral PFC of rhesus monkeys have been shown to induce locomotor hyperactivity, reminiscent of the increased activity found with PFC ablations (Ma *et al.*, 2005). These results in monkeys suggest that PFC dysfunction may contribute to the locomotor hyperactivity, as well as the impulsivity and poor attention regulation/working memory, which form the cardinal symptomology of ADHD. It is possible that some patients with genetic alterations of DBH have insufficient endogenous NA stimulation of alpha-2A-adrenoceptors, and thus exhibit behavioural changes similar to those observed with yohimbine infusions in PFC. This speculation is supported by recent findings that genetic alterations in DBH are associated with impaired sustained attention in ADHD (Bellgrove *et al.*, 2006).

(b)   Alpha-1-adrenoceptors

In contrast to the improvement observed with alpha-2A-adrenoceptor stimulation, high levels of NA release, e.g. during stress, impair PFC cognitive function via the engagement of lower affinity alpha-1-adrenoceptors (Birnbaum *et al.*, 1999). Thus, stimulation of alpha-1-adrenoceptors in PFC with infusions of agonists such as phenylephrine mimics the impairment observed with stress (Arnsten *et al.*, 1999; Mao *et al.*, 1999). At the cellular level, iontophoresis of phenylephrine markedly decreases delay-related PFC cell firing (Birnbaum *et al.*, 2004). This reduction in PFC neuronal response, and the impairment in working memory, are both mediated by increased phosphotidyl inositol intracellular signalling in PFC (Birnbaum *et al.*, 2004). Based on this research in animals, the alpha-1-adrenoceptor antagonist, prazosin is now being used to treat Post-Traumatic Stress Disorder (PTSD) (Raskind *et al.*, 2003). Prazosin may also be helpful in children with ADHD-like symptoms that are due to PTSD or other uncontrollable stressors.

(c) Beta-1-adrenoceptors

Very recent evidence suggests that NA can also impair PFC function through actions at beta-1-adrenoceptors (Ramos *et al.*, 2005). The beta-1 antagonist, betaxolol, improved spatial working memory in both rats and monkeys following intra-PFC infusion or systemic administration, respectively. However, the aged monkeys in this study developed serious pancreatic side effects, indicating that this agent may be inappropriate as a cognitive-enhancer. Betaxolol may improve PFC cognitive function by suppressing beta-1-adrenoceptor mediated production of cAMP.

In summary, moderate levels of catecholamines are essential to PFC cognitive function, while high levels impair these higher cognitive abilities.

14.6 MEDICATIONS USED TO TREAT ADHD MAY OPTIMISE CATECHOLAMINE MECHANISMS IN PFC

Most effective treatments for ADHD facilitate catecholamine transmission (see Solanto, Chapter 13, this volume). For example, methylphenidate (Ritalin) blocks DA and NA transporters, amphetamines (e.g. Adderall) block DA and NA transporters and increase catecholamine release, atomoxetine blocks NA transporters (which take up DA in PFC, thus effectively increasing the concentration of both catecholamines in the synapse and extrasynaptic space (Bymaster *et al.*, 2002)), and guanfacine mimics NA at alpha-2A adrenoceptors. Oral, low dose treatment with stimulants can enhance PFC cognitive function. For example, methylphenidate improves performance of PFC tasks in both normal college students (Mehta *et al.*, 2000) and in ADHD patients (Aron *et al.*, 2003). The alpha-2A agonist guanfacine has also been shown to improve performance of PFC tasks (Connors CPT, Stroop interference test) in children (Scahill *et al.*, 2001) and adults (Taylor & Russo, 2001) with ADHD.

Although much research has focused on the DA effects of stimulant medications, recent biochemical evidence from studies in rats indicates that low, oral doses of methylphenidate, that produce plasma levels similar to those observed in ADHD patients, have more effect on NA than on DA in subcortical structures (Kuczenski and Segal, 2002). Recent research in rats has shown that low, oral doses of methylphenidate increase both NA and DA release in the PFC (Berridge *et al.*, 2006) and improve spatial working memory performance (Arnsten and Dudley, 2005). These enhancing effects could be blocked by either a D1 or alpha-2 receptor antagonist, indicating that both DA and NA contribute to the PFC enhancing effects of methylphenidate in rats (Arnsten and Dudley, 2005).

Optimising catecholamine influences in PFC may ameliorate ADHD symptoms irrespective of the actual cause of the ADHD. It is logical that such treatments would be helpful if ADHD symptoms arose from inadequate catecholamine transmission in PFC, as suggested by the findings of Ernst *et al.* (Ernst *et al.*, 1998).

However, it is likely to be helpful under other conditions as well – e.g. slowed maturation of PFC circuits, smaller PFC volume – as long as there is sufficient PFC tissue available as a substrate for catecholamine actions.

14.7 SUMMARY

In summary, the PFC mediates executive abilities such as working memory, attention regulation, behavioural inhibition, planning and organisation that are impaired in patients with ADHD. Research in animals has shown that DA, via D1 receptors, and NA, via alpha-2A adrenoceptors, have critical beneficial actions in PFC. Many of the symptoms of ADHD, including impulsivity and hyperactivity, can be recreated by blocking NA alpha-2 receptors in the monkey PFC. The elucidation of catecholamine influences on PFC executive functioning provides a rational basis for understanding ADHD symptoms, and for the intelligent treatment of this disorder.

Acknowledgements

Research in this chapter was funded by PHS grants R37 AG06036, MH066393, and P50 MH068789.

14.8 REFERENCES

Anderson SW, Bechara A, Damasio H *et al.* (1999) Impairment of social and moral behavior related to early damage in human prefrontal cortex. *Nature Neuroscience* **2**: 1032–7.

Arnsten AFT, Cai JX, Goldman-Rakic PS (1988) The alpha-2 adrenergic agonist guanfacine improves memory in aged monkeys without sedative or hypotensive side effects. *J Neurosci* **8**: 4287–98.

Arnsten AFT, Dudley AG (2005) Methylphenidate improves prefrontal cortical cognitive function through a2 adrenoceptor and dopamine D1 receptor actions: relevance to therapeutic effects in Attention Deficit Hyperactivity Disorder. *Behavioral and Brain Functions (Biomed Central)* **1**: 2.

Arnsten AFT, Goldman-Rakic PS (1984) Selective prefrontal cortical projections to the region of the locus coeruleus and raphe nuclei in the rhesus monkey. *Brain Res* **306**: 9–18.

Arnsten AFT, Goldman-Rakic PS (1985) Alpha-2 adrenergic mechanisms in prefrontal cortex associated with cognitive decline in aged nonhuman primates. *Science* **230**: 1273–6.

Arnsten AFT, Goldman-Rakic PS (1998) Noise stress impairs prefrontal cortical cognitive function in monkeys: evidence for a hyperdopaminergic mechanism. *Arch Gen Psychiatry* **55**: 362–9.

Arnsten AFT, Li B-M (2005) Neurobiology of executive functions: catecholamine influences on prefrontal cortical function. *Biological Psychiatry* **57**: 1377–84.

Arnsten AFT, Mathew R, Ubriani R *et al.* (1999) Alpha-1 noradrenergic receptor stimulation impairs prefrontal cortical cognitive function. *Biol Psychiatry* **45**: 26–31.

Arnsten AFT, Steere JC, Hunt RD (1996) The contribution of alpha-2 noradrenergic mechanisms to prefrontal cortical cognitive function: potential significance to Attention Deficit Hyperactivity Disorder. *Arch Gen Psychiatry* **53**: 448–55.

Aron AR, Dowson JH, Sahakian BJ, Robbins TW (2003) Methylphenidate improves response inhibition in adults with Attention-Deficit/Hyperactivity Disorder. *Biol Psychiatry* **54**: 1465–8.

Aron AR, Robbins TW, Poldrack RA (2004) Inhibition and the right inferior frontal cortex. *Trends Cogn Sci* **8**: 170–7.

Avery RA, Franowicz JS, Studholme C *et al.* (2000) The alpha-2A-adenoceptor agonist, guanfacine, increases regional cerebral blood flow in dorsolateral prefrontal cortex of monkeys performing a spatial working memory task. *Neuropsychopharmacology* **23**: 240–9.

Barbas H, Medalla M, Alade O *et al.* (2005) Relationship of prefrontal connections to inhibitory systems in superior temporal areas in the rhesus monkey. *Cereb Cortex* Jan **5**; Epub ahead of print.

Barkley RA (1997) *ADHD and the Nature of Self-Control.* New York: Guilford Press.

Bartus RT, Levere TE (1977) Frontal decortication in rhesus monkeys: a test of the interference hypothesis. *Brain Res* **119**: 233–48.

Bates JF, Goldman-Rakic PS (1993) Prefrontal connections of medial motor areas in the rhesus monkey. *Journal of Comparative Neurology* **336**: 211–28.

Bedard AC, Ickowicz A, Logan GD *et al.* (2003) Selective inhibition in children with Attention-Deficit Hyperactivity Disorder off and on stimulant medication. *J Abnorm Child Psychol* **31**: 315–27.

Bellgrove MA, Domschke K, Hawi Z *et al.* (2005b) The methionine allele of the COMT polymorphism impairs prefrontal cognition in children and adolescents with ADHD. *Exp Brain Res* **163**: 352–60.

Bellgrove MA, Hawi Z, Gill M, Robertson IH (2006) The cognitive genetics of attention deficit hyperactivity disorder (ADHD): sustained attention as a candidate phenotype. *Cortex*, **42**: 838–45.

Bellgrove MA, Hawi Z, Lowe N *et al.* (2005a) DRD4 gene variants and sustained attention in attention deficit hyperactivity disorder (ADHD): effects of associated alleles at the VNTR and -521 SNP. *Am J Med Genet B Neuropsychiatr Genet* **136**: 81–6.

Berridge CW, Devilbiss DM, Andrzejewski ME *et al.* (2006) Methylphenidate preferentially increases catecholamine neurotransmission within the prefrontal cortex at low doses that enhance cognitive function. *Biological Psychiatry* **60**(10): 1111–20.

Birnbaum SG, Gobeske KT, Auerbach J *et al.* (1999) A role for norepinephrine in stress-induced cognitive deficits: Alpha-1-adrenoceptor mediation in prefrontal cortex. *Biol Psychiatry* **46**: 1266–74.

Birnbaum SB, Yuan P, Bloom A *et al.* (2004) Protein kinase C overactivity impairs prefrontal cortical regulation of working memory. *Science* **306**: 882–4.

Brown RM, Crane AM, Goldman PS (1979) Regional distribution of monoamines in the cerebral cortex and subcortical structures of the rhesus monkey: concentrations and in vivo synthesis rates. *Brain Res* **168**: 133–50.

Brozoski T, Brown RM, Rosvold HE, Goldman PS (1979) Cognitive deficit caused by regional depletion of dopamine in prefrontal cortex of rhesus monkey. *Science* **205**: 929–31.

Bunge SA, Kahn I, Wallis JD *et al.* (2003) Neural circuits subserving the retrieval and maintenance of abstract rules. *J Neurophysiology* **90**: 3419–28.

Bymaster FP, Katner JS, Nelson DL *et al.* (2002) Atomoxetine increases extracellular levels of norepinephrine and dopamine in prefrontal cortex of rat: a potential mechanism for efficacy in attention deficit/hyperactivity disorder. *Neuropsychopharmacology* **27**: 699–711.

Cai JX, Arnsten AFT (1997) Dose-dependent effects of the dopamine D1 receptor agonists A77636 or SKF81297 on spatial working memory in aged monkeys. *J Pharmacol Exp Ther* **282**: 1–7.

Cai JX, Ma Y, Xu L, Hu X (1993) Reserpine impairs spatial working memory performance in monkeys: reversal by the alpha-2 adrenergic agonist clonidine. *Brain Res* **614**: 191–6.

Carr DB, Sesack SR (2000) Projections from the rat prefrontal cortex to the ventral tegmental area: target specificity in the synaptic associations with mesoaccumbens and mesocortical neurons. *J Neurosci* **20**: 3864–73.

Casey BJ, Castellanos FX, Giedd JN *et al.* (1997) Implication of right frontostriatal circuitry in response inhibition and Attention-Deficit/Hyperactivity Disorder. *J Amer Acad Child Adolescent Psychiatry* **36**: 374–83.

Castellanos FX, Giedd JN, Marsh WL *et al.* (1996) Quantitative brain magnetic resonance imaging in attention deficit/hyperactivity disorder. *Arch Gen Psychiatry* **53**: 607–16.

Cavada C, Goldman-Rakic PS (1989) Posterior parietal cortex in rhesus monkey: II. Evidence for segregated corticocortical networks linking sensory and limbic areas with the frontal lobe. *J Comp Neurol* **287**: 422–45.

Chambers CD, Bellgrove MA, Stokes MG *et al.* (2006) Executive 'brake failure' following deactivation of human frontal lobe. *J Cognitive Neurosci*, **18**: 444–55.

Dias R, Roberts A, Robbins TW (1996) Dissociation in prefrontal cortex of affective and attentional shifts. *Nature* **380**: 69–72.

Druzin MY, Kurzina NP, Malinina EP, Kozlov AP (2000) The effects of local application of D2 selective dopaminergic drugs into the medial prefrontal cortex of rats in a delayed spatial choice task. *Behavioural Brain Res* **109**: 99–111.

Durston S, Fossella JA, Casey BJ *et al.* (2005) Differential effects of DRD4 and DAT1 genotype on fronto-striatal gray matter volumes in a sample of subjects with attention deficit hyperactivity disorder, their unaffected siblings, and controls. *Mol Psychiatry* **10**: 678–85.

Ernst M, Zametkin AJ, Matochik JA *et al.* (1998) DOPA decarboxylase activity in attention deficit disorder adults. A [fluorine-18]fluorodopa positron emission tomographic study. *J Neurosci* **18**: 5901–7.

Faraone SV, Perlis RH, Doyle AE *et al.* (2005) Molecular genetics of Attention-Deficit/Hyperactivity Disorder. *Biol Psychiatry* **57**: 1313–23.

Filipek PA, Semrud-Clikeman M, Steingard RJ *et al.* (1997) Volumetric MRI analysis comparing subjects having Attention-Deficit Hyperactivity Disorder with normal controls. *Neurology* **48**: 589–601.

Franowicz JS, Kessler L, Dailey-Borja CM *et al.* (2002) Mutation of the alpha2A-adrenoceptor impairs working memory performance and annuls cognitive enhancement by guanfacine. *J Neurosci* **22**: 8771–7.

French GM (1959) Locomotor effects of regional ablation of frontal cortex in rhesus monkeys. *J Comp Physiol Psychol* **52**: 18–24.

Funahashi S, Chafee MV, Goldman-Rakic PS (1993) Prefrontal neuronal activity in rhesus monkeys performing a delayed anti-saccade task. *Nature* **365**: 753–6.

Fuster JM (1973) Unit activity in prefrontal cortex during delayed response performance: neuronal correlates of transient memory. *J Neurophysiol* **36**: 61–78.

Fuster JM (1985) The prefrontal cortex, mediator of cross-temporal contingencies. *Human Neurobiol* **4**: 169–79.

Giedd JN, Blumenthal J, Molloy E, Castellanos FX (2001) Brain imaging of attention deficit/hyperactivity disorder. *Ann N Y Acad Sci* **931**: 33–49.

Godefroy O, Rousseaux M (1996) Divided and focused attention in patients with lesion of the prefrontal cortex. *Brain and Cognition* **30**: 155–74.

Goldman-Rakic PS (1987) Circuitry of the primate prefrontal cortex and the regulation of behavior by representational memory. In F Plum (ed.) *Handbook of Physiology: The*

Nervous System, Higher Functions of the Brain, pp. 373–417. Bethesda: American Physiological Society.

Goldman-Rakic PS (1995) Cellular basis of working memory. *Neuron* **14**: 477–85.

Granon S, Passetti F, Thomas KL *et al.* (2000) Enhanced and impaired attentional performance after infusion of D1 dopaminergic receptor agents into rat prefrontal cortex. *J Neurosci* **20**: 1208–15.

Gross CG (1963) Locomotor activity following lateral frontal lesions in rhesus monkeys. *J Comp Physiol Psychol* **56**: 232–6.

Gross CG, Weiskrantz L (1964) Some changes in behavior produced by lateral frontal lesions in the macaque. In JM Warren, K Akert (eds) *The Frontal Granular Cortex and Behavior* (pp. 74–101). New York: McGraw-Hill Book Co.

Henze DA, Gonzalez-Burgos GR, Urban NN *et al.* (2000) Dopamine increases excitability of pyramidal neurons in primate prefrontal cortex. *J Neurophysiol* **84**: 2799–809.

Hill DE, Yeo RA, Campbell RA *et al.* (2003) Magnetic resonance imaging correlates of Attention-Deficit/Hyperactivity Disorder in children. *Neuropsychology* **17**: 496–506.

Itami S, Uno H (2002) Orbitofrontal cortex dysfunction in Attention-Deficit Hyperactivity Disorder revealed by reversal and extinction tasks. *Neuroreport* **13**: 2453–7.

Iversen S, Mishkin M (1970) Perseverative interference in monkeys following selective lesions of the inferior prefrontal convexity. *Exp Brain Res* **11**: 376–86.

Jakala P, Riekkinen M, Sirvio J *et al.* (1999) Guanfacine, but not clonidine, improves planning and working memory performance in humans. *Neuropsychopharmacology* **20**: 460–70.

Jakala P, Sirvio J, Riekkinen M *et al.* (1999) Guanfacine and clonidine, alpha-2 agonists, improve paired associates learning, but not delayed matching to sample, in humans. *Neuropsychopharmacol* **20**: 119–30.

Jodo E, Chiang C, Aston-Jones G (1998) Potent excitatory influence of prefrontal cortex activity on noradrenergic locus coeruleus neurons. *Neuroscience* **83**: 63–79.

Kates WR, Frederikse M, Mostofsky SH *et al.* (2002) MRI parcellation of the frontal lobe in boys with attention deficit hyperactivity disorder or Tourette syndrome. *Psychiatry Res* **116**: 63–81.

Kennard MA, Spencer S, Fountain G (1941) Hyperactivity in monkeys following lesions of the frontal lobes. *J Neurophysiology* **4**: 512–24.

Kimberg DY, D'Esposito M, Farah MJ (1997) Effects of bromocriptine on human subjects depend on working memory capacity. *Neuroreport* **8**: 3581–5.

Knight RT, Scabini D, Woods DL (1989) Prefrontal cortex gating of auditory transmission in humans. *Brain Res* **504**: 338–42.

Konishi S, Nakajima K, Uchida I *et al.* (1999) Common inhibitory mechanism in human inferior prefrontal cortex revealed by event-related functional MRI. *Brain* **122**: 981–91.

Kuczenski R, Segal DS (2002) Exposure of adolescent rats to oral methylphenidate: preferential effects on extracellular norepinephrine and absence of sensitization and cross-sensitization to methamphetamine. *J Neurosci* **22**: 7264–71.

Li B-M, Mei Z-T (1994) Delayed response deficit induced by local injection of the alpha-2 adrenergic antagonist yohimbine into the dorsolateral prefrontal cortex in young adult monkeys. *Behav Neural Biol* **62**: 134–9.

Li B-M, Mao Z-M, Wang M, Mei Z-T (1999) Alpha-2 adrenergic modulation of prefrontal cortical neuronal activity related to spatial working memory in monkeys. *Neuropsychopharmacol* **21**: 601–10.

Ma C-L, Arnsten AFT, Li B-M (2005) Locomotor hyperactivity induced by blockade of prefrontal cortical alpha-2-adrenoceptors in monkeys. *Biological Psychiatry* **57**: 192–5.

Ma C-L, Qi X-L, Peng J-Y, Li B-M (2003) Selective deficit in no-go performance induced by blockade of prefrontal cortical alpha2-adrenoceptors in monkeys. *Neuroreport* **14**: 1013–16.

McLean A, Dowson J, Toone B *et al.* (2004) Characteristic neurocognitive profile associated with adult Attention-Deficit/Hyperactivity Disorder. *Psychol Med* **34**: 681–92.

Malmo RB (1942) Interference factors in delayed response in monkeys after removal of frontal lobes. *Neurophys* **5**: 295–308.

Manes F, Sahakian BJ, Clark L *et al.* (2002) Decision-making processes following damage to the prefrontal cortex. *Brain* **125**: 624–39.

Mao Z-M, Arnsten AFT, Li B-M (1999) Local infusion of alpha-1 adrenergic agonist into the prefrontal cortex impairs spatial working memory performance in monkeys. *Biol Psychiatry* **46**: 1259–65.

Mattay VS, Goldberg TE, Fera F *et al.* (2003) Catechol O-methyltransferase val158-met genotype and individual variation in the brain response to amphetamine. *Proc Natl Acad Sci USA* **100**: 6186–91.

Mehta MA, Owen AM, Sahakian BJ *et al.* (2000) Methylphenidate enhances working memory by modulating discrete frontal and parietal lobe regions in the human brain. *J Neuroscience* **20**: RC651–6.

Miller EK, Li L, Desimone R (1993) Activity of neurons in anterior inferior temporal cortex during a short-term memory task. *J Neuroscience* **13**: 1460–78.

Morita M, Nakahara K, Hayashi T (2004) A rapid presentation event-related functional magnetic resonance imaging study of response inhibition in macaque monkeys. *Neurosci Lett* **356**: 203–6.

Muir JL, Everitt BJ, Robbins TW (1996) The cerebral cortex of the rat and visual attentional function: dissociable effects of mediofrontal, cingulate, anterior dorsolateral, and parietal cortex lesions on a five-choice serial reaction time task. *Cerebral Cortex* **6**: 470–81.

Murphy BL, Arnsten AFT, Goldman-Rakic PS, Roth RH (1996) Increased dopamine turnover in the prefrontal cortex impairs spatial working memory performance in rats and monkeys. *Proc Nat Acad Sci USA* **93**: 1325–9.

Petrides M (1986) The effect of periarcuate lesions in the monkey on the performance of symmetrically and asymmetrically reinforced visual and auditory go, no-go tasks. *J Neuroscience* **6**: 2054–63.

Raine A, Lencz T, Bihrle S, Colletti P (2000) Reduced prefrontal gray matter volume and reduced autonomic activity in antisocial personality disorder. *Archives General Psychiatry* **57**: 119–27.

Rama P, Linnankoski I, Tanila H *et al.* (1996) Medetomidine, atipamezole, and guanfacine in delayed response performance of aged monkeys. *Pharmacol Biochem Behav* **54**: 1–7.

Ramos B, Birnbaum SB, Lindenmayer I *et al.* (2003) Dysregulation of protein kinase A signaling in the aged prefrontal cortex: new strategy for treating age-related cognitive decline. *Neuron* **40**: 835–45.

Ramos B, Colgan L, Nou E *et al.* (2005) The beta-1 adrenergic antagonist, betaxolol, improves working memory performance in rats and monkeys. *Biological Psychiatry* **58**: 894–900.

Ramos BP, Stark D, Verduzco L *et al.* (2006) Alpha 2A-adrenoreceptor stimulation improves prefrontal cortical regulation of behaviour through inhibition of cAMP signaling in aging animals. *Learning and Memory* **13**: 770–6.

Raskind MA, Peskind ER, Kanter ED *et al.* (2003) Prazosin reduces nightmares and other PTSD symptoms in combat veterans: a placebo-controlled study. *Am J Psychiatry* **160**: 371–3.

Rosenberg DR, Lewis DA (1994) Changes in the dopaminergic innervation of monkey preforntal cortex during late postnatal development: a tyrosine hydroxylase immunohistochemical study. *Biol Psychiatry* **36**: 272–7.

Rubia K, Smith AB, Brammer MJ, Taylor E (2003) Right inferior prefrontal cortex mediates response inhibition while mesial prefrontal cortex is responsible for error detection. *Neuroimage* **20**: 351–8.

Rubia K, Overmeyer S, Taylor E *et al.* (1999) Hypofrontality in Attention Deficit Hyperactivity Disorder during higher-order motor control: a study with functional MRI. *Am J Psychiatry* **156**: 891–6.

Sara SJ, Herve-Minvielle A (1995) Inhibitory influence of frontal cortex on locus coeruleus. *Proc Nat Acad Sci USA* **92**: 6032–6.

Sawaguchi T, Goldman-Rakic PS (1994) The role of D1-dopamine receptors in working memory: local injections of dopamine antagonists into the prefrontal cortex of rhesus monkeys performing an oculomotor delayed response task. *J Neurophysiol* **71**: 515–28.

Scahill L, Chappell PB, Kim YS *et al.* (2001) Guanfacine in the treatment of children with tic disorders and ADHD: A placebo-controlled study. *Amer J Psychiatry* **158**: 1067–74.

Selemon LD, Goldman-Rakic PS (1985) Longitudinal topography and interdigitation of corticostriatal projections in the rhesus monkey. *J Neurosci* **5**: 776–94.

Sowell ER, Thompson PM, Welcome SE *et al.* (2003) Cortical abnormalities in children and adolescents with Attention-Deficit Hyperactivity Disorder. *Lancet* **362**: 1699–1707.

Stuss DT, Gow CA, Hetherington CR (1992) 'No longer Gage': frontal lobe dysfunction and emotional changes. *J Consult Clin Psychol* **60**: 349–59.

Tanila H, Rama P, Carlson S (1996) The effects of prefrontal intracortical microinjections of an alpha-2 agonist, alpha-2 antagonist and lidocaine on the delayed alternation performance of aged rats. *Brain Res Bull* **40**: 117–19.

Taylor FB, Russo J (2001) Comparing guanfacine and dextroamphetamine for the treatment of adult Attention Deficit-Hyperactivity Disorder. *J Clin Psychopharm* **21**: 223–8.

Thompson-Schill SL, Jonides J, Marshuetz C *et al.* (2002) Effects of frontal lobe damage on interference effects in working memory. *Cogn Affect Behav Neurosci* **2**: 109–20.

Trommer BL, Hoeppner JA, Zecker SG (1991) The go-no-go test in attention deficit disorder is sensitive to methylphenidate. *J Child Neurol* **6**: 128–31.

Van Tol HHM, Bunzow JR, Guan H-C *et al.* (1991) Cloning of the gene for a human dopamine D4 receptor with high affinity for the antipsychotic clozapine. *Nature* **350**: 610–14.

Vijayraghavan S, Wang M, Williams GV, Arnsten AFT (2007) Dopamine D_1 receptor stimulation alters tuning of prefrontal cortical neurons during spatial working memory. *Nature Neuroscience* in press.

Wallis JD, Anderson KC, Miller EK (2001) Single neurons in prefrontal cortex encode abstract rules. *Nature* **411**: 953–6.

Wang M, Vijayraghavan S, Goldman-Rakic PS (2004) Selective D2 receptor actions on the functional circuitry of working memory. *Science* **303**: 853–6.

Wang X, Zhong P, Yan Z (2002) Dopamine D4 receptors modulate GABAergic signaling in pyramidal neurons of prefrontal cortex. *J Neuroscience* **22**: 9185–93.

Watanabe M (1986) Prefrontal unit activity during delayed conditional go/no-go discrimination in the monkey I. Relation to the stimulus. *Brain Res Rev* **382**: 1–14.

Wilkins AJ, Shallice T, McCarthy R (1987) Frontal lesions and sustained attention. *Neuropsychologia* **25**: 359–65.

Williams GV, Goldman-Rakic PS (1995) Blockade of dopamine D1 receptors enhances memory fields of prefrontal neurons in primate cerebral cortex. *Nature* **376**: 572–5.

Woods DL, Knight RT (19860) Electrophysiological evidence of increased distractability after dorsolateral prefrontal lesions. *Neurology* **36**: 212–16.

Yamaguchi S, Knight RT (1990) Gating of somatosensory input by human prefrontal cortex. *Brain Res* **521**: 281–8.

Yeo RA, Hill D, Campbell R *et al.* (2000) Developmental instability and working memory ability in children: a magnetic resonance spectroscopy investigation. *Dev Neuropsychol* **17**: 143–59.

Young CE, Yang CR (2004) Dopamine D1/D5 receptor modulates state-dependent switching of soma-dendritic Ca2+ potentials via differential protein kinase A and C activation in rat prefrontal cortical neurons. *J Neurosci* **24**: 8–23.

Zahrt J, Taylor JR, Mathew RG, Arnsten AFT (1997) Supranormal stimulation of dopamine D1 receptors in the rodent prefrontal cortex impairs spatial working memory performance. *J Neurosci* **17**: 8528–35.

15 Stimulant Response in ADHD and Comorbid Anxiety Disorder

ALASDAIR VANCE

Department of Paediatrics, University of Melbourne, Victoria, Australia

15.1 OVERVIEW

This chapter begins with an exploration of the definitions of attention deficit hyperactivity disorder (ADHD), anxiety disorder, comorbidity, the types of stimulant medication used and the understanding of treatment response versus non-response. Then a systematic, sequential overview follows of the key datasets that have informed our current understanding of the effect that comorbid anxiety disorder has on stimulant medication response in ADHD.

The chapter then selectively focuses on the phenomenology of ADHD, combined type (ADHD-CT) and anxiety symptoms in pre-pubertal children, in particular the further comorbid condition of dysthymic disorder that often accompanies anxiety disorder. A cognitive neuroscience construct, spatial working memory (SWM), with robust brain-behaviour relationships, is used to assess ADHD-CT and anxiety disorder and, separately, ADHD-CT and dysthymic disorder. Of particular interest is whether comorbid anxiety disorder differs from comorbid dysthymic disorder in its effects on SWM performance and the putative prefrontal cortical neural networks known to subserve this function.

The chapter ends with a summary of evidence suggesting that there is a subgroup of pre-pubertal children with ADHD-CT and anxiety disorder that have an attenuated response to stimulant medication. Further, this type of anxiety disorder may be driven by an underlying and unrecognised dysthymic disorder that is associated with SWM deficits independent of ADHD-CT. Future clinical and research implications are noted.

15.2 STIMULANT MEDICATION RESPONSE IN ADHD AND COMORBID ANXIETY DISORDER: INITIAL ISSUES REQUIRING CLARIFICATION

15.2.1 THE DEFINITION OF ADHD AND ANXIETY DISORDER

(a) ADHD

It is important to reflect on how recently the two major psychiatric disorder classificatory systems differed in their definition of ADHD. The International

Classification of Diseases, revision 9 (ICD-9) (World Health Organization, 1978) and *The Diagnostic and Statistical Manual of Mental Disorders*, 3rd edition (DSM-III) (American Psychiatric Association, 1980) led to reported point prevalence differences of as much as a factor of 20 (Taylor *et al.*, 1991). Recently, the development of the ICD-10 'hyperkinetic disorder' (World Health Organization, 1992) and DSM-IV 'Attention-Deficit/Hyperactivity Disorder' (American Psychiatric Association, 1994) diagnoses brought the World Health Organization and the American Psychiatric Association nosologies of childhood hyperactivity closer than they have been for almost three decades (Tripp *et al.*, 1999).

The major development is that both systems now agree that pervasiveness is a key diagnostic criterion, which means that the ADHD symptoms must occur in two or more settings. It is also clear that the absence of the symptoms under clinic observation does not necessarily exclude the diagnosis if, for example, the symptoms still exist in less structured environments (Tripp & Luk, 1997). However, there are still major differences between the two systems. DSM-IV (American Psychiatric Association, 1994) recognises three subtypes of ADHD: a predominantly inattentive type, a combined type, and a predominantly hyperactive-impulsive type, while ICD-10 (World Health Organization, 1992) requires both inattentive and hyperactive-impulsive behaviour to make the diagnosis of hyperkinetic disorder. As a result, DSM-IV (American Psychiatric Association, 1994) criteria identify a broader group of children than those identified by ICD-10 (World Health Organization, 1992; Tripp *et al.*, 1999). The validity of the predominantly hyperactive-impulsive group has not been established (Lahey *et al.*, 1994) while the predominantly inattentive group has been shown to be valid and is associated with higher levels of 'anxiety' (usually dimensionally defined by parent and/or child report), 'sluggish' cognitive tempo and a better prognosis than ADHD-CT (Cantwell & Baker, 1992). However, the DSM-IV (American Psychiatric Association, 1994) construct of ADHD-CT is now so similar to that of ICD-10 (World Health Organization, 1992) hyperkinetic disorder that meaningful comparison of studies using both diagnoses can occur (Vance & Luk, 2000).

There are additional reasons why it is important to limit the scope of this chapter to ADHD-CT. First, ADHD-CT in primary school-age children is a common presenting condition in public child mental health services (Jensen *et al.*, 1997; Zarin *et al.*, 1998). Anxiety is a frequent comorbid condition in these primary school-age children with ADHD-CT (Biederman *et al.*, 1991; Eiraldi *et al.*, 1997; Pliszka, 1998), yet there has been relatively little systematic research of the nature of this comorbid 'anxiety' (Jensen *et al.*, 1997; Pliszka, 1998; Willcutt *et al.*, 1999), while comorbid oppositional defiant disorder (ODD)/conduct disorder (CD) and language-based learning disorders have been more thoroughly investigated (Jensen *et al.*, 1997; Pliszka, 1998; Willcutt *et al.*, 1999). This relative paucity of research is incongruent with the average 25% prevalence of ADHD-CT and 'anxiety' in clinical and epidemiological samples (Biederman *et al.*, 1991).

Secondly, ADHD-CT is associated with increased rates of comorbid 'anxiety' compared to matched healthy control participants and this 'anxiety' does not appear to decrease with increasing age (Woolston *et al.*, 1989; Brown *et al.*, 1991; Walker *et al.*, 1991). In particular, increased rates of separation anxiety disorder have been reported with ADHD-CT, compared to ADHD inattentive type, and control subjects (Cantwell & Baker, 1992). Kashani and Orvaschel (1990) reported that adolescents aged 17 years with ADHD-CT (DSM-III-R equivalent) and 'anxiety' had significantly more ODD behaviours than those with ADHD-CT without 'anxiety'. This association was not apparent when children aged 8 years were assessed. Therefore, there is emerging evidence for a subgroup of primary school-age children with ADHD-CT and 'anxiety' who continue to experience ADHD-CT, ODD/CD symptoms, and anxiety symptoms into adolescence. This subgroup is different from the well-known association of primary school-age children with ADHD, inattentive type and 'anxiety' with decreased comorbidity rates of ODD/CD symptoms and a better prognosis in terms of educational achievement, occupational record, and established interpersonal relationships (Jensen et al., 1997; Pliszka, 1998).

(b) Anxiety disorder

Both the child and the parent report have been noted to be important in determining comorbid 'anxiety' associated with ADHD-CT. Significant clinical correlates, such as levels of self-confidence and impairments in activities of daily living, may be associated with the child report alone (Tannock, 1994). In addition, only approximately 50% of children with self-reported 'anxiety' have also been reported with 'anxiety' by their parents (Pliszka, 1992). Recently, March et al. (2000) have noted that the parent report of a given child's anxiety disorder(s) from the MTA study may represent this child's 'negative affectivity and associated behavioural problems' rather than 'neurotic anxiety suffered by children with anxiety disorders alone'. These findings are consistent with the known usefulness of the child's self-report of 'anxiety' in identifying internalising symptoms (Bird et al., 1992; Ialongo et al., 1994; Jensen et al., 1999).

Now, 'anxiety' is a heterogeneous construct, with many different forms (Silverman & Treffers, 2001) and hence defining which anxiety disorders will be studied is an essential initial step. From a categorical perspective, generalised anxiety disorder, separation anxiety disorder, social phobia and specific phobia are the four most common types of anxiety disorder in children (Silverman & Treffers, 2001). Historically, they all arose from what March et al. (2000) have termed 'true neurotic anxiety' and therefore can be considered as a group. They are readily distinguished from obsessive compulsive disorder, which has different, well-described fronto-striatal deficits (Silverman & Treffers, 2001) that underpin its greater-than-chance association with ADHD-CT, which also has well-described, but different, fronto-striatal deficits (Barkley, 1997) (see also Chapter 10). The remaining anxiety disorders (Panic Disorder, Agoraphobia, Post Traumatic Stress Disorder) are low prevalence and also have potentially different antecedents than the other anxiety disorders, noted above.

To date, ADHD-CT has been associated with greater-than-chance levels of generalised anxiety disorder, separation anxiety disorder, social phobia and specific phobia, consistent with their high point prevalence. Recently, we extended this finding by showing that after two years there was no decrease in the parent report but a significant decrease in the child report of these anxiety disorders, which supported the view that parent and child reported 'anxiety' may reflect both similar and different underlying processes (March et al., 2000; Vance et al., 2002).

15.2.2   ADHD-CT, ANXIETY DISORDER AND DYSTHYMIC DISORDER

Further, we investigated the association of anxiety disorders with ADHD-CT and dysthymic disorder because dysthymic disorder is often poorly recognised yet strongly associated with anxiety disorders. Dysthymic disorder in children is a mood disorder characterised by chronically depressed and/or irritable mood for more days than not, over a period of 1 or more years, with no remission longer than 2 months (American Psychiatric Association, 1994). The clinical validity of early-onset dysthymic disorder as a diagnostic construct has been established (Klein *et al.*, 1988) and high rates of co-occurring externalising disorders have been reported (Ferro *et al.*, 1994). Early clinical and epidemiological studies in children and adolescents found rates of co-occurrence with ADHD-CT from 0% to 57.1%, and with ODD/ CD from 21% to 83% (Angold & Costello, 1993). According to Kovacs *et al.* (1994), in a group of 55 children with dysthymic disorder, ADHD (predominately ADHD-CT) was the most prevalent pre-existing condition (24%). Dysthymic disorder lasts almost 2.5 years longer in the presence of a co-occurring externalising disorder (Kovacs *et al.*, 1997). Epidemiological studies report anxiety disorders in 30–75% of children and adolescents with dysthymic disorder (Angold & Costello, 1993), while Kovacs *et al.* (1994) report anxiety disorders at a rate of 40% in a clinical dysthymic disorder sample. The co-occurrence of depressive and anxiety disorders in children and adolescents has been associated with an increase in severity of 'depression' (Mitchell *et al.*, 1988), 'anxiety' (Strauss *et al.*, 1988), and both syndromes (Bernstein, 1991). We (Sanders *et al.*, 2005) found that generalised anxiety disorder and separation anxiety disorder were increased in the dysthymic disorder groups, whether ADHD-CT was present or not, consistent with emerging evidence that dysthymic disorder and 'anxiety' may represent a different phenotypic expression of a common underlying aetiological process, while the explanation for co-occurrence of ADHD-CT and anxiety disorders remains unclear.

15.2.3   THE BIOLOGICAL CORRELATES OF ADHD-CT AND ANXIETY

To date, there is some evidence of children with ADHD-CT and 'anxiety' being associated with decreased verbal working memory (Tannock *et al.*, 1995), increased noradrenergic hyper-reactivity (Urman *et al.*, 1995) and increased noradrenergic and adrenergic tonic activity (Pliszka *et al.*, 1994) compared to ADHD-CT alone. We extended these findings by demonstrating that child-reported 'anxiety' alone was associated with the postural blood pressure marker of autonomic instability in children with ADHD-CT (Vance *et al.*, 2002). Again, the studies vary in the rigour of the definition of both ADHD-CT and 'anxiety', particularly the exclusion of dysthymic disorder.

15.2.4   SUMMARY

ADHD-CT is important because it is similar to the ICD-10 construct of hyperkinetic disorder and has a greater-than-chance association with 'anxiety' that appears to not decrease with increasing age. Parent and child reported 'anxiety' are important because they reflect both similar and different underlying processes. Generalised anxiety disorder, separation anxiety disorder, social phobia and specific phobia are the most common forms of 'anxiety' in children and share antecedents, thus reflecting true neurotic anxiety (March *et al.*, 2000). Dysthymic disorder is associated with this 'true neurotic anxiety' but is often not recognised. Finally, ADHD-CT and 'anxiety' may be associated with impaired working memory and increased autonomic instability, although the existing studies have not carefully differentiated 'true neurotic anxiety' from that associated with dysthymic disorder.

15.2.5   THE IMPLICATIONS OF COMORBIDITY

Caron and Rutter (1991) suggested that comorbidity can imply a number of types of association with different implications for stimulant medication response. These include the chance co-occurrence of two separate disorders, a primary-secondary relationship between them, common risk factor(s) including genetic liability and a greater-than-chance hybrid where the unique elements of both disorders are expressed. It may be possible to differentiate between these associations using different methods. For example, at a phenomenological level, a hybrid comorbid relationship may be evident (see the description of our dysthymic disorder, 'anxiety' and ADHD-CT findings above), while at a molecular genetic level, a particular candidate gene polymorphism (for example, the 10-repeat allele of a variable number tandem repeat (VNTR) in the 3' untranslated region of the dopamine transporter) may be a common risk factor (Vance, 2004). Nevertheless, a careful study of comorbidity in ADHD-CT will be informative as our clinical phenotyping, cognitive neuroscience constructs and candidate gene polymorphisms become more specific. To date, a hybrid model of comorbidity best fits the existing data on ADHD-CT and 'anxiety'. This implies that stimulant medication may have a differential response in this comorbid group, or on closer examination, a subset of this comorbid group.

15.2.6   THE TYPE OF STIMULANT MEDICATION

There has been much debate about the clinical effects of dexamphetamine (short-acting) and methylphenidate, given their manifestly different mechanisms of action (see Chapter 13). However, qualitative and quantitative differences in positive and adverse effects have been negligible (Elia *et al.*, 1991; Vance & Luk, 2000), despite a few effects that seem to be due to the faster comparative excretion rate of methylphenidate (60–120 minutes; Pelham *et al.*, 1999). Therefore, short-term stimulant medication response in ADHD-CT and 'anxiety' can include treatment with either of these commonly used agents.

15.2.7   THE APPROACH TO DETERMINING STIMULANT MEDICATION TREATMENT RESPONSE VERSUS NON-RESPONSE

Given its clinical and research implications, a surprisingly limited range of approaches have been used to determine stimulant medication treatment response versus non-response in children with ADHD-CT. The majority have been 'one-tailed', as the data reported suggest that the measurement of a true worsening of response rather than a mere failure to improve sufficiently is rare (Mollica *et al.*, 2004). The simplest technique (Taylor *et al.*, 1987) involves a one-tailed statistical rule with an arbitrary 50% reduction in ADHD-CT symptoms due to drug effect, defined by the following equation:

$$\frac{\text{placebo score} - \text{drug score}}{\text{baseline score}} = 100$$

or a decrease of one standard deviation in drug score relative to baseline and placebo scores (Pliszka, 1989). The ADHD-CT symptoms are determined by clinical judgement and/or parent and teacher behavioural ratings (Aman & Turbott, 1991).

A more sophisticated two-tailed statistical rule is the 'reliability change index' (Jacobson & Truax, 1991), which is defined by (a) the change predicted by regression in the placebo condition being subtracted from that in the drug condition and (b) this change being significant beyond chance level when the mean of the dependent change variable is closer to the mean of the normal population than the mean of the ADHD-CT population. That is, the post- versus pre-treatment difference divided by the standard error is larger than 1.96 (Buitelaar *et al.*, 1995). Multiple regression techniques have also been used more recently (MTA Cooperative Group, 1999a, 1999b; March *et al.*, 2000). However, all these approaches are further limited by the need for control data from a healthy comparison group measured over the same time interval as the active treatment condition.

Recently, we developed a two-tailed repeated measures statistical rule that could be applied at single case or group levels to assess change in children with ADHD-CT (Mollica *et al.*, 2004). To avoid an inflated Type I error, we used Ingraham and Aitken's (1996) change rule requiring improvement greater than 1.50–1.65 standard deviations ($p < 0.05$ one-tailed) to retain a Type I error rate at less than 0.05, depending on the number of test measures (1.5: <10 measures; 1.65: 10 measures). Given the known increased intra-individual variability of performance in children with ADHD-CT, we did not use the reliability change index denominator of the standard deviation of difference scores (Rasmussen *et al.*, 2001). Rather, we submitted data from the multiple baseline conditions to a series of one-way Analyses of Variance (ANOVA) in order to determine the mean square residual (MSr) for a given measure. The square root of the MSr was then calculated to determine the within-subjects standard deviation (WSD; Bland & Altman, 1996). Performance for the average baseline condition was then subtracted from performance for the active treatment condition. This difference was expressed as a ratio of the WSD to determine the treatment response ratio. For the cognitive and behavioural measures, ratios greater than 1.65 ($p < 0.05$ one-tailed) were classified as a significant improvement, while those less than −1.65 ($p < 0.05$ one-tailed) were a significant deterioration. The advantages of such an approach are that (1) it can be used reliably at a single case level and at a group level, (2) it can be used to reliably assess change in cognitive and behavioural measures and (3) it can allow true as opposed to partial treatment response and non-response to be determined. This latter advantage may specifically aid ongoing research into ADHD-CT and 'anxiety' by improving the homogeneity of these response/non-response groups, thereby increasing the chance of determining true threshold effects with cognitive (for example, visuospatial working memory) and environmental cue (for example, parental interpersonal sensitivity) dependent measures.

15.3 STIMULANT MEDICATION RESPONSE IN ADHD AND COMORBID ANXIETY DISORDER: FURTHER SPECIFIC ISSUES REQUIRING CLARIFICATION

The consideration of stimulant medication response in children with ADHD and anxiety disorder requires a number of key issues to be examined. First, ADHD-CT is the most robust construct of ADHD and the careful categorical and dimensional examination of ADHD-CT and anxiety disorder requires multi-informant perspectives. Further, anxiety disorder should be defined by the 'true neurotic anxiety' disorders (March et al., 2000) of generalised anxiety disorder, separation anxiety disorder, social phobia and specific phobia. Dysthymic disorder is important to consider because it is associated with this 'true neurotic anxiety' but is often not recognised. The cognitive neuroscience construct of working memory may aid the differentiation of ADHD-CT and anxiety disorder. Secondly, a hybrid model of comorbidity best describes ADHD-CT and anxiety disorder and allows this comorbid group, or on closer examination, a subset of this comorbid group to have a differential response to stimulant medication. Thirdly, either dexamphetamine or methylphenidate may be used as short-term stimulant medication treatment in ADHD-CT and anxiety disorder, as their treatment response and side effect profiles are equivalent. Finally, a reliable two-tailed metric should be used to determine true responder and non-responder status, as this will maximise the homogeneity of these groups which will aid future investigation of putative threshold effects with cognitive and environmental cue dependent measures.

15.3.1 STIMULANT MEDICATION RESPONSE IN ADHD AND COMORBID ANXIETY DISORDER: AN OVERVIEW

Taylor et al. (1987) completed a three-week randomised controlled trial of methylphenidate in boys with ADHD-CT (DSM-III equivalent; American Psychiatric Association, 1980) and demonstrated that a good response to stimulant medication was predicted by the absence of overt emotional disorder, defined by semi-structured parent interview. The strengths of the study were the rigorous definition of response (see earlier review) and the test of the influence of overt emotional disorder on the medication-placebo difference. The primary weakness was the use of the parent alone to define overt emotional disorder, rather than the parent and child self-report, and the over-inclusiveness of the emotional disorder dimension that fails to differentiate anxiety from depressive disorder phenomena. Two years later, Pliszka (1989) published data that further focused this association, suggesting that the child self-report of comorbid generalised anxiety disorder (DSM-III-R equivalent; American Psychiatric Association, 1987) mediated 'significantly poorer response' to stimulant medication in children with ADHD-CT (DSM-III-R equivalent; American Psychiatric Association, 1987). These four week, randomised placebo controlled trial data also extended the association to girls (<10% of the sample). However, 'anxiety' was defined by clinical interview alone with no clear exclusion of depressive disorders, such as dysthymic disorder. Du Paul *et al.* (1994) provided further evidence for the association between broadly defined anxiety and depressive phenomena (internalising symptoms) and a 'significantly less positive response' to stimulant medication, after a one week randomised placebo controlled trial, although responder status was not defined. Buitelaar *et al.* (1995) replicated Taylor *et al.*'s (1987) findings in a sample of 6–13-year-old children (90% male) using a more careful two-tailed statistical rule – the reliability change index (Jacobson & Truax, 1991) – to define responder and non-responder status. They reported that low rates of parent reported child 'anxiety' predicted stimulant medication responder status during a four-week randomised placebo controlled trial. Again, they used a broad dimensional measure of 'anxiety' that did not differentiate anxiety from depressive disorder phenomena.

Two influential studies then challenged this emergent association between anxiety and depressive phenomena and diminished response to stimulant medication in children with ADHD. Firstly, Diamond *et al.* (1999) completed a four-month ran-domised placebo-controlled trial of stimulant medication in 6–12-year-old children (>70% male). They reported 'no differential response of the 'ADHD and anxiety' versus the 'ADHD without anxiety' groups with respect to core ADHD symptom reduction and side effect profiles'. Importantly, they defined their ADHD-CT (DSM-III-R equivalent; American Psychiatric Association, 1987) group categori-cally and dimensionally and excluded any clinically impairing depressive disorder (dysthymic and major depressive disorders) symptoms. This is the only extant study to have so rigorously defined their ADHD-CT with and without 'anxiety' groups. It suggests that the replicated diminished response to stimulant medication may be only associated with 'anxiety', when this 'anxiety' is associated with clinically impair-ing depressive disorder (dysthymic and major depressive disorders) symptoms.

Secondly, the Multimodal Treatment Study of Children with ADHD (MTA) (MTA Cooperative Group, 1999a, 1999b; March *et al.*, 2000) reported data from 7–9-year-old children (80% male) with ADHD-CT and found that comorbid anxiety disorder did not alter the response of the ADHD-CT group as a whole to stimulant medication over the 14 months of the randomised clinical trial. However, the behav-ioural treatment group had a significantly better outcome than the community care group and did not differ statistically from the medication alone and combined medication and behavioural treatment groups. Also, the combined medication and behavioural treatment group used significant less stimulant medication than the medication alone group. These data certainly support the effectiveness of stimulant medication in the longer-term treatment of children with ADHD-CT, but their interpretation with respect to stimulant medication response and ADHD-CT and comorbid 'anxiety' needs to be circumspect for the following reasons: (1) ADHD-CT was defined by categorical parent report alone and therefore reflects a broader phenotype of the disorder compared to the more rigorously defined ADHD-CT groups in the studies above; (2) 'anxiety' was defined broadly as part of the inter-nalising dimension from the parent and teacher report and more specifically from the child self-report, with only the parent report significantly moderating the better outcome with behavioural treatment and (3) the lack of a placebo condition meant that the effect of 'anxiety' on the medication–placebo difference could not be tested, unlike the replicated findings from the studies above (Taylor, 1999). Hence, the potential helpful and/or harmful roles of this type of 'anxiety' remains unclear with respect to (a) compliance with the medication treatment intervention and (b) the effect of the non-specific interpersonal aspects of the receiving and monitoring of stimulant medication (Taylor, 1999).

In summary, two clear messages emerge from the above studies. First, a broader phenotype of 'anxiety' is associated with a diminished response to stimulant medication in children with ADHD-CT. Secondly, this replicated attenuated response to stimulant medication may be only associated with 'anxiety', when this 'anxiety' is associated with clinically impairing depressive disorder (dysthymic and major depressive disorders) symptoms.

15.4   STIMULANT MEDICATION RESPONSE IN ADHD AND COMORBID ANXIETY DISORDER: TWO PHENOMENOLOGICAL STUDIES

The following two studies evince how comorbid anxiety and dysthymic disorder can have a differential influence on the spatial working memory ability of children with ADHD-CT. Study 1 and study 2 investigate the association of ADHD-CT with true 'neurotic' anxiety (March et al., 2000) and with dysthymic disorder, respectively. A cognitive neuroscience construct with robust brain-behaviour relationships, spatial working memory (SWM) (Barnett et al., 2001) is used to investigate ADHD-CT and anxiety disorder and, separately, ADHD-CT and dysthymic disorder. Of particular interest is whether comorbid anxiety disorder differs from comorbid dysthymic disorder in its effects on SWM performance and the putative prefrontal cortical neural networks known to subserve this measure. The extant literature suggests that comorbid anxiety disorder should have an independent impairing effect on SWM (Tannock et al., 1995), while to our knowledge there is no literature that supports a directional hypothesis for SWM function in dysthymic disorder, separate from major depressive disorder.

SWM is one of the most commonly investigated neuropsychological constructs of executive function (Goldman-Rakic, 1995) (see also Chapter 12). As this construct is largely non-verbal, models of the relationship between SWM and prefrontal cortical function are constrained by studies of single neuronal firing rates in alert primates (Goldman-Rakic, 1995), studies of behaviour following focal prefrontal cortical lesions in adult humans (Owen et al., 1993) and studies of patterns of regional cerebral blood flow in healthy humans performing SWM tests (D'Esposito et al., 1995). Furthermore, the experimental paradigms used in these studies can be applied unchanged to the study of executive function in young children where limited linguistic skills often preclude the assessment of other executive processes. For example, a recent study found that children as young as 4 years could perform a SWM test although test performance was correlated positively with age (Luciana & Nelson, 1998). In addition, the effect of amphetamine agonists and antagonists on models of SWM has been investigated at both the neuronal (Arnsten &

Goldman-Rakic, 1990) and behavioural level (Barnett *et al.*, 2001). The results from these studies therefore provide a sound theoretical framework within which the interaction between disorder, cognition and stimulant medication can be interpreted. Finally, recent studies have begun to decompose performance on SWM tasks and determine the extent to which different components are affected in different neuropsychiatric disorders (Pantelis *et al.*, 1997). We have extended the parsing of SWM processes in children with ADHD-CT and reported SWM deficits mediated by decreased spatial span that are ameliorated by stimulant medication (Barnett *et al.*, 2001). However, we have not separately examined ADHD-CT with anxiety disorder and ADHD-CT without anxiety disorder.

15.4.1   STUDY 1: ADHD-CT ALONE, ADHD-CT AND ANXIETY DISORDERS AND ANXIETY DISORDERS ALONE GROUPS

Seventy-five children aged from 7 to 12 years were identified in specialised clinics for ADHD and anxiety disorders in the Western region of metropolitan Melbourne, Australia, from a sample of 200 children consecutively referred. Twenty-five children had ADHD-CT alone (DSM-IV criteria; American Psychiatric Association, 1994), 25 had ADHD-CT and anxiety disorder(s) (N = 25), and 25 children had anxiety disorder(s) alone. ADHD-CT was defined through a semi-structured clinical interview (Silverman & Albano, 1996) with the child's parent(s) and by the parent and/ or teacher report of the subscale scores of the core symptom domains of ADHD-CT being greater than 1.5 standard deviations above the mean for a given child's age and gender (Conners, 1997). Anxiety disorders were defined as generalised anxiety disorder, separation anxiety disorder, social phobia and specific phobia (DSM-IV criteria; American Psychiatric Association, 1994), diagnosed through a semi-structured clinical interview with the child's parent(s) (Silverman & Albano, 1996) and by the parent and/or child report of the total anxiety scores being greater than 1.5 standard deviations above the mean for a given child's age and gender (Achenbach & Edelbrock, 1983; Reynolds & Richmond, 1985). The children were all stimulant, anxiolytic and antidepressant medication naïve and were consecutively referred for assessment because they were not responding to usual clinical psychological management approaches. The children met the inclusion criteria of living in a family home (and not in an institution) and attending normal primary schools. All had Intelligence Quotients above 70 (Wechsler, 1991) and none had identifiable learning disorders (Wilkinson, 1993), overt neurological disease, endocrine disease, depressive disorders, conduct disorder or psychotic symptoms. There was no refusal and parent(s) gave informed consent. Ethics committee approval was obtained for the study.

All groups were matched for age, gender, verbal/performance/fullscale IQ, spelling, arithmetic and social adversity (see Table 15.1).

(a)   Measures

Anxiety Disorders Interview Schedule for Children (A-DISC) (Silverman & Albano, 1996), Conners' Global Index (CGI) (Conners, 1997), Child Behaviour Checklist (CBCL) (Achenbach & Edelbrock, 1983), Revised Children's Manifest Anxiety

Table 15.1. Subject characteristics: ADHD-CT alone, ADHD-CT and anxiety disorders (ADs) and anxiety disorders alone groups

	1 ADHD-CT N = 25	2 ADHD-CT + ADs N = 25	3 ADs N = 25	F (2,72)	p
Age	111.88 (26.58)	109.92 (28.11)	116.25 (19.96)	0.17	0.84
Gender (M,F)	23,2	23,2	18,7	6.18#	0.06
CGI	21.86* (5.73)	21.69* (5.81)	7.04 (6.36)	41.54	**** 1 = 2 > 3
CBCL int	60.81 (8.98)	71.32* (10.72)	65.71* (7.51)	25.05	**** 2 = 3 > 1
RCMAS	53.97 (11.68)	65.24* (10.77)	66.13* (11.15)	21.63	**** 2 = 3 > 1
VIQ	94.62 (14.55)	94.13 (18.59)	96.33 (4.16)	0.03	0.98
PIQ	98.76 (14.80)	97.5 (16.44)	105.00 (12.65)	0.32	0.73
FSIQ	95.24 (13.43)	94.08 (14.70)	103.68 (8.25)	1.58	0.22
Spell	87.58 (17.02)	85.78 (11.91)	94.8 (17.31)	0.77	0.47
Arith	80.48 (19.44)	88.17 (19.75)	98.40 (7.02)	2.14	0.13
SAS	7.58 (1.77)	7.77 (1.90)	6.88 (1.15)	1.53	0.22

CGI = Conners' Global Index (Conners); CBCL int = CBCL internalising subscale T score; RCMAS = Revised Children's Manifest Anxiety Scale total anxiety T score; VIQ/PIQ/FSIQ = verbal/performance/fullscale IQ (WISC-3); Spell = Spelling standard score (WRAT-3); Arith = Arithmetic standard score (WRAT-3); SAS = social adversity status (PACS); # 3×2 χ^2; **** $p < 0.0005$; * = in clinical range.

Scale (R-CMAS) (Reynolds & Richmond, 1985), 3rd edition of the Wechsler Intelligence Scale for Children (WISC-3) (Wechsler, 1991), 3rd edition of the Wide Range Achievement Test (WRAT-3) (Wilkinson, 1993), Parental Account of Childhood Symptoms (PACS) (Taylor *et al.*, 1986) and the Cambridge Neuropsychological Test Automated Battery (CANTAB) are used to assess spatial working memory (SWM) and spatial memory span (SS) (Kempton *et al.*, 1999). The computerised tests are presented on a high resolution IBM monitor with a touch sensitive screen. All children reported previous experience with computers. The SWM task is a self-ordered searching task that measures working memory for spatial stimuli and requires the subject to use mnemonic information to work towards a goal. Subjects are required to search through boxes that appear on the screen with the aim of finding the 'blue tokens' hidden inside. The key instruction was that once a token had been taken out of a box, that box would not be used again to hide a token. After two practice trials with two boxes, there were four test trials with each of two, three, four, six and eight boxes. Returning to an 'empty' box already opened and a token removed on a previous search constituted a 'forgetting' or 'between search' error (BSE). A strategy score was calculated from subject's performance on the six and eight box levels, to reflect how often a searching sequence was initiated from the same box during a trial. Higher strategy scores represent low use of strategy (that is, many sequences beginning with a different box), and lower scores represent efficient use of strategy (that is, many sequences starting with the same box).

The Spatial Span task is a computerised version of the Corsi block tapping test (Kempton *et al.*, 1999) that assesses spatial short-term memory capacity. This task measures the ability to remember a sequence of squares presented on the screen. After an incorrect attempt at choosing the squares in sequence, the next trial remains at the same difficulty level. The spatial short-term memory span was calculated at the highest level at which the subject successfully remembered at least one sequence of boxes.

(b) Statistical analysis

Performance on the (1) BSE variable and (2) the Strategy and Spatial Span variables was compared between groups using respective (1) repeated measures two-factor design which included a between-subjects factor (group) and a within subjects factor (difficulty level) and (2) one-way analysis of variance. To protect against experiment-wise error, Type I error rates were set at $p < 0.01$. Where the omnibus F was significant, the *post-hoc* Studentized Newman-Keuls (SNK) procedure ($p < 0.01$) was conducted to determine the source of this significance. To investigate the contribution of spatial span and strategy to the number of between search errors (BSE), the inter-correlations between BSE and span and between BSE and strategy for all levels of difficulty were investigated for each group using Pearson product moment correlation coefficients (Kempton *et al.*, 1999). Finally, although the groups were matched for age, the relationship between age and BSE was investigated for each group by plotting and comparing the linear regressions of BSE and age for each group.

(c) Results

There was a significant effect of condition (BSE) (Wilks' $\lambda = 0.12$, $F(4, 69) = 82.87$, $p < 0.0005$) and group ($F(2, 72) = 6.01$, $p = 0.005$, partial $\eta^2 = 0.88$) with the ADHD-CT groups associated with increased BSE, whether 'anxiety' was present or not (Figure 15.1). Also, there was a significant interaction between BSE and group (Wilks' $\lambda = 0.65$, $F(8,138) = 2.73$, $p = 0.01$, partial $\eta^2 = 0.20$). Both Spatial Span ($F(2, 72) = 6.34$, $p = 0.003$) and Strategy ($F(2, 72) = 6.77$, $p = 0.002$) differed between the groups, with the ADHD-CT groups, whether 'anxiety' was present or not, having a worse Spatial Span and Strategy (Table 15.2).

The pattern of intercorrelations between BSE, Spatial Span and Strategy was qualitatively similar for the ADHD-CT alone (BSE: Spatial Span $r = -0.52$, $p = 0.02$; BSE: Strategy $r = 0.46$, $p = 0.04$), ADHD-CT and 'anxiety' (BSE: Spatial Span $r = -0.75$, $p = <0.0005$; BSE: Strategy $r = 0.60$, $p = 0.002$) and 'anxiety' alone groups (BSE: Spatial Span $r = -0.62$, $p = 0.001$; BSE: Strategy $r = 0.85$, $p = <0.0005$). For all groups, there was a medium–large strength positive correlation of strategy with BSE and negative correlation of spatial span with BSE.

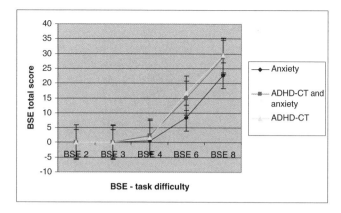

Figure 15.1. Between Search Errors (BSE) by task difficulty for ADHD-CT alone, ADHD-CT and anxiety and Anxiety alone groups

Table 15.2. Group performance on the spatial working memory task and the spatial span task: ADHD-CT alone, ADHD-CT and anxiety disorders (ADs) and anxiety disorders alone groups

	1 ADHD-CT N = 25	2 ADHD-CT + ADs N = 25	3 ADs N = 25	F (2,72)	p
Spatial working memory					
Total between-search errors	47.52 (14.24)	52.00 (21.54)	30.68 (14.68)	10.38	<0.0005 1 = 2 > 3
Strategy score	35.95 (5.56)	36.71 (4.14)	31.56 (5.95)	6.77	0.002 1 = 2 > 3
Spatial Span	5.00 (1.61)	4.15 (1.65)	6.16 (1.14)	6.34	0.003 1 = 2 < 3

BSE decreased in an age-independent linear fashion for all the groups, with anxiety disorder(s) alone associated with significantly less BSE than the ADHD-CT groups, whether anxiety was present or not (Figure 15.2).

(d) Discussion

These data suggest that, irrespective of whether comorbid anxiety was present or not, children with ADHD-CT have poorer spatial working memory, strategy use and spatial span than children with anxiety disorder. Further, children with ADHD-CT, with or without anxiety disorder, performed the spatial working memory task in the same way. As age increased, spatial working memory ability improved in all groups, although ADHD-CT had a worse spatial working memory performance,

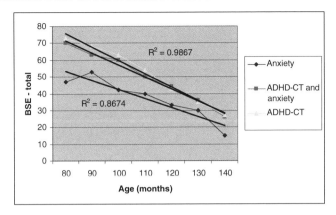

Figure 15.2. Linear regressions of BSE and age for ADHD-CT alone, ADHD-CT and anxiety and Anxiety alone groups

whether anxiety disorder was present or not. Our prior findings (Kempton *et al.*, 1999; Barnett *et al.*, 2001) of a significantly worse SWM performance in children with ADHD-CT compared to a healthy participant control group are consistent with the findings from the current study. Clearly we cannot comment on whether SWM performance in the anxiety disorder alone group is within normal limits in the absence of a healthy participant control group.

Spatial working memory relies on the integrity of the dorsolateral prefrontal cortex (DLPFC) in non-human primates and human beings (Goldman-Rakic, 1997), the spatial span component subserved by the ventrolateral prefrontal cortex (Brodmann Area (BA) 47) and the organising, executing and monitoring component associated with the mid-DLPFC (BA 46,9) (Owen *et al.*, 1996). Hence, the above findings suggest age-independent dysfunction involving these prefrontal cortical structures in children with ADHD-CT, whether 'anxiety' is present or not.

15.4.2 STUDY 2: ADHD-CT ALONE, ADHD-CT AND DYSTHYMIC DISORDER AND DYSTHYMIC DISORDER ALONE GROUPS

Seventy-five children aged from 7 to 12 years were identified in specialised clinics for ADHD and dysthymic disorders in the Western region of metropolitan Melbourne, Australia. Twenty-five children had ADHD-CT alone, 25 had ADHD-CT and dysthymic disorder, and 25 children had dysthymic disorder alone. ADHD-CT was defined as in Study 1. Dysthymic disorder was defined through a semi-structured clinical interview with the child's parent(s) and/or the child (Silverman & Albano, 1996) and by the parent (Achenbach & Edelbrock, 1983) and/or child report (Lang & Tisher, 1983) of the total depression scores being greater than 1.5 standard deviations above the mean for a given child's age and gender. The children were all stimulant, anxiolytic and antidepressant medication naïve and were consecutively referred for assessment because they were not responding to usual clinical psychological management approaches. The children met the inclusion criteria of living in a family home (and not in an institution) and attending normal primary schools. All had Intelligence Quotients above 70 (Wechsler, 1991)

Table 15.3. Subject characteristics: ADHD-CT alone, ADHD-CT and dysthymic disorder (DD) and dysthymic disorder alone groups

	1 ADHD-CT N = 25	2 ADHD-CT + DD N = 25	3 DD N = 25	F (2,72)	p
Age	111.88 (26.58)	114.16 (21.99)	127.8 (20.10)	0.63	0.24
Gender (M,F)	23,2	19,6	16,9	6.72#	0.06
CGI	21.86* (5.73)	23.54* (5.71)	11.48 (6.16)	32.37	**** 1 = 2 > 3
CBCL int	60.81 (8.98)	74.53* (11.44)	68.92* (7.83)	29.88	**** 2 = 3 > 1
CDS	3.44 (0.82)	8.17* (1.68)	8.49* (1.85)	24.65	**** 2 = 3 > 1
VIQ	94.62 (14.55)	91.29 (16.47)	99.92 (15.29)	1.84	0.18
PIQ	98.76 (14.80)	94.46 (16.01)	98.54 (15.44)	0.58	0.57
FSIQ	95.24 (13.43)	90.92 (15.86)	99.92 (14.99)	2.20	0.12
Spell	87.58 (17.02)	91.87 (13.03)	97.24 (18.42)	1.93	0.15
Arith	80.48 (19.44)	87.75 (17.14)	86.68 (12.18)	1.27	0.29
SAS	7.58 (1.77)	7.81 (1.92)	6.78 (1.35)	1.61	0.19

CGI = Conners' Global Index (Conners); CBCL int = CBCL internalising subscale T score; CDS = Children's Depression Scale decile score; VIQ/PIQ/FSIQ = verbal/performance/fullscale IQ (WISC-3); Spell = Spelling standard score (WRAT-3); Arith = Arithmetic standard score (WRAT-3); SAS = social adversity status (PACS); # 3×2 χ^2; ****$p < 0.0005$; * = in clinical range.

and none had learning disorders (Wilkinson, 1993), overt neurological disease, endocrine disease, conduct disorder, major depressive disorder or psychotic symptoms. There was no refusal and parent(s) gave informed consent. Ethics committee approval was obtained for the study.

All groups were compared for age, gender, verbal/performance/fullscale IQ, spelling, arithmetic and social adversity (see Table 15.3).

(a) Measures (additional to Study 1)

Children's Depression Scale (CDS) (Lang & Tisher, 1983).

(b) Statistical analysis

The Statistical Analysis is similar to Study 1.

(c) Results

There was a significant effect of condition (BSE) (Wilks' $\lambda = 0.08$, $F(4, 69) = 116.65$, $p < 0.0005$) while both group ($F(2, 72) = 1.56$, $p = 0.22$, partial $\eta^2 = 0.07$) and the interaction between BSE and group (Wilks' $\lambda = 0.77$, $F(8, 138) = 1.37$, $p = 0.22$, partial $\eta^2 = 0.12$) were non-significant. Both Spatial Span ($F(2, 72) = 1.68$, $p = 0.21$) and Strategy ($F(2, 72) = 0.83$, $p = 0.44$) did not differ between the groups: in short, the ADHD-CT and dysthymic disorder groups were unable to be differentiated (Table 15.4, Figure 15.3).

The pattern of intercorrelations between BSE, Spatial Span and Strategy was qualitatively different for the ADHD-CT alone (BSE: Spatial Span $r = -0.52$, $p = 0.02$; BSE: Strategy $r = 0.46$, $p = 0.04$), ADHD-CT and dysthymic disorder (BSE: Spatial Span $r = -0.56$, $p = 0.004$; BSE: Strategy $r = 0.23$, $p = 0.28$) and dysthymic disorder alone groups (BSE: Spatial Span $r = -0.36$, $p = 0.08$; BSE: Strategy $r = 0.73$, $p = <0.0005$). The dysthymic disorder alone group had a large positive correlation with strategy alone compared to the ADHD-CT alone group's medium–large positive correlation of strategy with BSE and negative correlation of spatial span with BSE. The ADHD-CT and dysthymic disorder group had a medium-large negative correlation with spatial span alone.

Table 15.4. Group performance on the spatial working memory task and the spatial span task: ADHD-CT alone, ADHD-CT and dysthymic disorder (DD) and anxiety disorders alone groups

	1 ADHD-CT N = 25	2 ADHD-CT + DD N = 25	3 DD N = 25	F (2,72)	p
Spatial working memory					
Total between-search errors	47.52 (14.24)	52.79 (18.05)	44.28 (17.47)	1.60	0.21
Strategy score	35.95 (5.56)	37.46 (2.95)	36.28 (3.85)	0.83	0.44
Spatial Span	5.00 (1.61)	4.58 (1.67)	5.36 (1.15)	1.68	0.20

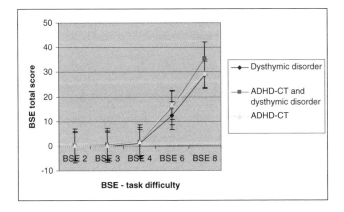

Figure 15.3. Between Search Errors (BSE) by task difficulty for ADHD-CT alone, ADHD-CT and dysthymic disorder and Dysthymic disorder alone groups

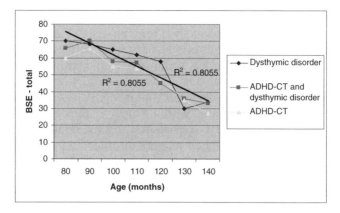

Figure 15.4. Linear Regressions of BSE and age for ADHD-CT alone, ADHD-CT and dysthymic disorder and Dysthymic disorder alone groups

BSE decreased in an age-independent linear fashion for all the groups, with dysthymic disorder alone associated with similar BSE to the ADHD-CT groups, with and without dysthymic disorder (Figure 15.4).

(d) Discussion

These data suggest that children with ADHD-CT and dysthymic disorder are indistinguishable on their spatial working memory performance but do differ in their approach to completing the spatial working memory task. The ADHD-CT group relies on spatial span and strategy while the dysthymic disorder group depends on strategy alone. As age increased, spatial working memory ability improved in all groups. As mentioned earlier in the *Discussion* of Study 1, the ADHD-CT data in this study are consistent with our previous studies (Barnett *et al.*, 1991; Kempton *et al.*, 1999). Given the absence of a healthy participant control group, we are unable to determine whether the spatial working memory performance in the dysthymic disorder group is truly aberrant. Nevertheless, the putative age-independent dysfunction involving the dorsolateral and ventrolateral prefrontal cortical structures (Owen *et al.*, 1996; Goldman-Rakic & Selemon, 1997) in children with ADHD-CT is indistinguishable from dysthymic disorder.

15.5   STIMULANT MEDICATION RESPONSE IN ADHD AND COMORBID ANXIETY DISORDER: A SUMMARY, RESEARCH AND CLINICAL IMPLICATIONS

15.5.1   SUMMARY

ADHD-CT is the focus of this chapter, despite the known association between ADHD, inattentive type and increased levels of anxiety, because ADHD-CT is the more robust construct, from an ICD-10 (World Health Organization, 1992) and DSM-IV (American Psychiatric Association, 1994) perspective. The importance of careful categorical and dimensional examination of ADHD-CT and anxiety disorder requiring multi-informant perspectives is emphasised. Further, specification of anxiety disorders, as the 'true neurotic anxiety' disorders of generalised anxiety disorder, separation anxiety disorder, social phobia and specific phobia, is recommended. Next, dysthymic disorder is necessary to consider because it is associated with these 'true neurotic anxiety disorders' but is often not recognised. The cognitive neuroscience construct of spatial working memory may aid the differentiation of ADHD-CT and anxiety disorder, consistent with a hybrid model of comorbidity, which best describes ADHD-CT and anxiety disorder and allows this comorbid group, or on closer examination, a subset of this comorbid group to have a differential response to stimulant medication. Dexamphetamine or methylphenidate provide equivalent short-term stimulant medication treatment response and side effect profiles in ADHD-CT and anxiety disorder. Finally, a reliable two-tailed metric should be used to determine true responder and non-responder status, as this will maximise the homogeneity of these groups which will facilitate future investigation of putative threshold effects with cognitive neuroscience (for example, visuospatial working memory) and environmental cue (for example, parental interpersonal sensitivity) measures.

A subsequent review of the existing literature emphasised that a broader phenotype of 'anxiety' is associated with a diminished response to stimulant medication in children with ADHD-CT: in particular, this replicated attenuated response to stimulant medication may be only associated with 'anxiety', when this 'anxiety' is associated with clinically impairing depressive disorder (dysthymic and major depressive disorders) symptoms. The empirical studies presented provide additional support for these different types of 'anxiety'; pure anxiety disorder does not add to the neurobiological vulnerability of prefrontal cortical dysfunction evident in children with ADHD-CT. In contrast, dysthymic disorder, which is often comorbid with anxiety disorder, is indistinguishable from ADHD-CT with respect to our robust cognitive neuroscience measure of prefrontal cortical dysfunction.

15.5.2   RESEARCH IMPLICATIONS

The finding of additional prefrontal cortical dysfunction associated with comorbid dysthymic disorder with ADHD-CT opens up a new area of enquiry. For example, dysthymic disorder may be associated with relatively more 'orbitofrontal' neural circuit dysfunction while ADHD-CT is associated with relatively more 'dorsolateral prefrontal' cortical dysfunction, using Alexander, DeLong and Strick's (1986) model. Further, such a neurobiological vulnerability may help explain why a subgroup of children with ADHD-CT and 'anxiety' (dysthymic disorder-related) have a diminished response to stimulant medication. The obvious next systematic step, given these data, is a randomised, placebo-controlled trial of stimulant medication in children with ADHD-CT alone, ADHD-CT and anxiety disorder and ADHD-CT and dysthymic disorder, as defined in the above studies. A two-tailed metric should then be applied to determine treatment responders and non-responders. Then, a range of the above independent variables can be altered to extend these findings to examine ADHD, inattentive type, other anxiety disorders such as obsessive compulsive disorder, panic disorder and post-traumatic stress disorder, major depressive disorder and the developmental stage, for example pre- and post-puberty to determine whether the findings are developmental stage independent or not. Subsequently, true threshold effects (Levy, 2004) may be investigated to illuminate aetiological pathways and suggest innovative medication and psychological treatments.

15.5.3 CLINICAL IMPLICATIONS

The recognition that comorbid 'anxiety', if associated with dysthymic disorder, carries additional prefrontal cortical neurobiological vulnerability to that of ADHD-CT is important. More careful parsing of such key comorbidities associated with ADHD-CT and their specific, targeted treatment are needed. Further, novel synergistic psychological and medication approaches need to be developed.

15.6 REFERENCES

Achenbach RM, Edelbrock CS (1983) *Manual for the Child Behaviour Checklist and Behaviour Profile*. Burlington: University of Vermont.

Alexander GE, DeLong M, Strick PE (1986) Parallel organization of functionally segregated circuits linking basal ganglia and cortex. *Annual Review of Neurosciences* **9**: 357–81.

Aman MG, Turbott SH (1991) Prediction of clinical response in children taking methylphenidate. *Journal of Autism and Developmental Disorders* **21**: 211–28.

American Psychiatric Association (1980) *Diagnostic and Statistical Manual of Mental Disorders*, 3rd edn (DSM-III). American Psychiatric Association, Washington, DC.

American Psychiatric Association (1987) *Diagnostic and Statistical Manual of Mental Disorders*, 3rd edn, revised (DSM-III-R). American Psychiatric Association, Washington, DC.

American Psychiatric Association (1994) *Diagnostic and Statistical Manual of Mental Disorders*, 4th edn (DSM-IV). American Psychiatric Association, Washington, DC.

Angold A, Costello EJ (1993) Depressive comorbidity in children and adolescents: empirical, theoretical, and methodological issues. *American Journal of Psychiatry* **150**: 1779–91.

Arnsten AFT, Goldman-Rakic PS (1990) Analysis of alpha-2 adrenergic agonist effects on the delayed nonmatch-to-sample performance of aged rhesus monkeys. *Neurobiology of Aging* **11**: 583–90.

Barkley RA (1997) Behavioural inhibition, sustained attention, and executive functions: constructing a unified theory of ADHD. *Psychological Bulletin* **121**: 65–94.

Barnett R, Vance ALA, Maruff P *et al.* (2001) Abnormal executive function in attention deficit hyperactivity disorder: the effect of stimulant medication and age on spatial working memory. *Psychological Medicine* **31**: 1107–15.

Bernstein GA (1991) Comorbidity and severity of anxiety and depressive disorders in a clinic sample. *Journal of the American Academy of Child and Adolescent Psychiatry* **30**: 43–50.

Biederman J, Newcorn J, Sprich S (1991) Comorbidity of attention deficit hyperactivity disorder with conduct, depressive, anxiety, and other disorders. *American Journal of Psychiatry* **148**: 564–77.

Bird HR, Gould MS, Staghezza B (1992) Aggregating data from multiple informants in child psychiatry epidemiological research. *Journal of the American Academy of Child and Adolescent Psychiatry* **31**: 78–85.

Bland JM, Altman DG (1996) Statistical notes: measurement error. *British Medical Journal* **313**: 744.

Brown RT, Maden-Swain A, Baldwin K (1991) Gender differences in a clinic-referred sample of attention deficit disordered children. *Child Psychiatry and Human Development* **22**: 111–28.

Buitelaar JK, Van-der-Gaag RJ, Swaab-Barneveld H, Kuiper M (1995) The prediction of clinical response to methylphenidate in children with attention deficit hyperactivity disorder. *Journal of the American Academy of Child and Adolescent Psychiatry* **34**: 1025–32.

Cantwell DP, Baker L (1992) Attention Deficit Disorder with and without hyperactivity: a review and comparison of matched groups. *Journal of the American Academy of Child and Adolescent Psychiatry* **31**: 432–8.

Caron C, Rutter M (1991) Comorbidity in child psychopathology: concepts, issues and research strategies. *Journal of Child Psychology and Psychiatry* **32**: 1063–80.

Conners CK (1997) *Conners' Rating Scales*, revised. New York: Multi-Health Systems.

d'Esposito M, Detre JA, Alsop DC *et al.* (1995) The neural basis of the central executive system of working memory. *Nature* **378**: 279–81.

Diamond IR, Tannock R, Schachar RJ (1999) Response to methylphenidate in children with ADHD and comorbid anxiety. *Journal of the American Academy of Child and Adolescent Psychiatry* **38**: 402–9.

DuPaul GJ, Barkley RA, McMurray MB (1994) Response of children with ADHD to methylphenidate: interaction with internalizing symptoms. *Journal of the American Academy of Child and Adolescent Psychiatry* **33**: 894–903.

Eiraldi RB, Power TJ, Nezu CM (1997) Patterns of comorbidity associated with subtypes of Attention-Deficit/Hyperactivity Disorder among 6- to 12-year-old children. *Journal of the American Academy of Child and Adolescent Psychiatry* **36**: 503–14.

Elia J, Borcherding BG, Rapoport JL, Keysor CS (1991) Methylphenidate and dextroamphetamine treatments of hyperactivity: are there true nonresponders? *Psychiatry Research* **36**: 141–55.

Ferro T, Carlson GA, Grayson P, Klein DN (1994) Depressive disorders: distinctions in children. *Journal of the American Academy of Child and Adolescent Psychiatry* **33**: 664–70.

Goldman-Rakic PS (1995) Architecture of the prefrontal cortex and the central executive. In J Grafman, KJ Holoyoak, F Boller (eds) *The Structure and Function of the Prefrontal Cortex, Vol. 769. Annals of the New York Academy of Sciences*. New York: New York Academy of Sciences, 71–83.

Goldman-Rakic PS, Selemon LD (1997) Functional and anatomical aspects of prefrontal pathology in schizophrenia. *Schizophrenia Bulletin* **23**: 437–58.

Ialongo N, Edelsohn G, Wertharner-Larsson L *et al.* (1994) The significance of self-reported anxious symptoms in first grade children. *Journal of Abnormal Child Psychology* **22**: 441–55.

Ingraham LJ, Aitken CB (1996) An empirical approach to determining criteria for abnormality in test batteries with multiple measures. *Neuropsychology* **10**: 120–4.

Jacobson NS, Truax P (1991) Clinical significance: a statistical approach to defining meaningful change in psychotherapy research. *Journal of Consulting and Clinical Psychology* **59**: 12–19.

Jensen PS, Martin D, Cantwell DP (1997) Comorbidity of ADHD: implications for research, practice and DSM-V. *Journal of the American Academy of Child and Adolescent Psychiatry* **36**: 1065–79.

Jensen PS, Rubio-Stipec M, Canino G *et al.* (1999) Parent and child contributions to diagnosis of mental disorder: are both informants always necessary? *Journal of the American Academy of Child and Adolescent Psychiatry* **38**: 1569–79.

Kashani JH, Orvaschel H (1990) A community study of anxiety in children and adolescents. *American Journal of Psychiatry* **147**: 313–18.

Kempton S, Vance ALA, Maruff P *et al.* (1999) Executive function and Attention Deficit Hyperactivity Disorder: stimulant medication and better executive function performance in children. *Psychological Medicine* **29**: 527–38.

Klein DN, Taylor EB, Dickstein S, Harding D (1988) The early-late onset distinction in DSM-III-R Dysthymia. *Journal of Affective Disorders* **14**: 25–33.

Kovacs M, Akiskal HS, Gatsonis C, Parrone PL (1994) Childhood-onset dysthymic disorder: clinical features and prospective naturalistic outcome. *Archives of General Psychiatry* **51**: 365–74.

Kovacs M, Obrosky DS, Gatsonis C, Richards C (1997) First-episode major depressive and dysthymic disorder in childhood: clinical and sociodemographic factors in recovery. *Journal of the American Academy of Child and Adolescent Psychiatry* **36**: 777–84.

Lahey BB, Applegate B, Barkley RA *et al.* (1994) DSM-IV Field trials for Attention Deficit Hyperactivity Disorder in children and adolescents. *American Journal of Psychiatry* **151**: 1673–85.

Lang M, Tisher M (1983) *Children's Depression Scale*. Melbourne: ACER.

Levy F (2004) Synaptic gating and ADHD: a biological theory of comorbidity and anxiety. *Neuropsychopharmacology* **29**: 1589–96.

Luciana M, Nelson CA (1998) The functional emergence of prefrontally guided working memory systems in four-to-eight-year-old children. *Neuropsychologia* **36**: 273–93.

March JS, Swanson JM, Arnold LE *et al.* (2000) Anxiety as a predictor and outcome variable in the multimodal treatment study of children with ADHD (MTA). *Journal of Abnormal Child Psychology* **28**: 527–41.

Mitchell J, McCauley E, Burke PM, Moss SJ (1988) Phenomenology of depression in children and adolescents. *Journal of the American Academy of Child and Adolescent Psychiatry* **27**: 12–20.

Mollica C, Maruff P, Vance A (2004) The development of a statistical approach to classifying treatment response using cognitive performance in individual children with ADHD. *Human Psychopharmacology* **19**: 1–12.

MTA Cooperative Group (1999a) A 14-month randomized clinical trial of treatment strategies for attention deficit hyperactivity disorder. *Archives of General Psychiatry* **56**: 1073–86.

MTA Cooperative Group (1999b) Moderators and mediators of treatment response for children with ADHD. *Archives of General Psychiatry* **56**: 1088–96.

Owen AM, Evans AC, Petrides M (1996) Evidence for a two-stage model of spatial working memory processing within the lateral frontal cortex: a positron emission tomography study. *Cerebral Cortex* **6**: 31–8.

Owen AM, Roberts AC, Hodges JR *et al.* (1993) Contrasting mechanisms of attentional set-shiftng in patients with frontal lobe damage or Parkinson's Disease. *Brain* **116**: 1159–75.

Pantelis C, Barnes TRE, Nelson HE *et al.* (1997) Frontal-striatal cognitive deficits in patients with chronic schizophrenia. *Brain* **120**: 1823–43.

Pelham WE, Gnagy EM, Chronis AM *et al.* (1999) A comparison of Adderall to methylphenidate in children with ADHD. *Pediatrics* **104**: 1300–11.

Pliszka SR (1989) Effect of anxiety on cognition, behaviour and stimulant response in ADHD. *Journal of the American Academy of Child and Adolescent Psychiatry* **28**: 882–7.

Pliszka SR (1992) Comorbidity of Attention Deficit Hyperactivity Disorder and Overanxious Disorder. *Journal of the American Academy of Child and Adolescent Psychiatry* **31**: 197–203.

Pliszka SR (1998) Comorbidity of Attention-Deficit/Hyperactivity Disorder with psychiatric disorder: an overview. *Journal of Clinical Psychiatry* **59**: 50–8.

Pliszka SR, Maas JW, Javors MA, Rogeness GA (1994) Urinary catecholamines in Attention Deficit Hyperactivity Disorder with and without comorbid anxiety. *Journal of the American Academy of Child and Adolescent Psychiatry* **33**: 1165–73.

Rasmussen LS, Larsen K, Houx P *et al.* (2001) The assessment of postoperative cognitive function. *Acta Anaesthesiolica Scandanavia* **45**: 275–89.

Reynolds CR, Richmond BO (1985) *Revised Children's Manifest Anxiety Scale: Manual.* Los Angeles, CA: Western Psychological Services.

Sanders M, Arduca Y, Karamitsios M *et al.* (2005) Characteristics of anxiety disorders in medication naïve, clinically referred children with attention deficit hyperactivity disorder, combined type (ADHD-CT) and dysthymic disorder (DD). *Australian and New Zealand Journal of Psychiatry* **39**: 359–65.

Silverman WK, Albano AM (1996) *Anxiety Disorders Interview Schedule for DSM-IV.* Texas: Graywind.

Silverman WK, Treffers PDA (eds) (2001) *Anxiety Disorders in Children and Adolescents.* Cambridge: Cambridge University Press.

Strauss CC, Last CG, Hersen M, Kazdin AE (1988) Association between anxiety and depression in children and adolescents with anxiety disorder. *Journal of Abnormal Child Psychology* **16**: 57–68.

Tannock R (1994) Attention deficit disorders and anxiety disorders. In TE Brown (ed.) *Subtypes of Attention Deficit Disorders in Children, Adolescents and Adults.* New York: American Psychiatric Press, pp. 125–70.

Tannock R, Ickowicz A, Schachar R (1995) Differential effects of methylphenidate on working memory in ADHD children with and without comorbid anxiety. *Journal of the American Academy of Child and Adolescent Psychiatry* **34**: 886–96.

Taylor E (1999) Development of clinical services for ADHD. *Archives of General Psychiatry* **56**: 1097–9.

Taylor E, Schachar R, Thorley G, Wieselberg M (1986) Separation of hyperactivity and anti-social conduct in British child psychiatric patients. *British Journal of Psychiatry* **149**: 760–7.

Taylor E, Schachar R, Thorley G *et al.* (1987) Which boys respond to stimulant medication? A controlled trial of methylphenidate in boys with disruptive behaviour. *Psychological Medicine* **17**: 121–43.

Taylor E, Sandberg S, Thorley G, Giles S (1991) *The Epidemiology of Childhood Hyperactivity.* Institute of Psychiatry Maudsley Monograph. London: Oxford University Press.

Tripp G, Luk ESL (1997) The identification of pervasive hyperactivity: is clinic observation necessary? *Journal of Child Psychology and Psychiatry* **38**: 219–34.

Tripp G, Luk SL, Schaughency EA, Singh R (1999) DSM-IV and ICD-10: a comparison of the correlates of ADHD and Hyperkinetic Disorder. *Journal of the American Academy of Child and Adolescent Psychiatry* **38**: 156–64.

Urman R, Ickowicz A, Fulford P, Tannock R (1995) An exaggerated cardiovascular response to methylphenidate in ADHD chidren with anxiety. *Journal of Child and Adolescent Psychopharmacology* **5**: 29–37.

Vance ALA, Luk ESL (2000) Heart of the matter review: Attention Deficit Hyperactivity Disorder: progress and controversies. *Australian and New Zealand Journal of Psychiatry* **34**: 719–30.

Vance ALA, Barnett R, Costin J *et al.* (2002) Characteristics of parent- and child-reported anxiety in psychostimulant medication naïve, clinically referred children with attention deficit hyperactivity disorder, combined type (ADHD-CT). *Australian and New Zealand Journal of Psychiatry* **36**: 234–9.

Vance ALA, Costin J, Maruff P (2002) Attention Deficit Hyperactivity Disorder, combined type (ADHD-CT): differences in blood pressure (BP) due to posture and the child report of anxiety. *European Child and Adolescent Psychiatry* **11**: 24–30.

Vance ALA (2004) The molecular genetics of depressive disorders pre- and post-puberty: where to from here? *Proceedings of the Contemporary Challenges in Clinical Psychiatry (CCCP) Conference.* Sydney: ProCom.

Walker JL, Lahey BB, Russo ME *et al.* (1991) Anxiety, inhibition and conduct disorder in children: 1. Relations to social impairment. *Journal of the American Academy of Child and Adolescent Psychiatry* **30**: 187–91.

Wechsler D (1991) *Wechsler Intelligence Scale for Children*, 3rd edition. Texas: The Psychological Co-operation.

Wilkinson GS (1993) *Wide Range Achievement Test-Revised.* Wilmington, DE: Jastak Assessment Systems.

Willcutt EG, Pennington BF, Chabildas NA *et al.* (1999) Psychiatric comorbidity associated with DSM-IV ADHD in a nonreferred sample of twins. *Journal of the American Academy of Child and Adolescent Psychiatry* **38**: 1355–62.

Woolston JL, Rosenthal SL, Riddle MA *et al.* (1989) Childhood comorbidity of anxiety/affective disorders and behaviour disorders. *Journal of the American Academy of Child and Adolescent Psychiatry* **28**: 707–13.

World Health Organization (1978) *Mental Disorders: Glossary and Guide to their Classification in Accordance with the Ninth Revision of the International Classification of Diseases.* Geneva: World Health Organization.

World Health Organization (1992) *ICD-10: The ICD-10 Classification of Mental and Behavioural Disorders: Clinical Descriptions and Diagnostic Guidelines.* Geneva: World Health Organization.

Zarin DA, Suarez AP, Pincus HA *et al.* (1998) Clinical and treatment characteristics of children with Attention-Deficit/Hyperactivity Disorder in psychiatric practice. *Journal of the American Academy of Child and Adolescent Psychiatry* **37**: 1262–70.

16 Avenues for Pharmacogenetic Research in ADHD

EDWINA BARRY[1], **ZIARIH HAWI**[1] **AND AIVEEN KIRLEY**[2]
1. School of Medicine and Health Sciences, Trinity College Dublin, Ireland;
2. Cluan Mhuire Service, Blackrock, Co. Dublin, Ireland

16.1 OVERVIEW

Pharmacogenetics refers to the study of hereditary variation in drug response (Weber, 1997). Optimal response to stimulant medication (methylphenidate or dextroamphetamine) is in the range of 70% for any one stimulant (Greenhill *et al.*, 1999). However the extent of response varies considerably with some children responding favourably to one stimulant but not another (Elia *et al.*, 1991). Factors accounting for this variability are poorly understood and there are no reliable methods to decide in advance which medication or dosage regimens will best suit an individual patient. Among other factors, individual genetic variation is thought to have a central role in determining the extent of response to an administered medication. Recent pharmacogenetic studies attempt to explore the relationship between genes and medication response. However, those genes involved in ADHD aetiology are not necessarily the same genes that influence medication response. While ADHD as a disorder may have large heritability values in the order of 75% (Biederman & Faraone, 2005), the measurement of pharmacogenetic traits is much more difficult and thus the heritability of medication response in ADHD is currently unknown. Pharmacogenetic studies aspire to lead to the development of personalised prescription regimens that improve symptom control and medication tolerance and ultimately produce improved compliance. In this chapter, recent advances in ADHD pharmacogenetics are discussed.

16.2 WHY IS PHARMACOGENETICS IMPORTANT IN ADHD?

Approximately 75% of ADHD children treated with a stimulant show favourable responses (Green, 1995) and among those positive responses, a spectrum of response exists. Some children respond extremely well while others benefit to a lesser extent. In addition, some children with ADHD respond favourably to one stimulant drug but less so or even not at all to another stimulant drug. In a double-blind crossover study, Elia *et al.* (1991) compared methylphenidate, dextroamphetamine and placebo in treating 48 males with a history of ADHD symptoms. The authors reported that 38 (79%) of subjects responded to methylphenidate and 42 (88%)

Handbook of Attention Deficit Hyperactivity Disorder. Edited by M. Fitzgerald, M. Bellgrove and M. Gill.
© 2007 John Wiley & Sons Ltd

responded to dextroamphetamine. Overall 46 (96%) of subjects had a positive response to one or both stimulant drugs versus placebo. The crucial point is that 25% of subjects demonstrated a selective response to a particular stimulant drug leading to subsequent speculation about genetic influence on stimulant response in ADHD. Elia *et al.* (1991) also distinguished between behavioural non-response and adverse effects, which few studies have done. While behavioural non-response to stimulants is rare when a wide range of doses are given, most subjects experience some adverse effects. During week 2 or 3 of treatment in the Elia *et al.* (1991) study, adverse effects required that titration of medication dose was slowed or reduced in 19 (40%) subjects. The authors noted that making a definitive clinical decision of improvement was often difficult because behavioural improvement had to be weighed against adverse effects, and different symptoms responded independently to dosage, setting and subject. It is unclear whether this variability in response and adverse effects is mainly pharmacokinetic or pharmacodynamic (Kimko *et al.*, 1999). There is some evidence that side effects occur less often with methylphenidate that with dextroamphetamine. Gross and Wilson (1974) reported that side effects were sometimes severe enough to make immediate discontinuation of stimulants necessary (1.1% of 377 patients for methylphenidate and 4.3% of 371 patients for dextroamphetamine). Pharmacogenetic studies of ADHD are important as the development of personalised prescription regimens will hopefully lead to improved symptom control, better tolerance of medication and in turn better compliance with medication over time.

As well as benefiting the individual, personalised prescription regimens will benefit society as a whole in terms of reducing the burden of ADHD (educational and occupational failure, family and marital dysharmony) and reducing the costs of treatment failure and drop out. Such regimens would provide reassurance both to parents and clinicians when prescribing stimulant medications to young children rather than the current situation where parents anxiously agree to blind medication trials. Dosreis *et al.* (2003) showed that 55% of parents attending paediatric primary care clinics in Baltimore were initially hesitant to use medication on the basis of information in the lay press. Knowledge of the clinical genetics of methylphenidate response will also assist the development of novel drug targets as well as information about possible adjustments that could be made to current drug treatments.

16.3 CURRENT PHARMACOTHERAPY IN ADHD

Kutcher *et al.* (2004) produced an international consensus statement on the treatment of ADHD and disruptive behavioural disorders at a meeting sponsored by Johnson and Johnson. The authors suggested that first-line treatment for ADHD without co-morbidity is stimulant medication aided by psychosocial intervention. For ADHD with co-morbid conduct disorder, a combination of pharmacotherapy and psychosocial intervention was suggested. For primary conduct disorder, first-line treatment is psychosocial intervention, with pharmacotherapy considered as adjunctive therapy if required. Taylor *et al.* (2004) published the European clinical guidelines for hyperkinetic disorder – first upgrade. These guidelines refer to the diagnosis of hyperkinetic disorder as well as its management covering psychological, educational, pharmacological and nutritional approaches. These guidelines are somewhat more conservative suggesting that pharmacological treatment of ADHD is indicated when the patient meets criteria for ADHD and psychological treatments alone are insufficient. These guidelines suggested that first-line pharmacological treatment of ADHD/HKD is a stimulant medication while the second-line pharmacological treatment is to switch to another class of stimulant medication. Third-line pharmacological treatment of ADHD/HKD suggested switching to another drug type, e.g. a noradrenergic reuptake inhibitor.

Stimulant medications are the most commonly prescribed psychotropic medication in children and concern has been expressed about the exponential increase in their use in recent decades. However, of all psychotropic medications prescribed for children, empirical data exist regarding their safety and efficacy. Three types of stimulant medications are available for clinical use: methylphenidate, dextroamphetamine and pemoline. Owing to hepatotoxicity associated with its use, pemoline has been removed from the market in many countries. An important development has been the release of long-acting preparations replacing thrice daily dosing schedules though these do not suit every child. Three published studies have used decision analytic modelling techniques to examine the cost effectiveness of methylphenidate in the treatment of ADHD and have concluded that it is a cost-effective treatment for children with ADHD (Matza *et al.*, 2005).

Although stimulant medications have been the cornerstone of ADHD pharmacotherapy for over 30 years, medications having a primarily noradrenergic effect also show efficacy in ADHD treatment. Several studies have shown that tricyclic antidepressants have a moderate response rate in the treatment of ADHD symptoms (Spencer & Biederman, 2002). A newer drug is atomoxetine, a highly selective noradrenergic reuptake inhibitor, shown to be effective in children (Michelson *et al.*, 2001) and adults (Michelson, 2003) with ADHD. Unlike tricyclic antidepressants, atomoxetine does not have anti-cholinergic side-effects and has a safe cardiovascular profile. Atomoxetine was the first non-controlled medication to gain approved by the US Food and Drug Administration for the treatment of ADHD. A clinical advantage of this drug is its lower abuse potential than stimulant drugs but adverse effects include weight loss, the potential for severe hepatic injury and suicidal ideation (Wooltorton, 2005).

Other medication types occasionally used in the treatment of impairing ADHD symptoms are MAO inhibitors (phenelzine and selegiline); alpha2 agonists (clonidine and guanfacine) and others, e.g. modafinil and bupropion.

16.4   PHARMACODYNAMICS OF ANTI-ADHD MEDICATIONS

Pharmacogenetic studies to date have mainly focused on methylphenidate, the main drug class used in the pharmacological treatment of ADHD. The precise mode of action of stimulant medications is not fully understood but considerable progress has been made in the study of stimulant actions (Solanto *et al.*, 2001). Methylphenidate probably acts primarily through inhibition of the dopamine transporter (DAT) which is a pre-synaptic inhibitory autoreceptor regulating activity in dopaminergic pathways. Increased availability of dopamine in the synapse in response to a neural impulse is hypothesised to enhance executive function and remediate deficits in inhibitory control and working memory in those children affected by ADHD (Douglas *et al.*, 1988). Methylphenidate also caused a calming effect in hyperactive DAT-knock out (DAT-KO) mice suggesting an important role for serotonergic modulation of catecholinergic neurotransmission (Gainetdinov *et al.*, 1999). Therefore the action of methylphenidate may be linked to the tonic and phasic control of dopamine and serotonin release. Unfortunately this hypothesis does not provide critical insight as the DAT-KO mouse is an imperfect model of human ADHD. However, further gene expression studies using animal models such as those involving the Spontaneous Hyperactive Rat (SHR) have the potential to provide new pharmacogenetic targets.

Neuroimaging studies have suggested that fronto-striatal areas in the brain, which are rich in dopaminergic innervation, may be affected in those with ADHD (Rubia *et al.*, 1997). Functional imaging studies have shown that dopamine transporter density is increased in ADHD patients compared to controls (Dougherty *et al.*, 1999) and that administration of methylphenidate reduces transporter density to near normal levels in ADHD (Krause *et al.*, 2000). It is not known whether raised DAT density is a state or trait feature of ADHD and indeed raised DAT density is not unique to ADHD (e.g. Brunswick *et al.*, 2003). In a recent study using PET to image the effects of methylphenidate in human brain, Volkow *et al.* (2005) replicated previous findings that methylphenidate blocks DAT but also found that extracellular dopamine levels were greater when the drug was given with a salient rather than a neutral stimulus, i.e. the effects of the drug were context dependent. The authors also found that methylphenidate-induced increases in extracellular dopamine were associated with enhanced perception of the stimulus as salient. Unfortunately there are no current ligands available for imaging of the noradrenaline (Norepinephrine or NET) transporter, therefore we do not know the noradrenergic effects of taking methylphenidate or atomoxetine in humans.

DAT and NET densities vary between brain regions (Madras *et al.*, 2005); DAT density is low while NET density is higher in the frontal cortex. The reverse applies in the striatum where DAT density is high and NET density is very low. Methylphenidate, amphetamine and atomoxetine all increase extracellular dopamine and noradrenaline levels in the frontal cortex, but only methylphenidate and dextro-amphetamine increase extracellular dopamine levels in the basal ganglia. The latter two stimulant drugs have different effects on DAT with methylphenidate hypothesised to block dopamine transport while amphetamine is a DAT substrate proposed to trigger dopamine release in the basal ganglia (amphetamine has a range of other dopamine-raising effects). However, the debate cannot be simplified to either dopamine or noradrenaline as the key neurotransmitter in ADHD as transporter – selective inhibitors such as atomoxetine are not transmitter-selective and in fact dopamine affinity for NET is greater than for DAT in the frontal cortex where NET density is higher (Madras *et al.*, 2005). These authors speculated that DAT/NET ratios in defined brain regions are likely to govern selective drug effects on catecholamine transport. It is also unknown if neuroadaptation in brain dopamine systems differs in response to different drug types.

16.5   PHARMACOKINETICS OF ADHD MEDICATIONS

Simulants show rapid absorption, low plasma protein binding and rapid extracellular and hepatic metabolism (Patrick *et al.*, 1987). A clinical effect can be seen in as little as 20 minutes after administration of the medication. Peak blood levels occur between 1 and 2.5 hours after administration and the serum half-life is around 2.5 hours (Winsberg *et al.*, 1982). The absorption of sustained-release methylphenidate is slower and produces a smaller peak concentration than an equivalent dose of standard methylphenidate. Methylphenidate is primarily metabolised by de-esterification to the inactive metabolite ritalinic acid which is in turn eliminated in urine. A new active metabolite has been identified in human volunteers given methylphenidate and ethanol, namely, ethylphenidate (Markowitz *et al.*, 2000) but its pharmacodynamic significance is unknown. Biotransformation through oxidative metabolism also occurs but there is no evidence to suggest methylphenidate is metabolised by the CYP2D6 enzyme. Amphetamine is primarily metabolised through oxidative deamination to form the inactive metabolites benzoic acid and hippuric acid. Aromatic hydroxylation occurs to a lesser extent and is subject to metabolism by the CDP2D6 enzyme. Therefore CYP2D6 inhibitors such as fluoxetine could alter amphetamine pharmacokinetics.

Atomoxetine is metabolised in the liver by the polymorphic CYP2D6 enzyme and poor metabolisers of this enzyme (an estimated 7% of the Caucasian population) experience higher peak concentrations of the drug. The latter may lead to higher rates of adverse effects such as weight loss. While routine laboratory tests are not currently recommended before commencing the drug, it is easy to see how an affordable, routinely available genetic test would aid the identification of those at higher risk of experiencing adverse effects.

16.6   PHARMACOGENETIC STUDIES IN ADHD

Clinical pharmacogenetic studies in ADHD have mainly investigated possible association of methylphenidate response and either dopaminergic receptor or transporter polymorphisms rather than drug metabolism polymorphisms. The majority of current studies have focused on DAT1, the main presumed site of action of methylphenidate. Current studies have also targeted response to medication in terms of reduction in core ADHD symptoms generally rated by parents over a specified time period rather than medication tolerance. For clarity of presentation, clinical studies are divided into studies examining methylphenidate response in relation to dopaminergic polymorphisms (Table 16.1), noradrenergic polymorphisms (Table 16.2) and the sole genome-wide scan testing linkage with methylphenidate response (Table 16.3).

16.6.1   DOPAMINERGIC SYSTEM

Molecular genetic studies in ADHD have examined for association between the disorder and the dopamine transporter (DAT), 5 post-synaptic dopamine receptors (DRD1-DRD5), and enzymes involved in the dopamine pathway including Tyrosine

Table 16.1. Studies of methylphenidate response and dopaminergic gene variants

Sample origin	Sample size	Study design	Definition of responder status	Findings	Study authors
African-American	30	Prospective open-label	ABRS score reduced from ≥1.5 to ≤1.0	Decreased response with 10-repeat allele homozygosity DAT1	Winsberg & Comings (1999)
Brazilian-European descent	50	Prospective open-label	50% reduction in mean basal scores of ABRS	Decreased response with 10-repeat allele homozygosity DAT1	Roman et al. (2002)
Irish	119	Retrospective report	Categorical subjective variable: very good/mediocre/poor response	Increased response with 10-repeat allele homozygosity DAT1	Kirley et al. (2003)
North American	47	Prospective double-blind	CGI-S score of ≤3	Increased response with one or two copies of the 10-repeat allele DAT1	Stein et al. (2005)
British	168	Retrospective report	'Very Improved' on the CGI-S	No effect of 10-repeat allele DAT1	Langley et al. (2005)
Canadian	140	Prospective, cross-over design	CGI-rated improvement	Increased response in heterozygotes DAT1	Joober et al. (2005)
Brazilian-European descent	8	SPECT scan	Moderate responders i.e. at least 30% reduction in ABRS scores from baseline	Higher rCBF in medial frontal and left basal g areas in 10-repeat homozygotes DAT1	Rohde et al. (2003)
Korean	11	[123I]IPT SPECT scan	50% reduction in ADHD RS-IV scores from baseline	Correlation between 10-repeat homozygosity DAT1, poorer response to medication and high DAT density in basal ganglia.	Cheon et al. (2005)

Ethnicity	N	Study design	Clinical finding	Genetic finding	Reference
African-American	30	Prospective open-label	ABRS score reduced from ≥1.5 to ≤1.0	No effect of DRD2 Taq 1 or DRD4*7	Winsberg & Comings (1999)
Turkey	111	Retrospective report	50% improvement in no. of symptoms and assoc. impairment	Association with transmission DRD4*7 when non-responders were excluded	Tahir et al. (2000)
German	47	Prospective open-label	Decreased serum prolactin and change in CGAS scores	Decreased response with DRD4*7 /5HTT LL genotype	Seeger et al. (2001)
Canadian	111	Prospective double-blind, placebo-controlled crossover trial	Change in parent and teachers Conners' scores	Increased response in T/T genotype of −521 C/T DRD4 polymorphism, DRD4*7 no effect	Ben Amor et al. (2004)
North American (Mixed African American and Hispanic ethnicity)	45	Prospective open-label	Dose of methylphenidate required to normalize Conners' global index scores	Higher doses required with DRD4*7 genotype	Hamarman et al. (2004)

ABRS = Conners' Abbreviated Rating Scale.
CGIS = Clinical Global Impression – Severity of Impairment Scale.
SPECT = Single Photon Emission Computerised Tomography.
RCBF = Regional Cerebral Blood Flow.
ADHD RS-IV = ADHD rating scale version IV.
SNAP IV = Swanson, Nolan and Pelham rating scale version IV.

Hydroxylase (TH), Dopamine Beta Hydroxylase (DBH) and Catechol-O-Methyltransferase (COMT). These genetic variants all represent potential targets for pharmacogenetic studies in ADHD. Please refer to Chapter 8 for further reading about these polymorphisms.

(a)   DAT1

In the first pharmacogenetic study of all child psychiatric disorders, Winsberg and Comings (1999) studied the role of the DAT1 polymorphism in predicting response to methylphenidate in a group of 30 African-American children meeting DSM-IIIR criteria for ADHD. All subjects were stimulant-naïve and were considered eligible if they achieved a score of greater than 1.5 on the Conners Abbreviated Rating Scale (ABRS) (Conners & Barkley, 1995). Methylphenidate was titrated upward until behavioural change was achieved but dose was restricted to no more than 60 mg/day or 0.7 mg/kg. Clinical response to medication was defined as a categorical variable (reduction in the mean score from greater than 1.5 to equal or less than 1.0 on 2 consecutive ABRS ratings by parents and teachers). There were 16 responders and 14 non-responders (i.e. 53% non-responders in contrast with 20–30% in Caucasian study samples). Notably all non-responders had received a minimum dose of methylphenidate 40 mg/day. Twelve of the 14 non-responders were homozygous for the DAT1 10-repeat allele compared with 5 of the 16 responders producing a chi^2 value of 6.9 (p = 0.008).

Roman et al. (2002) carried out a blind naturalistic study of methylphenidate response in 50 medication-naïve Brazilian boys meeting DSM-IV criteria for ADHD. The dose of methylphenidate was titrated up to 0.7 mg/day. A clinical response to medication was defined as a decrease of at least 50% in mean basal scores of ABRS, suggesting a robust improvement. 15 out of 20 (75%) youths who were heterozygous for the 10-repeat allele demonstrated a robust improvement in Conners ABRS scores while only 14 out of 30 (47%) of youths who were homozygous for the 10-repeat allele achieved a similar level of improvement (Fisher's exact test; one-tailed p = 0.04). In addition, 10-repeat allele heterozygotes had significantly higher improvement in global functioning than the homozygote group (U = 184; Z = −2.33; one-tailed p < 0.01).

In contrast, Kirley et al. (2003) collected retrospective parental ratings of methylphenidate response (i.e. categorically defined variable of very good/mediocre/poor response) in a sample of 119 Irish children. An association was found between parental transmission of the 10-repeat allele and 'very good' response status (chi^2 = 7.918, df = 1, p = 0.005). An advantage of this study is that the transmission disequilibrium test was used in the analysis, which limits population stratification bias, however, the retrospective nature of the study was a potential source of bias.

Stein et al. (2005) carried out a double-blind, placebo-controlled crossover trial of extended release methylphenidate in a group of 47 children. In this 4-week crossover study children underwent forced weekly dosage changes (placebo, 18 mg, 36 mg and 54 mg). Good response was defined as a score of less than of equal to 3 on the Clinical Global Impression – Severity of Impairment Scale. Subjects who were homozygous for the 9-repeat allele showed poorer response to medication at the 36 and 54 mg doses whereas those with one or two copies of the 10-repeat allele experienced better response to medication at the same doses (chi^2 = 6.92; p < 0.01).

Two studies failed to show any association between DAT1 and medication response. Langley *et al.* (2005) failed to find an association between the 10-repeat allele and retrospective parental ratings of methylphenidate response in 168 British children of Caucasian descent meeting ICD-10 criteria for hyperkinetic disorder. Subjects had received 3 or more months of treatment with methylphenidate and parental ratings were made retrospectively using the Clinical Global Impression Scale. No evidence was found for either association between DAT1 10-repeat allele and ADHD in the sample or with medication response (chi^2 = 1.63; df = 3; p = 0.65).

Joober *et al.* (2005) recruited 140 children with ADHD into a 2-week placebo-controlled cross-over prospective methylphenidate trial using methylphenidate 0.5 mg/kg/day. Outcome measures were based on the Conners' Global Index for parents and teachers at the end of each week. Carriers of the heterozygous genotype (9/10) showed the lowest improvement on placebo and the highest on methylphenidate based on parental ratings. Carriers of the 9/9 and 10/10 genotypes showed higher response to placebo and lower response to methylphenidate. Carriers of the 9/9 genotype showed a clinically (but not statistically) significant worsening of their symptoms on methylphenidate compared with placebo.

(b)   Functional studies of DAT1 polymorphisms and methylphenidate response

Rohde *et al.* (2003) carried out a pilot study investigating the relationship between DAT1 polymorphisms, methylphenidate response and cerebral blood flows during an attention test. Regional cerebral blood flow (rCBF) was measured using single photon emission computerised tomography (SPECT). Only medication-naïve boys who demonstrated a moderate response to methylphenidate (defined as improvement of at least 30% of the core ADHD symptoms) after 4 days of treatment with a dose of 0.70 mg/kg/day were included in the study. Boys homozygous for the 10-repeat DAT1 allele exhibited significantly greater rCBF measured after 4 days of treatment with methylphenidate in medial frontal and left basal ganglia areas than children without this genotype (Wilcox W = 10; z = –2.34; p = 0.02). The authors proposed that ADHD children with homozygosity for the DAT1 10-repeat allele (possibly encoding an overactive dopamine transporter) showed a higher cerebral blood flow (probably reflecting a higher dopamine activity level) in brain regions associated with working memory and inhibitory behaviour in order to achieve a response to methylphenidate. Limitations of this study and therefore aspects that future imaging studies must address are restriction to one gender and acute administration of methylphenidate versus chronic administration.

Cheon *et al.* (2005) tested for association between DAT density in the basal ganglia using [^{123}I]IPT SPECT imaging, 10-repeat DAT1 allele homozygosity and response to methylphenidate in 11 Korean methylphenidate-naïve children meeting criteria for DSM-IV combined type. The children were treated with methylphenidate for 8 weeks at doses up to 0.7 mg/kg/day before SPECT imaging. Of 7 children with the 10/10 genotype, only 2 (28.6%) showed good response to medication (defined as 50% decrease in ADHD RS-IV scores from baseline) compared to the

4 children without the 10/10 genotype who all responded well to medication (p = 0.06). In addition, children with the 10/10 genotype showed a significantly greater increase in DAT density in their basal ganglia than children without this genotype i.e. those who responded well to methylphenidate showed lower DAT density in bilateral basal ganglia areas after treatment with methylphenidate.

(c) DRD4

Winsberg and Comings (1999) utilised the sample study sample described earlier to examine the role of DRD2 and DRD4 alleles in predicting methylphenidate response. They studied the DRD2 Taq 1 A1/A2 polymorphism (Grandy *et al.*, 1989) and the DRD4 48 base pair repeat polymorphism (Van Tol *et al.*, 1992) but found no predictive effects.

   Tahir *et al.* (2000) tested for association of DRD4 and DRD5 with ADHD in a sample of 111 Turkish families (104 trios, 7 dyads) meeting DSM-IV criteria for ADHD. Increased transmission of the DRD4 7-repeat allele was found in the sample using TDT ($chi^2 = 2.79$; p = 0.047) and there was also a trend for linkage and association in the DRD5 polymorphism ($chi^2 = 2.38$; p = 0.06). When non-responders to methylphenidate were excluded from the analysis, transmission of the DRD4 7-repeat allele increased ($chi^2 = 4.48$; p = 0.017) and association with the DRD5 polymorphism became significant ($chi^2 = 4.9$; p = 0.013).

   Seeger *et al.* (2001) tested for gene-gene interactive effects in prediction of clinical response to treatment with methylphenidate in a group of 47 German children meeting ICD-10 criteria for Hyperkinetic Disorder. Decreased serum prolactin was used as a measure of physiological response as well as change in general functioning scores using the Children's Global Assessment Scale. Dopamine antagonises the release of prolactin and chronic methylphenidate treatment results in a decrease in basal prolactin levels (Weizman *et al.*, 1987). The children were treated as inpatients with methylphenidate 0.6–0.8 mg/kg for a week period. Children's DNA was genotyped for DRD4 7-repeat allele status and a functional polymorphism in the promoter region upstream from the coding region of the serotonin transporter (5-HTT). The latter polymorphism is an insertion/deletion of a 44 base pair sequence resulting in long (L) and short (S) alleles and affects serotonin transporter expression. The authors reported an association between the combination DRD4 7-repeat/5-HTT LL genotype and reduced improvement in general functioning (i.e. poor response). Poor responders to treatment also had higher prolactin levels.

   Ben Amor *et al.* (2004) carried out a 2-week double-blind, placebo-controlled crossover trial of low-dose methylphenidate (0.5 mg/day) in 111 6–12-year-old children meeting DSM-IV criteria for ADHD. Baseline evaluation and response to medication and placebo were assessed using Conners' Teacher and Parent Questionnaires. Three DRD4 polymorphisms were investigated, namely the 48 base pair VNTR in exon III, -521C/T substitution in intron I and a 120-base pair promoter region duplication. A significant effect of the -521C/T polymorphism was found in the Teachers Conners' scores with children with the T/T genotype responding better to medication than those with the C/T genotype (F1, 60 = 7.86, p = 0.006). No effect was found for the 48 base pair VNTR in exon III or the 120-base pair promoter region duplication.

Hamarman *et al.* (2004) carried out a prospective open-label trial of methylphenidate in 45 children meeting DSM-IV criteria for ADHD who were attending a child psychiatry service in New Jersey, USA. Subjects received increasing doses of methylphenidate until serial measures of the Conners' Global Index T-score normalised on parental ratings. Unlike the other studies, Hammarman did not set a predefined measure of medication response but instead analysed the effect of genotype on the dose of medication required to normalise Conners' Global Index T-scores (CGI-P). Subjects with the 7-repeat allele required a higher dose of methylphenidate (mean dose 47 mg or 1.7 mg/kg) to achieve normalisation of the CGI-P compared to subjects without the 7-repeat allele (man dose 31 mg or 0.79 mg/kg) (log rank = 14.17; df = 1; p = 0.0002).

16.6.2   SEROTONERGIC SYSTEM

Molecular genetic studies in ADHD have examined for association with genes coding for the serotonin transporter (5-HTT), tryptophan hydroxylase (TPH1 and TPH2) and the monoamine oxidases (MAO-A and MAO-B) (see also Chapter 8).

No pharmacogenetic study in ADHD has specifically examined medication response in relation to serotonergic polymorphisms, however, Seeger *et al.* (2001) tested for gene-gene interaction between the DRD4 7-repeat allele and a functional polymorphism in the 5-HTT promoter region as described earlier.

16.6.3   NORADRENERGIC SYSTEM

Molecular genetic association studies in ADHD have examined for association with NET and three adrenergic receptors, Adrenoceptor Alpha-2A (ADRA2A), Adrenoceptor Alpha-2C (ADRA2C) and Adrenoceptor Alpha-1C (ADRA1C) (see also Chapter 8).

(a)   NET

Yang *et al.* (2004) explored the association between alleles of the norepinephrine transporter gene (NET) and methylphenidate response in 45 Chinese Han youths

Table 16.2. Methylphenidate response and noradrenergic gene variants

Sample origin	Sample size	Study design	Definition of responder status	Findings	Study authors
Chinese Han	45	Prospective open-label	Change in ADHD RS-IV scores and subscales	Increased response in hyperactive/ impulsive symptoms in NET G allele homozygotes	Yang *et al.* (2004)
Brazilian of European descent	97	Prospective, open-label	Change in SNAP-IV scores	Reduced response in ADRA2A G allele homozygotes	Polanczyk *et al.* (2005)

ADHD RS-IV = ADHD Rating Scale Version IV.
SNAP-IV = Swanson, Nolan and Pelham rating scale version IV.

who met DSM-IV criteria for ADHD. All of the medication-naïve subjects were treated with methylphenidate in doses of 0.45 to 0.60 mg/kg/day, which was titrated weekly to optimal response, based on parental report of response and side-effects. Medication response was measured as the mean change in ADHD RS-IV symptom scores associated with each genotype with no predefined cut-offs. A significant association was found between NET gene G1287A genotypes and response to methylphenidate for hyperactive-impulsive subscale scores (mean score reduction for G/G genotype was 7.15; for G/A genotype was 6.94; for A/A genotype was 2.13; $p = 0.012$) but not for inattentive subscale scores. This finding of an association between NET gene polymorphisms and methylphenidate response awaits replication. Interestingly atomoxetine, a recently licensed drug for the treatment of ADHD, is a highly specific inhibitor of NET and no pharmacogenetic studies have yet been published in relation to atomoxetine response.

(b)   ADRA2A

In a review article by Polanczyk *et al.* (2005), findings were presented by the authors showing an association between methylphenidate response and an MspI polymorphism in the promoter region of the alpha2A-adrenoceptor gene (ADRA2A). Ninety-seven of 144 medication-naïve children meeting DSM-IV criteria for ADHD and treated with methylphenidate doses greater or equal to 0.3 mg/kg/day were genotyped for the MspI polymorphism. Response was measured as change after 4 weeks of treatment in parent and teacher rated SNAP IV scores from baseline. G allele homozygotes (14 of 97) were significantly younger than those with other genotypes ($p < 0.01$). G allele homozygotes showed higher total scores in the SNAP IV at 4-week review even after adjusting for age ($p = 0.04$). The study authors are currently analysing data in relation to NET1 and DBH SNPs and methylphenidate response.

16.6.4   GENOME-WIDE SCANNING

Van der Meulen *et al.* (2004) presented findings from the first genome-wide scan testing for linkage with methylphenidate response in a group of 102 Dutch sib-pairs with ADHD. The genome scan using Genehunter used 400 markers with an average distance of 10cM. A peak was found using quantitative trait locus (QTL) analysis on chromosome 7 with a maximum Z-score of 2.60 and a corresponding LOD-score of 2.63 in a traditional Haseman-Elston analysis. Smaller peaks with Z-scores of 2.72, 2.61 and 2.37 and corresponding LOD-scores of 1.95, 1.90 and 2.09 were found on chromosomes 3, 5 and 9 respectively. It must be noted that the threshold for

Table 16.3. Methylphenidate response and genome scan study

Sample origin	Sample size	Study design	Definition of responder status	Findings	Study authors
Dutch	102	Retrospective report	Change in SWAN scores	Largest peak on chrom. 7 LOD score = 2.84	Van der Meulen *et al.* (2004)

significance using genome-wide QTL analysis is generally held to be higher than any of the values achieved in this study.

16.7 SOURCES OF HETEROGENEITY IN PHARMACOGENETIC STUDIES IN ADHD

As can be seen from Tables 16.1–16.3, no clear consensus with regard to pharmacogenetic studies of methylphenidate in ADHD is emerging. Conflicting findings and non-replication of previous findings may relate to heterogeneity in study design but there may of course be an absence of a true effect for DAT1, for instance. Therefore the field requires well-powered, placebo-controlled trials in which a range of medication doses are administered before declaring non-response.

16.7.1 STUDY DESIGN

Review of Tables 16.1–16.3 demonstrates how a variety of methodological approaches have been used. Some studies were designed primarily as genetic association studies of ADHD in which retrospective data of methylphenidate response was collected (e.g. Tahir *et al.*, 2000; Kirley *et al.*, 2003; Langley *et al.*, 2005). The prospective studies have generally been open-label studies (i.e. patient and doctor know what medication is being taken) and only those of Ben Amor *et al.* (2004) and Stein *et al.* (2005) have employed more stringent double-blinded, cross-over designs. A variety of methylphenidate doses have been administered and some such as Ben Amor *et al.* (2004) were possibly sub-therapeutic potentially masking real effects. Most studies have relied exclusively on parental ratings of medication response, which may have introduced rater bias, particularly in open-label studies. The prospective studies have generally employed short-term follow-up periods and it would be worthwhile knowing if prediction effects are sustained after 6 months or 1 year of treatment.

16.7.2 SAMPLE SIZE

Sample size has been an issue across the board and this is not surprising given the expensive nature of sample collection for prospective studies. The planning of future international collaborative efforts is important in this regard as an amalgamation of the current data is restricted by wide variation in the definition of medication responder status and statistical analysis techniques in particular. Smits *et al.* (2005) reviewed methodological issues in pharmacogenetic studies favouring randomised clinical trial study designs and their paper provides a useful checklist of questions to be asked when designing and reporting on such studies. These authors also suggested that pharmacogenetic study findings usually presented in the form of relative risks and odds ratios should be translated into absolute risk and ultimately the number-needed-to-treat (NNT) to facilitate clinical decision analysis. These authors also clarified the difference between a prognostic factor (when a genotype predicts outcome) and an effect modifier (the genotype must be associated with differences in treatment effect). They commented that case only designs lacking a control group (as in the majority of pharmacogenetic studies in ADHD) cannot distinguish between the genotype as a prognostic factor or an effect modifier.

16.7.3   DEFINITION OF RESPONDER STATUS

Most studies have measured response to medication using standard rating scales that measure core ADHD symptoms of inattention, hyperactivity and impulsivity while some have used measures of overall functioning or the clinician's global impression of response. Measurement scales that take a broader view of the child with ADHD are arguably better as we must not forget the high prevalence of co-morbid disorders in ADHD. For instance, a child with ADHD and a co-morbid anxiety disorder may improve with stimulant treatment in terms of core ADHD symptoms but their overall functioning might have disimproved due to a worsening of their anxiety symptoms (see Chapter 15). Another not infrequent clinical scenario is where a parent reports the child's ADHD symptoms are much improved whereas the teacher reports that the child's hyperactivity/impulsivity symptoms are reduced while the child appears overmedicated at school. Therefore studies should have multiple raters of response using both ADHD symptom measures and global functioning measures of response over longer follow-up periods so that effects on co-morbid disorders can be assessed. Some studies have employed a definition of positive response as a 50% reduction in ADHD symptoms from baseline (e.g. Roman *et al.*, 2002) producing a categorical yes/no response variable. The clinical reality is that there is a spectrum of response and an ADHD symptom reduction of 20–30% is meaningful. Quantitative outcome measures reflect this reality more accurately while an alternative approach is that of Hamarman *et al.* (2004) examining the dose required to produce normalisation of symptoms or a percentage reduction in symptoms.

16.7.4   STATISTICAL ANALYSIS

Many studies have employed a categorical definition of responder status, e.g. good/poor and compared the distribution of genetic variants amongst those categories using the chi-square test or Fisher's exact test. Alternatively, other studies (Yang *et al.*, 2004) grouped the mean symptom change score after treatment according to genotype and compared using the parametric analysis of variance (ANOVA) or the non-parametric Kruskall-Wallis test. A further statistical analysis approach employs logistic regression TDT (Kirley *et al.*, 2003) which utilises quantitative outcome measures and has the advantage of avoiding population stratification that could otherwise produce spurious results.

16.7.5   ETHNICITY

Heterogeneity due to ethnic origin of the source populations may be an important source of variability in pharmacogenetic study findings. It is most significant in the Winsberg and Comings (1999) study that there was such a high rate of poor response to methylphenidate among African-American children. This clinically important finding warrants further studies specifically targeting recruitment of this group of children.

16.8 FUTURE PROSPECTS

All of the pharmacogenetic studies listed have focused on the degree of response rather than the prevalence of adverse events which is an equally important parameter as persistent side-effects such as weight loss or insomnia limit compliance and may even lead to withdrawal of medication if cost outweighs benefit. Pharmacogenetic studies to date have excluded atomoxetine; however, this may reflect the amount of time it takes to recruit an adequate sample size and obviously the follow-up period will need to be longer than for methylphenidate trials, given the slower onset of action of the drug. We anticipate pharmacogenetic studies of atomoxetine examining pharmacodynamic (e.g. NET) and pharmacokinetic (e.g. CYP2D6) genes. Ideally all clinical trials of novel anti-ADHD drugs would collect DNA to facilitate pharmacogenetic studies at some future date and this would help to reduce the exorbitant costs of clinical data collection. This will require collaboration between industry and academic researchers but could happen quickly if required by medication licensing authorities.

It is important to define and analyse further the function of specific DAT1 haplotypes in association studies and pharmacogenetic studies in ADHD. Existing neuroimaging studies of DAT which have produced diverging conclusions have employed different probes and population samples. Future studies would ideally recruit larger samples through collaboration between multiple centres using similar protocols and collecting more detailed clinical information. Brain imaging of NET in medication-naïve and medicated patients is also indicated. Madras *et al.* (2005) have proposed that genetic variants of trace amine receptors in ADHD warrant further investigation as well as DAT interaction with regulatory proteins such as PICK in the context of drug response in ADHD.

16.9 REFERENCES

Ben Amor L, Grizenko N, Schwartz G *et al.* (2004) Association between three polymorphisms in the dopamine receptor D4 (DRD4) gene and attention deficit hyperactivity disorder (ADHD): a pharmacogenetic study. *Proceedings of the XIIth World Congress of Psychiatric Genetics*, Dublin, Ireland.

Biederman J, Faraone SV (2005) Attention-deficit-hyperactivity disorder. *Lancet* **366**: 237–48.

Brunswick DJ, Amsterdam JD, Mozley PD, Newberg A (2003) Greater availability of brain dopamine transporters in major depression shown by [99mc]TRODAT-1 SPECT imaging. *Am J Psychiatry* **160**: 1836–41.

Cheon K-A, Ryu Y-H, Kim J-Wm, Cho D-Y (2005) The homozygosity for 10-repeat allele at dopamine transporter gene and dopamine transporter density in Korean children with attention deficit hyperactivity disorder: relating to treatment response to methylphenidate. *Eur Neuropsychopharmacol* **15**(1): 95–101.

Conners CK, Barkley RA (1985) Rating scales and checklists for child psychopharmacology. *Psychopharmacol Bull* **21**: 809–43.

Dougherty DD, Bonab AA, Spencer TJ *et al.* (1999) Dopamine transporter density in patients with attention deficit hyperactivity disorder. *Lancet* 18–25 Dec; **354**(9196): 2132–3.

Douglas VI, Barr RG, Amin K *et al.* (1988) Dose effects and individual responsivity to methylphenidate in attention deficit disorder. *J Child Psychol & Psych* **29**: 453–75.

Dosresis S, Zito JM, Safer DT *et al.* (2003) Parental perception and satisfaction with stimulant medication for attention deficit-hyperactivity disorder. *J Dev Behav Pediatr* **24**(3): 155–62.

Elia J, Borcherding BG, Rapoport JL, Kaysor CS. (1991) Methylphenidate and dextroamphetamine treatments of hyperactivity: are there true non-responders? *Psychiatry Res* **36**: 141–55.

Gainetdinov RR, Westel WC, Jones SR *et al.* (1999) Role of serotonin in the paradoxical calming effect of psychostimulants on hyperactivity. *Science* **283**: 397–401.

Grandy DK, Litt M, Allen L *et al.* (1989) The human dopamine D2 repector gene is located on chromosome 11 at q22-q23 and identifies a Taq IRFLP. *Am J Hum Genet* **45**: 778–85.

Green WH (1995) The treatment of Attention-Deficit Hyperactivity Disorder with non-stimulant medications. *Child Adolesc Psychiatr Clin N Am* **4**: 169–95.

Greenhill LL, Halperin JM, Abikoff H (1999) Stimulant medications. *J Am Acad Child Adolesc Psychiatry* **38**(5): 503–12.

Gross MD, Wilson WC (1974) *Minimal Brain Dysfunction*. New York: Brunner/Mazel.

Hamarman S, Fossella J, Ulger C *et al.* (2004) Dopamine receptor 4 (DRD4) 7-repeat allele predicts methylphenidate dose response in children with attention deficit hyperactivity disorder: a pharmacogenetic study. *J Child & Adolesc Psychopharmacol* **14**(4): 564–74.

Joober R, Grizenko N, Ben Amor L *et al.* (2005) A pharmaco-behavioral genetic study of the dopamine transporter gene (SLC6A3) in children with Attention Deficit Hyperactivity. *Am J Med Genetics* **138B**: 9.

Kimko HC, Cross JT, Abernethy DR (1999) Pharmacokinetics and clinical effectiveness of methylphenidate. *Clin Pharmacokinet* **37**: 457–70.

Kirley A, Lowe N, Hawi Z *et al.* (2003) Association of the 480 bp DAT1 allele with methylphenidate response in a sample of Irish children with ADHD. *Am J Med Genetics* **121B**: 50–4.

Krause KL, Dresel SH, Krause J *et al.* (2000) Increased striatal dopamine transporter in adult patients with attention deficit hyperactivity disorder: effects of methylphenidate as measured by singles photon emission computed tomography. *Neurosci Lett* **285**(2): 107–10.

Kutcher S, Aman M, Brooks SJ *et al.* (2004) International consensus statement on Attention-Deficit/Hyperactivity Disorder (ADHD) and disruptive behaviour disorders (DBDs): clinical implications and treatment practice suggestions. *European Neuropsychopharmacol* **14**(1): 11–28.

Langley K, Turic D, Peirce Tr *et al.* (2005) No support for association between the dopamine transporter (DAT1) gene and ADHD. *Am J Med Genet B Neuropsychiatr Genet* **139**: 7–10.

Madras BK, Mailler GM, Fischman AJ (2005) The dopamine transporter and Attention-Deficit/Hyperactivity Disorder. *Biol Psychiatry* **57**: 1397–1409.

Markowitz JS, DeVane CL, Boulton DW *et al.* (2000) Ethylphenidate formation in human subjects after the administration of a single dose of methylphenidate and alcohol. *Drug Metab Dispos* **25**: 620–4.

Matza LS, Paramore C, Prasad M (2005) A review of the economic burden of ADHD. *Cost Effectiveness & Resource Allocation* **3**: 5.

Michelson D, Adler L, Spencer T *et al.* (2003) Atomoxetine in adults with ADHD: two randomised, placebo-controlled studies. *Biol Psych* **53**: 112–20.

Michelson D, Faries D, Wernicke J *et al.* (2001) Atomoxetine in the treatment of children and adolescents with Attention-Deficit/Hyperactivity Disorder: a randomised, placebo-controlled, dose-response study. *Pediatrics* **108**: E83.

Patrick KS, Mueller RA, Gualtieri CT, Breese GR (1987) Pharmacokinetics and actions of methylphenidate. In HY Meltzer (ed.) *Psychopharmacology: The Third Generation of Progress*, 3rd edn, New York: Raven, 1387–95.

Polanczyk G, Zeni C, Genro JP *et al.* (2005) Attention-deficit/hyperactivity disorder: advancing on pharmacogenomics. *Pharmacogenomics* **6**(3): 225–34.

Rohde LA, Roman T, Szobot C *et al.* (2003) Dopamine transporter gene, response to methylphenidate and cerebral blood flow in Attention-Deficit/Hyperactivity Disorder: a pilot study. *Synapse* **48**: 87–9.

Roman T, Szobot C, Martine S *et al.* (2002) Dopamine transporter gene and response to methylphenidate in Attention-Deficit/Hyperactivity Disorder. *Pharmacogenetics* **12**: 497–9.

Rubia K, Overmeyer S, Taylor E *et al.* (1997) Inhibitory control of hyperactive adolescents in fMRI. In AW Toga, RSJ Frackowiak, JC Sazziotta (eds) *Neuroimage. Third International Conference on Functional Mapping of the Human Brain* (May 1997, Copenhagen, Denmark). New York: Academic Press.

Seeger G, Schloss P, Schmidt MH (2001) Marker gene polymorphisms in hyperkinetic disorder-predictors of clinical response in treatment with methylphenidate? *Neuroscience Letters* **313**: 45–8.

Smits KM, Schouten JS, Smits LJ *et al.* (2005) A review on the design and reporting of studies on drug-gene interaction. *J Clin Epidemiol* **58**: 651–4.

Solanto MV, Arnsten AFT, Castellanos FX (eds) (2001) *Stimulant Drugs and ADHD: Basic and Clinical Neuroscience.* Oxford: Oxford University Press.

Spencer T, Biederman J (2002) Non-stimulant treatment for Attention-Deficit/Hyperactivity Disorder. *J Attent Disord* **6**: 109–19.

Stein MA, Waldman ID, Sarampote CS *et al.* (2005) Dopamine transporter genotype and methylphenidate dose response in children with ADHD. *Neuropsychopharmacol* **30**(7): 1374–82.

Tahir E, Yazgan Y, Cirakoglu B *et al.* (2000) Association and linkage of DRD4 and DRD5 with attention deficit hyperactivity disorder (ADHD) in a sample of Turkish children. *Mol Psychiatry* **5**(4): 396–404.

Taylor E, Dopfner M, Sergeant J *et al.* (2004) European clinical guidelines for hyperkinetic disorder-first upgrade. *Eur Child & Adolesc Psychiatry* **13**(Suppl 1).

Van der Meulen E, Bakker SC, Pauls DL *et al.* (2004) A genome-wide quantitative trait locus analysis on methylphenidate response rate in Dutch sib pairs with Attention-Deficit Hyperactivity Disorder. *Proceedings of the 16th World Congress of the International Association for Child and Adolescent Psychiatry and Allied Professions*, Berlin, Germany.

Van Tol HHM, Wu CM, Guan H-C *et al.* (1992) Multiple dopamine D4 receptor variants in human population. *Nature* **358**: 149–52.

Volkow ND, Wang GJ, Fowler JS, Ding YS (2005) Imaging the effects of methylphenidate on brain dopamine: new model on its therapeutic actions for Attention-Deficit/Hyperactivity Disorder. *Biol Psychiatry* **57**: 1410–15.

Weber WW (1997) *Pharmacogenetics.* New York: Oxford University Press.

Weizman R, Dick J, Gil-AD I *et al.* (1987) Effects of acute and chronic methylphenidate administration on beta-endorphin, growth hormone, prolactin and cortisol in children with attention deficit disorder and hyperactivity. *Life Sci* **40**: 2247–52.

Winsberg BG, Comings DE (1999) Association of the dopamine transporter gene (DAT1) with poor methylphenidate response. *J Am Acad Child Adolesc Psychiatry* **38**(12): 1474–7.

Winsberg BG, Kupietz SS, Sverd J *et al.* (1982) Methylphenidate oral dose plasma concentrations and behavioural response in children. *Psychopharmacology* **76**: 329–32.

Wooltorton E (2005) Suicidal ideation among children taking atomoxetine (Straterra). *CMAJ* **173**(12): 1447.

Yang L, Wang Y-F, Li J, Faraone SV (2004) Association of norepinephrine transporter gene with methylphenidate response. *J Am Acad Child Adolesc Psychiatry* **43**(9): 1154–8.

III Treatment Perspectives

17 Cognitive Behavioural Treatment of ADHD

SUSAN YOUNG

*Department of Forensic Mental Health Science, Institute of Psychiatry,
King's College, London, UK*

17.1 OVERVIEW

The multiple problems and difficulties that people with ADHD face in their daily
lives have been consistently reported in the literature. These problems may be direct
consequences of ADHD symptoms or they may be more indirectly associated with
the disorder. This chapter briefly reviews a study that examined how people with
ADHD felt about receiving their diagnosis and their experience of taking medication. The findings suggest that receiving a diagnosis for the first time as adults
resulted in the individual engaging in an adaptive process and a period of psychological and emotional adjustment. Treatment with medication gave symptom relief
but not problem relief. The chapter outlines how the psychological needs of people
with ADHD can be met by discussing two psychological treatment programmes.
First, the Young-Bramham Programme which is a cognitive behavioural programme
specifically designed for adults with ADHD (Young & Bramham, 2007); and, secondly, a cognitive skills group programme suitable for people with ADHD and
antisocial behaviour problems, the R&R2: ADHD programme (Young & Ross,
2007).

17.2 BACKGROUND

In spite of the plethora of research reporting symptom-related and psychosocial
problems of children and adults with ADHD, little attention has been paid to the
coping strategies and mechanisms employed by them to cope with their problems.
This deficit in research and clinical practice most likely reflects an assumption that
pharmacological treatment is a panacea for ADHD. Of course pharmacological
treatment has been shown to be efficacious in symptom reduction for both adults
and children, but this does not necessarily lead to adaptive, functional improvement
in their daily lives. Furthermore, adults are different to children and they may be
more isolated. Children have somewhere to go every day (some form of educational
service whether this be mainstream school, special school or pupil referral units)
which provides them with a peer set to refer to. They are in environments that have

Handbook of Attention Deficit Hyperactivity Disorder. Edited by M. Fitzgerald, M. Bellgrove and M. Gill.
© 2007 John Wiley & Sons Ltd

rules and clear expectations for behaviour. Structure is imposed on them by the setting, whether this be educational services, youth offending teams, social services, foster care and/or parents. As these children grow up and mature they become responsible for their own lives. The structure that supports them disintegrates. Many youth quit school without gaining qualifications, are restricted in their occupational opportunities, and spend their time on the streets. The fast rewards of antisocial behaviour, whether these be financial or thrills, beckon the person who has lost their personal and social structure. There are no rules any more, only the moral rules they impose on themselves.

The ability to cope with problems and challenging situations is an important skill that may not have been learned along the way. The development of prosocial skills, critical reasoning and constructive problem-solving are skills that determine the outcome of how we deal with stressful events. There is very little research about the coping strategies of people with ADHD. Adolescent girls have been reported to use a wide variety of ineffective strategies during adolescence (Young *et al.*, 2005). Perhaps their lack of preferred coping strategies reflects an underlying uncertainty about how to respond, proceed or cope with stressful situations. Their problem-solving skills may be less developed compared with other teenagers as their thinking may be less organised schematically and they adopt a more haphazard cognitive approach.

It is possible that an adolescent repertoire of coping strategies that is inadequate or ineffective becomes further entrenched with maturity and develops into the adoption of maladaptive coping strategies in adulthood. A study of clinically referred adults found ADHD adults (mean age 25) favoured strategies of confrontation and avoidance (Young, 2005). Thus when faced with stressful situations, ADHD adults may respond by either aggressively confronting the situation or by employing avoidance strategies. Additionally, they lacked planful problem-solving, i.e. they lacked an ability to outline a plan of action and follow it. Thus they may be unable to think and plan ahead and, in response, adopt a haphazard, ad-hoc, spur-of-the-moment problem-solving strategy, perhaps becoming irritable and confrontational. Importantly, however, individuals tended to positively reappraise stressful situations, which is a constructive response, although this will clearly depend on the context of the situation. The study further suggested that the way young adults cope with stressful situations is determined by their cognitive ability. In particular, attentional problems were negatively associated with seeking advice and support from others.

The results of these studies need replication. However, they suggest that individuals whose ADHD symptoms persist into adulthood lack constructive coping strategies. This is an important indicator for psychological intervention. ADHD adults may misjudge situations as their impulse-driven nature leads them to make fast, decisive solutions based on much less information than those of their peers. Psychological interventions that target the accurate appraisal of events, the inhibition of rapid maladaptive responding, and the selection of appropriate coping mechanisms may help individuals learn to cope better with stressful situations. In turn this may have a positive impact on outcome and decrease the risk of psychiatric admission in later life (Dalsgaard *et al.*, 2002).

By adulthood, individuals with ADHD have frequently had many encounters with various education and mental health services (Young, Toone & Tyson, 2003), yet the diagnosis of ADHD has often not been made. Individuals diagnosed for the first time in adulthood may lack trust in services and feel they have been unfairly treated by a system that had previously failed to identify their problems.

When diagnosis is made for the first time in adulthood, ADHD adults report a difficulty adjusting to the diagnosis and their need to take medication. We have conducted in-depth interviews with our clients and their partners to ascertain their beliefs and feelings about receiving a diagnosis and being treated with medication. From the client interviews (Young et al., in press) three themes emerged: (1) feeling 'different' from others; (2) the psychological and emotional impact of the diagnosis; and (3) preoccupation about the future.

1. *Feeling 'different' from others.* Clients reported that they had lived through their childhood and adolescence with the feedback that they were 'problem children'. They grew up with a sense that they were continually being unfavourably compared with their peers (by family members, friends and teachers). Clients reported to respond in one of two ways; they either accepted the perspective of others or rejected it. For those who accepted it, they reported they recognised themselves that they were less able than others and ruminated about possible causes. They said they felt confused and frustrated, and this led them to have low self-esteem and low expectations of themselves and what they may achieve. Other clients responded differently and dismissed the negative feedback of others. Perhaps their cognitive problems played a protective role by distracting them from engaging in a process of rumination. An insight into their differences compared with others came later when, with greater years and maturity, they reflected back on past events and/or they recognised the similarities between their behaviour in childhood and that of their own child who had been diagnosed with ADHD.

2. *The psychological and emotional impact of the diagnosis:* Immediately after receiving their diagnosis, clients reported feeling a great sense of relief and elation that they were finally being 'heard' and understood. The diagnosis was a 'meaning maker' that provided an opportunity for them to re-evaluate the past and relocate blame for past difficulties and failures by shifting from an internal attribution ('it was all my fault') to an external attribution ('it wasn't my fault at all, there was a reason – the ADHD'). This meant that their long quest for an explanation of their lifelong difficulties had finally come to an end. There followed a period of adjustment, which was characterised by feelings of turmoil and confusion when individuals looked back and reframed past experiences in light of their new knowledge and understanding of themselves. We call this sense of emotional turmoil 'the silent problems' as clients described themselves engaging in a tumultuous internal process when they tried to makes sense of their feelings of relief, joy, elation, anger and anxiety. They ruminated about the past and felt angry that they had not been diagnosed earlier and when they were younger. They thought about how their life experiences might have been more positive and how, with earlier treatment, more successful. At the same time they also felt anxious about the future and what it meant to have a 'disease for life'. The process ended with personal acceptance that 'ADHD is a part of me'.

3. *Preoccupation about the future.* Clients reported that taking stimulant medication gave them a sense of normality, i.e. they no longer felt 'different' to others, as

they felt they were now able to function in the same way as 'normal' people who don't share their difficulties. Medication had a positive impact on their ability to function successfully in their everyday lives, both in a task-oriented way and from an interpersonal perspective. The medication meant that they were able to structure and prioritise tasks better. They believed it enhanced their creative skills. In the past they had always believed that they were underachieving their potential; following treatment with medication they believed they could reach their potential. This meant that they had a more positive attitude and felt hopeful about the future. However, clients reported that as their medication wore off, others began to notice their symptoms and gave negative feedback regarding their behaviour and attitude. Previously they would have ruminated about this feedback and felt a dip in mood and/or dismissed it, but now they reported to be more accepting of it and thought about it more constructively, e.g. thinking about what they could do to change their behaviour. However, when the effects of medication wore off, the rapid emergence of symptoms made clients realise that there is no 'miracle cure' for their problems and that medication does not solve all of their problems. Treatment with medication helped clients distinguish between problems that were strongly associated with their symptoms and those that were less influenced by the presence of symptoms. This meant they became motivated to engage in a process of change, especially with respect to symptoms and/or problems they perceived to be resistant to treatment with medication. Nevertheless the perception of others remained a concern of clients who worried about the stigma of ADHD and that this was perceived to be a convenient excuse for their behavioural problems, e.g. that they would be viewed as 'a problem person' and not a 'person with a problem'.

The interviews identified a clear role for psychological intervention in the treatment of adults newly diagnosed with ADHD. This must reflect the stage of acceptance in which the client is engaged and the needs of the individual at that time. This will be best achieved through the provision of a treatment process that includes components of psychoeducation; a reflective person-centred paradigm; cognitive behavioural treatment to teach coping strategies and skills; and cognitive remediation techniques to teach strategies to control core symptoms.

Psychological treatment for adults begins at the time they are diagnosed. The way that the diagnosis is communicated to the client will be an important determinant of their future adjustment to the diagnosis. Attentional problems and anxiety may mean that many individuals do not attend adequately to the information given in a feedback appointment and factual information regarding diagnosis and treatment should be supplemented in a written handout and reinforced at subsequent appointments.

Clients need to be supported through the process of adjustment while they come to terms with the diagnosis and the impact of the disorder on their lives. The initial sense of relief is usually quickly replaced by more negative feelings, e.g. anger, resentment, anxiety, and/or depression as clients reflect on past experiences and ruminate on these from a new perspective. Clients often report feelings of anger toward the numerous child and adult medical and mental health services to whom they have presented over the years and who had 'missed' the diagnosis. There is a risk that individuals may become depressed if they ruminate over past under-achievements and lost opportunities. Poor impulse control may mean they act on suicidal ideations. It is important that the therapist acknowledges the client's feelings of emotional turmoil and helps them reframe the past by guiding them to learn from the past and focus on the future in a constructive manner. The therapist can apply cognitive behavioural techniques to help the client control their emotional lability and process feelings of distress. Learning cognitive skills to help reduce restlessness and impulsiveness, and improve the ability to sustain attention will increase confidence by giving clients a sense of control, especially when the effect of medication starts to dissipate.

Psychological treatment can then shift to focus on skills development, e.g. social skills, time management and problem-solving skills, in order to help the client develop methods to structure daily living and improve interpersonal skills so they may function more successfully and achieve their potential (Young, 1999, 2002). Concern about the future and how they will be evaluated by others can be addressed by emphasising the positive aspects of the ADHD disorder (e.g. creativity) and, secondly, by teaching clients skills to anticipate future challenges and hurdles and apply appropriate coping strategies. Clients need to develop a sense of self-efficacy that they have the ability to reach their potential and succeed in the future.

17.3 PSYCHOLOGICAL TREATMENT

Individuals with ADHD require structure in terms of personal organisation and social boundaries and practical help to cope with everyday problems. These needs are best met in a cognitive-behavioural paradigm, either applied on an individual or group basis, because this model has a strong evidence base (Roth & Fonagy, 1996).

However, there are a number of challenges in the adaptation of cognitive behavioural therapy (CBT) for this client group. These vary from pragmatic difficulties, e.g. resistance to completing 'homework' tasks as this reminds them of school work and associated feelings of underachievement or failure, to generic problems, e.g. core symptoms limiting their ability to stay focused and learn new tasks or techniques. Psychological treatment therefore is most likely to be effective if this integrates aspects from psychoeducational and motivational interviewing paradigms with cognitive behavioural therapy.

17.3.1 PSYCHOEDUCATION

ADHD adults are not passive recipients of health services, they are individuals with enquiring minds and a thirst for knowledge about their condition and its treatment. Thus psychoeducation should be applied from the start of the diagnostic process (Jackson & Farrugia, 1997) to provide fundamental information about ADHD, its aetiology, prognosis, comorbid problems, cognitive deficits and their expression in daily living. In spite of information being widely available in the media and internet, there is still a surprising amount of erroneous 'lay' information that may mislead and/or confuse the client. Understanding that their problems have a neurobiological basis that is responsive to treatment with medication, and that many of the problems are associated with the syndrome and may be effectively reduced by psychological treatment will be an important step in repairing the self-esteem of people who have long believed themselves to be stupid, and/or who have been labelled as stupid or lazy by others.

Individuals with ADHD want to know about their treatment options so they can make informed decisions about how best to organise and manage their lives. They want to know about the different types of medications, doses and side-effects in order to play an active role in determining what suits them best. Some individuals want to receive psychological treatment as well as medication, others may not want medication at all and prefer to learn psychological strategies to help them. This may particularly be the case as symptoms remit and the need for medication reduces. What is important, however, is that through the provision of psychoeducation sessions, the client will acknowledge and understand their personal strengths and limitations. This means they are more likely to develop realistic expectations of self-performance and they will be less likely to set themselves unachievable over-arching goals which are bound to fail. Failure reinforces the negative schema. In order to make progress they need to develop adaptive coping skills that help them achieve tasks, reach set goals and enjoy the feeling of success.

17.3.2   MOTIVATIONAL INTERVIEWING

CBT emphasises action as a means of addressing change and a central tenet of treatment involves engagement and collaboration in treatment. Individuals who adopt an ambivalent attitude are unlikely to be successful. Ambivalence may arise from a sense of learned helplessness and/or failure which then participates in a feedback loop process of self-fulfilling prophecy. Most people with ADHD like the thought of change; however, there may be pockets of resistance for problems that are long-standing and seem insurmountable to the client ('it never works out . . . I can't be bothered'). These feelings can be overcome by introducing motivational interviewing techniques into treatment. Motivational interviewing is a means of communication that facilitates change by expressing empathy, highlighting discrepancies between current behaviour and important goals or values, and inviting new perspectives (Miller & Rollnick, 2002). It is important, however, to emphasise to the client that the therapist cannot wave a magic wand and change the client, but the role of the therapist is to facilitate change and support the client in the change process. The aim of using these techniques is to induce a belief that change is possible, to develop the client's confidence that they are capable of making positive change in their life and that they are able to overcome any obstacles they will meet that may hamper success.

17.3.3   COGNITIVE BEHAVIOURAL THERAPY

Cognitive treatment has been successfully applied to this client group even with minimal contact (Wilens *et al.*, 1999; Stevenson *et al.*, 2002). Cognitive behavioural treatment aims for people with ADHD to develop personal coping strategies to manage the symptoms of ADHD and their associated problems. This involves utilising various cognitive techniques including cognitive remediation; cognitive reframing of the past; cognitive restructuring; cognitive reasoning strategies; skills development and rationalisation; development of internal/external compensatory strategies and behavioural techniques. In particular, cognitive remediation strategies draw on techniques commonly applied in brain injury rehabilitation services to improve executive deficits (e.g. memory and attentional control; reduce impulsive responding). They are therefore very appropriate to use when treating the core symptoms of adult ADHD and one small study has reported success (Stevenson *et al.*, 2002). Weinstein (1994) suggests that they are an 'important active adjunct' to other psychological treatment interventions. Learning to apply strategies that directly address and/or compensate for the core symptoms of ADHD may help individuals develop better organisational skills and give them a greater sense of self-control. Furthermore it may decrease the likelihood that they work in a self-imposed chaotic environment and reduce learned helplessness.

A target of treatment is to enable the individual to develop self-efficacy and the confidence that change can be achieved, to develop strategies to effect positive lifestyle change and cope with challenges. This involves education about the disorder, adopting psychoeducational techniques, overcoming ambivalence drawing on motivational interviewing decisional balance, cognitive-restructuring and reframing the past by challenging negative automatic thoughts, self-monitoring performance, recognising errors in thinking and evaluating cognitive distortions and misattributions. Whenever possible, it will also be important to elicit core beliefs the individual holds about him/herself, other people and the world. Behavioural techniques such as graded task assignments, modelling and role-play need to be employed to develop and rehearse new skills.

In order to maintain focus and concentration on the sessions, it is important to apply a variety of techniques in sessions (shifting topics, visual aids, role-play, etc.). Specific tools such as worksheets, role-plays and exercises are presented as ways of maintaining attention and motivation, and reducing impulsivity. A fast-paced structure incorporating a variety of cognitive behavioural techniques (including practical exercises) will be attractive to individuals who have significant cognitive deficits, high intolerance and a low boredom threshold. Encouraging individuals to extend techniques learned in sessions into their daily lives will include helping them to impose structure on their day and utilise plans, lists and prioritise tasks. Because individuals with ADHD are motivated to satisfy a need for immediate gratification, it is important to introduce both immediate smaller rewards and larger delayed rewards for successfully completing tasks.

17.4 THE YOUNG-BRAMHAM PROGRAMME

The Young-Bramham Programme is a structured programme that draws on psychoeducation, motivational interview techniques, cognitive behavioural therapy and cognitive remediation techniques (Young & Bramham, 2007). The programme is modular so specific topics can be selected as appropriate. Alternatively the therapist can work through each module until the programme is completed. If modules are to be selected, we recommend these are chosen collaboratively with the client so s/he is empowered by the process. Due to attentional and working memory deficits, it is recommended that sessions allow additional time for consolidation of information and rehearsal of new material. It is recommended that 3–4 sessions are spent on each module, but this may be shortened or lengthened according to the need of the individual. However, due to the underlying need for immediate gratification, we suggest that no more than 6 sessions are spent on one module at any time. If the material is not fully covered or needs to be repeated, we suggest that this is re-introduced at a later stage and following alternative modules in order to avoid boredom and disengagement. Because of the Young-Bramham Programme's modular design, skills acquisition is cumulative. Thus if the client has difficulty with a module presented early in the programme, this can be revised at a later stage when new skills have been acquired. This may make it seem easier to understand.

The Young-Bramham Programme is supplemented by a companion website of psychoeducational material and practical exercises. These help the ADHD client and therapist determine individual needs and difficulties which will become the targets for intervention, as well as providing information handouts and useful exercises to use in the course of treatment.

There are two primary aims of psychological treatment in the Young-Bramham Programme:

1. *Change from the outside in:* helping the individual to make adaptations to their environment in order to optimise their personal, occupational and social functioning.
2. *Change from the inside out:* helping the individual to develop psychological strategies for adaptive functioning within different environments.

The Young-Bramham Programme has been written for delivery in individual sessions. However, we have successfully delivered it in a more intensive 'group workshop' format running it as a 3-day programme (i.e. one day per month for three months). In traditional group therapy, patients meet weekly for 1–2 hours over a set period, but we have found that a workshop paradigm appeals better to ADHD individuals who have difficulty with delayed gratification. They respond positively to the 'immediacy' of workshops which cover aspects of one module at a time (e.g. in half-day or one-day sessions) and they are not expected to commit to weeks of treatment. There are regular breaks introduced in the programme (e.g. ten minutes every 1½ hours) and participants are provided with detailed handouts or 'workbooks' that contain exercises to complete within the workshop and/or later at home to reinforce the techniques presented. Individual treatment can follow group workshops which have introduced the client to basic techniques and information.

The Young-Bramham Programme outlines specific interventions that will be helpful in ameliorating core deficits (impulsivity, inattention, time management, problem-solving) and associated problems (social relationship skills, anxiety, anger and frustration, depression, sleep problems, alcohol and drug misuse, antisocial behaviour) as follows:

17.4.1   COPING WITH INATTENTION AND MEMORY PROBLEMS

Attentional and memory impairments can lead to many problems in day-to-day functioning including difficulties listening, failure to finish tasks, being easily distracted and coming off-task. In addition to coping with feelings of restlessness, clients with ADHD usually experience one of two types of attentional problem: (1) external distraction, e.g. they notice irrelevant details; and (2) internal distraction, e.g. they have a strong urge to do something different and perhaps more stimulating. In order to overcome these problems, clients need to learn techniques to help them develop better self-control and stay on task and introduce methods to adapt their environment to minimise the opportunity for distraction. This involves selecting the most appropriate surroundings suitable for success and maximising their ability to sustain attention by employing techniques such as setting small achievable steps towards goals, introducing regular breaks and frequent rewards for success. The module also provides internal and external strategies that the client can apply to improve their memory, e.g. the use of visual cues, rehearsal and repetition of information, making lists, using a diary etc.

17.4.2   COPING WITH IMPULSIVITY

People with ADHD act without thinking. They do things on the spur of the moment and don't think about the potential outcomes of their behaviour. They have a preference for immediate reward and an inability to delay gratification. They may make rash decisions without first obtaining and assessing all the available information. Research has shown that their inability to inhibit a response means that they make a high number of errors (Young *et al.*, 2006). These errors can be costly, both financially and emotionally, if individuals jump to conclusions, misappraise situations and/or misjudge the intention of others as this means they may respond in an inappropriate and/or dysfunctional way. This module helps ADHD clients identify situations in which they may be vulnerable to responding in an impulsive way and determine appropriate strategies of self-monitoring and self-restraint. This includes the use of stop-and-think techniques, self-instructional training, the use of self-statements, role-plays that involve the consequential thinking (both personal and social), and techniques to distract themselves from impulsively coming off-task when engaged in tedious tasks.

17.4.3   TIME MANAGEMENT

Managing and structuring time is a particular challenge for people with ADHD. This is because they become easily distracted from the task at hand and tend to have lots of things on the go that they need to do. Thus they flit from task to task and end up with lots of half-finished tasks and unmet deadlines. This can be a particular problem when it comes to completing the more mundane, but necessary, chores. Because they do not finish projects on time, they get a reputation for being unreliable. This can be a source of frustration and distress to the individual which leaves them with a strong sense of having let people down and being a failure. This module presents ways of applying a methodical approach to make plans by reviewing goals (short-term and long-term goals), listing activities, devising a time schedule, sequencing and prioritising activities, and planning breaks and rewards. Methods are also outlined to help the individual maintain their attention to completion of a task, to adhere to a plan, evaluate progress and avoid procrastination.

17.4.4   PROBLEM-SOLVING

People with ADHD are often not very good at solving problems for many reasons. Their poor impulse control and attentional limitations may mean that they select an immediate solution without a full evaluation of the situation and consideration of alternative possibilities. They may worry unnecessarily about minor more immediate issues, focus on or anticipate a negative outcome and lose sight of the whole picture. The module proposes methods to train the client to perform a thorough and accurate appraisal of the problem or situation and avoid engaging in an inaccurate and rapid decision-making process by teaching the individual to generate multiple alternative solutions, evaluate these solutions and implement them. Methods for choosing solutions include applying techniques, such as rehearsing a solution to evaluate consequences and challenging distorted thinking.

17.4.5   SOCIAL RELATIONSHIP SKILLS

One reason that many people with ADHD have interpersonal relationship difficulties is because their symptoms are misinterpreted by others. For example, their difficulty sitting still and concentrating on an important conversation may be perceived as them being superficial, disinterested and/or fickle. Their impulsivity means that they may have difficulty observing social rules, such as turn-taking and reciprocity in conversation. The tendency to be hypersensitive about criticism may hamper personal and professional relationships, even when this is given in a friendly and constructive way, as the ADHD client may respond by getting irritated and impatient, throw a tantrum and storm off. In order to improve social skills, this module introduces techniques to increase self-awareness, develop the ability to take another's perspective and accurately perceive and respond to the social cues provided by others by monitoring their facial expressions, posture, voice quality and gestures. Clients are taught to attend to non-verbal communication as well as verbal communication skills and rehearse challenging situations to better develop conversation and listening techniques.

17.4.6   COPING WITH FEELINGS OF ANXIETY

One of the most commonly experienced sources of anxiety for people with ADHD is reported to be group settings, especially ones in which they are expected to follow a predetermined protocol of behaviour (e.g. formal meetings). It is possible that clients lack confidence in their ability to impose self-control in such situations and anticipate that they will speak out of turn, interrupt someone speaking, say something silly, and/or draw unnecessary attention to themselves. This seems paradoxical given their seemingly disinhibited gregarious nature. This module applies classic CBT for anxiety problems to be more appropriate for people with ADHD by introducing an immediate reward system into the programme and focusing on the types of situations most likely to be experienced as anxiety-provoking by people with ADHD. The module introduces techniques to evaluate thoughts, feelings and modify behaviour in varying social situations, including controlling the impulse to over-compensate for feelings of inadequacy by 'playing the fool' and/or engaging in inappropriate attention-seeking behaviour.

17.4.7   COPING WITH FEELINGS OF ANGER AND FRUSTRATION

People with ADHD have feelings of anger and frustration for one of two reasons. The first is 'state' anger and this is symptom related, as this causes clients to have a predisposition towards explosive outbursts of temperament. This is more likely to be expressed outwardly than inwardly suppressed, possibly due to their poor impulse control, irritability and a low boredom threshold. Other people perceive these emotional outbursts as a negative character trait and anticipate that the individual is unpredictable and/or, in some cases, dangerous. The second reason is that ADHD clients may have 'trait' anger, which is expressed by their irritability and dissatisfaction towards various professional services (education, health, social) for inadequately meeting their needs. Clients will be particularly disposed to ruminating about their dissatisfaction regarding past service-presentations if diagnosis and treatment is made in adulthood. This module examines the dysfunctional ways of managing anger and the reasons people with ADHD feel angry are reviewed, e.g. impatience, the desire for immediate gratification. The stages of anger are examined according to a cognitive behavioural model, especially physical signs of anger, as if these are noticed and recognised, an individual may disengage from an anger-escalation process. Methods to cope with insults and criticisms are also introduced.

17.4.8   COPING WITH FEELINGS OF DEPRESSION

There is an increased risk for people with ADHD to feel low and depressed because they experience many knock-backs in life, e.g. academic underachievement or failure, relationship difficulties, and financial problems. Their cognitive deficits may mean that low mood may rapidly escalate into depression because of a lack of opportunity to experience success and mastery, an inability to plan and structure their time well, poor motivation to start projects and/or difficulty finishing them. Depression in people with ADHD needs to be taken very seriously because of their difficulty with self-regulation and impulsiveness, which may mean they will act out on an impulse to self-harm. An important feature of this module is to raise the awareness of clinicians about the potential risk of self-harm and suicide in this population. Following treatment with medication, increases the risk of depression as they may develop better insight into past problems but ruminate more, i.e. with reduced distractibility, over past failures and maladaptive interpersonal relationships with important people in their lives (e.g. parents, siblings). The cognitive-behavioural model of depression is adapted to incorporate inattentive and impulsive features of negative thinking and thinking errors. Ways of breaking the cycle are presented including challenging negative thoughts that are commonly experienced by people with ADHD, reducing self-talk that perpetuates low mood and developing positive self-statements relating to ADHD strengths (e.g. resilience, creativity).

17.4.9   SLEEP PROBLEMS

People with ADHD often complain of sleep problems. Some sleep problems may be explained by their core symptoms resulting in the client having an incessant feeling of inner restlessness or ceaseless mental activity, which causes them to find it difficult to get to sleep at night. Alternatively sleep problems may be more akin to disturbances associated with affective disorders such as early wakening. A disturbance in sleep pattern may also be related to change in medication for treating ADHD, particularly following withdrawal of stimulant medication, e.g. drug holidays. This module reviews the different types of sleep problems that are commonly experienced by clients and discusses the interplay between core symptoms of ADHD and sleep disturbance. The client is taught techniques to manage and reduce sleep-related problems drawing on sleep hygiene and relaxation paradigms.

17.4.10   ALCOHOL AND DRUG MISUSE

People with ADHD may become involved with substances via two mechanisms. First, poor impulse control may lead them to act recklessly and engage in risk taking behaviours such as experimentation with drugs (which may lead to addiction). Secondly, many individuals may have misused substances (especially amphetamines) in the past in order to self-medicate. This is especially likely to have been the case for undiagnosed adults who describe a paradoxical calming response as opposed to a speed-buzz. The module reviews types of substance misuse and their relationship with ADHD, including alcohol; nicotine; cannabis; opiates; stimulants; hallucinogens; tranquilisers; solvents. The module applies motivational interviewing techniques to engage the client to enter a process of evaluation regarding their substance misuse. It outlines the vicious cycle of substance use which makes it difficult to stop misuse, and discusses dysfunctional beliefs which may have developed for adults with ADHD around substance misuse. Other techniques include emphasising the issue of 'choice' and 'control', raising self-esteem, identifying methods for coping with physical cravings and urges, such as distraction techniques and activity scheduling and using support with positive feedback.

17.4.11   THE FUTURE – LEARNING TO LIVE WITH IMPULSIVITY AND INATTENTION

This is the only module that is always included in the Young-Bramham Programme and it is always the last module in the programme. It draws on a relapse prevention model by summarising techniques introduced in previous modules, and drawing attention to those that have been particularly helpful. The module teaches the client to incorporate a plan for 'risk' situations and/or times when they are likely to feel vulnerable and slip back into old habits. By identifying such times/situations, the client can be prepared to apply learned techniques and avoid impulsive and/or dysfunctional automatic responses. Relapse plans need to include multiple options that can be applied as appropriate to a variety of situations, e.g. seeking social support, seeking professional advice, applying cognitive techniques, and avoidance of troublesome situations/persons. The module emphasises the positive aspects of having ADHD such as creativity, resilience, and flexibility and discusses how to apply these characteristics adaptively to achieve success in everyday tasks, as well as to achieve medium- and longer-term plans. In particular the module examines the influence of expectations of the self on future outcomes, i.e. the interrelationship between self-efficacy and a self-fulfilling prophecy. Through engaging in a process of reappraisal of what they have learned and applied this to make achievements during the Young-Bramham Programme, the client will develop a greater sense of self-efficacy and purpose.

17.4.12   FORMAT AND STRUCTURE OF TREATMENT SESSIONS

Treatment sessions are helpful both on an individual basis or in a group format. Individual treatment means a therapist may tailor the treatment according to the individual's specific needs, whereas group treatment encompasses more general problems and provides normalisation, mutual understanding and peer support. This is important since adults with ADHD often report feeling socially isolated and misunderstood by others. A group forum provides the opportunity to meet people with similar problems and to share strategies for coping with difficulties. Individuals can validate their own experiences by sharing their thoughts with other adults with ADHD (Hallowell, 1995). In addition it provides opportunities for acquiring and rehearsing key skills within a supportive non-critical environment.

(a)   Therapeutic alliance

People with ADHD have interpersonal relationship problems and many of their relationships have been somewhat intense and short-lived. This means that they may find it difficult to develop a trusting therapeutic relationship and they are likely to be hypersensitive to rejection. It is important that the client has confidence in the therapist and perceives that the therapist understands their problems. It is essential that the therapist and client collaborate together to identify clear goals of treatment and outline session plans that work towards them achieving their target. Aside from this helping to engage the client in the collaborative process, it additionally models the ethos of the Young-Bramham Programme 'in vivo'.

(b)   Structure

Concentration problems may mean that individuals have difficulty following a train of thought or developing a theme using cognitive techniques. They may have difficulty keeping to time limits and/or struggle to cope with one or half-day workshops. A few individuals may even have difficulty attending a fifty-minute individual session. Adaptations to the therapeutic process will need to take account of these problems by introducing shorter sessions, scheduled breaks, structured changes in topic and/or variety in treatment methods (e.g. switching between visual aids, written exercise and role plays within sessions). Additional techniques and teaching aids need to be introduced in order to shift attention and maintain interest and motivation e.g. inclusion of role plays and use of individual exercises. If treatment is being provided in a group format, then dividing the group to work in pairs or small groups as well as incorporating larger group discussion is helpful.

(c) Agendas

An agenda should be drawn up collaboratively at the beginning of each session. The agenda provides a structure to follow within the session. The therapist needs to ensure that sessions are not sabotaged by the client introducing various 'crises' that take over the session and distract them away from adhering to the agenda and treatment. This will provide a model for the client of how to deal with difficult situations in a rational and non-catastrophic manner. The agenda should always include a time for 'matters arising', however, so important issues that arise may be discussed in the session and these may be brought forward and/or used as a basis for homework assignments and discussed again in the following session(s), by which time the matter may no longer be perceived to be of such great significance.

(d) Goal setting

The Young-Bramham Programme is modular in its design which means that once the problems have been identified that the client wishes to work on, then the relevant modules are selected and goals for treatment determined. This methodological aspect of treatment will help the client categorise their difficulties and which in turn will help them feel that their difficulties are manageable. Without setting clear goals for treatment, sessions may be reduced to disorganised chaotic and emotional sessions, which will leave both the therapist and the client feeling dissatisfied. Goals must be specific and the way to reach them broken down into stages. It is important to avoid general goals such as 'I wish I could get on better with people' or 'I want to be rich'. In order to maintain focus, goals should be reviewed regularly in the sessions.

(e) Rewards

People with ADHD are motivated to seek immediate or short-term rewards and they are unable to delay gratification by succeeding in long-term goals. This is one reason that goals of treatment must be broken down into multiple small steps that can be achieved and then each point of success should be associated with an immediate reward. This is an important and primary adaptation of cognitive behavioural therapy for people with ADHD. Rewards may range from short breaks in periods requiring intense concentration, reading the newspaper, a drink, a walk around the block to larger rewards for the completion of chores for the day and/or finalising a task, going out with a friend, watching a movie. It will be important to develop collaboratively sets of small, medium and larger rewards that can be applied in the course of the sessions and for homework assignments. Some individuals will have difficulty operating the system at first because they may impulsively take their reward even if they are not entitled to it. It is therefore imperative that small rewards are frequently introduced, especially at first, so they get used to how it feels to be rewarded for even small gains.

(f) Homework assignments

It is important that clients learn to take responsibility for endorsing and rehearsing techniques learned in sessions in an applied setting and this is achieved by setting homework assignments at the end of each session. The course of changing learned patterns of behaviour requires the rehearsal of new actions that are positively reinforced until these become automatic. One way of recognising and reinforcing success is for the client to record identified behaviours and monitor change in homework tasks. Thus the use of rating scales to record change in attitude and confidence, and/or ratings of steps achieved towards a set goal are a tangible measure of success which will positively reinforce and motivate the client towards reaching their goal and even setting new ones within the programme. Resistance to homework tasks needs to be addressed by identifying and anticipating potential obstacles that will prevent the client completing homework tasks.

(g) Treatment termination

Once the individual has worked through the appropriate modules of the Young-Bramham Programme to achieve individual goals, the client will be ready to complete the final module of the Young-Bramham Programme (The Future – Learning to Live with Impulsivity and Inattention). It is recommended that this module is never omitted. It is based on a relapse prevention paradigm that will prepare the client for the end of treatment. Some clients may take longer than others to reach this point, depending on the number of modules required and the number of sessions required for each module as it will take some clients longer to acquire skills than others. The Future module will encourage the client to disengage from the support provided by the therapist and seek this independently, e.g. by external endorsement of success and achievement. By the end of the programme the client will have learned the techniques required to set and obtain life goals, and success will positively reinforce success. However, the transition from treatment to autonomy needs to be planned carefully with collaboration, for example, by reducing the frequency of sessions and/or conducting brief planned follow-up sessions in person or by telephone.

17.5 ADHD AND ANTISOCIAL BEHAVIOUR

Findings from a qualitative study of 'high risk' adolescent boys (age 10–17) who obtained positive ratings on teacher ratings for ADHD on the Conners' scales and living in a residential care setting (providing both open and secure care) have determined the need and importance of psychological intervention for youth in this environment (Chesney, 2004). Transcripts of in-depth interviews using Interpretive Phenomenological Analysis identified three main themes relating to: (1) feelings of loss and vindication; (2) the search for a sense of belonging, and (3) consolations of confinement. The boys struggled to articulate experiences, thoughts or feelings both from their own perspective and those of others. They held external attributions regarding their antisocial behaviour and drew upon experiences of abuse, bereavement and rejection to 'explain' their offending, conduct and attentional problems. Thus they did not take personal responsibility for their behaviour. Although, the boys identified themselves as 'victimised', they did not acknowledge or consider their own victims.

Thus for ADHD children and adults who are associated with forensic or 'high risk' services, a primary target will be to improve reflective skills and verbal expression. In order to interrupt the antisocial trajectory of many of these young people, it will also be necessary for them to shift attribution of blame for their antisocial behaviour from an external perspective and encourage them to take greater personal responsibility for their conduct. This will include the development of empathetic capacity for victims of antisocial behaviour and the development of the cognitive and social skills associated with prosocial behaviour. The provision of both pharmacological treatment to reduce symptoms and psychological treatment has been shown to be effective in a case study of a 23-year-old high-security hospital patient convicted for arson and detained under a legal classification of psychopathic disorder (Young & Harty, 2001). This case illustrated how identification and treatment of ADHD have profound implications in terms of symptom reduction and the ability to engage and benefit from other treatments, e.g. education, psychological interventions, and occupational therapy. In this case treatment led to a reduction of risk, shorter length of stay in high security and earlier discharge to lower security than anticipated. However, following pharmacological treatment and, as the patient's core symptoms improved, he began to be thoughtful and analyse prior events, lost opportunities and disrupted relationships. As a child he had frequent contact with the local health authority and social services and he felt angry that his diagnosis had not been made earlier. Instead of flitting from one interest to another he ruminated about past events in his life and felt depressed. The patient had a history of deliberate self-harm and there was concern that he would impulsively act out suicidal ideation.

Symptoms of ADHD (diagnosed or undiagnosed) may lead professionals to draw the incorrect conclusion that these individuals are untreatable. Ironically such individuals may actually be untreatable if their underlying ADHD symptoms are unrecognised as this means that interventions are unlikely to be appropriately designed to treat the underlying condition.

There are various cognitive programmes, e.g. Reasoning & Rehabilitation (R&R) (Ross, Fabiano & Ross, 1986) that are used to change the thinking styles of antisocial individuals and offenders and these programmes have been delivered in various settings (e.g. community, hospital, prison and probation settings). The R&R programme has been delivered to more than sixty thousand antisocial youths and adult offenders in seventeen countries over the past twenty years and its efficacy has been demonstrated in numerous independent international evaluations (Antonowicz, 2005). However, antisocial individuals who display evidence of ADHD symptoms require a *specialised* programme that provides psychological treatment to manage their core symptoms as this (together with treatment with medication if appropriate) will help them engage better in psychological interventions designed to provide prosocial cognitive skills, emotional skills and values.

A new edition of the R&R programme has been developed for antisocial youth and adults who have ADHD (R&R2 for ADHD Youths and Adults: Young & Ross, 2007). A specific advantage of the programme is that it is not limited to providing treatment to individuals with a diagnosis of ADHD but also aims to treat individuals with symptoms and problems associated with ADHD, or with remitting symptoms, and who have conduct/antisocial behaviour problems. The R&R2 for ADHD Youth and Adults includes specific training techniques that target the cognitive, attitudinal, emotional and behavioural characteristics that are associated with ADHD symptoms that limit such individuals' ability to acquire prosocial competence or prevent them from benefiting from programmes designed to help them acquire prosocial competence. The programme can be delivered in the community, prison, probation or hospital settings. The programme appeals to clients as it has an ethos of 'training' as opposed to 'therapy'. It is highly structured and therefore does not have to be delivered by 'Trainers' who are experts in ADHD. The programme employs a variety of training techniques to engage the individual and aims to make the 'training' fun by incorporating games, individual and group exercises, role play, brainstorming, audiovisual material and the use of participants' workbooks. The goal of the programme is to teach the individual psychological techniques to control core symptoms associated with ADHD, to identify thinking errors and engage in a process of critical reasoning, alternative and consequential thinking. This is achieved in the delivery of four modules presented over 15 sessions: a Neurocognitive Module that introduces techniques to improve attentional control, memory, impulse control and develop skills in constructive planning; a Problem Solving Module which engages the individual in a process of skilled thinking as opposed to automatic thinking, scanning for information, problem identification, generative alternative solutions, consequential thinking, managing conflict and making choices; an Emotional Control Module which includes managing thoughts and feelings of anger and anxiety; and a Social Skills module which includes the recognition of the thoughts and feeling of others, both verbal and nonverbal, social perspective taking and the development of empathy.

The programme has been designed to provide maximum flexibility for trainers so it may be applied at the most appropriate developmental level of the individual. It introduces a neurocognitive skills module that establishes specific training techniques to improve attentional control, memory, impulse control and develop strategies to achieve by learning constructive planning techniques. Thus learning and applying these target skills complements the overall aim of the Reasoning & Rehabilitation programme to develop prosocial competencies by predisposing better performance in the programme and increasing the likelihood of positive outcome. By learning behavioural control and through the development of listening skills, the participants will be better able to focus on other aspects of the core curriculum aimed to develop prosocial attitudes, skills and values. This is achieved through modules of social cognition that teach problem-solving skills, skills in emotion regulation, social skills and values, social perspective taking, the development of empathy, critical reasoning, negotiation skills and conflict resolution.

17.6 CONCLUSION

The Multimodel Treatment of Children with ADHD Study (MTA Cooperative Group, 1999) showed that a combination of pharmacological and psychological treatments was the most efficacious method of treating children with ADHD. However, adults with ADHD are not the same as children with ADHD and psychological interventions may play a greater role in the treatment of adults with the condition than has been established for ADHD children. Adults with ADHD may have long experienced problems at school and home, interpersonal relationship difficulties and lack of achievement. By adulthood, many of them have developed a schema of 'internalised failure'. Following diagnosis, psychological treatment will play an important part in their understanding of themselves and their interaction with the world. Although medication helps alleviate core symptoms of ADHD, psychological intervention will help treat comorbid psychiatric problems, psychosocial problems and skills deficits. Indeed there is a strong evidence base for psychological treatment of many psychiatric problems that are associated with the ADHD condition.

The chapter has introduced two cognitive behavioural programmes that have been developed to help treat the problems commonly experienced by people with ADHD. The Young-Bramham Programme is a modular programme that may be applied on a 'pick and mix' basis in order to meet the individual needs of adults who suffer with this heterogeneous syndrome and/or whose symptoms are in full or partial remission. The programme can be applied in individual or group format. For youth and adults with antisocial behavioural problems, a more suitable programme is the R&R2 for ADHD Youth and Adults which aims to address symptoms and problems associated with ADHD and reduce antisocial attitudes and behaviour by teaching prosocial thinking styles.

17.7 REFERENCES

Antonowicz DH (2005) The Reasoning and Rehabilitation Program: outcome evaluations for offenders. In M McMurran, J Maguire (eds) *Social Problem Solving and Offending: Evidence, Evaluation and Evolution*. Chichester: John Wiley & Sons.

Chesney S (2004) The experience of conduct and attention problems in five adolescent males confined in a young offender unit: a study using interpretative phenomenological analysis. Unpublished DClinPsy doctoral dissertation: Salomons Canterbury Christ Church University College.

Dalsgaard S, Mortensen PB Frydenberg M, Thomsen PH (2002) Conduct problems, gender and the adult psychiatric outcome of children with attention-deficit hyperactive disorder. *British Journal of Psychiatry* **181**: 416–21.

Hallowell EM (1995) Psychotherapy of Adult Attention Deficit Disorder. In K Nadeau (ed.) *A Comprehensive Guide to Attention Deficit Disorder in Adults*. New York: Brunner/Mazel Publishers.

Jackson B, Farrugia D (1997) Diagnosis and treatment of adults with Attention Deficit Hyperactivity Disorder. *Journal of Counselling and Development* **75**: 312–19.

Miller WR, Rollnick S (2002) *Motivational Interviewing: Preparing People to Change Addictive Behaviour* (2nd edn). New York: Guilford.

MTA Cooperative Group (1999) A 14-month randomized clinical trial of treatment strategies for attention-deficit/hyperactivity disorder. the multimodal treatment study of children with ADHD. *Archives of General Psychiatry* **56**(12): 1073–86.

Ross RR Fabiano E, Ross RD (1986) *Reasoning & Rehabilitation: A Handbook for Teaching Cognitive Skills.* Ottawa: Cognitive Centre of Canada (cogcen@canada.com)

Roth A, Fonagy P (1996) *What Works for Whom? A Critical Review of Psychotherapy Research.* London: Guildford Press.

Stevenson CS, Whitmont S, Bornholt L *et al.* (2002) A cognitive remediation programme for adults with Attention Deficit Hyperactivity Disorder. *Australian and New Zealand Journal of Psychiatry* **36**: 610–16.

Weinstein C (1994) Cognitive remediation strategies: an adjunct to psychotherapy of adults with attention deficit hyperactivity disorder. *Journal of Psychotherapy Practice and Research* **3**(1): 44–57.

Wilens T, McDermott S, Biederman J *et al.* (1999) Cognitive therapy for adults with ADHD: a systematic chart review of 26 cases. *Journal of Cognitive Psychotherapy: An International Quarterly* **13**(3): 215–26.

Young S (1999) Psychological therapy for adults with Attention Deficit Hyperactivity Disorder. *Counselling Psychology Quarterly* **12**(2): 183–90.

Young S (2002) A model of psychotherapy for with ADHD. In S Goldstein, A Teeter (eds) *Clinical Interventions for Adult ADHD: A Comprehensive Approach.* New York: Harcourt Academic Press.

Young S (2005) Coping strategies used by ADHD adults. *Personality and Individual Differences* **38**(4): 809–16.

Young S, Bramham J (2007) *ADHD in Adults: A Psychological Guide to Practice.* Chichester: John Wiley & Sons.

Young S, Bramham J, Gray K, Rose E (in press) The experience of receiving a diagnosis and treatment of ADHD in adulthood: a qualitative study of clinically referred patients using Interpretative Phenomenological Analysis. *Journal of Attention Disorders.*

Young S, Harty M (2001) Treatment issues in a personality disordered offender: a case of ADHD in secure services. *Journal of Forensic Psychiatry* **12**(1): 158–67.

Young S, Heptinstall E, Sonuga-Barke EJS *et al.* (2005) The adolescent outcome of hyperactive girls: interpersonal relationships and coping mechanisms. *European Child & Adolescent Psychiatry* **14**(5): 245–53.

Young S, Ross RR (2007) *R&R2 for ADHD Youths and Adults: A Handbook for Teaching Prosocial Competence.* Ottawa: Cognitive Centre of Canada (cogcen@canada.com).

Young S, Toone B, Tyson C (2003) Comorbidity and psychosocial profile of adults with Attention Deficit Hyperactivity Disorder. *Personality and Individual Differences* **35**(4): 743–55.

Young S, Morris RG, Bramham J, Tyson C (2006) Inhibitory dysfunction on the Stroop in adults diagnosed with Attention Deficit Hyperactivity Disorder. *Personality and Individual Differences.* **41**: 1377–84.

18 ADHD in the Classroom: Symptoms and Treatment

WILL WILKINSON[1] AND MALIE LAGENDIJK[2]

1. Boleybeg, Barna, Co. Galway, Ireland; 2. National University of Ireland, Galway, Ireland

18.1 OVERVIEW

Attention Deficit/Hyperactivity Disorder (AD/HD) represents one of the greatest impediments to the teaching–learning process. In this chapter, we emphasise how the behaviours associated with AD/HD impact classroom pedagogy. Subsequently, we cluster school-based interventions into three general domains: academic, behavioural, and cognitive–behavioural. A sample of topics include individualised education plans, technology applications, home–school liaise, applied behaviour analysis, self-monitoring, and social skills programmes. Specific techniques within each domain are illustrated with exemplary research bearing on the efficacy of the intervention.

18.2 INTRODUCTION

Being short, not quick of foot, and having poor eye–hand coordination would not predict success in basketball. Likewise, being quiet, reflective, and socially reticent would not auger well for success in sales or marketing. Fortunately, individuals who lack the requisite dispositions for careers in basketball and sales are free to choose any endeavour they desire, preferably one which matches their strengths and minimises weaknesses.

By contrast, imagine one who is involuntarily placed in a situation where a premium is placed on the very attributes the person does not possess. Further, consider that the one in question is a child and must endure, on a daily basis, the mismatch between what is expected and what the individual cannot deliver. This is precisely what occurs for a child with Attention Deficit/Hyperactivity Disorder (AD/HD) in the school classroom.

If one could pick, from all the variables of individual difference, the one most critical to basic survival in school, it would be difficult to select a variable more important than attention span, focus, and basic concentration. Regardless of general ability and attainment levels, a student who can pay attention, persist, listen, and remain on-task, will have the one basic tool necessary to follow classroom rules. Essentially, the concentrating child has the most basic, prerequisite tool to learn and progress.

Handbook of Attention Deficit Hyperactivity Disorder. Edited by M. Fitzgerald, M. Bellgrove and M. Gill.
© 2007 John Wiley & Sons Ltd

This is not the case with a child who presents with AD/HD. Take a core symptom like inability to withhold impulses, which any experienced teacher will re-frame as 'doesn't raise hand before answering questions'. Similarly, consider the idea of impatience, another core symptom, which is easily recognisable in the school environment as 'not waiting for his/her turn'. These problems alone can create significant discipline problems for the class teacher. And, if one considers the entire symptom spectrum that is AD/HD, it is amazing that a child with AD/HD can last a single day in the classroom. Certainly, teachers will be tested to the limits, and, at the very least, wonder why so many commonplace interventions have so little effect.

For example, consider the following case history as it relates solely to the child's educational history:

Table 18.1. A child with AD/HD in the school classroom

The child is a nine-year-old boy. The consistent report from teachers is that the child is very scattered: can't find necessary learning materials, leaves books/copies at home, forgets assignments, and spends an inordinate amount of time looking for required materials in his desk or school bag. If the child has all the prerequisite equipment, then he will play with pencils, erasers, paper, but not actually work on the assignment. Independent seatwork is rarely successful unless teachers can sit or stand next to the desk and monitor/prompt the child to stay on-task. If one-to-one supervision is not forthcoming, the child will invariably find some task-irrelevant behaviour, including looking at other students, staring out the window, whispering to another student, drawing on the paper, etc.

In the first few years of primary school, the child rarely stayed in his chair. He was often out of his seat to sharpen his pencil, ask classmates questions, look out the window, and anything but stay seated. He was always the first to check out an event, such as a child having a new toy, looking at somebody else's drawing, anything but remaining seated. If there was any noise in the room, the teacher always knew where to look. When he did do schoolwork, he tended to rush through it and make numerous careless mistakes.

He also had great difficulty waiting, and always interrupted teachers while they spoke to other students. During class discussions, the basic rule was to raise your hand before answering a question, and this child rarely did so. Instead, he blurted out a comment or response, despite frequent reminders not to.

In the end, teachers recognised that this child did not intend to be so active, inattentive, and impulsive. Teachers realised that the behaviour they observed was not intentional, but beyond the child's control. Even when the child was seemingly trying to follow class rules, something prevented him from doing so.

History shows no significant medical complications (e.g. no hospitalisations, accidents, injuries). Parents have told teachers that the child was a 'demanding' baby who slept little and was always very alert. He enjoyed Montessori school and no complaints were noted at this time. Difficulties came to serious attention when he started primary school (e.g. parents were told that he was very 'active' and tended to rush through schoolwork). Teachers note that the child has age standard ability and learning attainments. Rather, it is the child's behaviour that is becoming a source of concern for teachers and parents. Teachers, in reviewing previous reports, note the following consistent comments:

- not applying himself; not achieving to potential
- lazy, unmotivated
- rarely completes work; leaves assignments unfinished; won't finish work unless supervised
- extremely short attention span; easily distracted
- avoids any form of sustained mental work (e.g. reading, maths, writing)
- doesn't seem to listen to instructions; must continually repeat self
- inconsistent; some days better than others
- forgetful; leaves books/copies at home
- blurts out answers; trouble waiting his turn; interrupts others
- does not stay in chair; fidgets a lot

In general, AD/HD is a heterogeneous group of learning and behaviour disorders, characterised by a core triad of symptomatic behaviours including persistent overactivity, impulsivity, and difficulties in sustaining attention (Taylor, 1994). AD/HD, as defined by the American Psychiatric Association's Diagnostic and Statistical Manual of Mental Disorders (DSM-IV-TR, APA, 2000), is a 'persistent pattern of inattention and/or hyperactivity-impulsivity that is more frequent and severe than typically observed in individuals at a comparable level of development'. These dysfunctions are manifested in symptoms, such as aggression, poor rule-regulated behaviour, poor delay of gratification, behavioural disinhibition, learning difficulties, poor impulse control, and low motivation, that interfere directly with achievement of developmental tasks, academic performance, and social relationships (Cantwell, 1996). It is no wonder then that AD/HD represents a serious public health concern, accounting for the largest number of referrals to child mental health clinics of all psychiatric and behavioural problems of childhood (APA, 2000).

18.3   THE RATIONALE FOR SCHOOL-BASED INTERVENTIONS

AD/HD is an increasingly important educational issue. As noted earlier, children and adolescents with AD/HD are at high risk relative to the normal population with respect to scholastic and social failure in school settings (Weiss & Hechtman, 1993). A review of the literature suggests that the classroom context is a critical one for the development of interventions for children with AD/HD. After all, the classroom is the place where children of school age spend considerable time, and where the demands for attention, concentration, and impulse control are virtual requirements for school success (Drumm, 2004). Specifically, the classroom is a setting which requires a high degree of planning, coordination, control, and evaluation of procedures (e.g. in following rules), interacting adequately with peers and teachers, actively participating in the learning process, and avoiding the interruption of classmates' activities (Miranda, Presentacion & Soriano, 2002). It is for this reason that the classroom has been deemed an important and appropriate setting in which to introduce a variety of interventions, which will support the personal, social, and scholastic development of students with AD/HD.

Nearly all children with AD/HD have attainment problems in school, and co-morbid specific learning difficulties (such as Dyslexia) have been estimated to occur in 10 to 25 per cent of cases (Hinshaw, 1994). Such associated difficulties may require extra resources in the form of a special needs assistant, access to a special class, remedial intervention, and/or resource teacher support. In addition to the triad of primary symptoms displayed by children with AD/HD, such children often present with other important problems in adjustment, including difficulties in social relationships. (Frick & Lahey, 1991). Youngsters with AD/HD do not lack knowledge about social skills; rather they are unaware of their failure to use them (Carr, 1999). Social problems may interfere with routine functioning in a multiplicity of domains, such as difficulties in making and maintaining appropriate peer relationships (Sheridan & Dee, 1996).

In recent times, there has been a reported increase in the administration of psycho-stimulant medication for school-aged children with AD/HD (Cooper, 2001). Stimulant treatment seems to be the treatment of choice for children with AD/HD, because it has been found to improve such common deficits as impulsivity, inattention, and other executive functions dependent on behavioural inhibition (Miranda *et al.*, 2002). However, although some children display reductions in behavioural symptoms with the use of medication, it has not been shown that academic performance improves to the same level (Swanson *et al.*, 1995), nor has it been shown that psycho-stimulants produce long-term positive changes (Pelham, Wheeler & Chronis, 1998). Following a thorough review of the literature, Greenhill (1998) concluded that stimulant therapy is effective in 70% of cases in reducing the core symptoms of AD/HD, and that the most effective treatment overall involves the combination of medication and psychological intervention in the form of intensive behavioural treatments (Multimodal Treatment Study of Children with AD/HD Cooperative Group, 1999).

The use of stimulant medication is not a panacea, as it does not exclude the need for other interventions in targeting behavioural and academic difficulties (Sattler, 2002). There is therefore a real need for the implementation of psychosocial and psychoeducational treatments, as simply medicating children does not teach them the skills they need to improve their behaviour and academic performance. In light of the various difficulties such children must face, school professionals are thus in need of effective strategies for managing behaviour and enhancing academic performance for students with AD/HD. The aim of school-based interventions is to provide the child with an appropriate environment in which to learn (with suitable curriculum and level of teacher contact), a contingency-management programme to establish or reduce target behaviours, and self-management strategies that focus on teaching the child skills they need to improve their own behaviour and academic performance. It is important to note that not all students with AD/HD will respond favourably to the same interventions, thus one must determine what works for each individual student's learning needs.

In their meta-analytic study of school-based interventions, DuPaul and Eckert (1997) found school-based interventions to be effective in reducing AD/HD-related behaviours and, to a lesser extent, in enhancing academic performance. These same authors provided a useful way of classifying relevant studies into one of three categories, which will be used here for the purposes of clarifying the various school-based interventions found in the literature. These include:

(a) *Academic intervention:* This type of 'instructional management' intervention focuses primarily on manipulating antecedent conditions (i.e. academic instruction, materials, classroom structure), and requires the provision of efficient instructional resources adapted to the learning style of children with AD/HD.
(b) *Behavioural intervention*: This type of 'contingency management' intervention involves training teachers in the use of techniques, such as positive reinforcement to establish or reduce target behaviours, contingency contracting, token reward, time-out, response cost, planned ignoring, or losing privileges.
(c) *Cognitive-behavioural intervention*: This type of intervention (also referred to 'cognitive behaviour modification') refers to techniques designed to provide

individuals with the tools necessary to control their own behaviours (e.g. cognitive modelling, self-reinforcement, self-monitoring, self-instruction). It focuses on the development of self-control skills and reflective problem-solving strategies as a means of regulating an individual's behaviour.

18.4 ACADEMIC INTERVENTIONS

The aim of academic or 'instructional' interventions is to modify the school environment to draw out the child's strengths rather than their weaknesses. All too often weaknesses are drawn out due the rigidity of the classroom structure and environment, as well as the expectation that all children should attend to and concentrate on tasks, control their impulses, and achieve academic success through traditional forms of teaching. Academic interventions include the importance of psychoeducation and collaboration between home and school, modifying classroom structure, tailoring teaching techniques and task demands, and the more recent introduction of technology applications.

18.4.1 PSYCHOEDUCATION

The main aims of psychoeducation are to increase teachers' knowledge about AD/HD and to enable the teacher to respond to the educational needs of students with AD/HD. The educational success of children with AD/HD involves the presence of teachers actively and willingly engaged in the process of working with AD/HD students, and a supportive administration that recognises AD/HD as a condition in need of specialised accommodations, and provides training and resources necessary to adequately serve the special needs of these students (Pfiffner & Barkley, 1998). Empirical data suggest that lack of training and knowledge in the area of AD/HD is the barrier most frequently indicated by primary school teachers in the process of working with students with AD/HD (Reid *et al.*, 1994).

The teacher's knowledge of and attitude about AD/HD are critical. It is important that the teacher has knowledge and understanding about the nature and causes of AD/HD, and is willing to problem-solve and apply well-documented interventions to help children with AD/HD overcome their difficulties. Social perception and expectations may well play a large role in how children's behaviour is considered by school professionals: appreciating that children with AD/HD don't misbehave on purpose enables teachers to work more sensitively and carefully with them (Comfort, 1994). A positive teacher–student relationship, based on teacher understanding of the student and the disorder, enables improved academic and social functioning. Once aware of the difficulties such children have, educators can begin to meet these children at their level and to adapt the classroom environment to suit their individual learning needs.

18.4.2 COLLABORATION BETWEEN HOME AND SCHOOL

An important consideration for enhancing the effectiveness of school-based interventions is the relationship between home and school. When both teachers and parents are knowledgeable about AD/HD, have realistic goals, and are motivated to work with the child, effective collaboration may develop easily. However, this is not always the case as a negative cycle of communication may develop between home and school (Drumm, 2004), which compromises the student's progress. For example, parents may feel that the school system is failing to adequately address their child's needs, whilst teachers may believe that family difficulties are impacting on the child's symptoms, or that medication should be considered in lieu of accommodations in the classroom. Parents and teachers thus need to dispel notions of blame and to work toward improving the fit between the child's characteristics and the home and school environments (Pfiffner & Barkley, 1998).

The need to establish interventions in all settings in which difficulties occur is crucial as changes in one setting rarely generalise without intervention to other settings, an example being the effective use of home-based reward programmes as an adjunct to classroom-based interventions. In any case, there needs to be regular communication between home and school to ensure consistency across both settings in terms of addressing the child's learning needs, making it important to arrange structured fixed times for meetings, where parents and teachers can discuss concerns without an overly negative focus. Parents and teachers should meet on a regular basis to discuss the child's educational progress (the older child could attend some of these meetings), where clear roles are delineated for teacher, parent, and child, which presents a concrete method of developing an effective collaboration between home and school.

18.4.3   CLASSROOM STRUCTURE

In recent years, increased attention has been paid to the importance of the structure of the classroom environment, classroom rules, and the nature of task assignments for improving AD/HD children's school functioning. One of the most common modifications to the classroom environment involves moving the child's desk away from other children to an area closer to the teacher at the front of the classroom, but including them as part of the regular class seating. This reduces the child's access to peer reinforcement of disruptive behaviour, limits possibilities of distraction, and allows the teacher to better monitor the child's progress and behaviour, and to provide more frequent feedback. Altering seating arrangements in this manner may be as effective as a reinforcement programme in increasing appropriate behaviour (Pfiffner & Barkley, 1998).

It is essential for the classroom to be a place where activities are highly structured, well organised, and predictable, and where the teacher uses motivation-based strategies and a practical hands-on approach. Incorporating as much routine as possible into the school environment and establishing clear guidelines and limits for behaviour will help children know what is expected of them. Children with AD/HD may not handle change very well, so it is important to avoid too many transitions (i.e. change in teacher, physical relocation, schedule changes, and disruptions), and to ensure that children are prompted in advance of any transitions or shift in rules of conduct. Giving children with AD/HD choices in school is helpful to them because they need to learn how to make choices and to use their decisions wisely (Comfort,

1994). It is thus important to strike a balance between giving these students, on the one hand, much-needed structure and routine but, on the other hand, enabling them to be given a fair amount of independence and choice.

18.4.4 TASK DEMANDS

As with all children, academic tasks should be well matched to the child's abilities. In order to increase students' sense of success, academic assignments should be brief and presented one at a time, short time limits for task completion should be specified (e.g. use of timer), and feedback regarding accuracy of assignments should be immediate (i.e. as it is being completed). It is worth stressing that accuracy is more important than speed, and that quality is more important than quantity. When giving instructions, it is important to maintain eye contact, to use short and simple directions, to demonstrate and model what is expected, to alert students to critical information by using key phrases (e.g. 'this is important'), and to monitor frequently for understanding by asking students to repeat the instructions (Sattler, 2002).

It is important for children to feel comfortable with seeking assistance, and then for teachers to gradually reduce the assistance given, whilst keeping in mind that children with AD/HD may need more help for a longer period of time than the average child. Students may be encouraged to keep assignment logs, memory and visual reminder strategies (e.g. stop signs or big ears for 'stop, look, and listen'), and other organisational aids such as a daily assignment notebook, which may also be used for regular communication with parents (ERIC Digest, 1998). Consistent study habits are to be promoted, and a sense of responsibility for completing tasks (Lerner, 1997).

18.4.5 TEACHING TECHNIQUES

There are several ways in which teaching techniques may be modified to suit the needs of the student with AD/HD. First, children's attention during classroom lessons may be enhanced by delivering the lesson in an enthusiastic yet task-focused style, keeping it brief, and allowing frequent and active child participation. Interspersing classroom lessons with brief moments of physical exercise may also help diminish fatigue, as well as scheduling as many academic subjects in morning hours as possible, in light of the progressive worsening of the student's inattentiveness over the course of the day (Pfiffner & Barkley, 1998).

Further, varying the presentation format and task materials by using multisensory modalities and colourful, stimulating tasks (e.g. colour, shape and texture) may be useful in reducing activity level, enhancing attention, and improving the overall performance of children with AD/HD. For example, one may supplement traditional lectures with visual aids, video clips, demonstrations, and small-group activities (Sattler, 2002). Ideally, low-interest or passive tasks should be interspersed with high-interest or active tasks to optimise performance, as tasks requiring an active response may also allow hyperactive children to better channel their disruptive behaviours into constructive responses (Zentall, 1993). The use of computers may also be used to increase students' motivation, as will now be discussed.

18.4.6   TECHNOLOGY APPLICATIONS

One potentially effective tool for working with children with AD/HD is computer-based technology, which offers new options for the expansion and development of instructional interventions. Technology may be effective because a number of inherent features are closely associated with characteristics of effective instruction for children with AD/HD. For instance, the computer can provide step-by-step instruction, organise content into smaller chunks of information, wait for responses, offer immediate feedback and reinforcement, and allow repeated trials so students can begin to learn problem-solving techniques, and evaluate consequences in a safe environment.

Software may also be used to introduce new material with graphics, words, and sound, which tallies with the usefulness of multisensory approaches to increase the student's motivation. Although in theory computer-based technologies offer great promise for children with AD/HD, further research must be conducted to identify the most effective technologies and establish service delivery systems where teachers are adequately trained, with the aim of promoting large-scale implementation (Xu, Reid & Steckelberg, 2002).

A number of practical interventions (adapted from Comfort, 1994; Drumm, 2004) may be used effectively to enhance the classroom environment and enable the child with AD/HD to learn more effectively (Table 18.2).

Table 18.2. Practical interventions in the classroom

1. The classroom environment needs to be structured and predictable, with rules, timetables, and assignments clearly spelled out.
2. Seat the child close to the teacher, and limit possibilities of distraction.
3. Offer choice, and allow for flexibility within the structure.
4. Prepare the child for what will happen next.
5. Establish schedules that build in frequent and physically active breaks. Other activities given at regular intervals can help break up concentration time.
6. Instructions should be brief, clear, and repeated a number of times. They should be written down as well as given orally. Ask the child to repeat the instructions back to the person giving them.
7. Multisensory modalities (e.g. pictures) are recommended when teaching and explaining.
8. Be careful not to over-stimulate or to over-exhaust.
9. The child should be given extra time to complete tasks, length of assignments should be shortened or broken down into easily completed parts to increase success. After all, success is one of the best motivators.
10. Provide stepwise instruction and regular feedback. Praise the child and 'catch them' behaving appropriately.
11. Understand and tolerate mistakes, and use them as opportunities for learning.
12. Teach goal setting: Plan for and monitor realistic steps toward goal achievement.
13. Collaborate with students' parents by meeting with them on a regular basis and delineating clear roles for teacher, parent, and child.
14. Alter expectations for a child with AD/HD and increase awareness of the most effective interventions.

18.4.7 EFFECTIVENESS OF ACADEMIC INTERVENTIONS

In their study investigating the effectiveness of a school-based multi-component programme for the treatment of children with AD/HD, Miranda *et al.* (2002) found that academic performance (i.e. in mathematics and natural sciences) was enhanced by the implementation of instructional procedures or academic interventions. This finding is noteworthy, considering that neither behaviour modification, nor the use of psycho-stimulant medication, has previously been found to improve academic performance (DuPaul & Eckert, 1997). In addition to 'Academic Interventions', teacher-administered consequences continue to be the most commonly used psychosocial interventions with children with AD/HD.

18.5 BEHAVIOURAL INTERVENTIONS

In this group of interventions, we limit our discussion to consequences, or contingency management; that is, the group of teacher behaviours that immediately follow the child's behaviour. There is certainly partial overlap with the 'Academic Interventions' in that knowing how to manage consequences involves knowing what are the relevant antecedents (i.e. the context in which the behaviour occurs). However, behavioural interventions do not focus on the antecedents, instead they stress the consequence part of the A-B-C chain. It should be noted at the outset that behaviour researchers, or those in the 'applied behaviour analysis' camp, would beg to differ with the concept of AD/HD as a useful construct (Reid & Maag, 1998). Knowing that one has a short attention span does little to promote an effective intervention. That is, one of the key components of the behavioural interventions is not to refer to specific symptoms of AD/HD, but rather, to target specific behaviours directly observable in the classroom. For instance, in behavioural intervention studies, no reference is made to 'short attention span' or 'easily distracted'. Instead, the most common occurring dependent variable is 'off-task', as observers can more reliably record whether a child is on-task (e.g. sitting at desk doing independent seatwork) or off-task (e.g. looking out the window). Stated differently, 'short attention span' is a hypothetical construct, while 'on/off task' are observable behaviours.

Hence, effective behaviour management programmes not only aim to target directly the behaviours where change is desired, but also focus on teaching children a set of skills and adaptive behaviours to replace the problematic behaviour (DuPaul & Stoner, 1994). As stated, because behavioural improvement in the classroom may not necessarily be paralleled by improvement in academic functioning, increased attention is now being paid to the development of academic skills rather than just 'on-task' behaviour. More recently, investigators (e.g. Boyajian *et al.*, 2001) have studied methods to better link the selection of target behaviours with intervention for AD/HD through the use of functional assessment. The general procedure is also known as 'functional analysis', where various types of conditions (e.g. type of task, structure of class, etc.) are analysed with an eye to determining how these conditions influence behaviour. It is this type of careful analysis and subsequent intervention that is becoming increasingly salient with children in the school setting.

There are several differences in the use of contingencies with students who are diagnosed with AD/HD relative to a non-AD/HD cohort. For example, it is well known that children with AD/HD will not respond to contingencies unless these contingencies are powerful and immediate (Pfiffner & Barkley, 1998). While this is true of all children, the immediacy and potency of rewards are more an issue with AD/HD children relative to non-AD/HD samples. Another difference is the frequency of contingencies. Whereas children without AD/HD do not require consistent contingency management throughout the school day, children with AD/HD do in view of their motivational difficulties. Thus, when considering school-based contingencies, one must be able to implement these contingencies at any given time during the day.

Likewise, it is sometimes necessary to continue these contingencies at home, in order to provide an environmental constancy. This would not necessarily be the case in children who do not present with AD/HD. Thus, home-based reward programmes can be an effective adjunct to classroom-based interventions (Pfiffner & Barkley, 1998). For example, once children show that they can respond to a continuous reward system, written contingency contracts or behaviour modification charts may be used, where the child agrees to carry out certain agreed target behaviours, and in return the teacher and the parents agree to certain rewards if the targets are met and certain response costs where targets are not met. This helps give the child choice, encourages responsibility, and assists in developing an internal sense of self-control (Drumm, 2004).

When setting behavioural targets for which the child can earn reinforcers, the targets should be highly specific and typically centre on following instructions to behave in a positive way rather than cease behaviour in a negative way (e.g. 'I've noticed that you finished your task before the end of class today. Well done!'). Rewards that are employed must be changed or rotated more frequently for children with AD/HD, given their tendency for more rapid habituation to response consequences, to maintain the power of efficacy of the programme in motivating appropriate child behaviour. Finally, in most cases, individual contingency management programmes are more effective for AD/HD students relative to group contingency management. That is, the student with AD/HD is singled for particular consequences instead of consequences being delivered to the entire class, or to a larger group. When using individual contingencies, it may be more effective if this is conducted quietly and without drawing attention of the class to the process, since the class's response may make both receiving and losing points equally reinforcing (Carr, 1999), not to mention the possible social impact of singling out a child in the classroom.

In reviewing research on contingency management, the most frequently occurring teacher-based consequences are:

- *Positive reinforcement:* A consequence that directly increases the student's behaviour it follows.
- *Extinction* (also known as 'planned ignoring'): This is a consequence through which its purposeful withdrawal decreases the behaviour it follows.
- *Punishment* (e.g. 'response cost'): A negative consequence designed to decrease the behaviour it follows.

There are many examples from the behaviour literature, which can be squarely placed in each tradition. What follows are prototypical examples of each of the aforementioned consequences.

18.5.1 POSITIVE REINFORCEMENT

Because of their low levels of intrinsic motivation and their difficulty in sustaining effort when reinforcement is inconsistent and weak, children with AD/HD may be more dependent on external reinforcers and usually require more frequent and powerful reinforcement to modify classroom performance. Positive reinforcement comes in many forms (e.g. praise, tangible rewards, token economies). One of the most frequently cited forms of positive reinforcement is the already mentioned 'contingency contract', which was one of the interventions used by Flood and Wilder (2002). They recorded 'off-task' behaviour (e.g. looking away from the task for more than 3 seconds, not writing/rubbing out for 5 seconds etc.) during a no-treatment baseline condition for an 11-year old boy diagnosed with AD/HD. During the treatment condition, a contingency contract was implemented where the child could earn access to a desired item if a certain amount of academic work was completed. The results indicated a dramatic increase in on-task behaviour.

There are numerous other types of positive reinforcement programmes, ranging from structured formal systems, such as token economies (Reid & Maag, 1998) and automated classroom reinforcement (Evans et al., 1995), to less formal and non-structured positive reinforcement (e.g. teacher praise). Unfortunately, positive reinforcement, by itself, is usually insufficient in modifying AD/HD-type behaviour. Whereas the use of positive approaches is emphasised when working with children AD/HD, negative consequences are usually necessary. Therefore, positive reinforcement is often used in conjunction with response suppression contingencies. In reviewing the literature, the two most common types of response inhibition methods are extinction (also known as 'planned ignoring'), and a punishment paradigm known as 'response cost', which will be discussed in the next section.

18.5.2 PLANNED IGNORING (EXTINCTION)

Active ignoring requires the complete and contingent withdrawal of positive teacher attention to decrease inappropriate behaviour. Using a standard functional analysis paradigm in an experimental study of extinction, Edwards, Magee and Ellis (2002) examined the behaviour of a 10-year-old student with AD/HD. Of the four functional assessment conditions, the one relating to extinction was the 'attention condition', where every time a target behaviour occurred (e.g. aggression, non-compliance, or off-task behaviour), the adult immediately commented on the infraction and attended to the misbehaviour (e.g. 'You threw your book at the wall'). Results of the baseline attention condition indicated that aggression was especially high when immediately followed by contingent adult attention. To change this situation, the condition was modified into 'extinction', where the adult did not comment or pay any form of attention to aggressive behaviour (i.e. no eye contact, no verbal comment, etc.). This modified condition resulted in a dramatic decrease in aggressive behaviour.

It should be noted that these conditions were in an experimental setting (e.g. clinic room with one adult). However, the researchers exported these principles to the classroom setting by training the teacher to ignore the students' misbehaviour in the classroom (i.e. when misbehaviour occurred, the teacher immediately attended to another student or students, as if the infraction did not occur). This type of 'planned ignoring,' combined with a frequent positive reinforcement (e.g. teacher praise when appropriate behaviour occurred) resulted in a significant decrease in all misbehaviours, a decrease that was maintained long after the intervention was employed (Edwards *et al.*, 2002). As not all behavioural difficulties of children may be considered as purely bids for teacher attention, it is recommended that this strategy be used in tandem with praise.

18.5.3   RESPONSE COST

In general, 'response cost' refers to the loss of reward contingent on an inappropriate behaviour. For example, in a classroom token economy, a token (e.g. points, stars, beads, etc.) is earned when appropriate behaviour occurs (positive reinforcement) and removed when inappropriate behaviour occurs; removal refers to the child's behaviour (response) as costing a reward. This strategy is easy to use, convenient, and readily adapted to a variety of target behaviours and situations (Pfiffner & Barkley, 1998).

An interesting study by Carlson, Mann and Alexander (2000) shows how effective response cost can be in the classroom management of students with AD/HD. In this study, 40 children with AD/HD were compared with 40 non-AD/HD children in one of three conditions: reward only, response cost, and no contingency. In the reward condition, children earned tokens (which could be exchanged for money) for completion/accuracy of maths problems. In the response cost condition, children received all the tokens at the outset, and subsequently lost them if problems were not completed or not completed correctly. Obviously, tokens did not feature in the no-contingency group. Results indicated that AD/HD children's maths performance was significantly higher in the response cost group compared to the reward group. Even more impressive was that the response cost condition promoted 'intrinsic' motivation, and not the dependency on reward, or removal of same, that many feel is an inherent weakness in behaviour modification programmes.

18.5.4   EFFECTIVENESS OF BEHAVIOURAL INTERVENTIONS

A variety of teacher-administered behavioural interventions have proven effective during the course of research investigations, a number of which have been described. As discussed, a combination of positive consequences and negative consequences has been shown to be optimal. The challenge now lies in designing programmes that can be easily integrated with classroom instruction and are practical to use. The key question is whether these gains are maintained over time. There are key programming elements if one wishes to maintain behaviour improvements in the future. For example, lasting behaviour change is more likely if one gradually reduces the frequency of contingencies. Likewise, behaviour improvement is more likely to be noted in different settings (e.g. home) if similar management procedures are used across contexts, which once again highlights the importance of collaboration between home and school. Future research might also focus on increasing academic behaviours (e.g. completion of assignments), in addition to 'on-task' behaviour, although admittedly being 'on-task' is a prerequisite for academic performance. Still another key element in helping children with AD/HD to learn to manage their behaviour is via self-management, which is one of the key aspects of 'Cognitive-Behavioural Interventions'.

18.6 COGNITIVE-BEHAVIOURAL INTERVENTIONS

Cognitive-behavioural or self-management interventions, which include strategies such as self-monitoring, self-reinforcement, self-instruction and problem-solving approaches, were originally developed to target the impulsive, disorganised, and non-reflective manner in which children with AD/HD approach academic tasks and social interactions. Because of their emphasis on the development of self-control, it was believed that these interventions would reduce the need for external rewards, and would thereby result in better maintenance and generalisation of gains made by AD/HD children than achieved by more traditional behavioural interventions (Pfiffner & Barkley, 1998).

Examination of the literature shows that self-management strategies have been applied to children across all developmental levels, and have been shown to be effective with students with a wide variety of difficulties, including specific learning difficulties (Reid, 1996). It is helpful to conceptualise self-management interventions as existing on a continuum. At one end, the intervention is completely controlled by the teacher, who provides feedback regarding whether the student's behaviour met the desired criteria, followed by the appropriate consequences being administered. At the other end, it is the student who engages in evaluating his/her behaviour, without benefit of the teacher's input, and the student self-administers the appropriate consequences, much like the traditional behavioural interventions. In working with children with AD/HD, the objective is to move the student as far toward the self-management side of the continuum as possible (Shapiro, DuPaul & Bradley-Klug, 1998).

Self-management strategies can be dichotomised into procedures based on the principles of contingency-management or cognitive-control strategies. Techniques founded on the principles of contingency-management emphasise the relationship between responses and their consequences, and require the student to evaluate his/her own responses, after which the appropriate consequences are self-administered (e.g. self-monitoring, self-reward, self-recording). In contrast, cognitive-based self-management strategies emphasise the antecedents of responding, in that the student is required to examine the thought process that precedes the response, with the goal being to change the thought, with the hope of it resulting in a different outcome (e.g. self-instruction, problem-solving training; Shapiro *et al.*, 1998).

18.6.1 SELF-MONITORING AND SELF-REINFORCEMENT

Although a number of self-management strategies have fallen short of initial expectations, it has been shown that both self-monitoring and self-reinforcement strategies have had some success with AD/HD students. Such strategies involve children monitoring and evaluating their own academic and social behaviour, and rewarding themselves (e.g. with tokens or points) based on those evaluations, which are then compared with the teacher's ratings. Training involves teaching children how to observe, record, and evaluate their own behaviour to determine whether they deserve a reward, while such observations may be prompted by a periodic auditory signal or visual cue. In their study evaluating the effectiveness of self-management on 9-year-old children with AD/HD, Davies and Witte (2000) found such strategies useful for improving classroom behaviour, and noted that students find 'being in control' to be such a reinforcing activity that they become highly motivated to participate in self-monitoring. Davies and Witte also argued for the cost-effectiveness of such treatments and for its suitability for older students.

In their study investigating the application of self-monitoring and self-reinforcement on 7 to 10-year-old hyperactive children during individual seat work, Barkley, Copeland and Sivage (1980) found that 'on-task' behaviour did improve in this context, particularly with the older children, but that this improvement did not seem to generalise to the regular classroom environment. The combination of such strategies has also been used with some success to maintain gains from a token economy with secondary-level AD/HD students, for whom behavioural or contingency management procedures have often not been viewed as favourably by teachers or students (DuPaul & Stoner, 1994). In this study, students were trained to evaluate their own behaviour, after having achieved success in a standard teacher-administered token economy, which was gradually faded out over time. Although the fading of teacher involvement is emphasised in this procedure, the continued checking of student ratings and backup reinforcers appeared important in sustaining improvement.

18.6.2   SELF-INSTRUCTIONAL TRAINING AND PROBLEM-SOLVING STRATEGIES

Many cognitive training programmes involve teaching children self-instructional and problem-solving strategies in addition to self-monitoring and self-reinforcement. The prototypical programme involves teaching children a set of self-directed instructions to follow when performing a task. The model suggests that control is developed through three stages: firstly teachers control the child's behaviour through overt direction; then the child is instructed to control their behaviour through speech (i.e. making self-reinforcing positive statements out loud); and finally the child is encouraged to make the statements covert in the hope of the speech becoming internalised. Reinforcement is then typically provided to the child for following the procedure as well as selecting correct solutions.

Unfortunately, several studies have failed to show positive results when applying self-instructional and problem-solving strategies to children with AD/HD (e.g. Braswell *et al.*, 1997). It has been noted that when improvement does occur, it is when external or self-reinforcement is provided for accurate and positive self-evaluations in conjunction with self-instructional training. In fact, the effectiveness of these programmes may be more a result of reinforcement rather than cognitive self-instructions (Pfiffner & Barkley, 1998). This finding links in with the analysis of various studies by Abikoff (1985), who noted that the most successful self-management techniques used forms of contingency management rather than cognitive control. Such outcomes would actually be predicted by Barkley's (1994) conceptualisation of AD/HD, in that the inability to inhibit responding to the environment is viewed as a core deficit among AD/HD children, and such difficulties would not permit the students to even invoke the cognitive thought process that is the controlling variable in cognitive approaches to self-management (Shapiro *et al.*, 1998).

18.6.3   EFFECTIVENESS OF CBT INTERVENTIONS

Despite the range of difficulties for which self-management has been successful, substantial questions have been raised about the use of the technique with children with AD/HD. In sum, self-monitoring and self-reinforcement seem to be the most effective of the self-management interventions, although their effects are not as strong, as durable, or as generalisable as was once expected, and they have not been found to be superior to traditional behavioural programmes. The complete transfer of management from teacher to student of the programme is unrealistic as children continue to need adequate reinforcement for displaying self-control skills to maintain this type of behaviour, and their ratings require regular monitoring to ensure honest reporting (Pfiffner & Barkley, 1998).

However, some gains can be achieved from the use of self-management programmes (i.e. self-monitoring and self-reinforcement) as long as the training is of sufficient duration, and when there is some overlap between the skills taught during training and the requirements of the classroom environment. In addition, such programmes seem to facilitate partial fading of token programmes and, in particular, may be more acceptable to teachers than token programmes for use with older students (DuPaul & Stoner, 1994).

In a recent meta-analysis conducted by Robinson *et al.* (1999), which examined the outcomes of 23 studies that used cognitive-behaviour modification in school settings, evidence was provided for the efficacy of this type of intervention in reducing inappropriate and maladaptive behaviour. However, other studies have suggested that, although cognitive-behavioural strategies may help to improve the basic symptoms of AD/HD, improvements in academic performance were not shown (Miranda & Presentacion, 2000), nor did the strategies achieve the generalisation and maintenance of improvements over time (Braswell *et al.*, 1997).

18.7   OTHER INTERVENTIONS

The multisystemic management of AD/HD may also include other child-focused interventions such as social skills and anger management training, which aim to target the secondary difficulties associated with the diagnosis. For example, social skills training may help the child to learn new behaviours which are important in developing and maintaining social relationships, like waiting a turn, sharing toys, asking for help, and responding to teasing. A number of studies have found that combining social skills training with a behaviourally-based intervention (e.g.

self-monitoring) may be a highly effective way of helping youngsters to develop more accurate self-awareness concerning the degree to which they exhibit socially appropriate behaviour, as well as increasing the chances that the children will maintain and generalise the gains that they have made (Antshel & Remer, 2003).

Controlling impulses, particularly aggressive impulses, may underpin some of the peer-relationship difficulties shown by youngsters with AD/HD. Designed to increase the child's ability to manage and cope with anger and frustration, anger management training typically involves education about anger/frustration, instruction in recognising anger signals, and training in relaxation and de-escalation methods. Hinshaw (1996) has shown that anger management training may be effective in reducing impulsive aggression amongst youngsters with AD/HD.

18.8 CONCLUSION

As noted at the outset, attention span and concentration are perhaps the most fundamental building blocks of classroom learning. And, it is fair to say that attention span is one of the most complex variables of all teaching-learning processes. Connor (1997) summarises the situation cogently when he states that attention may be influenced by many factors including 'the nature of the task; the nature of the previous task; the child's particular interest; the child's learning style; the child's ability and experiences; the time of day; the mood of the child, peers, teacher, etc., etc.'.

Complexity aside, what is obvious is that a child with AD/HD is at risk for failure in the classroom. Yet, there are many strategies available for educators to increase the chance of success. In this chapter, a number of interventions were explored which promote classroom success in children with AD/HD. As mentioned, the need to develop programmes to enhance maintenance and generalisation of teacher-administered interventions continues to be critical (Pfiffner & Barkley, 1998).

It is becoming increasingly clear that the choice of intervention should be based on the factors Connor (1997) mentions, as well as careful analysis of behaviour in the classroom (i.e. 'functional analysis'). Such an assessment goes well beyond a diagnosis of AD/HD, in that it aims to provide a useful mechanism for tailoring interventions to individual children, as well as helping to predict which of many classroom-based interventions will have the greatest impact on changing problematic behaviours, and ultimately, academic performance.

As a result of such interventions requiring a considerable amount of time and resources to implement properly, one must also consider the broader context beyond the school classroom. Where children with AD/HD are included in regular classes, particularly if they present with co-morbid learning difficulties, remedial instruction may be required in specific skill areas (e.g. reading, writing, spelling, and maths), as well as aiding in planning and developing a modified teaching curriculum and using structured classroom-based interventions. Although the importance of the teacher's role was highlighted throughout the chapter, a responsibility also lies with governmental education departments in providing adequate resourcing to meet the complex needs of children with AD/HD.

In any case, schools, educators, governments, professionals, and parents alike share a mutual responsibility for children who have difficulties in adapting to the classroom environment. As mentioned previously, it is not fair to expect the same from a child with AD/HD, compared to a child without the condition. Therefore, it is vital for us to try to understand and to accommodate the needs of children with AD/HD so that they may be able to get the most out of their education. After all, altering our own expectations for these children can facilitate their ability to succeed and can improve their self-esteem through achievement and positive adaptation, as well as help children cope with the syndrome without developing secondary conduct and emotional difficulties.

18.9 REFERENCES

Abikoff H (1985) Efficacy of cognitive training interventions in hyperactive children: a critical review. *Clinical Psychology Review* **5**: 479–512.

American Psychiatric Association (2000) *Diagnostic and Statistical Manual of Mental Disorders – Text Revision* (4th edn).Washington, DC: American Psychiatric Association.

Antshel KM, Remer R (2003) Social skills training in children with attention deficit/hyperactivity disorder: A randomized controlled clinical trial. *Journal of Clinical Child & Adolescent Psychology* **32**: 153–65.

Barkley RA (1994) Impaired delayed responding: a unified theory of attention deficit/hyperactivity disorder. In DK Routh (ed.) *Disruptive Behaviour Disorders in Childhood* (pp. 11–57). New York: Plenum.

Barkley RA, Copeland A, Sivage C (1980) A self-control classroom for hyperactive children. *Journal of Autism and Developmental Disorders* **1**: 75–89.

Boyajian AE, DuPaul GJ, Handler MW *et al.* (2001) The use of classroom-based brief functional analyses with preschoolers at-risk for attention deficit/hyperactivity disorder. *School Psychology Review* **30**(2): 278–93.

Braswell L, August GJ, Bloomquist ML *et al.* (1997) School-based secondary prevention for children with disruptive behaviour: initial outcomes. *Journal of Abnormal Child Psychology* **25**: 197–208.

Cantwell DP (1996) Attention deficit disorder: a review of the past ten years. *Journal of the American Academy of Child and Adolescent Psychiatry* **35**: 978–87.

Carlson CL, Mann M, Alexander DK (2000) Effects of reward and response cost on the performance and motivation of children with AD/HD. *Cognitive Therapy & Research* **24**(1): 87–98.

Carr A (1999) *The Handbook of Child and Adolescent Clinical Psychology: A Contextual Approach.* London: Brunner-Routledge.

Comfort RL (1994) Students with AD/HD need balance of structure in classroom. *Brown University Child & Adolescent Behaviour Letter* **10**(9): 1–3.

Connor MJ (1997) Making judgements about attention and concentration levels: how do we know what to expect? *Emotional and Behavioural Difficulties* **2**: 14–20.

Cooper P (2001) Understanding AD/HD: a brief critical review of the literature. *Children & Society* **15**: 387–95.

Davies S, Witte R (2000) Self-management and peer-monitoring within a group contingency to decrease uncontrolled verbalizations of children with attention deficit/hyperactivity disorder. *Psychology in the Schools* **37**(2): 135–47.

Drumm M (2004) Multisystemic and multicomponent treatment for attention deficit/hyperactivity disorder (AD/HD). *The Irish Psychologist* **30**(12): 292–9.

DuPaul GJ, Eckert TL (1997) School-based interventions for students with attention deficit/ hyperactivity disorder: a meta-analysis. *School Psychology Review* **26**: 5–27.

DuPaul GJ, Stoner G (1994) *AD/HD in the Schools: Assessment and Intervention Strategies.* New York: Guilford Press.

Edwards WH, Magee SK, Ellis J (2002) Identifying the effects of idiosyncratic variables of functional analysis outcomes: a case study. *Education and Treatment of Children* **25**(3): 317–30.

ERIC Digest (1998) *Teaching Children with Attention Deficit/Hyperactivity Disorder: Update September 1998.* Reston, VA: Educational Resources Information Centre.

Evans JH, Ferre L, Ford LA, Green JL (1995) Decreasing attention deficit/hyperactivity disorder symptoms utilizing an automated classroom reinforcement device. *Psychology in the Schools* **32**: 210–19.

Flood WA, Wilder DA (2002) Antecedent assessment and assessment-based treatment of off-task behaviour in a child diagnosed with attention deficit/hyperactivity disorder (AD/ HD). *Education and Treatment of Children,* **25**(3): 331–8.

Frick PJ, Lahey BB (1991) The nature and characteristics of attention deficit/hyperactivity disorder. *School Psychology Review* **20**: 163–73.

Greenhill L (1998) Childhood attention deficit/hyperactivity disorder: pharmacological treatments. In P Nathan, J Gorman (eds), *A Guide to Treatments that Work* (pp. 42–64). New York: Oxford University Press.

Hinshaw S (1994) *Attention Deficits and Hyperactivity in Children.* Thousand Oaks, CA: Sage.

Hinshaw S (1996) Enhancing social competence: integrating self-management strategies with behavioural procedures for children with AD/HD. In E Hibbs, P Jensen (eds) *Psychosocial Treatments for Child and Adolescent Disorders: Empirically Based Strategies for Clinical Practice* (pp. 285–309). Washington, DC.: American Psychiatric Association.

Lerner JW (1997) Attention deficit disorder. In JW Lloyd, DJ Kameenui, D Chard (eds), *Issues in Educating Children with Disabilities* (pp. 27–44). Mahwah, NJ: Erlbaum.

Miranda A, Presentacion MJ (2000) Efficacy of cognitive-behavioural therapy in the treatment of children with AD/HD, with and without aggressiveness. *Psychology in the Schools* **37**: 169–82.

Miranda A, Presentacion MJ, Soriano M (2002) Effectiveness of a school-based multicomponent program for the treatment of children with AD/HD. *Journal of Learning Disabilities* **35**(6): 546–62.

Multimodal Treatment Study of Children with AD/HD Cooperative Group (MTA) (1999) A 14-month randomized clinical trial of treatment strategies of Attention Deficit/Hyperactivity Disorder. *Archives of General Psychiatry* **56**: 1073–86.

Pelham WE, Wheeler T, Chronis A (1998) Empirically supported psychosocial treatments for attention deficit/hyperactivity disorder. *Journal of Clinical Child Psychology* **27**: 190–205.

Pfiffner LJ, Barkley RA (1998) Treatment of AD/HD in school settings. In RA Barkley (ed.) *Attention Deficit/Hyperactivity Disorder: A Handbook for Diagnosis and Treatment* (2nd edn., pp. 458–90). New York: Guilford Press.

Reid R (1996) Research in self-monitoring with students with learning disabilities: the present, the prospects, and the pitfalls. *Journal of Learning Disabilities* **29**(3): 317–31.

Reid R, Maag JW (1998) Functional assessment: a method for developing classroom-based accommodations and interventions for children with AD/HD. *Reading & Writing Quarterly* **14**(1): 9–42.

Reid R, Vasa SF, Maag JW, Wright R (1994) An analysis of teachers' perceptions of attention deficit/hyperactivity disorder. *Journal of Research and Development in Education* **27**: 196–202.

Robinson TR, Smith SW, Miller MD, Brownell MT (1999) Cognitive behaviour modification of hyperactivity impulsivity and aggression: a meta-analysis of school-based studies. *Journal of Educational Psychology* **91**: 195–203.

Sattler JM (2002) *Assessment of Children: Behavioural and Clinical Applications* (4th edn). San Diego: Sattler.

Shapiro ES, DuPaul GJ, Bradley-Klug KL (1998) Self-management as a strategy to improve the classroom behaviour of adolescents with AD/HD. *Journal of Learning Disabilites* **31**(6): 545–55.

Sheridan SM, Dee CC (1996) A multimethod intervention for social skills deficits in children with AD/HD and their parents. *School Psychology Review* **25**: 57–83.

Swanson JM, McBurnett K, Wigal T *et al.* (1993) Effect of stimulant medication on children with attention deficit disorder: a 'review of reviews'. *Exceptional Children* **60**: 154–62.

Taylor E (1994) Syndromes of attention deficits and overactivity. In M Rutter, E Taylor, L Hersov (eds) *Child and Adolescent Psychiatry: Modern Approaches* (3rd edn, pp. 285–307). London: Blackwell.

Weiss G, Hechtman L (1993) *Hyperactive Children Grown Up: AD/HD in Children, Adolescents, and Adults* (2nd edn). New York: Guilford Press.

Xu C, Reid R, Steckelberg A (2002) Technology applications for children with AD/HD: assessing the empirical support. *Education and Treatment of Children* **25**(2): 224–48.

Zentall S (1993) Research on the educational implications of attention deficit/hyperactivity disorder. *Exceptional Children* **60**(2): 143–53.

19 Psychosocial Treatments for Adults with ADHD

SAM GOLDSTEIN[1] **AND ROBERT BROOKS**[2]

1. University of Utah School of Medicine, Salt Lake City, Utah, USA; 2. Harvard Medical School, Needham, Mass, USA

19.1 OVERVIEW

There is an increasing recognition that psychosocial treatments, when applied through research proven methods, are effective in the treatment of adult ADHD (Rostain and Ramsay, 2006; Safren, Perlman, Sprich and Otto, 2005). This chapter provides an overview of risks and outcome issues facing adults with ADHD. First the basic characteristics and mindset of adults with ADHD are outlined, focusing on core symptoms related to impulsivity, low frustration tolerance, moodiness, disorganisation, rigidity, inflexibility, insatiability and an unfortunate dearth of empathy. The chapter then reviews the unfortunate mindset that develops for many adults with ADHD and provides a series of assessment questions to pose in an interview format to understand the mindset of adults with ADHD. Finally, the chapter concludes with an overview of psychosocial treatment and a set of guidelines to incorporate into the counseling process.

The existence of ADHD as a clinically impairing condition is irrefutable (Goldstein & Goldstein, 1998; Barkley, 2005). Though the etiology of the condition and precise symptom profile remain debatable concepts, presenting symptoms and impairing consequences are easily observed and measured. In light of current theories portraying ADHD as a condition of impaired development, it should not be a great philosophical nor academic leap to accept the condition as present throughout the lifespan (Barkley, 1997, 2005; Goldstein & Goldstein, 1998; Goldstein, 1999). Yet scientific method requires more than just hypotheses and theory before belief can confidently be described as fact. Though thousands of peer-reviewed studies dealing with ADHD in childhood have been published, the literature still contains less than 150 peer-reviewed articles dealing with ADHD in adults. The number of studies has been increasing significantly year by year, including the ongoing, reported results from longitudinal studies following children with ADHD into their adult years. As with any emerging condition, each published study holds the promise of new data, insight, and perhaps a new path to follow in regards to ADHD in the adult years. Time will determine which paths bear fruit and which may result in dead ends.

In the last 15 years, the biopsychosocial nature of this condition across the lifespan has become increasingly apparent. Epstein *et al.* (1997) demonstrated that

Handbook of Attention Deficit Hyperactivity Disorder. Edited by M. Fitzgerald, M. Bellgrove and M. Gill.
© 2007 John Wiley & Sons Ltd

adults with ADHD presented with a longer delay when their attention was misdirected with cues in a reaction-time task measuring hemispheric control. Those with ADHD had difficulty switching when misdirected by cues to the right visual field when the target presented in the left visual field. Gansler *et al.* (1998) administered a battery of neuropsychological tests to thirty adults with ADHD. They found that this population, in comparison to a normal sample, experienced specific problems with the skills necessary to perform test tasks involving visual tracking, auditory attention, and visual continuous performance. Deficits on these tasks suggest problems with executive control, likely linked to a dysregulation of the frontal lobes. This pattern of problems, though not always the consensus reached by other researchers, has provided consistent evidence of deficits in a variety of tasks sensitive to executive function and self-regulation (Holdnack *et al.*, 1995; Jenkins *et al.*, 1998).

Although some authors have suggested that ADHD may reflect the development of a pattern of adaptive skills based upon an evolutionary model (Hartmann, 1993), the emerging research literature is sobering. Not a single childhood nor adult study exists to suggest those with ADHD hold any type of advantage over individuals without this condition (Goldstein & Barkley, 1998). Further, the increased recognition that ADHD reflects not so much a problem sitting still or paying attention but rather a problem of self-regulation or self-control, provides a workable hypothesis to explain the myriad of problems currently identified for adults with histories of ADHD. This plausible theory for ADHD explains that rather than representing an adapted or evolved set of valuable qualities, individuals with ADHD suffer from weaknesses in the development of efficient self-regulatory and executive functions. These cognitive functions fall on a normative curve, much akin to height or weight. Qualities of ADHD appear to place individuals at the lower tail of an adaptive Bell Curve for these skills.

Readers should consider this chapter a work in progress. Given the nearly exponential growth in interest and peer-reviewed published research dealing with adult ADHD as well as the time span between the completion of the chapter and the publication of this text, approximately thirty to fifty additional research studies exploring symptom, problems, outcome, and, most importantly, treatment of ADHD in adults will be published. Nonetheless, the available research suggests a consistent pattern of emerging trends. This chapter will briefly review these trends to set a foundation for the need to develop effective psychosocial treatment. We will then offer a best practice model of psychosocial treatment based on available science for individuals with ADHD.

19.2 OUTCOME OF ADHD IN THE ADULT YEARS

The body of literature attesting to the emotional, cognitive, vocational, academic, substance use, and criminal risks of the condition are growing. It has been estimated from available literature that approximately one-third of adults with ADHD progress satisfactorily into their adult years, another one-third continues to experience some problems while the final one-third continues to experience and often develops significant problems (for review, see Goldstein, 1995; Goldstein and Teeter-Ellison,

2002; Hechtman, 2000; Barkley, 2005). By combining a number of outcome studies it is reasonable to conclude that 10–20% of adults with histories of ADHD experience few problems. Sixty per cent continue to demonstrate symptoms of ADHD and experience social, academic, and emotional problems to at least a mild to moderate degree and 10–30% develop anti-social problems in addition to their continued difficulty with ADHD and other comorbid problems (Satterfield, Hoppe & Schell, 1982; Gittelman *et al.*, 1985; Cantwell & Baker, 1989; Barkley, 1990; Weiss & Hechtman, 1993; Herrero, Hechtman & Weiss, 1994). Interestingly, many of these negative outcomes are linked to the continuity, severity, and persistence of ADHD symptoms.

There are very limited data to suggest that females at outcome when controlling for initial presentation are at a more reduced risk for antisocial problems than males with ADHD (Herrero, *et al.*, 1994). It is fair for clinicians to assume that the absence of significant comorbid disruptive behavioural problems during the childhood years is a good predictor for the absence of the development of antisocial disorders in adulthood. Clinicians should be cautioned, however, that the presence of such problems in childhood is not necessarily predictive of anti-social outcome for all cases (Werner & Smith, 2001). In their follow-up study, Weiss and Hectman (1993) found only 11% of adults with ADHD to be symptom free, with 79% experiencing some type of internalising problem and 75% experiencing interpersonal problems. In this cohort, 10% had attempted suicide, and 5% were dead from either suicide or accidental injury.

The continuity of the condition in the form of similar symptoms but different consequences has been well demonstrated by Millstein *et al.* (1997) in their study of clinically referred adults with ADHD. Ninety-eight per cent reported difficulty following directions; 92% reported poor sustained attention; 92% trouble shifting activities; 88% reported being easily distracted; 80% losing things; 70% not listening, fidgeting, interrupting, and speaking out of turn.

Arthur Robin and colleagues (Robin, Bedway & Tzelepis, 1998) demonstrated that beyond the risk of clinical comorbidity and the life impairment, adults with ADHD appear to be at greater risk to develop dysfunctional personality styles. Fifty per cent of individuals with ADHD in their follow-up study, in comparison to 5% of normals, demonstrated a personality style characterised by pessimism, helplessness, and disorganisation. In comparison, only 44% of those with ADHD, in comparison to 88% of the normal group demonstrated a personality style consistently with empathy, extroversion, and motivation.

19.2.1 PSYCHOLOGICAL/EMOTIONAL

As the number of research studies in adults with ADHD is increasing, the increased vulnerability of a range of psychiatric problems that ADHD correlates with and may in fact mediate continues to grow. Mannuzza *et al.* (1993) in their longitudinal study, reported that at 24 years of age, those with ADHD demonstrated a higher incidence of antisocial personality disorder as well as alcohol and substance abuse. Though these authors did not report a higher incidence than controls for mood or anxiety disorders in this population, others have. For example, Millstein *et al.* (1997) in their adult sample reported that adults with the Combined Type of Attention Deficit Hyperactivity Disorder demonstrated a 63% incidence of Major Depression;

23% Dysthymia; 17% Bipolar Disorder, 11% Panic Disorder; 12% Simple Phobia; 21% Generalized Anxiety Disorder; and 7% Obsessive/Compulsive Disorder. Even adults meeting only the Inattentive Criteria in this study were not immune from fairly similar rates of depression yet appeared to experience less problems with bipolar and anxiety disorders. The true risk of ADHD in contributing to bipolar illness has yet to be defined.

In contrast to Millstein, *et al.* (1997), Sachs and Baldassano (2000) found only 8 out of a group of 56 adults with bipolar disorder demonstrating a history of ADHD. These 8 were compared with 8 without a history of ADHD. The age and onset of the first affective episode were lower for the subjects with bipolar disorder and ADHD (mean age 12 years) than for those without a history of ADHD in childhood (mean age 20 years). Though research on adult females is as sparse as the research literature in pertaining to female children with ADHD, at least one study has demonstrated that 70% of females with adult-diagnosed ADHD experience a history of depression and 62% experience a history of anxiety (Rucklidge & Kaplan, 1997). The incidence of these two conditions in the general population reported in this study, though not insignificant (33% depression; 17% anxiety), is still dramatically less than in the clinical group.

The diverse risks of ADHD into adulthood have been well demonstrated. In 1998 Vitelli studied the relationship between childhood conduct disorder, ADHD, and adult antisocial personality disorder in a sample of maximum security inmates. The results confirmed that childhood Conduct Disorder and ADHD were significantly related to adult antisocial personality disorders, psychopathy, and impulsivity. The combination of childhood Conduct Disorder and ADHD appeared to predict significantly worse outcome in regards to problems related to adult violence, substance abuse, and institutional misconduct.

19.2.2   SUBSTANCE USE AND DEPENDENCE

In 1990, Shekim reported 34% of a population of 56 adults with ADHD demonstrated alcoholism, while 30% demonstrated drug abuse. An inpatient study completed by Milin *et al.* (1997) with a clinical sample of 36 adults, many of whom met criteria for a diagnosis of ADHD found those with symptoms of ADHD tended to be more likely to have a history of alcohol combined with drug use disorders. The authors further reported that symptoms of anti-social personality disorder were far more prevalent in substance abusers with a history of both childhood and adult ADHD than those without this condition. In 1999, Coure *et al.*, reported histories of substance use in adults in an inpatient setting. In this setting there were significant differences in the percentage of those presenting with ADHD between the substance use disorders groups divided by drug of choice. Of the ADHD subtypes, subjects with Combined and Inattentive Types were significantly more likely to have ADHD symptoms continue into adulthood than the Hyperactive/Impulsive subtype. Those with cocaine use were more likely to have a history of ADHD in childhood when compared to those with alcohol or combined substance abuse in groups.

Wilens, Biederman and Mick (1998) examined the rates of remission and duration of substance abuse in individuals with histories of ADHD. The duration of substance abuse was over 37 months longer in a population of adults with ADHD versus those without ADHD. The median time to remission was more than twice as long in ADHD as in controls (144 versus 60 months). The authors reported a need to replicate their data but suggested that ADHD is not only a risk factor for the early initiation and a specific pathway for substance abuse but is also associated with longer duration and a significantly slower remission rate.

Finally, the rate of cigarette smoking in adults with ADHD has also been demonstrated as increased relative to the general population (Pomerleau *et al.*, 1995). In a population of 71 individuals with ADHD with a mean age of nearly 34 years, 42% of the males were current smokers, 13% ex-smokers and 45% had never smoked. Comparative figures for males in the normal population were 28%, 29%, and 42% respectively. Thirty-eight per cent of females in this group with ADHD were current smokers, 31 ex-smokers and 31% had never smoked as compared to 23.5%, 19% and 57.5% respectively in the general population. Smokers experienced greater symptoms of ADHD as children than non-smokers and scored higher on measures of childhood and adult psychiatric comorbidity. The authors suggested that smokers with ADHD may need treatment with a stimulant and sustained nicotine replacement therapy before they can actually quit smoking.

19.2.3   SYMPTOM PRESENTATION AND DEFINITION

In an effort to understand the meaning and course of symptoms of ADHD into adulthood, Murphy and Barkley (1996) collected symptom report data on 720 adults of at least 17 years of age. The adults were obtained by soliciting volunteers from among individuals entering one of two sites of the Department of Motor Vehicles in Massachusetts to apply for or renew their driver's licence. These authors constructed two rating scales using the 18 DSM-IV symptom list for ADHD. The authors correlated the data, collecting six scores. The first three were summations of the item scores calculated separately for the inattention, the hyperactive-impulsive, and the total ADHD item list. The second three were symptom counts of the number of positively endorsed items calculated separately within the inattention, hyperactive-impulsive, and total ADHD item list. Creating the symptom counts, the authors considered a symptom as present if the answer given to the item was often or very often (score of 2 or 3).

Murphy, Gordon and Barkley (2000) extended this work by completing a statistical re-analysis of the original Murphy and Barkley data. In this re-analysis a number of trends were examined. Almost 80% of the sample endorsed six or more of the 18 items as having surfaced during their early lives. Nearly 75% of the sample reported they were currently experiencing six or more symptoms of ADHD at least sometimes. Murphy *et al.* point out these data powerfully demonstrate the commonality of some ADHD complaints in the general population that may occur independent of possessing the clinical condition. Further, even when more stringent criteria for symptom frequency are applied, 25% endorsed having at least six of the 18 symptoms often or very often during childhood. Twelve per cent endorsed having at least six symptoms often or very often in their current lives. The authors further note that almost half of the sample reported that they had failed to give close attention to details or made careless mistakes in their work at least sometimes when they were younger. Nearly a quarter of the sample reported these symptoms occurred often or very often. Over a third reported they frequently had difficulty organising tasks and activities in childhood. A similar percentage lost things necessary for tasks or activities and reported feeling as if they were driven by a motor. As Murphy, *et al.* point out, 'these data provide powerful testament to the universality of ADHD symptomatology' (p. 4).

Clinicians should be cautioned that if 10–20% of the normal population endorses symptoms of ADHD, the ADHD diagnosis based largely on self-report in the absence of significant impairment can lead to substantial over-diagnosis. Further, the risk for misjudgment increases given that according to these data 25% of the population characterised themselves as having had at least six symptoms of ADHD during childhood. Thesc data argue against clinicians making diagnoses in the absence of corroborating data. These authors have undertaken a comprehensive epidemiologic study beginning with a large symptom pool of DSM-IV descriptors, complaints, and problem consequences of ADHD in an effort to arrive at a statistically sound set of symptom criteria and a threshold of symptoms as well as impairment in making the diagnosis of ADHD in adults. Initial findings reflect significant problems with executive functions in adults with ADHD (Barkley and Murphy, 2006). These include problems with organisation, follow-through, impulse control and poor decision-making. A very similar pattern of data has been reported with a population of nearly 400 college students (Lewandowski *et al.*, 2000). On the basis of their findings and previous research, these authors suggest that self-report alone of symptoms of ADHD may be a reasonable initial threshold for assessment but should not be used as confirming criteria.

19.3   THE CHARACTERISTICS AND MINDSET OF ADULTS WITH ADHD

Adults with the diagnosis of ADHD are not a homogeneous group. Their cognitive styles and behaviours vary. A diagnosis of ADHD does not define their entire functioning or existence. However, there are certain core behaviours that many possess that distinguish them to a greater or lesser degree from individuals without ADHD. These behaviours elicit responses from others, responses that contribute to the formation of their mindset. Unfortunately, in far too many instances the mindset of individuals with ADHD is filled with negativity. The following represent a selected list of those behaviours that exert the strongest adverse impact on their lives:

19.3.1   IMPULSIVITY

One of the most prominent characteristics of individuals with ADHD is their impulsivity. They are often described as acting before they think, of failing to consider the consequences of their behaviours. As children they are likely to blurt out answers in a classroom, or push their peers out of the way to be first in line, or place their finger in a light socket to see what happens, or climb a tall tree without considering the dangers. Adults will remind them how to behave in certain situations and they will agree. However, moments later they seemingly forget what they have just been taught, behaving in ways that are in stark contrast to what they have been told. It is easy to interpret their behaviours as manipulative or oppositional but as Barkley (1995) and others observe, it is not that they don't know what to do but rather they are so impulsive that they don't use what they know.

One observes similar patterns of behaviours in adults with ADHD. They may rush through tasks, or fail to demonstrate social skills by saying things that others experience as abrasive, or engage in risk-taking activities. Impulsivity is often reflected in a lack of self-discipline or self-control. Goleman (1995) has highlighted self-discipline as a major ingredient of emotional intelligence, which he defines as 'being able to motivate oneself and persist in the face of frustrations; to control impulse and delay gratification; to regulate one's moods and keep distress from swamping the ability to think; to empathise and to hope' (p. 34). Goleman's definition of emotional intelligence has direct bearing on other features of adults with ADHD as well.

19.3.2   LOW FRUSTRATION TOLERANCE

Closely linked to an impulsive style is how quickly adults with ADHD become frustrated and angry. This frustration is evident in many situations. If a task is difficult and not very interesting they are quick to give up. If someone doesn't respond to what they want, they are quick to anger. Adults with ADHD have difficulty tolerating their own shortcomings as well as the shortcomings of others. It is not unusual for them to cast blame on others when things do not go well. They often expect others to change but may not be as willing to change themselves. On the surface this unwillingness may appear as a statement that they are right and others wrong but often their reluctance to change is rooted in feelings of helplessness. As one woman with ADHD commented, 'I just felt I couldn't change my angry outbursts at my kids. I felt terrible but I blamed them and told them that if they met their responsibilities and treated me with more respect, I wouldn't have to shout at them or spank them. But I didn't take any responsibility for my own behavior.' Her insight was to be the first step towards change.

19.3.3   MOODINESS

Many adults with ADHD are burdened by fluctuations in mood. One moment they may feel happy only to have feelings of sadness dominate a few moments later. Some clinicians contend that the depression is primarily biologically based while others feel that it is in response to years of frustration and failure. As with any affective disorder, most likely both biology and environment interact to different degrees with different individuals to contribute to the moodiness and depression. These shifts in mood are burdensome not only to adults with ADHD but also to those who interact with them.

19.3.4   DISORGANISATION

One of the most frequent complaints about individuals with ADHD is their difficulty with organisation. As children and adolescents, their school desks look as if a tornado has struck, whose three-ring binders that appeared so neat the first day of school quickly fall prey to different subjects being mixed together, who fail to complete homework assignments, who finally finish assignments that somehow are lost or misplaced on the way from home to school (for many of these children it seems that a black hole exists between home and school, sucking up assignments and papers with great regularity), and who constantly search for lost socks, shoes, coats, and book bags.

This pattern typically follows them into their adult years. They lose things, forget where they placed their keys, cannot locate bills to pay, neglect to jot down an important appointment in their book, or fail to complete a project at work because they have misjudged the time required or become distracted with two other projects. Needless to say, their time management skills leave much to be desired.

19.3.5   RIGIDITY, INFLEXIBILITY, AND INSATIABILITY

The other side of the coin of impulsivity and disorganisation is the lack of flexibility that many adults with ADHD demonstrate. Someone observing their behaviour might be puzzled how someone can be so impulsive and disorganised at one moment and so rigid the next. On the one hand this rigidity may exemplify, in part, a desperate attempt to cope with the disorganisation and lack of control in one's life, but it also seems to be another example of a failure of self-regulation.

Children with ADHD manifest this pattern by having difficulty with transitions. Thus, in school they take a great deal of time to get started with an activity. When the teacher informs the class it is time to stop this activity and begin a new one (e.g. shifting from reading to math), they will not want to stop the first activity until they have completed it. If they are involved with a game or task at night, they do not want to go to bed until they have finished it, much to the frustration of their parents.

This characteristic of inflexibility will frequently be manifested in the difficulty children with ADHD have in accepting 'no' as an answer to a request (demand?) they have made. Their cognitive style does not leave room for compromise. They believe that their requests are reasonable and that when adults do not comply, the adults are being unfair and arbitrary. They frequently perceive only one solution to the problem, namely, that others comply with their wishes and when this does not occur they often experience meltdowns with accompanying tantrums (Greene, 1998).

A feature closely linked to inflexibility and a failure to compromise is what might be labelled 'insatiability'. This inborn feeling of insatiability, which is not easily quenched, leads to the perception that the world is unfair. When insatiability, inflexibility, and rigidity become interwoven into a cognitive and emotional tapestry, which is not unusual in children with ADHD, the end result are children who are demanding, unhappy, difficult to soothe, and unable to compromise. While this may seem an overly bleak picture, it is found in many youngsters with so-called 'difficult' temperaments (Brooks & Goldstein, 2001; Chess & Thomas, 1987). Children with ADHD typically fall under the category of temperamentally 'difficult.'

In adults, insatiability and inflexibility are displayed in many aspects of their lives. They are seldom satisfied even when they succeed. Enjoyment is fleeting at best. In couples therapy, when one member of the couple has ADHD, it is not surprising to hear the other describe his or her spouse as difficult to please, unhappy, always seeing the glass as half empty, possessing an intense need to be right, perceiving compromise as giving in, and frequently not paying attention. Often, the spouse with ADHD minimises these descriptions by saying he or she would feel fine if other people were more giving and considerate. In their parenting roles, the inflexibility may be expressed in an authoritarian style replete with anger. It is little wonder that tension and friction become dominant features of families where one or more members have ADHD.

19.3.6   A DEARTH OF EMPATHY

Clinicians often observe that many individuals with ADHD struggle to be empathic. While this difficulty with empathy is closely linked to other characteristics, given its importance in our day-to-day interactions it deserves special mention. Goleman (1995) has highlighted empathy as a major ingredient of emotional intelligence. In simple terms empathy may be defined as the capacity to put oneself inside the shoes of other people and to see the world through their eyes. Empathic people are able to take the perspective of others even when they disagree with these others. They attempt to understand how their words and deeds are experienced and how others would describe them. They reflect upon and take responsibility for their behaviour. They are able to realistically assess and appreciate the 'social scene'.

Cognitive and emotional skills are necessary for empathy to develop. Examining the characteristics of children and adults with ADHD quickly leads to an appreciation that their empathy is often compromised. It is a great struggle to take the perspective of another when we are impulsive, frustrated, or moody, when we quickly interpret the actions of others as withholding or unfair, when we believe that others are not listening to us, and when we feel we are being cheated.

19.4   THE UNFORTUNATE MINDSET OF ADULTS WITH ADHD

If impulsivity, low frustration tolerance, moodiness, disorganisation, rigidity, inflexibility, insatiability, and a lack of empathy are the possible manifestations of the biological underpinnings of ADHD in adults, as we have already seen, these characteristics will impact on almost all aspects of a person's life. They will serve as a major influence in determining the ways in which we respond to others, how they respond to us and how successful we are in the many personal and professional activities in which we engage.

From childhood, the particular style of many individuals with ADHD as described above results in poor peer relationships as well as compromises in school and subsequent work performance. Slowly, negative assumptions or perceptions about oneself and others take shape, becoming an integral part of an individual's mindset. In turn, this mindset plays a powerful role in determining one's behaviours in a wide spectrum of situations, generating a cycle of negative beliefs, a loss of hope, and self-defeating behaviours.

The following are several of the main interrelated features of this negative mindset with suggestions at the end of this section of ways that clinicians might assess this mindset via interview questions. Also, questionnaires such as Seligman's (1990) 'learned optimism' scale may be used in conjunction with interview material to evaluate the positive or negative qualities of an individual's mindset.

19.4.1 'I DO NOT HAVE A GREAT DEAL OF CONTROL OF MY LIFE'

One of the hallmarks of a positive mindset is feeling a sense of control over what transpires in one's life together with a realistic appraisal of those areas over which one has control and those that are beyond one's influence. As Covey (1989) has eloquently noted, all people have 'circles of concern' but effective people recognise and use their time and energy to focus on their 'circles of influence', that is, they are proactive rather than reactive. Stress is frequently linked to the belief, 'I have little say or control over the important things that occur in my life.'

The very nature of the characteristics of ADHD contributes to a feeling of not being in control. For example, if one behaves impulsively without considering the consequences, negative results are likely to follow that are often interpreted as a lack of control of one's actions. A woman with ADHD commented, 'I always yell at my kids. I tell myself not to but then when they don't do what I want them to do I get so frustrated so quickly that I scream. I feel terrible afterwards.' A man with ADHD said, 'No one really listens to me. Nothing I do seems to work.'

Or as another example, if one is insatiable, constantly seeking unobtainable gratification, then continued hunger and frustration are the likely outcome as is the feeling that 'nothing I do is enough to get what I want' or 'people won't give me what I deserve.'

19.4.2 'WHEN I AM SUCCESSFUL IT IS BASED ON LUCK OR CHANCE'

Whether aware or not, when we succeed or fail at things in life we offer ourselves different explanations for these successes and failures. As suggested by attribution theory (Weiner, 1974), these explanations are linked to our self-esteem and sense of optimism. Attribution theory has been studied relative to individuals with attentional and learning problems as a target population (Canino, 1981; Licht, 1983; Brooks, 1999). Children and adults with high self-esteem perceive their successes as based in great part on their own efforts or abilities. These individuals assume realistic ownership for their achievements. They believe they are active participants in their own success.

In contrast, individuals with low self-esteem typically attribute success to things outside of their control such as luck, chance, or fate. An adult with ADHD vividly said that her success in life was like 'a house made out of cards'. She added, 'I feel that if any kind of wind comes along, my entire facade of success will crumble.'

If you believe that your success is not rooted in your resources and effort but rather in luck or chance or things beyond your control, then it is difficult to be confident about experiencing success in the future. In such a case, a loss of hope becomes a dominant feature of one's life.

19.4.3 'FAILURE INDICATES MY INADEQUACY AS A PERSON'

Just as attribution theory highlights differences in how individuals understand the successes in their lives, so too does it clarify how failure is perceived. Children and adults with high self-esteem typically believe that mistakes are experiences from which to learn rather than feel defeated. Mistakes are attributed to variables that can be modified, such as a lack of adequate effort when engaged in reaching a realistically attainable goal or the use of ineffective strategies when studying for a test. A child requesting assistance to learn the strategies involved in solving math problems or an adult registering for a computer course in response to struggles to master the computer represent examples of taking positive action to confront mistakes.

In contrast, individuals with low self-esteem are vulnerable to thinking that they cannot correct the situation or overcome the obstacle. They view mistakes as a consequence of factors that are not modifiable, such as a lack of ability or intelligence, and this belief breeds a feeling of helplessness and hopelessness. They begin to believe regardless of what they do, few, if any, positive outcomes will appear. The probability of future success is diminished because these people expect to fail and thus, retreat from the challenges at hand. As clinicians, we have seen this pattern with a number of adults with ADHD.

19.4.4 'I'M LESS WORTHY THAN OTHERS'

If one encounters many failure situations, it is not difficult to understand how self-esteem is adversely affected. True self-esteem or what Lerner (1996) calls 'learned self-esteem' is based on realistic accomplishment. Each success serves as a step up the ladder of future success. However, when mistakes, failure, and negative feedback are major parts of a person's landscape, there is little room for high self-esteem or confidence.

Self-doubts appear early in the lives of many children with ADHD and continue into their adulthood. Sentiments such as 'I can't do that, it's too tough' or 'This is stupid' (the child in fact feels stupid) are voiced by children as young as five and six. Just as each success serves as the foundation for future success so too does each setback serve as a reinforcement of the idea, 'I am not very capable.'

A man with ADHD reported, 'If I have any doubts about my ability to do something, these doubts quickly multiply and interfere with my ever being able to succeed. I see myself as klutzy and I have trouble concentrating. The other day I went to assemble a toy we had bought for my son. The moment I saw the number of parts and the directions I told myself, "I'll never be able to do that. I can't understand directions. I bet I'll have pieces left over." And guess what? When I finished, the toy didn't work and I had pieces left over.' With much insight he added, 'The moment I told myself I couldn't do it, the outcome was no longer in question.' These negative feelings of low self-worth trigger coping strategies that often exacerbate rather than improve the situation.

19.4.5 'THE WORLD IS UNFAIR'

Individuals with ADHD often believe that situations and people are unfair. The characteristics of ADHD noted earlier such as insatiability, inflexibility, and low frustration tolerance reinforce the feeling that things are not fair. The sense of unfairness is manifested in other ways during one's youth. One middle school boy with ADHD was angry with a teacher who gave him a D grade for the semester. On five tests he had received 3 Fs, 1 D, and 1 B. In actuality, the teacher might have been justified in giving him a failing grade. The boy complained that he deserved a B as a grade since one of his test scores was a B. When we pointed out that the teacher was probably basing the grade on all five tests, the boy persisted, 'But I got a B on a test!'

At first we thought that he realised that he did not deserve a B but was attempting to convince himself or us that he did. However, we soon appreciated that his seeming distortion of the situation actually reflected a number of the characteristics associated with ADHD. One, he was conditioned to perceive things as unfair when he did not get what he wanted and two, his cognitive style was to view situations in a rigid, black and white fashion, not allowing him to assume another perspective. Once he felt he deserved a B, there was no room for a different view.

This feeling of unfairness, which becomes an ongoing, emotional strain, is also apparent in adults with ADHD. They harbor constant complaints about employers, spouses, and salespeople who they believe are not fair. While at times there may be justification to these complaints, frequently they represent anger at feeling misunderstood and not having demands met.

19.4.6 'PEOPLE SEEM ANGRY WITH ME'

Closely related to this last point but deserving separate mention is the sense that others are angry with you. This perception, although exaggerated at times, does have some basis in reality. People do not find it easy to be with someone who comes across as self-centred, impulsive, demanding. Annoyance and frustration often pervade relationships, contributing to the feeling that the other people are angry with me. Unfortunately, if empathy is lacking, the response to this feeling is to become angry in return rather than attempt to resolve the conditions that are reinforcing the anger.

A woman with ADHD reported that her brother and sister were always 'ganging up' on her and calling her 'inconsiderate' and 'selfish'. She said that she let them know in 'No uncertain terms' that they were the selfish ones and should go see a therapist. She was unable to consider the possibility that her siblings were accurate about her behaviour, instead feeling that they were angry because of their 'personality problems' and their 'jealousy' of her talents.

19.4.7 'I HAVE LITTLE, IF ANYTHING, TO OFFER THE WORLD'

A sense of self-esteem and dignity is nurtured when individuals feel that they are making a contribution to their world, that their actions make a positive difference (Brooks, 1991; Brooks & Goldstein, 2001, 2003). This hypothesis was supported by narrative research the second author conducted with adults asked to identify one of the most positive moments they had in school. The most frequent answer received concerned when they were asked to help out in some manner (e.g. painting a mural on the wall, watering plants, tutoring younger children). The act of assisting others typically reinforces the belief, 'I am worthwhile. I have something positive to offer others.' Many adults with ADHD who possess a negative mindset view themselves as adding little, if anything, to the lives of others. The belief that one has little to contribute to others lessens feelings of competence and a sense of worth and dignity. One man we saw with ADHD summed up his feelings when he reported with great honesty, 'I think the only thing I have ever given others is heartache.'

19.4.8 'I AM PESSIMISTIC THAT THINGS WILL IMPROVE'

This feature of a negative mindset is also understandable given the other beliefs that many individuals with ADHD hold. It is difficult to be optimistic when people feel little control of their lives, when they have difficulty taking ownership for success, when they believe people are unfair and angry, and when they are unable to see any ways in which they make a positive difference in their world. Pessimism about future success and happiness often results in a self-fulfilling prophecy for failure. If you expect that you will continue to experience unhappiness and failure, subtly or not so subtly your actions will lead to these expectations being realised. An ongoing cycle of expected failure and actual failure is a very powerful force in contributing to a pessimistic outlook that is devoid of a sense of hope.

This sense of pessimism and loss of hope was poignantly reflected in the writings of a young man with ADHD explaining why he dropped out of high school. 'My alarm goes off and I awake to a new day. At 7:00 in the morning my stomach is queasy and my head hurts. "Oh God, another day of school." Too sick to eat breakfast, I stand in the shower saying, "Maybe it will be a good day," but deep inside I know it will be the same.' Given these strong beliefs it is little wonder that he perceived that his only way of coping was to leave school.

19.5 ASSESSING THE MINDSET OF INDIVIDUALS WITH ADHD

It is important to emphasise that while not all adults with ADHD develop a negative mindset, many appear to possess some if not all of these characteristics. Before examining the coping strategies used by adults with ADHD and the ways in which a clinician can help replace a negative mindset with a mindset that is filled with more positive and resilient beliefs, it may be helpful to articulate the kinds of questions that clinicians can raise to assess the mindset of individuals with ADHD.

While paper and pencil procedures have been developed to evaluate a person's self-esteem, sense of competence, and optimism or pessimism, as clinicians we have found that interview questions remain the best resource for obtaining revealing information. Interview questions permit a more in-depth view of an individual's perspective and they allow you to follow-up and elaborate on particular points. The following represent a sample of questions that may be raised (see Table 19.1). It is important to remember that many of these questions serve as a springboard to further questions and discussion, helping us to understand the mindset of adults with ADHD.

All of these questions tap into the views that people have of themselves, of others, of their competencies and vulnerabilities, of their relationships, of their hopes for the future, of their beliefs if they can bring about change. In essence, the answers to these questions represent a mindset or a set of assumptions about oneself and

Table 19.1. Sample assessment questions

How does having ADHD affect your life?
  What are the negative and positive aspects of having ADHD?
  What things would you like to see changed in your life?
  What have you attempted to do to change any of these things?
  In what areas have you been successful?
  Why do you believe you have been successful?
  In what areas have you been unsuccessful?
  What do you think has contributed to your not being successful?

When you are not successful at a certain task, what is your usual response? Would you give a few examples.
  Are there people who are trying to be of help to you?
  Who are they?
  How do you know they are trying to be of help?
  What is one of the most helpful things someone did for you?

Are there any people who actually seem to be interfering with your chances for success?
  In what way are they behaving to keep you from being successful?
  What is one of the least helpful or even hurtful things someone did to you?

If you could change one or two things about yourself beginning tomorrow, what would they be?
  How would you start?
  Looking a year or two ahead, how do you see your life changing?

For things to improve, do you think others have to become more tolerant of your having ADHD or do you feel you have to begin to make some changes or is it a combination of the two?

---

others. Understanding and changing this mindset form the foundation for a psychosocial treatment plan for ADHD. Following is a brief overview of various areas addressed in psychosocial interventions for ADHD; subsequent to this overview, the remainder of this chapter is devoted to offering guidelines for facilitating positive change in this mindset.

19.6   PSYCHOSOCIAL TREATMENT PLAN FOR ADHD

There is a small but increasing body of literature to supporting psychosocial interventions, including counselling, life coaching, marital, and vocational therapies for adults with ADHD (Nadeau, 2002; Young, 2002; Rostain and Ramsey, 2006). Nadeau (2002) notes that the orientation for psychosocial interventions with ADHD must be 'neuropsychological' in nature. This requires a much more active, directive role for therapists and a multi-level approach focused on helping individuals with ADHD improve cognitive function, develop internal and external compensatory strategies and re-structure their physical and social environment to meet daily demands and maximise functioning. Nadeau refers to this as a 'three-prong' approach (Nadeau, 2002). It is important to also recognise that the treatment of ADHD may in an indirect way benefit individuals suffering from comorbid conditions such as depression or anxiety, but it is more likely than not that these conditions when present require direct treatment.

Issues related to self-esteem, relationships, and work place problems comprise the focus of a psychosocial model. Young (1999, 2002) suggests that cognitive behavioural therapy can be adapted to meet the needs of adults with ADHD. There is a small but emerging body of literature supporting this theory (Wilens *et al.*, 1999; Rostain and Ramsey, 2006). Young suggests that the aim of psychosocial treatments for adults with ADHD must focus on environmental adaptation and the development of life skills. The model reviewed in this chapter to shift negative into positive mindsets in adults with ADHD is consistent with a cognitive behavioural therapy model.

Psychosocial intervention for ADHD can also include efforts to facilitate daily activities through a coaching model (Ratey, 2002), parenting (Phelan, 2002), relationship issues (Kilcarr, 2002), and vocational support (Crawford & Crawford, 2002). Interested readers are referred to these authors for in-depth discussion of these issues.

19.7 STEPS FOR CHANGING NEGATIVE INTO POSITIVE MINDSETS

As clinicians, one of our main roles when working with individuals with ADHD burdened by a negative mindset and accompanying self-defeating coping behaviours, is to help them replace negative feelings and thoughts with an optimistic, positive outlook and more adaptive ways of managing stress and pressure. Clinicians must serve as a catalyst to generate a positive cycle in which the individual engages in activities that lead to fulfillment, satisfaction, and success. As each success chips away at negative feelings, realistic risk-taking and the confronting of challenges are likely to follow. As noted earlier, success breeds success.

19.7.1 DEMYSTIFYING MINDSETS

An initial step in changing negative mindsets is to help individuals define and understand (a) the assumptions that they have about themselves (including ADHD) and others and (b) how these assumptions prompt certain behaviours and self-defeating coping strategies. In essence, this first step emphasises the strengthening of self-awareness, which Goleman (1995) views as a basic component of emotional intelligence.

The questions outlined earlier to assess the mindset of adults with ADHD can serve as the catalyst for demystifying ADHD and promoting greater self-awareness. As an example, when asked to describe both a successful and unsuccessful experience from his life, a man with ADHD answered as if he had read and decided to adhere to the tenets of attribution theory. The successful experience he recounted was of a tennis match against a friend who was a good tennis player. He won the match and reported, 'I was lucky. My friend didn't play at his best. I even wondered if he was trying to let me win since he had beaten me so often.'

As an unsuccessful experience, he recalled an incident from college when he failed the initial exam given in a mathematics course. His first thought was, 'I'm really stupid in math. I'll never pass.' He dropped the class. He then confided, 'After I dropped the class, I started to blame the teacher and thought, "If the teacher were a better teacher, I would have been able to handle the material in the class and pass it."' He used two main coping strategies to deal with his sense of failure, the first 'quitting' and the next 'rationalising/externalising'.

Although it may seem very obvious to the reader that this man with ADHD had a negative mindset, that he was unable to take credit for his success and felt like he would never learn from his failure, he was unaware of his assumptions and how they affected his life. In therapy he offered a number of other examples of this way of thinking. To assist him to become more cognisant of these negative assumptions and to begin to challenge him to change, a technique described by solution-oriented therapists, namely to elicit 'exceptions' to typical ways of behaving and thinking, was used. Exceptions pertain to situations in which certain problems do not occur or occur less frequently (de Shazer, 1991; Murphy, 1997).

Individuals are asked to think of times that they were successful in a certain domain rather than focusing on when the problem did not occur. This man with ADHD was asked to reflect upon times that he was successful and attributed his success to his own resources and of times he made mistakes and was able to learn from these mistakes. He struggled at first to think of examples but with some encouragement was able to do so. Both illustrations involved the actions of a coach. He recalled as a young teenager playing in a youth basketball league; he almost single-handedly won a playoff game by making two steals and three baskets in the last minute. 'When the game was over and my coach congratulated me, I said, "I was really lucky." My coach said really strongly, "It wasn't luck, it was your determination and skill." The way he said it made me believe him.'

He also recalled that from the first day of practice this coach actually told the team that if they thought their success was based on luck, they did not realise the benefits of practice, hard work, and teamwork. 'I also remember when I had a bad game and was really feeling down. The coach put his hand on my shoulder and said even the pros have bad games. He reminded me of my good games and then pointed out how I wasn't following through on my shot. I wish I could have remembered this coach's lessons. During the year he was my coach I felt more confident than ever before but unfortunately the feeling didn't last long.'

He then described the coach he had the following year who 'believed in sarcasm and putdowns and never seemed to offer encouragement'. He continued, 'I remember one game where we were losing by one point. A teammate threw the ball to me with a few seconds to go and it went off my hands and out of bounds. We lost the game. I don't know if the throw to me was too hard or I was just too anxious to get it and shoot. I felt terrible and then even worse when the coach said in front of everyone that I missed the ball because "I didn't have good hands". Can you imagine that? I wasn't that secure to begin with and his remark made me feel like I would never be good. After that anytime someone threw the ball to me I felt uncomfortable. I'm still upset with myself that I let his remark have such a negative impact on me.'

These examples, especially the 'exceptions' to his current mindset, helped him to appreciate and understand the assumptions that directed his way of thinking and behaving and set the stage for the second step involved in developing a more positive mindset, namely, articulating the components of this mindset. This articulation provides clinicians with a compass in guiding interventions to nurture a resilient mindset.

19.7.2   DEFINING THE MAIN COMPONENTS OF A POSITIVE, RESILIENT MINDSET

In many ways the features of a positive mindset are the mirror image of the earlier description of a negative mindset. They include:

(a)   'I will learn to distinguish what I have control over from that which I do not. I will focus my time and energy on those things on which I have control since I am the author of my life.'

As was noted earlier, one of the hallmarks of effective people is their belief that they are masters of their own destiny. Research focusing on successful adults with learning and attentional difficulties found that they did not adhere to a martyr role. They never asked, 'Why me?' but instead believed, 'I had no control of being born with ADHD, but what I do have control over is learning how to deal with ADHD.'

Gerber, Ginsberg and Reiff (1992) studied the ways in which successful adults with learning disabilities view themselves (we believe the same is true for adults with ADHD) and emphasise the importance of feeling in control when they write:

> Control is the key to success for adults with learning disabilities . . . Control meant taking charge of one's life and adapting and shaping oneself in order to move ahead . . . Control was the fuel that fired their success (p. 479).

The sense of being in control is associated with the attitude that if changes are to occur in my life, I must take responsibility for these changes and not wait for others to come to my rescue or immediately satisfy my needs. Such a perspective not only lessens the sense that the world is unfair and ungiving but also places responsibility for change within oneself.

(b)   'Success can be based on my own strengths and resources'

This feature of a resilient mindset is closely aligned with feeling a sense of control of one's life. While effective people will give credit to individuals who contributed to their success, they also believe that their success rests largely on their own efforts. In essence, they assume ownership for what occurs in their lives.

A woman with ADHD constantly downplayed any of her accomplishments, an attitude that not only diminished her enjoyment when she succeeded, but also lessened the probability of future achievement. Adhering to a negative script, she had the following knee jerk reaction to success: 'I was lucky this time. It probably won't happen again.' Each success elicited the same thoughts. In her case, she segregated one success from the next, so that they did not build upon each other to change her negative mindset. As she became more aware of this self-defeating attitude, she was able to adopt a realistic outlook in which she could say, 'I did well because I planned what I was going to do and worked hard.'

(c) 'I possess islands of competence'

We all have areas of strength or what we refer to as 'islands of competence'. However, as we have seen, a number of adults with ADHD fail to acknowledge or appreciate their strengths. People with a more positive, resilient mindset are able to identify their islands of competence. It is for this reason that we ask individuals to report what they view as their strengths and how they use these strengths in their daily lives. It is also why we use the technique of searching for 'exceptions' when people respond that they don't feel they are very good at anything. We want to begin to plant the seeds that will flower into areas of competence.

(d) 'I believe that mistakes are opportunities for learning and growth'

No one is really thrilled when they make mistakes or fail. However, as clinicians we recognise that one of our most important tasks is to help people feel less intimidated by mistakes. When mistakes are viewed as situations from which to learn, people are more willing to take realistic risks rather than backing away from challenges. They do not expend an inordinate amount of time and energy fleeing from possible setbacks. Rather, their efforts are directed towards developing plans of action to succeed; if they do not succeed, they reflect upon what they have learned and what they can do differently next time. Their outlook is optimistic.

(e) 'I make a positive difference in the world'

A basic component of emotional well-being appears to be the belief that one's actions benefit others (Brooks & Goldstein, 2003). As therapists we have witnessed countless examples of individuals, many with ADHD, who engage in activities that make a positive difference (e.g. being involved in a charity, serving as a coach in a youth sports league, helping at a senior citizen centre); in the process their own sense of dignity and self-worth is enhanced and the roots of a resilient mindset are secured.

19.7.3   DEVELOPING A PLAN OF ACTION FOR CHANGE

Once clinicians help adults with ADHD gain a clearer picture of what ADHD entails, and once these adults can appreciate the assumptions that characterise their mindset and guide their behaviours, the next step is to articulate a problem-solving model for change. The model we predicate interventions upon, developed by psychologist Myrna Shure for children and adolescents, appears equally relevant for adults (Shure, 1994, 2000). Our modification of Shure's basic model includes the following components, all of which we believe have a commonsense, achievable quality to them.

(a)   Articulate both short-term and long-term goals for change

If adults with ADHD have developed a negative mindset that offers little hope for the future and we have helped them to understand that mindsets can be changed, a first step is to have them begin to articulate the changes they would like to see occur in their lives. It is often helpful to divide these changes into short-term and long-term goals, with the short-term goals contributing to the realisation of the long-term goals.

(b)   Select a few goals to address

We have discovered that while some adults with ADHD struggle to articulate goals (as therapists we can help them to do so), others are able to generate a long list. However, sometimes their impulsivity and low frustration tolerance prompt them to begin to work on all of these goals at once, almost a certain prescription for failure. Instead, as therapists we must assist them to prioritise their goals and to select one or two on which to give initial focus (O'Hanlon, 1999). We want to maximise the probability that the goals they have selected are achievable so that success will be more likely. Once we have selected the areas they wish to address, we can help to articulate both the short-term and long-term components of these goals.

As an example, in our sessions with adults with ADHD we take out a sheet of paper and ask them what they would like to see changed in their lives. We write down their responses and then select one or two areas on which to focus. The very exercise of examining and selecting these one or two areas serves several purposes. It helps to define precise and realistic goals. In addition, it serves to challenge and modify various components of a negative mindset such as feelings of low self-esteem and not having control over one's life.

The second author once worked with a man with ADHD who defined as two of his goals 'strengthening his marital relationship' and 'focusing on his physical health' (he was overweight). We discussed both of these goals, which at first were cast in somewhat general terms. While describing his marital relationship, aspects of a negative mindset were immediately apparent. He initially placed responsibility for change on his wife contending that 'she was not as supportive and loving as she could be' and he also felt that she was unfair in what she expected him to do around the house.

The characteristics of a negative mindset, especially the sense that he had little, if any, control of his life, were also operating when we discussed the issue of his physical health. He complained that he had a 'poor metabolism', noting that 'I can just smell food and I put on weight.' He also said that his job demands made it almost impossible to engage in a regular exercise routine. In essence, he was erecting obstacles to the achievement of goals before they were well-defined and planned. He externalised responsibility by arguing his wife needed to be more supportive and that she should not expect too much of him since he had ADHD; he blamed his poor fitness on his metabolism and job schedule. While there might be some truth in all of these assertions, if he continued to adhere to these obstacles to success, it would keep him from asking the following question, 'Even given these obstacles, what is it that I can do to slowly begin to deal with the problems at hand?'

In the role as a therapist, Dr Brooks pointed out in an empathic way the self-defeating patterns he had established and reframed his goals in the following way:

Improving his marital relationship was set as his long-term goal. Short-term goals involved spending more time with his wife, being less critical of her, and fulfilling two designated household responsibilities on a regular basis. Improving his physical fitness was set as his long-term goal. His short-term goal was to go on a healthy diet, begin exercising on a regular basis, and lose a pound each week until he had shed 20 pounds.

(c)   Develop realistic, achievable plans to reach designated goals

Given the impulsivity, poor planning skills, and low frustration tolerance evident in even medicated adults with ADHD, designing a realistic plan of action is of paramount importance. For example, we once worked with a woman with ADHD, who similar to the man in the last example, wanted to lose weight through diet and exercise. However, she was in such a 'rush' to do so that she went on what could be seen as a starvation diet and she immediately engaged in doing several hours of exercise a day, having done little exercise previously. She began to lose weight quickly but her initial exuberance and feeling of success were soon replaced by exhaustion and not feeling well physically. Before long, she resorted to her old habits, asserting, 'This diet and exercise stuff really doesn't work.' As obvious as it may appear to the reader that this woman's approach was doomed to failure, the possibility of failure was not at first evident to her.

(d)   Have criteria for evaluating the success of a plan of action

Another key issue involved when developing a strategy to reach one's stated goals is the criteria to use to assess whether the plan is working effectively. In some instances, the criteria are very concrete such as weight loss and greater fitness (e.g. losing a certain amount of weight in a specified time period or being able to jog two miles within a month). In other instances, an assessment of effectiveness may require more work in defining criteria for success such as when the goal is 'an improved relationship with one's spouse'.

(e)   Consider possible obstacles to the goals being achieved as well as how these obstacles will be handled

In addition to developing criteria to assess the effectiveness of different strategies, we have found that it is important to discuss openly the possibility that a plan may not work. It should be routine to inquire after a plan is considered, 'What if it doesn't work?' This comment is not offered as a self-fulfilling prophecy for failure since we then add, 'Some plans seem great in my office but they don't work outside the office. So let's think of possible back-up plans should the first one prove ineffective.'

It is it important in advance to acknowledge that some courses of action will prove ineffective but that we can learn from these. When we do not discuss the possibility of failure, the reaction of many adults with ADHD to a plan that proved unsuccessful may be to view it as another indication of their ineffectiveness. It may lower even further their sense of self-worth, trigger feelings of sadness, prompt anger towards themselves or their therapist, and reinforce a more pessimistic view of what they could accomplish to change their lives. However, by proactively considering possible obstacles as well as subsequent strategies, these adults will be less vulnerable to feelings of failure and better equipped to handle disappointments. By possessing back-up plans they also are likely to feel more in control of their lives rather than victims and martyrs. Given the negative mindset of many adults with ADHD that assumes the worst and takes each failure as an indication of how unworthy they are, it is critical to build in this step of anticipating interventions not working and designing alternative strategies.

(f)   Change the goals if repeated efforts at success do not work

If our strategies to reach particular goals continue to lead to failure, it is often a signal that the goals may need to be changed. Goals that appear reasonable may actually turn out to be too ambitious or other unanticipated factors may interfere with their success. When this occurs, it is important to review and modify the original goals.

A woman with ADHD set as one of her goals spending a half-hour each evening playing the piano, an activity she not only enjoyed but which helped to relax her. In our sessions she decided that if this goal of playing piano a half-hour each evening didn't work her back-up plan was to practise every other evening. Given her other responsibilities, she found it difficult to set aside a half-hour every evening to play piano. She resorted to the back-up plan, namely, to practise every other evening. She discovered much to her dismay that she began to miss some of her practices every other evening. She said to us, 'Another example of my not being able to follow through on things.'

We asked what she thought would help her find time to play the piano, especially since it was an activity that brought her enjoyment. At first she fell prey to a negative mindset and contended that 'probably nothing would work. I can't even succeed at something I enjoy doing.' However, with some encouragement she offered an interesting observation together with a revised goal. 'A half-hour doesn't seem like much but maybe it is. I wonder what would happen if I began by setting aside 15 minutes each evening.' While some may judge this modification of a goal as simplistic, we viewed it as a major step forward in terms of indicating that she was altering her negative mindset. The very task of contemplating and implementing a new goal was a reflection that she was moving beyond the feeling that she was helpless, that the situation was hopeless, and that she did not have the resources to find an alternative solution. She discovered much to her delight that 15 minutes a night of practice was achievable for her. Not surprisingly, she frequently extended the 15 minutes to 20 or 25 minutes once she was seated at the piano. She perceived this additional time as a 'bonus'.

(g)   As goals are reached, add new goals to reinforce a positive mindset and be aware of the negative thoughts that may serve as obstacles to future growth

After one month of practising piano for 15 minutes the woman in the previous example moved to her next goal – playing 20 minutes each evening. The seemingly small accomplishment of playing 15 minutes a night was like climbing Mt. Everest for her. She found that true success is based on realistic accomplishment and that each success reinforces a positive mindset thereby setting the stage for future success. Feeling more confident she added a new goal, namely, taking piano lessons once a week to strengthen her skills. She felt that she had achieved a certain level of discipline and commitment to take these lessons.

(h) As new goals are added, continue to develop more effective ways of coping that will help to maintain a positive mindset and strengthen the gains that have been made

Replacing a negative mindset takes ongoing work and effort. Until a more positive mindset is firmly rooted, there will be many occasions when the old mindset rears its ugly head and begins once again to be a dominating force. For this reason it is important to help adults with ADHD recognise (a) the feelings and beliefs that signal the possibility that a negative mindset is taking hold (e.g. believing 'I am stupid' or 'I am worthless' or 'I will always fail' or as the woman we described earlier told us that her success in life was like 'a house made of cards. I feel that if any kind of wind comes along, my entire facade of success will crumble'); (b) the different coping strategies that are being used to manage these feelings and which ones are actually counterproductive; (c) the need for more realistic goals and plans of action; and (d) the acceptance of one's strengths and vulnerabilities.

19.8   SUMMARY

In this chapter we have reviewed findings from an increasing number of studies that focus on ADHD in adults, including the presence of co-morbid conditions and symptom presentations. We have outlined key behaviours associated with many adults with ADHD and how these behaviours serve to reinforce a negative mindset, one that interferes with achievement and happiness in personal and professional life. We have introduced the range of psychosocial treatments for ADHD. Finally, we have offered a strength-based framework together with strategies that clinicians can use to assist adults with ADHD to replace a mindset filled with self-doubt and pessimism with one filled with realistic hope and optimism. As clinicians we can serve a significant role in nurturing resilience in adults with ADHD, offering them a more promising, satisfying lifestyle.

19.9   REFERENCES

Barkley RA (1990) A critique of current diagnostic criteria for attention deficit hyperactivity disorder: Clinical and research implications. *Journal of Developmental and Behavioral Pediatrics* **11**: 343–52.
Barkley RA (1995) *Taking Charge of ADHD: The Complete, Authoritative Guide for Parents*. New York, NY: Guilford.
Barkley RA (1997) *The Nature of Self-Control*. New York, NY: Guilford.

Barkley RA (2005) *Attention Deficit Hyperactivity Disorder* (3rd edn). New York, NY: Guilford.

Barkley R, Murphy K (2006) Identifying new symptoms for diagnosing ADHD in adulthood. *ADHD Report* **14**: 7–12.

Brooks R (1991) *The Self-Esteem Teacher: Seeds of Self-Esteem.* Loveland, OH: Treehaus Communications.

Brooks R (1999) Fostering resilience in exceptional chidlren: the search for islands of competence. In V Schwean, D Saklofske (eds) *Handbook of Psychosocial Characteristics of Exceptional Children* (pp. 563–86). New York, NY: Kluwer Academic/Plenum Press.

Brooks R, Goldstein S (2001) *Raising Resilient Children.* Chicago, IL: Contemporary.

Brooks R, Goldstein S (2003) *Nurturing Resilience in Our Children.* New York, NY: McGraw-Hill.

Canino FJ (1981) Learned-helplessness theory: Implications for research in learning disabilities. *Journal of Special Education* **15**: 471–84.

Cantwell DP, Baker L (1989) Stability and natural history of DSM-III childhood diagnoses. *Journal of the American Academy of Child and Adolescent Psychiatry* **28**: 691–700.

Chess S, Thomas A (1987) *Know Your Child.* New York, NY: Basic Books.

Coure C, Brady K, Saladin M, *et al.* (1999) Attention deficit hyperactivity disorder and substance use: Symptoms, patterns and drug choice. *American Journal of Drug and Alcohol Abuse* **25**: 441–8.

Covey SR (1989) *The 7 Habits of Highly Effective People.* New York, NY: Simon & Schuster.

Crawford R, Crawford V (2002) Career impact: finding the key to issues facing adults with ADHD. In S Goldstein, A Teeter Ellison (eds) *Clinician's Guide to Adult ADHD.* New York, NY: Academic Press.

de Shazer S (1991) *Putting Difference to Work.* New York, NY: Norton.

Epstein JM, Conners CK, Earhardt D *et al.* (1997) Asymmetrical hemispheric control of visual-spatial attention in adults with ADHD. *Neuropsychology* **11**: 467–73.

Gansler DA, Fucetola R, Krengel M *et al.* (1998) Are there cognitive subtypes in adult ADHD? *Journal of Nervous and Mental Disease* **186**: 776–81.

Gerber PJ, Ginsberg R, Reiff HB (1992) Identifying alterable patterns in employment success for highly successful adults with learning disabilities. *Journal of Learning Disabilities* **25**: 475–87.

Gittelman R, Mannuzza S, Shenker R, Bonagura N (1985) Hyperactive boys almost grown up: I. Psychiatric status. *Archives of General Psychiatry* **42**: 937–47.

Goldstein S (1995) *Understanding and Managing Children's Classroom Behavior.* New York, NY: Wiley.

Goldstein S (1999) Attention deficit hyperactivity disorder. In S Goldstein, C Reynolds (eds) *Handbook of Neurodevelopmental and Genetic Disorders in Children.* New York, NY: Guilford.

Goldstein S, Barkley RA (1998) ADHD, hunting and evolution: 'Just so' stories (commentary). *The ADHD Report* **6**(5): 1–4.

Goldstein S, Goldstein M (1998) *Managing Attention Deficit Hyperactivity Disorder in Children: A Guide for Practitioners* (2nd edn). New York, NY: Wiley.

Goldstein S, Teeter-Ellison A (2002) *Clinician's Guide to Adult ADHD.* New York: Academic Press.

Goleman D (1995) *Emotional Intelligence.* New York, NY: Bantam Books.

Greene RW (1998) *The Explosive Child: A New Approach for Understanding and Parenting Easily Frustrated, Chronically Inflexible Children.* New York, NY: HarperCollins.

Hartmann T (1993) *Attention Deficit Disorder: A Different Perception.* Novato, CA: Underwood Miller.

Hechtman L (2000) Subgroups of adult outcome of Attention Deficit Hyperactivity Disorder. In T Brown (ed.). *Attention Deficit Disorders and Comorbidities in Children, Adolescents and Adults.* Washington, DC: American Psychiatric Press (pp. 437–54).

Herrero ME, Hechtman L, Weiss G (1994) Antisocial disorders in hyperactive subjects from childhood to adulthood: Predictive factors and characterization of subgroups. *American Journal of Orthopsychiatry* **64**: 510–21.

Holdnack JA, Noberg PJ, Arnold SE *et al.* (1995) Speed of processing and verbal learning deficits in adults diagnosed with ADHD. *Neuropsychiatry, Neuropsychology and Behavioral Neurology* **8**: 282–92.

Jenkins M, Cowan R, Malloy P *et al.* (1998) Neuropsychological measures which discriminate among adults with residual symptoms of ADHD and other attentional complaints. *Clinical Neuropsychologist* **12**: 74–83.

Kilcarr P (2002) Making marriages work for individuals with ADHD. In S Goldstein, A Teeter Ellison (eds) *Clinician's Guide to Adult ADHD.* New York, NY: Academic Press.

Lerner B (1996) Self-esteem and excellence: the choice and the paradox. *American Educator* **20**: 14–19.

Lewandowski L, Codding R, Gordon M *et al.* (2000) Self-reported LD and ADHD symptoms in college students. *The ADHD Report* **8**: 1–4.

Licht BG (1983) Cognitive-motivational factors that contribute to the achievement of learning-disabled children. *Journal of Learning Disabilities* **16**: 483–90.

Mannuzza S, Gittelman-Klein R, Bessler AA *et al.* (1993) Adult outcome of hyperactive boys: education achievement, occupational rank, and psychiatric status. *Archives of General Psychiatry* **50**: 565–76.

Milin R, Loh E, Chow J, Wilson A (1997). Assessment of symptoms of ADHD in adults with substance use disorders. *Psychiatric Services* **48**: 1378–80.

Millstein RB, Wilens TE, Biederman J, Spencer TJ (1997) Presenting ADHD symptoms and subtypes in clinically referred adults with ADHD. *Journal of Attention Disorders* **2**(3): 159–66.

Murphy JJ (1997) *Solution-Focused Counseling in Middle and High Schools.* Alexandria, VA: American Counseling Association.

Murphy K, Barkley R (1996) Updated adult norms for the ADHD Behavior Checklist for adults. *The ADHD Report* **4**: 12–16.

Murphy K, Gordon M, Barkley R (2000) To what extent are ADHD symptoms common? A reanalysis of standardization data from a DSM-IV checklist. *The ADHD Report* **8**(3): 1–5.

Nadeau KG (2002) The clinician's role in the treatment of ADHD. In S Goldstein, A Teeter Ellison (eds) *Clinician's Guide to Adult ADHD.* New York, NY: Academic Press.

O'Hanlon B (1999) *Do One Thing Different and Other Uncommonly Sensible Solutions to Life's Persistent Problems.* New York, NY: William Morrow.

Phelan TW (2002) Families and ADHD. In S Goldstein, A Teeter Ellison (eds) *Clinician's Guide to Adult ADHD.* New York, NY: Academic Press.

Pomerleau OF, Downey KK, Stelson FW, Pomerleau CS (1995) Cigarette smoking in adult patients diagnosed with attention deficit hyperactivity disorder. *Journal of Substance Abuse* **7**: 373–8.

Ratey N (2002) Life coaching for adult ADHD. In S Goldstein, A Teeter Ellison (eds) *Clinician's Guide to Adult ADHD.* New York, NY: Academic Press.

Robin AL, Bedway M, Tzelepis A (1998) Understanding the personality traits of Adults with AD/HD: a pilot study. *Attention* **4**(4): 49–55.

Rostain AL, Ramsay JR (2000) A combined treatment approach for adults with ADHD. *Journal of Attention Disorders* **10**: 150–9.

Rucklidge JJ, Kaplan BJ (1997) Psychological functioning of women identified in adulthood with Attention Deficit Hyperactivity Disorder. *Journal of Attention Disorders* **2**(3): 167–76.

Sachs GS, Baldassano CF (2000) Comorbidity of attention deficit hyperactivity disorder with early- and late-onset bipolar disorder. *American Journal of Psychiatry* **157**: 466–8.

Safren SA, Perlman CA, Sprich S, Otto MW (2005) *Mastering Your Adult ADHD: A Cognitive Behavioral Treatment Program.* Oxford: Oxford University Press.

Satterfield JH, Hoppe CM, Schell AM (1982) A prospective study of delinquency in 110 adolescent boys with attention deficit disorder and 88 normal adolescent boys. *American Journal of Psychiatry* **139**: 795–8.

Seligman M (1990) *Learned Optimism: How to Change Your Mind and Your Life.* New York, NY: Pocket Books.

Shekim WO (1990, Spring/Summer) Adult attention deficit hyperactivity disorder, residual state. *CH.A.D.D.ER Newsletter*: 16–18.

Shure MB (1994) *Raising a Thinking Child.* New York, NY: Holt.

Shure MB (2000) *Raising a Thinking Pre-Teen.* New York, NY: Holt.

Vitelli R (1998) Childhood disruptive behavior disorder and adult psychopathology. *American Journal of Forensic Psychology* **16**: 297–37.

Weiner B (1974) *Achievement, Motivation and Attribution Theory.* Morristown, NJ: General Learning Press.

Weiss G, Hechtman L (1993) *Hyperactive Children Grown Up* (2nd edn). New York, NY: Guilford.

Werner EE, Smith RS (2001) *Journeys from Childhood to Midlife: Risk, Resilience, and Recovery.* Ithaca, NY: Cornell University Press.

Wilens TE, Biederman J, Mick E (1998) Does ADHD affect the course of substance abuse. *American Journal on Addictions* **7**: 156–63.

Wilens TE, McDermott SP, Biederman J, Abrantes A (1999) Cognitive therapy in the treatment of adults with ADHD: a systematic chart review of twenty-six cases. *Journal of Cognitive Psychotherapy* **13**: 215–26.

Young SJ (1999) Psychological therapy for adults with attention deficit hyperactivity disorder. *Counseling Psychology Quarterly* **12**(2): 183–90.

Young SJ (2002) A model of psychotherapy for adults with ADHD. In S Goldstein, A Teeter Ellison (eds). *Clinician's Guide to Adult ADHD.* New York, NY: Academic Press.

20 Avenues for the Neuro-Remediation of ADHD: Lessons from Clinical Neurosciences

REDMOND G. O'CONNELL,[1] **MARK A. BELLGROVE**[2] **AND IAN H. ROBERTSON**[1]

1. School of Psychology and Institute of Neuroscience, Trinity College Dublin, Ireland; 2. School of Psychology and Queensland Brain Institute (QBI), University of Queensland, Brisbane, Australia

20.1 OVERVIEW

There is now a wealth of evidence to suggest that at least a significant proportion of those diagnosed with ADHD suffer from a prominent disturbance of executive functions linked to abnormalities in frontal-subcortical circuitry (see Chapters 10, 11 and 12 for a full review). ADHD is primarily a behavioural disorder but executive functions such as working memory, inhibition and attention are integral to cognitive development and may also play a causal role in the emergence of behavioural symptoms in ADHD (Barkley, 1997; Nigg, 2001; Castellanos & Tannock, 2002; Sonuga-Barke, 2003). It is surprising therefore that there is such a dearth of research investigating treatments for ADHD that would directly target neuropsychological deficits.

At present, there are just two well-established, 'evidence-based', treatments for ADHD: psychostimulant medication and behaviour therapy. Psychostimulant treatments have proven efficacy in dealing with the behavioural features of ADHD and in fact also lead to significant improvements in cognitive performance (Tannock, Ickowicz & Schachar, 1995; Overtoom et al., 2003; Schweitzer et al., 2004; Shafritz et al., 2004) but these changes are achieved by increasing extracellular levels of dopamine without directly altering affected cortical networks in a lasting manner (e.g. Schweitzer et al., 2004). A number of highly effective behavioural interventions have also been developed for ADHD and have been reliably associated with reductions in primary and secondary behavioural symptoms (MTA Cooperative Group, 2004; Pelham, Wheeler & Chronis, 1998). Once again, however, improvements are achieved without addressing neuropsychological abnormalities. This may explain, in part, why despite long-term treatment, both neuropsychological and neurological abnormalities associated with ADHD persist into adulthood in a significant proportion of cases (e.g. Woods, Lovejoy & Ball, 2002; Castellanos et al., 2002; Ernst et al., 2003). As a result there is still a need for the development of new interventions that can directly target these deficits and bring about lasting improvements.

Handbook of Attention Deficit Hyperactivity Disorder. Edited by M. Fitzgerald, M. Bellgrove and M. Gill.
© 2007 John Wiley & Sons Ltd

Based on a growing understanding of the capacity of the human brain for plasticity and self-repair there is now strong evidence to suggest that neuropsychological functions can be improved by carefully structured cognitive training. In the present chapter we will explore the hypothesis that experience-dependent changes in brain structure and function can provide a new avenue for the remediation of ADHD.

20.2   CAPITALISING ON NEURAL PLASTICITY

Research with both animal and human models has shown that normal associative learning and experience evoke important changes in cortical sensory and representational fields, synaptic connectivity, dendritic arborisation and axonal sprouting. The brain modifies itself at the level of the synapse, constantly establishing and strengthening connections between neurons through the basic process of Hebbian learning (Hebb, 1949). Co-activation of neurons or networks of neurons strengthens the connections between them and improves their efficiency. With continued activation these simple changes at the synaptic level can eventually lead to experience-dependent dendritic/axonal sprouting and even neurogenesis (Cotman & Neito-Sampedro, 1982; Kempermann, Brandon & Gage, 1998; Gould *et al.*, 1999). Thus different patterns of behaviour and experience will have tangible effects on neural circuitry.

Experience-dependent changes in synaptic connectivity can occur within a matter of minutes (Dinse, Recanzone & Merzenich, 1993) but over much longer periods of time changes in large-scale neural networks and brain structures can be observed. For example, Munte, Altenmuller & Jancke (2002) found increases in grey and white matter volume in several brain regions of highly experienced musicians while London taxi drivers show structural differences in the hippocampus associated with their increased use of spatial representations during navigation (Maguire *et al.*, 2000). Hence the classical view that infancy and adolescence represent a critical period for brain development after which neural pathways become fixed and immutable has been replaced by an understanding that the human brain is amenable to change.

Importantly it is thought that the same mechanism which underlies the processes of experience-dependent plasticity also promotes both spontaneous and guided recovery following brain injury (Robertson & Murre, 1999). That is, if a damaged brain area is regularly stimulated, be it directly or indirectly, there is the potential for lost functions to be restored by re-establishing damaged neural connections or by forming new compensatory connections (Seltzer, 1998). As with natural experience dependent-changes, functional recovery after brain injury can be seen in a matter of hours and further improvement can occur over weeks, months or even years (see Eslinger, 2002, for more discussion). The potential for massive cortical reorganisation is not always beneficial as in the case of phantom limb sensation in which deafferented cortical circuits are gradually activated by adjacent areas of the cortex leading to the sensation that the lost limb is actually present (Ramachandran, Stewart & Rogers-Ramachandran, 1992). As a result, functional recovery will only occur in the context of particular patterns of behaviour. Our understanding of how areas of the brain collaborate to perform various functions is therefore crucial in allowing us to hypothesise novel methods for targeting damaged networks.

We are only beginning to identify mechanisms by which experience-dependent plasticity may be helped or hindered but increasingly, researchers and clinicians have been able to make use of the ideas emerging from the field of neuroscience to develop ingenious methods for improving or restoring brain function. In the field of cognitive rehabilitation researchers have combined what we know about neuroplasticity with knowledge of how sensory, motor and cognitive functions are achieved by the normal brain in order to develop highly structured training schedules designed to stimulate the affected brain area and thus re-establish or strengthen neural connections. For example Robertson, Hogg and McMillan (1998) showed that unilateral neglect was significantly reduced by simply encouraging patients to make voluntary contralesional hand movements. This approach was informed by previous work demonstrating the existence of multiple representations of space in the brain that interact to produce a coherent spatial reference system (Rizzolatti & Camarda, 1987). As a result of the interconnections between these representations when the somatosensory spatial map is activated by limb movement, the damaged peripersonal spatial map will also be simultaneously activated. Through repeated indirect activation of the damaged circuit neural connections are re-established and the lost function gradually returns. In this manner a detailed understanding of the neural processes underlying functional impairments resulting from brain injury has paved the way for the emergence of novel strategies for behaviourally inducing plastic reorganisation of lesioned brain systems in a variety of disorders including hemiparesis, phantom limb sensation and apraxia.

While it was initially thought that the principles of guided recovery applied only to low-level sensory, perceptual and motor functions, it has become apparent that high-level cognitive functions such as attention, memory and language may also be amenable to experience-dependent restitution. One common approach used to improve or rehabilitate high-level cognitive impairments has been direct training of specific processes through intensive, highly structured practice. The rationale is simple: repeated use of particular cognitive processes during training stimulates plastic changes in the underlying neural circuitry leading to increased neural efficiency and a consequent increase in cognitive capacity. A key prediction arising from the process-specific approach is that improvements in training should transfer to unpractised tasks that require the same underlying cognitive function. The aim is to restore the lost function so that therapeutic gains can be applied to many facets of daily life. Limb activation training for unilateral neglect produces generalised improvements without the need for training to be repeated in every different context within which the patient operates (Robertson *et al.*, 2002). If process-specific training effects are not restricted to the training tasks themselves, then improvements should be seen on untrained tasks that recruit the targeted process. Processes such as attention and working memory are supportive processes that underpin a number of cognitive functions. These fundamental processes should provide the foundation upon which broader improvements in cognitive functioning can be built and have been the most common targets of process-specific training.

Cognitive deficits in patients with brain abnormalities have also been successfully treated by implementing compensatory strategies. These strategies involve the use of environmental modifications, residual abilities and self-management strategies designed to bypass the defective cognitive processor (e.g. see Manly *et al.*, 2002; Eslinger, 2002). This represents another substantial and interesting area of research; however, in this chapter we focus exclusively on restorative strategies that are designed to capitalise on neural plasticity as a potential avenue for neuropsychological remediation in ADHD. Here we review a few illustrative examples of process-specific neuro-cognitive training in healthy and brain-injured populations that are most pertinent to our discussion of ADHD.

20.3   TRAINING OF HIGH-LEVEL COGNITIVE FUNCTIONS

20.3.1   COGNITIVE REHABILITATION

At the outset it is important to note that proper evaluation of the efficacy of the process-specific approach in clinical groups has been hampered by great variation between studies in the intensity, duration and content of training schedules as well as important methodological weaknesses (see Park and Ingles, 2001). Nevertheless the possibility of restoring lost brain function through neuro-cognitive training has gained support from a limited number of well-designed studies.

Attention problems are among the most common consequences of brain damage and perhaps as a result, the majority of direct training studies have targeted aspects of attention. Several studies targeting different components of attention have been conducted, of which a number have shown positive effects of training with brain-injured participants on both practised and unpractised psychometric measures (Ben-Yishay, Piasetsky & Rattock, 1987; Sohlberg & Mateer, 1987; Neimann, Ruff & Baser, 1990; Sohlberg *et al.*, 2000; Stablum *et al.*, 2000).

Much of the published research on direct cognitive training of brain injured patients has focused on Attention Process Training (APT) developed by Sohlberg and Mateer (1987). APT consists of a set of tasks and drills of increasing difficulty in which participants respond to visual or auditory stimuli, designed to exercise the sustained, selective, alternating (i.e. switching) and divided components of attention separately. The basic assumption here is that discrete components of attention can be targeted through repeated individual stimulation. Tasks are organised around a hierarchical model of attention such that demands are placed on increasingly complex attentional processes. The training tasks range from simply pressing a buzzer when the number 3 is heard to complex semantic categorisation. Each task is performed until mastery has been accomplished. A major advantage of programmes like APT is that therapy can be adapted to the individual according to their abilities from the outset.

Sohlberg and colleagues (2000) compared APT training with an educational and support method using a basic crossover design. Two randomly assigned groups were differentiated by the order in which they received APT (24 hours per week over 10 weeks) and a placebo intervention consisting of brain injury education and supportive listening (10 hours per week over 10 weeks). In this kind of design each participant serves as their own control while between-groups comparisons are made by analysing performance after each treatment block. Participants were two groups of 7 individuals with acquired brain injury between 18 and 60 years of age who were at least one year post-injury. Treatment effects were assessed on the basis of untrained neuropsychological tests probing aspects of attention and working memory as well as questionnaires and structured interviews asking participants about their day-to-day functioning. The authors found that self-reported changes in attention and memory functioning, as well as improvement on neuropsychological tests of attention and executive functioning were greater after APT than after therapeutic support. Importantly, improvements on neuropsychological tasks that were not primarily attentional in nature (including Stroop, Trail Making Test, and memory for locations) indicated a generalisation of learning. It is thought that training a core, supportive process such as attention, has generalised effects by improving overall input to cognitive processing thus providing a more stable and effective substrate for other cognitive abilities (Sohlberg & Mateer, 2001).

A study by Sturm et al. (1997) evaluated the effects of a more dynamic computerised attention training. In this study all participants completed two training periods of 14 one-hour sessions and were assessed on a standardised computerised battery of attention tests comprising separate tests for sustained, selective, alternating and divided attention. The authors manipulated the order in which participants were exposed to high- and low-level attention training tasks. It was found that prior training on the most basic aspects of attention led to significant improvements on higher aspects whereas no such improvements were found in basic attention when the order was reversed. Additionally, the authors found improved performance on other computerised tests on which they had not been trained, but that were specific to the type of attention trained in each case. This finding is consistent with evidence indicating that there are separable neural circuits underlying different attentional processes (Posner & Peterson, 1990) and has clear implications for the structuring of rehabilitative training schedules.

In the study by Sohlberg et al. (2000) the authors noted that the vigilance level of individual patients influenced the extent of improvement with therapy on several tests of executive attention. Only patients who had poor vigilance levels showed improvement in basic attentional skills and only patients with higher vigilance levels showed improvement on more demanding attentional or working memory tasks. This finding suggests that patients with brain injury require training that is tailored to their specific needs. Other rehabilitation studies have tended to include patients with brain injuries of widely varying severity in the same treatment group which may explain, in part, why the results of direct-process training have been inconsistent thus far (Park & Ingles, 2001). Sohlberg et al. (2000) recommend that future studies should delineate specific patient profiles in order to determine who is likely to benefit from a particular training programme.

Recent literature searches by Limond and Leeke (2005) and by Penkman (2004) yielded few studies that have examined the effectiveness of process-specific training techniques with paediatric groups (excluding ADHD) and these studies were hampered by serious methodological issues. One of the more methodologically sound studies was conducted by Butler and Copeland (2002) who examined the contribution of a broad cognitive rehabilitation programme for 21 children and young adults (aged 6–22 years) with attention deficits arising from cancer treatment. A waiting list control group of 10 children and young adults was used but there was no control for non-specific treatment effects such as child–adult interaction. The multi-component programme included APT, a variety of meta-cognitive strategies from the educational field and cognitive-behavioural interventions. Significant improvement for the experimental group was found on three attention/concentration measures (digit span, continuous performance task, sentence memory) but not on an arithmetic measure included to assess generalisation. Unfortunately it is not possible to determine how much of these benefits can be attributed to APT as opposed to the other components of the intervention as each participant was administered all three components. The absence of a non-specific effects control group also limits the drawing of any firm conclusions. Further empirical investigation using more rigorous experimental designs will be necessary before the efficacy of cognitive training for children with acquired brain injury can be properly evaluated.

The precise neural mechanisms underlying functional recovery with direct process training have yet to be firmly established but a small number of functional imaging studies have begun to shed some light on this issue (Wexler *et al.*, 2000; Sturm *et al.*, 2004). Sturm and colleagues (2004) conducted a PET and fMRI activation study of the effects of alertness training on patients with alertness deficits due to right-hemisphere vascular brain damage. The computerised training procedure required participants to drive a simulated vehicle as quickly as possible while looking out for occasional obstacles on the road. The difficulty level of the training was increased as each participant's performance improved. Previous work has established a right lateralised fronto-parietal alertness network (Posner & Peterson, 1990; Paus *et al.*, 1997). Before training none of the patients activated the right superior, middle or dorsolateral frontal cortex implicated in the maintenance of an alert state. After training, however, patients who exhibited significant behavioural improvements in alertness showed reactivation of these right frontal regions. These results are therefore indicative of a functional reorganisation of the alertness network. Importantly, patients who were included in a memory training control group did not show the same pattern of right hemisphere activations post-training.

In another study, Wexler *et al.* (2000) used fMRI to study 8 patients with schizophrenia before and after 10–15 weeks of verbal working memory exercises. It had previously been shown that poor performance on these tasks by patients with schizophrenia was accompanied by lower than normal activation of the left inferior frontal cortex (Stevens *et al.*, 1998). The degree of functional improvement on the memory tasks after training was significantly correlated with the percentage-change increase in left inferior frontal activation (see Figure 20.1). These studies have provided some of the first evidence that improved cognitive performance in patients with neurological abnormalities is associated with a recovery of the affected neural networks.

Recent reviews by the Brain Injury Interdisciplinary Special Interest Group (BI-ISIG) of the American Congress of Rehabilitation Medicine (ACRM) concluded that there is sufficient empirical evidence to recommend direct-attention training for TBI or stroke during the post-acute phase of recovery and rehabilitation (Cicerone *et al.*, 2000, 2005). However, only a small number of training studies have included real-life measures of treatment efficacy and as a result a justified criticism of the direct-process approach to the remediation of higher cognitive function has been that there is little evidence of treatment effects beyond such proximal

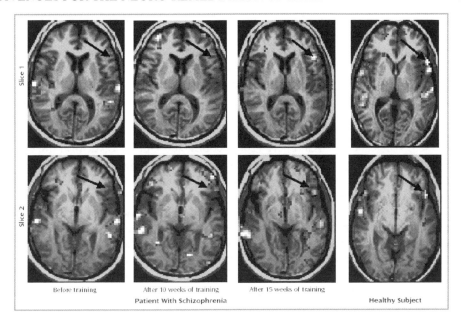

Figure 20.1. Images from functional MRI before and after training for a patient with schizophrenia performing a memory task and for a healthy subject performing the same task

Note: The arrows in slice 1 point to the left inferior frontal gyrus, where task-related activation is clearly evident in the patient after 15 weeks of training and in the healthy subject. The arrows in slice 2 point to the left lateral orbital gyrus, where activation is again clearly present in the healthy subject and in the patient after 15 weeks of training. Some evidence of activation is also present in the patient at the end of 10 weeks of training, but none before the beginning of the exercises.

Source: Wexler *et al.*, 2000.

Reprinted with permission from the *American Journal of Psychiatry*. American Psychiatric Association.

outcomes as training tasks or very similar untrained neuropsychological tasks (Park & Ingles, 2001; Wexler, in press). Transferring therapeutic gains to complex everyday life situations may be particularly difficult for patients with severe impairments. In fact as we will see, direct-process training may be most suited to individuals who maintain strong residual functions in the targeted area.

20.3.2   NEURO-COGNITIVE TRAINING OF HEALTHY INDIVIDUALS

Studies with healthy participants have revealed that attention and working memory capacities may not necessarily be fixed, but may be amenable to significant change with experience. A recent review of the practice-effects literature by Kelly and Garavan (2005) highlights the major changes in neural activity that can occur with intensive practice on a cognitive task. With sufficient practice, the normal brain is capable of enhancing its efficiency by increasing or decreasing activations within a neural network, by improving connectivity between brain regions and even by reorganising the cortical areas that are employed during the execution of a cognitive skill. These processes may be particularly important with respect to ADHD as they suggest that the benefits of process-specific neuro-cognitive training may not necessarily be limited to the recovery of dramatic losses of function but could also be effective in the remediation of subtle cognitive impairments. A large number of fMRI and PET studies have explored the neural correlates of practice on cognitive tasks (as reviewed by Kelly and Garavan 2005). In addition, a small number of studies have examined the effects of extensive cognitive training on normal healthy individuals.

Olesen, Westerberg & Klingberg (2004) conducted an fMRI study on the effects of extended working memory practice in healthy adults. Participants practised 90 trials per day for 5 weeks on three visuo-spatial working memory tasks and were compared with an un-trained control group. Training improved performance on un-trained measures of working memory and was associated with significantly increased scores on measures of inhibition (Stroop) and general fluid intelligence (Raven's Advanced Progressive Matrices). Participants were scanned while performing a working memory task. After training there were clear increases in brain activity in the middle frontal gyrus and inferior parietal cortices. Previous work has shown that there is a positive correlation between levels of activity in these regions and working memory capacity (Rypma & d'Esposito, 2000; Klingberg, Forssberg & Westerberg, 2002a). Thus, significant and generalised improvements in cognitive capacity are possible even in the undamaged brain.

Research with healthy adults tells us that changes in brain activation with cognitive training follow a complex time-course. Another imaging study of working memory training by Hempel and colleagues (2004) suggested that training-related activation changes in fronto-parietal working memory regions were best described by an inverse U-shaped quadratic function with initial activation increases at the time of improved performance giving way to decreases after consolidation of performance gains (see Figure 20.2). Kelly and Garavan (2005) note the common process of 'scaffolding' in which activity in frontal control areas (prefrontal cortex, anterior cingulate and posterior parietal cortex) gradually decreases after a task has been well rehearsed. Deactivation of frontal regions is associated with attainment of automatic or asymptotic performance and a decreased demand on control or attentional processes. Ensuring that task difficulty is increased as performance improves (not done in the study by Hempel *et al.*) appears to be crucial to maintaining demands on high-level executive processes.

Few studies have examined cognitive training in healthy children. One recent and well-designed study by Rueda and colleagues (Rueda *et al.*, 2005) examined the influence of a computerised training programme for executive attention that was specifically adapted for children. Each exercise was divided into a number of levels and gains to the next level were made upon achieving a criterion level of performance. Each training task exercised a particular executive process such as anticipation, conflict resolution, inhibitory control or stimulus discrimination and involved cartoon characters and concepts that were familiar to children. Training was administered over five sessions, within a two to three-week period, to two groups of normally developing children who differed in age (4 and 6 years). In order to control for number of sessions involving child–adult interaction, a second group of children watched popular videos during which at varying intervals the video was paused and

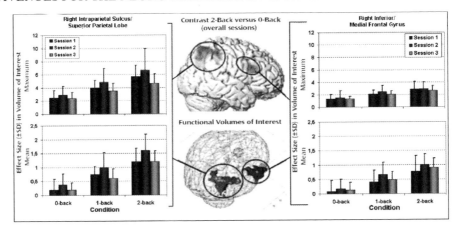

Figure 20.2. Training related cerebral activation changes in nine normal subjects during performance of a working memory task

Note: Maximum and mean effect sizes of the volumes of interest (intraparietal sulcus/superios parietal lob, 206, voxels, inferior frontal gyrus/medial frontal gyrus, 42 voxels) during the three different task conditions at baseline and after 2 and 4 weeks (sessions 1–3, respectively) of training.

Source: Hempel *et al.*, 2004.

Reprinted with permission from the *American Journal of Psychiatry*. American Psychiatric Association.

the image of a fish appeared on screen: the control children had to press a button to restart the video. Training resulted in reduced difficulty in resolving conflict and exerting executive control. Two further effects of this brief training were particularly interesting. First, electrophysiological data suggested that in the 4-year-old group, training produced an EEG pattern for conflict resolution similar to untrained 6-year-olds. For 6-year-olds the effect of training was to produce a more adult-like pattern of activity. Second, the authors also found evidence of generalisation of training benefits to measures of intelligence and reasoning ability. These data indicate that process-specific training at an early age may accelerate the development of attentional networks.

In sum, we have outlined some of the strongest available evidence that experience dependent plasticity can be exploited to improve cognitive function in both brain injured and healthy populations. Research with healthy participants indicates that gains in cognitive ability can be made with appropriately targeted training.

20.4 IS ADHD A CANDIDATE FOR NEURO-COGNITIVE REMEDIATION?

As reviewed in Chapter 12, ADHD is associated with a range of neuropsychological impairments. In particular, converging evidence points to prominent deficits in executive functions such as response inhibition (Oosterlaan, Logan & Sergeant,

1998; Nigg, 2001), working memory (Martinussen *et al.*, 2005), sustained attention (Manly *et al.*, 2001; Shallice *et al.*, 2002; O'Connell *et al.*, 2004) and temporal processing (Barkley, Murphy & Bush, 2001; Mullins *et al.*, 2005). These deficits have been reliably demonstrated in children but a number of recent reviews show similar problems in adults with ADHD (Woods, 2002).

Executive functions such as working memory, sustained attention, response inhibition and temporal processing are all dependent on communication between subcortical and frontal regions and imaging studies have consistently identified dysregulation of predominantly right hemispheric fronto-striatal circuitry in ADHD (reviewed by Bush, Valera & Seidman, 2005). Sowell *et al.* (2003) carried out detailed spatial mapping of cortical morphology and grey-matter density in children with ADHD and found clear structural abnormalities in dorsolateral prefrontal cortex, lateral temporal regions and inferior parietal regions. These areas are strongly interconnected and are thought to form a broad attention-action system that is critical for the maintenance of inhibitory and attentional control. Thus there are clear commonalities between the neural structures underpinning executive functions and the structural and functional brain changes in ADHD. Consequently several of the most prominent theoretical models of ADHD have proposed that neuropsychological impairments play a causal role in the development of this behavioural syndrome (Barkley, 1997; Nigg, 2001; Castellanos & Tannock, 2002; Sonuga-Barke, 2003). Research has shown that non-affected relatives of patients with ADHD also show performance deficits on neuropsychological measures and that risk-genes for ADHD may also impair neuropsychological function in ADHD (e.g. Bellgrove *et al.*, 2005, see also Chapter 12). These findings provide further evidence that neuropsychological deficits in ADHD are the result of genetically linked neural impairment. It can be hypothesised, therefore, that remediation of neuropsychological deficits in ADHD would have two potential benefits: improvement of cognitive function itself and an associated reduction in behavioural symptoms.

In a major structural imaging study by the National Institutes of Mental Health in the US developmental changes in brain volumes were examined by scanning 152 children and adolescents with ADHD and 139 controls over a ten-year period (Castellanos *et al.*, 2002). The volume of cerebral white and grey matter of children and adolescents with ADHD was on average 3–4% smaller than that of children without the condition and the greater the severity of symptoms the greater the discrepancy in the size of various brain areas. Importantly, the white and grey matter volumes of the ADHD group followed the same maturational trajectories as their healthy counterparts. Furthermore, participants who were receiving medication showed the same structural abnormalities as unmedicated participants. Thus, although normal maturational processes are taking place, an abnormality at some early stage of development appears to place children with ADHD at a persistent disadvantage. This presents the possibility that intensive neuro-cognitive training could remediate this developmental lag and lead to lasting improvements in cognitive and behavioural function in children with ADHD. Process-specific training of key neuropsychological impairments may provide one avenue for non-pharmacological remediation in ADHD.

20.5 NEURO-COGNITIVE REMEDIATION STUDIES OF ADHD

We are aware of only a small number of studies that have attempted process-specific remediation of neuropsychological function in ADHD. One of the first steps in this direction was taken by Semrud-Clikeman and colleagues (1999) who examined the efficacy of the APT programme in treating attention deficits in children with ADHD. A treatment group of 21 children with ADHD was compared to a waiting list ADHD group and a separate control group without attentional difficulties. At post-test, the intervention group showed normalised performance on un-trained visual cancellation and auditory attention tasks relative to the non-ADHD participants. In addition qualitative interviews with teachers indicated increases in attentive on-task behaviour in class. However, non-specific effects could not be ruled out in this study as only a waiting list control group was included. Furthermore APT was administered in combination with instruction in problem-solving and therefore it is not clear how much of the observed improvements can be attributed to increases in attentional capacity *per se*.

In order to overcome these limitations Kerns, Eso and Thomson (1999) conducted a further examination of APT in a group of 14 children (average age 9 years) diagnosed with ADHD. In this study, the treatment group was trained on a new version of APT, named 'Pay Attention', that was specifically designed for use with children. Children were seen after school twice a week for eight weeks. A carefully matched control group engaged in a variety of computer-based games and puzzles in order to rule out the influence of one-on-one contact with the therapist and other non-specific factors. Pre-post measures included seven psychometric tests of attention and executive control, a measure of academic performance (age-appropriate arithmetic problems) and home and school versions of an ADHD symptom questionnaire. Significant treatment effects were found for the Mazes sub-test of the WISC-III, the Day-Night Stroop Task, the Attentional Capacity Test (ACT) and sections of the Underlining Test (a measure of sustained visual attention). Some generalisation of training benefits was indicated by improved scores on the academic task and a marginally significant improvement in inattentive and impulsive behaviour noted by the teachers. Another interesting detail of this study was that five children in each group were receiving medication at the time of training indicating that medication does not necessarily preclude neuro-cognitive training. The possibility that medication might provide the appropriate setting conditions for effective participation in a neuro-cognitive training programme is in need of further investigation.

A different approach was taken by Shaffer and colleagues (2000) who developed Interactive Metronome® Training. The severity of inattentive symptoms in boys with ADHD is a significant predictor of motor coordination difficulties (Piek, Pitcher & Hay, 1999) and fronto-striatal regions are associated with both high-order motor control and ADHD (Rubia *et al.*, 1999). This evidence fuelled the hypothesis that training aspects of motor regulation such as planning, sequencing, timing and rhythmicity may play a concomitant role in improving the capacity to attend. During the training procedure children perform a series of prescribed movements in time with a steady metronome reference-beat sound heard in headphones.

Movements are registered by special sensors placed on the hands, the thighs and on the floor. The Interactive Metronome (IM) analyses the temporal accuracy of each movement and provides feedback to the participant in the form of spatially and tonally-changing guide sounds. Successful performance of this kind of training requires the participant to focus without interruption for extended periods of time. A matched random assignment process, based on medication dosage, age and baseline attentional ability was used to assign 56 boys, aged between 6 and 12 and diagnosed with ADHD to three groups: an IM group, a video-game practice placebo group and a waiting-list control group. Each participant underwent 15 one hour IM treatment sessions per day over a 3–5 week period. Fifty-eight pre-test factors assessing attention, clinical functioning and academic skills were used to examine treatment effects. Test-retest analyses revealed that the IM group had a significantly stronger improvement pattern than the video-game group, showing improvements over 53 test scores compared with 40 in the video-game group and 23 in the waiting-list group. The IM group made significantly larger gains in areas of attention, motor control, language processing, reading and aggressive behaviour than either the video-game or waiting-list groups. The comparatively strong improvements in the video-game group underlines the need for the inclusion of appropriate placebo conditions in any examination of ADHD interventions.

Working memory deficits in ADHD have also been targeted for process-specific training. As discussed earlier, Olesen and colleagues (2004) found that plastic changes in the neural networks underlying working memory could be encouraged by systematic training in normal, non-impaired adults. The commonalities between the cortical areas involved in working memory and those thought implicated in ADHD provided a neuroanatomical rationale for a series of studies conducted by Klingberg and colleagues. Based on a training regime previously used to induce cortical plasticity in sensory and motor cortices, Klingberg, Forssberg and Westerberg (2002b) developed a computerised working memory training programme in which task difficulty was closely matched to the individual's performance on a trial-by-trial basis in order to maximise the training effect. Four subtests were presented during each training session: a visuo-spatial working memory task, backwards digit span, a letter-span task and a choice reaction time task. Task difficulty was adjusted by changing the number of stimuli to be remembered. Participants in the treatment group (7 children, mean age 11.0) were trained at a children's hospital for at least 20 minutes per day, 4–6 days a week, for at least 5 weeks. Participants in the control condition (7 children, mean age 11.4) were trained on a placebo programme that included the same working memory tasks but without adjustment of difficulty level and for less than 10 minutes per day. The study was designed as a double-blind study.

Comparison of pre- and post-intervention measures indicated a significant treatment effect for the practised visuo-spatial working memory task, an unpractised and non-computerised visuo-spatial working memory task, a measure of impulsivity (Stroop accuracy), a measure of reasoning ability (Raven's Progressive Matrices, RPM) and for the number of head movements made during testing. Correlational analyses revealed that improvement on RPM was correlated with improvement on the trained working memory task. The latter relationship is consistent with the view that working memory facilitates higher-order processes such as reasoning ability by allowing information to be stored and manipulated on-line. The reduction in head movement was highly correlated with improvements on both the trained working memory task and RPM. As the authors note, the gradual improvement in working memory over a number of weeks is reminiscent of the slow re-acquisition of a perceptual or motor skill and the fact that each of the pre/post tests is dependent on prefrontal cortex may indicate that training did induce change at the neural level. The clear evidence of generalisation to non-working memory tasks (Stroop, RPM) is particularly encouraging and provides strong evidence that training a fundamental process such as working memory can lead to a general improvement in cognitive capacity.

Building upon these strong findings Klingberg and colleagues (2005) conducted one of the most thorough trials of a cognitive training programme designed for children. Fifty-three unmedicated children with ADHD, aged 7–12 (mean 9.8) were recruited from four clinical sites and randomly assigned to a treatment or comparison group. The authors employed the same double-blind design as in their initial study however this time participants in the control condition (working memory training without adjustment of difficulty) were trained for the same duration as the intervention group. In addition, symptom ratings of ADHD were included in the outcome measures and there was a 3-month follow-up to assess persistence of treatment effects. The training materials were saved on compact disc, allowing the children to complete the intervention independently either at home or at school. After training, participants in the treatment group significantly outperformed the comparison group on each of the executive outcome measures (Span Board, Stroop, Digit-Span, RPM) and these differences remained at follow-up 3 months later. Importantly, the effect size for improvement on the untrained working memory task (0.93 on Span Board) represented a strong clinical effect and compares very favourably to those previously reported for stimulant medication. A comparison with previous studies of working memory and response inhibition indicated that, post-training, the spatial working memory and Stroop performance of the children was 0.3 standard deviations or less below normative levels. Most importantly, there was also a strong and specific clinical effect on parent ratings of ADHD symptoms using both DSM-IV criteria and the Conners' Parent Rating Scale. Effect sizes of 1.21 for parent-rated attention and 0.47 for parent-rated hyperactivity/impulsivity are particularly impressive given that all participants were unmedicated. Again, these differences were still evident at follow-up. These results represent some of the strongest evidence to date that direct neuro-cognitive training in ADHD leads to generalised improvements in both the short and longer term that extend to unpractised cognitive tasks and aspects of every-day behaviour.

There is thus good initial evidence that process-specific neuro-cognitive training can be an effective treatment for ADHD (see Table 20.1 for summary). Each of the studies reviewed above has implemented sound methodology and produced encouraging levels of improvement especially considering the comparatively limited success with paediatric and adult brain-injured patients. We have cited evidence from research with brain injured and healthy groups that training related improvements in cognitive performance are accompanied by plastic changes in underlying neural networks although the neural consequences of cognitive training in ADHD have yet to be explored. Nevertheless we can draw three tentative conclusions from

Table 20.1. Summary of ADHD cognitive training studies reviewed

Study	N[a]	Treatment	Control procedure	Neuropsychological generalisation	Everyday life improvement
Semrud-Clikeman et al. (1999)	21 (12)	Attention/Executive Control Practice	Waiting list	Not measured	Not measured
Kerns et al. (1999)	7 (7)	Attention/Executive Control Practice	Video game practice	Measure of academic performance	Behavioural reports (teacher)
Shaffer et al. (2000)	19 (18)	Attention/motor coordination training	Video game practice + waiting list control	Language processing	Reading and aggressive behaviour
Klingberg et al. (2002b)	7 (7)	Working Memory Practice	Working memory practice without adjustment of difficulty	Stroop, Raven's matrices, reduced head movement	Not measured
Klingberg et al. (2005)	27 (26)	Working Memory Practice	Working memory practice without adjustment of difficulty	Stroop, Raven's matrices	Behavioural reports (parent and teacher)

[a]Number of participants in treatment group (control group).

the studies conducted so far. First, direct process-specific training of attention and working memory leads to significant improvements in the targeted cognitive function on trained and untrained tasks even after controlling for non-specific effects. Secondly, these improvements appear to generalise to other cognitive tasks that bear little relation to the practised tasks but depend in some way on the same fundamental process. Thirdly, cognitive training of ADHD leads to reductions in behavioural symptoms supporting the notion of a causal role for neuropsychological deficits in ADHD.

As such, these first studies have yielded encouraging results and will surely stimulate many more studies to explore this approach. The clinical division of the American Psychological Association has proposed operational criteria for a treatment to be considered 'well-established': two or more studies must show that the treatment is superior to medication, placebo, or an alternative treatment or that it is equivalent to an already established treatment (Hoagwood *et al.*, 2001). A series of case studies showing equivalence or superiority is also deemed acceptable. Therefore more studies of the kind carried out by Klingberg *et al.* (2005) will be required before cognitive training of ADHD can be established as an evidence-based treatment. Developing an effective non-pharmacological intervention for ADHD that can be carried out easily at home or at school with a minimum of participation from the clinician is an exciting prospect that may be particularly desirable to the patient for its convenience and cost-effectiveness.

20.6   FUTURE CONSIDERATIONS

Finally we wish to highlight a number of issues that should be considered in future studies of neuro-cognitive remediation in ADHD (see also Box 20.1).

20.6.1   ELUCIDATION OF NEURAL PROCESSES UNDERLYING COGNITIVE TRAINING

We have cited evidence from research with brain-injured and healthy participants that improvements following process-specific training are accompanied by plastic changes in underlying neural networks. Individuals with ADHD appear to use alternative strategies and more diffuse networks of brain regions while performing neuropsychological tasks (e.g. Durston, 2003; Schweitzer *et al.*, 2004; Tamm *et al.*, 2004). It is not clear whether cognitive training consolidates compensatory activation patterns or causes a reorganisation of the process-related network. Imaging the neural correlates of training in ADHD will be essential for a better specification of treatment effects.

20.6.2   DURATION, INTENSITY AND MAINTENANCE

The literature on cognitive training is characterised by huge variation in the duration and intensity of the programmes that are employed. For example, in just five studies of ADHD treatment intensity varied from 60 minutes twice a week (Semrud-Clikeman *et al.*, 1999) to 40 minutes per day 4–6 days a week (Klingberg *et al.*, 2005)

Box 20.1. Steps in the development of an effective neuro-cognitive remediation strategy.

Steps (A, B and C). A detailed understanding of the neural processes underlying cognitive function is necessary for the development of effective training strategies. For example, frontal control regions tend to deactivate as performance reaches asymptotic levels therefore if these regions are being targeted then training difficulty must increase as performance improves. In addition, studies by Shaffer et al (2001) and by Klingberg et al (2005) have demonstrated how a knowledge of the overlap in brain areas employed for separate neuropsychological functions allowed them to hypothesise generalised improvements.

Step 1. Treatment effects will be maximised by establishing patient profiles and applying cognitive training only to those patients who have demonstrated a deficit in the targeted process.

Step 2. A crucial step in establishing neuro-cognitive training as an effective treatment will be the provision of appropriate comparison groups. A non-specific comparison group should control for possible confounds including interaction with the therapist, positive feedback, spontaneous improvement and practice effects. Neuro-Cognitive training strategies should also be pitted against existing treatments to establish their unique effects.

Step 3. A complete assessment of neuro-cognitive training effects should include neuropsychological and functional imaging measures assessing the targeted cognitive function but, most importantly, transfer of training benefits to everyday life function should be assessed.

Step 4. A final step in the development of cognitive training will be to investigate different treatment intensities and durations and their effect on maintenance of improvements. In addition cognitive training may be an effective component within a multimodal treatment framework.

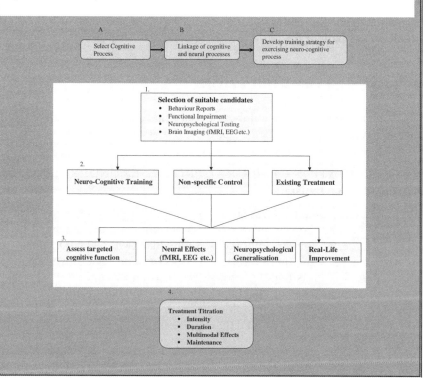

and treatment duration varied from 3 weeks (Shaffer *et al.*, 2000) to 8 weeks (Kerns *et al.*, 1999). An important question that will need to be answered with respect to training of cognition in ADHD is, how much and for how long? At what point does intensive cognitive training cease to be beneficial? Does training have to be repeated to maintain improvements in the longer term? Studies that employ identical training programmes but vary their duration and intensity will be required before we can obtain a definitive answer. The relationship between maintenance of treatment effects and intensity requirements will be particularly important for cost-benefit analyses.

20.6.3 NEUROPSYCHOLOGICAL HETEROGENEITY

A recent paper by Nigg *et al.* (2005) has drawn attention to the fact that the performance distributions of neuropsychological tests overlap substantially in ADHD and control participants. The authors tested a sample of 887 children with ADHD-combined type on a range of executive functions and found that no more than half of the children could be classified as impaired (using the 90th percentile as a cut off) on any given measure. Thus in any given sample a certain proportion of children with ADHD will perform within or above the normal range on neuropsychological tasks suggesting that executive deficits measured by these tasks do not contribute causally to ADHD in *all* cases. However, by reviewing studies that have examined neuropsychologically-impaired children with ADHD in isolation, the authors did uncover convincing evidence of an etiologically distinct ADHD-subgroup in which neuropsychological deficits do appear to play a central role.

In clinical and neuropsychological terms, heterogeneity is the rule rather than the exception in ADHD (Greene & Ablon, 2001). Matching a treatment to individual needs may be as important as the actual components of the treatment itself. Careful titration of medication significantly enhances treatment effects (MTA, 2004) and the same rigour should be applied to non-medical interventions. Using molecular genetics may provide a means of reducing heterogeneity by identifying sub-groups for whom a particular genotype is associated with a distinct neuropsychological profile (e.g. Bellgrove *et al.*, 2005, see also Chapter 12). Carefully matching cognitive treatments to individual impairments in this manner may be one way of maximising treatment effects in future studies. In addition, studies of neuro-cognitive training in ADHD are once again well placed to potentially clarify the role of neuropsychological deficits by comparing treatment effects in neuropsychologically impaired and unimpaired ADHD children.

20.6.4 MULTIMODAL TREATMENT

In recent years there has been an increasing consensus that treatments for ADHD should be targeted at more than one domain and this line of thinking has led to the development of large-scale multimodal treatment programmes (Wells *et al.*, 2000; Hechtman *et al.*, 2004). The studies reviewed above suggest that neuro-cognitive training may be effective both with (Kerns *et al.*, 1999) and without medication (Klingberg *et al.*, 2005). However, ADHD involves a range of primary and secondary behavioural and self-regulatory difficulties that are unlikely to be fully eradicated by a purely cognitive treatment. Behavioural therapies provide important feedback and instruction where ADHD may have hindered the development of adaptive patterns of behaviour. Pharmacological treatments may provide the focus required to facilitate participation in a neuro-cognitive remediation programme but there is also evidence that medication acting upon neurotransmitter systems can influence recovery from brain injury (Barrett & Gonzalez-Rothi, 2002) and that dopaminergic projections to prefrontal cortex play a critical role in neurogenesis (Rubia *et al.*, 2000). This leads us to the hypothesis that pharmacological and neuro-cognitive interventions may have synergistic effects on neural plasticity. While single component analyses of process specific training remain a priority in the short term, an interesting challenge for future work will be to investigate the potential adjunctive or synergistic effects that medical, behavioural and neuro-cognitive treatments have in combination.

20.6.5   DEVELOPMENTAL CONSIDERATIONS

Knowledge of the timing of normal neuropsychological development may be helpful in maximising the effectiveness of neuro-cognitive treatments. While certain neuropsychological abilities are in place from early infancy, others are not performed efficiently until adulthood when the protracted development of frontostriatal circuitry is finally complete. Prefrontal white matter matures slowly throughout childhood and adolescence and this maturation is accompanied by steady improvements in cognitive function (Liston *et al.*, 2005; Paus, 2005). In particular, developmental studies indicate that there is a dramatic leap in the ability to maintain attention and exert executive control between the ages of 3 and 8 (Luciana & Nelson, 1998; Rueda *et al.*, 2004; Paus, 2005). This is also the age group at which symptoms of ADHD begin to become apparent (Drechsler *et al.*, 2005) and may therefore represent a sensitive period during which neuro-cognitive training would be most beneficial. It would be of particular interest to explore the effects of a child's age on the extent of change effected by neuro-cognitive training. In addition, given the clear evidence of neural plasticity in the adult brain, remediation programmes aimed at adults with ADHD would also be desirable.

Castellanos and colleagues (2002) have shown that although structural abnormalities are apparent in children with ADHD from an early age, patterns of brain maturation do not seem to be affected. It has been suggested that acquired brain injury (ABI) in children may have a cumulative effect on ongoing development where specific cognitive deficits only become apparent years later at the stage when they would normally be expected to mature (Limond and Leeke, 2005). Parallels can therefore be drawn between ABI and ADHD. There is growing evidence that structured practice on cognitive tasks promotes plastic changes in the brain leading to enhanced efficiency of neural networks and cognitive function. The studies conducted so far with normal and impaired children indicate that process-specific training essentially accelerates development in the targeted areas. Therefore the early measurement and remediation of neuropsychological deficits at this stage may be critical in altering abnormal developmental trajectories in ADHD by encouraging maturation in key cognitive processors. Future work should investigate whether extensive training from an early age can lead to neural and behavioural improvements that last throughout and beyond development.

20.7   REFERENCES

Barkley RA (1997) Behavioral inhibition, sustained attention, and executive functions: constructing a unifying theory of ADHD. *Psychological Bulletin* **121**(1): 65–94.

Barkley RA, Murphy KR, Bush T (2001) Time perception and reproduction in young adults with Attention Deficit Hyperactivity Disorder. *Neuropsychology* **15**(3): 351–60.

Barrett AM, Gonzalez-Rothi LJ (2002) Theoretical bases for neuropsychological interventions. In P Eslinger (ed.) *Neuropsychological Interventions: Clinical Research and Practice*. London: Guilford Press.

Bellgrove MA, Hawi Z, Lowe N *et al.* (2005) DRD4 gene variants and sustained attention in attention deficit hyperactivity disorder (ADHD): effects of associated alleles at the VNTR and -521 SNP. *Am J Med Genet B Neuropsychiatr Genet*, Epub ahead of print.

Ben-Yishay Y, Piasetsky EB, Rattock J (1987) A systematic method for ameliorating disorders in basic attention. In MJ Meyer, AL Benton, L Diller (eds) *Neuropsychological Rehabilitation*. Edinburgh: Churchill.

Bush G, Valera EM, Seidman LJ (2005) Functional neuroimaging of Attention-Deficit/Hyperactivity Disorder: a review and suggested future directions. *Biol Psychiatry* **57**(11): 1273–84.

Butler RW, Copeland DR (2002) Attentional processes and their remediation in children treated for cancer: a literature review and the development of a therapeutic approach. *Journal of the International Neuropsychological Society* **8**: 115–24.

Castellanos FX, Lee PP, Sharp W *et al.* (2002) Developmental trajectories of brain volume abnormalities in children and adolescents with Attention-Deficit/Hyperactivity Disorder. *JAMA* **288**(14): 1740–8.

Castellanos FX, Tannock R (2002) Neuroscience of Attention-Deficit/Hyperactivity Disorder: the search for endophenotypes. *Nature Reviews* **3**: 617–28.

Cicerone KD, Dahlberg C, Kalmar K *et al.* (2000) Evidence-based cognitive rehabilitation: recommendations for clinical practice. *Arch. Phys. Med. Rehabil.* **81**: 1596–615.

Cicerone KD, Dahlberg C, Malec JF *et al.* (2005) Evidence-based cognitive rehabilitation: updated review of the literature from 1998 through 2002. *Arch. Phys. Med. Rehabil.* **86**: 1681–92.

Cotman CW, Nieto-Sampedro M (1982) Brain function, synapse renewal and plasticity. *Annual Review of Psychology* **33**: 371–401.

Dinse HR, Recanzone GH, Merzenich MM (1993) Alterations in correlated activity parallel ICMS-induced representational plasticity. *NeuroReport* **5**(173–6).

Drechsler R, Brandeis D, Foldenyi M *et al.* (2005) The course of neuropsychological functions in children with attention deficit hyperactivity disorder from late childhood to early adolescence. *J Child Psychol Psychiatry* **46**(8): 824–36.

Durston S (2003) A review of the biological bases of ADHD: what have we learned from imaging studies? *Ment. Retard. Dev. Disabil. Res. Rev.* **9**(3): 184–95.

Ernst M, Kimes AS, London ED *et al.* (2003) Neural substrates of decision making in adults with attention deficit hyperactivity disorder. *Am. J. Psychiatry* **160**(6): 1061–70.

Eslinger PJ (ed.) (2002) *Neuropsychological Interventions: Clinical Research and Practice*. London: Guilford Press.

Gould E, Beylin A, Tanapat P *et al.* (1999) Learning enhances adult neurogenesis in the hippocampal formation. *Nat Neurosci* **2**(3): 260–5.

Greene RW, Ablon JS (2001) What does the MTA study tell us about effective psychosocial treatment for ADHD? *Journal of Clinical Child Psychology* **30**(1): 114–21.

Hebb DO (1949) *The Organisation of Behaviour: A Neuropsychological Theory*. New York: Wiley.

Hechtman L, Abikoff H, Klein RG *et al.* (2004) Academic achievement and emotional status of children with ADHD treated with long-term methylphenidate and multimodal psychosocial treatment. *J. Am. Acad. Child Adolesc. Psychiatry* **43**(7).

Hempel A, Gisel FJ, Garcia Caraballo NM *et al.* (2004) Plasticity of cortical activation related to working memory during training. *American Journal of Psychiatry* **161**(4): 745–7.

Hoagwood K, Burns B, Kiser L *et al.* (2001) Evidence-based practice in child and adolesecent mental health services. *Psychiatric Services* **52**(9).

Kelly AMC, Garavan H (2005) Human functional neuroimaging of brain changes associated with practice. *Cereb. Cortex* **15**(8): 1089–1102.

Kempermann G, Brandon EP, Gage FH (1998) Environmental stimulation of 129/SvJ mice causes increased cell proliferation and neurogenesis in the adult dentate gyrus. *Current Biology* **8**(16): 939–42.

Kerns KA, Eso K, Thomson J (1999) Investigation of a direct intervention for improving attention in young children with ADHD. *Developmental Neuropsychology* **16**(2): 273–95.

Klingberg T, Fernell E, Olesen PJ *et al.* (2005) Computerized training of working memory in children with ADHD – a randomized, controlled trial. *Journal of the American Academy of Child and Adolescent Psychiatry* **44**(2): 177.

Klingberg T, Forssberg H, Westerberg H (2002a) Increased brain activity in frontal and parietal cortex underlies the development of visuo-spatial working memory capacity during childhood. *Journal of Cognitive Neuroscience* **14**: 1–10.

Klingberg T, Forssberg H, Westerberg H (2002b) Training of working memory in children with ADHD. *Journal of Clinical and Experimental Neuropsychology* **24**(6): 781–91.

Limond J, Leeke R (2005) Practitioner review: cognitive rehabilitation for children with acquired brain injury. *J. Child Psychol. Psychiatry* **46**(4): 339–52.

Liston C, Watts R, Tottenham N *et al.* (2005) Frontostriatal microstructure modulates efficient recruitment of cognitive control. *Cereb. Cortex.*

Luciana M, Nelson CA (1998) The functional emergence of prefrontally-guided working memory systems in four- to eight-year-old children. *Neuropsychologia* **36**(3): 273–93.

Maguire EA, Gadian DG, Johnsrude IS *et al.* (2000) Navigation-related structural change in the hippocampi of taxi drivers. *Proc. Natl. Acad. Sci. USA* **97**: 4398–403.

Manly T, Anderson V, Nimmo-Smith I *et al.* (2001) The differential assessment of children's attention: The Test of Everyday Attention for Children (TEA-CH), normative sample and ADHD performance. *Journal of Child Psycol. Psychiat.* **42**(8): 1065–81.

Manly T, Hawkins K, Evans J *et al.* (2002) Rehabilitation of executive function: facilitation of effective goal management on complex tasks using periodic auditory alerts. *Neuropsychologia* **40**: 271–81.

Martinussen R, Hayden J, Hogg-Johnson S, Tannock R (2005) A meta-analysis of working memory impairments in children with Attention-Deficit/Hyperactivity Disorder. *Journal of the American Academy of Child and Adolescent Psychiatry* **44**(4): 377–84.

Mateer CA, Sohlberg MM, Youngman P (1990) The management of acquired attention and memory disorders following mild closed head injury. *Cognitive Rehabilitation in Perspective*. London: Taylor & Francis.

MTA Cooperative Group (2004) National Institute of Mental Health Multimodal Treatment Study of ADHD follow-up: changes in effectiveness and growth after the end of treatment. *Pediatrics* **113**(4): 762–9.

Mullins C, Bellgrove MA, Gill M, Robertson IH (2005) Variability in time reproduction: difference in ADHD combined and inattentive subtypes. *J. Am. Acad. Child Adolesc. Psychiatry* **44**(2): 169–75.

Munte TF, Altenmuller E, Jancke L (2002) The musician's brain as a model of neuroplasticity. *Nature Rev. Neurosci.* **3**: 473–8.

Neimann H, Ruff RM, Baser CA (1990) Computer-assisted attention retraining in head-injured individuals: A controlled efficacy study of an outpatient program. *Journal of Consulting and Clinical Psychology* **58**: 811–17.

Nigg JT (2001) Is ADHD a disinhibitory disorder? *Psychological Bulletin* **127**(5): 571–98.

Nigg JT, Willcutt EG, Doyle AE, Sonuga-Barke EJ (2005) Causal heterogeneity in Attention-Deficit/Hyperactivity Disorder: do we need neuropsychologically impaired subtypes? *Biol Psychiatry* **57**(11): 1224–30.

O'Connell RG, Bellgrove MA, Dockree P, Robertson IH (2004) Reduced electrodermal response to errors predicts poor sustained attention performance in Attention Deficit Hyperactivity Disorder. *NeuroReport* **15**(16): 2535–8.

Olesen PJ, Westerberg H, Klingberg T (2004) Increased prefrontal and parietal activity after training of working memory. *Nature Neuroscience* **7**(1): 75–9.

Oosterlaan J, Logan GD, Sergeant J (1998) Response inhibition in ADHD, CD, comorbid ADHD + CD, anxious and normal children: a meta-analysis of studies with the stop task. *Journal of Child Psychol. Psychiat.* **39**: 411–26.

Overtoom CCE, Verbaten MN, Kemner C *et al.* (2003) Effects of methylphenidate, desipramine, and L-dopa on attention and inhibition in children with ADHD. *Behavioural Brain Research* **145**: 7–15.

Park NW, Ingles JL (2001) Effectiveness of attention rehabilitation after an acquired brain injury: a meta-analysis. *Neuropsychology* **15**(2): 199–210.

Paus T (2005) Mapping brain maturation and cognitive development during adolescence. *Trends in Cognitive Sciences* **9**(2): 60–8.

Paus T, Zatorre RJ, Hofle N *et al.* (1997) Time-related changes in neural systems underlying attention and arousal during the performance of an auditory vigilance task. *Journal of Cognitive Neuroscience* **9**(3): 392–408.

Pelham WE Jr, Wheeler T, Chronis A (1998) Empirically supported psychosocial treatments for attention deficit hyperactivity disorder. *J. Clin. Child. Psychol.* **27**(2): 190–205.

Penkman L (2004) Remediation of attention deficits in children: a focus on childhood cancer, traumatic brain injury and attention deficit disorder. *Pediatric Rehabilitation* **7**(2): 111–23.

Piek JP, Pitcher T, Hay DA (1999) Motor coordination and kinaesthesis in boys with Attention-Deficit/Hyperactivity Disorder. *Developmental Medicine and Child Neurology* **41**: 159–65.

Posner MI, Peterson SE (1990) The attentional system of the human brain. *Annu. Rev. Neurosci.* **13**: 25–42.

Ramachandran VS, Stewart M, Rogers-Ramachandran DC (1992) Perceptual correlates of massive cortical reorganisation. *NeuroReport* **3**: 583–6.

Rizzolatti G, Camarda R (eds) (1987) *Neural Circuits for Spatial Attention and Unilateral Neglect*. Amsterdam: North Holland Press.

Robertson IH, Hogg K, McMillan TM (1998) Rehabilitation of unilateral neglect: reducing inhibitory competition by contralesional limb activation. *Neuropsychological Rehabilitation* **8**: 19–29.

Robertson IH, Murre JJ (1999) Rehabilitation of brain damage: brain plasticity and principles of guided recovery. *Psychological Bulletin* **125**(5): 544–75.

Robertson IH, McMillan TM, MacLeod E *et al.* (2002) Rehabilitation by Limb Activation Training (LAT) reduces impairment in unilateral neglect patients: a single-blind randomised control trial. *Neuropsychological Rehabilitation* **12**: 439–54.

Rubia K, Overmeyer S, Taylor E *et al.* (1999) Hypofrontality in Attention Deficit Hyperactivity Disorder during high-order motor control: a study with functional MRI. *American Journal of Psychiatry* **156**(6): 891–6.

Rubia K, Overmeyer S, Taylor E *et al.* (2000) Functional frontalisation with age: mapping neurodevelopmental trajectories with fMRI. *Neuroscience & Biobehavioral Reviews* **24**(1): 13–19.

Rueda MR, Fan J, McCandliss BD *et al.* (2004) Development of attentional networks in childhood. *Neuropsychologia* **42**: 1029–40.

Rueda MR, Rothbart MK, McCandliss BD *et al.* (2005) Training, maturation, and genetic influences on the development of executive attention. *Proc. Natl. Acad. Sci. USA* **102**(41): 14931–6.

Rypma B, d'Esposito M (2000) Isolating the neural mechanisms of age-related changes in human working memory. *Nature Neuroscience* **3**: 509–15.

Schweitzer JB, Lee DO, Hanford RB *et al.* (2004) Effect of methylphenidate on executive functioning in adults with Attention-Deficit/Hyperactivity Disorder: normalization of behavior but not related brain activity. *Biological Psychiatry* **56**(8): 597–606.

Seltzer M (1998) Regeneration and plasticity in neurologic dysfunction. In R Lazar (ed.) *Principles of Neurologic Rehabilitation*. New York: McGraw-Hill.

Semrud-Clikeman M, Nielsen KH, Clinton A *et al.* (1999) An intervention approach for children with teacher- and parent-identified attentional difficulties. *Journal of Learning Disabilities* **32**(6): 581–90.

Shaffer RJ, Jacokes LE, Cassily JF *et al.* (2000) Effect of interactive metronome training on children with ADHD. *The American Journal of Occupational Therapy* **55**: 155–62.

Shafritz KM, Marchione KE, Gore J *et al.* (2004) The effects of methylphenidate on neural systems of attention in Attention Deficit Hyperactivity Disorder. *Am. J. Psychiatry* **161**(11): 1990–7.

Shallice T, Marzocchi GM *et al.* (2002) Executive function profile of children with ADHD. *Developmental Neuropsychology* **21**(1): 43–71.

Sohlberg MM, McLaughlin KA, Pavese A *et al.* (2000). Evaluation of attention process training and brain injury education in persons with acquired brain injury. *Journal of Clinical and Experimental Neuropsychology* **22**(5): 656–76.

Sohlberg MM, Mateer CA (1987) Effectiveness of an attention training program. *Journal of Clinical and Experimental Neuropsychology* **19**: 117–30.

Sohlberg MM, Mateer CA (2001) Improving attention and managing attention problems: adapting rehabilitation techniques to adults with ADD. *Annals New York Academy of Sciences* **931**: 359–75.

Sonuga-Barke EJS (2003) The dual pathway model of AD/HD: an elaboration of neuro-developmental characteristics. *Neuroscience & Biobehavioral Reviews* **27**(7 SU-): 593–604.

Sowell ER, Thompson PM, Welcome SE *et al.* (2003) Cortical abnormalities in children and adolescents with Attention-Deficit Hyperactivity Disorder. *The Lancet* **362**: 1699–707.

Stablum F, Umilta C, Mogentale C *et al.* (2000) Rehabilitation of executive deficits in closed head injury and anterior communicating artery aneurysm patients. *Psychological Research* **63**(3–4): 265–78.

Stevens AA, Goldman-Rakic PS, Gore JC *et al.* (1998) Cortical dysfunction in schizophrenia during auditory word and tone working memory demonstrated by functional magnetic resonance imaging. *Arch. Gen. Psychiatry* **55**: 1097–103.

Sturm W, Longoni F, Weis S *et al.* (2004) Functional reorganisation in patients with right hemisphere stroke after training of alertness: a longitudinal PET and fMRI study in eight cases. *Neuropsychologia* **42**(4): 434–50.

Sturm W, Wilmes K, Orgass B, Hartje W (1997) Do specific attention deficits need specific training? *Neuropsychological Rehabilitation* **7**(2): 81–103.

Tamm L, Menon V, Ringel J, Reiss AL (2004) Event-related FMRI evidence of frontotemporal involvement in aberrant response inhibition and task switching in Attention-Deficit/Hyperactivity Disorder. *J. Am. Acad. Child Adolesc. Psychiatry* **43**(11): 1430–40.

Tannock R, Ickowicz A, Schachar R (1995) Differential effects of methylphenidate on working memory in ADHD children with and without comorbid anxiety. *Journal of the American Academy of Child and Adolescent Psychiatry* **34**: 886–96.

Wells KC, Pelham WE, Kotkin RA *et al.* (2000) Psychosocial treatment strategies in the MTA study: rationale, methods and critical issues in design and implementation. *Journal of Abnormal Child Psychology* **28**(6): 483–505.

Wexler BE (in press) Cognitive remediation and vocational rehabilitation for schizophrenia. *Schizophrenia Bulletin*.

Wexler BE, Anderson M, Fullbright RK, Gore JC (2000) Preliminary evidence of improved verbal working memory performance and normalization of task-related frontal lobe activation in schizophrenia following cognitive exercises. *American Journal of Psychiatry* **157**: 1094–7.

Woods SP, Lovejoy DW, Ball JD (2002) Neuropsychological characteristics of adults with ADHD: a comprehensive review of initial studies. *The Clinical Neuropsychologist* **16**(1): 12–34.

IV Concluding Thoughts

21 Evolutionary Aspects of ADHD

ESTER I. KLIMKEIT AND JOHN L. BRADSHAW
Centre for Developmental Psychiatry and Psychology, School of Psychology, Psychiatry and Psychological Medicine, Monash University, Australia

21.1 OVERVIEW

Attention Deficit/Hyperactivity Disorder (ADHD) is unusual in that, as an externalising disorder, it impacts far more heavily upon others than upon the individual concerned. This is also true of many of the comorbid conditions and behaviours often co-occurring with the disorder, e.g. oppositional-defiant syndrome and frank sociopathy; however, other common comorbidities such as anxiety, depression, Tourette's syndrome and even co-occurring obsessive compulsive features certainly impact heavily on the individuals themselves. In pure form, ADHD may even be regarded by some more in terms of a personality bias than as an outright pathology. As such, in certain historical periods, social contexts or environmental conditions, the cognitive and attentional features (risk taking, diffuse attentional focus) may even be adaptive, and have been selected for, such that a population includes a certain number of individuals peculiarly fitted for a military or explorational career.

21.2 INTRODUCTION

Whereas somatic diseases such as cancer are 'real' disorders which can be seen and identified by conducting a variety of laboratory tests, there are no laboratory tests that are diagnostic of psychiatric disorders. Classification systems for mental disorders, such as the *Diagnostic and Statistical Manual of Mental Disorders* (DSM-IV), define mental disorder as a 'clinically significant behavioural or psychological syndrome or pattern that is associated with present distress or disability or with a significantly increased risk of suffering death, pain, disability or an important loss of freedom' (American Psychiatric Association, 1994, p. xxi). This definition emphasises the social dimension of psychiatric disorders, in that persons around the individual must view the condition as distressing or disabling. What may be viewed as inappropriate or 'sick' in one sociocultural environment may not be in another (Thakker & Ward, 1998). While some psychiatric disorders involve behaviour that is clearly deemed 'abnormal' by some (but not necessarily all) cultures, such as conditions involving hallucinations, other conditions are characterised simply by 'inappropriate levels' of 'normal' behaviour. Individuals with Attention Deficit/

Handbook of Attention Deficit Hyperactivity Disorder. Edited by M. Fitzgerald, M. Bellgrove and M. Gill.
© 2007 John Wiley & Sons Ltd

Hyperactivity Disorder (ADHD) for example, are thought to display excessive levels of inattention, hyperactivity and impulsivity, which are behaviours common to all individuals.

Prima facie it appears difficult for evolutionary theory to encompass psychiatric conditions, because by definition they disable individuals and do not have a clear survival advantage. However, persuasive Darwinian explanations can be given for disease states (Nettle, 2004). In some cases, the same genes may be adaptive for relatives, but not the affected individual, as in the case proposed for homosexuality, which may not offer a reproductive advantage for the individual, but is associated with higher fecundity in female maternal relatives (Camperio-Ciani, Corna & Capiluppi, 2004). Partial syndromes or 'small doses' of the same condition may also offer a fitness advantage by protecting against even more deleterious circumstances. For example, while sickle cell anaemia is a disease state detrimental to well-being, being a mere carrier of this disease is protective against malaria. In other cases maladaptations can arise when a population is adapting to a complex environment and trading off various features against each other (Nettle, 2004). Nettle (2004) gives the example of increased levels of maternal death during childbirth in the human primate, which may be a by-product from earlier selection to increase brain size. It is also possible that a certain level of genetic variation is adaptive in certain environmental conditions but not others, resulting in a 'mismatched environment' for those individuals (Carrey, 1998). It is also important to recognise that genetics do not fully account for psychopathology. Genes are moderated by environmental circumstances and by experience.

In this chapter we will explore how in certain historical periods or environmental conditions, behaviours indicative of ADHD may be adaptive, and may have been selected for. ADHD can be classified as an externalising disorder, where the characteristic behaviours are often seen as more distressing for parents, siblings or fellow students than the affected child. The prevalence of ADHD is estimated at 3–5% in school-aged children (American Psychiatric Association, 1994), and is persistent into adolescence in 50–80% of childhood diagnoses, and to adulthood in 30–50% of cases (Barkley, 1997). ADHD is a major risk factor for later personality and psychiatric disorders, delinquency, substance abuse, driving accidents and speeding violations, difficulties in adult social relationships, marriage and employment (Barkley, 1997; Sagvolden & Sergeant, 1998; Wilens, Biederman & Spencer, 2002; Barkley *et al.*, 2004). Most of these developmental risks are exacerbated by the presence of comorbid aggression/conduct problems (Barkley, 1997; Dalsgaard *et al.*, 2002).

Between 50% and 80% of children with ADHD also meet diagnostic criteria for other disorders (Tannock, 1998; Wilens *et al.*, 2002). Generally, the presence of a comorbid disorder indicates a more serious problem and worse prognosis (Weiss, 1996). The most frequent comorbid disorders are other externalising disorders such as oppositional defiant disorder and conduct disorder, followed by internalising disorders like mood disorders, anxiety disorders and specific learning disorders (Tannock, 1998). Language and speech disorders, Tourette's syndrome and obsessive compulsive disorder also appear comorbidly with ADHD (Cantwell & Baker, 1992; Comings, 1995; Peterson *et al.*, 2001).

21.3 IS ADHD A PERSONALITY BIAS RATHER THAN OUTRIGHT PATHOLOGY?

Some researchers argue that psychiatric disorders are mostly the expression of an extreme form of personality bias (Nigg *et al.*, 2002). One of the most common links between personality and psychopathology in the literature is the study of abnormal behaviour traits in normal populations. As Maher and Maher (1994) point out, these studies typically investigate the presence of psychopathological symptoms in a normal population (usually undergraduate students), in the belief that these findings can be transferred to our understanding of psychopathology. Parker, Majeski and Collin (2004) for example, investigated ADHD symptoms and personality traits in university students. This approach assumes that at least some symptoms of psychopathology are merely an exaggeration of normal traits (Maher & Maher, 1994). Both psychopathology and personality traits show substantial genetic heritability (Nigg *et al.*, 2002). A large genetic twin study of ADHD suggests that ADHD is best characterised as a normally distributed trait (Levy *et al.*, 1997).

There appears to be some connection between temperament which is considered an early precursor to personality traits (Nigg *et al.*, 2002) and psychiatric disorders, because difficult-temperament children are over-represented in psychiatric populations (Maziade *et al.*, 1990). However, difficult temperament predicts the presence of psychiatric conditions in preadolescence and adolescence (predominantly externalising disorders) only when family functioning (dysfunctional behaviour control) is also taken into account (Maziade *et al.*, 1990). This suggests that extreme temperament is not automatically equivalent to a clinical behaviour disorder, and reflects the importance of taking into consideration gene–environment interactions.

Most researchers agree that the heterogeneity of ADHD suggests multiple pathways, with genes and environment interacting to produce the profile of behaviours seen in this disorder (Faraone & Biederman, 1998; Johnston & Mash, 2001). Thus family difficulties may arise as a consequence of the child's ADHD which results in a decline in parenting and family functioning, or as a consequence of shared genetic vulnerability among family members. In other words, the child can influence parent behaviour and parenting can influence the presentation of the child. Family functioning may interact with a child's predisposition and exacerbate the severity of ADHD symptoms, or in some instances of a chaotic family environment where the child has relatively little predisposition, the family dysfunction may in itself elevate ADHD behaviours to a problematic level. Alternatively, a highly functioning family may serve as a protective factor that may reduce the level of ADHD behaviours.

Temperament or personality may predispose an individual to a particular disorder, or gene–environment interactions with personality may predispose individuals to certain psychopathology (Nigg & Goldsmith, 1998). There were initial reports that the dopamine receptor gene (DRD4) was related to novelty seeking (Ebstein *et al.*, 1996) and to ADHD (LaHoste *et al.*, 1996). While not all studies have supported the involvement of dopamine genes in ADHD (e.g. Castellanos *et al.*, 1998), meta-analyses have supported this association (e.g. Faraone *et al.*, 2001; Maher *et al.*, 2002). Evidence for the relationship between dopamine receptor genes and novelty seeking has, however, been more mixed and not supported by meta-analysis (Malhortra & Goldman, 2000; Kluger, Siegried & Ebstein, 2002; Strobel *et al.*, 2003). If a relationship between the dopamine receptor gene and novelty seeking could be substantiated, this would demonstrate that the same genes are involved in both ADHD and personality, thus providing some evidence for the association between personality and psychopathology. In a recent study (Lynn *et al.*, 2005) examining the link among ADHD in adults, novelty-seeking temperament and dopamine D4 receptor gene variant, it was found that novelty seeking predicted ADHD diagnosis (explaining 26% of the variance), while dopamine gene variant predicted ADHD ($r^2 = 5\%$) but not novelty seeking. Thus while both novelty seeking (to a greater extent) and dopamine receptor genes (to a lesser extent) were associated with a lifetime history of ADHD, the association between novelty seeking and ADHD may not be due to variation in the DRD4 gene.

Sensation seeking is a personality trait characterised by the need for varied, novel and intense experiences and the willingness to take risks for these experiences (Cronin, 1991). In a study of young adults Shaw and Giambra (1993) found that those with diagnoses of ADHD as children had higher levels of sensation seeking than those that did not have this childhood diagnosis. Research has shown that high sensation seekers engage in high risk activities such as hang-gliding (Straub, 1982) and mountain climbing (Cronin, 1991). Sensation seeking has also been associated with alcohol and drug use, impulsivity, excessive gambling (Roberti, 2004) and reckless behaviour in driving, sexual behaviour, minor criminal acts and aggression (Arnett, 1996). Some researchers have examined other personality factors to distinguish between socially acceptable and antisocial ways of meeting sensation-seeking needs. For example, Goma-I-Freixanet (1995) found that prisoners, risky-sport participators, and males in risky prosocial jobs differed from controls in terms of being thrill and adventure-seeking and extraverted. However, the prisoners could be discriminated from the other groups by poor socialisation, disinhibition and impulsiveness. Others have suggested that in societies that cannot provide adventure and stimulation for sensation-seeking young people, crime and drugs may meet their needs (Zuckerman, 1983).

Some researchers propose that inheritance of general personality factors may predispose individuals to the risk of developing one or more of a range of possible maladaptive (or even adaptive) behaviours depending on the individual's environment (Legrand, Iacono & McGue, 2005). The environment (e.g. parenting) may modify actual gene expression and the nature of the resulting behaviour. Thus the inheritance risk of hyperactivity, conduct problems and drug and alcohol problems is non-specific, and the inherited risk corresponds to externalising tendencies (Legrand *et al.*, 2005). The externalising disposition increases the risk of demonstrating problematic behaviour, but these tendencies could alternatively be expressed in more positive ways: fire fighters, rescue workers, test pilots and entrepreneurs may show moderate externalising tendencies (Legrand *et al.*, 2005). Under this model, a mother with antisocial traits does not pass on genes that code simply for antisocial behaviour, but rather general externalising tendencies. Thus her child may not have problems with antisocial behaviour, but rather, drug and alcohol problems. The same genes are expressed differently under different environmental conditions, and predispose on the one hand both to antisocial behaviour and drug and alcohol problems, and on the other to otherwise useful, if risky or dangerous, occupations.

There have been some attempts to measure personality traits in individuals with ADHD. Individuals with ADHD and individuals with antisocial personality disorder score low on the personality variables of conscientiousness, low on agreeableness and high on neuroticism. In addition, those with antisocial personality disorder also score high on extraversion (Nigg *et al.*, 2002). Symptoms of inattention are associated with low conscientiousness and to a lesser extent, neuroticism, whereas hyperactivity-impulsivity and oppositional behaviours correlate with low agreeableness (Nigg *et al.*, 2002). Parker *et al.* (2004) found that the Big-Five personality traits (Goldberg, 1990) accounted for less than half of the variance in total ADHD symptom scores in university students. A low score in conscientiousness was the most powerful predictor for inattention scores and a low score in agreeableness the most powerful predictor for hyperactivity-impulsivity scores. This finding suggests that other factors such as personality may predispose someone to, or moderate, ADHD symptom expression.

21.4 ARE BEHAVIOURS SUCH AS DIFFUSE ATTENTIONAL FOCUS, IMPULSIVITY AND HYPERACTIVITY ADAPTIVE IN CERTAIN HISTORICAL PERIODS?

Brown and Braithwaite (2004) found that despite variability in both groups, on average, fish in high predation environments tended to be more bold (showing a greater propensity to take risks and greater exploratory behaviour) than fish (from the same founder species) from low predation sites. Presumably it is advantageous for high-predation fish to thoroughly explore a new environment to become aware of escape routes and to ensure that no predators are present. Thus temperamental traits appear to be selected for, often in a very short time period, if they are advantageous in a particular environment. It could be argued that ADHD must have had a selective advantage at least in our human ancestors otherwise it would no longer persist in the genome. Behaviours adaptive for our hunter-gatherer existence may have ceased to be adaptive in our present environment. Our current-day environment favours problem solving and analytic strategies, focusing of attention, and restraint of impulsivity (Jensen *et al.*, 1997). The fact that the majority of individuals diagnosed with ADHD are also diagnosed with comorbid disorders suggests that it is perhaps not just the ADHD which is in some way adaptive, but perhaps also, or even instead, the other co-occurring conditions.

Comorbid aggression may have been adaptive for our ancestors when competing for food or mates and fighting off predators. Low mood or depression may also be adaptive (Keller & Nesse, 2005). It has been suggested that the genes associated with depression exist to tune affective circuits so as to heighten responses to negative emotional scenes or faces signalling threat, which may be adaptive in dangerous environments (Hamman, 2005). Given that depressive disorders are higher in women than men and most prevalent during early productive years, it has been proposed that in evolutionary terms it may be conducive for women to stay quietly out of danger in a sheltered place (Niculescu, 2001; Keller & Nesse, 2005). As women are involved in child rearing it made sense historically for women to manifest more of this trait then men. While dysthymic traits may be adaptive for sheltering women from danger in order to bear and care for children, it may not have been adaptive for the hunter-man. Thus a predisposition to dysthymia may have been selected for in women and against in men over time. The increased incidence of depression in the first trimester and postpartum, suggests that lower activity of the mother at these critical periods may have been reproductively advantageous (Niculescu, 2001).

Jensen *et al.* (1997) argue that rapid attentional switching, hyperactivity and impulsivity may have conveyed advantages in our ancestral environments. Increased activity is postulated to be useful in a hunter-gatherer environment, in terms of foraging, spotting new opportunities and potential dangers. Additionally it may also stimulate development of muscle and motor skills. This may be especially important for those who have comorbid motor coordination problems, which is a relatively common comorbid condition in individuals with ADHD (Voeller, 2004). Impulsive hair-trigger responsiveness – pouncing quickly on potential prey or fleeing from a potential predator – is seen by these authors as adaptive in resource-scarce environments. Similarly over-focused sustained attention may have been maladaptive in high threat or novel environments. Attentional capture by sudden-onset events in the periphery may be greater when attention is unfocused. As reviewed in Chapters 11 and 12, children with ADHD have significant problems in sustaining attention. Indeed, recent studies suggest that this deficit relates to variation in dopaminergic genes (Bellgrove, Gill *et al.*, 2005; Bellgrove, Hawi *et al.*, 2005). Aggression and risk-taking may also have been useful on primitive battlefields, but maladaptive in our recently safer resource-rich current environment. Other authors, however, argue that the executive dysfunctions associated with ADHD reduce fitness (Brody, 2001). They speculate that waiting, planning, cooperation and rehearsal are all important elements of an effective hunter (Brody, 2001).

21.5   IS ADHD ADAPTIVE IN CERTAIN MODERN-DAY ENVIRONMENTAL OR SOCIAL CONTEXTS?

Our current-day environment has changed from the days of our ancestors, and appears to be associated with the increase in diagnosis of psychiatric conditions such as depression, ADHD, drug and alcohol abuse (Timimi, 2004). As psychiatric conditions are subjective social constructs, this increase in diagnosis may reflect problems in our social environment or change in cultural expectations of children. Our current western economies require ever higher levels of education, social competence and self-organisation, which unfortunately are areas impaired by ADHD (McArdle, 2004). It could be argued that recent culture has come to disadvantage such children. While the prevalence of ADHD genetically may not have changed, what we might be witnessing is the decline in the capacity of western culture to cope with and raise these children (McArdle, 2004; Timimi, 2004). Thus it is conceivable that ADHD conveyed valuable qualities in different times, but among today's communities affected by globalisation, ADHD is associated with impairments to well-being and health.

Cultural factors may influence the prevalence and severity of ADHD (McArdle, 2004), because cultural and societal tolerance for different behaviours vary. Watching a videotape of the same child, Chinese and Indonesian clinicians have been shown to give the child higher ratings of hyperactivity than clinicians from Japan and the US (Mann *et al.*, 1992). Using the same cut-off rates on a behaviour teacher rating scale produces different rates of hyperactivity in different countries (e.g. Scotland – 4.5% versus Spain – 16%; Gingerich *et al.*, 1998). It may indeed be more useful to measure gene distribution in different populations, in order to obtain a more objective measure of ADHD prevalence, and that of other neuropsychiatric or neurodevelopmental disorders.

Personality traits and behaviours, as we have seen, may be adaptive in the right context. Sih *et al.* (2004) suggest that aggressive individuals, for example, may do well in certain situations (competition for food or mates) but not in others (e.g. in parental care). This notion that individuals do well in some contexts and poorly in others could help to explain the maintenance of individual variation in behaviour. Thus apparently maladaptive behaviour may be an otherwise adaptive behavioural tendency that is carried over different contexts. A range of different behavioural tendencies may be adaptive given suitable variation in environments. Species can persist if they have large between-individual variation so that there are always some individuals able to respond appropriately to environmental changes. This may explain the success of the human race, high levels of both inter-individual genetic, and intra-individual behavioural, variability.

While a certain condition may not be adaptive for the particular individual, it may be adaptive for that individual's relatives. According to the Darwinian argument, if homosexual men have fewer children, then the homosexuality gene should quickly disappear from the population. However, a recent study (Camperio-Ciani *et al.*, 2004) has suggested that the gene which predisposes men to homosexuality may increase a woman's chances of having more children. The study found that female maternal relatives of homosexual men had higher fecundity than female maternal relatives of heterosexuals. Thus the gene has a reproductive advantage in female relatives, although not for the (homosexual male) individual. Most of the studies investigating relatives of individuals with ADHD investigate negative attributes such as psychopathology. To our knowledge, there are no studies investigating the prevalence of positive attributes such as skill at extreme sports, creativity, or fecundity of the relatives of individuals affected with ADHD. This may be an interesting avenue for future research.

There are many similarities between various psychiatric states and normal adaptive behaviours. Psychopathology may represent the extreme end of a continuum of normal adaptive behaviour. Thus optimum levels of the behaviour may indeed be adaptive. Fear, for example, allows one to achieve balance among exploration and protection behaviours (Jones & Blackshaw, 2000). Obsessional behaviour may be advantageous if the behaviour selected has previously been successful for task completion, and disadvantageous in a rapidly changing environment where more flexibility is needed (Jones & Blackshaw, 2000). The adaptiveness of depressed mood proposed in the literature includes communicating a need for help, signalling withdrawal in a hierarchy conflict, not challenging authority, and disengaging from unreachable goals (Nesse, 2000). Just as anxiety may inhibit dangerous actions, depression is thought to inhibit futile efforts. However, at a certain level, or of a certain type, depression may inevitably be considered to be maladaptive (Nesse, 2000). A similar argument can be made for the case of ADHD, where a number of studies have found that unaffected sibling of children with ADHD also have attentional and response inhibition deficits that fall somewhere in the middle of that of their ADHD affected siblings and controls (Crosbie & Schachar, 2001; Schachar *et al.*, 2005). It is possible that response disinhibition, or an impulsive style in reduced form, may facilitate certain activities such as being able to take advantage of unexpected opportunities, and thus be adaptive.

As Bradshaw and Sheppard (2000) point out, many individuals with Tourette's syndrome are skilled in music, art, athletics and games, while individuals with bipolar disorder tend to be creatively gifted, especially in poetry, writing and visual arts. Autism is associated with good attention to detail and at times with unusual islands of exceptional ability, involving for example, rote memory, musical, artistic or computational capacities. Indeed, even clinically unaffected relatives may tend to cluster in occupations such as engineering, computing or architecture. The paranoia and suspicion characteristic of schizophrenia, may be in lower levels adaptive in dangerous times. A similar argument can be made for personality traits. Schizotypal personality disorder, which may be seen as a mild version of some schizophrenia symptoms, is associated with good performance on tests of creativity (Gosline, 2004). Like anxious and depressed individuals, individuals with ADHD tend to score high on the personality trait of neuroticism. While high neuroticism is associated with poor outcome (mental health, social relationships), it is also associated with increasing competitiveness and is a predictor of success in certain populations (e.g. university students), who are perhaps resilient enough to cope with its negative effects. Thus higher neuroticism may be selected for because it has beneficial effects until the point where the negative effects of mental illness outweigh the benefits (Nettle, 2004).

ADHD behaviours may be more adaptive in environments that are dangerous and resource-scarce. However, many modern occupations also demand ice-age impulsivity and response readiness, for example, those of the soldier, air traffic controller, entrepreneur, emergency ward physician or salesperson (Bradshaw, 2001). It should also be noted that not all impulsive and risk-taking behaviours are disadvantageous (Evenden, 1999). Impulsive people may be well placed to take advantage of unexpected opportunities, while others' impulsive choice may lead to drug addiction in which addicts affect their health for the immediate rewards of the drug (Evenden, 1999; Cardinal, 2004).

Longitudinal adult outcome studies of children with ADHD typically find that those with a childhood diagnosis of ADHD show lower educational achievement and lower occupational rank (Weiss *et al.*, 1985; Mannuzza *et al.*, 1993). Mannuzza *et al.* (1993) found that the greatest disparity occurred among the higher ranking positions, with 21% of the controls employed as professionals compared to 4% of the clinical sample. However, rates were comparable for lower-ranking positions and among skilled workers. The top occupations of the clinical males were tradesperson, small business owner, salesperson or serviceman, sanitation or warehouse worker, manager or producer, police or fireman, and messenger or cashier. The authors noted that one-fifth of the clinical sample owned and operated their own business compared to 5% of controls. The authors speculated that this may reflect individuals wanting to work without close supervision, in a non-sedentary activity. Further, their high impulsivity levels were speculated to perhaps render these individuals less likely to be able to keep a typical nine to five job. This finding could also indicate that individuals with ADHD may be more focused on the immediate rewards of having their own business, rather than delayed rewards associated with slowly working their way up in someone else's company, which is consistent with the motivational/delay aversion accounts of the disorder (Sonuga-Barke *et al.*, 1992; Sonuga-Barke, 2002). This finding is, importantly, also consistent with suggestions that individuals with ADHD may be favoured in the occupation of entrepreneur (Jensen *et al.* 1997; Bradshaw & Sheppard, 2000).

While to our knowledge there are no direct studies investigating the prevalence of ADHD in different occupational groups, it is possible that these individuals may be over-represented in careers such as the military or in explorers. There is some indirect evidence that suggests that this hypothesis is worthy of further exploration. Williams, Bell, and Amoroso (2002) for example, who investigated drinking and risk-taking behaviours of enlisted male soldiers in the US army, found that enlisted army males were of greater risk for unhealthy drinking habits compared to civilians. In addition, these high risk drinkers wore seatbelts less frequently, drove over the speed limit more and smoked more cigarettes per day. While these behaviours may be a response to stressful working conditions, they are also remarkably similar to the greater driving accidents and speed violations, cigarette smoking and substance use documented in ADHD (Sagvolden & Sergeant, 1998; Wilens *et al.*, 2002).

There is also some evidence that by adulthood, individuals with ADHD have more children than controls (Weiss *et al.*, 1985), and are more likely to have fathered children in young adulthood (Hansen, Weiss & Last, 1999). It is likely that greater impulsivity results in riskier sexual practices and consequently greater fecundity, which may explain why this condition persists and may even be increasing in incidence. Conversely, however, autism and schizophrenia persist in the population at a fairly constant level, despite the generally reduced opportunities for procreation in these groups.

21.6 CONCLUSION

The evidence suggests that diffuse attentional focus, impulsivity and hyperactivity may have been adaptive in historical resource-scarce, dangerous environments. ADHD may also have adaptive aspects in today's environment, in terms of greater fecundity and perhaps for modern-day occupations such as soldier and entrepreneur. In addition, its comorbid conditions may also offer certain benefits such as the enhanced performance in music, art, athletics and games often associated with Tourette's syndrome. It may be refreshing for parents to reframe their child with ADHD, as Jensen *et al.* (1997) do, in terms of being response-ready, experience-seeking, and curious.

21.7 REFERENCES

American Psychiatric Association (1994) *Diagnostic and Statistical Manual of Mental Disorders-IV*. Washington, DC: APA.

Arnett JJ (1996) Sensation seeking, aggressiveness, and adolescent reckless behavior. *Personality and Individual Differences* **20**(6): 693–702.

Barkley RA (1997) Behavioral inhibition, sustained attention, and executive functions: constructing a unifying theory of ADHD. *Psychological Bulletin* **121**(1): 65–94.

Barkley RA, Fischer M, Smallish L, Fletcher K (2004) Young adult follow-up of hyperactive children: antisocial activities and drug use. *Journal of Child Psychology and Psychiatry* **45**(2): 195–211.

Bellgrove MA, Gill M, Hawi Z *et al.* (2005) Dissecting the attention deficit hyperactivity disorder (ADHD) phenotype: sustained attention, response variability and spatial attentional asymmetries in relation to dopamine transporter (DAT1) genotype. *Neuropsychologia* **43**(13): 1847–57.

Bellgrove MA, Hawi Z, Lowe N *et al.* (2005) DRD4 gene variants and sustained attention in Attention Deficit Hyperactivity Disorder (ADHD): effects of associated alleles at the VNTR and -521 SNP. *American Journal of Medical Genetics: Part B Neuropsychiatric Genetics* **136**(1): 81–6.

Bradshaw JL (2001) *Developmental Disorders of the Frontostriatal System: Neuropsychological, Neuropsychiatric and Evolutionary Perspectives*. Philadelphia: Psychology Press.

Bradshaw JL, Sheppard DM (2000) The neurodevelopmental frontostriatal disorders: evolutionary adaptiveness and anomalous lateralization. *Brain and Language* **73**: 297–320.

Brody JF (2001) Evolutionary recasting: ADHD, mania and its variants. *Journal of Affective Disorders* **65**: 197–215.

Brown C, Braithwaite VA (2004) Effects of predation pressure on the cognitive ability of the poeciliid Brachyraphis episcopi. *Behavioral Ecology* **16**(2): 482–7.

Camperio-Ciani A, Corna F, Capiluppi C (2004) Evidence for maternally inherited factors favouring male homosexuality and promoting female fecundity. *Proceedings of the Royal Society of London* B., **271**: 2217–21.

Cantwell DP, Baker L (1992) Attention deficit disorder with and without hyperactivity: a review and comparison of matched groups. *Journal of the American Academy of Child and Adolescent Psychiatry* **31**(3): 432–8.

Cardinal RN (2004) Waiting for better things. *The Psychologist* **17**(12): 684–7.

Carrey N (1998) ADHD as a disorder of adaptation. *Journal of the American Academy of Child and Adolescent Psychiatry* **37**(8): 797.

Castellanos FX, Lau E, Tayebi N *et al.* (1998) Lack of an association between a dopamine-4 receptor polymorphism and Attention-Deficit/Hyperactivity Disorder: genetic and brain morphometric analyses. *Molecular Psychiatry* **3**: 431–4.

Comings DE (1995) Tourette's Syndrome: a behavioral spectrum disorder. In WJ Weiner, AE Lang (eds) *Behavioral Neurology of Movement Disorders* (Vol. 65, pp. 293–303). New York: Raven Press.

Cronin C (1991) Sensation seeking among mountain climbers. *Personality and Individual Differences* **12**(6): 653–4.

Crosbie J, Schachar R (2001) Deficient inhibition as a marker for familial ADHD. *American Journal of Psychiatry* **158**(11): 1884–90.

Dalsgaard S, Mortensen PB, Frydenberg M, Thomsen PH (2002) Conduct problems, gender and adult psychiatric outcome of children with Attention-Deficit Hyperactivity Disorder. *British Journal of Psychiatry* **181**: 416–21.

Ebstein RP, Novick O, Umansky R *et al.* (1996). Dopamine D4 receptor (D4DR) exon III polymorphism associated with the human personality trait of novelty seeking. *Nature Genetics* **12**: 78–80.

Evenden JL (1999) Varieties of impulsivity. *Psychopharmacology* **146**: 348–61.

Faraone SV, Biederman J (1998) Neurobiology of Attention-Deficit Hyperactivity Disorder. *Biological Psychiatry* **44**: 951–8.

Faraone SV, Doyle A, Mick E, Biederman J (2001) Meta-analysis of the association between the 7-repeat allele of the dopamine D4 receptor gene and attention deficit hyperactivity disorder. *American Journal of Psychiatry* **158**(7): 1052–7.

Gingerich KJ, Turnock P, Litfin JK, Rosen LA (1998) Diversity and Attention Deficit Hyperactivity Disorder. *Journal of Clinical Psychology* **54**(4): 415–26.

Goldberg LR (1990) An alternative 'description of personality': The Big Five factor structure. *Journal of Personality and Social Psychology* **59**: 1216–29.

Goma-I-Freixanet M (1995) Prosocial and antisocial aspects of personality. *Personality and Individual Differences* **19**(2): 125–34.

Gosline A (2004) Creative spark can come from schizophrenia. *New Scientist* **24**(July): 14.

Hamman S (2005) Blue genes: wiring the brain for depression. *Nature Neuroscience* **8**(6): 701–3

Hansen C, Weiss D, Last C (1999) ADHD boys in young adulthood: psychosocial adjustment. *Child and Adolescent Psychiatry* **38**(2): 165–71.

Jensen PS, Mrazek D, Knapp PK *et al.* (1997) Evolution and revolution in child psychiatry: ADHD as a disorder of adaptation. *Journal of the American Academy of Child and Adolescent Psychiatry* **36**(12): 1672–81.

Johnston C, Mash EJ (2001) Families of children with Attention-Deficit/Hyperactivity Disorder: review and recommendations for future research. *Clinical Child and Family Psychology Review* **4**(3): 183–207.

Jones I, Blackshaw JK (2000) An evolutionary approach to psychiatry. *Australian and New Zealand Journal of Psychiatry* **34**: 8–13.

Keller MC, Nesse RM (2005. Is low mood an adaptation? Evidence for subtypes with symptoms that match precipitants. *Journal of Affective Disorders* **86**: 27–35.

Kluger AN, Siegried Z, Ebstein RP (2002) A meta-analysis of the association between DRD4 polymorphism and novelty seeking. *Molecular Psychiatry* **7**(7): 712–17.

LaHoste GJ, Swanson JM, Wigal S *et al.* (1996) Dopamine D4 receptor gene polymorphism is associated with attention deficit hyperactivity disorder. *Molecular Psychiatry* **1**: 121–4.

Legrand LN, Iacono WG, McGue M (2005) Predicting addiction. *American Scientist* **93**(2): 140–8.

Levy F, Hay DA, McStephen M *et al.* (1997) Attention-deficit hyperactivity disorder: a category or a continuum? Genetic Analysis of a large-scale twin study. *Journal of the American Academy of Child and Adolescent Psychiatry* **36**(6): 737–44.

Lynn DE. Lubke G, Yang M *et al.* (2005) Temperament and character profiles and the dopamine D4 receptor gene in ADHD. *American Journal of Psychiatry* **162**(5): 906–14.

McArdle P (2004) Attention-deficit hyperactivity disorder and life-span development. *British Journal of Psychiatry* **184**: 468–9.

Maher BA, Maher WB (1994) Personality and psychopathology: a historical perspective. *Journal of Abnormal Psychology* **103**(1): 72–7.

Maher BS, Marazita ML, Ferrell RE, Vanykov MM (2002) Dopamine system genes and attention deficit hyperactivity disorder: a meta-analysis. *Psychiatric Genetics* **12**(4): 207–15.

Malhortra AK, Goldman D (2000) The dopamine D4 receptor gene and novelty seeking. *The American Journal of Psychiatry* **157**(11): 1885.

Mann EM, Ikeda Y, Mueller CW *et al.* (1992) Cross-cultural differences in rating hyperactive-disruptive behaviors in children. *American Journal of Psychiatry* **149**: 1539–42.

Mannuzza S, Klein RG, Bessler A *et al.* (1993) Adult outcome of hyperactive boys: educational achievement, occupational rank and psychiatric status. *Archives of General Psychiatry* **50**(7): 565–76.

Maziade M, Caron C, Cote R *et al.* (1990a) Extreme temperament and diagnosis. *Archives of General Psychiatry* **47**: 477–84.

Maziade M, Caron C, Cote R *et al.* (1990b) Psychiatric status of adolescents who had extreme temperaments at age 7. *The American Journal of Psychiatry* **147**(11): 1531–6.

Nesse RM (2000) Is depression an adaptation? *Archives of General Psychiatry* **57**(1): 14–20.

Nettle D (2004) Evolutionary origins of depression: a review and reformulation. *Journal of Affective Disorders* **81**: 91–102.

Niculescu AB (2001) Sex hormones, Darwinism, and depression. *Archives of General Psychiatry* **58**(11): 1083–4.

Nigg JT, Goldsmith HH (1998) Developmental psychopathology, personality and temperament: reflections on recent behavioral genetics research. *Human Biology* **70**(2): 387–412.

Nigg JT, John OP, Blaskey LG *et al.* (2002) Big five dimensions and ADHD symptoms: links between personality traits and clinical symptoms. *Journal of Personality and Social Psychology* **83**(2): 451–69.

Parker JDA, Majeski SA, Collin VT (2004) ADHD symptoms and personality: relationships with the five-factor model. *Personality and Individual Differences* **36**: 977–87.

Peterson B, Pine DS, Cohen P, Brook JS (2001) Prospective, longitudinal study of tic, obsessive-compulsive, and Attention-Deficit/Hyperactivity Disorders in an epidemiological sample. *Journal of the American Academy of Child and Adolescent Psychiatry* **40**(6): 685.

Roberti JW (2004) A review of behavioral and biological correlates of sensation seeking. *Journal of Research in Personality* **38**: 256–79.

Sagvolden T, Sergeant JA (1998) Attention deficit/hyperactivity disorder – from brain dysfunctions to behaviour. *Behavioural Brain Research* **94**: 1–10.

Schachar RJ, Crosbie J, Barr CL *et al.* (2005) Inhibition of motor responses in siblings concordant and discordant for Attention Deficit Hyperactivity Disorder. *American Journal of Psychiatry* **162**(6): 1076–82.

Shaw GA, Giambra LM (1993) Task unrelated thoughts of college students diagnosed as hyperactive in childhood. *Developmental Neuropsychology* **9**: 17–30.

Sih A, Bell AM, Johnson JC, Ziemba RE (2004) Behavioral syndromes: an integrative overview. *The Quarterly Review of Biology* **79**(3): 243–77.

Sonuga-Barke EJS (2002) Psychological heterogeneity in ADHD – a dual pathway model of behaviour and cognition. *Behavioural Brain Research* **130**: 29–36.

Sonuga-Barke EJS, Taylor E, Sembi S, Smith J (1992) Hyperactivity and delay aversion – I. The effect of delay on choice. *Journal of Child Psychology and Psychiatry* **33**(2): 387–98.

Straub WF (1982) Sensation seeking among high and low-risk male athletes. *Journal of Sport Psychology* **4**: 246–53.

Strobel A, Spinath FM, Angleitner A *et al.* (2003) Lack of association between polymorphisms of the dopamine D4 receptor gene and personality. *Neuropsychobiology* **47**: 52–6.

Tannock R (1998) Attention deficit hyperactivity disorder: advances in cognitive, neurobiological, and genetic research. *Journal of Child Psychology and Psychiatry* **39**(1): 65–99.

Thakker J, Ward T (1998) Culture and classification: the cross-cultural application of the DSM-IV. *Clinical Psychology Review* **18**(5): 501–29.

Timimi S (2004) A critique of the international consensus statement on ADHD. *Clinical Child and Family Psychology Review* **7**(1): 59–63.

Voeller KKS (2004) Attention-Deficit Hyperactivity Disorder (ADHD). *Journal of Child Neurology* **19**(10): 798–814.

Weiss G (1996) Attention Deficit Hyperactivity Disorder. In M Lewis (ed.) *Child and Adolescent Psychiatry* (2nd edn, pp. 544–77). Baltimore: Williams & Wilkins.

Weiss G, Hechtman L, Milroy T, Perlman T (1985) Psychiatric status of hyperactives as adults: a controlled prospective 15-year follow-up of 63 hyperactive children. *Journal of the American Academy of Child and Adolescent Psychiatry* **24**: 211–20.

Wilens TE Biederman J, Spencer TJ (2002) Attention deficit/hyperactivity disorder across the lifespan. *Annual Review of Medicine* **53**: 113–31.

Williams JO, Bell NS, Amoroso PJ (2002) Drinking and other risk taking behaviors of enlisted male soldiers in the US army. *Work* **18**: 141–50.

Zuckerman M (1983) Sensation seeking and sports. *Personality and Individual Differences* **4**(3): 285–93.

22 Future Directions in ADHD Research and Clinical Practice

MARK A. BELLGROVE[1] AND ERIC T. TAYLOR[2]

1. *School of Psychology and the Queensland Brain Institute (QBI) at the University of Queensland, Brisbane, Australia;*
2. *Department of Child & Adolescent Psychiatry, Institute of Psychiatry, King's College, London, UK*

22.1 OVERVIEW

The preceding chapters of this book have reviewed the impressive gains that have been made in our understanding of ADHD across clinical, neurobiological and treatment levels. This chapter commences with a selected overview of the main advances in our knowledge of the neurobiology of ADHD that are currently driving the field forward. The current era of neurobiological research into ADHD is one that embraces collaboration between disciplines and recognises the need for analysis of the ADHD phenotype at multiple levels. Today we see cognitive neuroscientists, molecular geneticists and psychiatrists, among others, working together like never before. Yet in other areas of research into ADHD, scientific advances have been less rapid. In the remainder of the chapter we focus on issues of clinical nosography, comorbidity, diagnostic thresholds and the possibilities for minimising the influence of known risk factors.

22.2 ADVANCES IN NEUROBIOLOGICAL RESEARCH IN ADHD

The last decade has seen a rapid increase in our knowledge of how disruption to discrete neurobiological systems might give rise to the behavioural phenomena that we now recognise as core to ADHD. In this section we selectively review important advances in the fields of neuropsychology, neuroimaging and genetics that are currently driving the field forward. In reviewing these fields, we also identify a number of areas where knowledge is either incomplete or inconsistent.

22.2.1 THE NEUROPSYCHOLOGY OF ADHD

Neuropsychological investigations of ADHD commenced with observations that damage to the human prefrontal cortex resulted in symptoms of distractibility, impulsivity and hyperactivity that resembled in large part, the symptoms displayed

Handbook of Attention Deficit Hyperactivity Disorder. Edited by M. Fitzgerald, M. Bellgrove and M. Gill.
© 2007 John Wiley & Sons Ltd

by children with hyperkinesis (Mattes, 1980). The ensuing years gave rise to an impressive body of worked that has unequivocally established the generality that as a group, children with ADHD, display neuropsychological impairment, relative to matched controls. Given the clinical similarity between the behaviour of patients with prefrontal syndromes and individuals with ADHD, it is not surprising that the bulk of this literature is devoted to documenting the performance of the latter group on tests that are sensitive to frontal lobe function. Thus, for example, children, adolescents and adults have been shown to be impaired on a range of so-called executive tasks, that require them to sustain attention, inhibit, plan, problem solve or use memory to guide future action (Pennington & Ozonoff, 1996; Seidman, 2006).

While few theorists would disagree that deficits on such tasks support the involvement of prefrontal dysfunction in ADHD, disagreement has existed over the centrality of a generalised executive disturbance (Pennington & Ozonoff, 1996) versus a more specific deficit in behavioural inhibition (Barkley, 1997; Nigg, 2001), versus a basic problem in the regulation of arousal (Sergeant, Oosterlaan & van der Meere, 1999; Sergeant, 2000) or dysfunction within reward systems (Sonuga-Barke, 1994; Sonuga-Barke, Saxton, & Hall, 1998; Sagvolden et al., 2005). Implicit within each of these unitary accounts is the assumption that dysfunction within the neural circuits supporting a process, such as behavioural inhibition, is causally related to the development of ADHD. Recent commentary, however, has emphasised the influence of neuropsychological heterogeneity with only approximately 50% of children with ADHD presenting with impaired performance on, for example, response inhibition tasks. An even smaller percentage of ADHD children display a pervasive executive function impairment across a number of tasks (Nigg et al., 2005). This raises serious questions about the unitary nature of inhibitory deficits, for example. In recent times, however, there has been a rapprochement of unitary accounts of ADHD, such as behavioural inhibition and delay aversion. This has led to the development of a dual-pathway model under which deficits of *either* behavioural inhibition or delay aversion might give rise to ADHD (Sonuga-Barke, 2003) (see also Chapter 11). This move signals a recognition that no one account is likely to be sufficient to describe a complex and heterogeneous condition like ADHD and that dysfunction within multiple neural systems may co-exist within an individual, with each ascribing its own 'flavour' to the disorder (see also Castellanos & Tannock's (2002) aetiological model of ADHD incorporating deficits of reward and temporal processing and working memory). Empirically, a dual-pathway model may be supported by data showing that a combination of executive (e.g., response inhibition) and reward (e.g. delay aversion) measures may better predict ADHD status than either measure alone (Solanto et al., 2001). As reviewed by Kelly and colleagues (Chapter 11) executive and reward circuitry may be dissociated at the level of the striatum, with the ventral striatum (nucleus accumbens) associated with reward processes and the dorsal striatum (caudate and putamen) associated with an executive system. Although a dual-pathway model of ADHD has appeal, as yet there is little evidence to explicitly link dysfunction within the ventral striatum to ADHD, whereas robust evidence exists for disruption to the dorsal striatum (Casey et al., 1997; Castellanos et al., 1994; Konrad et al., 2005). Further, the model seems better able to account for the hyperactive/impulsive, rather than inattentive, symptoms of the disorder, perhaps restricting its explanatory power.

Despite these advances there are a number of significant limitations to the neuropsychological literature of ADHD. First, although meta-analyses tell us that executive deficits are robustly seen across the lifespan in individuals with ADHD (Seidman, 2006) and adequately discriminate ADHD from non-ADHD participants, there has been a general failure to link cognitive impairment to symptom severity. There may be a number of valid reasons for this lack of correlation, including a poor correspondence between behavioural and laboratory measures of attention, significant heterogeneity which washes out any correlation that might otherwise exist, and the inherent weakness of DSM-based scales that measure ADHD symptoms. Nevertheless, this link is a logical requirement if one posits that dysfunction within a given process is causally related to the development of ADHD. Should not those individuals who show greater symptom severity also display greater cognitive impairment, for example? A cursory review of the neuropsychological literature will demonstrate that for most cognitive measures correlations with symptom measures are either absent or low. For example, a wealth of evidence suggests that, as a group, children with ADHD experience profound difficulties when required to inhibit automatic or prepotent responses (i.e., problems of behavioural inhibition). Meta-analyses of performance indices deriving from the stop-signal task, such as stop-signal reaction time (SSRT), show that 82% of studies report a significant group difference, relative to matched controls (Willcutt et al., 2005). Response inhibition deficits also appear robustly associated with the adult form of the disorder (Lijffijt et al., 2005). Deficient response inhibition has been proposed as the experimental analogue of problems of hyperactivity and impulsivity. Indeed some evidence in healthy children and adults shows that SSRT may be moderately correlated with global measures of impulsivity (Logan, Schachar & Tannock, 1997; Avila et al., 2004). Yet when studies examine the correlation between dimensional measures of hyperactivity/impulsivity and SSRT in ADHD populations correlations are invariably low or absent (Solanto et al., 2001; Schachar et al., 2005). This weakens an otherwise promising convergence between the clinical presentation, cognitive-neuroscientific models of response inhibition (Aron et al., 2003; Chambers et al., 2006) and pathophysiological findings which suggest disruption to neural substrates of response inhibition (inferior frontal gyrus) in ADHD (Rubia et al., 1999; Durston et al., 2003; Sowell et al., 2003).

One potential source of error variance in establishing robust clinical-experimental correlates for cognition in ADHD, may have been the field's over-reliance on global measures of frontal function, such as the Wisconsin Card Sorting Task, Trail-Making Tests and tests of planning (Tower of Hanoi; Tower of London) (Willcutt et al., 2005). These tasks are complex and multi-componential and inevitably provide a 'global' measure of frontal functioning, rather than a measure of dysfunction within a discrete neural system. In our view, the development of a valid neuropsychology of a neurodevelopmental disorder such as ADHD requires that the signs and symptoms of the disorder should be understood in terms of psychological processes and that these in turn, should be related to discrete brain systems. In this endeavour, much may be gained from adopting the methods and paradigms from cognitive neuroscience, with its emphasis on how the brain represents and implements discrete aspects of cognition. When such methods have been applied to ADHD, promising results have emerged. For example, Konrad et al. (2006) employed the Attention Network Test (ANT) within a functional brain imaging study of medication-naïve boys with ADHD. The ANT task derives from Posner and Peterson's model of attention which emphasises separable components of attention (alertness, conflict and spatial orienting) which are subserved by distinct neural systems (Posner & Peterson, 1990). Behaviourally children with ADHD showed evidence of impairment in resolving conflict between competing stimuli and, to a lesser extent, in orienting their attention to locations in space. The neural correlates of impaired conflict resolution were a reduction in the activity with the putamen and precentral gyrus, whereas the control children showed increased activation in these areas when required to resolve conflict. Importantly, although there were no significant correlations between symptom severity and behavioural indices, significant correlations were found between symptom severity and neural indices. Specifically, ADHD children who had higher symptom levels, activated the putamen less during trials on which they were required to resolve conflict (Konrad et al., 2005). The results of this study therefore suggest that neural indices may have greater sensitivity to detect clinical-experimental correlations than traditional behavioural measures of reaction time and accuracy, for example.

There are a number of other limitations within the extant neuropsychological literature that provide challenges for future research. First, as reviewed in Chapter 2, evidence exists that ADHD combined and inattentive subtypes are distinct in terms of their associated patterns of comorbidity, educational achievement and social functioning (Milich, Balentine & Lynam, 2001). Neuropsychology has, however, generally failed to find a robust distinction between the cognitive profiles of children with ADHD combined and inattentive types. Although an executive dysfunction hypothesis was originally proposed for the combined-subtype (Barkley, 1997), robust subtype differences on executive measures have not been found. For example, Geurts et al. examined executive and non-executive task performance as a function of DSM-IV sub-type. Although children with ADHD-combined type differed from controls on a range of tasks related to inhibition, they did not differ with respect to children with ADHD-inattentive type (Geurts et al., 2005). Nigg et al. reported a complex interaction with gender, such that boys with ADHD combined type differed from those with the inattentive type on measures of response inhibition, but these differences did not exist for girls (Nigg et al., 2002). Isolated reports of sub-type differences have nevertheless been published. Mullins et al. (2005) examined time reproduction in children with ADHD combined and inattentive subtypes. Although the two subtypes did not differ in terms of the absolute magnitude of their time reproduction errors, children with the combined subtype showed significantly greater variability in their reproductions than children with the inattentive subtype. O'Driscoll et al. (2005) employed oculomotor paradigms to investigate motor planning (predictive saccades) and motor inhibition (antisaccades) in ADHD. These authors found greater deficit in adolescents with ADHD combined-type than in ADHD inattentive-type on both these measures. The study by O'Driscoll et al. highlights a theme of this chapter that behavioural paradigms that are tightly linked to underlying physiological systems may have greater utility in elucidating the neural substrates of ADHD than global measures of cognition that are themselves multi-componential.

The failure to identify a distinct cognitive profile for the inattentive subtype may also reflect an inherent recruitment bias with the majority of neuropsychological studies recruiting children with the combined-type form of the disorder. This bias is further reflected in theorising, with most explanatory accounts of ADHD focusing on the combined-type form of the disorder (Barkley, 1997; Sagvolden *et al.*, 2005). Future studies should endeavour to recruit samples of both predominantly combined- and inattentive-type children, bearing in mind the likely small effect size of any cognitive differences between the subtypes.

22.2.2   NEUROIMAGING OF ADHD

Here we briefly review the main advances made within the structural and functional brain imaging literatures of ADHD. The interested reader is referred to a number of recent and excellent reviews of both structural (see Seidman *et al.*, 2005) and functional (see Bush *et al.*, 2005) brain imaging in ADHD. Most of what we know regarding structural changes in the brains of individuals with ADHD has arisen from studies that have employed magnetic resonance imaging (MRI) in children to examine total cerebral volume or the volume of an individual cerebral territory. The main practical advantage of MRI, relative to older structural imaging techniques, such as computerised tomography (CT), is its greater spatial resolution. MRI also has established test-retest reliability allowing it to be used in both cross-sectional and longitudinal designs. The latter design is particularly interesting in light of the persistence of ADHD symptoms from childhood to adulthood in 30–60% of cases. Functional imaging techniques include single photon emission computed tomography (SPECT), positron emission tomography (PET) and functional MRI (fMRI). The former techniques (SPECT and PET) are invasive as they require the injection or inhalation of radioactive materials. fMRI on the other hand, is non-invasive and does not require exposure to ionising radiation allowing it to be employed in longitudinal studies of functional brain activity. Further, relative to both SPECT and PET, fMRI has superior temporal and spatial resolution, making it suitable for studying a disorder such as ADHD, where deficits occur in both time and space. Despite the limitations of SPECT, it has, however, made an important contribution in the area of in vivo neuroreceptor imaging of, for example, dopamine transporter densities in individuals with ADHD (see Spencer *et al.*, 2005). These findings have provided vital clues for genetic studies of ADHD and will be discussed further below.

(a)   Structural brain imaging in ADHD

The most consistent and reliable finding in the structural brain imaging literature of ADHD is a reduction in total brain volume of around 3–5%. This reduction has been seen in seven out of twelve reports and may be particularly pronounced in the right-hemisphere of the brain (Seidman, Valera & Makris, 2005). This reduction in cerebral volume contrasts, for example, with an overall increase in cerebral volume that is seen in autism (Brambilla *et al.*, 2003) and stands as a point of difference between two disorders which have significant clinical and neurobiological overlap (see Chapter 5).

Widespread regional volume reductions have also been observed in children and adolescents with ADHD. As noted throughout this book, prefrontal theories of ADHD are predominant. Consistent with this theorising, the majority of MRI studies have identified reduced volumes of the prefrontal cortex, including the dorsolateral prefrontal cortex in ADHD (Castellanos *et al.*, 1996, 2001, 2002; Filipek *et al.*, 1997; Mostofsky *et al.*, 2002). Also consistent with fronto-striatal accounts of the disorder, a number of studies have noted smaller volumes within striatal (caudate and putamen) and basal ganglia regions (Castellanos *et al.*, 1996; Pliszka *et al.*, 2006). Reports of smaller volumes in the right hemisphere are consistent with behavioural deficits of response inhibition, for example, which shows reliance upon the right hemisphere. Indeed Casey *et al.* (1997) provided an important structure-function correlate showing that performance on three response inhibition tasks correlated with anatomic measures of prefrontal cortex and caudate nuclei, particularly in the right hemisphere. Nevertheless, it should be noted that volume reductions in the left striatum and basal ganglia but not the right, have been reported (Aylward *et al.*, 1996).

The cerebellum has also emerged as an important structure in pathophysiological models of ADHD. The cerebellum receives input from cortical association areas (frontal, parietal, temporal) and interfaces with fronto-striatal circuits at the level of the thalamus, providing feedback to the cortex via the thalamocortical projection. A number of studies in children with ADHD have indicated volume reduction in the posterior inferior lobules, VIII to X, of the cerebellar vermis in both boys and girls (Seidman *et al.*, 2005). Although a reduction in the volume of the cerebellum has been associated with increased attentional problems, at this stage of the literature, the functional consequences of cerebellar abnormality for behaviour and cognition in ADHD remain unclear.

A number of other important findings have emerged from the structural imaging literature of ADHD. First, Castellanos and colleagues (2002) conducted the largest MRI study of children with ADHD (n = 152) and healthy controls (n = 139) who were scanned up to 4 times over a decade. At initial scan, participants with ADHD had an overall reduction in total cerebral volume of 3.2%, after accounting for significant co-variates. Significant reductions in grey and white matter volumes were also seen across frontal, parietal, temporal and occipital cortices as well as in the caudate and cerebellum. These findings challenge 'fronto-centric' views of ADHD pathophysiology that have dominated the literature. Indeed, after adjusting for total brain volume differences, only the volume reduction in the cerebellum remained significant. Compared with controls, previously unmedicated children with ADHD had smaller total cerebral volumes and smaller cerebellar volumes. Unmedicated children also had smaller total white matter volumes compared to controls and medicated children with ADHD. Importantly, volume reductions in frontal and temporal grey matter volume and caudate and cerebellar volume were significantly correlated with the clinician-rated Clinical Global Impressions rating and parent-rated child behaviour checklist attention problems. At follow-up, developmental trajectories for nearly all areas, with the exception of the caudate, remained parallel to those seen in the healthy control groups. As Castellanos and colleagues suggest, this finding suggests that 'neuropsychiatric symptoms appear to reflect fixed earlier neurobiological insults or abnormalities' (p. 1747), but that later developmental processes occurring during late childhood and early adolescence are essentially intact. An interesting avenue for future research will be to examine whether cognitive remediation techniques can promote plastic changes in the brain and thus change aberrant developmental trajectories in ADHD (see also O'Connell *et al.,* Chapter 20).

A second area in which the application of MRI may hold particular promise for ADHD is in the area of imaging genetics. Although this field is in its infancy, there have been a number of published examples that suggest that an MRI-based phenotype may be appropriate for genetic studies. For example, Castellanos *et al.* (2003) studied caudate volumes in monozygotic twins discordant for ADHD. The affected twins were found to have significantly smaller caudate volumes than their unaffected co-twins. Durston *et al.* (2004) conducted two MRI-based studies in which brain volumes were compared between children with ADHD and their unaffected siblings. In this design the unaffected siblings were used as a proxy for familial risk, since siblings have 50% of their genes in common. In their first study Durston *et al.* reported that both children with ADHD and their unaffected siblings displayed reductions in right prefrontal grey matter and left occipital grey and white matter, relative to controls. Reductions in the volume of the right cerebellum were seen only in children with ADHD, relative to controls, but not the unaffected siblings. These findings suggest that prefrontal volumes might show a familial-risk profile whereas reduced right cerebellar volumes may be somewhat disorder-specific. In a second study, Durston *et al.* (2005) employed the same sib-pair design but partitioned their data according to the presence or absence of the 'risk' alleles of either the dopamine D4 receptor (DRD4) polymorphism or the dopamine transporter (DAT1) polymorphism (see also Chapters 8 and 12). There was a significant effect of the DAT1 genotype on caudate volume, with individuals who were homozygous for the risk variant (10-repeat) having smaller caudate volumes than those carrying an alternative repeat variant (9-repeat). This effect was most pronounced in children who had ADHD. By contrast, DRD4 genotype was associated with volume reductions only in prefrontal grey matter; this effect was most pronounced in unaffected siblings. An earlier report, however, found no influence of DRD4 genotype on brain anatomic measures (Castellanos *et al.*, 1998). These findings provide preliminary evidence that an MRI-based phenotype may be sensitive to genetic susceptibility to ADHD, however further confirmation studies are required.

(b) Functional brain imaging in ADHD

As reviewed in this chapter and elsewhere in this book, fronto-striatal dysfunction has been the predominant and guiding aetiological account of ADHD in recent times. Perhaps not surprisingly then, early attempts to examine the functional neuroanatomical correlates of ADHD used cognitive probes arising from cognitive psychology and neuropsychology. Thus, the Go/No-go or stop-signal paradigms have been used extensively to probe the neural bases of behavioural inhibition. To date, 10 studies have employed fMRI while ADHD and control subjects performed response inhibition tasks (Vaidya *et al.*, 1998, 2005; Rubia *et al.*, 1999, 2005; Teicher *et al.*, 2000; Durston *et al.*, 2003; Schulz *et al.*, 2004; Tamm *et al.*, 2004; Booth *et al.*, 2005; Pliszka *et al.*, 2006). In general these studies converge upon a view of response inhibition, particularly in children with ADHD, which is characterised by dysfunctional frontostriatal inhibitory networks. Structural and functional deficits within the IFG, caudate and basal ganglia are reliably observed and may form the pathophysiological substrate of response inhibition deficits in ADHD. Functional deficits within this inhibitory network may require the recruitment of additional and compensatory brain areas by children and adolescents with ADHD (Durston *et al.*, 2003; Tamm *et al.*, 2004; Vaidya *et al.*, 2005).

Electrophysiological data also speak to the issue of the primacy of response inhibition deficits in ADHD. For example, studies that have recorded event-related potentials (ERPs) while ADHD and non-ADHD participants perform either Go/No-go or stop-signal paradigms have reliably found group differences in components relating to response inhibition, such as the N2 and P3. However, robust electrophysiological differences have also been found in components relating to the ongoing allocation of attentional resources, response preparation and orienting of attention to the No-go stimulus (see Kenemans *et al.*, 2005). Since these differences occur earlier in time than the inhibitory response, they indicate that a basic problem of state regulation and/or attentional orienting may contribute to later problems of response inhibition. These ERP findings therefore augment those obtained using fMRI and further question unitary accounts of ADHD.

An emerging theme within the functional neuroimaging literature of ADHD is the role of the anterior cingulate in the cognitive and motivational disturbances of the disorder. In a seminal study Bush and colleagues (Bush *et al.*, 1999) asked adults with ADHD and healthy controls to perform a cognitive interference task (Counting Stroop). Stroop-type tasks have been repeatedly shown to robustly activate the dorsal anterior cingulate. Bush *et al.* noted that, relative to controls, the ADHD participants displayed significant hypoactivation in the dorsal anterior cingulate. A number of the response inhibition tasks noted above also found hypoactivation in the anterior cingulate in ADHD participants (Rubia *et al.*, 1999; Durston *et al.*, 2003; Tamm *et al.*, 2004). The study by Rubia *et al.* alternated experimental (No-Go) and control (Go) conditions. Under these circumstances activation seen during the No-Go condition could be due to a number of processes other than response inhibition. One important candidate might be error processes associated with commission errors. The influence of error processes may be particularly relevant to ADHD where participants reliably make more commission errors, for example. The consequence of this might be that activation patterns seen during No-Go blocks are unduly influenced by post-error processes, rather than reflecting response inhibition deficits, *per se*. This explanation may not, however, account for hypoactivation seen in the anterior cingulate in studies where only correct trials are analysed (i.e. post-error processes cannot contaminate activation maps (Durston *et al.*, 2003)). Nevertheless, the influence of error processing in fMRI studies of ADHD should be borne in mind and may help to explain contradictory findings in the literature (see Bush, Valera & Seidman, 2005). Within the cognitive neuroscience literature, error processing has recently attracted much interest. Error processing may call on at least two distinct systems: one to monitor performance and detect the occurrence of an error and another to implement the necessary cognitive control required to adjust behaviour. Much evidence from fMRI and event-related potentials suggests an important role for the anterior cingulate in error detection, while the dorsolateral prefrontal cortex may play a role in subsequent performance adjustments (Garavan *et al.*, 2002; Garavan *et al.*, 2003). One possibility is that the executive deficits that are so reliably reported in ADHD could be underpinned by a basic problem in either detecting errors or making the appropriate performance adjustments subsequent to an error. A number of behavioural studies do suggest aberrant error processing in ADHD (Schachar *et al.*, 2004) and preliminary neuroimaging work suggests that medication-naïve adolescents with ADHD show less activation in the posterior cingulate than controls on trials on which they may make an error (Rubia *et al.*, 2005).

Given the primacy of response inhibition accounts of ADHD and fronto-striatal pathophysiological models, it is perhaps unsurprising that cerebral regions outside this system have attracted less interest from fMRI researchers. One such region that in our opinion may come to prominence in ADHD is the parietal lobe. Although a number of structural imaging studies have noted abnormalities in the parietal lobe in ADHD (Sowell *et al.*, 2003; Makris *et al.*, 2006), it is only relatively recently that functional imaging studies have begun to use activation probes that may reliably activate this region. Much research from cognitive neuroscience shows that the parietal lobe is important for aspects of attention including sustained attention and spatial selective attention (Husain & Rorden, 2003) where in the latter case, attention serves to enhance the perceptual processing of stimuli at particular locations in space. The parietal lobe also plays an important role in spatial working memory, where some have conceptualised spatial rehearsal as being achieved by attention shifts between objects in space (Awh & Jonides, 2001). Although preliminary, hypoactivation has been reported in the superior parietal lobule in ADHD children during a selective attention task (Booth *et al.*, 2005). Silk *et al.* (2005) also reported marked hypoactivation in the superior parietal lobule in children with ADHD, relative to controls, while participants performed a mental rotation task requiring spatial working memory. These imaging studies are consistent with behavioural data showing robust deficits in spatial working memory in ADHD and somewhat less consistently, impairments in spatial selective attention.

22.2.3 GENETICS OF ADHD

A large amount of data from twin, family and adoption studies suggests a large genetic component to ADHD, with heritability estimates in the range of 0.6–0.9 (see Chapters 8 and 10). Like most complex diseases which do not show a Mendelian inheritance pattern, the most likely genetic model for ADHD is one in which a number of genes each confers a small amount of 'risk' or susceptibility to the disorder. The last 10 years has seen a massive research effort aimed at identifying the behaviour (see Bennett *et al.*, Chapter 7) and molecular genetics of ADHD (see Hawi *et al.*, Chapter 8). Here we summarise the main findings from molecular genetics, demonstrating how psychiatric genetics is interfacing with neuropsychology, neuroimaging and pharmacology.

The workhorses of molecular genetic studies of ADHD have been the methods of genetic-linkage and genetic-association. Linkage attempts to examine the segregation of the disorder with polymorphic genetic markers using either large family pedigrees or multiple smaller families in an attempt to localise a disease gene to a chromosomal region. Linkage studies of ADHD have met with some success and have identified a number of chromosomal locations that may harbour susceptibility genes, including areas of chromosomes 4, 5, 11, 16 and 17 (Smalley *et al.*, 2002; Arcos-Burgos *et al.*, 2004). Linkage studies, are nonetheless, often under-powered to detect genes of small effect and so researchers have turned to studies of genetic association which typically employ a candidate-gene approach.

The candidate-gene approach to ADHD follows hypotheses that derive primarily from the efficacy of stimulant medications in the treatment of ADHD. Since stimulants, such as methylphenidate and amphetamine, are known to act on dopaminergic systems within the brain, initial efforts were aimed at isolating DNA variants of genes that were involved in dopamine signalling. The best replicated of these associations are with DNA variants of the dopamine D4 and D5 receptor genes (DRD4, DRD5) and the dopamine transporter gene (DAT1) (Faraone *et al.*, 2005). To illustrate the candidate gene approach and to highlight the ways in which this approach may interface with other areas of neuroscience, we focus here on the DAT1 gene. A fuller discussion of the candidate gene approach to ADHD can be found in Chapter 8 by Hawi and colleagues.

A number of lines of evidence suggested that the dopamine transporter gene (DAT1) might be an important candidate gene for ADHD. First, stimulants, such as methylphenidate, act by inhibiting the dopamine transporter (Madras, Miller & Fischman, 2005) and lead to increased processing efficiency within fronto-striatal circuits (Vaidya *et al.*, 1998). Secondly, a number of functional imaging studies using SPECT have also shown that dopamine transporter densities in the striatum of both children (Cheon *et al.*, 2003) and adults with ADHD are elevated but that these levels may be normalised with methylphenidate (Dougherty *et al.*, 1999; Dresel *et al.*, 2000; Krause *et al.*, 2000).

Accordingly, a number of studies investigated whether DNA variants of the DAT1 gene were associated with ADHD; that is whether a particular DNA variant was observed more frequently in cases with ADHD than in controls, for example. A large number of studies have tested for association with a variable number of tandem repeat (VNTR) polymorphism within the 3′ untranslated region of the DAT1 gene. The 10-repeat allele of this polymorphism appears to have functionality and has been associated with ADHD in a number of studies (Faraone *et al.*, 2005). As is often the case in genetic association studies, however, non-replications do exist and suggest genetic heterogeneity between study populations. Brookes *et al.* (2006) recently observed that the 10-repeat allele of the 3′ VNTR was in linkage disequilibrium with the 3-repeat allele of an Intron 8 marker and together these formed a common haplotype that was associated with ADHD. Haplotypes represent sets of closely linked DNA variants that can be used to very accurately map disease causing variants. Interestingly, these authors also reported a gene–environment interaction between the presence of the 'risk' haplotype and the presence of maternal drinking during pregnancy, such that the association between DAT1 variants and ADHD was stronger in the ADHD children of mothers who drank.

As reviewed by Barry and Gill in Chapter 9, heritability estimates for ADHD that are less than perfect imply some contribution from non-genetic factors. In the study by Brookes *et al.* (Brookes *et al.*, 2006) a gene–environment interaction was present as the association with DAT1 variants was only seen in the ADHD children of mothers who drank alcohol. Increasingly, molecular genetic studies of ADHD will need to move beyond examining main effects of genotype towards examining gene–environment interactions with key environmental factors. A limitation in this endeavour is that exposure to environmental agents is often measured in imprecise ways (i.e., how many drinks per week did you have during pregnancy?). The result of imprecise measurement is that very large samples may be required if false positive findings are to be avoided. Caspi and Moffitt (Caspi & Moffitt, 2006) recommend that once gene–environment interactions have been discovered by genetic epidemiologists, neuroscientists may be able to elucidate the neural mechanisms of these interactions using precise control over exposure to pathogens.

The DAT1 10-repeat allele of the 3′ VNTR has also been shown to influence cognitive performance in a number of studies of ADHD (Loo *et al.*, 2003; Bellgrove *et al.*, 2005; Bellgrove, Gill, *et al.*, 2005). The approach of linking a candidate gene to an intermediate phenotype, or 'endophenotype', has attracted much interest in the literature. Endophenotypes are intermediate phenotypes which relate to the disorder, are heritable and demonstrate familial-risk profiles. The assumption of the endophenotype approach is that the genetic architecture of the endophenotype will be less complex than that of the clinical phenotype. Studies that employ endophenotypes should then have greater power to detect genes of small effect. As reviewed in Chapter 12 by Bellgrove *et al.*, the study of suitable endophenotypes for ADHD is in its infancy. With respect to the DAT1 10-repeat allele, a number of studies have reported that 10-repeat homozygotes perform more poorly on tests of sustained and spatial attention and have more variable reaction times (Bellgrove *et al.*, 2005; Loo *et al.*, 2005). The 10-repeat allele was also associated with response inhibition deficits in children who rated highly for ADHD symptoms within an epidemiological sample (Cornish *et al.*, 2005). A reviewed earlier, an influence of the 10-repeat DAT1 allele on the volume of the caudate was also documented in children with ADHD (Durston *et al.*, 2005). To date, no studies have integrated molecular genetics with fMRI within an ADHD population, although a number of groups around the world are working towards this goal.

The candidate gene approach may also interface with psychopharmacology, as discussed in this book by Barry and colleagues in Chapter 16. Pharmacogenetics is the study of how individual differences in drug response may be conditional upon an individual's genotype. Again, the DAT1 gene has proved an attractive candidate for pharmacogenetic studies since the mainstay treatment for ADHD, stimulants, act in large part by inhibiting the dopamine transporter. One pathophysiological hypothesis of ADHD asserts that the 10-repeat allele of the DAT1 gene increases expression of the gene and is thus associated with higher levels of DAT (Heinz *et al.*, 2000; Kirley *et al.*, 2003). It is therefore proposed that methylpenidate will be most efficacious in those who possess the 10-repeat allele. To date empirical support for this hypothesis has been inconsistent with some studies reporting an enhanced response to methylphenidate as a function of the 10-repeat DAT1 allele (Kirley *et al.*, 2003; Stein *et al.*, 2005), whereas other studies have reported a poorer response (Winsberg & Comings, 1999; Roman *et al.*, 2002; Rohde *et al.*, 2003; Cheon *et al.*, 2005). Potential confounds within this literature include the recruitment of children with ADHD who are medication naïve versus medication withdrawn. Ideally, all studies of this nature would be conducted prospectively by following a cohort that was medication naïve at intake. However, since stimulant medications are not disorder-specific and improve cognition and attention in non-ADHD populations, it may be possible to conduct pharmacogenetic studies using methylphenidate doses in the therapeutic range even in healthy adult populations. Further, the neural mechanisms of drug action could also be probed in healthy adults, with respect to genotype, using modern imaging techniques. For example, since SPECT relies upon the use of radioactive materials, it may be unethical to employ such measures in healthy or disordered children. These concerns, however, may be somewhat reduced in healthy adults. Using SPECT to examine transporter densities as a function of genotype and medication status (on vs. off) would provide vital information regarding the biological subtrates of stimulant-response. Alternatively, fMRI could be used to examine the effect of genotype and medication status on key cognitive parameters that are known to be impaired in ADHD (e.g. spatial working memory). In this way, biological pathways of direct relevance to ADHD could be mapped in healthy individuals. Of course in order to be relevant to childhood ADHD, this approach needs to assume some continuity between the neural systems mediating stimulant response in children and adults. Evidence does exist, however, that stimulants achieve comparable effects on behaviour and cognition in both children and adults with ADHD.

It should be apparent from the above brief discussion of the neuropsychology, neuroimaging and genetics literatures of ADHD that great strides have indeed been made towards defining the neurobiological mechanisms of ADHD. The last 10 years have seen a rapid development in our understanding of the biological contributions to ADHD, facilitated in large part, by a co-operative research community that recognises the need for collaboration, replication and the benefit of multi-modal approaches. In this way, we believe that empirical work in ADHD may provide a model for research into other neurodevelopmental disorders where gains in knowledge have been less rapid. In the remainder of this chapter we review areas of research relevant to treatment and clinical practice in ADHD where we believe further advances might still be made.

22.3   FUTURE DIRECTIONS IN CLINICAL PRACTICE AND THE IMPLICATIONS OF NEUROBIOLOGICAL ADVANCES

22.3.1   TRANSLATIONAL RESEARCH

The rapid advances in genetics, neuroscience and cognitive psychology have raised hopes for clinical and educational progress, but have not yet satisfied them. Clinical practice has not changed in nature over the last 30 years. Stimulant medication and behaviour therapy are still, as they were then, the major interventions; public controversy about their legitimacy persists; the long-term outcome for mental health remains rather poor. There have been advances, however: more children are recognised and treated (some would say too many), services in many countries have developed correspondingly, adults are beginning to receive diagnosis and treatment, long-acting formulations of stimulant drugs have increased their acceptability, and a non-stimulant drug (atomoxetine) has been introduced and licensed. These advances have not been driven solely by neurobiological knowledge, but future advances may well be. Which diagnostic concepts need to be recognised, the overlap with other conditions, the threshold for diagnosis, and the possibilities for reducing risk factors or providing protection against them are all calling for further research and application.

22.3.2 CLINICAL NOSOGRAPHY

Growing neurobiological knowledge might be expected to modify the diagnostic concepts that are used by clinicians. What will the taxons of classification look like in the future?

The history of clinical classification in ADHD research has for the last 30 years been one of retreat from neurobiological theory. As reviewed in Chapter 1 by Sharkey and Fitzgerald, there used to be etiologically based concepts for classifying disorders such as 'Minimal Brain Dysfunction' or 'Continuum of Reproductive Casualty'. These concepts foundered, however, when classical epidemiological research on children who had brain lesions emphasised that there was nothing very characteristic about their presentations, that brain-behaviour correlations were on the whole remarkable for their absence, and that the main effect of neurological compromise was to increase the risk for a wide range of psychiatric presentations (Rutter *et al.*, 1970). It followed that the presence of a brain cause could not usually be inferred from the form of the psychiatric presentation alone.

Other etiological influences, such as those of disrupted attachment in early life, also proved to have rather complex and widespread effects. The notion of specific diseases in child mental health had to be abandoned. Furthermore, reliability studies of the diagnosis of ADHD found a worrying lack of agreement between clinicians, partly because of differing opinions about which aspects of a mixed case should be considered primary (e.g. Prendergast *et al.*, 1988). A major advance therefore came when the classifications, such as DSM-III and ICD-10, abandoned explanatory causes, and moved towards a classification simply at the level of behavioural description. 'ADHD' remains a concept defined at this behavioural level.

However, it was never the intention that classification should remain merely at the level of description. Researchers have been led to seek a more precise classification by the frequent lack of robustness in neurobiological findings and the suspicion that this may spring from an inadequately defined phenotype. Clinicians have hoped for a diagnosis based upon neurophysiological disturbance – not least because of the uncertainties of diagnoses when so much depends upon the evaluation of children's behaviour by parents and other people who are emotionally involved with them (Taylor, 1998).

Could a genetic classification replace the present behaviour-based system? Based on our current understanding of ADHD this seems unlikely for several reasons. First, the findings presented in this book seem to point to multiple interacting genetic influences, each of small effect, that interact not only with each other but also with environmental risks. It could turn out to be the case that single genes will code powerfully for particular forms of psychiatric presentation, but so far the evidence has not suggested it. Secondly, the etiology is not necessarily the main thing that clinicians wish to characterise. Throughout medicine the key concern for any illness is the physiological processes that are altered and cause harm to the individual. This pathogenetic process may well be the result of several different etiologies, but it is likely to be the key level at which intervention can be effective. The effect of genetic studies may well be to spur research that clarifies the neurophysiological and neuropsychological processes involved, but it may not prove to be more potent than them in defining disease. Thirdly, it is important to remember that classifications do not only serve the purpose of aiding biological and clinical science – they must also help in education, in public understanding, and in determining the economic basis of services. Homogeneity at the level of practical consequences is therefore at least as important as homogeneity at the level of basic cause.

If future advances find altered neurobiological processes, and adopt them as the basis of classification, what might they look like? The research findings reviewed in this book have not established the notion that biological markers will be found for a single, unitary illness of ADHD. In all tests of brain structure and function there is considerable overlap between ordinary people and those with ADHD. In addition, heterogeneity among those with ADHD is considerable. There is now a wide variety of theoretical formulations for the underlying neuropsychological basis of ADHD. Indeed, as discussed above, recent reviews suggest that several processes are involved (Nigg *et al.*, 2005; Sonuga-Barke *et al.*, 2005; Castellanos *et al.*, 2006). Delay aversion and rapid delay of reward gradients can give a persuasive account of impulsive behaviour in motivational terms; but disinhibitory failures of response suppression can also give plausible accounts, as can executive failures of decision-making between alternatives. Furthermore, these pathophysiological processes may interact with each other. A child unable to analyse time-delayed sequences of stimuli might well become motivationally averse to doing so. Genetic analysis may well help to disentangle which patterns of cognitive alteration share genetic variance with hyperactive behaviour and which are epiphenomena of the underlying pathology.

It may well be this heterogeneity of processes that creates the greatest scope for the application of neurobiological findings to practice. If it were possible to analyse the component dysfunctions in behavioural presentations of inattentiveness, then it might well be helpful to assign individual children to specific types of neurocognitive change, with corresponding implications for cause, associations and intervention.

22.3.3 'COMORBIDITY'

Can the recent neurobiological advances shed light on the frequent clinical problem that many apparently diverse symptoms can be exhibited by the same child? Considerable progress has already been made, and to appreciate this it is helpful to summarise some of the key reasons that apparently different disorders may occur together. It is possible, for example, that the classification schemes makes false divisions and that 'disorders', such as ADHD and conduct disorder, frequently occur together simply because they are manifestations of a single underlying condition. Twin analyses have suggested, for example, that the genetic influences acting upon conduct disorder in school children are to a large extent the same as those that operate on ADHD (Nadder *et al.*, 2002). Does this mean that the distinction between ADHD and oppositional/conduct problems is false? The answer is probably not since neurobiological distinctions can be drawn between these two disorders. Children with ADHD and no conduct disorder tend to show a range of other neurodevelopmental delays, such as motor clumsiness and the cognitive changes already discussed; children with oppositional or conduct disorder, but no hyperactivity, do not (Banaschewski *et al.*, 2005). This dissociation has sometimes been missed in experimental surveys because mixed cases have been included with conduct disorder; children with mixed problems – who show the combination of conduct problems and hyperactivity – do indeed show the neurobiological associations of those with hyperactivity alone. One conclusion for classification drawn from this is that the mixed state should be classified with ADHD (or 'hyperkinetic disorder') rather than with conduct disorder alone – as is incorporated in the ICD-10 classification.

It is noteworthy that the genome scans carried out in sib-pair studies for autism have identified several of the same positional loci as those emerging from the genome scans for ADHD (Faraone *et al.*, 2005). This may well imply that there are general genetic influences creating a risk for a variety of neurodevelopmental influences; but it is far from suggesting that autism and ADHD should be classified as one. Different findings regarding brain size, neuropsychological function, and risks for later problems such as epilepsy further distinguish these two disorders and have been reviewed elsewhere (Banaschewski *et al.*, 2005) (see also Chapter 5). To take yet a third example from the same review, ADHD and reading disorders will often occur together, and one positional locus on chromosome 6 has been associated with both reading and attention problems. Nevertheless, the conditions can be differentiated in important respects such as the response to medication (or in the case of reading problems the lack of it) and the dissociation between executive function deficits in ADHD and problems such as those of phonological coding that characterise dyslexia.

Neurobiological investigations have therefore been powerful in discounting the idea that comorbidity of disorders reflects a single brain disposition. They have if anything pointed up the necessity for clinicians to evolve sharper and more precise tools for the distinction between different patterns of overactive and inattentive behaviour. Can they go further and clarify clinical controversies? To take an instance of this, consider the case of the overlap between the core ADHD symptoms of inattentiveness, impulsiveness and overactivity and the alterations of emotional adjustment that frequently coexists. Clinically, several patterns of emotional disturbance can be encountered in people with ADHD. Some show persisting worries about the future or fears of present activity – the kind of classical symptomatology that is usually called 'anxiety'. Others may have episodes of depression or euphoria that meet conventional criteria for a diagnosis of bipolar disorder. Others again show a pattern of very rapidly volatile emotion – often irritable – and this emotional lability has been regarded by many as a variant form of bipolar disorder – 'Juvenile Bipolar Disorder (JBD)'. Neurobiological investigations of the brain's activity during different states of emotional tension seem well placed to clarify whether those with JBD have changes characteristic of ADHD, or rather those of BPD or another disorder entirely. At present it is too soon to give a definitive answer, but the comparison of clinical groups differing in details of their presentation should continue to be a powerful research design. In a similar way we can foresee studies of how people with Tourette disorder normally inhibit tics, or how those with epilepsy normally inhibit seizures, and whether this inhibitory pathology in ADHD weakens the resistance against these conditions and contributes to their association with ADHD.

22.3.4   DIAGNOSTIC THRESHOLDS

Clinicians and families are often puzzled by borderline cases. If some, but not all of the features of the disorder are present, should a diagnosis be made or not? Neurobiological studies have not solved this, but they have clarified the nature of the difficulty. Twin studies do not suggest that there is a discrete disorder of ADHD. Genetic influences on the range of ADHD-like behaviours in the ordinary populations are similar in strength and kind to those that determine the differences between those with diagnosed ADHD and controls (Curran *et al.*, 2003). The picture that emerges is one of a continuum of biological risk. It is therefore clear that there will be some arbitrary element in the decision about where to put the precise cut-off. In practice, therefore, the criteria for diagnoses are arrived at rather pragmatically. For example, the DSM-IV threshold is based upon the levels that characterised children referred to clinics in the USA. The tautology for diagnosis, and the possible problems in application to other countries, are clear. A better threshold would be that which predicts impairment, either in social functioning, or in important neuropsychological processes. We expect the controversies about the legitimacy of clinical diagnoses to generate more research about the relationships between neurocognitive change and impairment.

22.3.5   DEVELOPMENTAL ISSUES

The discourse of clinicians and researchers is sometimes curiously uninformed by developmental change. Case-control studies are the rule, in which age is a factor to be controlled out of the investigation rather than systematically included within the design. When it is included, it is often illuminating.

Volumetric studies of children's brains at different ages have given a picture of a rather constant difference between ADHD and controls (Castellanos *et al.*, 2002). That is to say, brain structures are growing in size at a similar rate in both groups but those in ADHD remain smaller through development. This is, of course, a very simple account of a very complex process. Different parts of the brain grow at different rates; myelin increases during adolescence while grey matter declines; the microstructure will vary from region to region (Giedd *et al.*, 1999). Nevertheless, the pattern does help to distinguish this model of 'developmental difference' from others, such as those in which the difference gradually disappears during development, or in which brain development stops earlier or later in the group with disorder. Much more, however, remains to be done. At the level of simple description, we need to know about trajectories in functional localisation. One might, for example, expect that functions, such as attention, develop in a modular fashion as the brain becomes more expert in handling task demands. One might predict a process of encephalisation, in which (for instance) striatal involvement in the inhibition of reward is progressively taken over by prefrontal brain areas to allow more complex analyses of the situations in which response suppression is called for. It may be that genetic or environmental factors can moderate these influences, or even be manipulated. Much remains to be learned.

The development of structure and function over time needs to be not only described but also understood in its course and its implications. Major behavioural changes take place as affected individuals enter adult life (Taylor et al., 1996). Some develop major complications during adolescence, such as substance abuse or recidivist offending. Others outgrow their disabilities and take unexceptional places in society. Does this reflect brain change, and how is it influenced? There is already some evidence that there are genetic influences upon the course of disorder as well as upon its initiation (Kuntsi et al., 2005; Price et al., 2005). The characterisation of those influences may yield new treatments. There are also known environmental influences upon the cause. For example, high levels of critical expressed emotion in the family predict a transition from pure ADHD into a combined form of ADHD with oppositional/conduct problems (Rutter et al., 1997). Does this psychosocial influence have biological consequences upon brain function? Does it operate only upon genetically susceptible groups? Is the environmental influence under genetic control?

22.3.6 ETIOLOGY

Neurobiological findings have not only shown the strength of genetic influences; they are clarifying how environmental influences may operate. There are many associations between ADHD and environmental adversity; the difficulty has been unravelling the etiological pathways.

Sometimes, the environmental pathogen may be simply an association of the genetic risk. Knopik et al. (2006) have recently reported a powerful twin design to clarify the effects on the foetus of exposure to alcohol because of maternal drinking. They studied not only the offspring of mothers who had drunk alcohol, but also the children of those mothers' monozygotic (identical) twins who had, in spite of their genetic liability, not taken alcohol in pregnancy. The offspring of the co-twins then shared half their genes but not their uterine environment; yet they were indeed at risk for the development of ADHD. If this finding is replicated, it will weaken the public health arguments against the hazards of drinking small amounts of alcohol in pregnancy (though not of course dispute the existence of a foetal alcohol syndrome); and discourage clinicians from attributing the child's problems to the mother's drinking.

Sometimes, however, the strength of the environmental influence may only be fully appreciated when it is appreciated that it acts on genetically vulnerable populations. The interaction between low birth weight and an allele of a gene for COMT (an enzyme that breaks down neurotransmitters in the brain) is a case in point (Thapar et al., 2005): the risk of low birth weight may be a weak one across the whole population, but it is substantial when the baby is vulnerable. The continuing search for gene–environment interactions is likely to raise all sorts of ideas about how environmental adversity affects brain development. The goal is to clarify possible preventive strategies and develop treatments in embryonic or early postnatal life to protect against the environmental risks.

22.4 DEVELOPMENTS IN CLINICAL PRACTICE

The easiest prediction to make is that new drugs will become available, that they will have different profiles of action, and that therapeutic choice will be enlarged. The industry is already in the progress of seeking licences for drugs such as modafinil; nicotine analogues and drugs affecting GABA are in the pipeline; and in the longer term drugs affecting new learning are being developed, such the antagonists and agonists of CREBs (cAMP response element binding proteins).

These developments will bring more choice, some of it difficult. Cognitive enhancers may well have effects that are not confined to those with ADHD. Will it be seen as a form of cheating to take such drugs to enhance school or work performance – as with steroids taken by athletes – or as a legitimate method of self-improvement? When a range of first-line drugs is available, it should be possible to match the treatment more closely to the individual. Studies of the neurobiological action of new drugs (for instance, their effect on activation in neuroimaging paradigms) should therefore go together with the randomised clinical trials of efficacy, effectiveness and cost-effectiveness.

It is harder to foresee the course of psychological interventions. So far cognitive approaches have been disappointing, but this may be because they have targeted non-essential aspects of the symptom complex. As new psychological paradigms are shown to yield abnormalities in children with ADHD (or its successor concepts), greater weight should be given to small-scale and proof-of-concept studies on the effects of training the deficient abilities or devising learning schemes that bypass them (see O'Connell *et al.*, Chapter 20).

Earlier identification of children at risk is likely to become feasible – for instance, by foetal DNA analysis. Whether this leads on to screening programmes and early interventions will depend on many factors still to be researched – not only the positive and negative predictive value of screening tests, but the cost and effectiveness of interventions and their public acceptability.

Perhaps the biggest impact so far of neurobiological studies has been intangible: the provision of a validity to the concept of ADHD that has disarmed some of society's fears about the over-medicalisation of children's problems. The apparent validation is, in part, spurious. A genetic origin of behaviours clearly does not of itself imply their pathological nature. Nevertheless, it has had powerful effects – sometimes helpful, as in liberating the problem-solving abilities of parents when they feel no longer culpable; sometimes unhelpful, as when teachers construe the problems of ADHD as medical and therefore outside their scope. It will increasingly be necessary for scientists to engage in debate and discussion with the public and consider the social impact of their discoveries.

22.5 REFERENCES

Arcos-Burgos M, Castellanos FX, Pineda D *et al.* (2004) Attention-deficit/hyperactivity disorder in a population isolate: linkage to loci at 4q13.2, 5q33.3, 11q22, and 17p11. *Am J Hum Genet* **75**(6): 998–1014.

Aron AR, Fletcher P, Bullmore ET *et al.* (2003). Stop-signal inhibition disrupted by damage to the right inferior frontal gyrus in humans. *Nature Neuroscience* **6**(2): 115–16.

Avila C, Cuenca I, Felix V *et al.* (2004) Measuring impulsivity in school-aged boys and examining its relationship with ADHD and ODD ratings. *J Abnorm Child Psychol* **32**(3): 295–304.

Awh E, Jonides J (2001) Overlapping mechanisms of attention and spatial working memory. *Trends Cogn Sci* **5**(3): 119–26.

Aylward EH, Reiss AL, Reader MJ *et al.* (1996) Basal ganglia volumes in children with Attention-Deficit Hyperactivity Disorder. *Journal of Child Neurology* **11**(2): 112–15.

Banaschewski T, Hollis C, Oosterlaan J *et al.* (2005) Towards an understanding of unique and shared pathways in the psychopathophysiology of ADHD. *Dev Sci* **8**(2): 132–40.

Barkley RA (1997) Behavioral inhibition, sustained attention, and executive functions: constructing a unifying theory of ADHD. *Psychological Bulletin* **121**(1): 65–94.

Bellgrove MA, Gill M, Hawi Z *et al.* (2005) Dissecting the Attention Deficit Hyperactivity Disorder (ADHD) phenotype: sustained attention, response variability and spatial attentional asymmetries in relation to Dopamine Transporter (DAT1) Genotype. *Neuropsychologia* **43**(13): 1847–57.

Bellgrove MA, Hawi Z, Kirley A *et al.* (2005) Association between Dopamine Transporter (DAT1) genotype, left-sided inattention, and an enhanced response to methylphenidate in Attention-Deficit Hyperactivity Disorder. *Neuropsychopharmacology* **30**(12): 2290–7.

Booth JR, Burman DD, Meyer JR *et al.* (2005) Larger deficits in brain networks for response inhibition than for visual selective attention in attention deficit hyperactivity disorder (ADHD). *J Child Psychol Psychiatry* **46**(1): 94–111.

Brambilla P, Hardan A, di Nemi SU *et al.* (2003) Brain anatomy and development in autism: review of structural MRI studies. *Brain Res Bull* **61**(6): 557–69.

Brookes KJ, Mill J, Guindalini C *et al.* (2006) A common haplotype of the dopamine transporter gene associated with Attention-Deficit/Hyperactivity Disorder and interacting with maternal use of alcohol during pregnancy. *Arch Gen Psychiatry* **63**(1): 74–81.

Bush G, Frazier JA, Rauch SL *et al.* (1999) Anterior cingulate cortex dysfunction in Attention-Deficit/Hyperactivity Disorder revealed by fMRI and the Counting Stroop. *Biol Psychiatry* **45**(12): 1542–52.

Bush G, Valera EM, Seidman LJ (2005) Functional neuroimaging of Attention-Deficit/Hyperactivity Disorder: a review and suggested future directions. *Biol Psychiatry* **57**(11): 1273–84.

Casey BJ, Castellanos FX, Giedd JN *et al.* (1997) Implication of right frontostriatal circuitry in response inhibition and Attention-Deficit/Hyperactivity Disorder. *Journal of the American Academy of Child & Adolescent Psychiatry* **36**(3): 374–83.

Caspi A, Moffitt TE (2006) Gene-environment interactions in psychiatry: joining forces with neuroscience. *Nat Rev Neurosci* **7**(7): 583–90.

Castellanos FX, Giedd JN, Berquin PC *et al.* (2001) Quantitative brain magnetic resonance imaging in girls with Attention-Deficit/Hyperactivity Disorder. *Archives of General Psychiatry* **58**(3): 289–95.

Castellanos FX, Giedd JN, Eckburg P *et al.* (1994) Quantitative morphology of the caudate nucleus in attention deficit hyperactivity disorder. *Am J Psychiatry* **151**(12): 1791–6.

Castellanos FX, Giedd JN, Marsh WL *et al.* (1996) Quantitative brain magnetic resonance imaging in Attention-Deficit Hyperactivity Disorder. *Archives of General Psychiatry* **53**(7): 607–16.

Castellanos FX, Lau E, Tayebi N *et al.* (1998) Lack of an association between a dopamine-4 receptor polymorphism and Attention-Deficit/Hyperactivity Disorder: genetic and brain morphometric analyses. *Mol Psychiatry* **3**(5): 431–4.

Castellanos FX, Lee PP, Sharp W *et al.* (2002) Developmental trajectories of brain volume abnormalities in children and adolescents with Attention-Deficit/Hyperactivity Disorder. *Journal of the American Medical Association* **288**(14): 1740–8.

Castellanos FX, Sonuga-Barke EJ, Milham MP, Tannock R (2006) Characterizing cognition in ADHD: beyond executive dysfunction. *Trends Cogn Sci* **10**(3): 117–23.

Castellanos FX, Tannock R (2002) Neuroscience of Attention-Deficit/Hyperactivity Disorder: the search for endophenotypes. *Nat Rev Neurosci* **3**(8): 617–28.

Chambers CD, Bellgrove MA, Stokes MG *et al.* (2006) Executive 'brake failure' following deactivation of human frontal lobe. *Journal of Cognitive Neuroscience* **18**(3): 444–55.

Cheon KA, Ryu YH, Kim YK *et al.* (2003) Dopamine transporter density in the basal ganglia assessed with [123I]IPT SPET in children with attention deficit hyperactivity disorder. *Eur J Nucl Med Mol Imaging* **30**(2): 306–11.

Cheon KA, Ryu YH, Kim JW, Cho DY (2005) The homozygosity for 10-rcpeat allele at dopamine transporter gene and dopamine transporter density in Korean children with attention deficit hyperactivity disorder: relating to treatment response to methylphenidate. *Eur Neuropsychopharmacol* **15**(1): 95–101.

Cornish KM, Manly T, Savage R *et al.* (2005) Association of the dopamine transporter (DAT1) 10/10-repeat genotype with ADHD symptoms and response inhibition in a general population sample. *Mol Psychiatry* **10**(7): 686–98.

Curran S, Rijsdijk F, Martin N *et al.* (2003) CHIP: Defining a dimension of the vulnerability to attention deficit hyperactivity disorder (ADHD) using sibling and individual data of children in a community-based sample. *Am J Med Genet B Neuropsychiatr Genet* **119**(1): 86–97.

Dougherty DD, Bonab AA, Spencer TJ *et al.* (1999) Dopamine transporter density in patients with attention deficit hyperactivity disorder. *The Lancet* **354**: 2132–3.

Dresel S, Krause J, Krause KH *et al.* (2000) Attention deficit hyperactivity disorder: binding of [99mTc]TRODAT-1 to the dopamine transporter before and after methylphenidate treatment. *European Journal of Nuclear Medicine* **27**(10): 1518–24.

Durston S, Fossella JA, Casey BJ *et al.* (2005) Differential effects of DRD4 and DAT1 genotype on fronto-striatal gray matter volumes in a sample of subjects with attention deficit hyperactivity disorder, their unaffected siblings, and controls. *Mol Psychiatry* **10**(7): 678–85.

Durston S, Hulshoff Pol HE, Schnack HG *et al.* (2004) Magnetic resonance imaging of boys with Attention-Deficit/Hyperactivity Disorder and their unaffected siblings. *J Am Acad Child Adolesc Psychiatry* **43**(3): 332–40.

Durston S, Tottenham NT, Thomas KM *et al.* (2003) Differential patterns of striatal activation in young children with and without ADHD. *Biol Psychiatry* **53**(10): 871–8.

Faraone SV, Perlis RH, Doyle AE *et al.* (2005) Molecular genetics of Attention-Deficit/Hyperactivity Disorder. *Biol Psychiatry* **57**(11): 1313–23.

Filipek PA, Semrud-Clikeman M, Steingard RJ *et al.* (1997) Volumetric MRI analysis comparing subjects having Attention-Deficit Hyperactivity Disorder with normal controls. *Neurology* **48**(3): 589–601.

Garavan H, Ross TJ, Kaufman J, Stein EA (2003) A midline dissociation between error-processing and response-conflict monitoring. *Neuroimage* **20**(2): 1132–9.

Garavan H, Ross TJ, Murphy K *et al.* (2002) Dissociable executive functions in the dynamic control of behavior: inhibition, error detection, and correction. *Neuroimage* **17**(4): 1820–9.

Geurts HM, Verte S, Oosterlaan J *et al.* (2005) ADHD subtypes: do they differ in their executive functioning profile? *Arch Clin Neuropsychol* **20**(4): 457–77.

Giedd JN, Blumenthal J, Jeffries NO *et al.* (1999) Brain development during childhood and adolescence: a longitudinal MRI study. *Nat Neurosci* **2**(10): 861–3.

Heinz A, Goldman D, Jones DW *et al.* (2000) Genotype influences in vivo dopamine transporter availability in human striatum. *Neuropsychopharmacology* **22**: 133–9.

Husain M, Rorden C (2003) Non-spatially lateralised mechanisms in hemispatial neglect. *Nature Reviews Neuroscience* **4**: 26–36.

Kenemans JL, Bekker EM, Lijffijt M *et al.* (2005) Attention deficit and impulsivity: selecting, shifting, and stopping. *International Journal of Psychophysiology* **58**(1): 59–70.

Kirley A, Lowe N, Hawi Z *et al.* (2003) Association of the 480 bp DAT1 allele with methylphenidate response in a sample of Irish children with ADHD. *Am J Med Genet* **121B**(1): 50–4.

Knopik VS, Heath AC, Jacob T *et al.* (2006) Maternal alcohol use disorder and offspring ADHD: disentangling genetic and environmental effects using a children-of-twins design. *Psychol Med* **36**(10): 1461–71.

Konrad K, Neufang S, Hanisch C *et al.* (2006) Dysfunctional attentional networks in children with Attention Deficit/Hyperactivity Disorder: evidence from an event-related functional magnetic resonance imaging study. *Biol Psychiatry* **59**(7): 643–51.

Krause KH, Dresel SH, Krause J *et al.* (2000) Increased striatal dopamine transporter in adult patients with attention deficit hyperactivity disorder: effects of methylphenidate as measures by single photon emission computed tomography. *Neuroscience Letters* **285**: 107–10.

Kuntsi J, Rijsdijk F, Ronald A *et al.* (2005) Genetic influences on the stability of Attention-Deficit/Hyperactivity Disorder symptoms from early to middle childhood. *Biol Psychiatry* **57**(6): 647–54.

Lijffijt M, Kenemans JL, Verbaten MN, van Engeland H (2005) A meta-analytic review of stopping performance in Attention-Deficit/Hyperactivity Disorder: deficient inhibitory motor control? *J Abnorm Psychol* **114**(2): 216–22.

Logan GD, Schachar RJ, Tannock R (1997) Impulsivity and inhibitory control. *Psychological Science* **8**(1): 60–4.

Loo SK, Specter E, Smolen A *et al.* (2003) Functional effects of the DAT1 polymorphism on EEG measures in ADHD. *J Am Acad Child Adolesc Psychiatry* **42**(8): 986–93.

Loo SK, Teale PD, Reite ML (1999) EEG correlates of methylphenidate response among children with ADHD: a preliminary report. *Biol Psychiatry* **45**(12): 1657–60.

Madras BK, Miller GM, Fischman AJ (2005) The dopamine transporter and Attention-Deficit/Hyperactivity Disorder. *Biological Psychiatry* **57**(11): 1397–409.

Makris N, Biederman J, Valera EM *et al.* (2006) Cortical thinning of the attention and executive function networks in adults with Attention-Deficit/Hyperactivity Disorder. *Cereb Cortex* Aug. 18 [Epub ahead of print].

Mattes JA (1980) The role of frontal lobe dysfunction in childhood hyperkinesis. *Compr Psychiatry* **21**(5): 358–69.

Milich R, Balentine AC, Lynam DR (2001) ADHD combined type and ADHD predominantly inattentive type are distinct and unrelated disorders. *Clinical Psychology* **8**(4): 463–88.

Mostofsky SH, Cooper KL, Kates WR *et al.* (2002) Smaller prefrontal and premotor volumes in boys with Attention-Deficit/Hyperactivity Disorder. *Biological Psychiatry* **52**(8): 785–94.

Mullins C, Bellgrove MA, Gill M, Robertson IH (2005) Variability in time reproduction: difference in ADHD combined and inattentive subtypes. *J Am Acad Child Adolesc Psychiatry* **44**(2): 169–76.

Nadder TS, Rutter M, Silberg JL *et al.* (2002) Genetic effects on the variation and covariation of attention deficit-hyperactivity disorder (ADHD) and oppositional-defiant disorder/conduct disorder (ODD/CD) symptomatologies across informant and occasion of measurement. *Psychol Med* **32**(1): 39–53.

Nigg JT (2001) Is ADHD a disinhibitory disorder? *Psychological Bulletin* **127**(5): 571–98.

Nigg JT, Blaskey LG, Huang-Pollock CL, Rappley MD (2002) Neuropsychological executive functions and DSM-IV ADHD subtypes. *J Am Acad Child Adolesc Psychiatry* **41**(1): 59–66.

Nigg JT, Willcutt EG, Doyle AE, Sonuga-Barke EJ (2005) Causal heterogeneity in Attention-Deficit/Hyperactivity Disorder: do we need neuropsychologically impaired subtypes? *Biol Psychiatry* **57**(11): 1224–30.

O'Driscoll GA, Depatie L, Holahan AL *et al.* (2005) Executive functions and methylphenidate response in subtypes of Attention-Deficit/Hyperactivity Disorder. *Biol Psychiatry* **57**(11): 1452–60.

Pennington BF, Ozonoff S (1996) Executive functions and developmental psychopathology. *Journal of Child Psychology and Psychiatry* **37**(1): 51–87.

Pliszka SR, Glahn DC, Semrud-Clikeman M *et al.* (2006) Neuroimaging of inhibitory control areas in children with attention deficit hyperactivity disorder who were treatment naive or in long-term treatment. *Am J Psychiatry* **163**(6): 1052–60.

Pliszka SR, Lancaster J, Liotti M, Semrud-Clikeman M (2006) Volumetric MRI differences in treatment-naive vs chronically treated children with ADHD. *Neurology* **67**(6): 1023–7.

Posner MI, Peterson SE (1990) The attention system of the human brain. *Annual Review of Neuroscience* **13**: 35–42.

Prendergast M, Taylor E, Rapoport JL *et al.* (1988) The diagnosis of childhood hyperactivity. A U.S.-U.K. cross-national study of DSM-III and ICD-9. *Journal of Child Psychology & Psychiatry & Allied Disciplines* **29**(3): 289–300.

Price TS, Simonoff E, Asherson P *et al.* (2005) Continuity and change in preschool ADHD symptoms: longitudinal genetic analysis with contrast effects. *Behav Genet* **35**(2): 121–32.

Rohde LA, Roman T, Szobot C *et al.* (2003) Dopamine transporter gene, response to methylphenidate and cerebral blood flow in Attention-Deficit/Hyperactivity Disorder: a pilot study. *Synapse* **48**(2): 87–9.

Roman T, Szobot C, Martins S *et al.* (2002) Dopamine transporter gene and response to methylphenidate in Attention-Deficit/Hyperactivity Disorder. *Pharmacogenetics* **12**: 497–9.

Rubia K, Overmeyer S, Taylor E *et al.* (1999) Hypofrontality in attention deficit hyperactivity disorder during higher-order motor control: a study with functional MRI. *American Journal of Psychiatry* **156**(6): 891–6.

Rubia K, Smith AB, Brammer MJ *et al.* (2005) Abnormal brain activation during inhibition and error detection in medication-naive adolescents with ADHD. *Am J Psychiatry* **162**(6): 1067–75.

Rutter M, Graham P, Yule W (1970) *A Neuropsychiatric Study in Childhood*. London: Heinemann Medical; Philadelphia: JB Lippincott Co.

Rutter M, Maughan B, Meyer J *et al.* (1997) Heterogeneity of antisocial behavior: causes, continuities, and consequences. *Nebr Symp Motiv* **44**: 45–118.

Sagvolden T, Johansen EB, Aase H, Russell VA (2005) A dynamic developmental theory of Attention-Deficit/Hyperactivity Disorder (ADHD) predominantly hyperactive/impulsive and combined subtypes. *Behav Brain Sci* **28**(3): 397–419.

Schachar RJ, Chen S, Logan GD *et al.* (2004) Evidence for an error monitoring deficit in attention deficit hyperactivity disorder. *J Abnorm Child Psychol* **32**(3): 285–93.

Schachar RJ, Crosbie J, Barr CL *et al.* (2005) Inhibition of motor responses in siblings concordant and discordant for Attention Deficit Hyperactivity Disorder. *Am J Psychiatry* **162**(6): 1076–82.

Schulz KP, Fan J, Tang CY *et al.* (2004) Response inhibition in adolescents diagnosed with attention deficit hyperactivity disorder during childhood: an event-related FMRI study. *Am J Psychiatry* **161**(9): 1650–7.

Seidman LJ (2006) Neuropsychological functioning in people with ADHD across the life-span. *Clin Psychol Rev* **26**(4): 466–85.

Seidman LJ, Valera EM, Makris N (2005) Structural brain imaging of Attention-Deficit/Hyperactivity Disorder. *Biol Psychiatry* **57**(11): 1263–72.

Sergeant J (2000) The cognitive-energetical model: an empirical approach to Attention-Deficit Hyperactivity Disorder. *Neuroscience & Biobehavioral Reviews* **24**: 7–12.

Sergeant J, Oosterlaan J, van der Meere J (1999) Information processing and energetic factors in ADHD. In H Quay, A Hogan (eds) *Handbook of Disruptive Behavior Disorders* (pp. 75–103). New York: Kluwer Academic.

Shaw P, Lerch J, Greenstein D *et al.* (2006) Longitudinal mapping of cortical thickness and clinical outcome in children and adolescents with Attention-Deficit/Hyperactivity Disorder. *Arch Gen Psychiatry* **63**(5): 540–9.

Silk T, Vance A, Rinehart N *et al.* (2005) Decreased fronto-parietal activation in Attention Deficit Hyperactivity Disorder, combined type (ADHD-CT): an fMRI study. *British Journal of Psychiatry* **187**(3).

Smalley SL, Kustanovich V, Minassian SL *et al.* (2002) Genetic linkage of Attention-Deficit/Hyperactivity Disorder on chromosome 16p13, in a region implicated in autism. *Am J Hum Genet* **71**(4): 959–63.

Solanto MV, Abikoff H, Sonuga-Barke E *et al.* (2001) The ecological validity of delay aversion and response inhibition as measures of impulsivity in AD/HD: a supplement to the NIMH multimodal treatment study of AD/HD. *J Abnorm Child Psychol* **29**(3): 215–28.

Sonuga-Barke EJ (1994) On dysfunction and function in psychological theories of childhood disorder. *J Child Psychol Psychiatry* **35**(5): 801–15.

Sonuga-Barke EJ (2003) The dual pathway model of AD/HD: an elaboration of neuro-developmental characteristics. *Neuroscience & Biobehavioral Reviews* **27**: 593–604.

Sonuga-Barke EJ, Auerbach J, Campbell SB *et al.* (2005) Varieties of preschool hyperactivity: multiple pathways from risk to disorder. *Dev Sci* **8**(2): 141–50.

Sonuga-Barke EJ, Saxton T, Hall M (1998) The role of interval underestimation in hyperactive children's failure to suppress responses over time. *Behavioural Brain Research* **94**(1): 45–50.

Sowell ER, Thompson PM, Welcome SE *et al.* (2003) Cortical abnormalities in children and adolescents with Attention-Deficit Hyperactivity Disorder. *Lancet* **362**(9397): 1699–1707.

Spencer TJ, Biederman J, Madras BK *et al.* (2005) In vivo neuroreceptor imaging in Attention-Deficit/Hyperactivity Disorder: a focus on the dopamine transporter. *Biol Psychiatry* **57**(11): 1293–1300.

Stein MA, Waldman ID, Sarampote CS *et al.* (2005) Dopamine transporter genotype and methylphenidate dose response in children with ADHD. *Neuropsychopharmacology* **30**(7): 1374–82.

Tamm L, Menon V, Ringel J, Reiss AL (2004) Event-related FMRI evidence of frontotemporal involvement in aberrant response inhibition and task switching in Attention-Deficit/Hyperactivity Disorder. *J Am Acad Child Adolesc Psychiatry* **43**(11): 1430–40.

Taylor E (1998) Clinical foundations of hyperactivity research. *Behav Brain Res* **94**(1): 11–24.

Taylor E (1999) Developmental neuropsychopathology of attention deficit and impulsiveness. *Dev Psychopathol* **11**(3): 607–28.

Taylor E, Chadwick O, Heptinstall E, Danckaerts M (1996) Hyperactivity and conduct problems as risk factors for adolescent development. *J Am Acad Child Adolesc Psychiatry* **35**(9): 1213–26.

Teicher MH, Anderson CM, Polcari A *et al.* (2000) Functional deficits in basal ganglia of children with Attention-Deficit/Hyperactivity Disorder shown with functional magnetic resonance imaging relaxometry. *Nature Medicine* **6**(4): 470–3.